Volume I

THE CHALLENGE
TO ISOLATION

THE CHALLENGE
TO ISOLATION

The World Crisis of 1937-1940 and
American Foreign Policy

VOLUME I

by
William L. Langer
and
S. Everett Gleason

GLOUCESTER, MASS.

PETER SMITH

1970

CONTENTS

VOLUME I

Volume II

PREFACE

Ever since the intervention of the United States in the First World War a "great debate" on American foreign policy has agitated the country. For a generation Americans have been trying to make up their minds whether and to what extent they should assume responsibility for affairs beyond their own frontiers. In the absence of any general scholarly study of American policy during the first great conflict, the issue was at that time left to partisan controversialists. Popular disillusionment with the fruits of victory was followed by confusion of mind, and in the end many Americans became firmly convinced that their grand crusade had in fact been engineered by munitions makers, international bankers and foreign propagandists.

The mounting international tension and the growing danger of renewed conflict in the late 30's was bound to add fuel to the hot debate between the "isolationists" and the "interventionists," that is, between those determined to stand aloof from foreign wars at all costs and those convinced that the United States could not escape the effects of foreign quarrels and that therefore the country should take a hand in them if only to protect itself and its national interests. The attack on Pearl Harbor brought the controversy to a temporary close, but since 1945 it has flared up anew, despite the fact that the world position of the United States and, in fact, the entire international alignment have been fundamentally transformed in the interval. It was perhaps inevitable that under the circumstances the policies of President Roosevelt before and during the Second World War should be repeatedly examined by partisans on both sides. The last few years have seen the publication of a number of highly critical volumes, along with several books and essays vindicating the late President's views and policies.

Holding this development probable, the Council on Foreign Relations, a nonpartisan organization for the study of international affairs, laid plans early in 1946 for the writing and publication of an extensive, scholarly history of American foreign policy in the period just before and during the Second World War, in the hope that a thorough analysis of all the circumstances and developments would aid the American public in understanding and evaluating the historical forces underlying past and current problems. The Council received from the Rockefeller Foundation a substantial grant of money with which to finance the project, and thereupon invited the undersigned to undertake the task. In the intervening five years we have enjoyed the full support of the Council's Committee on Studies, but have been given all latitude in the planning and execution of the enterprise. At the very outset we decided not to rely on a large staff, but to do the research and writing ourselves. Happily we found ourselves in general agreement on all essential questions of form and interpretation, and years of close professional collaboration have deepened a friendship that reaches far into the past.

As trained historians we were fully aware of the magnitude of our undertaking. All research in recent history is hampered as well as aided by the superabundance and variety of the records. Had we relied only on published materials, we should still have had an arduous task, considering the vast number of published papers and the volume of periodical literature and newspaper reports. We could not, however, foresee in the beginning the veritable deluge of records and memoirs that has flooded the bookshops in the few years since the end of the war. The papers and other evidence adduced at the Nürnberg and Tokyo war crimes trials alone are staggering in number and variety. Yet to these must be added the voluminous proceedings of important government investigations, like those of Norway, Sweden, the Netherlands and Belgium; the records of numerous treason trials in France and elsewhere; the imposing array of war memoirs, ranging from those of Mr. Hull, Mr. Churchill and M. Reynaud to those of relatively minor officials and commanders; and finally the almost countless government and private studies of many phases of political and military activity. It may be said without fear of contradiction that at least so far as European affairs are concerned, most of the important historical data have already come to light in one way or another. It goes without saying, however, that the sifting and analysis of this mountainous mass of evidence has in itself been a task of formidable proportions.

Our objective has been to examine the development of American policy not as a thing in itself, but in the context of the world events which conditioned that policy. For that reason we have examined the larger part of the literature on the war period from foreign as well as from domestic sources. Furthermore, we realized that an authoritative account of American policy would require full use of the official American records. We therefore requested Secretary of State Dean G. Acheson (in 1946 Under Secretary of State) for permission to consult the files of the State Department. That permission was given, and we have, over the years of the project, had free access to these invaluable records. They have formed the backbone of our entire account, and in the course of the study here presented, all sources not otherwise identified are to be taken as coming from the State Department files.

Through the interest of Fleet Admiral William D. Leahy (at that time Chief of Staff to the Commander in Chief) we were granted permission also to consult such military records as bore on the formulation and execution of American foreign policy. Also, in the course of conversations with statesmen and diplomats who participated in the events of those critical years, we secured access to many private papers. Thus we were able to utilize the vast files accumulated by former Secretary of the Treasury Henry Morgenthau, Jr.; the unpublished diary of the late Secretary of War Henry L. Stimson; the similar diary of former Ambassador Joseph C. Grew, who also put at our disposal the diary of his son-in-law, the late Ambassador Pierrepont Moffat; the diaries and papers of former Assistant Secretary of State Adolf A. Berle, Jr.; certain letters of the late Secretary of the Navy Frank Knox to Mrs. Knox; papers of former Postmaster General Frank C. Walker, bearing on Far Eastern affairs; the files of Major General William J. Donovan; and the records of Mr. Grenville Clark as they bear on the introduction of Selective Service, and of Mr. Francis P. Miller with respect to the organization and activity of the so-called Century Group. The writers are deeply indebted also to Mr. Wayne C. Grover, the Archivist of the United States, and to Mr. Herman Kahn, the Director of the Franklin D. Roosevelt Memorial Library, for permission to consult many of the Roosevelt Papers at Hyde Park, which proved extremely valuable for the light they threw on the late President's views and purposes. Through the courtesy of the office of Alien Property they have been enabled to use and occasionally quote from the diaries of Colonel General Alfred Jodl and of Colonel General Franz Halder (copyright 1945 and 1946, respectively, by the Attorney General of the United States).

In lieu of the historical perspective which can come only with the passage of years, we have enjoyed the opportunity of consulting and discussing various problems with those who were most directly concerned with them. Many of these men have not only given us generously of their time, but have also taken the trouble to read either the whole or part of the present volume. Among State Department officials we are under particular obligation to former Under Secretary of State Sumner Welles, to Deputy Under Secretary of State H. Freeman Matthews, to former Ambassadors Joseph C. Grew, William C. Bullitt, Joseph P. Kennedy, William Phillips, H. F. Arthur Schoenfeld, Spruille Braden, Wallace Murray, and the late Laurence A. Steinhardt. Many officials of the State Department have helped us with information or advice, among them Messrs. John D. Hickerson, George F. Kennan, Maxwell M. Hamilton, Joseph W. Ballantine, Carlton Savage, G. Frederick Reinhardt, Charles E. Bohlen, Elbridge C. Durbrow and Max Bishop. Outside the State Department we have enjoyed the interest and aid of Fleet Admiral William D. Leahy, Justice Robert H. Jackson and Lieutenant General Stanley D. Embick. Captain Tracy B. Kittredge of the Historical

Section of the Joint Chiefs of Staff, Dr. Stetson Conn, Dr. Ray S. Cline and Mr. Mark S. Watson, all of the Historical Division of the Department of the Army, have read large parts of the manuscript and have made valuable suggestions. Robert E. Sherwood, author of *Roosevelt and Hopkins*, Professor Samuel E. Morison of Harvard University, and Professor Samuel F. Bemis of Yale University, have also read parts or all of the manuscript and have offered useful criticism. Finally, we are deeply grateful to Dr. Joseph Willits of the Rockefeller Foundation, and to Allen W. Dulles, Walter H. Mallory, Hamilton Fish Armstrong, and Dr. Henry M. Wriston of the Council on Foreign Relations for their unflagging interest and advice.

Originally we had hoped, in the four years allotted to the project, to complete the history of American policy from 1939 to 1945 in perhaps three or four volumes. But in view of the almost unmanageable mass of materials, both published and unpublished, it soon became evident that the achievement of that objective was out of the question. At the end of the four years, work was not yet completed on the first two volumes, covering the period from September, 1938 to December, 1941. A further grant, this time from the Sloan Foundation, made possible the continuance of the enterprise and the conclusion of the work on these first volumes. One, complete in itself, is presented to the public herewith; a second will follow.

We are more conscious than perhaps others could possibly be of the questions left unanswered by our narrative. For all their bulk, even the official records leave many issues obscure and, as we have set forth in the introduction to the present volume, there are many matters which probably will remain forever shrouded in uncertainty and doubt. But within the limits of the possible we have tried to give a complete account of the world crisis and the American response to it, and to set forth the complicated interrelationships of many aspects of the global conflict. It is hardly necessary to say that as professional historians we have tried to keep an open mind and to adduce all the evidence that appeared relevant. It is equally unnecessary to say that we have retained complete freedom in the interpretation and presentation of the materials. The manuscript has been checked by the State Department, but exclusively with an eye to safeguarding American relations with other countries and to protecting the national security. No one, in the State Department or elsewhere, has made the slightest effort to influence our views or to shade our conclusions. This book is in no sense an official or even a semi-official account, nor is it one in the publication of which we have any financial interest. All royalties from the sale of the volume accrue to the Council on Foreign Relations, to be used in the furtherance of other studies. In short, this is an entirely independent, scholarly study, and one for which we alone assume responsibility.

In conclusion we take pleasure in acknowledging the technical aid received from Dr. G. Bernard Noble and the staff of the Division of Historical Research of the State Department, as well as from the staffs of the libraries of the Council on Foreign Relations and of Harvard College. We are indebted also to Mrs. Arline Van Blarcom Pratt, our very competent research assistant, whose familiarity with the State Department files proved invaluable, to Miss Marie Carney, our able and devoted secretary, and finally to our respective wives who, throughout strenuous years of travel, study and writing, have aided in every possible way and have contributed particularly to the preparation and review of the manuscript.

WILLIAM L. LANGER

S. EVERETT GLEASON

UXORIBUS · NOSTRIS · CARISSIMIS

INTRODUCTION

Under a democratic form of government the formulation and conduct of foreign policy are bound to be at best complicated and arduous, for they involve at every stage the expressed or implied assent of Congress and the support of public opinion. The United States Constitution has little to say of the management of such affairs, though it explicitly assigns to the President responsibility for the determination and direction of the country's foreign relations. From this it follows that the methods of procedure, both on the executive and the legislative side, have had to be worked out over an extended period of time and through long practice in meeting concrete situations and problems. The role of Congress in foreign policy has been and still is a matter for lively debate, while the task of informing and educating the people so as to make its will effective continues to be one of the difficult aspects of the general problem of democratic control of international relations.

The various facets of this problem inevitably call for attention in a study of American foreign policy in any given period. For the most part they can be adequately treated only in the course of the ensuing narrative. However, in view of the dominant position of the Chief Executive, a few introductory observations on the role of President Roosevelt may serve as a useful guide to the complexities confronting the reader. Under the American system the character and conduct of foreign policy necessarily reflect the training, methods, temperament and objectives of the Chief Executive, limited always by the domestic political considerations that condition all phases of government in a democracy. They are affected also by the President's choice of assistants and advisers, and by his general ability as an administrator. Finally, the President's views and practices will also determine the character of the records with which the historian is obliged to work. For that reason, if for no other, it is desirable to give some attention to these rather elusive aspects of the subject.

Among American Presidents, Franklin D. Roosevelt was certainly one of the best fitted by background, education and experience, as well as by interest and temperament, to understand world conditions and to sense their implications for the national interest and security. His consuming interest in geography and his almost passionate devotion to the Navy were only among the more obvious manifestations of his concern for world affairs. True, in the early years of his Administration he was so engrossed with the problems of the New Deal that he had relatively little time for international issues. But by the year 1937 that was no longer the case. The New Deal had been fairly launched and, as the situation in the Far East and in Europe became dangerously acute, Mr. Roosevelt concentrated his attention more and more on external problems. While he occasionally spoke of himself as his own Secretary of State, he meant by this no more than that he personally considered all matters of importance and made all major decisions, as by the Constitution he was called upon to do, though he necessarily left much of the detailed formulation and actual operation of policy to his appointed subordinates.

Having stated these generalities, it must be confessed at once that it is well-nigh impossible to penetrate beyond them and determine or demonstrate the President's outlook, reasoning and attitude on specific questions or policies. Former Cabinet officers who were close to Mr. Roosevelt, like Miss Perkins and Mr. Morgenthau, have described him as a most complicated human being—a man of bewildering variety of moods and motives. That being so, future biographers of the late President are bound to find their subject baffling and elusive, while for the present writers, neither of whom knew Mr. Roosevelt personally, it would be foolhardy to attempt more than a brief comment on that complex character. Suffice it to remark, as of significance in the context of foreign policy, that the President, for all his apparent sociability, joviality and even frivolity, was essentially a reserved and self-sufficient figure. In the years just preceding Pearl Harbor no man stood in such close relationship to him as had Louis Howe earlier. Harry Hopkins no doubt was more fully initiated into Mr. Roosevelt's thoughts than anyone else, but even Hopkins, who spoke of himself as merely an errand boy, was rather an executive agent than a confidential adviser. He never claimed to read the President's inmost thoughts and indeed was probably not equipped by training or temperament to appreciate or criticize them.

Much less were others in a position of complete confidence. Mr. Roosevelt inspired intense loyalty in his associates, who admired his indomitable courage, his unshakable hopefulness, and his wholehearted devotion to the good of the public and the cause of humanity. But none of them had the conviction of understanding the man or grasping his thought processes. In varying degrees they may have deluded themselves into thinking that they inspired or influenced him in one direction or another, but for the most part the President undoubtedly made up his mind quite independently. Mrs. Roosevelt, who characteristically disclaims knowledge of her husband's deeper reasoning, has declared that she never knew anyone really less influenced by others.

Mr. Roosevelt was at all times mindful of his great prerogatives. He was jealous of them and utterly confident of his ability to discharge them. Impatient of formality, not to say order, and much averse to administrative red tape, he preferred to deal with people and problems directly. As Chief Executive of a powerful nation he regarded himself as fully the equal of foreign royalty. He corresponded personally with kings and heads of states, not to mention foreign statesmen and diplomats. His intense efforts, in 1939 and 1940, to assure the safety of European royalty and refugee leaders are enlightening evidence of his sense of responsibility toward his equals. His persistent predilection for personal conferences with foreign statesmen is yet another indication of his sense of exalted position and of his almost unlimited confidence in his personal influence and ability. At the beginning of the period here under discussion he was wedded to the idea of a grand assembly, at which the responsible heads of government might thresh out their differences and arrive directly at agreement. Subsequently he was much intrigued by the notion of a personal conference with Mussolini, and later he was sorely tempted to accept the invitation to meet with Prince Konoye. He derived manifest satisfaction from his close relationship to Prime Minister Mackenzie King of Canada and to Prime Minister Churchill, and in his closing years was obviously gratified to sit at the table in personal conference with Churchill and Stalin. All in all, the evidence is unmistakable of his great faith in the efficacy of direct discussion at the highest level, where decisions could be reached without the intervention of subordinates.

Personal conferences with foreign leaders were necessarily exceptional, but even at a lower level Mr. Roosevelt regularly employed the same procedure. He kept himself fully posted on foreign affairs by reading important telegrams at breakfast each day. He reinforced his knowledge by maintaining unusually close contact with foreign representatives in Washington and by not infrequently sending special emissaries—personal representatives—to foreign capitals. There can be no doubt that he transacted important business by telephone calls to Mr. Churchill or to the American Ambassadors in London and Paris, or by frequent conversations with diplomats accredited to Washington. This practice certainly facilitated and speeded action, but inevitably produced administrative complications, if not confusion, the more so as the President was not always mindful of the need for keeping his subordinates fully and promptly informed.

For the historian as well, Mr. Roosevelt's methods have created certain difficulties. Since the late President left relatively little in the way of notes, diaries, or memoirs, and since his closest associates concede their ignorance of his inmost thoughts, reliable and detailed information on the motivation of his foreign policy will in all probability remain forever lacking. This is the more true since Mr. Roosevelt, despite his keen interest in history and his obvious solicitude for his place in it, refused to keep a systematic record of his telephone conversations or conferences with foreign representatives. In these respects the American records are far less complete than those, for instance, of the British. From the records of foreign governments, if and when they are published, it will undoubtedly be possible to cull much information on American foreign policy as revealed in the reports of ambassadors on their talks with the President. A few bits of such data have already become available in British and French publications and give clear indication of the value of such records. But for the time being the American historian is obliged to content himself with occasional revelations in the President's correspondence, in his marginal annotations and chits, and in the memoranda of conversations made by government officials when they were present at White House conferences.

Jealousy of his prerogatives and preference for personal contact made Mr. Roosevelt averse to effective staff work. His immediate assistants were, for the most part, able and energetic men who served primarily in an executive capacity and played but a minor role, if any, in the formulation of policy. The Roosevelt Cabinet, at best an amorphous institution, provided no adequate forum for discussion and deliberation. It was notorious that many members of the official family were mutually antipathetic, not to say hostile, to each other. Many of them were enthusiastic New Dealers and as such were more interested in domestic than in foreign problems. Some, indeed, were almost isolationist in their attitude toward involvements abroad which might jeopardize the cause of social reform. In view of the competition for power so characteristic of the loosely knit Roosevelt administration, leakages of information from Cabinet meetings were deplorably common. It was therefore understandable that neither the President nor his Secretaries were much disposed to raise important, confidential issues at the weekly Cabinet meetings. At the suggestion of the President, one member or another might report on a current situation or problem, but even then only in a fairly superficial, circumspect and noncommittal fashion. Only on the rarest occasions was a matter of real moment in foreign policy discussed freely by the Cabinet, and then chiefly with reference to its domestic political implications. Records of Cabinet meetings would therefore be of relatively minor importance to the historian, even if they existed. As a matter of fact, Mr. Roosevelt objected strongly to notes being taken by those present. Apparently most members respected his wishes, and reliable reports of Cabinet debate are therefore rarities.

In this respect, too, the British system was more methodical and effective, for control over foreign policy was concentrated in the restricted War Cabinet. President Roosevelt certainly knew about British methods and procedures, and he was often urged by associates and friends to set up something like a War Cabinet which would relieve him of some responsibility and at the same time provide much-needed coördination in formulating foreign policy. But the President turned a deaf ear to all such suggestions. Far from shirking responsibility, he positively enjoyed it, and therefore refused to delegate any significant part of it. Just as he declined for a long time to vest extensive authority over war production in any one man, so he rejected proposals for the formal association of even his chief advisers in a body, like the present-day National Security Council, which might infringe on his complete freedom in planning and operation. It was not that he failed to confer or to hear the opinions of others. On the contrary, he was avid of information and eager to hear varying views. But always he sought private discussion with one or at most a few individuals, avoiding general debate or acriminious controversy, and above all reserving the ultimate decision for himself.

Mr. Roosevelt may have rationalized his attitude by reference to his multifarious duties and functions as Chief Executive and by argument that no one else could hope to grasp all the widely ramified aspects of a particular problem. For one thing, he was obliged to keep constantly in view the domestic reaction to foreign policy. Like all successful Presidents, he was of course an adroit and accomplished politician and never left Congress or the country out of his calculations. He realized that any foreign policy, if it were to succeed, must have the declared or at least tacit approval of Congress and the support of the public. Hostile writers have tried to prove him a would-be dictator and have emphasized his allegedly insidious maneuvers to steer the country into a policy bound to end in war. The record suggests, however, that while the President certainly gave intellectual leadership in arousing the country to the dangers of the world situation, he was often a temporizer when it came to action. Mrs. Roosevelt has commented on her late husband's keen sense of timing and on his ability to await patiently the arrival of what seemed to him the most auspicious moment. She has remarked also on his feeling that no leader could afford to get too far ahead of his followers, and on his wholesome respect for the opinion of Congress as expressive of the popular sentiment.

These points seem to be well taken. Mr. Roosevelt certainly kept his political ear to the ground and at a rather early date decided for himself that systematic public-opinion polls were not sufficient for his purposes. He read a number of important newspapers every morning, including the most hostile. Knowledgeable citizens from all parts of the country were received with pleasure and treated as important sources of information. Finally, he relied on his much-traveled wife to provide detailed reports on all sorts of conditions and trends throughout the land.

In retrospect, indeed, there is real ground for thinking that the President tended to underestimate popular support for his foreign policy and that his occasional reluctance to act or to act openly may have been occasioned by his misgivings about Congress, for which he evidently had an almost inordinate concern. It was, of course, true that in the years before Pearl Harbor there was in Congress much determined and bitter opposition to the Administration, on the score of both domestic and foreign policy. Nonetheless, on reviewing the record it is hard to escape the impression that the President was inclined to exaggerate the strength and cohesion of this opposition. For the most part the votes on vital measures of foreign policy left him with more than a merely comfortable margin, and in some instances, notably the Destroyer Deal and Lend Lease, the crippling opposition he so much dreaded never materialized at all. Such fears as the President suffered from appear to have been inspired largely by his antagonists on "the Hill."

Closer and more continuous contact between the executive and the legislature would almost certainly have taken some of the edge off the situation. Mr. Roosevelt did, on occasion, invite opposition as well as administration leaders to confer with him, but these consultations were episodic and generally concerned with political tactics rather than with the substance of policy. Whether from fear of leakages or from other considerations, Mr. Roosevelt did not, in the pre-Pearl Harbor years, take Congressional leaders into his confidence so far as foreign relations were at issue. His feeling seems to have been that the isolationists were irreconcilable and that therefore on questions of foreign policy there was little middle ground between evasion and pitched battle. His practice, in the latter alternative, was to appeal, not to the good sense of Congress, but to that of the country at large. It is well known that he put great store by his public utterances and press conferences. The latter gave him an opportunity to present matters in a highly informal, not to say homely, fashion, which probably appealed to the common man though it estranged many people by the frequent frivolity of tone. The President's major addresses were all based on his own outlines. They were drafted and redrafted as many as ten or a dozen times, sometimes in the State Department, sometimes by his personal assistants, often by both, while Mr. Roosevelt himself gave them the finishing touches. The summation—the "snapper," as he called it—was invariably his own contribution, as were many of the choicest and most effective phrases.

In the formulation and execution of foreign policy the President's chief collaborators were, naturally, the Secretaries of State, War and Navy, to whom must be added, for the period here under consideration, Secretary of the Treasury Morgenthau. Mr. Morgenthau was a neighbor and personal friend of the President and a man peculiarly devoted to the Roosevelt policies. He saw more of Mr. Roosevelt than did other Cabinet officers and was ever ready to serve in any capacity, including that of whipping boy. He administered his own department with exemplary efficiency, yet always seemed to have time and energy to spare. In order to reduce jurisdictional disputes and get on with things, the President gave him general charge of foreign orders for munitions, thereby according him, prior to Lend Lease, a substantial part in the implementation of a vitally important foreign policy.

It goes without saying that this arrangement annoyed other Cabinet members and created considerable friction between the State Department and the Treasury. Mr. Morgenthau made no secret of his belief that the State Department was an antiquated, unwieldy and inefficient institution, ill-equipped to arrive at clear and prompt decisions and therefore an obstructive rather than a contributing force. Secretary of State Hull, on the other hand, suspected his Treasury colleague of a desire to take over vital functions of the State Department and warmly resented what he regarded as unwarranted interference in his own domain. The voluminous records collected by Mr. Morgenthau provide a vivid though hardly edifying picture of this administrative duel. It was the kind of conflict all too common in Rooseveltian Washington, resulting almost invariably from the President's indifference to sound administration, his haphazard way of trying to get things done, and lastly his notable disinclination ever to make a final choice between rival members of his official family.

Secretary of State Hull was a man older than the President and of very different origin and background. Prior to his appointment in 1933 he had served long and successfully in Congress and had interested himself particularly in problems of international trade and tariff policy. Even earlier than Mr. Roosevelt, he had sensed the dangers in the world situation and had warned the country of them. As a man of great integrity and high principle he was especially disturbed by the rapidly progressing breakdown of international law and morality. His prescription against this menace was reaffirmation of traditional standards of justice and fair dealing, insistence on the value of peaceful methods to settle international differences, and return to more liberal trade relations as the only way to alleviate the existing world tension. His was a somewhat rigid, doctrinaire approach, criticized by those who felt that his constant harping on general principles revealed a disinclination to come to grips with concrete, practical problems. Mr. Hull was a man of the people and as such easily moved to that moral indignation characteristic of the American people when confronted by the iniquities of foreigners. With much vigor and in highly picturesque language he would lecture and at times berate foreign diplomats, without necessarily making progress toward the solution of existing issues.

Temperamentally the President and Mr. Hull had almost nothing in common. In contrast to Mr. Roosevelt, the Secretary was extremely serious, cautious, and hesitant, making an intimate relationship difficult. The evidence indicates that the President had a high regard for Mr. Hull; that he relied greatly on his Congressional experience and his continued close contacts with former colleagues. He respected and subscribed to Mr. Hull's principles and valued his ability to spot possible objections to any proposed course. Fundamentally the two men were agreed on major policies and there was no acrimonious debate between them. It may be that at times Mr. Roosevelt lost patience with the Secretary's caution and deliberation, but the record does not substantiate the oft-repeated charge that the President ignored Mr. Hull or by-passed the State Department. The Secretary was kept as fully informed as the President's habits permitted, and his views carried great weight with his chief. Actually the two men, one daring and pliable, the other circumspect and inflexible, made a good team.

Unhappily the relations between the President and his Secretary of State were even in this period somewhat clouded by the presence of Mr. Sumner Welles, the Under Secretary of State and therefore the acting Secretary in Mr. Hull's absences. Mr. Welles was a Presidential appointee and a man after the President's heart. Of highly cultured background, he was a skillful diplomat and a man of great knowledge, quick and incisive intelligence, ready ideas, and almost boundless energy. Much of the direction of the Good Neighbor Policy toward Latin America was left in his hands, but the President, who saw him informally at frequent intervals, tended to look to him also for advice and action on European affairs. It was, under the circumstances, perhaps inevitable that tension should develop between the Secretary of State and his chief subordinate. Mr. Hull resented the confabulations in the White House and suspected the Under Secretary of awaiting his (Hull's) absence in order to railroad through decisions on vital matters. Mr. Welles, in turn, may have found the hesitancy and delays of his chief trying, but was powerless to change a situation which was not of his making. However, there is nothing in the record to suggest that the personal differences between Mr. Hull and Mr. Welles had a decisive effect on the form or content of American policy.

Toward the State Department as an institution the President's attitude was not gracious. He felt that the Department and more particularly the Foreign Service contained much deadwood, by which he meant there were many men who had been appointed for social rather than for more practical considerations, who were unfriendly to his foreign as to his domestic policies, and who were not beyond making unauthorized disclosures to opposition circles. Such was certainly not in general the case, and both Secretary Hull and Under Secretary Welles tried on occasion to argue the President out of his prejudice. The State Department was, it is true, notorious for its leakage of information, but this was probably the result more often of loose organization and carelessness than of ulterior motives. It would in fact be a mistake to underline the President's suspicions. Many American Ambassadors and State Department officials were men of high caliber on whose information and judgment he counted heavily. If at times he transmitted important messages through the Navy rather than through the State Department, it was merely because of the greater security of the Navy codes; and if he transacted business directly with foreign ambassadors or leaders, it was because that was his nature. The charge of systematically circumventing the State Department is largely devoid of foundation. On the contrary, the President tried to pass along virtually all important information to Secretary Hull or his subordinates, and almost all key documents, even the President's letters to foreign potentates, were ordinarily drafted in the Department.

Within the State Department the Secretary ruled supreme. Mr. Hull liked and admired his staff and saw no need for major changes. The Department was still a relatively small organization in which the so-called "political desks" played the dominant role. In order to relieve the administrative pressure on certain chief officials, a number of them had been appointed advisers, notably for Far Eastern, Latin American, and European affairs, and for economic and legal affairs. But in this period there was still no provision for genuine staff work. On Sunday mornings the Secretary would meet with a group of officials for informal discussion and consultation. These meetings were free and easy and gave ample opportunity for the presentation of divergent views. But they were quite unsystematic, for the Secretary himself decided, on each occasion, who should be asked to attend and the selection at times was a rather baffling one. Coördination between various divisions of the Department was left largely to chance. Incoming and outgoing messages were still handled by a complicated system of distribution and required a great deal of time and energy before action could be decided and taken.

From the standpoint of the historian the records of the State Department, for all their bulk and variety, are almost as deficient as those of the White House. The reports from abroad were, to be sure, complete and, contrary to popular belief, of very high quality. Care was taken to record at once all conversations between State Department officials and the representatives of foreign governments. Consequently it is comparatively easy to determine what was known to the Department at any time and what action was taken on the basis of such knowledge. But of the reasoning that produced the decisions there is hardly a trace. The British Foreign Office practice of writing "minutes," or comments—sometimes at great length—on incoming telegrams and despatches was not followed in the State Department. No official record was kept of the Secretary's staff meetings and almost none of conferences between various divisions of the Department or between State Department officials and members of other government agencies. Excepting relatively few departmental memoranda, there is little to reflect conflicting views or register the course of debate leading to the ultimate resolution. There is slight prospect that this vital gap will ever be bridged. Since in any modern government foreign policy is closely intertwined with military and economic considerations, at least brief reference to the problem of administrative coördination is desirable. The President took no initiative to effect such coördination, being quite content, so it seems, to call in military or other experts as the occasion required. The only systematic consultation between the State, War and Navy Departments was at first provided by the Standing Liaison Committee, composed of Under Secretary Welles, the Chief of Staff of the Army, and the Chief of Naval Operations. Though this committee, which for the most part met regularly, marked a promising beginning, it soon tended to confine its deliberations to problems of hemisphere relations. It certainly did not fill the need for close contact and integrated action in foreign and defense policy. Mr. Stimson, when he became Secretary of War in June, 1940, was appalled by the President's "happy-go-lucky" methods of conducting important business. He objected particularly to the Liaison Committee, which, though not composed of the responsible departmental chiefs, reported directly to the President. Mr. Stimson therefore arranged with Secretaries Hull and Knox for meetings and discussions at the highest level.

By the beginning of 1941 this arrangement had become permanent, the three Secretaries foregathering regularly once a week. Somewhat later the group was enlarged to include Secretary Morgenthau and became known as the Cabinet Defense Council. In other words, some provision had been made, in the months preceding the Pearl Harbor attack, for a reasonable exchange of information and for mutual consultation between those primarily concerned with foreign policy and national defense. But the process of integration was far from complete and did not extend below the surface. Secretary Stimson and others despaired of ever breaking the President of his slipshod practice of conferring directly with individuals as the mood dictated. Mr. Roosevelt's was indeed not an orderly administration. Unhappily it took the tragedy of Pearl Harbor to throw the needed light, somber though it was, on the urgent necessity for closer and more effective coördination of the national security effort.

CHAPTER I

American Attitudes and Policies

1. THE POPULAR TEMPER

President Roosevelt's address at Chicago on October 5, 1937, is generally regarded as having marked an important departure in American foreign policy. By suggesting a "quarantine" against powers threatening and disturbing the peace of the world, the President for the first time during his administration had advanced a positive program. On the other hand, the violently negative reaction of the public to his suggestion furnishes the best possible proof of the unwillingness of the American people at that time to consider any degree of involvement in world affairs or any measure of participation with others in preventing the spread of conflict. The significance of this attitude requires no particular emphasis in view of the fact that by then Mussolini had already devoured Ethiopia; Hitler had reoccupied the Rhineland; Italy, Germany and Soviet Russia were intervening actively in the Spanish Civil War; and the Japanese armies were invading China. The spread of aggression was alarming, yet the American people refused to entertain any proposals for action with other nations to check the rapid deterioration of the international situation.

This negative stand was certainly not due either to ignorance or lack of interest in foreign affairs. Never before in their history had Americans been so well informed about events abroad and never before had they followed them so closely. Hundreds of thousands of young Americans had seen military service in Europe during the First World War, and further thousands had visited abroad during the prosperous twenties. The American press was represented throughout the world by able and alert correspondents. Through newspapers, magazines, books and radio the public had ample opportunity to learn of foreign developments, while countless groups for the study of world affairs had sprung up after 1920 and provided excellent forums for debate of international issues.

11

Being promptly and generally well informed, the American public—in so far as it took an interest in world affairs at all—tended to react strongly against the aggressive policies of the Fascist powers. By the autumn of 1937 hardly a trace of intellectual or spiritual neutrality remained. In the previous decade the attitude toward Mussolini and his brand of Fascism had been rather condescending and indulgent, but after the advent of Hitler in Germany (1933), Americans were quick to sense the character of the National Socialist Revolution. They seem to have grasped instinctively that what had happened in Germany was of infinitely greater import than what had taken place in Italy. Furthermore, Hitler's program from the outset had been based on racial discrimination and persecution, so that the innate dislike of Americans for all forms of totalitarianism and dictatorship was at once reinforced by strong and active hatred of racial and religious intolerance. The tragedy of the German Jews was bad enough, but the Nazi brutalities against Socialists, Communists, Catholics and dissenters of every stripe served to confirm the conviction that Nazism was a creed basically incompatible with American ideals and traditions. As a nation Americans had long had to deal with despotic governments without feeling any obligation or desire to fight them. But the Nazi phenomenon was something new and clearly struck at fundamental beliefs and traditions. In the United States the feeling spread rapidly and soon became almost universal that Fascism of the German type violated basic moral codes, Christian values, and indeed the ordinary "decencies" by which all civilized peoples aimed to abide.

Efforts were not lacking to draw conclusions from the state of affairs abroad. While American diplomats from the very beginning reported confidentially that Nazi Germany threatened to become a menace to world peace, newspaper correspondents were soon trumpeting the same warnings into the public ear and competent writers were cautioning their readers that ultimately not even remote America would be able to evade the issue.[1] But the country at large was unimpressed or at least unconvinced. Despite the activities of Huey Long and the agitation of Father Coughlin, there seemed little prospect of a rise of Fascism in the United States and, as most people preferred to think, little danger from Fascism or Nazism abroad. In the economic sphere, foreign trade was regarded as in no sense vital to the United States, and even some of the most prominent economists looked with half-amused skepticism upon the barter miracles that Dr. Hjalmar Schacht was performing for his Nazi masters. The best answer to the Nazi economic offensive, they argued, was extension of the American reciprocal trade

[1] Merely by way of illustration, reference may be made to the discerning reports of Consul General Messersmith in Berlin (excerpts in *Peace and War*, Washington, 1943, 192, 246), to William L. Shirer: *Berlin Diary* (New York, 1941), and to Hamilton Fish Armstrong: *We or They: Two Worlds in Conflict* (New York, 1936).

program. And as for a military threat, that appeared altogether beyond the limits of the plausible. At an even much later date an eminent military analyst was to declare that "Any invasion of our borders in force, even by a combination of Powers, becomes virtually impossible in the foreseeable future."[2] Colonel Charles A. Lindbergh, despite his exceptional knowledge of German air power, expressed the conviction, as late as 1941, that the United States was in no danger provided it did not waste its planes and other equipment on the British. Relying, quite naturally, on such authoritative assurances, most Americans felt secure enough and beguiled themselves with arguments supplied them in quantity by some of their most respected public figures: war is inherently evil and settles nothing in any case; being not immediately menaced, the first duty of Americans is to maintain their unique civilization and protect it from foreign contamination; the best way, therefore, to deal with Fascism and Nazism is to stay away from them and concentrate all efforts on the solution of national social and economic problems, so as to preserve intact the great stronghold of democracy.

It is a commonplace to say that isolationism was at this time rampant. For a short time during and after the First World War the American tradition of separateness, aloofness and nonentanglement with foreign powers had begun to weaken. There had sprung up some realization of the interdependence of modern nations, of the implications of foreign conflict for the American national interest, and of the need for the United States to assume a full share of responsibility for international organization and collective security. But the aftermath of the great conflict proved altogether disillusioning. The Senate rejected membership in the League of Nations and for years thereafter it was regarded as politically impossible to induce the American people to subscribe to any form of political commitment beyond that of the Monroe Doctrine. To be sure, there were throughout the entire interwar period political leaders of both parties, influential organizations, clergymen, teachers, writers and commentators who never abandoned the campaign for American participation in international organization, for collective action, and for the assumption of specific obligations to aid in forestalling aggression and war. But public sentiment was against them and became rabidly so with the onset of the great depression and the subsequent development of international tension. The economic collapse tended to throw people back on their own immediate problems, while the course of events abroad made association with other powers all the more unpalatable. Having waged a war to make the world safe for democracy, the country watched with bitter disillusionment the rise of dictatorships and the ensuing recrudescence of aggression and conflict. On all sides it was felt again that the European system was basically

[2] Hanson W. Baldwin: "Our New Long Shadow" (*Foreign Affairs*, April, 1939).

rotten, that war was endemic on that continent, and that somehow the Europeans had only themselves to blame for their plight.

In this mood, Americans were all too ready to abandon the foreigner to his own folly or iniquity, and to forswear all further crusading. It has been aptly observed that Americans, having once believed, erroneously, that war would settle everything, were now disposed to endorse the reverse fallacy that war could settle nothing. Starting from diverse premises, representatives of widely differing opinions—pacifist and imperialist, liberal and conservative, educated and ignorant—arrived at the same conclusion. By 1937 public-opinion polls indicated that a large majority of Americans believed our participation in the First World War had been a mistake. A few months later, in January, 1938, the much-debated Ludlow Amendment, which would have required a popular referendum before a declaration of war, was defeated in the House by a narrow margin of twenty-one votes, despite all efforts of the Administration to mobilize opposition against it.[3]

The prevalent aversion to foreign involvement and the determined opposition to any form of political or military commitment found their most eloquent expression in the effort to insure the United States against being drawn into another conflict, that is, in the extraordinary neutrality legislation of the years 1935-1937, which represented a startling break from the traditional adherence to established international law. The Congressional Investigating Committee under Senator Nye's chairmanship had just demonstrated to the satisfaction of most Americans that the First World War had resulted chiefly from the mad imperial ambitions of the European antagonists, and that the United States had been sucked into the conflict through insidious propaganda and the machinations of powerful munitions-making interests. The new neutrality laws were designed to forestall a repetition of such a calamity. They therefore established rigid government control over the shipment of munitions abroad, prohibited the export of arms to belligerent nations, forebade private loans or credits to nations at war, and authorized the President to forbid travel by Americans on the ships of warring states. Seemingly no loophole had been left through which the country could again be drawn into the conflicts of other nations. Here, indeed, was isolationism in action. Though cogent arguments were advanced against so startling a break and ,against the whole notion that the United States could or should in all cases remain neutral, it can hardly be disputed that public opinion warmly supported the neutrality legislation and expected highly beneficial results from it.[4]

A prominent American historian, who was at the same time one of the

[3] *Public Opinion Quarterly,* October, 1939, 599; Francis S. Wickware: "What We Think about Foreign Affairs" (*Harper's Magazine,* September, 1939); Cordell Hull: *Memoirs* (Macmillan, New York, 1948), I, 364.

[4] A telling critique of the entire program was that of Allen W. Dulles and Hamilton Fish Armstrong: *Can We Be Neutral?* (New York, 1936).

intellectual leaders of what he chose to call "nationalism," once conveniently defined isolationism as including rejection of membership in the League of Nations; nonentanglement in the political controversies of Europe and Asia; nonintervention in the wars of those continents; neutrality, peace and defense for the United States through measures appropriate to those purposes; and the pursuit of a foreign policy friendly to all nations disposed to reciprocate. To this he added, however, that "An isolationist may favor promotion of good-will and peace among nations by any and all measures compatible with nonentanglement in any association of nations empowered to designate 'aggressors' and bring engines of sanction and coercion into action against them."[5] This last remark will serve to recall the fact that the American people was at all times willing, short of commitments to act with others, to contribute in every way possible to improve the world and to prevent hostilities. In the decade after the First World War it had accomplished miracles in the way of relief· and had contributed heavily to the economic reconstruction of Europe. It had hailed with enthusiasm the conclusion of the Kellogg-Briand Pact which outlawed war, believing only too gladly that beyond this nothing was necessary. And it had applauded the efforts of its Government to further the work of disarmament initiated at the Washington Conference of 1921-1922. Those who, like Secretary of State Hull, were quick to express condemnation of injustice and aggression, to preach respect for law and order, and to plead for the peaceful settlement of disputes between nations were sure of warm support from the American public. But beyond that popular sentiment would not go. The dominant feeling was overwhelmingly opposed not only to any involvement in foreign quarrels but to participation in any collective action to prevent or settle such quarrels. Behind the high wall of neutrality the American people felt reasonably secure to pursue its own good despite all the storms that might rage abroad.

2. The President's Plan

It is well worth recalling that even before the advent of the Roosevelt Administration in 1933 the American Government had begun to appreciate the implications of the international situation, and that Mr. Henry L. Stimson, as Secretary of State under President Hoover, had made a valiant effort to establish joint action between Britain and the United States to check Japanese aggression in Manchuria. It is altogether probable that positive action at that time would have been approved by the American public and that thereby the system of collective security might have been saved. The British Government, unfortunately, failed to make the most of the opportunity and thereby assumed the chief responsibility for what in retrospect appears as little short of a tragedy. Nonetheless, the United States

[5] Charles A. Beard: *American Foreign Policy in the Making* (Yale University Press, New Haven, 1946), 17, note.

at that time advanced the doctrine of nonrecognition of territorial changes brought about by force and thereby set up a deterrent to aggression which, while obviously not decisive, was far from being a negligible factor in international relations.[6]

As for Mr. Roosevelt, his debut in matters of foreign affairs was in no sense a promising one. At the time of his inauguration he had already ceased to profess support for the League of Nations, and it has often been pointed out that, as a political realist, he had made up his mind to avoid anything like the disaster that befell President Wilson. One can understand that in the initial hectic months of his first term he was so preoccupied with domestic problems that he had little time or energy for the consideration of foreign affairs. Nevertheless, his handling of the London Economic Conference of 1933 was certainly a case of almost unpardonable bungling. Its effect seems to have been to disgust Mr. Roosevelt with European affairs. During the next several years he seems to have assumed a generally negative attitude and apparently shared the opinion that the solution of America's problems would constitute the most effective contribution he could make toward a new and better world system. Naturally a major power like the United States could not stand wholly aloof from all the great issues that agitated the world. The American Government, with the full support of the public, continued to use its best influence in the cause of disarmament, in the direction of more liberal trade policies, and in general in behalf of the peaceful settlement of international disputes. But its action in the matter of sanctions against Italy during the Ethiopian crisis lacked clarity, not to say vigor, while the policy pursued in the course of the Spanish Civil War could hardly be described as a contribution to the strengthening of democracy abroad.

It is true that the President commented adversely on the "inflexible provisions" of the neutrality legislation of 1935-1937, but there is no evidence that he disapproved its general purpose. He was merely echoing the popular sentiment when he declared that his Administration was "definitely committed to the maintenance of peace and the avoidance of any entanglements which would lead us into conflict." Even though he might, from time to time, call attention to the dangers of the European situation, he drew no new conclusions with respect to American policy. As late as August, 1936, he stated in his Chautauqua speech: "We shun political commitments which might entangle us in foreign wars; we avoid connection with the political activities of the League of Nations. . . . We are not isolationists except in so far as we seek to isolate ourselves completely from war."[7]

[6] See especially Henry L. Stimson: *The Far Eastern Crisis* (New York, 1936).

[7] Much pertinent material was assembled, for critical purposes, by Charles A. Beard: *American Foreign Policy in the Making*, 13, 134 ff., 165, 171-74; but on the President's early attitude see also William C. Bullitt: "How We Won the War and Lost the Peace" (*Life*, August 30, 1948).

Secretary Hull, perusing daily the many well-informed and discerning telegrams that flowed into the State Department from American representatives abroad, was probably more keenly aware than the President of the evil omens over Europe and perhaps more fully convinced that the United States could not afford to stand completely aloof. But the Secretary had no more thought than the President of committing this country to any positive course of political or military action. His concern was largely with the moral content and principles of international relations and how these could be saved from complete destruction. In July, 1937, he had advanced eight basic principles, to which some sixty nations hastily paid lip service. Only one Government, as Mr. Hull recalls in his *Memoirs*, had demurred at what it termed "these vague formulae." To the Secretary they were much more: "solid, living, all-essential rules . . . as vital in international relations as the Ten Commandments in personal relations."[8] Mr. Hull had long advocated disarmament and never ceased to plead for more liberal trade relations as the most promising approaches to a more prosperous and therefore more peaceful world. He clearly believed that the United States should contribute to the commonweal through economic concessions and support, and he favored coöperation with other nations at least to the extent of consultation and the exercise of moral pressure. But from long Congressional experience he was exceedingly sensitive to the feeling of the legislature and the country. He was, in fact, prone to overestimate the isolationist attitude of the nation and to underrate the chances of executive leadership. Quick to see potential objections to any positive program, he was inclined to argue that too bold a course would only serve to provoke serious dissension at home which, in turn, would be exploited by the dictators.

The Administration, having picked its way somehow through the stormy Ethiopian crisis and the initial phase of the Spanish Civil War, found itself confronted, in the summer of 1937, by the formidable though undeclared war of Japan against China. By this time the British, more directly menaced by aggression than the Americans, had reversed themselves to the extent of proposing "joint action" to induce the Japanese to cease hostilities and accept a peace settlement. Such coöperative action would certainly have been more acceptable to the American public in the Far East than in Europe, partly because American sympathy for China and dislike of Japan went far beyond merely material considerations and partly because Japanese aggression against China involved out-and-out violation of international agreements to which the United States was a party. To this should be added the fact that Japanese power was not held in high regard by Americans and that therefore it was thought that a strong stand would be less risky than a firm attitude toward the European dictators. The Japanese advance

8 Hull: *Memoirs*, I, 535-36.

into China had evoked at once a vigorous demand for an embargo on war supplies to Japan, by the shipment of which, it was reiterated, the United States was positively supporting the Japanese campaign.[9]

But despite the fact that American isolationism was never as uncompromising on Far Eastern issues as on European, the Administration gave no indication of readiness to depart from the established pattern of policy. The reply to the British suggestion of joint action was that the course thus far pursued by the two governments on "parallel lines" had been truly coöperative and that "both Governments should again, each in its own way, urge upon the Japanese and the Chinese Governments the importance of maintaining peace."[10] This document, while expressing readiness to act, left no hope whatever that the United States Government would join in any mutual or collective steps, or indeed proceed on any basis other than that of complete independence of action.

Nonetheless, the situation in the Far East was fraught with danger and it seemed desirable to Secretary Hull that the nation be alerted to the possible need for a strong stand by its Government. The Secretary and his close friend and adviser, Mr. Norman Davis, therefore suggested to the President that, in the course of a visit to the Middle West, he make a public address designed to counteract the prevalent isolationism. This was the background of the famous Quarantine Speech at Chicago on October 5, 1937, the text of which had been in part prepared in the State Department and with the collaboration of Mr. Davis. But in the final version the President decided on his own to go far beyond what had been submitted to him. In effect, he broke with isolationism, discarded the policy of strict neutrality, and stepped forward as an advocate of collective security. Calling attention to the significance of developments abroad, he admonished his listeners against supposing that the United States could remain immune from attack:

> Peace-loving nations must make a concerted effort in opposition to those violations of treaties and those ignorings of humane instincts which today are creating a state of international anarchy and instability from which there is no escape through mere isolation or neutrality. . . . There is a solidarity and interdependence about the modern world, both technically and morally, which makes it impossible for any nation completely to isolate itself from economic and political upheavals in the rest of the world, especially when such upheavals appear to be spreading and not declining.

Ninety percent of the world's people, the President insisted, desired peace; there must be some way of making their will prevail:

---

[9] Details in Herbert Feis: *The Road to Pearl Harbor* (Princeton, 1950), 10-11.

[10] Memo from the British Embassy, July 20, 1937, and the State Department reply, July 21, 1937; also memo of conversation between Mr. Hornbeck and the British Ambassador, July 21, 1937. See further Hull: *Memoirs*, I, 538-39.

When an epidemic of physical disease starts to spread, the community approves and joins in a quarantine of the patients in order to protect the health of the community against the spread of the disease. . . . War is a contagion, whether it be declared or undeclared. . . . We are determined to keep out of war, yet we cannot insure ourselves against the disastrous effects of war and the dangers of involvement. We are adopting such measures as will minimize our risk of involvement, but we cannot have complete protection in a world of disorder in which confidence and security have broken down.

Just what Mr. Roosevelt meant by "quarantine" was not revealed at the time, but according to later well-informed writers his idea was that an aggressor should be defined as any nation which, like Japan, had sent its troops on to the territory of another nation and that, once a nation had been so stigmatized, all others should pledge nonintercouse with it. In short, what he had in mind was an extreme form of sanctions.[11] For such a drastic departure neither the President's advisers nor the country at large were prepared. Mr. Hull and Mr. Davis were shocked beyond words by the President's daring improvisation. Years later, when writing his memoirs, Mr. Hull reiterated his conviction that the unfortunate "quarantine" utterance had set back the campaign for collective action by at least six months.[12] Mr. Roosevelt's address did in fact produce a strong and country-wide protest, among Democrats as among Republicans, which serves well as evidence of the popular aversion to any program of common action with other nations. Many efforts were made to smoke the President out and to discover just what he had in mind. But Mr. Roosevelt refused to be drawn. To reassure the country he stated on October 12, 1937, that sanctions against Japan were not being considered and that the purpose of the forthcoming Brussels Conference was to seek an agreement between Japan and China. Nevertheless, he insisted that he had a plan, though he refused to divulge it.[13]

It was commonly supposed at the time that the President himself recognized that he had gone too far and that, on the advice of Secretary Hull, he decided to let the whole incident sink into oblivion. The contrary, however, was the fact. Mr. Roosevelt had for some time been thinking of arranging a dramatic meeting of the world's statesmen at sea, but had now settled down to a somewhat less spectacular program, evidently inspired by Under Secretary Welles, and seemingly intended to support international action at the Brussels Conference. In the record the plan appears

[11] Joseph Alsop and Robert Kintner: *American White Paper* (New York, 1940), Appendix ii. This account was based on materials and information supplied by the White House and the State Department.
[12] Hull: *Memoirs,* I, 544 ff.
[13] Sumner Welles: *The Time for Decision* (Harper, New York, 1944), 61 ff.; Beard: *American Foreign Policy in the Making,* 184 ff.; Basil Rauch: *Roosevelt, from Munich to Pearl Harbor* (New York, 1950), 46 ff.

first in the form of a memorandum by Mr. Welles to the President, dated October 6, 1937, the very day following the President's Chicago speech. Basing his argument on certain passages of that address, Mr. Welles reasoned as follows:

No one can today affirm that such a thing as international law exists or that there is any common agreement on the part of the so-called civilized nations of the world upon the fundamental standards which should and must govern the relations between nations if world order is to be restored.

Is it not possible that before any definite progress can be made towards a solution of the innumerable and grave ills with which the world today is afflicted—and by this I mean the solution of all pending political, armament, financial and economic problems which must be solved if world peace is to be attained—that an attempt should be made to secure general international agreement as to the fundamental norms which should govern international conduct?

If such bases were to be agreed upon by common international consent, is it not likely that that agreement upon common standards will both expedite and facilitate the practical agreements necessary to reëstablish peace in the world?

I therefore suggest for the President's consideration that he inquire of the other governments of the world whether they will be willing to take part in a world conference which he will be prepared to call because of the reasons above indicated for the purpose of attempting to achieve a common agreement upon the following questions:

1. The basic principles which should be observed in international relations (as, for example, noninterference in the internal affairs of other nations).

2. The laws and customs of land warfare.

3. The laws and customs of naval warfare.

4. The rights and obligations of neutrals both on land and at sea, except in so far as they may be restricted by existing international agreements.

5. The right of freedom of access on the part of all peoples to raw materials.

The first of these five points covers by implication the whole field of international law. I do not suggest that any attempt be made at the conference proposed to undertake the codification of international law. This might well be delegated by common agreement to expert committees appointed for that purpose. What I do suggest is that this first point embrace those principles which are of primary and present importance.

If this suggestion is given consideration, it should be made clear beyond any doubt that the proposal envisages solely the reaching of common agreement upon standards of international conduct and does not embrace either political, economic or financial adjustments.

On this basis I should assume that the non-dictatorial governments would be willing to coöperate. I should likewise assume that Germany and Italy would find it to their advantage to coöperate. Under present circumstances it would appear improbable that Japan would take part.

From the standpoint of an improved world psychology it would appear to me that a very great advance would be attained if the overwhelming majority of the nations could reach an agreement upon such principles, because of the inherent need for the reëstablishment of those principles, and that, in addition thereto, the mere fact that the nations of the world today could by concerted action agree upon anything of vital importance would in itself be a material step forward.[14]

This plan could hardly be described as daring or heroic. Its extreme modesty simply reflected once more the circumspection of official American thinking. But at any rate it was a plan and that was what the President felt he needed. He responded at once, but directed that in the first instance the five points be submitted to other governments through diplomatic channels. If they acknowledged the need for international agreement, the United States Government should then announce its willingness to work with a restricted number of other Governments in determining the principles and standards believed desirable and necessary. Thereupon the findings should be reported to the other Governments and "if it is then ascertained that the great majority of the Governments of the world are in accord, it will be determined whether this agreement shall be ratified by means of a world conference called specifically for that purpose or whether formal agreement shall be arrived at through diplomatic channels."[15]

It will be seen at once that Mr. Roosevelt, far from inflating the Welles proposal, decided for an even less pretentious program. And yet, during the ensuing couple of weeks, he evidently changed his mind and determined to make a grand gesture. The documentary record is so scant that it is impossible to retrace the discussions that must have taken place between the President and Mr. Welles or to specify the factors that may have influenced them to change their approach. It may be noted, however, that in the interval two episodes occurred which may well have swayed the President. On October 11, 1937, Assistant Secretary Messersmith, who had been recalled from Vienna on the grounds that his great knowledge of Central European affairs would be more valuable in Washington, presented Secretary Hull with a long memorandum covering the current world situation. The heart of Messersmith's argument was that, although the Far Eastern and Mediterranean problems for the moment held the center of the stage, the crux of the world problem was still Germany: "With the German problem settled and a government there with which the United States and other countries could deal in a normal way, the difficult questions in the Far East and in the Mediterranean, as well as the general European question, would permit of a fairly ready, gradual and reasonable settlement." The Assistant Secretary warned particularly of the dangers of the appeasement policies which were being followed by the European democracies: "There is no logical escape from the fact that, if the lawless nations continue to gain their ends through force, or through

[14] Memo of Welles to the President, October 6, 1937 (*Roosevelt Papers:* Secretary's File, Box 62).

[15] Memo of Welles to the President, October 9, 1937, summarizing the President's desires as expressed to Welles on the preceding day (*Roosevelt Papers:* Secretary's File, Box 62).

the threat of force, or if too dangerous compromises continue to be made as they have been in recent years, disintegration will proceed inexorably and to the point at which the peace of the world will be definitely endangered and catastrophic war the sole outcome."[16]

This memorandum was taken to the President by Mr. Hull and may well have persuaded him of the need for expanding his program. He had already heard from Paris that the French Premier, M. Chautemps, had expressed eagerness "to sit down quietly with President Roosevelt and ask exactly what he, the President, had in mind when he spoke of the peace-loving nations making a 'concerted effort' in opposition to violations of treaties."[17] And in this connection it was also noteworthy that on October 11, 1937, the German Ambassador in Washington indicated to Mr. Welles that his Government aimed at the solution of its claims through peaceful methods of negotiation, rather than through force.[18] All told, there was at least some ground for thinking the time auspicious for a spectacular move on the President's part.

Mr. Roosevelt hit upon the idea of inviting all diplomatic representatives in Washington to meet with him at the White House on the afternoon of Armistice Day (November 11), on which occasion he would read them a message which, at the same time, would be presented to all chiefs of state through American representatives abroad. In substance he was to propose an effort to reach agreement on the following four matters:

1. The essential and fundamental principles which should be observed in international relations.

2. The methods through which all peoples may obtain the right to have access upon equal and effective terms to raw materials and other elements necessary for their economic life.

3. The methods by which international agreements may be pacifically revised.

4. In the unhappy event of war, the rights and obligations of neutrals both on land and at sea, except in so far as in the case of certain nations they may be determined by existing international agreements; and the laws and customs of warfare whose observance neutrals may be entitled to require.

As in the earlier version of the plan, the United States Government was to offer to confer with a number of other Governments and then submit the findings to all.[19]

16 Memo of Messersmith to Hull, October 11, 1937; also letter from Mr. Messersmith to the authors, July 9, 1950.
17 Telegram from Wilson (Chargé d'Affaires at Paris), October 7, 1937.
18 Memo of conversation between Welles and Ambassador Dieckhoff, October 11, 1937; similarly, memo of conversation between Mr. Hugh Wilson and Ambassador Dieckhoff, October 13, 1937.
19 Letter of Welles to the President, October 26, 1937, to which two drafts are attached. These differ from each other only inasmuch as one stresses the urgent need for reduction of armaments and points out that this could be more easily attained after agreement "upon practical foundations for peace" (Roosevelt Papers: Secretary's File, Box 23).

It will be observed at once that, in comparison with the original project, the new program gave more prominence to economic questions and above all to the problem of treaty revision. In fact, the final draft of the proposal included this significant statement by the President:

I recognize that however essential it may be for the nations of the earth to reach a joint accord as to these norms of international conduct, such agreement alone may not necessarily secure the maintenance of peace. It is possible that before the foundations of a lasting peace can be secured, international adjustments of various kinds may be found in order to remove those inequities which exist by reason of the nature of certain of the settlements reached at the termination of the Great War. The traditional policy of freedom from political involvement which the Government of the United States has maintained and will maintain is well known. In the determination of political readjustments the Government of the United States can play no part. But it has seemed to me that every kind of adjustment, if undertaken, might perhaps be more readily arrived at if all nations come to a common agreement as to the principles upon which healthy international relationships should be based.

This passage, though it does not propose a policy of appeasement and though it scrupulously repeats the American abstention in political matters, nevertheless recognizes the "inequities" of the peace settlements and admits the possible need for concessions by others. In his letter to the President, Mr. Welles not only pointed out that the dramatic meeting at the White House would strengthen the position of the democracies at the Brussels Conference and would put an end to misinterpretation of the Quarantine Speech in the United States, but added significantly: "The reference in the suggested draft to the probable need for readjustment of the settlements arrived at after the conclusion of the World War would, I think, almost inevitably create a favorable reaction on the part of Germany."

Historically this plan is of great interest as an expression of the President's and Mr. Welles's current thinking on American participation in collective action to ensure peace. Practically it came to nothing because of what Mr. Welles has described as the almost hysterical opposition of some of the President's chief advisers. This refers especially to Secretary Hull, who has confessed his objections to the scheme, but without making clear the grounds for his position. In view of the Secretary's great concern for the principles of international intercourse, he might have been expected to subscribe wholeheartedly to an effort at agreement on such principles. As a matter of fact, Mr. Welles reported to the President as late as October 26, 1937, that Secretary Hull had read the draft and considered it "entirely sound." His opposition must therefore have come at the last moment, and one can only surmise that he lost heart. After the violent reaction to the Quarantine Speech, he probably feared that the President's powerful initiative would evoke a storm of protest in Congress and throughout the country, to say nothing of the fact that, in the event of failure, the Administration and the nation would suffer a serious loss of prestige. At the very least Mr. Hull felt that the support of Britain or France should be secured before any move was made.[20]

Though for the time being he shelved his plan, the President remained firmly convinced that the United States, in its own interest, could no longer stand wholly aloof from the world crisis. In conversation with a visiting French statesman he expressed serious doubt whether the policy of neutrality at any price would give the United States the security it desired. On the contrary, he voiced the opinion that such a policy was full of danger and might lead to war. He conveyed to his visitor the impression that he was intent on arousing the American public and on developing international coöperation in the effort to save the peace.[21] Such action appeared all the more urgent as the Brussels Conference of November, 1937, failed completely to advance a settlement of the Far Eastern problem or even to check the victorious movement of the Japanese troops into China. The shocking and ominous Japanese attack on the USS *Panay* in December, 1937, brought the United States to the verge of war and certainly helped to illuminate the explosive character of the international situation as it touched even the American people.

Strangely enough it was not this crisis but the evolution of the situation in Europe that inspired the President to resume his plan in January, 1938. During the preceding month Lord Halifax had paid a visit to Berlin and had made it clear to Hitler that the British Government was prepared to embark on a policy of appeasement in the hope of arriving at a settlement of differences. Obviously after discussion with the President, Under Secretary Welles on January 10, 1938, drew up a memorandum outlining the procedure for implementation of the October plan, and specifying particularly the methods for selecting nine representatives to work with the United States Government in drafting the bases of agreement. The Latin American governments were to name two delegates and Sweden, the Netherlands, Belgium, Switzerland, Hungary, Yugoslavia and Turkey were each to be invited to nominate one. These details, though interesting, are not important. The instructive sections of the Welles memorandum were those bearing on larger considerations, which deserve quotation at least in part:

[20] See Hull: *Memoirs*, I, 546; Welles: *The Time for Decision*, 64 ff.; and Welles's later account: "Thwarted Peace Plan" (*Washington Post*, May 4, 1948).

[21] Report of the French Chargé d'Affaires in Washington, M. Henry, of November 7, 1937, and letter from Henry to the Director of the French Foreign Office, November 18, 1937. These documents were captured by the Germans in 1940 and published in an article entitled: "Roosevelt's Kriegswille gegen Japan" (*Berliner Monatshefte*, February, 1943, 53-60).

It is my belief that the proposal in itself will lend support and impetus to the effort of Great Britain, supported by France, to reach the bases for a practical understanding with Germany both on colonies and upon security, as well as upon European adjustments. Great Britain and France are now equally persuaded that no approach to Italy is feasible unless this prior understanding with Germany is successfully attained.

Should this practical readjustment be discussed and pushed during the period when the recommendations envisaged in this Government's proposal are being determined, it is obvious that each of the two parallel negotiations will be guided in part by the decisions arrived at in the other; this Government serving as a channel of information, and no more, insofar as the negotiations between and among the great powers of Europe are concerned. It is, however, probable that the influence of this Government with regard to the problem of limitation of armaments in both parallel negotiations would be helpful.

In this connection it is important to remember that in the Hitler-Halifax conversations Hitler expressed his willingness to agree immediately to the elimination of offensive armaments. It is equally important to recall that Mussolini six months ago publicly suggested that the President take the leadership in a move for immediate limitation and eventual reduction of armaments.

If the German and Italian Governments do not reach a practical understanding with Great Britain and France as a result of their parallel negotiations above mentioned, it is possible that they will not acquiesce in the recommendations formulated as a result of the initiative of the United States. In such event, which would seem to be the worst of possible contingencies, this Government would at least have obtained the support of all the Governments of the world, other than those inseparably linked with the Berlin-Rome axis, for practical recommendations which would insure world peace and which would safeguard modern civilization. The rallying of public opinion on a world scale to those policies which alone can make for peace and economic progress would in itself be productive of practical good because of its inevitable repercussions on the German and Italian populations, as well as upon those smaller countries of Europe which have been feeling increasingly during these past three years that the great democracies have surrendered their leadership and that consequently they themselves, as a means of self protection, must align themselves with Rome and Berlin.

Finally, if Germany and Italy solve their practical problems with Great Britain and France, it would seem probable that their present support of Japan will be very greatly weakened—at least to an extent sufficient to obligate Japan to make peace with China upon terms not inconsistent with the principles of the Nine Power Treaty.[22]

From the foregoing it is plain that the President's project, only slightly expanded, was now intended to buttress the attempt of Britain to reach agreement with Germany. Though involving no approval of British appeasement, it certainly implied acceptance of it. In the event of failure, it was thought that the plan would have at least the moral effect of rallying

[22] Memo of Welles to the President, January 10, 1938. The substance of the argumentation is given also in Welles: *The Time for Decision*, 66 ff.

world opinion. Though Mr. Norman Davis urged that France, Germany and Italy as well as Britain should be sounded out beforehand, Mr. Roosevelt confined himself to Mr. Hull's original suggestion that the London Government be approached first. On January 11, 1938, the President sent a confidential message to Prime Minister Chamberlain outlining the plan, while Mr. Welles indicated to the British Ambassador that failure of his Government to respond favorably might result in the destruction of American confidence in Britain.[23]

Despite this admonition, Mr. Chamberlain would have nothing of the American proposal, partly no doubt because he was impressed with the strength of isolationist sentiment in the United States and had convinced himself that the Washington Government could not be counted on for anything beyond mere words, and partly because, in the words of Mr. Churchill, he "was imbued with a sense of a special and personal mission to come to friendly terms with the dictators of Italy and Germany, and he conceived himself capable of achieving this relationship."[24] Fearing lest American intervention jeopardize the negotiations on which he had already embarked, he undertook to dispose of the matter at once. Without consulting Foreign Secretary Eden, who was abroad, he replied to the President (January 13, 1938) expressing appreciation for having been consulted and for the President's willingness to take "a courageous initiative" in world affairs. But, he explained, the British Government was hopeful of appeasing Italy and Germany and was, in fact, prepared to recognize the Italian conquest of Ethiopia if the Italian Government gave evidence of a "desire to contribute to the restoration of confidence and friendly relations." Under the circumstances he suggested that Mr. Roosevelt might wish to consider "whether there is not a risk of his proposal cutting across our efforts here." The President's intervention, he thought, might lead the dictators to reject a solution, or at any rate to raise their price.[25]

This reply must have struck the White House like a bombshell, not only because it constituted a none too polite rejection of the President's proposal, but because it put British policy into an entirely new light. It had been the belief of the State Department that the British would try to negotiate first with Hitler, and with regard to "injustices" of the peace settlements. It now emerged that they were directing their efforts toward Italy and that they were about to recognize recent aggression, ignoring entirely the established American policy in such matters. After discussion

[23] Winston S. Churchill: *The Gathering Storm* (Houghton Mifflin, Boston, 1948), 251. The text of the President's message has not been found in the State Department archives, nor in the Roosevelt papers.

[24] Churchill: *The Gathering Storm*, 221, 242; Keith Feiling: *The Life of Neville Chamberlain* (Macmillan, New York), 322-25, quoting private letters of October, 1937, and of February, 1938.

[25] Message of Mr. Chamberlain to the President, January 13, 1938 (received in Washington on January 14, 1938).

with Mr. Hull and Mr. Welles, the President on January 17, 1938, replied to Mr. Chamberlain, saying that he had no alternative but to postpone his plan "for a short while," pending the outcome of the British efforts. In grave terms he indicated his uneasiness about the British course:

A surrender by His Majesty's Government of the principle of non-recognition at this time would have serious effect upon public opinion in this country. Public opinion in the United States will only support this Government in measures of pacific coöperation with the other peace-loving nations of the world, provided these measures of coöperation are destined to reëstablish and maintain principles of international law and morality. The recognition of the conquest of Ethiopia, which at some appropriate time may have to be regarded as an accomplished fact, would seem to me to be a matter which affects all nations which are committed to the principles of non-recognition and which should consequently be dealt with as an integral part of the measures for world appeasement, in which all the nations of the world have previously demonstrated their common interest and their willingness to bear their individual responsibility.

In conversation with the British Ambassador, Mr. Hull minced no words in referring to the projected recognition of Italian conquests: "The desperado nations would capitalize it as a virtual ratification of their policy of outright treaty wrecking and the seizure of land by force of arms. . . . The repercussions in the Pacific area might be very serious," and in the United States the British step would "rouse a feeling of disgust, which would revive and multiply all fears of pulling the chestnuts out of the fire; it would be represented as a corrupt bargain completed in Europe at the expense of interests in the Far East in which America was intimately concerned."[26]

Thus far the President's initiative, far from establishing "parallel action" in support of the British appeasement negotiations, seemed likely to create serious disagreement between London and Washington. But in the meanwhile (January 15, 1938) Mr. Eden had returned to London and had insisted on reconsideration of the whole matter by the Cabinet. As a result Mr. Chamberlain sent a new and more cordial message to the President on January 21, 1938, in which he not only explained that British recognition of Italy's Ethiopian conquest would be extended only as part of a general settlement, but also stated that he had now come to the conclusion that he should welcome the President's initiative, to the success of which the British would contribute to their utmost, whenever Mr. Roosevelt decided to go on with it.[27]

[26] Message of the President to Mr. Chamberlain, January 17, 1938; memo of conversation between Hull and the British Ambassador, January 17, 1938; Churchill: *The Gathering Storm*, 252-53.

[27] The text of this message has not been found in the official American records, but it is summarized by Churchill: *The Gathering Storm*, 253, and by Welles: *The Time for Decision*, 68. See further Feiling: *The Life of Neville Chamberlain*, 336, and Hull: *Memoirs*, I, 573, 579-81.

That decision Mr. Roosevelt never quite managed to reach. On February 2, 1938, he replied to British inquiries that he would give some indication of plans in the next few days, but a week later Mr. Welles explained to the British Ambassador that the military crisis in Germany (resignation of General von Fritsch, dismissal of General von Blomberg, assumption of the supreme command by Hitler himself) required further clarification, but that the President intended to proceed with his plan "in the relatively near future" and was awaiting British comments and suggestions. Before any such could be submitted, Mr. Eden resigned in protest against the Cabinet's Italian policy, and early in March, 1938, Hitler's occupation of Austria disillusioned the British in their hopes of appeasing the Nazi leader. Thereafter the President's plan faded from the picture.[28] The only significant feature of the closing phase of the conversations was the British misunderstanding, possibly intentional, of the American attitude toward appeasement. This is a matter of some importance and therefore warrants particular attention.

The British Ambassador in Washington reported to his Government that on January 22, 1938, Under Secretary Welles had told him that "the President regarded recognition (of the Italian conquest of Ethiopia) as an unpleasant pill which we should both have to swallow, and he wished that we should both swallow it together."[29] If accurately reported, this statement was certainly compromising. Actually it is hardly plausible, for there was no reason why the United States Government should ever swallow the pill of recognition, and the President had stated his position clearly in his message to Mr. Chamberlain on January 17, 1938. When, on February 2, 1938, Sir Ronald Lindsay inquired of Mr. Welles whether the President had anything further to say on the subject in view of Mr. Chamberlain's explanations (message of January 21, 1938), he was told that Mr. Roosevelt had expressed himself with "complete and entire clarity" in his first reply to the Prime Minister and that obviously there was nothing to add.[30]

The suspicion that Ambassador Lindsay did not always convey the substance of Washington conversations faithfully is strengthened by further records. According to a State Department memorandum of conversation between Mr. Welles and Sir Ronald on February 25, 1938, the Ambassador inquired about the American reaction to recent events in England which had led to the resignation of Mr. Eden. Mr. Welles's notes were as follows:

I said that I could only answer in very general terms, namely, that I trusted that the realistic and energetic efforts which the British Prime Minister was making towards reaching a peaceful solution to the various political adjustments in

---

[28] Memos of conversation between Welles and Ambassador Lindsay, February 2 and 9, 1938.

[29] Churchill: *The Gathering Storm*, 253.

[30] Memo of conversation between Welles and Ambassador Lindsay, February 2, 1938.

Europe might meet with success and that there might result therefrom the opportunity for a general world appeasement which would once more make possible the
reëstablishment of those principles of international conduct to which this Government is so firmly committed and without which it did not believe any permanent
peace could be found.[31]

This statement speaks for itself, leaving no doubt that American official
opinion wished the British success in their efforts, but without prejudging
their methods, without taking a stand on any specific issue, without assuming any responsibility. The British reaction therefore came as a disagreeable surprise. Early in March, 1938, Mr. Welles received from the new
Foreign Secretary, Lord Halifax, a message of which the salient passages
were these:

> I am very much gratified to learn that the President and Administration
> consider the procedure of His Majesty's Government to be right and I trust
> they may be justified in thinking that prospects are favourable. I am confident
> of their desire to help and we shall be sustained in our efforts by the knowledge
> that we have the sympathy of the United States.
>
> For any real and lasting betterment of the situation it will doubtless be
> desirable to seek some scheme of general coöperation in Europe both political
> and economic. If the United States Government could at any time see their
> way to assist or encourage such a development, that would evidently be of the
> greatest value. It is for that reason I propose to keep the United States Govern-
> ment informed of the progress of our negotiations so that they may, if they will,
> help us with their advice or criticism, and so that the President may, if he is
> so disposed, judge whether at any point it might be opportune for him to take
> independent but correlated action. I trust he would be willing to give us some
> warning of any initiative which he may contemplate.

Mr. Welles, undoubtedly after consultation with the President, at once
challenged this statement, whereupon the Ambassador admitted that he
had probably overemphasized the Under Secretary's earlier remarks and that
Lord Halifax in turn had read more into the report than had been intended. The occasion was such that Mr. Welles thought it well to restate
the American position explicitly:

> I said that I felt it necessary in the most friendly way to make it clear that I
> had never indicated in our previous conversation that the President or any
> responsible officials of this Government had undertaken to determine or much
> less to say to the British Government that they considered its procedure "to be
> right." I had said that this Government was, of course, adopting an attitude of
> contemplation and that it hoped that the British Government in its endeavor
> to find a solid foundation for a political appeasement in Europe would meet
> with a complete measure of success. I said that as the Ambassador knew from his

[31] Memo of conversation between Welles and Ambassador Lindsay February 25, 1938.

knowledge of the proposal which the President had had under consideration for some time that the President frankly recognized that certain political appeasements in Europe with which this Government had no direct concern and in which this Government could not participate were evidently an indispensable factor in the finding of bases for world peace; that in that sense and in that spirit I had said to the Ambassador that this Government trusted the negotiations for these political appeasements would prove completely successful, but that I wanted to make it very clear that this Government had not attempted to pass upon the methods of approach determined upon by Mr. Chamberlain nor in any other way to offer advice or counsel as to the manner in which the negotiations were being conducted.

In conclusion the Under Secretary noted:

I reminded the Ambassador that the President had made it emphatically clear that this Government did not intend to participate in any way in the questions of European political appeasement and that the only initiative which the President had contemplated was that concerning which the British Government had been fully informed. I said that for the time being the President had determined to hold that initiative in abeyance as the British Government had already been advised and that as the Ambassador had been informed, the British Government would be informed should the President at some subsequent date determine that it was desirable to take any action of the kind which he had previously contemplated.[32]

Even this very complete restatement of the American position did not deter the British from further efforts to associate the United States with the appeasement policy. On April 14, 1938, Lord Halifax sent a message announcing the forthcoming signature of the agreement with Italy and expressing the hope that the President would share the British view that the agreement embodied "a real contribution towards world appeasement." In that case, he added, the British Government would be grateful if the President could give "some public indication of his approval of the agreement itself and of the principles which have inspired it." Mr. Roosevelt was evidently not very enthusiastic, for he wrote Mr. Welles, in Secretary Hull's absence: "I suppose the last paragraph needs some answer." Thereupon the Under Secretary drafted a rather cool press statement, which was released on April 19, 1938, with only slight change by the President. After recalling the American faith in the promotion of world peace through solution of controversies by peaceful negotiation and through means of economic appeasement, the statement continued: "It [the Government] does not attempt to pass upon the political features of accords such as that recently reached between Great Britain and Italy, but this Government has

[32] Memo of conversation between Welles and Ambassador Lindsay on March 7, 1938 (dated March 8); message from Welles to the President reporting on the matter.

seen the conclusion of an agreement with sympathetic interest because it is proof of the value of peaceful negotiations."[33]

It is quite possible that the President's hesitancy about going on with his plan was due to anxiety lest the United States become too deeply involved with the British appeasement policy. Even though nothing came of the plan, it is patently important as reflecting Mr. Roosevelt's first positive program for collective action to forestall aggression and war. Mr. Churchill, indeed, has attached the utmost significance to it and to Mr. Chamberlain's unfortunate reaction. In his own words: "We must regard its rejection— for such it was—as the loss of the last frail chance to save the world from tyranny otherwise than by war. . . . That Mr. Chamberlain, with his limited outlook and inexperience of the European scene, should have possessed the self-sufficiency to wave away the proffered hand stretched out across the Atlantic leaves one, even at this date, breathless with amazement."[34] This is, of course, the view of a statesman whose great objective, then and later, was to associate the United States with the world crisis on almost any terms and who was therefore bound to consider the negative treatment of any American initiative a major blunder. On the other hand, Mr. Welles feels that if the President had not yielded to Mr. Hull's advice to sound out the British first, his plan would have made such an impression on the whole world that neither the British nor the Axis powers could have refused to lend at least apparent coöperation.[35]

And yet the question may be raised whether in fact the plan held so much promise. It must be remembered that the program was a very modest, very general one, like the statement of principles by Secretary Hull, to which almost all Governments had promptly assented. If put into effect, the Roosevelt plan would certainly have given rise to much discussion, but even if agreement had been eventually reached, it is not at all certain that such agreement would have advanced the settlement of burning specific issues. Since the publication of Axis records captured during the war, it has become perfectly patent that the ambitions of the Nazi leaders went far beyond what reasonable statesmen in other countries would have thought possible at the time, and that therefore the move contemplated by Mr. Roosevelt, like the appeasement efforts of Mr. Chamberlain, would probably have been doomed to failure. Conceivably, a really strong stand by the United States Government in support of the British might have changed the course of events, but the foregoing narrative should suffice to

[33] Text in *Documents on American Foreign Relations*, I, 276. For the background we have used the message from Halifax, transmitted in a telegram from Kennedy (London), April 15, 1938; the memo from the President to Welles, April 18, 1938; the letter from Welles to the President, submitting a draft, April 18, 1938. See also Hull: *Memoirs*, I, 579-80.

[34] Churchill: *The Gathering Storm*, 254 ff.

[35] Welles: *The Time for Decision*, 67.

show that nothing of the kind was even remotely envisaged in Washington. Mr. Roosevelt and his advisers sympathized with the British and wished them well in whatever efforts they felt constrained to make in the direction of peaceful adjustment, but there was never any question of approving or supporting their specific policy and certainly no thought of assuming any political or military commitment in connection with it. Under the circumstances Hitler was perfectly safe in discounting the influence of the United States.

3. Munich Crisis

Throughout the dispute that arose in the summer of 1938 over the German claims against Czechoslovakia, the United States Government maintained its "attitude of contemplation," which Mr. Stimson once stigmatized as "the policy of amoral drift." The country knew nothing of the President's grand conference plan, and he himself made no important pronouncement on foreign affairs until he issued his famous declaration of solidarity with Canada in the Kingston address of August 18, 1938. As the European tension developed the American public followed the situation with rapt attention, but gave little indication of desiring or approving any intervention by the United States.

Hitler's absorption of Austria and his dragooning of the Czechoslovak Government certainly aroused indignation and fanned the flames of hatred for the Nazi regime, but it was hardly suggested that the United States should do anything practical about it. The American Ambassadors in London and Paris were kept fully informed of developments and reported in detail to Washington, but Mr. Chamberlain at least cherished no hope of American action and was determined, like M. Bonnet on the French side, to go to almost any lengths, at the expense of the Czechs, to avoid the outbreak of hostilities with Germany. As the crisis came to a head in September, 1938, Lord Halifax from time to time inquired as to the President's attitude, but without ever making a formal request. In reply the State Department simply referred to a radio speech delivered by Secretary Hull on August 16, 1938, and to the President's address at Kingston, Ontario, two days later. But while these pronouncements restated the dangers of isolation and called upon the American people to coöperate with other nations in efforts to check lawlessness and preserve peace, they drew the line at foreign entanglements. The British could derive little comfort from them, or from the State Department's position "that it would not be practicable to be more specific as to our reaction in hypothetical circumstances."[36]

Bonnet, to be sure, tried to go farther. He suggested (September 8) that

---

[36] Telegrams from Johnson (London), August 24, 1938; from Kennedy (London) August 31, 1938; to Kennedy, September 1, 1938; from Kennedy, September 10, 1938; from Kennedy, September 14, 1938.

in case of dire necessity the President might act as arbiter and (September 12) that the United States Government might speak out in Berlin against the use of force, but these ideas were given no encouragement.[37] Not until the tension reached the breaking point (after September 23), did the President bestir himself. On September 24, Ambassador Bullitt had cabled urging that if the British and French decided to reject the German demands of September 23, the President should appeal to the chiefs of state of Britain, France, Germany, Italy and Poland to send representatives to The Hague to discuss ways and means of preserving peace, and that he should offer to send an American representative as well.

Apparently Mr. Roosevelt adopted this proposal with some enthusiasm and even contemplated including an offer to act as arbitrator. But there was some opposition on the part of his advisers, probably of Secretary Hull, who argued that the Germans were armed to the teeth, that they were clearly set on aggression, and that nothing short of a display of adequate force would deter them.[38] The President therefore dropped the idea of arbitration, for fear lest it have "untoward domestic effects," as Mr. Welles explained to Ambassador Bullitt. On the morning of September 26, he sent messages to Chancellor Hitler, President Beneš, Prime Minister Chamberlain and Premier Daladier pointing out the dangers of a rupture, recalling the Kellogg-Briand Pact and other provisions for peaceful settlement, expressing confidence that the existing differences could be settled by resort to reason, and urging that negotiations looking to a "peaceful, fair and constructive settlement" be continued. Hitler, as well as the other addressees, responded immediately, but with a long and windy exposition and vindication of the German claims.

Thereupon the State Department invited all other Governments to support the American appeal and the President personally besought the aid of Mussolini in behalf of continued negotiations. In a second message to Hitler (September 27), the President reiterated his view that existing differences could and should be settled by pacific methods and that the use of force might lead to a general war "as unnecessary as it is unjustifiable." If there were need to supplement the current negotiations, he suggested an immediate meeting in some neutral European city, which "would offer the opportunity for this and correlated questions to be solved in a spirit of justice, of fair dealing, and, in all human probability, with greater permanence." But to forestall criticism at home, Mr. Roosevelt took care to add: "The Government of the United States has no political involvements in Europe, and will assume no obligations in the conduct of the

---

[37] Telegrams from Bullitt (Paris), September 8, 12, 1938; memos of conversation between Mr. Moffat and the French Ambassador, September 13, 15, 1938.
[38] Telegram from Bullitt, September 24, 1938; Hull: *Memoirs*, I, 588 ff.

present negotiations. Yet in our own right we recognize our responsibilities as a part of a world of neighbors."[39]

The President's proposal, as made to Hitler, was couched in minimum terms. The idea of offering himself as arbitrator had been dropped, and Bullitt's suggestion that a stern warning against sending troops across the frontiers had been discarded. Above all, nothing was said of sending an American representative to the projected conference, while the American policy of noninvolvement was explicitly restated. All these items reflect the President's caution and his anxiety not to offend the American public. It so happened that on this occasion it made little difference, for there is no reason to suppose that the President's appeal influenced Hitler in his decision to call the Munich Conference.[40]

Immediately after it was known in Washington that Mr. Chamberlain had, accepted Hitler's invitation, the President instructed Ambassador Kennedy to transmit to the Prime Minister a laconic message: "Good man."[41] This somewhat indiscreet step need not, however, be taken to mean more than approval of Mr. Chamberlain's decision to negotiate further, a decision which afforded the greatest relief on both sides of the Atlantic and unleashed "a wild scramble for stocks" on the New York Stock Exchange. Mr. Roosevelt's congratulation had nothing to do with the specific terms agreed on between Chamberlain and Hitler on September 30, 1938, and the State Department hastened to announce that while that settlement had brought "a universal sense of relief," the United States Government would

[39] All these messages are printed in *Peace and War*, 425 ff. We have used further a memo from Moffat to Welles, September 26, 1938, reporting a transatlantic telephone conversation with Ambassador Bullitt; a memo of telephone conversation between Welles and Bullitt, September 26, 1938; a tel. from Bullitt, September 27, 1938; a memo of telephone conversation between Welles and Bullitt, September 27, 1938; and a memo of telephone conversation between Welles and Kennedy, September 27, 1938.

[40] Although at the time the British tended to give the President credit for Hitler's decision, it appears that Mussolini's favorable intervention was due rather to Chamberlain's appeal, transmitted through Lord Perth, than to the President's message. Nonetheless, it is worth noting that the Roosevelt message to Mussolini was known to the Italian Foreign Office before Lord Perth communicated the Chamberlain message (10:30 A.M. on September 28, 1938) and may therefore have had a bearing on the Duce's decision to intervene. At what time Hitler received the President's appeal could not be determined. On this point we have used tels. from Phillips, September 28, 29, October 1, and Phillips's letter to the President, October 6, 1938; tel. to Phillips, September 30, 1938; letter of the President to Phillips, October 17, 1938 (this item in *F.D.R.: His Personal Letters, 1928-1945*, Duell, New York, 1950, 818-19); tel. to Wilson (Berlin), October 18, 1938, and tels. from Wilson, October 20, 21, 1938.

[41] Tel. to Kennedy, sent about 1 P.M. on September 28, 1938, and received in London at 8 P.M. Kennedy reported that he delivered the message to Chamberlain fifteen minutes later. Hitler's invitation was communicated to Chamberlain while he was making a statement in Parliament. He at once announced his acceptance. Since the proceedings were broadcast by radio, this fact was known in Washington at 10:30 A.M. Kennedy's report was not received until 3:30 P.M. and therefore had no direct bearing on the President's congratulatory telegram.

not undertake "to pass upon the merits of the differences to which the Four-Power Pact signed at Munich on yesterday related."[42] That had been the official position throughout the appeasement negotiations, and there is no reason to suppose that the President at that or any other time took a stand with regard to the Chamberlain program. The only available evidence on this point is a telegram from the President to the Prime Minister of October 5, 1938, suggesting that he use his personal contact with Hitler to bring about an alleviation of the racial persecution in Germany. This message begins thus:

I fully share your hope and belief that there exists today the greatest opportunity in years for the establishment of a new order based on justice and on law. Now that you have established personal contact with Chancellor Hitler, I know that you will be taking up with him from time to time many of the problems which must be resolved in order to bring about that new and better order.[43]

This passage admits of no doubt that Mr. Roosevelt at least momentarily shared the Prime Minister's optimism about future relations with Germany; in other words, that he still placed some reliance on the Fuehrer's assurances and promises. Like Mr. Chamberlain and the whole world, he was soon to be disabused, but for the moment he rejoiced that peace had been preserved, that the dispute, whatever its merits, had been settled, and that there had been no occasion to transgress the bounds so clearly set by American opinion. Those bounds the President had observed scrupulously. He had advanced a program of collective action to determine principles, but in view of Mr. Chamberlain's fear lest that program jeopardize his efforts at appeasement, Mr. Roosevelt had held it in abeyance and had left the Prime Minister a free field. Relatively unconcerned with the terms of appeasement so long as they did not touch American interests (like the proposed recognition of Italian conquests), he hoped for British success and at the height of the Munich crisis used all his influence to ensure further negotiation. The settlement of disputes by peaceful methods was his dominant objective, so much so, in fact, that he persuaded himself that the Munich agreement opened vistas to a new and better order.

4. DAWN OF DISILLUSION

In many years the American public had not been so deeply stirred by foreign affairs as by the crisis of September, 1938. Day after day excited radio commentators had provided an hour-by-hour account of the dramatic and frightening developments. When it was all over, the feeling of relief was general, but almost from the beginning that feeling had been tinged with

---

[42] Press release of September 30, 1938 (*Peace and War*, 430).
[43] Tel. to Kennedy, October 5, 1938, instructing him to deliver the message orally to Chamberlain.

regret and indignation. Conservative, isolationist circles might put the whole incident aside as another demonstration of the ruthless realism of European politics, but moderate opinion deplored the submission of the democracies under threat, and among liberals and radicals there was vociferous protest against abandonment of the Czechs and surrender to the detested Hitler. Critics pointed out that the Munich settlement was a disaster for the democracies and warned that it did not promise the elimination of war, but only its postponement. There was much talk of Hitler's "bluff" and of the pathetic failure of Britain and France to call it. The democracies, it was argued, could have defeated the Nazis and should obviously have accepted the challenge, calling on Soviet Russia to join in combined and irresistible pressure on Germany. American pundits were as profuse in advice as they were in denunciation of Allied pusillanimity. Implicit in their position was the idea that Britain and France had, by their refusal to fight, let down America and betrayed the democratic cause.

During the succeeding few months the feeling against Hitler and the Nazis continued to grow apace. When, in November, 1938, the assassination of a German diplomat in Paris by a Polish Jew provoked a new and unprecedentedly violent outbreak of organized persecution in Germany, Americans felt justified in concluding that the Nazis were nothing but barbarians, if not demons. The President echoed a universal feeling when he expressed his amazement that "such things could occur in a twentieth-century civilization." He at once withdrew the American Ambassador from Berlin "for consultation," while in the country at large much sentiment developed for a boycott of all German goods. Yet for all the excitement, resentment and moral indignation, there was no public clamor for intervention in the European imbroglio. Even those who demonstrated the hopelessness of relying on Britain and France to check Hitler, for the most part avoided any suggestion that the United States assume any part of that assignment. According to the Gallup polls, about 95 percent of the population was opposed to American participation in another war, while two thirds of those consulted professed to favor a policy of refusing to sell munitions and war materials to either side. The mentality of "drifting isolation" was clearly as strong as ever, and one is tempted to say that the worse the situation appeared in Europe, the more determined became the American people to keep out of it.[44]

For at least a short time after the crisis American diplomats and correspondents abroad remained undecided whether the Munich settlement presaged a new era of peace or merely provided a short interlude between Axis aggressions. But Mr. Roosevelt was very soon disabused of any op-

[44] The polls for this period are well analyzed in Philip E. Jacobs: "Influences of World Events on U.S. 'Neutrality' Opinion" (*Public Opinion Quarterly*, March, 1940).

timism he may at first have entertained. On October 3, 1938, Ambassador Bullitt reported a conversation with M. Daladier, who expressed fear that Mr. Chamberlain had been taken in by Hitler and confessed that he did not believe a word of all the Nazi assurances for. the future. The French Premier thought that within six months Britain and France would be confronted with new German demands and remarked "that in his opinion the single thing which counted today was not diplomatic negotiations but strengthening of the military forces of France, especially in the field of air armament." By way of summary Mr. Bullitt reported: "Daladier sees the situation entirely, clearly, realizes fully that the meeting in Munich was an immense diplomatic defeat for France and England, and recognizes that unless France can recover a united national spirit to confront the future, a fatal situation will arise within a year."[45]

Following this disheartening conversation, which included extended discussion of France's requirements for air power, Ambassador Bullitt departed for home. But before he could reach Washington, Hitler reinforced Daladier's impressions by delivering a public speech in which he called for additional German armament on the plea that Mr. Chamberlain's promises could not be relied upon, in view of the possibility that he might be replaced by men like Churchill and Duff Cooper, who had roundly denounced the Munich settlement. In response to these ominous remarks, the President at once (October 11, 1938) announced an increase of American armaments to the tune of $300,000,000 for purposes of national defense. In an interview-with Mrs. Anne O'Hare McCormick he indicated his intention of concentrating on hemisphere defense: "all signs point 'Home.' "[46] This was a line bound to appeal to Americans of all shades, and it is worth noting that the opinion polls of the time reflected a striking rise in the President's popularity.

But if Mr. Roosevelt ever thought sincerely that American interests would be adequately served by a stronger home defense alone, Ambassador Bullitt's arguments certainly recalled him to his larger responsibilities. Bullitt stressed the fact that war in Europe must be expected in the not very distant future; that any war in Europe was bound to affect American interests, even if the United States succeeded in staying out of the conflict; that therefore it was decidedly America's business to do everything possible to prevent hostilities; that if, nevertheless, a clash proved unavoidable, Britain and France would constitute the first line of defense for the United States and the Western Hemisphere; and that, finally, we should support the European democracies, not only with words, but with the implements of war. Above

[45] Tel. from Bullitt, October 3, 1938.
[46] Anne O'Hare McCormick: "As He Sees Himself" (*The New York Times Magazine,* October 16, 1938).

all, the Ambassador expounded the grievous need of the French for planes, underlining the crucial importance of modern air power.[47]

From this point onward Mr. Roosevelt began to evolve plans for a huge air force and above all for the development of American plane-production facilities. He thought first of a force of 10,000 planes and an annual output of 15,000, but soon raised his estimates to 20,000 planes and a production capacity of 20,000 annually. From his discussion with Army and Air Corps officers it is reasonably clear that the President was intent on two things: he wanted a huge number of planes, not only for defense of the nation and the hemisphere, but to impress and possibly deter Hitler; and he insisted on an immense expansion of output in order that the United States might supplement the insufficient production of Britain and France. As yet he showed little appreciation for the need of building up American air power as part of an integrated, balanced rearmament program and was impatient when the War Department proposed to spend large parts of its appropriations on airfields, training facilities, etc. He could not, he is said to have remarked, impress Hitler with barracks and runways, but only with planes.

In an important military conference of November 14, 1938, the President explained that Germany could produce 12,000 planes per year as against British construction of 4,800 and French of 3,600. The United States, he added, must be prepared to resist assault on the hemisphere "from the North to the South Pole." What was needed was an air force of 20,000 planes and annual production of 24,000, though he confessed doubt whether Congress would vote funds for more than half these figures. In any event he felt that private industry should be supplemented by government facilities. Debate on these matters continued until presentation of the President's program to Congress in January, 1939, but even these preliminary, necessarily vague and confused estimates suffice to reflect the President's thinking in the autumn of 1938.[48]

The question has often been raised and debated why, if the President was aware of the dangers inherent in the European situation after Munich, he did not state them publicly and use his tremendous influence and prestige to induce a change in American opinion. The answer is not a simple one

---

[47] No record of Bullitt's long conference with the President on October 13, 1938, and his later discussions in Washington has been found, but the substance is adequately reflected in other documents, notably in the official study of Mark Watson: *The United States Army in World War II: The War Department, Chief of Staff: Pre-war Plans and Preparations* (Washington, 1950). See also Joseph Alsop and Robert Kintner: *American White Paper,* which was based on information from the White House and the State Department.

[48] Mark Watson: *Chief of Staff: Pre-war Plans and Preparations* (Washington, 1950), 126, 131-39; General Arnold's first report, in *The War Reports,* 307-8; William Frye: *Marshall, Citizen Soldier* (New York, 1947), 249-54. The account of a conference on September 28, 1938, in General H. H. Arnold: *Global Mission* (New York, 1949), 173, 177, is probably erroneously dated and refers clearly to the conference of November 14, 1938.

and has at least a number of different facets. For one thing, it is almost certain that if the President and his advisers recognized the threat of a war in Europe and discerned its probable repercussions on the United States, they had at most only the vaguest notion that the country might eventually have to intervene by force of arms. They clearly hoped that, in the long run, Britain and France would be able to defeat their opponents, especially if they could draw on the United States for material aid. The immediate need, then, seemed less for a reversal of the established attitude than for a modification of it in the sense of converting it to a stronger American initiative in the effort to prevent war and to win approval of a policy of aiding the European democracies in preparation for hostilities. This Mr. Roosevelt apparently hoped to accomplish without provoking too much public controversy, avoidance of which seemed to him at the time to be absolutely essential.

It must be remembered, in this connection, that the President's political position in the late months of 1938 was weaker than it had been at any time since he had taken office. The violent opposition to the New Deal and the widespread personal animus against the President had been climaxed by Mr. Roosevelt's attempt to "pack" the Supreme Court and perhaps even more by his avowed program of "purging" Democratic members of Congress who failed to support his policies. For a time there was real danger of a split in the Democratic Party, and in the elections of November, 1938, the Republicans gained eight seats in the Senate and eighty-one in the House, along with eleven governorships. Even though the Administration party still commanded a comfortable majority in Congress, there was so much bad feeling and dissension in its ranks that it could not be counted on for united support of the President. Many Democrats in Congress and almost all Republicans were isolationist in foreign affairs. Congress was in a "nasty" mood and to a large extent eager for a chance "to clip the President's wings." According to Vice President Garner, the next few months were to give Mr. Roosevelt "his roughest legislative ride." He felt impelled to promise cessation of New Deal legislation and was understandably intent on avoiding a major debate on the ticklish subject of foreign policy. With the disaster that had befallen President Wilson always prominently in mind, Mr. Roosevelt was determined not to repeat his predecessor's mistake or to jeopardize his program through his own political death.[49]

5. TAKING A STAND

While the temper of the country and the attitude of Congress dictated caution with respect to the affairs of Europe, the President could reckon on a large measure of support, even from the isolationists, for a program of

[49] This side of the problem is discussed ably and at much greater length in Basil Rauch: *Roosevelt, from Munich to Pearl Harbor*, Chapter IV.

national and hemisphere defense. His own utterances make it perfectly clear that his famous address at Kingston, Ontario (August 18, 1938), in which he gave assurance "that the people of the United States will not stand idly by if domination of Canadian soil is threatened by any other Empire," was directed not only to the Canadians, but also to the Nazis, by way of warning that aggression in the New World would find all the nations of the hemisphere united. As expected, the President's commitment was acclaimed throughout the United States, for the defense of Canada obviously concerned its neighbor and at bottom continentalism was nothing more than nationalism writ large. To Americans of all stripes it made good common sense to assure Canada of full support in the event of an attack.

The same reasoning inspired American thinking with respect to Latin America, for even though there was less affinity, less knowledge, and less sense of immediacy about that area than about Canada, the Monroe Doctrine had stood for more than a century as a pillar of American policy and the public was fully prepared to subscribe to the President's proposition that, if all else failed, the Western Hemisphere at least should remain a strong citadel wherein civilization might flourish unimpaired. The Good Neighbor Policy toward Latin America had been initiated by the Hoover Administration, but had been named by Mr. Roosevelt and had been developed by him despite all temptations to deviate from it. By 1938 it had already borne fruit in the form of greater confidence and more sincere coöperation. At the Buenos Aires Conference of 1936 the American States had accepted the principle of consultation in case of a threat to the peace of the Americas, and thereby the Monroe Doctrine had, to all intents and purposes, been transformed from a unilateral declaration into a multilateral pact.[50]

The results of the Buenos Aires Conference, though gratifying, had fallen short of the President's and Secretary Hull's hopes at the time, while during the succeeding years the need for more effective machinery for common action had made itself ever more keenly felt. The growth of Nazi and Fascist organizations in Latin American countries, the rapid expansion of foreign propaganda, and the extraordinary efforts of the Germans to develop trade had caused increasing uneasiness in Washington. In April, 1938, Secretary Hull had proposed the establishment of an interdepartmental committee, to be composed of Assistant Secretaries of State, to deal in coördinated fashion with these problems, but the President had insisted that the Chief of Staff and the Chief of Naval Operations be included, and what finally emerged was the Standing Liaison Committee, consisting of the Under Secre-

[50] For an authoritative account see Samuel F. Bemis: *The Latin American Policy of the United States* (New York, 1943), Chapters XVI ff. The subject was well reviewed also by Stephen Duggan: "The Western Hemisphere as a Haven of Peace?" (*Foreign Affairs*, July, 1940), and by Dexter Perkins: "Bringing the Monroe Doctrine up to Date" (*ibid.*, January, 1942).

tary of State, the Chief of Staff and the Chief of Naval Operations. During the summer and autumn of 1938 this committee met frequently and concerned itself chiefly with hemisphere problems. Its records reveal much anxiety about the numerous German and Italian military missions in Latin America, about German control of commercial air lines in Brazil and Colombia, and particularly about German arms shipments to Brazil, Uruguay, and the Argentine. The committee thereupon made efforts to strengthen American military representation at key capitals of Latin America and drafted legislation which would enable the American Republics to purchase arms and other matériel in the United States. Ways and means of superseding Nazi control of South American aviation were discussed, and finally the War and Navy Department planners were instructed by the Joint Board (November 12, 1938) to block out a program of hemisphere defense.[51]

In December, 1938, the President agreed that Secretary Hull should attend in person the regularly scheduled Inter-American Conference at Lima, Peru. Mr. Hull's objective was to induce the various American governments to bind themselves to resist any threat, direct or indirect, to their peace, safety or territorial integrity as it came from any non-American country, to agree to recognize such a threat to any one of them as a matter of concern to all, and to proclaim their determination to act in concert to resist it. As on previous occasions, the Argentine Government, always suspicious and resentful of United States leadership and ever intent upon not offending its important European customers, objected to far-reaching comprehensive commitments. Mr. Hull has related at length in his memoirs the complicated maneuvers through which the Buenos Aires Government was eventually brought partially into line. Agreement was ultimately reached on the Declaration of Lima, which, if it fell short of United States hopes, nevertheless represented a substantial advance.

Under the Declaration the American Republics reaffirmed their continental solidarity and their determination to collaborate in maintaining the principles upon which that solidarity rested. They engaged to defend these principles against all foreign intervention and activity that might threaten them, and recognized that any act menacing the peace, security, or territorial integrity of any one of them was a concern of all. In such case they undertook to "coördinate their respective sovereign wills by means of the procedure of consultation," but with the careful proviso that they would "act independently in their individual capacity, recognizing fully their juridical equality as sovereign states." The language was painfully guarded, yet the fact remained that for the first time the nations of the New World had declared their agreement to consider themselves a unit in their relation-

[51] *Minutes of the Liaison Committee*, May 25, June 20, July 11, November 14, 1938; Watson: *Chief of Staff: Pre-war Plans and Preparations*, 89-90; and the MS. study by Captain Tracy Kittredge, USNR: *United States-British Naval Coöperation, 1939-1942* (Naval Historical Monograph, Office of Naval History).

ships with the rest of the world. Secretary Hull was no doubt wise in relying on the spirit of the Declaration and in accepting a wordy compromise in preference to a bitter showdown on behalf of an agreement with sharper teeth. For the time being the demonstration of friendship and solidarity at Lima was sufficient.[52]

Even with regard to the Far East the American public was more amenable to a firm and positive policy than with respect to Europe. The relentless advance of the Japanese armies enhanced popular sympathy for the suffering Chinese people, while the ruthless disregard of the Japanese military leaders for American rights and interests fanned the flames of agitation for some form of retaliation. Officially the United States Government had taken its stand by the Washington Treaties and had adhered steadfastly to the nonrecognition doctrine established at the time of the Manchurian Incident. It had, furthermore, made an effort to uphold the principle of the Open Door in China and had exerted itself to protect American lives and property. But it had taken no effective steps to defend the independence and territorial integrity of China or to put any formidable obstacles in the way of the Japanese advance. On its part the Tokyo Government had pursued its own course at its own rate, paying little heed to American protests. By November, 1938, Prime Minister Konoye was ready to proclaim publicly the long-range Japanese program. He forecast a Greater East Asia Co-Prosperity Sphere based on a league of Japan, Manchukuo and China under Tokyo's leadership but ostensibly designed for mutual benefit. Konoye left no doubt of the fate envisaged for the Open Door policy, or indeed for all foreign interests and enterprises in China. The United States, along with Britain, France and other non-Asiatic powers, was admonished to recognize the changing conditions in Asia and to accept the inevitable.[53]

In response to this challenge, the State Department entered upon a lively debate with Tokyo which revealed more clearly than ever before the wide gulf separating the two Governments. In the course of the argument the Japanese Foreign Minister, Mr. Arita, stated frankly that his Government had associated itself with the Open Door policy because, at the turn of the century, other powers were carving out spheres of influence in China, while Japan was then too weak to do likewise. But his Government, he continued, had come to the conclusion, after the signature of the Washington Treaties of 1922, that the real purpose of the powers, in their support of the Open Door, was to exploit China as they were exploiting Africa. More recent events provided no reason for modifying this view; indeed, Mr. Arita "won-

[52] Hull: *Memoirs*, I, Chapter XLII; A. A. Berle: *New Directions in the New World* (New York, 1940), Chapter II; Welles: *The Time for Decision*, Chapter V.
[53] Japanese Government statement of November 3, 1938 (*Foreign Relations of the United States: Japan*, I, 477 ff.).

dered" whether the Open Door policy applied any longer to any region of
the world excepting possibly the Congo Basin.

The Foreign Minister then advanced to a second point: America and
Britain, he suggested, were great "have powers," self-contained and rich in
the resources needed for effective national defense. Japan, on the other
hand, was less advantageously situated. Since economic sanctions were as
serious a threat to Japan as military sanctions, the Tokyo Government felt
obliged to put the country, by its own efforts, beyond the pale of danger.
That, he explained, was the motive behind the "bloc" (Arita preferred the
term "economic coöperation") of Japan, Manchukuo and China. The sole
purpose of this combination was to assure Japan an economic position comparable to that of America or Britain. Obviously, however, the analogy
would not hold for the political sphere, nor need the economic bloc necessarily involve the exclusion of American or other foreign capital from its
domain. Indeed, continued Arita, Prince Konoye's statement of November
3, 1938, was not intended to announce any change in Japanese policy.
The Prime Minister was not shutting the Open Door or repudiating the
assurances given by his predecesors. But it should be remembered that such
assurances had never been meant to be unconditional, "for the reason that
the time had passed when Japan could give an unqualified undertaking to
respect the Open Door in China. . . ." Even though the earlier assurances
had been given in good faith, Japan could not now repeat them. The
Foreign Minister felt it would be useless and mischievous to attempt to
reconcile the principle of the Open Door as understood in the United States
and elsewhere abroad with the "new situation" which Japan was trying to
bring about, and equally futile to air publicly the disagreement on this
score. The sensible thing, he suggested, would be to open the way "for a
solution on some practical basis by arriving at a new definition of the
Open Door which would be mutually acceptable."[54]

To these ominous utterances the State Department replied first in an
"oral statement" and later in a detailed and reasoned note of December 30,
1938. The United States Government denied that it had been or then was
using the Open Door as a method of exploiting China, and insisted once
more that its advocacy of the principle of equality of commercial opportunity derived not only from considerations of material gain but also from
the conviction that the principle was most likely to provide economic and
political stability in China. Furthermore, the Japanese Government had not
only approved the principle, but was committed to it by treaty. The United
States did not propose to allow itself to be deprived of its rights and regarded it as "highly paradoxical" that recognition of American rights and
interests in China should be made contingent upon recognition of a "new
order" or "new situation" in the Far East. The United States found it im-

[54] *Foreign Relations of the United States: Japan*, I, 801-6.

possible to regard Japan as an "agent of destiny" in areas of the world not under its sovereignty. It did not insist on the maintenance of the *status quo,* but did insist that changes be made on an orderly, legal basis and by peaceful negotiation and agreement. It was prepared to give full consideration to any proposals designed to solve Far Eastern problems in a manner satisfactory to all concerned, but in the meanwhile would stand on its established rights.[55]

The wide divergence in view between the two Governments warranted little hope of an acceptable adjustment. By the autumn of 1938 the Washington Government had, in fact, already lost faith in securing respect for American rights through protests and warnings alone. For some months the question of economic retaliation had been under discussion, with particular reference to the desirability of denouncing the commercial treaty of 1911.

Closely linked with the problem of relations with Japan was the question of further aid to Nationalist China in its efforts to check the Japanese invasion. Since July, 1938, the Chinese Government had been pressing for a further credit, and in September a special mission had been sent to Washington in the hope of closing a deal. Both the President and Secretary of the Treasury Morgenthau were sympathetic to an arrangement by which China should be given a credit of twenty-five or thirty million dollars against shipments of tung oil over a period of some years, provided Chiang Kai-shek gave assurances that the Chinese resistance would continue. The Generalissimo showed no hesitation about making a declaration to this effect.[56]

At this point the State Department, engaged in its debate with Tokyo, began to raise objections based upon general considerations of Far Eastern policy. Secretary Hull wrote the President that Japan would certainly interpret the credit to China as something more than a commercial transaction and sense that its intent was to aid China in military resistance again Japan. The effect, therefore, might be increased attacks on American interests and not inconceivably eventual American involvement in hostilities. Mr. Hull's chief advisers on Far Eastern affairs argued eloquently that in this instance the game would not be worth the candle. In dealing with the Far Eastern crisis they thought a policy of pressure on Japan would be much more effective than one of aid to China. Rather than proceed by piecemeal, haphazard measures, they urged the desirability of plotting a consistent course of action, for which the support of Congress and the country would

[55] *Foreign Relations of the United States: Japan,* I, 806-26.
[56] Tel. from Bullitt, July 26, 1938; memos of conversation between Mr. Hull and the Chinese Ambassador, August 3, 11, September 15, 1938; memo of Mr. Feis to Mr. Hull, September 22, 1938, reporting conferences at the Treasury; memo of conversation between Mr. Moore and Mr. Feis and the Chinese Ambassador, September 24, 1938; memo of Mr. Feis to Mr. Hull, November 12, 1938, reporting on the status of the affair.

have to be obtained.[57] But State Department objections were overruled. The President felt committed by his earlier statements and on December 15, 1938, the credit to China ($25,000,000) was announced by the Reconstruction Finance Corporation.[58]

Meanwhile the larger question of retaliation on Japan for the violation of American rights and interests continued to receive attention in the State Department. Every possible method of economic pressure was carefully analyzed, but after much deliberation it was decided that a comprehensive and thoroughgoing program of reprisal was not desirable at the time, though it might be advisable to frame such a program for future use and to consider the denunciation of the commercial treaty of 1911 as an indispensable preliminary step. It was suggested that such a move might be tied up with the important note to Japan of December 30, 1938, but eventually it was decided to defer action pending Secretary Hull's return from Lima.[59] For the time being nothing concrete was done, chiefly, as the records show, for fear of going too far, provoking Japanese counteraction, and possibly becoming involved in hostilities. The concluding months of the year 1938 nevertheless marked a stiffening of the American attitude toward Japan, a firm and explicit statement of position with respect to Tokyo's pretensions, and at least the serious contemplation of practical measures to secure respect for American rights and interests in China. Though the skirmish was still largely one of words, the issue had been joined and the ground prepared for a more positive American policy.

6. Methods Short of War

As the President and his advisers felt their way toward a program of supporting the European democracies in rearmament and in eventual hostilities, it became increasingly clear that some revision of the neutrality laws would be essential. Under existing legislation there was nothing to prevent foreign powers from purchasing munitions in the United States in times of peace, provided they paid cash. But the law forbade supply of such matériel once the President had recognized a state of war. In January, 1938, Baron de La Grange, member of the French Senate and of that body's Commission de l'Air and a personal friend of Mr. Roosevelt, had come to the United

[57] Memo of Secretary Hull to the President, November 14, 1938, based on memos from Mr. Hamilton to Mr. Hull (November 13, 1938) and from Mr. Hornbeck to Mr. Hull (November 14, 1938).

[58] Tel. from Welles to Hull (en route to the Lima Conference), December 2, 1938; tel. from Hull to Welles, December 4, 1938, repeating his objections; memo by Welles, December 9, 1938; tel. to Grew (Tokyo), December 15, 1938.

[59] A long and detailed memo from the Division of Far Eastern Affairs, December 5, 1938; memo by Mr. Hornbeck, December 22, 1938; and a memo digesting the materials and entitled *Narrative of Developments Leading to the Giving of Notice by the United States of an Intention to Terminate the Japanese-American Commercial Treaty of 1911*, dated April 30, 1940.

States to place contracts with American manufacturers for large numbers of planes, engines and machine tools, these orders to be greatly increased in the event of war. His efforts were viewed sympathetically by the President and by the State Department, but every care was taken to disabuse him and the French Government of the idea that in the event of hostilities the American Government would lend itself to any subterfuges in order to enable the French to secure planes.[60]

In the course of the year (1938), Mr. Roosevelt himself dealt with most questions of French plane purchases. Several air missions were sent to the United States and in a few instances French pilots were permitted to fly planes of the United States Army and Navy, despite the misgivings of the Services about disclosing secret devices. Actually the French, hoping to increase their own production substantially, ordered only one hundred pursuit planes in June, 1938, though after Munich they began to plan for much larger contracts, especially for engines. Since American production capacity was at this time very small—hardly more than one hundred planes per month—the issue of plant expansion soon became an urgent one. Realizing the advantages that would accrue from such expansion, the War Department was willing to agree that the French should have a share of the output proportionate to their orders. General Arnold, commanding the Army Air Corps, used his influence to induce American manufacturers to increase their production facilities even without guaranteed orders. The story is a long and complicated one, the details of which are of little importance for the present study. On December 17, 1938, however, the President assigned to Secretary Morgenthau the task of dealing with all foreign orders for munitions, thereby laying the foundation for coördinated treatment of what was to become the major problem of aid to the European democracies.[61]

While it was possible for Mr. Roosevelt to smooth the way for the peacetime purchase of munitions by the French and British without making his efforts public, the larger issue of revising the neutrality laws could obviously be disposed of only after a mobilization of popular sentiment. With the opening of the New Year (1939), Mr. Roosevelt therefore suggested his program to the country. His message to Congress was a carefully prepared document, scrupulously designed to say what was necessary without saying too much—in other words meticulously aimed at securing approval for the essentials without provoking a possibly disastrous conflict with isolationism.

[60] Memo of conversation between Mr. Green and Baron de La Grange, January 18, 1938; tels. from Bullitt, January 24, February 23, May 17, 1938; tel. to Bullitt, May 18, 1938.

[61] The *Morgenthau Diaries (MS.)*, Vols. 172, 173, and 174 contain an extraordinarily complete record of the negotiation of the French orders. The question of permitting French pilots to test the P-36 pursuit plane and other Army and Navy planes occasioned an extended correspondence, which is contained in the State Department files. The State Department supported the French requests and early in October, 1938, the President gave informal permission.

Prefacing his remarks with a reference to the Munich crisis, the President reminded the Congress and the country that while a war which threatened to envelop the world in flames had been averted, it had since become increasingly clear that peace had not been assured. In many places undeclared wars were already raging, menacing three institutions regarded by Americans as essential: freedom of religion, democracy, and international good faith. "We know," he continued, "what might happen to us of the United States if the new philosophies of force were to encompass the other continents and invade our own. We, no more than other nations, can afford to be surrounded by enemies of our faith and our humanity." Fortunately the ideals of the whole Western Hemisphere were those of the United States also: "That hemisphere, that peace, and that ideal we propose to do our share in protecting against storms from any quarter. Our people and our resources are pledged to secure that protection. From that determination no American flinches." But this, Mr. Roosevelt emphasized, did not imply a stand by the Americas aloof from the rest of the world. The United States stood ready, as ever, to help the cause of peace and to take counsel with other nations to end aggression, to check the armaments race, and to encourage trade.

After these preliminary statements, the President turned to the constructive part of his message. Once again he pointed out that "the world has grown so small and weapons of attack so swift that no nation can be safe in its will to peace so long as any other single powerful nation refuses to settle its grievances at the council table." It was therefore imperative to embark upon a program of national defense and to do so in good time:

We have learned that God-fearing democracies of the world which observe the sanctity of treaties and good faith in their dealings with other nations cannot safely be indifferent to international lawlessness anywhere. They cannot forever let pass, without effective protest, acts of aggression against sister nations—acts which automatically undermine all of us.

Obviously they must proceed along practical, peaceful lines. But the mere fact that we rightly decline to intervene with arms to prevent acts of aggression does not mean that we must act as if there were no aggression at all. Words may be futile, but war is not the only means of commanding a decent respect for the opinions of mankind. There are many methods short of war, but stronger and more effective than mere words, of bringing home to aggressor governments the aggregate sentiments of our own people.

At the very least, we can and should avoid any action, or any lack of action, which will encourage, assist, or build up an aggressor. We have learned that when we deliberately try to legislate neutrality, our neutrality laws may operate unevenly and unfairly—may actually give aid to an aggressor and deny it to the victim. The instinct of self-preservation should warn us that we ought not to let that happen any more.[62]

[62] *The Public Papers and Addresses of Franklin D. Roosevelt, 1939,* 1-12.

This passage serves an as excellent demonstration of the President's circumspection. While upholding the American refusal to intervene with arms to prevent aggression, the only specific method "short of war" which he proposed was revision of the neutrality laws, in what respect he did not indicate. Ostensibly the emphasis throughout was on national and hemisphere defense, for which he could be certain of full support. The annual budget message of January 5, 1939, requested nearly one and one third billion dollars for defense, and was followed on January 12 by a special message asking a supplementary appropriation of over half a billion, primarily for the purchase of planes for the Army and Navy. Once more the President warned that the nation could not expect in the future to have a full year, as in 1917, to gear for war. But he still went out of his way to stress the purely defensive character of the proposed preparations: "calling attention to these facts does not remotely intimate that the Congress or the President have any thought of taking part in another war on European soil . . ."[63]

The public was quite amenable to the President's contention that his program was one of minimum requirements. The sum asked for the Navy, large though it was, would only permit maintenance of existing sea power in relation to the British, Japanese and others. As for the Army, the vastly increased appropriation was intended primarily for strengthening the Air Corps. The ground forces were to be enlarged only from about 180,000 to 220,000. Clearly there was to be no imitation of the highly mobile and flexible *Reichswehr,* or indeed anything that might suggest a nuclear expeditionary force. Only the air forces were to be greatly expanded, the Army to have ultimately 5500 planes and the Navy 3000. These figures were impressive, even by European standards, and led some commentators to remark that the projected forces were "really more than seems dictated by sound requirements of home defense." Already there was some suspicion that the objective was to build a reserve of planes on which the British and French might draw in case of emergency. But on the whole the notion of air power appealed to the public and there was no danger of strong opposition to the President's program.[64]

All promised well until, on January 23, 1939, there occurred one of those "untoward events" which punctuate the pages of history. On that day the news broke that one of the newest American bombers, engaged in a test flight in California, had crashed with the loss of several lives, including an official of the French Air Ministry. Thus the Congress and the country learned for the first time that foreigners were being permitted to fly United States Army aircraft and acquaint themselves with highly secret equipment.

[63] *Public Papers and Addresses, 1939,* 13 ff.
[64] An excellent analysis of the program was Hanson W. Baldwin's "Our New Long Shadow" (*Foreign Affairs,* April, 1939).

Vigorous protests were lodged at once, especially by isolationists who thought they scented a secret alliance. The Army was severely criticized and in self-defense put the responsibility on Secretary Morgenthau. Before long the controversy became so violent that the President announced publicly (January 27, 1939) that he himself had approved the sale of planes to France. A few days later he invited members of the Senate Military Affairs Committee to the White House and explained to them confidentially the reasons for his policy. Though apparently sworn to secrecy, one or more members of the group allowed the newspapers to learn that the President had referred to the American frontier as lying in France, or on the Rhine. In great resentment, Mr. Roosevelt branded this story as a deliberate lie, thereby in turn outraging some of his visitors, who let it be known that the President had left no doubt in their minds that he intended to pursue a policy directed against aggressors, despite the existing neutrality laws.[65]

The effect of this unfortunate incident was to throw suspicion on the President's plans and to build up opposition to the projected revision of the neutrality laws. Even among the President's supporters there was much criticism of his secrecy. The wise thing, it was argued, would have been to expound the situation to the country and to explain in detail that the one hopeful method of stopping Hitler was to make clear to him that in case of further aggression all the resources of the United States would be at the disposal of his opponents. This was the line recommended by former Secretary of State Stimson when, on March 6, 1939, he called for a direct military understanding between the United States, Britain and France.[66]

It remains a moot question whether, if the President had adopted a more daring course, he would not have brought equally or even more bitter accusations upon his head. In any case, he was now obliged to pick his way in foreign affairs through a fog of distrust. In an effort to dispel the public uneasiness, Mr. Roosevelt therefore attempted, in a press interview of February 3, 1939, to restate fundamentals. His policy, he said, had been thoroughly, completely and adequately presented in his annual message to Congress. It had not changed and was not going to change. By way of clarification, he offered the press "a simple statement of the policy":

1. We are against any entangling alliances, obviously.
2. We are in favor of the maintenance of world trade for everybody—all nations —including ourselves.
3. We are in complete sympathy with any and every effort to reduce or limit armaments.

[65] This entire episode was well summarized by D. F. Fleming: "Our Choice in Foreign Policy" (*Events*, March, 1939, 161 ff.), but see also "The Morgenthau Diaries, IV" (*Collier's Magazine*, October 18, 1947), and H. H. Arnold: *Global Mission*, 185 ff.

[66] Henry L. Stimson: letter to *The New York Times*, March 6, 1939. See also the criticisms in *The New York Times*, January 31 and February 3, 1939, the latter by Arthur Krock.

4. As a nation—as American people—we are sympathetic with the peaceful maintenance of political, economic and social independence of all nations in the world.[67]

This simple and apparently straightforward statement may have done much to reassure the country, for the Gallup polls of that period showed a majority of 65 per cent as approving the sale of planes to Britain and France and 44 percent as favoring discriminatory legislation on this score against Germany. But none of this meant that the President's opponents in Congress would not make the most of the issue. The indications all pointed to a full-dress debate on foreign policy, the proposed revision of the neutrality laws serving as a point of departure. In order not to give the opposition an opportunity to clip his wings, the President, in consultation with Secretary Hull, decided to leave the whole question of revision in the hands of Congress. Senator Pittman was to handle the matter in the Upper House and was profuse in assurances that he could achieve the desired end.

Yet in the course of the next three months no progress could be recorded. Though by March, 1939, no fewer than thirty-three different proposals lay before Congress, there was no prospect of early agreement on any one of them. Most important, from the Administration standpoint, was the Thomas Resolution, which in general corresponded with the President's desires. It would have authorized him, at the outbreak of war, to place an embargo on all American exports of arms, ammunition, implements of war and, logically, on certain other materials useful in war. The President, together with Congress, was then to determine the aggressor, after which the embargo would be lifted from the victim. The aggressor was to be defined as that state which resorted to war in violation of a treaty to which the United States was a party, including the Kellogg-Briand Pact of 1928. It is quite possible that with some public endorsement and support from the White House this resolution might have found acceptance. But the President scrupulously avoided any expression of opinion and studiously abstained from all interference. The result was that when Hitler, in mid-March, 1939, made his next dramatic move against Czechoslovakia, the basic neutrality policy of the United States still stood unchanged.[68]

The position of the United States in the spring of 1939 may therefore be summarized as follows: according to the Gallup polls less than half of the population (44 percent) was as yet convinced that war would break out in Europe in the course of the year. As between the probable antagonists there was no doubt whatever as to which enjoyed American sympathies. Hitler and all his works were abominated and many people expressed themselves

[67] *Public Papers and Addresses, 1939,* 110 ff.

[68] F. O. Wilcox: "The Neutrality Fight in Congress, 1939" (*American Political Science Review,* October, 1939, 811 ff.) provides an admirable analysis of the various proposals before Congress.

in favor of a boycott of all German goods, presumably in complete oblivion of the possible implications of economic sanctions. Half the population, at least, was agreeable to helping the British and French through the sale of planes and other munitions, though there was little if any sentiment for repeal of the Johnson Act, which prohibited loans to countries which were in default on their war-debt payments. But the most striking feature of the public attitude was the continuing and almost unanimous opposition to any involvement in another war. Everyone approved of efforts to prevent war, but hardly any would entertain the notion of participation under any circumstances or in any degree. As the international scene grew darker and darker, the American people looked anxiously to its own defenses and to those of the hemisphere, but beyond that the public refused to raise its sights.

The President and his advisers, on the other hand, had by this time convinced themselves that war in the near future was not at all improbable, and that the aggressors in Europe might well link their efforts with those of the imperialists of Asia. It was perfectly clear to them that in that event the United States would be deeply affected, to say the least, and that eventually a war abroad might be positively disastrous for their country. It appears that at this time Mr. Roosevelt still largely shared the prevalent opinion that if it came to war in Europe, the British and French would win, even though the conflict might be protracted. He therefore saw no need for preparing the United States for an intervention that would not be required. There was some reason to fear Nazi intrigue and activity in Latin America, but an attack on the United States appeared beyond the range of possibility.

The real issue, then, was threefold: in the first place to plan and execute what has been called a psychological offensive against Germany, making clear the attitude of the United States toward Nazi policies and suggesting that in the event of further aggression and war the United States would participate at least to the extent of making its enormous resources available to Britain and France; in the second place, to support the rearmament of the democracies by expanding American plane production and facilitating British and French orders; and, finally, as a last resort, to secure revision of the neutrality laws so that, if war came, the United States could throw its economic weight on the Allied side. By March, 1939, the Administration program had thus been mapped and a positive policy existed in embryo. But the implementation remained for the future and would depend largely on the impact of further developments abroad.

CHAPTER II

Farewell to Appeasement

1. FOG OF UNCERTAINTY

As the Roosevelt Administration, early in 1939, groped its way toward a policy of supporting the European democracies in their contest with Nazi Germany, it was constantly distracted by evil omens in the Far East. There was no evidence that the Tokyo Government had been moved by American protests or arguments or that it proposed to modify its aims and policies. The Japanese armies in China continued to disregard foreign rights and interests, while the Japanese seizure of Hainan Island (February, 1939), followed by the occupation of the Spratly Islands (March, 1939), clearly indicated designs for expansion far beyond anything involved in the settlement of the China Incident. The State Department queried Tokyo on the meaning of these moves, but probably without hope of more than the wholly evasive reply that was given.[1]

Japan's flagrant and brazen disregard of American rights quite naturally revived the discussion of possible retaliation. Nelson T. Johnson, the United States Ambassador to Chungking, was among those who urged that the Government show its teeth and demonstrate that it meant business. But even though certain high officials of the State Department shared this view, the prevailing opinion was still that the time had not yet come for a policy of systematic reprisal which, after all, might well lead to war. Even so logical and justifiable a step as the denunciation of the commercial treaty of 1911 was therefore eschewed.[2]

There were at least two good reasons why, at the time, it seemed essential to avoid any measure that might seriously antagonize Japan. In the first place American military authorities had come to the firm conviction that it

---

[1] *Foreign Relations of the United States: Japan*, I, 830 ff.
[2] Letter from Ambassador Johnson to the President, February 27, 1939 (*Roosevelt Papers:* Secretary's File, Box 43); memo of the Far East Division (April 30, 1940) reviewing the developments which led to the termination of the commercial treaty.

would be impossible for the United States to carry on effective operations in both the western Pacific and the Atlantic, that Hitler was potentially the more powerful and dangerous enemy, and that therefore everything should be done to prevent a crisis in the Far East until the situation in Europe had been further clarified.[3] In the second place the American Government was much preoccupied with the possibility that Germany, Italy and Japan, already united in the Anti-Comintern Pact of 1936, might reinforce their partnership by concluding a full-blown military alliance. On February 8, 1939, Ambassador Grew reported from Tokyo that negotiations to this end were already under way. He had even then learned the crucial fact that while the Japanese Government desired an agreement with Germany and Italy for mutual aid in the event of war with Soviet Russia, the Nazis on their side insisted on an agreement directed also against other powers, like Britain, France and the United States. The Ambassador lost no time in suggesting informally to the Japanese Foreign Minister that the Tokyo Government might do well, before concluding an alliance with Germany and Italy, to consider the probable effect of such a move on American public opinion. There the matter rested for the time being, but the possible linkage of the aggressive forces in Europe and Asia could no longer be overlooked and became of necessity a matter of major importance in the deliberations of the Washington Government.[4]

Though the Japanese program was fairly clear and though the danger of a military pact between Germany and Japan had already become recognizable, Hitler's intentions continued to be shrouded in complete obscurity. From the now available German records the Fuehrer's plans can be reconstructed without difficulty. The minutes of his conferences with the German military leaders in November, 1937 (that is, ten months before the Munich crisis), leave no doubt that only force, or at least an impressive and convincing show of force, could have stopped that demonic genius; that every concession, far from gratifying him, only whetted his appetite; and that every sign of yielding simply strengthened his conviction of his opponents' weakness and timidity. By the time of his epoch-making success at Munich, Hitler had already reached such an advanced stage of megalomania that he regretted not having insisted on much more, even at the cost of a great war. He had become obsessed with the idea that the Western democracies were soft and degenerate, that they could be imposed upon indefinitely, and that he had a divine mission to secure for the Germans, at the expense of others, what he himself chose to describe as "adequate" living space. The complete liquidation of Czechoslovakia had been on his books for some time, as had

[3] This viewpoint was cogently presented in the first draft (January, 1939) of a planning paper that was to provide the basis for the Rainbow war plans (Watson: *Chief of Staff: Pre-war Plans and Preparations*).

[4] Grew's telegram of February 8, 1939, is printed in *Foreign Relations of the United States: Japan*, II, 161 ff. See further Hull: *Memoirs*, I, 627-28.

the "settlement" of the Danzig and Corridor questions with Poland. Beyond these objectives he saw opening before him bright vistas of further expansion over the boundless plains of the Ukraine and Russia.[5]

But in 1939 few people in the democracies took Hitler's famous book —*Mein Kampf*—seriously and nothing, of course, was known of the nefarious schemings in secret Nazi conclaves. No responsible statesman claimed to know what the Fuehrer's next move would be. If the Munich crisis left a trail of disillusionment, it ushered in also a period of the utmost anxiety and suspense. American diplomatic reports from Europe revealed the widest divergence of opinion in responsible circles and stressed the utter perplexity and even hopelessness which tended to paralyze policy on many sides. Even minor developments were watched in the desperate hope of finding some indications of the future. Europe was flooded with rumors of coming Nazi action, ranging all the way from a campaign against the Ukraine to a sudden and unannounced air attack on Britain. As late as February, 1939, the American Chargé d'Affaires in Berlin, Mr. Gilbert, was expatiating on the futility of trying to determine the Nazi plans. At the cost of laboring the point he felt constrained to recall that all decisions rested in the hands of Hitler and that Hitler remained "inscrutable."[6]

On one point, however, there was general agreement: that a Nazi move of some kind was not far in the offing. In a great speech of October 5, 1938, Winston Churchill had pointed out the enormity of the Munich settlement and had stressed that the only concession Mr. Chamberlain had been able to secure from the Fuehrer was that the latter "instead of snatching the victuals from the table, has been content to have them served to him course by course." The fate of Czechoslovakia as an independent entity, he added prophetically, had already been sealed: "I think you will find that in a period of time which may be measured by years, but may be measured only by months, Czechoslovakia will be engulfed in the Nazi regime." The conclusion seemed to Mr. Churchill obvious: "We are in the presence of a disaster of the first magnitude which has befallen Great Britain and France. Do not let us blind ourselves to that. It must now be accepted that all the countries of Central and Eastern Europe will make the best terms they can with the triumphant Nazi power." Since real friendship between Britain and the existing Nazi Government was unthinkable, the only remedy was to hasten and expand rearmament for defense against the evil day that was coming: "Do not suppose that this is the end. This is only the beginning of the

---

[5] The record of the conference of November, 1937—the so-called Hossbach Minutes— is printed in *Nazi Conspiracy and Aggression* (Office of the United States Chief of Counsel for Prosecution of Axis Criminality, Washington, 1946), III, 295 ff.

[6] Despatch from Gilbert, February 24, 1939 (not received in the State Department until March 14, 1939). It is, of course, impossible to itemize separately the many messages which are summarized above, but mention might be made of a long British memorandum of January 24, 1939, in which all the numerous contingencies were catalogued.

reckoning. This is only the first sip, the first foretaste of a bitter cup which will be proffered to us year by year unless, by a supreme recovery of moral health and martial vigor, we arise again and take our stand for freedom as in the olden time."[7]

These views were shared fully by men like Mr. Eden and Mr. Duff Cooper, and soon made converts even in the ranks of erstwhile appeasers. Lord Halifax, the Foreign Secretary, seems to have urged upon the Prime Minister the need for reorganizing the Cabinet so as to include some of these dissident Conservatives and to enlist the united strength of the party. But Mr. Chamberlain refused to compromise with his opponents. It is probably not true that he put great store by the Anglo-German declaration signed at the time of Munich, or that he had much faith in Hitler's good behavior. He was satisfied, however, that he had done the right thing at Munich and that he must continue to exert his best effort in the direction of appeasement, if only in the hope that time might be gained and that popular sentiment, even in the totalitarian countries, might be aroused in behalf of peace. During the winter the Prime Minister made a particular effort to induce the French to consider concessions to the Italians, on the chance that Mussolini might thereby be enlisted to exercise a deterrent influence on his Nazi partner. The Paris Government was prepared to make some minor concessions for the good cause, but in France as in Britain there was a rising tide of opposition to the appeasement policy and Premier Daladier, for one, was determined not to yield to blackmail or to surrender any advantages at gun point. Actually the British Prime Minister, for all his talk of appeasement, himself favored increased armament and was more and more inclined to acknowledge the danger of serious complications in the near future.[8]

On all sides, therefore, speculation centered on the probable direction of Hitler's next venture. According to *Mein Kampf* the ultimate objective was to be the Ukraine, and this thesis was, in fact, frequently discussed in the Nazi press during the winter of 1938-1939. As viewed from London or Paris the project made perfectly good sense, for Soviet Russia was believed to be worn out by the Five Year Plans and militarily much weakened by the spectacular purges of 1937-1938. Furthermore, the Munich deal had left the Soviet Government completely isolated. At the time and ever since, the attitude and policy of the Kremlin with regard to the Czech crisis have been a subject of protracted but generally inconclusive argument. Foreign Commissar Litvinov certainly did his utmost to propagate the idea that if France observed its obligations to the Czechs, the Soviet Government would

---

[7] Winston S. Churchill: *Blood, Sweat and Tears* (Putnam, New York, 1941) , 55-66.

[8] On the British side one of the most enlightening treatments is that of Keith Feiling: *The Life of Neville Chamberlain*, Chapter XXX. Georges Bonnet: *Fin d'une Europe* (Paris, 1948), Chapter III, expounds his views as French Foreign Minister. The Franco-Italian issue was reported on at some length by Bullitt in telegrams of March 3, 8, 11, 1939.

do its share in defense of the threatened state. But since Russia and Germany had no common frontier it seemed highly unlikely that in any case the Soviets could or would afford more than limited air support. There was talk about the transport of troops by way of Rumania, but it is practically certain that Rumania, like Poland, would have resisted such a move. The issue is far too complicated to be examined in detail here, but it is relevant to point out that the recently published German and British documents for the period leave no doubt that the Germans were highly skeptical about Soviet aid to the Czechs and that the British shared their attitude. From the existing evidence it seems altogether likely that the policy of the Kremlin was to encourage the French to fight and draw the British into the struggle, thereby diverting the Nazi threat from the East.[9]

Conversely the statesmen of the democracies have been repeatedly charged by Soviet leaders and publicists with having deliberately attempted to divert Hitler to the East, with the thought that in the event of a conflict between the totalitarian states both would be seriously weakened, and with the further and perhaps more important thought that a Nazi victory over Russia would at least remove the ominous threat of a world social revolution. Such notions were certainly dear to the Conservative clique known as the Cliveden Set, and were probably not foreign to Prime Minister Chamberlain himself. The point need not be labored, for it is perfectly understandable that the powers at either extreme of Europe should have hoped that the dynamism of the Nazi Revolution might strike in a direction other than their own. The significant thing is that the governing classes of both Britain and France had no faith in Soviet aims or policies, and therefore raised no objection to the exclusion of the Soviet Government from the Munich Conference and bent their efforts toward appeasement of the Nazi dictator. Since the Kremlin was thereby isolated, it was entirely reasonable to suppose that Hitler might take advantage of the situation to further his Eastern plans.[10]

[9] The recent documentary evidence is briefly summarized by Gordon A. Craig: "High Tide of Appeasement: the Road to Munich, 1937-1938" (*Political Science Quarterly*, LXV, March, 1950), and rather extensively analyzed by Max Beloff: "Soviet Foreign Policy, 1929-41: Some Notes" (*Soviet Studies*, October, 1950). To these may be added a tel. from Bullitt, September 8, 1938, reporting Daladier's belief that the Russians might march through Rumania, even though Rumania and Poland would probably declare war; tel. from Bullitt, September 12, 1938, reporting Bonnet as saying that the Russians would probably send planes across Rumania, but that transport by land would be impossible; memo of conversation between Welles and the Polish Ambassador, October 10, 1938, in which the latter stated that the Polish Government was convinced that the Russians would not have sent more than a few planes and that they had made no preparations whatever along the Polish frontier.

[10] Feiling: *The Life of Neville Chamberlain*, 407, specifically denies that Chamberlain thought in the terms described, but quotes ample evidence of the Prime Minister's deep-seated distrust of the Soviet Government. Ambassador Kennedy, who was much in Chamberlain's confidence in those days, is convinced that he hoped Hitler might be diverted to the East. On the other side the Soviet official publication *Falsificators of*

Yet at the turn of the year the agitation in Italy for the retrocession of Nice and Corsica raised the tension in Franco-Italian relations to the point where it appeared more likely that Hitler might try first to provoke a conflict in the Mediterranean, with the objective of engaging the Western Powers and so securing a free hand in the East or possibly settling the score with the democracies before committing himself against Russia. Since the famous Maginot Line was regarded as almost impregnable, it seemed likely that the Nazi hordes would drive through the Low Countries or Switzerland. To meet such an eventuality the British and French promised the Dutch and Swiss support in resistance. The Brussels Government, for its part, declined any arrangement that might be interpreted as compromising the absolute neutrality it had proclaimed in 1936.[11]

Curiously enough, on the very eve of Hitler's *coup de grâce* against mutilated Czechoslovakia there was a certain relaxation of the fear and trembling in the western capitals. Hitler's high-handed attitude toward Prague, his public warnings to the Western Powers against interference in the affairs of Central and Eastern Europe, and his barefaced evasion of the promised guarantee of "Czechia's" revised frontiers made it all too probable that the end of that victimized state was not far off. On the other hand, weeks and months had passed since Munich. The armaments of the Western Powers were progressing and Paris was standing firm in the face of Fascist demands. Even Mr. Churchill, ordinarily so prone to fear the worst, saw a faint glimmer of hope on the horizon. Speaking to an American businessman in February, 1939, he expressed full confidence in the readiness of the British and French people to resist further demands even at the cost of war. Mr. Chamberlain himself, he opined, was being pushed further and further in the direction of adopting the Churchillian recipe. It was fully to be expected that Germany and Italy would provoke a series of crises designed to break the morale of the democracies and there was, he thought, more than a 50 percent chance of war. But if it came, the fighting would be chiefly in the Mediterranean, for the Maginot Line would keep the Germans out of France. It was Churchill's conviction that the British and French Fleets could bottle up Italy completely, in which case the Germans would be forced to use their slender reserves to bolster their ally. Meanwhile the Germans would doubtless bomb London, but even this might have the advantage of arousing American opinion and bringing the United States into the conflict. Furthermore, Mr. Churchill envisaged Turkey, Russia, and Rumania joining the British-French coalition and thought Yugoslavia, Poland and even

History (Soviet Embassy, Washington, D.C., February, 1948) reiterates the charges in vehement fashion. On this whole subject see the dispassionate analysis in Max Beloff: *The Foreign Policy of Soviet Russia*, II (New York, 1949), Chapter X.

[11] Letter of Welles to the President, January 30, 1939; two personal messages from Halifax to the President, February 7, 1939 (*Roosevelt Papers:* Secretary's File, Boxes 44, 53). See also Bonnet: *Fin d'une Europe*, 126 ff.

Czechoslovakia might eventually do likewise. All in all, he failed to see how Germany could win in the long run.[12]

Lest it be thought that these were only the views of a private person, though an influential one, it should be noted that the London and Paris Governments saw the situation in much the same light. In a British memorandum of February 28, 1939, submitted to the State Department for the President, it was stated that reports were less pessimistic than they had been. There were some which suggested German plans for the occupation of what remained of Czechoslovakia, but it was doubted in London that Hitler would precipitate a crisis. It seemed that the firm stand of the French against Italian claims and the steady rearmament of the British had really impressed him.[13]

Unfortunately it is not easy to determine the President's reaction to the many reports from Europe which reached him during those days. If he sympathized with Mr. Chamberlain's action at Munich, he veered soon afterward in the Churchillian direction. According to former Secretary Morgenthau, the President was irritated by Ambassador Kennedy's close association with the Cliveden Set and believed the British Prime Minister to be slippery—ready for peace at any price.[14] Even though this may be an overstatement, it is quite likely that Mr. Roosevelt was affected by the strong American reaction against the Munich settlement, and that he was influenced by the eloquent radio address of Mr. Churchill, broadcast to the United States on October 16, 1938. The reports submitted by Ambassador Bullitt during his visit to Washington in October, 1938, probably clinched the matter and dispelled all further hopes of success through appeasement. It may be taken for granted, therefore, that the President's message to Congress (January 4, 1939) was in part intended to impress upon Europe and the world that, in the event of war, the United States would support the European democracies at least in a material way.[15]

[12] Report of a conversation between Mr. Churchill and Mr. William S. Wasserman, February 10, 1939, sent to the President by Secretary Wallace on February 27, 1939 (*Roosevelt Papers:* Secretary's File, Box 41). Churchill spoke in a similar vein to Ambassador Kennedy as late as March 2 (tel. from Kennedy).

[13] Letter from Welles to the President (March 4, 1939) transmitting a memo from the British Embassy February 28 (*Roosevelt Papers:* Secretary's File, Box 44); tel. from Bullitt, March 11, 1939, reporting Bonnet's optimism. See also Feiling: *Life of Neville Chamberlain*, 394-96, for evidence of Chamberlain's rising confidence during February.

[14] "The Morgenthau Diaries" (*Collier's*, October 18, 1947). The *Moffat Diary (MS.)*, February 9, 1939, records Secretary Hull's suspicion that Ambassador Kennedy was not adequately representing the American viewpoint to Mr. Chamberlain.

[15] According to the *German White Paper* (New York, 1940) Polish diplomats in Paris and Washington reported Ambassador Bullitt as saying that the President opposed further concessions to the dictators and as indicating that the United States would enter the war if there were danger of Britain and France being defeated. This evidence, however, must be excluded in view of the fact that the authenticity of the documents published by the Germans has been categorically denied by Mr. Bullitt and by the Polish diplomats in question, namely Count Potocki and M. Lukasiewicz.

The American stand certainly heartened the statesmen of London and Paris and may even have troubled Hitler to some extent. On the one hand Prime Minister Chamberlain stated frankly that the President's annual message and the American rearmament program had, in his opinion, brought about Hitler's "quieting down," while Mr. Churchill told an American visitor that "the very best thing the United States could do was to keep on beating the drums and talking back to the dictators. The one thing that might make them hesitate in plunging the world into war was the fear that the United States would soon be in it in a big way."[16] On the other hand Lord Halifax reported that the German Ambassador had admitted to him that the Germans were greatly disturbed by the "almost weekly utterances" of the President and had convinced themselves that the United States would come to the aid of England and France, not in two years, but probably in two days.[17] Whether or not the relaying of these remarks was intended by the British to encourage the President, it is worth noting that, according to Ambassador Biddle, Polish official opinion placed a high value on the President's stand: it had acted as a "stop, look and listen" sign to the dictators and had obliged them to reëxamine their position vis-à-vis the West; it had stiffened London and Paris; it had consolidated the British Dominions in support of a stronger British stand; it had "gingered up" the French and counteracted a feeling of defeatism; and finally it had dampened Rome's "war-mongering boisterousness."[18]

The "quieting down" of Hitler in February and early March, 1939, attributed by London and Paris, at least in part, to the firmer attitude of the United States Government, gave rise to an entirely unwarranted optimism. As the vituperation of the Italians began to subside, it seemed ever more likely that the Fuehrer, if he resumed his policy of expansion at all, would direct it toward the East, either toward the Ukraine or the Balkans. It is not clear how much the Western capitals may have known of the negotiations between Berlin and Poland from October, 1938, to January, 1939. But on the American side Ambassador Biddle, though at first unable to make much sense of a host of contradictory rumors, was in a position, at the end of November, 1938, to indicate that the Germans were suggesting a bargain to the Poles and that, if the latter proved recalcitrant, Hitler might propose to the Soviet Government a deal which would involve the recognition of mutual spheres of influence.[19] Somewhat later Colonel Beck,

[16] Tel. from Kennedy, February 17, 1939, reporting the remarks of the Prime Minister; memo of a conversation between Mr. Churchill and Mr. Wasserman, February 10, 1939 (*Roosevelt Papers:* Secretary's File, Box 41).

[17] Tel. from Kennedy, February 23, 1939; tel. from Bullitt, February 27, 1939, reporting what a friend of Lord Halifax had told him of the interview.

[18] Letter from Biddle to the President, March 4, 1939 (*Roosevelt Papers:* Secretary's File, Box 53).

[19] Despatch from Biddle, November 26, 1939.

the Polish Foreign Minister, gave the Ambassador a detailed account of his visit to Berlin (January 5, 1939), at which the question of the Ukraine had been discussed at some length. Still later, after Ribbentrop's disillusioning visit to Warsaw (January 25, 1939), Biddle was able to report on the recall of a German trade commissioner who had already reached the Polish capital on his way to Moscow.[20]

Despatches from Warsaw were necessarily slow in reaching Washington and there is no evidence that they were given urgent treatment.[21] It is probably safe to assume that news of friction between Germany and Poland was taken everywhere in the West as a welcome promise that Hitler would turn his attention eastward. As for the ominous suggestions of a possible deal between the Nazis and the Soviets, they were not taken seriously, in view of the violent and long-drawn ideological conflict between the two countries. Joseph E. Davies, former United States Ambassador to Moscow, warned that the Fuehrer might well shelve his antagonism to Moscow and try to associate the Kremlin in a grand assault on the Western democracies.[22] But there is no evidence that these admonitions made an impression. Neither were the responsible statesmen of London and Paris moved by rumors current at the time. After a long conversation with Mr. Chamberlain, Ambassador Kennedy reported:

> Chamberlain does not take the possibility of a Russian-German alliance seriously. He says they are both so distrustful of each other that it would never work out; and that it is Hitler's hope of course to stir up enough trouble in the Ukraine so that he can point out how badly the Russians are treating the Ukrainians and that he could go in if he wanted to and in this way get some more concessions without any strain on his resources.

French Foreign Minister Bonnet was equally skeptical of alleged negotiations between Germany and Russia.[23]

And yet there was good reason to pay attention to the Soviet position. On February 22, 1939, Foreign Commissar Litvinov, in conversation with the British and French Ambassadors, criticized bitterly the policy of appeasement which, he said, had brought with it the collapse of the system of collec-

---

[20] Despatches from Biddle, November 26, 1938, January 13, and February 16, 1939; also a long review of the development of the German-Polish conflict by Ambassador Biddle, dated February 3, 1940. The Polish and German records on these vital negotiations may be found in the *Polish White Book* and in the *German Documents on the Outbreak of the War*; see also *Nazi Conspiracy and Aggression*, VII, No. L-151.

[21] Biddle's despatch of November 26, 1938, did not reach the Department ·until December 10; that of January 13, 1939, not until January 27; and that of February 16 until March 15. The second was sent to the President on February 16 and the third on March 15, 1939.

[22] Davies had meanwhile been appointed Ambassador to Brussels. See his reports of January 18 and March 21, 1939, in his *Mission to Moscow* (New York, 1943), 433 ff., 439. We have used also his unpublished tel. of February 9, 1939.

[23] Tel. from Kennedy, February 17, 1939; tel. from Bullitt, February 28, 1939.

tive security. Soviet Russia, he added, obviously could not carry on this system alone, but was prepared to help revive it provided the Western Powers would do their part sincerely and wholeheartedly. What exactly provoked these remarks is not known, but the French Ambassador was much impressed by them. In his report he stressed the thought that the Soviet Government felt itself at the crossroads. If Britain and France were to take a strong stand against Germany and Italy, he was persuaded that the Moscow Government could be counted on to do likewise.

If, on the other hand [he continued], we decline the Russian offer, we run the risk of seeing Russia follow a policy of organizing a system of security on her western and northwestern frontiers which would be her own. This system might provide for technical and economic collaboration with Germany, assisted by Poland and perhaps Rumania, which would free the Reich from all fear in the East and which, through the intermediary of Poland, the Baltic States and Rumania, would furnish Germany with raw materials and such freedom of movement as would be indispensable for settling accounts with the West.[24]

Whether or not the report of this conversation made an impression in London or Paris cannot be said. Presumably it did not evoke a favorable response, for on March 10, the very eve of Hitler's final blow at Czechoslovakia, Stalin himself astounded the world by a brutally outspoken address to the Eighteenth Congress of the Communist Party. The Soviet leader began by contrasting the economic crisis of the Western world with the steady, ordered progress of the Soviet Union. He thereupon reviewed the new cycle of "imperialist" wars which was already encompassing the world. A new division of the globe and of colonial spoils seemed to him the inevitable outcome. The system of collective security had broken down and the aggressors were in full career. For all this Stalin bitterly castigated the Western Powers which, though stronger than their opponents, were ready to yield all along the line. Fear of revolution resulting from war, he asserted, had wedded them to nonintervention and appeasement, and their one great hope was "of egging the Germans on to march farther East, promising them easy pickings and prompting them: 'Just start a war on the Bolsheviks, and everything will be all right.'" But, he insinuated, the aggressors had played the appeasers false. Nothing had come of all the ballyhoo about an invasion of the Ukraine and now Europe was stricken with fear, not knowing where the next move would lead. In the midst of all this uncertainty, said Stalin, Soviet policy remained clear and explicit:

We stand for peace and the strengthening of business relations with all countries. . . . We stand for peaceful, close and friendly relations with all the neighboring countries which have common frontiers with the U.S.S.R. . . . We stand for the support of nations which are the victims of aggression and are fighting

[24] *OSS Files:* tel. from the French Ambassador at Moscow, February 24, 1939.

for the independence of their country. . . . We are not afraid of the threats of aggressors, and are ready to deal two blows for every blow delivered by the instigators of war who attempt to violate the Soviet borders.

How to read this extraordinary statement was hard to say. The violent diatribe against the appeasing democracies and the suggestion of friendly relations with neighboring countries hinted the possibility of a Soviet-Nazi deal. On the other hand, the declaration of support for the victims of aggression and the warning against any assault on the Soviet Union appeared directed against Hitler's Germany. One thing, however, was inescapable, and that was substantially what Litvinov had told the Ambassadors: if Britain and France persisted in the policy of appeasement, the Soviet Government might be obliged to devise for itself some other system of security. In any event, it would not remain passive in the midst of crisis. A decision would have to be made.

With that, the confused and uncertain weeks of early 1939 drew to a close. On the Ides of March, Hitler ended the suspense and forced decisions that could no longer be avoided.

2. END OF CZECHOSLOVAKIA

After the foregoing exposition of the doubt and perplexity that beset the Western Governments in the early months of 1939, the question may well be asked: what, actually, were Hitler's immediate plans? Strangely enough, this query cannot be answered with assurance despite the vast quantities of evidence from the German side that have become available in recent years. However, nothing in the existing record indicates that the Fuehrer's basic aim—territorial conquest in Eastern Europe—was in any way changed. There is no good reason to doubt his oft-repeated assertion that he desired peace and friendship with Britain and, by derivation—since London and Paris were so closely linked—with France also. But this proposition was always based on the assumption that the Western democracies would leave Germany a free hand in Central and Eastern Europe. Hitler never tired of pointing out that Britain and France had no business to interfere in what was of right Germany's sphere, and that, if it came to the ultimate test, he would not tolerate such interference. Since, however, both the British and the French were reluctant to accept this basis for a settlement, it behooved Hitler to lay his plans in such a way that his opponents would prove unable to obstruct him. The first step, obviously, was to undermine the French alliance system in Central and Eastern Europe. At the beginning of 1939 that objective had already been largely attained. Poland, by the agreement of 1934, stood rather more in the Nazi camp than in the French; the entire Danubian region had already been brought into economic dependence on Germany; and by the Munich settlement Czechoslovakia had been eliminated as a military power and left at the mercy of its powerful neighbor. Even so, it may be observed that the Fuehrer was far from satisfied. Despite his triumph at Munich, he was determined to wipe out the Czechoslovak state completely and his plans were laid for action at the opportune time.

Within the wider circle of Hitler's thought the situation seems to have shaped up somewhat as follows: Poland, which had already taken part in the spoliation of Czechoslovakia, was to be enlisted in the campaign against Soviet Russia. In return for this privilege and as compensation for large prospective gains, Poland was to abandon Danzig to Germany and agree to the construction of an extraterritorial road across the Corridor to East Prussia. This proposition, first advanced to the Poles in October, 1938, and again in January, 1939, was later frequently referred to by the Germans as an almost unbelievably generous offer—so generous in fact that only a leader of Hitler's prestige and popular following could ever have made it palatable to the Germans. No doubt it so appeared to the Fuehrer, for he was thinking in world terms, in comparison to which Danzig and a road to East Prussia were trivial items indeed. In any case, the deal with Poland was on the books and by it the approach to Russia was to be laid open.

The Soviet Union, however, was a huge country which, inefficient though its Government may have been, would always be able to throw vast quantities of manpower into a struggle and, furthermore, might be supported by Britain and France, which, in their turn, might receive aid from the United States. The only counterweight to this coalition was the association of Japan with the Berlin-Rome Axis in a firm military pact. This global aspect of Hitler's policy has not, perhaps, been sufficiently stressed. Too frequently the European and Far Eastern problems are dealt with separately and, even when their interrelationship is sensed, it is not clearly elaborated. In treating this preliminary period the problem need not be analyzed in detail. The documentation is so extensive that even a sketch of the development can be made reasonably accurate.

Germany, Italy and Japan were already bound by the so-called Anti-Comintern Pact of 1936, which, though ostensibly directed against the spread of communism, was rightly suspected by the Soviet Government of containing secret clauses aimed at Russia itself.[25] Even in 1936 the Japanese High Command seems to have been intent on concluding a more specific military agreement and, acting through General Oshima, the Japanese Military Attaché in Berlin, several times broached the subject to the Nazi Government. At first the Germans turned a deaf ear, evidently fearing serious involvement before they were prepared for it. But when the suggestion was renewed in June, 1938, the Foreign Minister, Ribbentrop, took it up with

[25] *Cf.* Litvinov's speech of November 28, 1936, as quoted by Arthur U. Pope: *Maxim Litvinov* (New York, 1943), 405-6. The secret clauses are quoted by Dewitt C. Poole: "Light on Nazi Foreign Policy" (*Foreign Affairs,* October, 1946).

some enthusiasm and recommended it to the Italians. His proposal envisaged a defensive pact providing for consultation in case one of the signatories were to find itself in political difficulty; for political and economic support in case one of them were confronted with a threat from another power; and for military aid in case one of them were to suffer an unprovoked attack. The German view from the outset was that the arrangement should be directed against any and all powers. The Japanese, on their part, desired a pact aimed at Russia, though they were willing to accept a more general agreement provided Russia were put in a special category. There were long discussions about the exact wording of the text, but at the Munich Conference Ribbentrop was able to show Mussolini a preliminary draft. The Italian dictator was skeptical of the project, which he considered premature, but Ribbentrop continued to press for it. During his visit to Rome at the end of October, 1938, he explained to Mussolini that the situation was such that war with Britain and France within a few years was inevitable. In such an event, Japanese aid would be valuable, the more so as it would probably frighten the United States into ever deeper isolation. But the Duce remained unconvinced and reserved his decision till after the New Year.

Then, suddenly, Mussolini decided to take the plunge. On January 2, 1939, the Germans were informed that Italy would sign, and for these reasons: it was now clear that Britain and France were bound by a military pact and that French circles were accepting the possibility of war; furthermore, that the United States was embarking upon a program of rearmament which was patently designed "to furnish men and above all materials to the Western democracies in case of necessity." Ribbentrop was delighted and agreed that the papers should be signed at the end of January. But, unhappily for the Germans, at this very time (January 5) the Japanese Cabinet of Prince Konoye gave way to a new government under Baron Hiranuma, which insisted on reconsidering the matter and held innumerable conferences before making up its mind. By the end of January no decision had been reached. Instead of replying to the German proposal, the Tokyo Government announced its intention of sending a special mission to Berlin, which would arrive only at the end of February. Ribbentrop was furious and Mussolini disgusted, but the matter was not to be taken lightly, for the German Ambassador at Tokyo reported that while the Army staunchly favored the agreement, the Imperial Court and the Navy, as well as several high civilian officials, were opposed to anything that might estrange or provoke Britain and the United States. When at last the Japanese mission reached Berlin at the beginning of March, it reported that the Japanese Government would agree to mutual aid only in the event of war with Soviet Russia. There were heated confabulations. Oshima offered to return to Tokyo and threatened, if his government remained refractory, to resign.

Ribbentrop himself talked of taking a plane for Tokyo. He would hear nothing of Mussolini's suggestion of a separate German-Italian military alliance. Only a triple alliance which included Japan, he argued, would serve to deter the United States from support of the democracies. There the matter rested at the time of the March crisis. All depended on Tokyo's reaction to the protests and pressures of Ribbentrop, Oshima and Shiratori, the Japanese Ambassador at Rome.[26]

Here, then, was Hitler's grand design for isolating Russia, for neutralizing Britain and France, and for forestalling American interference on behalf of the democracies. The Japanese were to be assigned a heavy burden and it is no wonder that they hesitated to serve as shock absorbers. The entire project still hung in the balance when, on the night of March 14-15, Hitler dragooned President Hácha of Czechoslovakia into submission and then proceeded to the occupation of the rump Czech state. The complete liquidation of Czechoslovakia had long been foreseen by men like Churchill and the technique employed was the familiar one of subversion and threat.[27] So far as other powers were concerned, there was nothing to be done. Czechoslovakia itself had been rendered helpless at Munich and neither Britain nor France was therefore in a position to take effective action. To quote Churchill once again: "It is no use going to their aid when they are defenseless, if we would not go to their aid when they were strong. Therefore I agree entirely with those who think we should not intervene at the present time. We cannot. That is the end of it."[28]

Nevertheless, the Nazi occupation of Prague was to have repercussions of a revolutionary nature. The Fuehrer had for the first time flagrantly violated the principle of nationality, which theretofore had proved so effective an instrument of his policy. Furthermore, he had disregarded specific international obligations and flouted his own solemn promises. From that moment there was little room for doubt that no reliance could be placed on his word. It was clear to most people that his ambitions knew no limit and

[26] The most valuable evidence on these negotiations is to be found in the *Tokyo War Crimes Documents*, as follows: interrogation of Oshima (Documents 2156D and 4121) and affidavit by Oshima (Document 2862); affidavit by Shiratori (Exhibit 3595); memo by Prince Konoye (Defense Document 1580); deposition of Marquis Kido (Defense Document 2502); affidavit of Heinrich Stahmer (Exhibit 2744); a tel. from Ribbentrop to Ott, April 29, 1939, reviewing the entire matter from the German side (Document 4035). See further *The Ciano Diaries* (Doubleday, New York, 1946), entries for January-March, 1939, and *Ciano's Diplomatic Papers* (Odhams Press, London, 1948), 242 ff., 258 ff. This whole problem is discussed by Elizabeth Wiskemann: *The Rome-Berlin Axis* (New York, 1949), 123, 133-35, but far and away the best single treatment, making use of some unpublished Italian materials, is that of Mario Toscano: *Le Origini del Patto d'Acciaio* (Florence, 1948), 3-4, 12, 19, 26, 29 ff., 43 ff., 55-74 *passim*.

[27] Among recent accounts those of John W. Wheeler-Bennett: *Munich: Prologue to Tragedy* (New York, 1948), 331 ff., and of L. B. Namier: *Diplomatic Prelude, 1938-1939* (London, 1948), Chaps. II, III, can be highly recommended.

[28] Speech at Waltham Abbey, March 14, 1939 (Churchill: *Blood, Sweat and Tears*, 95-97).

that, unless stopped, he would use all available means to extend his power and control. To be sure, the question still remained open what direction the next Nazi thrust would take, but Slovakia's declaration of "independence," prompted by Nazi pressure, made it seem likely that the Germans, in conjunction with the Hungarians, would next turn to the rich oil and wheat fields of Rumania. In Britain excitement ran high. On all sides there were strident demands that something be done at once to check further Nazi aggression.

In the midst of the popular furore the Prime Minister, however, remained a puzzling figure. In the House of Commons on March 15 he explained that it had been impossible to reach agreement on a guarantee of Czechoslovakia's frontiers, as envisaged at Munich. The declaration of Slovak independence had then "put an end by internal disruption to the state whose frontiers we had proposed to guarantee," and consequently the British Government could not longer hold itself bound. With respect to the general situation, Mr. Chamberlain declared:

> It is natural that I should bitterly regret what has now occurred. But do not let us on that account be deflected from our course. Let us remember that the desire of all the peoples of the world still remains concentrated on the hopes of peace and a return to the atmosphere of understanding and good will which has so often been disturbed. The aim of the Government is now, as it has always been, to promote that desire and to substitute the method of discussion for the method of force in the settlement of differences.

Here, indeed, was no clarion call to action, either in support of Hitler's latest victim or against further aggression on his part. Churchill and no doubt many others could only conclude that the Prime Minister proposed to accept what had happened "with the best grace possible."[29]

In Washington the excitement was much greater than in London. State Department officials were divided in their opinions. "No one here," noted one of them, "has any illusions that the German Napoleonic machine will not extend itself almost indefinitely." But the character of the next German move was as enigmatic as ever. Some thought that Hitler, now that he had eliminated Czechoslovakia, would feel free to turn on the West, while others believed he might shelve his Ukrainian plans and try for an economic and political agreement with Soviet Russia before challenging Britain and France, and still others held that he would continue his advance to the East.[30] On the evening of March 14, 1939, Ambassador Bullitt telephoned the President from Paris and urged him first to make a ringing denunciation of Nazi aggression and then go to Congress with a request for

[29] Churchill: *The Gathering Storm*, 343-44. In this connection see the controversy between former Ambassador Kennedy and Mr. Churchill in *The New York Times*, September 26, 1948, and October 17, 1948.

[30] *Moffat Diary (MS.)*, March 14, 1939; *Berle Diaries (MS.)*, March 16, 1939.

repeal of the neutrality laws. But Mr. Roosevelt suspended judgment. He was convinced that Hitler would embark on his Eastern venture and suspected that economic and other strains might make the going hard for him. "He was not particularly bothered by it," and, like many Englishmen, may have calculated that a German advance to the East would at least afford relief to the European democracies.[31]

But in the State Department officials were agreed that something must be done. For weeks there had been much argument as to the advisability or inadvisability of having Mr. Hugh Wilson, the American Ambassador, return to his Berlin post. That idea was now definitively buried and the discussion then turned on the desirability of severing relations with Germany completely. But that move, too, was finally abandoned in the thought that it might not only irritate the Germans unnecessarily, but even encourage the British and French to think that in the last resort the United States would go to war. Ultimately it was decided that Mr. Welles (Acting Secretary in Mr. Hull's absence) should make a public statement, which the President approved on March 17, 1939, and which was given to the press on the same day. The text ran as follows:

The Government of the United States has on frequent occasions stated its conviction that only through international support of a program of order based upon law can world peace be assured.

This Government, founded upon and dedicated to the principles of human liberty and of democracy, cannot refrain from making known this country's condemnation of the acts which have resulted in the temporary extinguishment of the liberties of a free and independent people with whom, from the day when the Republic of Czechoslovakia attained its independence, the people of the United States have maintained specially close and friendly relations.

The position of the Government of the United States has been made consistently clear. It has emphasized the need for respect for the sanctity of treaties and of the pledged word, and for nonintervention by any nation in the domestic affairs of other nations; and it has on repeated occasions expressed its condemnation of a policy of military aggression.

It is manifest that acts of wanton lawlessness and of arbitrary force are threatening world peace and the very structure of modern civilization. The imperative need for the observance of the principles advocated by this Government has been clearly demonstrated by the developments which have taken place during the past three days.[32]

The second item on the program was in many ways even more eloquent than these forceful words. For some months the Secretary of the Treasury, Mr. Morgenthau, had been pointing out that the Germans were bestowing

[31] *Berle Diaries (MS.)*, March 16, 17, 1939.
[32] Text in *Peace and War*, 454-55. For the details we have relied on the *Moffat Diary (MS.)*, March 15, 17, 1939; and on the *Berle Diaries (MS.)*, March 16, 17, 1939. See also Hull: *Memoirs*, I, 615.

something in the nature of a bounty on certain items of German-American trade and that, under the law, he was entitled if not obligated to levy countervailing duties. The State Department had raised a number of objections to this course and the President had agreed that the step might have undesirable political repercussions. But the question had been reopened in a Cabinet meeting on March 10, 1939, at which time the President had changed his mind and decided to ask the Attorney General for an opinion. Before this was forthcoming, news arrived of the German action against Czechoslovakia. Mr. Welles, who was "hopping mad," argued that the time had now come to take the debated measures. The decision was reached in the Cabinet meeting of March 17, 1939, whereupon Mr. Welles at once informed the German Chargé d'Affaires of the new policy.[33] The President furthermore cast about for some way of blocking Czech funds in the United States, though both Secretary Morgenthau and Acting Secretary Welles discouraged the idea, in view of its implications and probable complications. Eventually Mr. Roosevelt decided not to recognize the German absorption of Czechoslovakia, but to continue to deal with the Czech representative in Washington. All in all, the American Government, acting strictly on its own, left no shred of doubt as to its reaction to Hitler's latest achievement.

It is unlikely that the American attitude had an influence on the British Prime Minister comparable to the pressure of the British public, the Foreign Office, and his own party colleagues, which induced him to shift his position when he delivered his famous address at Birmingham on March 17, 1939. Mr. Chamberlain on that occasion explained that he had spoken so softly two days before because at that time he had had insufficient information. He hoped to correct the impression that he did not feel strongly about what had happened. Thereupon he launched forth on an extended and vehement defense of his Munich policy and recalled Hitler's assurances of six months before: the Sudetenland would be the last territorial claim he had to make in Europe; once it was settled, he would no longer be interested in the Czech state; he did not want any Czechs in the German Reich. All these assurances had now been scrapped and the Prime Minister made much of the personal affront he had suffered. Only toward the end of his address did he come down to the question of future policy, asking certain very pertinent questions:

[33] Memo from Hugh Wilson to Mr. Sayre, December 3, 1939, to which are attached the minutes of a State Department meeting of December 5, 1939, and the draft of a letter to the President, December 6, 1939, which was not sent; memo of conversation between Welles and the German Chargé d'Affaires, March 17, 1939. This issue is fully documented in the *Morgenthau Diaries (MS.)*, Vols. 169, 170, 200, *passim*. We have used also the *Berle Diaries (MS.)*, March 22, 1939; the *Moffat Diary (MS.)*, March 17, 1939; and Hull: *Memoirs*, I, 615.

Is this the end of an old adventure, or is it the beginning of a new?

Is this the last attack upon a small state, or is it to be followed by others? Is this, in fact, a step in the direction of an attempt to dominate the world by force?

Those are grave and serious questions. I am not going to answer them tonight. But I am sure they will require the grave and serious consideration not only of Germany's neighbors, but of others, perhaps even beyond the confines of Europe.

Britain itself, he continued, would have to review its entire position:

I do not believe there is anyone who will question my sincerity when I say there is hardly anything I would not sacrifice for peace. But there is one thing that I must except, and that is the liberty that we have enjoyed for hundreds of years, and which we will never surrender. That I, of all men, should feel called upon to make such a declaration—that is the measure of the extent to which these events have shattered the confidence which was just beginning to show its head and which, if it had been allowed to grow, might have made this year memorable for the return of all Europe to sanity and stability.

It seemed to him incredible, he said, that Europe should face the challenge of an effort to dominate the world by force, but, in case the challenge should be made, he felt impelled to voice a warning:

I feel bound to repeat that, while I am not prepared to engage this country by new unspecified commitments operating under conditions which cannot now be foreseen, yet no greater mistake could be made than to suppose that, because it believes war to be a senseless and cruel thing, this nation has so lost its fibre that it will not take part to the utmost of its power in resisting such a challenge if it were ever made.[34]

While Chamberlain was delivering his Birmingham address the British Foreign Office was already in possession of most alarming new intelligence. On that very day the Rumanian Minister in London had reported that the Germans had demanded of his Government a monopoly of exports (chiefly oil and wheat) and the acceptance of measures of industrial restriction, in return for which Hitler was prepared to guarantee Rumania's frontiers. The Bucharest Government, he added, was inclined to regard these demands "as in the nature of an ultimatum." The matter was one of "extreme urgency," and the Minister desired to know what position the British Government would take in the event of German aggression. Thereupon Lord Halifax had at once consulted both the French and Russian Ambassadors and had instructed the British envoys in Warsaw, Belgrade, Bucharest, Athens and Ankara to sound out those Governments as to their

[34] Text in *Documents Concerning . . . the Outbreak of Hostilities Between Great Britain and Germany* (so-called *Blue Book*), 5 ff. For the circumstances and for an evaluation of the speech see Churchill: *The Gathering Storm*, 344 ff., and the detailed analysis in Wheeler-Bennett: *Munich*, 355 ff. We have used also Ambassador Kennedy's tel. from London, March 18, 1939.

attitude. During the next several days replies came in which covered the whole gamut of evasion. The Polish Government questioned the story of a German ultimatum and stated that it would have to consult with Bucharest before making up its mind. Prince Paul of Yugoslavia expressed willingness to consider British proposals if and when they were made. Greece fell back on its limited obligations under the Balkan Pact, but was ready to consider a joint Greek-Turkish-Yugoslav guarantee of Rumania's frontiers if Bucharest asked for it. The Turks were sympathetic but also limited themselves to the Balkan Pact and desired to wait and see what Britain would do. The Rumanians themselves desired to avoid provoking Germany and were interested only in British-French support if they decided to offer armed resistance to German pressure.

There remained the question of the French and Russian attitudes. The Paris Government, and particularly the Premier, M. Daladier, were fully prepared to take a strong line to check Germany. While thoroughly skeptical about the German "ultimatum" and not at all sure that the Rumanians would resist in a crisis, the French were heartily in favor of "drumming up support for Rumania from the four corners of the earth." In a conversation with Ambassador Bullitt, M. Daladier said that M. Herriot was eager to go to Moscow to negotiate "a firm and absolute military understanding with the Soviet Union." Mr. Bullitt expressed doubt whether Russian promises could be relied upon, but agreed that in the existing situation no stone should be left unturned "even though one might expect to find vermin under it." He recommended that Herriot be accompanied by someone as unscrupulous as the Bolsheviks themselves, but pointed out that it was most improbable that either the Rumanians or the Poles would accept Soviet aid in an emergency. As Daladier saw it, the situation was black: Hitler, in conjunction with the Hungarians, would first move against Rumania; then would come Poland's turn; and meanwhile Mussolini would probably submit unacceptable demands to France. In his view war was fast approaching. Diplomacy had almost ceased to count and the great problem now was to find armaments and allies. With this Bullitt agreed.[35]

To the Kremlin the British approach must have come as something of a surprise, considering Stalin's violent castigation of the Western democracies in the speech he had delivered only a few days before. But since, on that same occasion, the Soviet leader had promised Russian support to victims of aggression, it probably seemed to London not entirely paradoxical to inquire of Moscow what the Soviet Government might do in the

[35] The foregoing is based chiefly on personal messages from Halifax to the President, March 21, 23, 1939 (*Roosevelt Papers:* Secretary's File, Box 44), but also on tels. from Kennedy, March 18, 20, 22; tels. from Bullitt, March 18, 20; and on Bonnet: *Fin d'une Europe*, 154 ff.

event of a Nazi attack on Rumania. On the whole, the Soviet reply was not discouraging. Litvinov expressed surprise that the Rumanians, if actually threatened, should not have approached the Soviets themselves. However, he continued, since the British had not indicated their own intentions, the Soviet Government suggested that a six-power conference of Britain, France, Russia, Poland, Rumania and Turkey be convened at Bucharest to arrange a program of mutual protection. This proposal was at once discarded by the British as being "premature," probably because the replies of the Balkan Governments to the original British inquiry had not yet been received.[36] In the sequel the Soviet Government and Soviet sympathizers were to make much capital of the allegedly cavalier treatment accorded their proposal, which on the surface at least seemed altogether in line with Litvinov's plea to the British and French Ambassadors (February 22, 1939) for a strong and united stand against aggression. But there is no reason to suppose that the British Government had any nefarious purpose in view. At the time the situation was utterly confused and the replies from the other Governments were being awaited. Furthermore, it had become apparent that the Rumanian report of a German "ultimatum" had been exaggerated. Under the circumstances, and in consideration of the well-known aversion of powers like Poland and Rumania to any dealings with the Kremlin, the London Government may well have felt that the Soviet proposal was not only premature but far too pretentious and dangerous.[37]

What particularly confused the issue was a second move of the British Government, taken on March 19, 1939, before all the Governments consulted on March 17 had had a chance to respond. London now proposed to France, Russia and Poland that they agree to a public declaration, drafted by the British, that in the event of a threat to the independence of any European state, the four signatory powers would at once consult on measures to be taken in order to organize common resistance. M. Bonnet, the French Foreign Minister, who was in London at the time with President Lebrun, at once expressed his assent, though pointing out the probable difficulty of bringing both Russia and Poland into the same alignment. Litvinov, who, according to the official Soviet account, had been assured by the British Ambassador that the declaration would involve almost no commitments, promised that the Soviet Government would sign if France and Poland did likewise, but at the same time expressed disappointment at the rejection of the Kremlin's proposal for a six-power conference.

[36] Tels. from Kennedy, March 18, 20; tels. from Bullitt, March 20, 22, 1939. See also the reports of Walter Duranty from Moscow, in *The New York Times,* March 21, 22, 1939.

[37] The Soviet interpretation is forcefully presented in *Falsificators of History.*

It remained for the Poles, therefore, to give the project the *coup de grâce.* Foreign Minister Beck indicated that his Government might be willing to join with Britain and France, but that any association with Soviet Russia would be as unpleasant as it would be dangerous: it would provoke Hitler and perhaps lead to war.[38]

As an alternative to the British proposal, the Poles suggested that Britain and Poland conclude a secret agreement along the lines of the suggested declaration, without prejudice to a later decision about the projected public statement. Colonel Beck evidently did not see fit to inform either London or Paris that on March 21, 1939, Hitler had resubmitted to Warsaw his proposals for a settlement of the Danzig and Corridor problems. Obviously this ominous development must have influenced Polish policy. Hitler's ultimatum to Lithuania on March 22, 1939, which resulted in the retrocession of Memel to the Reich, could only be taken as further indication that the Fuehrer's eyes were directed to the East. The Poles, unwilling in any case to consider Soviet aid, could no longer hope to remain on the fence. Colonel Beck, who only a few weeks before had expressed the greatest distrust of British policy and had voiced the conviction that in a crisis the London Government would always fall back on appeasement, was now obliged to look to the West and to exert his best efforts to secure firm assurances of support against German demands.[39]

The argument of the British, in turn, appears to have been on this order: in the event of further German aggression it was of great importance that Rumania or Poland, as the case might be, should offer armed resistance. These two states had signed a treaty of mutual assistance in case of attack by Soviet Russia. If possible, the Poles were to be induced to extend this obligation to cover the eventuality of aggression by Germany. In view of the known opposition of both Poland and Rumania to any suggestion of Soviet aid, the attitude of Moscow in such a contingency seemed relatively unimportant. Furthermore, the British Government had little faith in the sincerity of Soviet policy and small respect for Soviet military power: "I must confess to the most profound distrust of Russia," wrote Mr. Chamberlain on March 26, 1939. "I have no belief whatever in her ability to maintain an effective offensive, even if she wanted to. And I distrust her motives, which seem to me to have little connection with our ideas of liberty, and to be concerned only with getting everyone else by the ears."[40]

These ideas were shared by other members of the Cabinet, who regarded Poland as a more formidable military power than the Soviet Union. Under

[38] Tels. from Kennedy, March 20, 22, 23, 24, 1939; messages of Lord Halifax to the President, March 21, 25, 1939; Bonnet: *Fin d'une Europe,* 161 ff.; Feiling: *Life of Neville Chamberlain,* 420 ff.; *Falsificators of History.*

[39] Despatch from Biddle, March 3, 1939, reporting Beck's comments on British policy and his determination to "wait and see."

[40] Feiling: *Life of Neville Chamberlain,* 403; Bonnet: *Fin d'une Europe,* 166.

the circumstances it seemed best to the British to make sure of Poland and more particularly to enlist Polish aid for Rumania, so that a line might be established in Eastern Europe beyond which Hitler could advance only at the risk of war.[41]

Hitler seems to have believed that the Poles would presently yield to his "generous and modest" proposals. On March 25, 1939, he explained to one of his generals that he did not want to solve the Danzig problem by force and thereby drive Poland into the arms of Britain. A military occupation of Danzig was to be considered only if the Poles indicated that such action would make it easier for them to accept the inevitable loss of the city. The larger question of Poland's future, which involved eliminating that state completely and annexing a large part of its territory, was to be left for a time when the political situation was particularly favorable.[42]

The Fuehrer's calculations were, however, doomed to immediate and bitter disappointment. On March 26, 1939, the Warsaw Government flatly rejected his proposals and warned him that "any further pursuance of these German plans, especially where the return of Danzig to the Reich was concerned, meant war with Poland."[43] This momentous decision was taken by the Warsaw Government without reference to the Western Powers, for Colonel Beck was still fearful lest the British renew their suggestions of the past that Poland make concessions to Germany on the Danzig issue. The Polish Ambassadors in Paris and London did not learn of the great decision until some days later, partly no doubt because the Poles knew that the Germans had broken their codes and therefore preferred to communicate by letter. To be sure, rumors of the German-Polish negotiations appeared in the press, but the British Foreign Office was skeptical of all such reports, probably recalling the recent flare-up over the German "ultimatum" to Rumania.[44]

In ignorance, then, of these ominous developments, the British Government continued its deliberations and, on the evening of March 27, 1939, decided to make Warsaw a firm offer. This decision meant relegation of Soviet Russia to "a second line of defense." According to Ambassador Kennedy it was obvious that the British and French did not expect Russia "to make any substantial contribution to the problem of common security."

[41] Tel. from Biddle, March 22, 1939, reporting the remarks of Robert H. Hudson, the British Under Secretary for Overseas Trade, who was visiting Warsaw. Hudson stated that the British Government felt impelled to disabuse the eastern states of the idea that Britain would not offer armed resistance until Hitler approached the Dardanelles.

[42] *Nazi Conspiracy and Aggression,* VIII, No. R-100.

[43] *Polish White Book,* No. 66; *German Documents on the Outbreak of the War,* Nos. 203, 208.

[44] Biddle reported the facts on March 25, 1939, in a tel. which was followed by another on March 26, 1939. In the former he stated that Beck had informed the British Ambassador that Hitler was pressing for a settlement of the Danzig question. Bullitt, in a telegram of March 25, 1939, reported that the French Foreign Office had information indicating German-Polish negotiations. Kennedy (March 27, 1939) reported Halifax's skepticism.

The French Government fell in line with the British proposal and on March 29, 1939, after a long Cabinet meeting, the British Government sent notes to Warsaw and Bucharest embodying the following proposition: If Poland and Rumania were to fight to defend their independence, Britain and France would give aid, provided Poland helped Rumania if necessary. In return Poland was to promise to support Britain and France in case of attack by Germany or in case they went to war to resist German aggression against Western countries (the Netherlands, Belgium or Switzerland) or against Yugoslavia. Britain and France, it was added, would maintain friendly contact with Soviet Russia to prevent that power from relapsing into isolation and to assure its benevolent neutrality and possible support in the way of supplying war materials.[45]

It is impossible to escape the conclusion that Colonel Beck cleverly maneuvered the British and French into their fateful offer. The Poles had rejected Hitler's proposals and were determined to fight for Danzig. They wanted the aid of the Western powers, but they would have nothing to do ·with a pact that included the Soviet Union. By their evasive replies to the British suggestion for a four-power declaration and by omitting to inform the British of their decision to defy Hitler, they left the London Government in doubt whether in fact they would resist Nazi aggression. Thereupon the Chamberlain Government, in its anxiety to have both Rumania and Poland offer resistance and to make sure that Poland supported Rumania against Germany as well as against Russia, was induced to make an offer that was heavily weighted in Poland's favor.[46]

Small wonder, therefore, that Colonel Beck, faced with the prospect of serious difficulties with Germany, made up his mind at once—"between two flicks of his cigarette ashes," as the story goes. He accepted the British-French proposal at least in general terms and gave his assent to a British declaration of guarantee, though clearly much of the detail was left for discussion during the Polish Foreign Minister's projected visit to London during the coming week. Prime Minister Chamberlain, for his part, did not await the final settlement. On March 31, 1939, he announced the guarantee to Parliament: ". . . In the event of any action which clearly threatened Polish independence, and which the Polish Government accordingly considered it vital to resist with their national forces, His Majesty's Government would feel bound at once to lend the Polish Government all support in their power."[47]

The British guarantee to Poland has been described as "one of the most

[45] Tel. from Kennedy, March 28, 1939; message from Halifax to the President, March 29, 1939; Bonnet: *Fin d'une Europe*, 168-69.

[46] Tel. from Kennedy, March 28, 1939, reporting the illuminating remarks of the Polish Ambassador; tel. from Bullitt, March 29, 1939, reporting from the Polish Ambassador the substance of a letter received by the latter from Beck.

[47] Full text in *British Blue Book*, No. 17. For the rest see Bonnet: *Fin d'une Europe*, 169-70; Namier: *Diplomatic Prelude*, 107 ff.

remarkable public declarations in the history of British foreign policy," inasmuch as it completely reversed Chamberlain's stand of March 17, 1939, against "new unspecified commitments operating under conditions which cannot be foreseen," and left the Warsaw Government to decide whether Britain should be involved in war. One writer has remarked with bitterness that the Prime Minister, having abandoned Czechoslovakia, then proceeded to guarantee one of Czechoslovakia's despoilers.[48] The explanation for this extraordinary turn is hard to find. According to Ambassador Kennedy, the Prime Minister was most reluctant about the commitment and fully sensed its implications, but felt impelled to act by popular protest against continuance of the appeasement policy, by public demand for an effective peace front, and by fear of American criticism. Whatever Mr. Chamberlain's reservations may have been, Lord Halifax and indeed most of the Cabinet had come to favor a positive, active policy, designed to deter Hitler and perhaps even to create among the Germans a revulsion against the Nazi leadership. Furthermore, the Prime Minister's declaration, widely interpreted as the death knell of appeasement, was welcomed and cheered by the British public, as well as by political leaders of all hues, from Churchill and Lloyd George to the Labour Party chieftains. The one criticism was that Soviet Russia had been left out of the new alignment. "To halt with the guarantee to Poland," declared Churchill, "would be to halt in No Man's Land under fire of both trench lines and without the shelter of either." More pointedly Lloyd George remarked: "If we go in without the help of Russia, we shall be walking into a trap. It is the only country whose armies can get there [i.e. to Poland] and who has got an air fleet which can match Germany's."[49]

Even at the time it was fully realized that an important turning point in international relations had been reached. On all sides it was felt that the years of appeasement had brought Britain to the verge of bankruptcy. Mr. Churchill has summed up the situation in a few eloquent lines:

History, which we are told is mainly the record of the crimes, follies and miseries of mankind, can be scoured and ransacked to find a parallel to this sudden and complete reversal of five or six years' policy of easy-going, placatory appeasement, and its transformation almost overnight into a readiness to accept an obviously imminent war on far worse conditions and on the greatest scale.[50]

3. THE PRESIDENT'S MESSAGE

The foregoing rather lengthy disquisition on the European crisis of March, 1939, is indispensable for the understanding of American policy, for it is impossible to appraise the reaction of the President and his advisers without rather full knowledge of the situation as they saw it. Conversely it

[48] Wheeler-Bennett: *Munich*, 374.

[49] Debate in Parliament, April 3, 1939 (see *The New York Times*, April 4, 1939); Churchill: *The Gathering Storm*, 346. We have used also a dispatch from Ambassador Davies (Brussels), April 4, 1939, reporting his talks with Churchill and Lloyd George.

[50] Churchill: *The Gathering Storm*, 347.

should not be forgotten that the course of events abroad was influenced, though not determined, by the attitude of Washington. For Hitler it was clearly of great importance to know whether, if he continued on his course of aggression, the United States would support the Western democracies and if so, whether merely by material aid. For London and Paris the line of American policy was even more crucial, for it might well mean the difference between defeat and victory. It was not astonishing, therefore, that almost every chancellery in Europe, with the exception of the German and Italian, made a point of keeping the President and the State Department fully advised. Even the Soviet Government, from time to time, saw fit to express itself on current developments.[51] Mr. Roosevelt and Mr. Hull were therefore promptly and fully informed. It is hardly an exaggeration to say that they were better placed than other statesmen to see all aspects of the situation and, if they deemed it desirable, to exercise great influence.

The reaction of the President and his advisers to the German absorption of Czechoslovakia has already been discussed. There is but scant evidence of their attitude toward the further developments of the crisis. Mr. Roosevelt apparently drew nothing but pessimistic conclusions from Hitler's latest coup and convinced himself once more that the chances of stopping further Nazi aggression through a policy of appeasement were just about nil. There is nothing in the record to indicate that the President did not sympathize with the British-French efforts to strengthen resistance to Hitler's advance and, if possible, to build up a peace front. Ambassador Bullitt certainly favored such a course and did what he could to encourage Prime Minister Daladier and the French Government to persevere. Ambassador Kennedy, in turn, was close to the British Prime Minister and reflected the latter's viewpoint. The Ambassador regarded war in the near future not only as a possibility, but as a probability, and made no secret of his belief that the British as well as the Americans should keep aloof from it. His thesis was that the Poles, if left to themselves, would feel obliged to make a deal with Hitler which would then enable the Nazis to pursue their objectives in the East. The conflict between the two leading totalitarian powers would then take care of itself, to the great benefit of the whole Western world. Among other things, the democracies and the United States would gain time for rearmament, the need for which Mr. Kennedy never tired of stressing.[52]

The President and the State Department had, however, no part in the British program of stiffening the Poles and Rumanians. From the diary of one high official it appears that the State Department had as much difficulty as the newspapermen in interpreting the British maneuvers. The

[51] *Moffat Diary (MS.)*, March 18, 19, 24, 1939, recording conversations with Oumansky, at that time Soviet Chargé d'Affaires.

[52] Much of this is based on conversations of the authors with Ambassador Kennedy, June 30, 1949. Needless to say, the Ambassador's opinions were clearly expressed also in his contemporary reports.

initial inquiry addressed to the Balkan and East European Governments, followed so quickly by the proposal for a public declaration, seemed "curiously inept" and raised the question whether the British effort to make Poland and Rumania "lie down" with Russia, which they were known to hate slightly more than Germany itself, was not like inviting Eastern Europe to accept German aggression more indulgently. Nonetheless, the British guarantee to Poland was taken as marking a step forward, inasmuch as it committed Britain to positive action in Eastern Europe.[53]

Another aspect of the Chamberlain policy, however, evoked greater enthusiasm in the White House. On March 20, 1939, the Prime Minister wrote to Mussolini, recalling their recent conversations in Rome and adumbrating the possibility of a settlement of outstanding issues. It was known that Mussolini had been surprised by the German occupation of Prague and that he was anything but pleased by his Nazi colleague's highhanded and independent action.[54] If the effort to wean the Duce from his German connection succeeded, it would exorcise the threat of a Mediterranean war between France and Italy, which would provide the Germans with a free hand for an assault upon Britain and the Low Countries.

The British move seemed one to which the President thought he might lend a helping hand. Ambassador Kennedy had recently paid a visit to Italy and had reported that the Italians wanted to avoid war and were, in fact, quite unprepared for it. He had discovered that the Italians put great store by American friendship and that the Rome Government listened anxiously whenever the President spoke.[55] Lord Halifax had inquired what the American viewpoint was with respect to Italy and immediately thereafter Ambassador Davies had telegraphed from Brussels urging Mr. Roosevelt to communicate with Mussolini either through Ambassador Phillips or through the Italian Ambassador in Washington. Davies's argument was that Hitler would not risk war unless he were certain of Italian support, that Mussolini might yet be deterred, and that perhaps he could be shown that he had much more to lose than to gain by throwing in his lot with the Germans.[56] The idea appealed to Mr. Roosevelt, who decided at once to try his hand.

On March 22, 1939, the President received the new Italian Ambassador, Prince Colonna, at the White House. The Ambassador, who had no reason to expect more than the usual formalities, must have been greatly surprised when Mr. Roosevelt began to deliver himself of a "curtain lecture." The President, following closely the suggestions of Ambassador Davies, warned Colonna that, despite all the American newspapers might say, the American

[53] *Moffat Diary (MS.)*, March 23, 24, 31, 1939.
[54] Tel. from Kennedy, March 20, 1939; tel. from Bullitt, March 20, 1939, reporting Foreign Minister Bonnet's readiness to make some concessions to Italy.
[55] Tel. from Kennedy, March 17, 1939.
[56] Tel. from Davies, March 21, 1939.

people was united in its sympathies and would, if war broke out between the dictators and the democracies, side overwhelmingly with the latter. This, he explained, was not because the American people wanted to dictate to others their form of government, but simply because they were opposed to policies of military domination which might threaten the peace of the world. It seemed to him, said the President, that Signor Mussolini had a great opportunity to prevent war:

In the first place, there was no question that the neutrality legislation in the United States would be speedily amended, and that should war break out for the reasons he had previously indicated, the people of the United States would certainly insist that such assistance as this country could render the countries which were the object of aggression in Europe be rendered to the fullest extent possible.

He then admonished Colonna that Europe had no room for two overlords and that Hitler, whenever it suited him, would throw the Duce over. If Signor Mussolini were to use his influence to defer the crisis, he would be given credit for averting war and would have a chance to secure concessions through discussions around the conference table. What the President envisaged was not anything as pretentious as the peace conferences of Versailles or Vienna, but rather:

. . . discussions among a limited number of people, and that, while he himself would not take the initiative because he did not desire to have it thought by the European powers that the United States was "butting into" European affairs, he did feel that Mussolini himself should take the initiative. He would lend him his support in finding "a reasonable solution" in every possible way.[57]

Nothing is known of Mussolini's reaction to the President's unconventional *démarche*, nor for that matter of the further history of Mr. Chamberlain's advances. It seems likely that M. Daladier, ever the opponent of any but the most modest concessions to Italy, objected to the price the British were prepared to pay. On March 29, 1939, the Premier, speaking over the radio, scotched all thought of substantial French concessions to Italy. He ridiculed talk of France's weakness and rejected out of hand the claims advanced by the Fascist press: "I said, and I maintain," he declared, "that we will not cede a foot of our land nor one of our rights."[58] Mussolini's reply was to proceed, on April 7, 1939, to the long-projected Italian occupation of Albania, by which he demonstrated the same disregard for solemn promises that marked Hitler's action of three weeks before. Albania, to be sure, meant little in terms of European politics, but the Duce's action at

[57] Memo by Welles of the President's talk with Prince Colonna, March 22, 1939 (*Roosevelt Papers:* Secretary's File, Box 53). On April 4, 1939, the President asked that copies be sent to Ambassadors Phillips, Bullitt and Kennedy, and also to Mr. Chamberlain and Lord Halifax (*F. D. R.: His Personal Letters*, II, 876).

[58] Tels. from Bullitt, March 18, 20, 27, 1939, reflecting his encouragement of Daladier in this stand. For the British position see Feiling: *Life of Neville Chamberlain*, 413.

once raised the question whether he would move next against Greece or join with Hitler in an assault first on Yugoslavia and then on Rumania. In view of Hitler's demands on Poland with respect to Danzig there could be little doubt that the two dictators had linked their forces for the realization of a combined program.[59]

This newest development was a severe blow to the President and his associates, who could not help seeing the situation in the darkest colors. On April 1 Hitler had delivered a threatening speech at Wilhelmshaven and Lord Halifax had informed the President that he had intelligence from a reliable source that Hitler proposed to reply to the British guarantee policy by delivering a lightning attack on the British Fleet in the hope of striking a knockout blow. Ambassador Bullitt had similar information from German sources and reported further that M. Daladier expected war by May 1.[60]

Under these circumstances it was more than an academic question what the United States should do. Thus far the country had expressed vigorous condemnation of aggression and had voiced sympathy with the victims and with the Western democracies. Could anything further be done? Was there, for example, any method of throwing American influence into the scales by assuring the democracies of material support? This was the question that plagued the White House and the State Department and to which the answer was difficult to find. The public opinion polls revealed that the American people, though deeply outraged by recent events in Europe, was still far from envisaging anything like military involvement. Only 16 or 17 percent of those questioned were in favor of intervention in case of need. On the other hand, the polls reflected a growing majority in favor of the supply of planes and other matériel to the British and French, and in fact of a revision of the American neutrality legislation.[61]

It will be recalled that Mr. Roosevelt, in his conversation with Prince Colonna on March 22, 1939, had expressed himself as confident of the early revision of the neutrality laws through Congressional action. In this he proved to be entirely too optimistic, for the Administration's program continued to run into endless difficulties. Ever since January, 1939, the matter had been under debate. Senator Pittman, who was to pilot the bill through the Senate, had taken the stand at the outset that outright repeal would be impossible and that nothing more than certain changes in the existing law should be proposed. Furthermore, he was exceedingly apprehensive lest the debate reopen the highly controversial issue of American policy toward the Spanish Civil War and lest the project for revision be lost

[59] *Berle Diaries (MS.)*, entry for April 7, 1939.

[60] Message from Halifax for the President, April 5 (*Roosevelt Papers:* Secretary's File, Box 44); tel. from Bullitt, March 25, 1939; *Berle Diaries (MS.)*, entry for April 5, 1939.

[61] In March, 1939, 52 percent favored the supply of planes and matériel; in April, 1939 the figure was 66 percent. The April poll recorded 57 percent as favoring revision of the neutrality laws.

in the morass of partisan conflict. It had therefore been agreed that the Administration's efforts should be concentrated on repeal of Article I (the arms embargo), but with the provision that exports of war materials to belligerents be put on a "cash and carry" basis. The President was to be given discretionary power to keep American citizens and ships out of zones of war as defined by him.[62]

The State Department thereupon prepared for Senator Pittman a draft bill incorporating the ideas to which the President had assented. By mid-March, 1939, the Spanish Civil War was drawing to a close and the moment for action seemed to have arrived. But by that time Pittman had become much concerned about the provision of discretionary power for the President, fearing lest the opposition in the Senate torpedo the entire bill rather than give the President any leeway "to ease us into war."[63] Nonetheless, the Senator on March 20, 1939, at last introduced his bill, describing it as the Peace Act of 1939. The so-called isolationists and interventionists at once took position, but the battle, which promised to be hotly contested, was yet again postponed when it was discovered that the proposed "cash and carrry" provision would apply in favor of Japan against China. The President took this occasion to repeat to Senator Pittman that "the existing neutrality act should be repealed *in toto* without any substitute," but the Senator refused to undertake so large an assignment.[64]

The hearings before the Senate Committee on Foreign Relations opened on April 5, 1939, with testimony by former Secretary of State Henry L. Stimson, who presented so strong a case for repeal that he threw a bad scare into both Pittman and Secretary Hull. The Secretary was extremely nervous about the whole strategy and day after day conferred with his subordinates in an effort to draft a statement which he might make to the Senate Committee. It was perfectly obvious to all that there was strong feeling in the Senate against according the President discretionary powers and against any move that might lead the country nearer war. Mr. Hull's inclination was to confine his statement to general terms, but it soon became evident that the isolationist leaders were spoiling for a chance to ask him a number of highly embarrassing questions. For days on end a half dozen of the highest officials of the Department worked to arrive at a satisfactory statement. Meanwhile the isolationists were prolonging the hearings of the committee and Pittman felt that he was losing control.

[62] Memo of a conversation between Senator Pittman, Judge Moore of the Department of Justice, and Mr. Carlton Savage of the State Department, February 10, 1939; memo by Mr. Savage, February 17, 1939, reporting on Judge Moore's conference with the President. Further: *Moffat Diary (MS.)*, January 20, 23, February 17, 1939.

[63] Memo by Carlton Savage of talks with Pittman, March 17, April 3, 1939; memo of conversation between Judge Moore and Pittman, March 18, 1939. See also Hull: *Memoirs*, I, 612 ff.

[64] Note of the President to Secretary Hull, March 28, 1939 (*Roosevelt Papers:* Secretary's File, Box 52).

On May 1, 1939, the "cash and carry" provisions of the existing law expired; thenceforth the British and French, if involved in war, would be unable to buy and transport American arms and munitions even in their own ships. Action on revision had become even more urgent and Secretary Hull therefore girded himself for the Congressional ordeal. But on May 8, 1939, Senator Pittman came down to the Department. Having read the Secretary's painfully elaborated statement, he remarked acidly that it would not do at all, for the committee was all set to quiz Mr. Hull on the Administration's commitments to Britain and France, on the relations of Japan to the United States and to the Axis, and other leading issues. The committee would not even agree to hear the Secretary in executive session. Evidently there was such a storm brewing that Mr. Hull decided against appearing for the time being at least.[65]

Months of planning, drafting and maneuvering had led to nothing but deadlock. The President desired the complete repeal of the existing law and, according to the opinion polls, a distinct majority of the population favored at least such revision as was necessary to enable the European democracies to secure arms and munitions in the United States. Yet the strong isolationist group, especially in the Senate, gave every indication of readiness to disregard public sentiment and of determination not to grant the President further power, if only from fear lest he use it to commit the country to some form of involvement in a future foreign war. The President was clearly unwilling to supply public leadership because he wanted to avoid further stirring up of political antipathies and desired above all to prevent a debate which would reveal to the world the strength of isolationist sentiment. Secretary Hull, too, was extremely apprehensive of the opposition in Congress and quite unwilling to face cross-examination on the real purposes of the Administration's policy. The matter had therefore been left to Senator Pittman, who proved a weak reed to lean upon. Pittman began by insisting on a compromise proposal, which, he declared, he could certainly pilot through the Upper House. But once the committee hearings began, he quickly lost heart. All told, the Administration forces found themselves in a sorry plight at the beginning of May, 1939.

The failure to secure Congressional action to provide the European democracies with material support in the event of further crisis deprived the President of the most effective means to impress or deter Hitler. Apparently all other possible courses of action were explored, including the perennial notion of calling a conference. Ambassador Bullitt, who was con-

---

[65] The day-by-day development of the issue is carefully recorded in the *Moffat Diary (MS.)*, April 5-10, 12, 17, 24, May 3, 5, 8, 1939. We have used also a memo by Carlton Savage, April 13, 1939. See further Hull: *Memoirs*, I, 641 ff.; Alsop and Kintner: *American White Paper*, 40-43; Whitney H. Shepardson and William O. Scroggs: *The United States in World Affairs, 1939* (New York, 1940), 72 ff.; Basil Rauch: *Roosevelt: from Munich to Pearl Harbor*, 114 ff.

vinced of the need for some overt action on the President's part, urged that, after the occupation of Albania, Italian funds in the United States be frozen. But this proposal was rejected for fear of seeming to align the country irrevocably against the Axis. Secretary Morgenthau suggested the possibility of forming a league of nonaggressor states with the idea of restricting the export of strategic raw materials to the Axis countries. But this, again, was considered too risky, the more so as its success would have required the coöperation of Soviet Russia.[66]

There remained to the President no weapon but the spoken word. There was a feeling, probably shared by Mr. Roosevelt himself, that too many statements had been issued in recent years, but there was always the chance that words might make an impression abroad. Indeed, the question arose whether it might not be possible to appeal, if only in veiled fashion, to the peoples of the world rather than to the governments. Some suggestion of this approach was contained in the statement of condemnation which Secretary Hull issued on the day after the Italian action against Albania:

> The forcible and violent invasion of Albania is unquestionably an additional threat to the peace of the world. It would be shortsighted not to take notice of this further development.
>
> Any threat to peace seriously concerns all nations and violates the will of all peoples in the world that their governments shall lead them, not toward war, but along paths of peace.
>
> It is scarcely necessary to add that the inevitable effect of this incident, taken with other similar incidents, is further to destroy confidence and to undermine economic stability in every country in the world, thus affecting our own welfare.[67]

The President was at this time recuperating at Warm Springs, where an "authoritative spokesman" expressed Mr. Roosevelt's full approval of the Hull statement. The same "spokesman" made clear that in the President's opinion the security of the United States itself was imperiled by each new act of Nazi-Fascist aggression, hastening the day when America might have to choose between available "economic weapons." There was no suggestion that the United States throw its military forces into a struggle against aggression, but the "spokesman" left no doubt that the Government stood behind Britain and France in their efforts to stop Hitler.[68]

Unfortunately Mr. Roosevelt himself spoiled the effect of this solemn warning by making a characteristically flippant remark as he left Warm

---

[66] *Berle Diaries (MS.)*, April 2, 5, 1939, including a long memo reviewing all possible courses of action. On the Treasury suggestion we have used a memo from Harry White to Secretary Morgenthau, which the latter presented to the President on April 10, 1939; tel. from Bullitt, April 10, 1939, urging the freezing of Italian funds.

[67] Text in *Documents on American Foreign Relations*, I, 305; Hull: *Memoirs*, I, 619. The background is given in the *Moffat Diary (MS.)*, April 8, 9, 1939.

[68] Belair, in *The New York Times*, April 9, 1939; Canham in *Christian Science Monitor*, April 10, 1939.

Springs on April 9, 1939: "I'll be back in the autumn if we don't have a war." These ill-considered words quite naturally aroused a storm of isolationist indignation. They were taken as certain proof of the President's determination to take the country into war and, what was worse, to commit the crime frivolously. Senator George rebuked the President in these pontifical words: "I venture the statement, Mr. President, and I venture it without fear or hesitancy: if we let Europe alone, there will be no war."[69] It was the use of the word "we" that gave rise to most speculation and impelled Mr. Roosevelt to restate his thought. According to an inspired editorial in the *Washington Post* (April 11, 1939), the "we" obviously meant Western civilization. The United States was certainly included in the threat of war. Conflict was not inevitable, but it could be prevented only if the United States made a show of preponderant force. It was crucial that the country declare its position before it became too late. Mr. Roosevelt at once endorsed this editorial and added an expression of his belief that it was essential for the United States to support British-French efforts to check the Axis.[70]

These rather startling statements were only the prelude to a much more imposing theme. Mr. Roosevelt, when he returned to Washington, had already made up his mind to speak out. In his Pan American Day address (April 14, 1939) he stressed the policy of hemisphere solidarity and defense:

> The American peace which we celebrate today has no quality of weakness in it! We are prepared to maintain it, and to defend it to the fullest extent of our strength, matching force to force if any attempt is made to subvert our institutions or to impair the independence of any one of our group.

But he also appealed to the Old World to emulate the Good Neighbor Policy: let the European nations adopt pledges against aggression similar to those which bound the twenty-one American Republics. Such pledges, along with the "open door of trade and intercourse," would make dreams of conquest appear "ridiculous and criminal" to Europeans as to Americans. "Do we really have to assume," queried the President, "that nations can find no better methods of realizing their destinies than those which were used by the Huns and the Vandals fifteen hundred years ago?" Axis complaints of "imprisonment" and "encirclement" were groundless. In conclusion Mr. Roosevelt urged the Europeans to "break the bonds of the ideas that constrain them toward perpetual warfare." He warned the whole world of the American position: "We, too, have a stake in world affairs."[71]

The Pan American Day address was patently directed to the peoples of

[69] *The New York Times*, April 14, 1939.
[70] *Washington Post*, April 11, 1939. See also the comment by Arthur Krock in *The New York Times*, April 14, 1939, and by Mr. Harsch in the *Christian Science Monitor*, April 14, 1939.
[71] Full text in *Public Papers and Addresses*, VIII, 195 ff.

the world and should be read in connection with the President's much more pretentious move, the "Saturday surprise" message to Hitler and Mussolini of April 15, 1939. The origin of this famous document is still somewhat obscure. Possibly it was inspired by telegrams or telephone conversations from Ambassador Bullitt, who was reporting genuine alarm on the part of the French Government and was continually urging the President to do something. Bullitt was certainly thinking of something more than another verbal effort, for on April 10, 1939, he telegraphed that words would have no effect on the dictators and that only action would count.[72] But words were the only weapon at the President's disposal and he may well have reckoned that a personal appeal from himself, as the head of a powerful nation, might yet make an impression; in any case it would keep the record clear and might gain time for Britain and France to rearm and construct a peace front.[73]

The President brought the first draft of the message back with him from Warm Springs and showed it to Secretary Hull on the evening of April 10, 1939. It is quite likely that even then Mr. Hull was not enamored of the idea, which further met with scant enthusiasm on the part of some State Department officials. Assistant Secretary Berle advocated expanding the original text and giving it the character of an appeal to the German and Italian peoples, rather than to their leaders. During the night he wrote an impassioned and eloquent message, making the words "sing." After some hours of discussion on the morning of April 11, the Berle text was submitted to Mr. Roosevelt, who evidently preferred his own version and adopted only passages of the Berle draft. For the next two days there was more debate, if not on the wording, at least on the timeliness, of the message. Secretary Hull urged that some passages be changed and the issuance of the message delayed. It was not until the afternoon of April 13, 1939, that Under Secretary Welles effected a compromise between the conflicting views. On the evening of April 14, 1939, the message was put on the wires and on the next day published to the world.[74]

In its final form the famous message was not at all "purple." In fact, it was a rather prosaic document. The argument, briefly, was this: the nations of the world were living in fear of war and, if war came, all nations—victors and vanquished and neutrals—would suffer. It was in the power of the leaders to spare their peoples the disaster that impended. Mr. Roosevelt

---

[72] Tel. from Bullitt, April 10, 1939. In the light of this telegram Hull's statement (*Memoirs*, I, 620), that the idea of the message was inspired by Bullitt, must be corrected.

[73] Alsop and Kintner: *American White Paper*, 36, supplemented by a conversation of the authors with Mr. Welles, May 27, 1947.

[74] Technically the President sent the message only to Hitler, as chief of the German State. The message to Mussolini, as head of the Italian Government, went out over Mr. Hull's signature. The various drafts are in *Roosevelt Papers*: Secretary's File, Box 45; and also in the *Berle Diaries (MS.)*, April 10-13, 1939. The *Berle Diaries* and the *Moffat Diary (MS.)*, April 10-15, 1939, both throw much light on the genesis and drafting of the message.

made it plain that in his opinion the threat came from Germany and Italy, and he called upon the leaders of those countries to demonstrate the sincerity of their oft-repeated statements that they did not desire war. International problems, he argued, could still be solved around the council table:

It is therefore no answer to the plea for peaceful discussion for one side to plead that unless they receive assurances beforehand that the verdict will be theirs, they will not lay aside their arms. In conference rooms, as in courts, it is necessary that both sides enter upon the discussion in good faith, assuming that substantial justice will accrue to both; and it is customary and necessary that they leave their arms outside the room where they confer.[75]

The heart of the President's proposal was that the dictators should give assurance that for a period of at least ten years they would not attack any one of a list of thirty-one independent nations, covering the whole of Europe and the Near East.[76] This period of peace would give ample opportunity to negotiate a settlement of outstanding problems, in which the United States would aid—within limits:

I propose that if it [the assurance] is given, two essential problems shall promptly be discussed in the resulting peaceful surroundings, and in those discussions the Government of the United States will gladly take part.

The discussions which I have in mind relate to the most effective and immediate manner through which the peoples of the world can obtain progressive relief from the crushing burden of armament which is each day bringing them more closely to the brink of economic disaster. Simultaneously the Government of the United States would be prepared to take part in discussions looking towards the most practical manner of opening up avenues of international trade to the end that every nation of the earth may be enabled to buy and sell on equal terms in the world market as well as to possess assurance of obtaining the materials and products of peaceful economic life.

At the same time, those Governments other than the United States which are directly interested could undertake such political discussions as they may consider necessary or desirable.[77]

This extraordinary and spectacular move on the President's part met with a surprisingly favorable response from the American public. Extremists

---

[75] This passage was particularly dear to the President. The far more picturesque version of the original text was toned down at Mr. Hull's advice. It read: "It is equally clear to me that no solution can be arrived at by council and negotiation if one party to the conversation carries a gun in one hand and a grenade in the other. In the pioneer days of America, courts of justice followed the frontiersman, but it was a well-established rule that all arms were left outside the courtroom."

[76] Psychologists may be able to deduce some conclusions from the fact that the President, in his first draft, inadvertently omitted the Soviet Union, which appears in the final text as "Russia."

[77] Text in *Public Papers and Addresses of Franklin D. Roosevelt*, VIII, 201-5; *Documents on American Foreign Relations*, I, 306-9.

among the isolationists might denounce it as meddling in other peoples' affairs, as a reprehensible effort to stir the Germans and Italians to revolt, and as a dastardly attempt to fan the flames of hatred. But many of those who on principle objected to any involvement in European matters were ready to applaud a noncommittal appeal to reason and an invocation to peace. Mr. Roosevelt had taken the precaution to head off any distorting criticism. On the morning of April 15 he had explained his message paragraph by paragraph to the Washington correspondents, watering it down as much as possible. He had called attention to the fact that he had offered to act, not as mediator, but only as intermediary: "I am the post office, the telegraph office—in other words, the method of communication." As for his offer to participate in discussions of disarmament and liberalization of trade, "there is nothing, absolutely nothing, new that we have not been doing right along." And lastly he noted that he had specifically excluded the United States from political discussions, by which he meant "boundaries and territories and so forth and so on." We would not have anything to do with such: "We do not, of course, enter into that type of discussion. We have not done it since Paris, and there is no prospect of our doing it." In closing the President took care to dismiss any talk of conspiracy with Britain or France. He told his listeners that there had not been any consultation with the Latin American or any other governments: "Great Britain, France or any other nation in the world was not consulted in any way and did not know anything about it."[78]

So it was made clear that no insidious motives underlay the message and that no new commitments were implied. The country at large accepted this explanation, while the interventionists rejoiced that the President had stressed the American interest in peace abroad and had "put the dictators on the spot" by identifying them as the only aggressors and by placing the responsibility clearly on their shoulders if they resorted to war.[79]

The President's message had been broadcast over all major networks and to all parts of the world. It evoked a tremendous popular response. The Latin American countries and governments reacted enthusiastically, as did also the peoples of Europe, with the exception of those dominated by the Axis. The British and French were overjoyed, feeling that the President had now definitely taken a stand against the Axis and that, in an emergency, he would surely find ways and means of implementing his decision. Even the Soviets voiced their approval. There could be no doubt that the message

[78] *Public Papers and Addresses*, VIII, 208-17.

[79] See the editorial in *The New York Times*, April 15, and the comments by Krock (*ibid.*, April 16) and by Canham (*Christian Science Monitor*, April 17, 1939). There is a good summary of the public reaction in D. F. Fleming: "Roosevelt and the Dictators" (*Events*, June, 1939).

had made a deep impression. Presumably the Germans and Italians, though unable to express themselves, were also somewhat moved.[80]

The acid test, of course, was to be the rejoinder of the addresses. The controlled press of Germany and Italy boiled with rage, scorn and vituperation, no doubt reflecting sentiments in high circles. It so happened that at the time Marshal Goering was paying a visit to Rome. In his conversation with the Duce on April 16, 1939, the President's message was the first item to be considered. Goering remarked that the document suggested an incipient brain malady, to which Mussolini added characteristically that it might be a case of creeping paralysis. The two paladins agreed that it might be best to reply only through the press, but that nevertheless the implications of the message deserved careful consideration. In other words, the importance of the American attitude was not at all overlooked by Berlin and Rome. Goering particularly stressed its influence on world opinion and even then speculated on the advantages of Roosevelt's possible non-reëlection in 1940.[81] The French Foreign Office learned from a high German source that the Fuehrer's fury, too, was directed chiefly against the President personally, and that his first reaction was to refuse a reply to "so contemptible a creature." But the strength of the impression made on the public by the message was so great that some official response appeared advisable.[82]

Mussolini gave the first indication of the Axis stand in a speech of April 20, when he stated his refusal to be influenced by "press campaigns, convivial vociferations, or Messiah-like messages." The suggestion of a ten-year truce he characterized as "absurd," while participation of the United States in any future conference on disarmament or trade would reveal the American Government restricted to "its customary role of distant spectator."[83] This was all that was heard from the Duce, who must have been even more aware than Ambassador Phillips of the aversion of the Italian people to any war. In any event, it was fully realized everywhere that not the Duce but the Fuehrer would make the decisions, and that therefore everything hinged on Hitler's reply.

Just what response the President expected to a message that combined sharp recrimination with fervent appeal is not entirely certain, but the

[80] In the *Roosevelt Papers:* Secretary's File, Box 45, there is a complete digest of the reactions of foreign governments and a comprehensive collection of news reports and kindred materials. See also Pertinax in *The New York Times,* April 17; report from London in *New York Herald Tribune,* April 20; Matthews in *The New York Times,* April 19, 1939.

[81] *Ciano Diaries,* entry for April 15; memo of conversation between Mussolini and Goering, April 16 (*German Foreign Office Documents*); letter of Ambassador Phillips to the President, April 20, 1939 (*Roosevelt Papers:* Secretary's File, Box 45); Tolischus, in *The New York Times,* April 17, 1939.

[82] Tel. from Bullitt, April 18, 1939.

[83] Text in *Documents on American Foreign Relations,* I, 325 ff.

violence of his antipathy to the dictators may be deduced from the following episode: Secretary of Agriculture Henry Wallace, no doubt quite ignorant of the President's plan, had proposed that he himself despatch an
appeal to the dictators. On April 14, 1939, Mr. Roosevelt wrote discouraging the idea:

> The two madmen respect force and force alone. They will try to disparage the
> [Wallace] note. There is danger that people in foreign lands and even some in
> the United States will look on your effort as being in the same category as delivering
> a sermon to a mad dog. The prestige of your name is so important in world affairs
> that it should not, in my opinion, be risked at this time. At the present time the
> most feasible way out is to use methods which would tend to drive a wedge
> between the two madmen.[84]

Having himself appealed to the "madmen," Mr. Roosevelt can hardly
have expected a soft reply. Mussolini's statement must have extinguished,
for the time being at least, any hope of undermining the Axis. Meanwhile
it became known to the State Department that Hitler had sent inquiries to
the Governments mentioned by the President, asking whether in fact they
felt menaced by Germany. According to reports, the Fuehrer proposed to
make capital of the replies in preparing a great public address scheduled for
April 28, 1939. To meet this unpleasant contingency, the President hit upon
the idea of approaching these same Governments and inviting statements
approving his message. His plan was to reveal these statements to the world
in a speech to be delivered on the very eve of Hitler's address. Actually the
duel of words did not take place, for the President and his advisers decided
to wait and see what Hitler might suggest and, if necessary, to address the
public later.[85]

When at last the Fuehrer appeared in splendor before the Reichstag
(April 28, 1939), it was to deliver one of his interminable harangues. Much
of his address was devoted to European affairs, including the denunciation
of the German-Polish Agreement of 1934 and of the Anglo-German Naval
Agreement of 1935. The reply to the President came at the very end and
was cleverly contrived. Sensing that Mr. Roosevelt's message might have the
effect in America of rallying public opinion in support of the democracies
and more particularly of working in favor of repeal of the neutrality laws,
Hitler rehearsed almost all the favorite arguments of American isolationists.
He violently denied past aggressions or future offensive plans. Furthermore,
he reported that he had canvassed the Governments listed by the President

---

[84] *Roosevelt Papers:* Secretary's File, Box 41.

[85] *Berle Diaries (MS.),* April 20, 24, 25, 1939; *Moffat Diary (MS.),* April 20, 26, 28,
1939. In the President's entourage there was evidently some fear lest Hitler propose
another Munich and lest the British Government show itself receptive. In that event the
President probably intended to express a strong adverse stand.

and had found that none of them felt any need for the assurances which the President had suggested. With ostensible modesty he therefore announced that the German Government was "prepared to give each of the States named an assurance of the kind desired by Mr. Roosevelt, provided that the State wishes it and itself addresses to Germany a request for such an assurance." But, he continued, "I should not like to let this opportunity pass without giving above all an assurance regarding those territories which would, after all, give him [the President] most cause for apprehension, namely the United States itself and the other states of the American Continent." As for the proposals to discuss disarmament and freer trade, the Fuehrer expressed skepticism but remained noncommittal. It occurred to him that the United States might well make a start by reducing its own tariff barriers.[86]

Hitler's reply amounted to a contemptuous rejection of the President's proposals, coupled with an attempt to cut the ground from under his feet by appealing to American isolationist sentiment. Within a few days the German press was crowing that the Fuehrer's speech had had a greater effect on American internal politics than any previous one. The rising opposition, especially Republican, was carefully noted and hopes for its success in the 1940 elections were fervently expressed.[87] Rabid American isolationists did in fact derive real satisfaction from the Fuehrer's sarcasm. This, they said, was the President's reward for meddling and for being so intolerably cocksure of himself. "He asked for it," was the unfeeling comment of Senator Nye.[88]

Of the official Washington reaction relatively little can be said. State Department members spent hours in rumination, trying to decide whether Hitler had meant to leave the door an inch ajar or slam it shut and turn the key. In reply to diplomatic inquiries it was stated that at the very worst the President's message had gained time and provided opportunity for reflection.[89] Mr. Roosevelt himself took Hitler's offensive remarks as a personal affront and was highly indignant. But he did nothing further to prolong the argument, possibly because it had become clear to him that the revision of the neutrality laws would be a long and arduous business and that therefore he had no effective instrument for exerting pressure on the dictators.[90]

---

[86] The full text in Adolf Hitler: *My New Order*, ed. Raoul de Roussy de Sales (New York, 1941), 630-77. The section containing the reply to the President, which is much too long to abstract in detail, is included in *Documents on American Foreign Relations*, I, 309-25.

[87] Deuel, in *Chicago Daily News*, May 10, 1939.

[88] See especially Mark Sullivan, in *The New York Herald Tribune*, May 3, 1939.

[89] *Moffat Diary (MS.)*, April 28, May 1, 1939.

[90] Conversation of the authors with Mr. Welles, May 27, 1947; see also Harsch, in *Christian Science Monitor*, April 28, 1939.

Even in retrospect it is difficult to assess the significance of the President's "Saturday surprise." That the famous message was sent in response to alarming reports from Europe is beyond dispute. Mr. Roosevelt had been told over and over again by foreign statesmen that his annual message to Congress in January, 1939, had, by indicating American support of the democracies, exercised a salutary influence. It is true that the German liquidation of Czechoslovakia and the Italian seizure of Albania belied these statements, but the President had almost unlimited confidence in his personal popularity with the masses and in his prestige as the head of a great and powerful nation. His move was highly dramatic and unconventional, while the message itself was a curious medley of condemnation and appeal, at one and the same time a plea to the dictators to behave and an attempt to arouse their peoples to protest.

Hitler's reply was both cunning and stinging. At the time it was hard to escape the conclusion that he had cleverly turned the tables and gotten the better of the argument. Yet on the long term it would appear that the President's message had really important repercussions, both at home and abroad. It certainly helped to stir the American people to a realization of the imminence of danger, and it provided a clear statement of the American stake in the preservation of peace. It stigmatized the dictators as aggressors and put on them in advance the responsibility for war, if and when war came. Unquestionably it did much—perhaps too much—to hearten the governments and peoples of non-Axis Europe and to sanction the efforts to check Nazi-Fascist expansion. The President thenceforth stood out as the moral leader in the crusade against war and thereby helped to dispel the almost universal feeling of hopelessness and despair. Such effects can not be measured with a yardstick, nor can they be documented. Yet when viewed in the large, it is clear that the Roosevelt message struck to the heart of the public throughout the world and that it served as an effective antidote to the disillusionment and demoralization of the Munich period.

CHAPTER III

The Play for Position

1. The European Peace Front

Two weeks after the announcement of the British guarantee to Poland, the London and Paris Governments issued a statement (April 13, 1939) that they would support Greece and Rumania in the event those countries resisted an action clearly threatening their independence. This declaration was the immediate result of the Italian occupation of Albania and marked the second stage in the development of the peace front envisaged by the Western democracies. Coming on the eve of President Roosevelt's message to Hitler suggesting that the German Government give assurances against aggression, it reveals the close synchronization of events on either side of the Atlantic, even though there was no planned linkage of policies between the Western Powers and the United States.

The British obligation to Poland was at first a purely unilateral one, undertaken in a moment of supposed crisis, but with the idea that it would be completed by further arrangements to be made with Colonel Beck during his visit to London in the first week of April, 1939. The larger British aim was not only to put the agreement with Poland on a basis of mutual aid, but to link up Poland with Rumania and if possible to strengthen this defensive bloc by enlisting the support of Greece, Turkey and even Bulgaria. Such a combination would indeed have presented a rather formidable obstacle to Nazi expansion into the Balkans, the more so in view of the assurances of British-French assistance.[1]

Beck's visit to London (April 3-7, 1939) went off very well so far as the externals were concerned. The Polish Foreign Minister had long been regarded in the West as generally unprincipled and unreliable, if not indeed

[1] Telegram from Atherton (Sofia), March 24, 1939, reporting the approaches of British and French representatives to the Bulgarian Government and the latter's refusal to entertain them.

a henchman of Hitler. He was more than surprised by the rousing reception accorded him and realized, probably for the first time, that he was something of a hero.[2] Nonetheless, he obliged the British Government to engage in prolonged discussions before even partial agreement was reached on political issues. There was no trouble about Poland's accepting the obligation to aid Britain in the event of a German attack, but the Chamberlain Government desired to have the Polish commitment extended to the eventuality of Britain's supporting the Low Countries or Switzerland in resistance to Germany. Beck felt that he had no authority to thus engage his government and in fact refused to do so until he had returned to Warsaw and consulted his colleagues. Similarly he evaded the proposal that Poland conclude a military alliance with Rumania for mutual support in case of attack by Germany or Hungary. Poland's relations with Hungary were good, he said, and it would be foolhardy for Poland to take sides between Hungary and Rumania in view of the burning conflict of territorial claims between those two states. The Polish Government still hoped to effect a settlement between the two disputants, pending which a Polish-Rumanian alliance would only drive Hungary into Hitler's arms and perhaps precipitate a war.

Beck was equally deaf to any suggestion that Soviet Russia be associated with the budding peace front, and argued that such a move would certainly drive the Nazis into war: "While Hitler will be roaring mad at Poland's action in tying up with Great Britain, he will not be as mad as if Russia were in with Poland too." Besides, he reasoned, the support of Russia was unnecessary, for if Poland took a firm stand against German claims, Hitler would not dare pursue his plans too far in the face of a Polish-British-French coalition. And finally, Moscow was not to be trusted and in any case would be unable to furnish much aid, even in the way of supplies. Chamberlain and Halifax tried to persuade their visitor that good relations with the Kremlin were nevertheless important, but at heart Chamberlain sympathized with Beck's viewpoint: "I confess," he noted, "I very much agree with him, for I regard Russia as a very unreliable friend . . . with an enormous irritative power on others." So it was more or less agreed that the Soviets should be left out of the picture.[3]

Hardly had the Polish Foreign Minister left London when Mussolini again jolted Europe by his action against Albania. The Greeks were in panic, fearing an almost immediate Italian attack on Corfu. At midnight

---

[2] Ambassador Bullitt rode with Beck, on the latter's return, from Calais to Lille. In a tel. of April 7, 1939, Bullitt reported that he could hardly exaggerate the impression the London visit had made on the Polish Foreign Minister.

[3] Feiling: *Life of Neville Chamberlain*, 408; message of Halifax to the President, April 8, 1939 (*Roosevelt Papers*: Secretary's File, Box 44); tels. from Kennedy, April 6, 1939; tels. from Bullitt, April 7, 9, 10, 17, 1939, reporting his conversations with Beck, with the Polish Ambassador to Paris, and with officials of the French Foreign Office.

(April 8, 1939) they summoned the British Minister, who had already retired. The Greek dictator, Metaxas, almost with tears in his eyes, expressed his people's determination to resist and begged the Minister to telegraph London, which he did. Meanwhile the Italian Government gave both the British and the Greeks assurances that no action against Greece was contemplated. In communicating this news to the Greek Government, on the morning of April 10, 1939, the British Minister indicated that the British and French Governments would not permit an Italian attack on Corfu. Therewith the Athens Government regained some composure.[4]

Apparently the British put little more stock in the Italian assurances than did the Greeks, for the Foreign Office at once approached Paris with the question whether the French Government would join in giving Greece a guarantee like that already extended to Poland. Thus far the French had not been directly involved, for their obligations to Poland had already been defined by existing treaties. Foreign Minister Bonnet had had no faith in the original British scheme for public declarations and had proposed that Britain and France both guarantee Poland and Rumania as preliminary to an invitation to Russia to support those countries in case of attack.[5] While perfectly agreeable to the guarantee to Poland, the French Foreign Office was convinced that Hitler's next move would be against Rumania, if only because the Rumanian oil supply was indispensable to the Nazi military machine. Therefore, when the British proposed a guarantee to Greece, the French insisted on a similar guarantee to Rumania. To this the London Government objected, on the plea that it would ruin the chances of Poland's accepting a military alliance with Rumania against Germany. But the time was short and the British, much concerned about the position in the eastern Mediterranean, decided to yield. On April 13, 1939, the two Governments announced publicly that they would feel bound to give full support to Greece and Rumania "in the event of any action being taken which clearly threatens the independence of Greece or Rumania and which the Greek and Rumanian Governments respectively considered it vital to resist with the national forces." The Greeks were delighted and the Rumanians grateful, but the Poles were so irritated that in the sequel they showed little inclination to close the Balkan front by negotiating a further alliance with Rumania.[6]

Despite such contretemps, the British Government felt that good progress was being made in the construction of a peace front. In return for the heavy

[4] Despatch from MacVeagh (Athens), April 10, 1939; letter from Ambassador Lindsay to Mr. Dunn of the State Department, April 12, 1939, communicating a British tel. to Washington of April 9, 1939.

[5] Tel. from Bullitt, March 25, 1939, reporting Bonnet's account of his discussions in London.

[6] Tels. from Bullitt, April 10, 12, 13, 15, 25, 28, 1939; tel. from Kennedy, April 13, 1939; tel. from Gunther (Bucharest), April 15, 1939.

burden it had assumed, it could hope that at least three countries of Eastern Europe would actively resist Nazi or Fascist aggression. But there remained the question how Britain and France were to lend effective assistance to countries like Poland or Rumania. The answer, it was thought, might be found in associating Turkey and Soviet Russia with the peace bloc, so that the Dardanelles might be opened to the British Fleet and contact established between the British and the Soviet forces. On April 12, 1939, the London Government proposed to the Turks that they join in the guarantee to Greece and that they conclude with Britain a treaty of mutual assistance in the event of an Italian attack on either. This latter proposal the Turks were quite willing to accept, but in their reply of April 25, 1939, they raised a number of related problems and made clear that they could not assume obligations with regard to the Balkans unless their own national interests were affected. They suggested, furthermore, that they would have to discuss various aspects of these problems with their Soviet neighbor and would therefore prefer to await the outcome of the negotiations between the British and French, on the one hand, and the Russians on the other.[7]

After the first approaches to the Kremlin in March, 1939, nothing more had been done to draw the Soviet Government into the discussions. Once again Soviet diplomats were complaining that their country was being treated as a pariah.[8] Such was certainly not the intent of the French Foreign Office. Both Premier Daladier and Foreign Minister Bonnet got along poorly with the Poles and evidently had far less faith in Polish military strength than the British. Their view was definitely that Soviet Russia was essential to the peace front and that the main task was to ensure Soviet aid for the Poles and Rumanians without informing them. On April 15, 1939, M. Bonnet, omitting prior consultation with London, proposed to the Soviet Ambassador that in case Britain and France should become involved in war with Germany as a result of their support of Poland or Rumania against German aggression, Soviet Russia should at once come to their assistance. The same was to hold, in reverse, if Russia became involved in war with Germany. Furthermore, the three governments (British, French, Soviet) were to take steps immediately to ensure that their mutual aid should be effective; that is, they should enter upon military conversations.[9]

While awaiting the reply to this concrete proposition, the French Government was horrified to learn that two days later (April 17, 1939), the British Government had submitted to the Soviets a very different project, which reflected all too clearly the reluctance of Prime Minister Chamberlain to bring the Kremlin into the picture. Apart from his general distrust and underestimation of Soviet Russia, Mr. Chamberlain was extremely fearful

[7] Tel. from Kennedy, April 12, 1939; tel. from Bullitt, April 28, 1939; memo from the British Embassy in Washington, April 29, 1939; tel. from Kennedy, April 28, 1939.

[8] Tel. from Bullitt, April 14, 1939, reporting the remarks of Soviet Ambassador Suritz.

[9] Bonnet: *Fin d'une Europe*, 180; tel. from Bullitt, April 18, 1939.

lest any association with the Kremlin antagonize the Poles and Rumanians and estrange other countries like Spain and Portugal and Japan.[10] But the Prime Minister was exposed to determined pressure both inside and outside the Cabinet. According to a public opinion poll taken in April, 1939, 92 percent of the British public expressed itself in favor of alliance with Russia. Conservative as well as Liberal and Labour Party leaders clamored for such a policy. Many years later Mr. Churchill still maintained, as he did at the time, that "the alliance of Britain, France and Russia would have struck deep alarm into the heart of Germany in 1939, and no one can prove that war might not even then have been averted."[11]

Since a majority of the Cabinet favored the same line, Mr. Chamberlain yielded to the extent of authorizing a very cautious move. On April 17, 1939, a note was sent to Moscow which recalled Stalin's promise, made in his address of March 10, 1939, that the Soviet Government would aid the victims of aggression. Since the British and French Governments were pursuing exactly that policy, the British note suggested that the Kremlin, on its own initiative, issue a public declaration stating that if any country adjoining the Soviet Union were to become the victim of aggression and were to fight for its independence, the Moscow Government would come to its assistance "if so desired and in such form as might be suitable."[12]

The French thought this note "a most terrible diplomatic blunder," since it might well antagonize Poland and Rumania. They felt unable to refuse to associate themselves with it, but hoped to high heaven that Stalin would decline the one-sided British suggestion.[13] Their hopes were soon fulfilled, for the Soviet reply of April 19, 1939, ignored the British proposal and in fact went beyond the French plan. The Moscow Government accepted the idea of mutual aid in the event of aggression by Germany on any one of the three powers, but insisted that the contracting powers should also guarantee all other European countries, including specifically the Baltic States and Finland, against aggression.[14]

The far-reaching Soviet proposal was to provoke much soul-searching in both London and Paris and to reveal the fundamental difference of view between the two Governments. Mr. Chamberlain, if not his Cabinet, was still loath to be carried into deep waters, while the French were eager to go the limit in the effort to secure the adherence of the Kremlin to the defensive front against Hitler. This basic divergence of view quite naturally raises the question whether in fact the Soviet Government had any genuine desire, in the spring of 1939, to join with the Western democracies in a

[10] Feiling: *Life of Neville Chamberlain*, 408; tel. from Kennedy, April 17, 1939.

[11] Churchill: *The Gathering Storm*, 362-63. See also Wheeler-Bennett: *Munich*, 394.

[12] Tel. from Bullitt, April 18, 1939; Bonnet: *Fin·d'une Europe*, 180; and the Soviet official statement: *Falsificators of History*.

[13] Tel. from Bullitt, April 18, 1939.

[14] Bonnet: *Fin d'une Europe*, 182; Gafencu: *Derniers jours d'Europe*, 164; *Falsificators of History*; also tels. from Bullitt, April 19, 21, 1939.

defensive coalition directed against Germany, or whether it was merely intent on exploiting the international situation with a view to inducing Hitler to make terms with the Kremlin. On both sides the argument has been a heated one and yet has produced nothing approaching agreement. In view of the almost complete lack of official Soviet records, it seems unlikely that the issue will be decided in the foreseeable future. The historian is therefore thrown back on the difficult task of putting events into their proper sequence and attempting a just appraisal of evidence that is admittedly deficient.

The key to Soviet foreign policy in the 1930's was probably to be sought in the outspoken and virulent enmity of Hitler and his Nazi revolution to Russia. The close political and economic relationship between Germany and Soviet Russia during the preceding decade was brought to an abrupt close in 1933 by Hitler's commitment to the struggle against communism and by his proclamation of designs on Soviet territory.[15] Since this was a period of Soviet isolation and of economic and military weakness, it is understandable that for a number of years the Kremlin, through Foreign Commissar Litvinov, had made itself the champion of collective security and of action through the League of Nations. The failure of that system was, of course, due in large part to conditions and policies unconnected with Soviet Russia, but it is nevertheless important to remember that despite all the ostensible idealism of the Soviet program, the European Governments generally continued to harbor profound suspicions of the Kremlin's aims and motives. It could be argued with considerable cogency that there was no reason to suppose that the Soviet leaders had given up their hopes for world revolution or their interest in fomenting unrest and disorder in the capitalist countries. Nor was there any ground for believing that the Soviet Government had reconciled itself to the loss of extensive territories regarded as indispensable to its security on the West. Its long-term aims may well have been shelved against a more propitious situation, but they had never been disavowed. Under the circumstances other governments could hardly be blamed if they regarded Litvinov's eloquent advocacy of collective security as designed primarily to tide his country over a particularly critical period. Soviet Russia, patently weakened by the great purges of 1937-1938, exposed to the possibility of a joint German-Polish attack in Europe and threatened by Japan in the Far East, was certainly in a dangerous position.[16]

---

[15] Of many treatments of this general topic, the following can be recommended: E. Fraenkel: "From Brest-Litovsk to Moscow" (Review of Politics, II, 1940, 43-62); John W. Wheeler-Bennett: "Twenty Years of Russo-German Relations, 1919-1939" (Foreign Affairs, October, 1946, 23-43); Dewitt C. Poole: "Light on Nazi Foreign Policy" (ibid., 130-54).

[16] The Soviet championship of collective security is most carefully analyzed by Max Beloff: The Foreign Policy of Soviet Russia, II (New York, 1949), supplemented by the same author's article, "Soviet Foreign Policy, 1929-1941: Some Notes" (Soviet Studies, October, 1950, 123-37).

As the men in the Kremlin watched Hitler and Mussolini march from one triumph to another, while Britain and France sought desperately to appease them, they must have feared that ultimately the much-touted four-power pact between the opposing parties might become a reality. Such a development would almost certainly have meant a free hand for Hitler in the East and would have almost inevitably brought a Nazi advance in its train. The abject surrender of the democracies at Munich marked the high-water stage of this development and helps to explain the apparent efforts of the Soviets to induce the French and British to stand firm even at the cost of war with Germany. It is therefore not at all difficult to believe that Stalin and his associates should have come to look upon Chamberlain, the architect of appeasement, as their chief enemy, or that they should have distrusted British and French policy as a matter of principle.[17]

In so critical a situation the Moscow Government determined to do its utmost to safeguard its own security against possible Nazi attack. The Soviet Union was particularly exposed on the side of Finland, a country which was proposing to refortify the Åland Islands with the consent of Sweden. The Kremlin seems to have suspected that the project was inspired from Berlin and in any case refused to consent to the refortification of the "Baltic Gibraltar" without prior assurances of Finland's attitude. It therefore proposed to Helsinki that Russia participate in the project and that, more importantly, Finland agree to accept Soviet aid in the event of a German attack. The suspicious Finns refused to go beyond a reaffirmation of their strict neutrality and for a time the subject was dropped. But in March, 1939, after the Nazi recovery of Memel, the issue was regarded in Moscow as a burning one. Negotiations were reopened in Helsinki, the Soviets offering to assent to the fortification of the Åland Islands and to cede to Finland a strip of territory in East Karelia in return for the cession or lease of four islands at the east end of the Gulf of Finland, commanding the sea approaches to Leningrad. Once again the Finns declined to go beyond a guarantee to remain neutral in a European war and to defend themselves to a man in case of attack. Under Soviet pressure the Helsinki Government eventually appealed to the United States to use its influence in Moscow, but this *démarche* proved entirely futile, for it elicited from Secretary Hull nothing more than a succinct statement of the established American policy: that the United States "has a traditional policy of not undertaking to interfere in political controversies across the seas; that we only speak about polit-

---

[17] We are here using an excellent contemporary analysis by Alexander Kirk, at that time United States Chargé d'Affaires at Moscow, dated April 6, 1939; and also a discerning memorandum by Loy Henderson, dated July 22, 1939. See also Sumner Welles: *The Time for Decision*, 322; Arthur U. Pope: *Maxim Litvinov*, 428 ff., Walter Duranty, in *The New York Times*, April 2, 1939.

ical conditions when they become so acute and dangerous as to constitute a definite threat to the peace of the world."[18]

Of similar pattern were the Soviet discussions with the Governments of the Baltic States. On March 28, 1939, notes were sent to Estonia and Latvia pointing out that the Soviet Government could not remain passive if the independence of those states were infringed upon, whether by their own consent or under pressure. But in these instances, too, the responses were negative. The Baltic Governments replied that they could not accept any restriction of their sovereignty and must reserve the right to judge for themselves when their sovereignty was being endangered.[19] The Kremlin had clearly failed in these first moves, but they serve to illustrate Soviet objectives at the very time when Britain and France were making the first effort to associate Russia with the projected peace front.

It might be argued that the Soviets, confronted by the danger of Nazi attack and at the same time threatened by Japan in the Far East, should have embraced the opportunity for a coalition with Britain and France.[20] But aside from the Kremlin's profound distrust of British-French policy there was another line of Soviet policy which began to emerge at this point. According to some commentators Stalin had long seen through the Nazi propaganda and had for some time been angling to revive Russia's traditional and highly advantageous tie with Germany.[21] It was noted that there was a marked lull in the Russian-German press war after the Munich crisis and that in February, 1939, a German trade expert had set out for Moscow. In the diplomatic field, too, there were indications that the Kremlin might be taking soundings looking toward a deal. Mr. Joseph E. Davies, the American Ambassador to Brussels and former Ambassador to Moscow, repeatedly warned of the possibility of an economic and even of a political agreement and argued that since Stalin's main objective must be to keep Soviet Russia out of war, he might well "take Hitler as the best bet for his security."[22]

[18] Tels. from Schoenfeld (Helsinki), February 1, April 4, 12, 1939; despatch from Kirk (Moscow), March 1, 1939; Moffat Diary (M.S.), April 10, 1939; memorandum of conversation between Mr. Hull and the Finnish Minister, April 10, 1939; The New York Times, April 21, 1939. See also the interesting book Finland and World War II, edited by John H. Wuorinen (New York, 1948), 44-47, which traces the Soviet proposals as far back as the spring of 1938.

[19] Tel. from Leonard (Tallinn), April 19, 1939, and despatch of April 25, 1939.

[20] In this connection it should be remembered that Berlin and Japan were linked by the Anti-Comintern Pact of 1936 and that the Soviet Government almost certainly knew, through its Tokyo spies, of the negotiations under way for a German-Japanese military alliance. On this see the report of the U. S. Department of the Army entitled The Sorge Spy Ring (February 10, 1949) and The New York Times, February 11, 1949.

[21] See the astounding article by the former Soviet secret agent W. G. Krivitsky: "Stalin Appeases Hitler" (Saturday Evening Post, April 29, 1939), and the prophetic article by Henry C. Wolfe: "Europe's Secret Nightmare" (Harper's Magazine, June, 1939). Substantially the same argument is advanced by A. Rossi: Deux ans d'alliance germanosoviétique (Paris, 1949), 14-15.

[22] Despatch from Davies (Brussels), February 9, 1939. See further his book Mission to Moscow (New York, 1943), 433 ff., 439-40, 442; and the memoirs of the French Ambassador

Stalin's famous address to the Supreme Soviet on March 10, 1939, may well have been a landmark in what was to be a startling diplomatic revolution. The ambiguity of his utterance was such that it could hardly have been accidental. Actually it served the purpose of leading on both parties to the dispute. The British read it as an expression of readiness to aid the victims of aggression and therefore to join a united front. On the other hand, the Germans took it as an invitation to bury the hatchet and restore good neighborly relations. Though proof is impossible, it does seem that the Soviet plan was to negotiate with the Western Powers in the hope of making Hitler amenable to a bargain with Russia, and at the same time to conjure up the specter of a Soviet-Nazi pact to impress the democracies. The Soviet apologia leaves little doubt that the Kremlin's great fear was that Britain and France might, even at a very late date, revert to a policy of appeasement. It was therefore important for the Soviet leaders to encourage London and Paris in their hopes for a peace front to block further Nazi expansion, at least until such time as a pact with Germany could be concluded on Soviet terms. It cannot be stated categorically that the long-drawn negotiations between London, Paris and Moscow in the spring and summer of 1939 were nothing but a ruse on the Kremlin's part, but such a conclusion suggests itself from a reading of the evidence.

It stands to reason that Stalin's fine-spun plan, if such it was, could succeed only if there was, on Hitler's part, some disposition to abandon the much-vaunted anti-Bolshevik policy. In this respect the moment was certainly opportune, for by April, 1939, German hopes of bringing Japan into an alliance with Germany and Italy were fading, while the efforts of the democracies to construct an anti-German front seemed to promise well. Ribbentrop, if not Hitler himself, began to toy with the idea of a *rapprochement* with the Kremlin, so that Soviet advances had at least some prospect of success. It is noteworthy that on April 17, 1939, the very day on which the British made their proposal to the Soviet Government, the Soviet Ambassador in Berlin sought a conference with Baron Weizsäcker, the State Secretary of the German Foreign Office. His ostensible purpose was to discuss Russian orders held by the Czech Skoda Works, but he soon turned the conversation to the subject of Nazi-Soviet trade relations and, according to Weizsäcker's record, ended on a suggestive political note:

Russian policy [remarked the Soviet diplomat] had always moved in a straight line. Ideological differences of opinion had hardly influenced the Russian-Italian relationship, and they did not have to prove a stumbling block with regard to

---

Robert Coulondre: *De Staline à Hitler* (Paris, 1950), 171. Among unofficial warnings may be mentioned H. R. Knickerbocker: "Soviet-German Alliance" (*Review of Reviews*, July, 1937); Stephen H. Roberts: *The House that Hitler Built* (New York, 1937), and Demaree Bess: "Spotlight on the Russian Bear" (*Saturday Evening Post*, December 24, 1938). This subject is well treated in Meno Lovenstein: *American Opinion of Soviet Russia* (Washington, 1941), Part IV.

Germany either. Soviet Russia had not exploited the present friction between Germany and the Western democracies against us, nor did she desire to do so. There exists for Russia no reason why she should not live with us on a normal footing. And from normal, the relations might become better and better.[23]

This was at best but an adumbration of Soviet desires, but is worth mentioning as background to the Kremlin's reply of April 19, 1939, to the British and French proposals. The Soviet note had set forth the idea of an out-and-out military alliance providing for mutual assistance in case one of the three partners was attacked by Germany or became involved in war with Germany as a result of support given any state which became the victim of German aggression. In Paris as in London this was regarded as a large order, but beyond that the views of the two Governments diverged. M. Bonnet, intent on a military alliance with Russia that would impress and possibly deter Hitler, was prepared to overlook Soviet designs in the Baltic and even convinced himself that in a crisis the Poles and Rumanians would agree to accept Soviet material aid.[24] After valiant efforts to find an appropriate formula, the French Government on April 29, 1939, suggested to Moscow a slightly modified version of the Soviet note of April 19: the three powers were to lend each other assistance if any one of them became involved in war with Germany as a result of action taken "to prevent any modification by force of the *status quo* in Central or Eastern Europe."

Bonnet had made every effort to induce the British to associate themselves with this proposal, but in vain. The London Government was anxious to avoid any move that might provoke a final division of Europe into two hostile camps or that might precipitate an immediate Nazi attack on Poland or Rumania. It may be taken for granted that Hitler's denunciation of the Anglo-German naval agreement of 1935 in his speech of April 28, 1939, served to strengthen British unwillingness to accept the far-reaching and somewhat suspect proposals of the Kremlin. In its note to Moscow of April 29, 1939, the Foreign Office therefore stuck by its original view that the Soviet Government should guarantee only "certain countries of Eastern Europe."[25]

[23] Department of State: *Nazi-Soviet Relations, 1939-1941*, edited by Raymond J. Sontag and James S. Beddie (Washington, 1948), 1-2; Ernst von Weizsäcker: *Erinnerungen* (Munich, 1950), 230-31; Peter Kleist: *Zwischen Hitler und Stalin* (Bonn, 1950), 26 ff. The development of the Nazi-Soviet pact has been traced by Harold C. Deutsch: "Strange Interlude: The Soviet-Nazi Liaison of 1939-1941" (*The Historian*, Spring, 1947, 107-36), and more recently by E. H. Carr: "From Munich to Moscow" (*Soviet Studies*, I, Nos. 1 and 2, June, October, 1949).

[24] The Rumanian Foreign Minister, Grigoire Gafencu, visited Paris at the end of April, 1939, and told Ambassador Bullitt that it might become vital for Rumania to receive war supplies from Russia (tel. from Bullitt, April 28, 1939).

[25] Tels. from Bullitt, April 21, 24, 25, 28, 29, May 1, 1939; memo of Ambassador Lindsay to Mr. Dunn, May 1, 1939. See also Bonnet: *Fin d'une Europe*, 182-83; Gafencu: *Derniers jours de l'Europe* (Paris, 1946), 165-67; *German White Paper*, No. 14 (report of the Polish Ambassador in London, April 26, 1939).

Both the British and the French notes of April 29, 1939, appear to have been informal suggestions rather than formal replies. They registered little progress and promised almost nothing in terms of eventual agreement, considering the fact that not even the two Western partners could unite on a single line. If one assumes that the Kremlin was honest in its proposals, one must also assume that it must have been disappointed in the results. On the other hand, if it was merely maneuvering to impress Hitler, Moscow's immediate aim had been attained; for no secret had been made of the negotiations, and there were indications that the Germans had indeed taken notice of the prospective alignment. To understand fully the further evolution of the international system, it is important to understand the frustration of Nazi hopes in the spring of 1939 and the ensuing reorientation of German policy.

2. GERMANY AND JAPAN

The world of 1939 watched with awe and fear the almost unbroken series of Nazi successes and knew next to nothing of the significant disappointments which, like ordinary mortals, Hitler, too, suffered. Poland provided one of them, for it is certain that the Fuehrer for years set great store by his agreement with his eastern neighbor and envisaged an ultimate partnership in the "settlement" of the Soviet problem. The Poles had managed to evade so dangerous a commitment and had tried to balance between East and West until, in March, 1939, Colonel Beck had flatly rejected the Nazi propositions.[26] The Nazi occupation of Prague blasted the British-French policy of appeasement, which had served the Fuehrer so well, while almost simultaneously the Nazi proposals to Poland led to the alignment of that power with the Western democracies. Hitler could no longer hope to secure Danzig without fighting, nor could he delude himself with thoughts of a German-Polish crusade against Soviet Russia. Thenceforth he must have considered it unwise to take action against the West so long as an untrustworthy Poland faced him on the East. He therefore shifted his ground and decided that the "settlement" of the Polish problem must come first. On April 3, 1939, he issued the first directive for the preparation of plans for an attack on Poland, the operation to be scheduled for any date after September 1, 1939.[27]

The German General Staff did not consider Poland by itself a serious military problem, for it did not share either Colonel Beck's high opinion of Polish strength and valor or the wildly exaggerated estimates of some British

[26] *Polish White Book*, Nos. 44, 48, 53; *German Documents on the Outbreak of the War*, Nos. 197, 198, 200, 201, 202; Stanislaw Mackiewicz: *Colonel Beck and His Policy* (London, 1944), 130.

[27] Peter de Mendelssohn: *Design for Aggression* (New York, 1946), 81. See also Hitler's explanations to his generals on May 23 and August 22, 1939, in *Nazi Conspiracy and Aggression*, III, 798-PS and VII, L-79, and Dewitt C. Poole: "Light on Nazi Foreign Policy" (*Foreign Affairs*, October, 1946).

circles. Furthermore, Hitler was probably little moved by the British-French guarantee, for the Western Powers could hardly give Poland much practical aid and there was always the possibility that, in a crisis, the Chamberlain Government would leave the Poles in the lurch and accept a new settlement in the Munich tradition.[28] Nonetheless, it was obviously in the German interest to avoid intervention by the West, if only for fear that the British might bomb the key industrial areas of the Ruhr. Even more important was the frustration of a coalition between the Western Powers and Soviet Russia which would have presented the Germans with the danger of a war on two fronts.[29]

In the preceding chapter it was pointed out that Hitler's recipe was to neutralize the British and French and discourage the United States by linking up with Japan and so distracting the democracies by the prospect of an acute crisis in the Far East. Japanese military circles were perfectly ready to conclude a military alliance, but the negotiations, which at first had promised well, soon threatened to founder on the opposition of the Japanese Cabinet, supported by the Navy and by big business interests. Outside Army circles there was little inclination in Japan to antagonize Britain and France and even less disposition to arouse the hostility of the United States. Ambassador Grew, it will be remembered, had warned explicitly of the probable reaction of a German-Japanese alliance on American public opinion, and the Japanese Government was evidently impressed by this admonition. Though the Japanese expressed to the Germans a readiness to conclude a military pact directed against Soviet Russia, Hitler refused to consider anything less than a pact which would include powers like Britain and France as well.

Throughout the spring months conflict over this issue raged unabated in Japanese Government circles. The Emperor, supported by Prince Saionji, the last remaining Elder Statesman, was opposed to an inclusive military pact and feared lest, in the event of a German victory, Japan be treated as a Nazi vassal. Within the Cabinet the Minister of War, General Itagaki, was the leading champion of the alliance, while the Minister of Marine, Admiral Yonai, was an uncompromising opponent. Baron Hiranuma, the Prime Minister, was inclined to yield to military pressure, but the Foreign Minister, Mr. Arita, refused to give way. As though this sharp division of opinion were not enough, the situation was further aggravated by the high-handed procedure of General Oshima, the Ambassador to Berlin, ardently supported by Mr. Shiratori, the Ambassador to Rome. These two men represented the most extreme military viewpoint and made valiant efforts to

[28] *Cf.* Ribbentrop's conversation with the Hungarian Prime Minister, May 1, 1939 (*Nazi Conspiracy and Aggression*, VII, D-738). The attitude of the British Ambassador in Berlin probably reinforced the Germans in this view (*German Documents, etc.*, Nos. 304-7).

[29] Hitler revealed his fears to his commanders on May 23, 1939 (*Nazi Conspiracy and Aggression*, VII, L-79).

railroad the Tokyo Government into the agreement desired by Berlin. Oshima assured Ribbentrop that if Germany became involved in war with any other power, Japan would "probably" join. In response to protests from home, the Ambassador and his colleague threatened again and again to resign and so provoke a Cabinet crisis.

To recount all the phases of this epic struggle would be as futile as it would be tedious. The upshot of it was that by early June, after innumerable formulas and proposals had been debated, the Japanese Government informed the Germans that they would, of course, commit themselves in every way against Soviet Russia and that they would participate in a war against another power to the extent of not remaining neutral. They were willing to accept the principle of mutual aid, but only on the understanding that the character and extent of such aid would have to be decided in each circumstance and that military aid would be given only "if possible." This decision was of small comfort to the Nazis and particularly to Ribbentrop, who had been wildly enthusiastic about the project and had persisted in his hope that some satisfactory solution could be found. For the time being, at least, the Germans had to admit their failure.[30]

The Tokyo Government was undoubtedly influenced in its discussions by the published reports of the British-French negotiations with Soviet Russia and perhaps even more by the attitude and action of the United States Government. The British, to be sure, made a point of telling Tokyo that the projected arrangements with Moscow had no reference to the Far East, but the Japanese were naturally disturbed by the prospect of a combination of three great powers, all of which had major interests in Asia.[31] Even more ominous were the indications of a stronger stand by Washington. The United States Government lodged a firm protest against Japanese occupation of the Spratly Islands (March 31, 1939) and in general became more insistent in its demands for explanation of the bombing of

[30] The development of the situation in Tokyo can be followed in minute detail in the *Saionji-Harada Memoirs* for March, April and May, 1939. Valuable material is contained also in the *Tokyo War Crimes Documents* as follows: deposition of Marquis Kido (Defense Document 2502); tel. from Ribbentrop to Ott, April 26, 1939 (Doct. 4035); message from Hiranuma to Hitler, May 4, 1939 (Docts. 4043B and D); tel. from Ott to Ribbentrop, May 6, 1939 (Doct. 4043C). We have used also tels. from Grew (April 26 and May 5, 1939), and a memo by Hornbeck, May 11, 1939. Interesting information may be derived from the reports of Hugh Byas in *The New York Times*, March 23 and April 28, 1939, and of Wilfrid Fleischer in the *New York Herald Tribune*, March 23, 24, 30, April 13, 1939. The fullest account of the negotiations is that of Mario Toscano: *Origini del Patto d'Acciaio* (Florence, 1948), 100 ff., which should now be supplemented by Herbert Feis: *The Road to Pearl Harbor* (Princeton, 1950), 29 ff.

[31] Sir Robert Craigie: *Behind the Japanese Mask* (New York, 1946), 70 ff. See also Grew's report of Arita's strong language on this subject, May 18, 1939 (*Foreign Relations of the United States: Japan*, II, 1 ff.).

American properties in China and of discriminatory trade regulations.[32] As yet the State Department confined itself to verbal warfare and hesitated about taking any really drastic steps. It continued to discuss the possible denunciation of the trade treaty of 1911, but still considered it inadvisable to resort to retaliatory measures. Small wonder that a proposal by the Chinese National Government that Britain and France take part in the Far Eastern war and that the United States take "parallel measures" was given little if any serious consideration.[33]

Meanwhile, however, the President took a significant step of a different kind. On April 15, 1939, within a half hour after the announcement of the President's message to Hitler, the United States Navy ordered the Fleet, which had been concentrated in the Atlantic for maneuvers, to return to its regular base at San Diego. This move was directly connected with the critical world situation. It had been suggested by Lord Halifax on March 21, 1939, as one way of quieting Australian uneasiness at a time when the British felt unable to send warships from the Mediterranean to Singapore.[34] Apparently no action was decided upon at that time, but in the days immediately following the Italian occupation of Albania, the French Government was extremely anxious about further Italian action against Greece and was greatly upset by the alleged intention of the British to send part of their Fleet from the Mediterranean to the Far East.[35] Since the President and his military advisers shared the view that it was more important to hold the Mediterranean than to strengthen the defenses of the Far East, the decision was taken to order the United States Fleet into the Pacific in order to lighten the pressure upon the British.[36]

The reappearance of the American Fleet in the Pacific probably made a deeper impression on the Tokyo Government than all the notes and protests of the preceding months. The President's message to Hitler and the simultaneous shifting of the Fleet must have been taken as two expressions of one and the same policy of supporting the European democracies. According to the inspired Tokyo press the Japanese Government suspected, with some justice, that the British and Americans had some understanding

[32] *Foreign Relations of the United States: Japan*, I, 642 ff., 831 ff.; II, 280-81.

[33] Memo entitled *Narrative of Developments Leading to the Giving of Notice by the U. S. of an Intention to Terminate the Japanese-American Commercial Treaty of 1911* (dated April 30, 1940). On the Chinese proposal we have used several memoranda of April, 1939, as well as a tel. from Bullitt, April 18, 1939. The proposal was presented to the British and French on April 4, and to the State Department on April 14, 1939. The American reply of May 1, 1939, was oral and stated merely that the American attitude with respect to coöperation and parallel action was well known.

[34] Tel. from Kennedy, March 22, 1939.

[35] Tels. from Bullitt, April 10, 11, 1939.

[36] *Berle Diaries (MS.)*, April 13, 1939; *Moffat Diary (MS.)*, April 15, 1939; Hull: *Memoirs*, I, 630. We have used also the MS. study by Captain Tracy Kittredge, USNR, on *Anglo-American Naval Coöperation, 1938-1941*.

for common action in the Pacific. For that reason, no doubt, Admiral Yonai, the Minister of Marine, spoke to Mr. Dooman, the Counselor of the American Embassy, assuring him that the United States need have no concern about a German-Japanese alliance and bespeaking the restoration of good relations between Japan and the United States.[37] It can hardly be far-fetched to suppose that the President's decision with respect to the Fleet strengthened the position of those elements in Tokyo which opposed the military pact with Germany. Ambassador Grew's warnings, in conversation with various Japanese, that if a general war broke out in Europe the United States would probably find it impossible to stay out, must have contributed to the same end. Mr. Grew had reason to believe that his remarks had been reported to the Emperor himself and that they had served a good purpose.[38]

3. THE SOVIETS AND THE WESTERN POWERS

As Hitler's grand design for a German-Italian-Japanese alliance thus began to fail, the Fuehrer was confronted with the problem of finding some other solution of his problem, which in essence was to forestall a coalition of Britain, France and Soviet Russia which would make it highly dangerous if not impossible for him to settle the score with Poland. A new prospect opened before him when, on May 3, 1939, the Kremlin announced that Maxim Litvinov, for many years Commissar for Foreign Affairs, had been relieved of his duties and that Vyacheslav Molotov would take over his position. Throughout the world this item of news created a sensation. It seemed obviously important, though utterly baffling. In diplomatic circles there was little inclination to accept Soviet statements that the change implied no shift in policy. Neither was it thought that Litvinov's reputed ill-health supplied an adequate explanation. What seemed most significant was that Litvinov was a Jew, that he was notoriously anti-German, and that for years he had been the vociferous champion of a system of collective security. The least that could be expected was that his dismissal presaged the abandonment of the policy or tactics theretofore supported by the Soviet leaders. The question of the hour was, then, what form future Soviet policy was apt to take.

Little was known of Molotov, the new Commissar for Foreign Affairs. Thus far he had not been concerned with Soviet foreign relations, but he was said to be very close to Stalin and to be hard and realistic in his approach to Soviet problems. Most noteworthy of all was the fact that Molotov, unlike Litvinov, was a member of the powerful Politburo. Indeed, he was the first Foreign Commissar in Soviet history to be a member of the inner governing group. It was therefore highly improbable that he

---

[37] *Grew Diary (MS.)*, April 19, 1939. See also Wilfrid Fleischer in *New York Herald Tribune*, April 19, 1939.
[38] *Grew Diary (MS.)*, May 15, 1939.

would assume control of the Foreign Office unless some major policy change was being contemplated. The only official explanation ever vouchsafed by the Kremlin was provided after the Second World War, and in these terms:

In a complex situation, when Fascist aggressors were preparing the Second World War, when Great Britain and France, backed by the United States, were plainly abetting the aggressors and spurring them on to start a war against the U.S.S.R., it was necessary to have in such a responsible post as that of People's Commissar of Foreign Affairs a political leader with greater experience and greater popularity in the country than Litvinov.[39]

This belated statement, of course, avoids the issue. At the time it was hoped in some quarters that Molotov, with his greater prestige and influence, might carry on the negotiations with Britain and France more vigorously. Others, including statesmen who knew Russia, suspected that the new commissar would prove himself an isolationist; that he would devote himself to the task of keeping Soviet Russia free of all involvement in the "imperialist" war that was threatening. Still others interpreted the dismissal of Litvinov, the Jew and enemy of Germany, to mean that the Soviets intended a gesture of good will toward Nazi Germany and therefore anticipated a Soviet move toward agreement with Hitler, either in order to frighten the democracies into acceptance of the Soviet terms or for its own sake as a means of disposing of the Polish problem to the mutual satisfaction of both Hitler and Stalin. Though a final judgment is even now impossible, it should be noted that from the time of Molotov's appointment onward the Soviet negotiations with Britain and France were paralleled by Soviet discussions with Germany. It is certainly safe to say that if the Kremlin had not definitely decided one way or the other in early May, 1939, it was at any rate in the unusual and enviable position of being able to turn either way as the circumstances dictated.[40]

No less an authority than Mr. Churchill has recorded his opinion that the appointment of Molotov reflected the despair of the Soviets with regard to the negotiations with Britain and France: "From the moment when Molotov became Foreign Commissar," he comments, "he pursued the policy of an arrangement with Germany at the expense of Poland."[41] Although

[39] *Falsificators of History.*

[40] Litvinov's resignation had been rumored ever since the time of the Munich crisis: tels. from Kirk (Moscow), October 31, 1938, and February 22, 1939. The foregoing discussion is based on numerous reports of American diplomats, notably a tel. from Kirk, May 4, 1939; a tel. from Davies (Brussels), May 10, 1939; and a tel. from Gunther (Bucharest), May 8, 1939. We have used also a memo by Loy Henderson, May 4, 1939. Among printed materials see Augur in *The New York Times,* May 4, 1939, and Walter Duranty in *The New York Times,* May 5, 1939; Bonnet: *Fin d'une Europe,* 184; Coulondre: *De Staline à Hitler,* 269-70; Gafencu: *Derniers jours de l'Europe,* 200 ff.; *Nazi-Soviet Relations,* 2-3.

[41] Churchill: *The Gathering Storm,* 369.

this assertion cannot be proved, it is altogether credible that the Kremlin was disappointed by the British proposals to date and it is important to consider that Hitler's speech of April 28, 1939, must have caused some concern in Moscow. That speech had revealed to the whole world the rift between Germany and Poland and had opened the prospect that Hitler would solve the Danzig problem even at the cost of war. If Poland were then eliminated, Russia would find itself face to face with Germany, which in the interval might have allied itself with Japan. To be sure, Hitler's denunciation of the Anglo-German naval agreement of 1935 might have been taken as marking a break between the two powers, but there is evidence to show that the Kremlin still and for some time to come suspected the British of readiness to return to appeasement on the slightest provocation. That the Soviet leaders were genuinely worried about German policy would seem to be indicated by their renewal of proposals to the Baltic States at this time. Indeed, it was reported that the Soviet Government had notified Berlin that if the independence or integrity of Finland, Estonia, Latvia or Lithuania were threatened, Russia would at once send troops to safeguard its own security.[42] At the very same time M. Potemkin, the Vice Commissar for Foreign Affairs, was returning from a visit to Turkey and making stops at Sofia, Bucharest and Warsaw. His objective had been to revive the Soviet-Turkish relationship and to draw the Eastern countries together in a common defensive front. The fact that he assured Colonel Beck that Russia would maintain a benevolent attitude toward Poland if the latter were attacked by Germany, and that he even indicated that Russia would furnish war supplies, all suggests that early in May, 1939, the Kremlin was still intent on making provision against German aggression.[43]

Since it is quite impossible to fathom the thinking of Stalin and Molotov, it must suffice to record that the first conversations of the British and French Ambassadors with the new Commissar for Foreign Affairs were cordial and even promising. Molotov made it plain that he preferred the French proposal to the British and "bombarded" the British representative with questions about his Government's policy which were hard to answer. But there was nothing to indicate that existing differences could not be compromised. In Paris M. Bonnet was highly optimistic and revived his hopes that Russia, Turkey, Poland and Rumania could all be brought into a common front with Britain and France.[44]

[42] Tel. from Bullitt, April 21, 1939. See also Kluckhohn in *The New York Times*, May 7, 1939; and Lias in *Christian Science Monitor*, May 10, 1939.

[43] On Potemkin's visits we have used tel. from MacMurray (Ankara), May 3, 1939, and his despatch of May 16, 1939; tel. from Biddle (Warsaw), May 10, 1939, and despatch May 12, 1939; tel. from Gunther (Bucharest), May 12, 1939; tel. from Atherton (Sofia), May 23, 1939. See also Gafencu: *Derniers jours de l'Europe*, 200 ff.; Bonnet: *Fin d'une Europe*, 208-10; and Joseph Growski: "L'année brillante de la politique des Soviets" (*La voix de Varsovie*, I, November 15, 1939).

[44] Tel. from Bullitt, May 10, 1939.

No doubt the French Foreign Minister was deluding himself, for neutral observers could not help noting the continuing Soviet distrust of the democracies, and the later Soviet justification commented suspiciously on the British proposal: "It is easy to see that actually the British proposal was addressed not so much to Moscow as to Berlin. The Germans were invited to attack the Soviet Union, and were given to understand that Britain and France would maintain neutrality if only the Germans attacked through the Baltic States."[45] In keeping with this mentality, Molotov on May 16, 1939, produced his reply to London and Paris. In the bluntest and most uncompromising terms he insisted that the projected pact must be completely reciprocal, that it must be fortified by a military convention, and that it must include guarantees to Finland, Estonia and Latvia, as well as to Poland and Rumania.[46]

This stiff note brought to a head the dispute between London and Paris and at the same time produced serious disagreement in British political circles. The French Government, already much concerned over Britain's unwillingness "to face realities" and agree to a military alliance, was even more distressed by rumors that Hitler was about to negotiate a deal with the Soviets. On May 7, 1939, the French Ambassador in Berlin reported at length on statements made by a German high in the Nazi councils. Whether wittingly or unwittingly this source imparted ominous information: Hitler was determined to secure Danzig and reunite East Prussia with the Reich, but would bide his time until the conditions were favorable; meanwhile he would seek an agreement with Soviet Russia so as to obviate intervention by the Western Powers and perhaps effect a fourth partition of Poland. The French Ambassador, M. Coulondre, was inclined to believe that Hitler had not yet reached a final decision, but was nonetheless disturbed. Prime Minister Daladier and Foreign Minister Bonnet, though they rarely saw eye to eye, were at least at one in thinking that a pact with Russia was essential if Hitler was to be stopped. They were prepared to guarantee the Baltic States on the theory that if these states were attacked by Germany, Poland would surely intervene in their behalf and Britain and France would thereby become involved. The French statesmen considered the temporizing attitude of the British dangerous and therefore used every ounce of their influence to persuade them.[47]

Prime Minister Chamberlain was quite impatient with such arguments.

[45] *Falsificators of History;* we have used also a tel. from Grummon (Moscow), May 9, 1939, and the report by Stoneman in the *Chicago Daily News*, May 8, 1939.

[46] Tels. from Kennedy, May 16, 1939, and from Bullitt, May 16, 1939. See also Kelley in *New York Herald Tribune*, May 16, 1939.

[47] *French Yellow Book*, Nos. 123, 125, 127; Coulondre: *De Staline à Hitler*, 270-71; Pertinax in *The New York Times*, May 20, 1939. We have used also tels. from Bullitt, May 15, 16, 22, 1939, and a State Department memo entitled *Information in Possession of the Department with Regard to the Recent German-Soviet Rapprochement* (August 31, 1939).

Having started with the idea that the Soviets were so weak that they would welcome an agreement on almost any terms, he was probably incensed by the tone of their reply. His distrust of the Kremlin ran deep and he was much impressed by the fact that many other Governments had voiced the hope that Britain would not associate itself with Soviet Russia. The Soviet insistence on guarantees for the Baltic States seemed to him to reveal designs in that region to which he would never consent to become a party. Like Shakespeare he may have felt that there is little choice in rotten apples, but that on balance Communist domination of Europe would be even worse than Nazi control. His personal adviser, Sir Horace Wilson, made no bones about saying that his chief put little store by the Soviet connection and still hoped to arrive at an economic accord with Germany, which is exactly what the Kremlin suspected. According to Sir Horace, Soviet military power was rated very low and it was doubted whether Moscow would be willing to risk sending troops across its own frontiers. If an agreement were made with the Soviets, Hitler would at once persuade the Germans that Britain was bent on their annihilation. No stock was to be put in the talk of a Nazi-Soviet deal, though it was possible that the Soviet leaders might try to bluff by playing this card.[48]

While Mr. Chamberlain stood his ground, the British public clamored for a pact with Moscow. On May 19, 1939, a rather acrimonious debate developed in Parliament, in the course of which Mr. Lloyd George warned against underestimating Soviet power and stressed the importance of a full-fledged alliance with Russia: "For months," he complained, "we have been staring this powerful gift horse in the mouth." Churchill, too, declared that "without an effective eastern front, there can be no satisfactory defence of our interests in the West, and without Russia there can be no effective eastern front." To which the Prime Minister replied that he simply could not help feeling "that there is a sort of veil, a sort of wall" between the British and the Soviet Governments, which he found it extremely difficult to penetrate. Under the circumstances he must walk warily. It was important not to divide Europe into two hostile blocs and it was equally important to consider the objections of other states. Though Mr. Churchill tried to brush aside these refinements and admonished the Government that if it cast aside the indispensable aid of Soviet Russia it would lead the country "in the worst of all ways into the worst of all wars," there was no sign that Mr. Chamberlain would yield to public pressure.[49]

On May 20, 1939, Lord Halifax stopped at Paris on his way to the meeting of the Council of the League of Nations at Geneva. He had hoped to find Mr. Molotov at the meeting, but at the last minute the Kremlin had

[48] Tels. from Kennedy, May 10, 16, 19, 1939. See also Sir Nevile Henderson: *Failure of a Mission* (New York, 1940), 229-30, 250 ff.

[49] Namier: *Diplomatic Prelude,* 165 ff.; Churchill: *The Gathering Storm,* 374 ff.

instructed Mr. Maisky, the Soviet Ambassador in London, to substitute. After conferences first with M. Bonnet and later with Mr. Maisky, the British Foreign Secretary convinced himself that an arrangement with Russia was essential and that it would probably have to be concluded on Soviet terms. On his return to London he secured support in the Cabinet and Mr. Chamberlain reluctantly agreed to accept the Soviet proposal in substance. To save face, however, the British decided to put the whole project under the League Covenant and to mask the phraseology. Their new proposal, dispatched on May 25, 1939, was that the three contracting powers, acting in accordance with the principles of the League, should lend each other immediate assistance (1) if any one of them became involved in war because of aid given a European country which they had guaranteed against aggression; (2) if any one of them became involved in war because of aid rendered a nonguaranteed country which, being the victim of aggression, defended itself and requested aid; (3) if any European power attacked one of the contracting parties while the latter was engaged in taking action in accord with Article XVI of the Covenant. The signatories were to consult whenever circumstances threatened to call for the implementation of these pledges.[50]

The French Foreign Office, while recognizing the imperfections of this compromise, thought the new note covered the essential points and hoped for the conclusion of the pact within a week. But Molotov refused to reduce his demands by even one tittle. He objected to bringing in the League, but above all insisted that Soviet aid to the Baltic States could not be left to the latters' own discretion. According to the later Soviet thesis, the Western Powers were trying "to drown the major issues in a swamp of minor amendments and innumerable versions," knowing full well that these would be unacceptable to Moscow. The same Soviet account reports that on May 27, 1939, Molotov told the British and French representatives that their countries seemed less interested in the pact than in talk about the pact. A few days later (May 31, 1939), the Foreign Commissar addressed the Supreme Soviet and reported on the negotiations. He voiced his suspicion that the Western Powers were not yet ready to abandon the policy of nonresistance to aggression, or at best were prepared only to resist in certain regions so as to divert the aggressor to other quarters. He then restated the Soviet demands and described them as absolutely minimal. In concluding he reminded his listeners (and indirectly the British and French) that the Moscow Government had no intention of renouncing business ties

[50] Tels. from Kennedy, May 24, 25, 1939; tels. from Bullitt, May 22, 23, 24, 25, 30, 1939; tel. from Grummon, May 24, 1939. Also Bonnet: Fin d'une Europe, 185. According to the former Rumanian Minister to London, Mr. Tilea, the Rumanian Government at this time agreed to the transit of Soviet troops provided Rumania's independence and integrity were guaranteed (letter to The New York Times, May 12, 1948).

with other countries: trade discussions with the Germans had taken place in the early spring and they would probably be resumed.[51]

This speech came to the British public and Government like a cold and disagreeable douche. Mr. Chamberlain, who no doubt felt that he had made a great concession, had announced on May 24, 1939, that he hoped for agreement within ten days and had thereby evoked tremendous popular enthusiasm. Now there was nothing to show but a prospect of Nazi-Soviet understanding. The disillusioned public was filled with misgivings and already began to fear lest Stalin sell out to the highest bidder.[52]

But the issue was now fairly joined. Clearly the Soviet Government would not adhere to the peace front unless Britain and France, as well as Russia, guaranteed the independence of the Baltic States, along with Poland and Rumania. On its face this seemed a reasonable proposition, but it understandably confirmed the British Government in its conviction that the Kremlin had designs on these lost territories and that, if it chose to conclude that their independence was threatened by Germany, it would proceed to occupy them militarily. As matters stood at the beginning of June, 1939, they were well summed up in a State Department memorandum:

> The question, therefore, presents itself as to whether the demands are made [by the Soviet Government] for the purpose of gaining greater security, or in order to effect a breakdown in the negotiations which would result in the Soviet Union being able, for an indefinite period, to play off the so-called democratic block against the Axis.[53]

Much criticism was at the time and later leveled at Mr. Chamberlain for his inept handling of the negotiations with Moscow. They were, in fact, marked by unwillingness and hesitation and showed little trace of clarity in conception or planning. But if British policy was maladroit, it seems reasonably clear that Soviet policy was dishonest. Once again it must be said that final proof is impossible. Nonetheless it appears almost certain that if Stalin meant to conclude an agreement with the democracies at all, it was only on the basis that Soviet Russia be given what amounted to a free hand in the Baltic States and Finland. Assuming that Soviet leaders did not expect Britain to make such a concession, one is forced to the conclusion that the chief purpose of the negotiations, from the Soviet standpoint, was to use them as a lever to move the Germans. The first discussions between Moscow and Berlin, in April and May, 1939, tend to support that thesis.

4. Origins of the Nazi-Soviet Pact

The German records leave no doubt that the Soviet Government, soon after the appointment of Molotov as Foreign Commissar, took the initiative

[51] *Falsificators of History;* Bonnet: *Fin d'une Europe,* 186-87.

[52] Kuhn in *The New York Times,* May 25, 1939; Philip, *ibid.,* June 2, 1939; Denny, *ibid.,* June 4, 1939.

[53] Memo by the Division of European Affairs, June 2, 1939.

toward an improvement of German-Russian relations. The first moves were extremely cautious and noncommittal. On May 5, 1939, the Soviet Chargé d'Affaires in Berlin, Mr. Astakhov (reputedly a favorite of Stalin) discussed with an official of the German trade division the possibility of renewing commercial negotiations and incidentally sounded out his interlocutor as to whether the change in the Soviet Foreign Office was likely to induce an alteration of the Nazi attitude toward the Kremlin. On the very next day Berlin was flooded with rumors of a forthcoming Nazi-Soviet agreement, for which the dismissal of the Jew Litvinov was said to have been the indispensable preparation. These insinuations were obviously inspired by the Nazi Government, possibly to test the popular reaction to so revolutionary a departure, but perhaps even more to impress and intimidate the Western Powers. The French, at least, took the matter seriously, but the British dismissed the whole thing as a clumsy maneuver.[54]

Nothing daunted by the Nazi exploitation of the situation, Mr. Astakhov on May 17, 1939, again raised the subject of Nazi-Soviet relations. There were, he remarked, no conflicts of foreign policy between the two countries and therefore no reasons for continued enmity between them. Though the Kremlin had a distinct feeling that it was menaced by Germany, he thought this sentiment could be allayed.[55]

This preliminary sparring was followed (May 20, 1939) by the first discussion between Count von der Schulenburg, the German Ambassador at Moscow, with Commissar Molotov. The Ambassador indicated that his Government was prepared to reopen trade discussions and suggested that an emissary be sent to Moscow for the purpose. But Molotov struck a cool note. The earlier trade talks, he recalled, had evidently not been seriously intended by the Berlin Government and therefore the Kremlin "could only agree to a resumption of the negotiations if the necessary 'political basis' for them had been constructed." He refused to clarify his ideas further, but remarked that the matter was one that ought to be considered.[56]

The Nazi Government had been thinking about it. In fact, the problem had been carefully analyzed during the second half of May. It will be remembered that by this time Hitler's great scheme for a military alliance with Japan had begun to look hopeless. Ribbentrop had already begun to generate enthusiasm for the idea of a Nazi-Soviet pact, and Goering, during a visit to Rome in mid-April, had expounded the idea to Mussolini, pointing out that such a pact might soften up the Poles and at the same time deter the Soviets from accepting the offers of the British and French.[57]

[54] *Nazi-Soviet Relations*, 3; Tolischus in *The New York Times*, May 7, 9, 1939; *French Yellow Book*, Nos. 123, 124, 125; David J. Dallin: *Soviet Russia's Foreign Policy* (New Haven, 1942), 26 ff.
[55] *Nazi-Soviet Relations*, 4-5.
[56] *Nazi-Soviet Relations*, 5-7.
[57] Memo of conversation between Mussolini, Goering and Ciano, April 16, 1939.

No doubt there were others who saw the advantages to the Nazi of a coalition with the detested Communists, but it seems that Hitler himself was reluctant to change his ideas or his plans. It may well be that the ideological aspect troubled him more than his lieutenants, and that he had doubts of his ability to convert his fanatical followers. Furthermore, he was probably loath to sacrifice his designs on Soviet territory. And finally, the Fuehrer seems to have been almost as distrustful of the Soviet Government as was Chamberlain. He had to ask himself whether the Kremlin was not plotting to involve Germany in war with the West and whether the Soviets might not make use of the negotiations to disillusion the Japanese about the German connection.[58]

For a time Hitler hesitated and awaited developments. But by the end of May, 1939, the Germans had decided that the negotiations of the Western Powers with Soviet Russia might prove successful. To forestall such an eventuality it was thought wise to let the Kremlin know that Berlin was not uninterested in its suggestions. On May 30, 1939, State Secretary Weizsäcker, on instructions from Ribbentrop, broached the matter to Astakhov. He expressed agreement with Molotov's contention that economic and political affairs could not be kept entirely distinct, but indicated that German policy would be governed by the course of Soviet negotiations with other powers. In the most discreet way he called attention to the fact that the development of German-Polish relations had freed German policy in the East, and finally came to the main point. To quote his own record:

I did not know whether there still was any room at all for a possible gradual normalization of relations between Soviet Russia and Germany, now that Moscow had perhaps already listened to the enticements of London. At any rate, however, since the Chargé and his Ambassador had talked so frankly in the Foreign Ministry, I would like to spare myself the reproach that we ask anything from Moscow; we did not desire anything from Moscow, but neither did we want to be told by Moscow at a later date that we had erected between us an impenetrable wall of silence.[59]

Apparently some expression of German interest was all that the Kremlin wanted for the time being. Even on the assumption that the Soviet leaders were more intent on an agreement with Germany than on anything else, it was patently to their interest to strike a bargain on the best possible terms. If Nazi uneasiness over the discussions between London, Paris and Moscow could be further stimulated, Hitler might in the end pay a high price for a pact. Whether or not this was Stalin's reasoning, he made no

[58] Kleist: *Zwischen Hitler und Stalin*, 38 ff.; Erich Kordt: *Nicht aus den Akten* (Stuttgart, 1950), 307 ff.
[59] *Nazi-Soviet Relations*, 7-17; Weizsäcker: *Erinnerungen*, 231; *French Yellow Book*, No. 127, reporting information from a high German source. We have used also two excellent tels. from Grummon (Moscow), May 20, 22, 1939.

further advances to Germany during June and most of July, 1939, but on the contrary awaited the next moves of the Nazis. The Germans, badly in need of raw materials for war purposes, were quite ready to reopen trade negotiations and offered to send one of their experts to Moscow for the purpose. But the Soviet Commissar for Foreign Trade intimated that certain political questions would first have to be considered and in general gave the German Ambassador the impression that the Russians suspected Berlin of wanting to make political capital out of any further trade discussions. By the end of June, 1939, the German Foreign Office was beginning to despair of progress along strictly economic lines. And yet, as the Nazi leaders pressed forward with their military plans against Poland, it became increasingly clear to them that an understanding with Moscow was essential.

On June 29, 1939, Count Schulenburg, returning to Moscow after extended conferences in Berlin, had a second interview with Molotov, during which the Ambassador made a concerted effort to open up the larger problem. He told the Soviet Commissar that Germany would welcome a "normalization" of relations and mentioned, as proof that Hitler had no hostile plans against the Soviets, the reserve shown by the German press, the conclusion of nonaggression pacts between Germany, Estonia and Latvia, and the continuing German desire to resume trade negotiations. To complete his argument he recalled that the German-Soviet treaty of friendship and nonaggression of 1926 was still in force.

Molotov listened attentively and voiced his satisfaction. The Soviet Government, he remarked, aimed at the cultivation of good relations with all its neighbors, but of course only on the basis of reciprocity. Becoming more pointed, he confessed that the Kremlin had had doubts of the validity of the treaty of 1926 in view of the hostile attitude of the Nazi Government and added acidly that with respect to the German nonaggression pacts with the Baltic States, "Germany had concluded them in her own interest, and not out of love for the Soviet Union." Furthermore, he queried the value of such agreements, considering Poland's recent experience with the German-Polish pact of 1934. It was exceedingly rare for German diplomats in the heyday of Nazi power to have to listen to such comments. Schulenburg was unable to hold out much hope to his Government. He was much impressed with Molotov's distrust of Germany, though he believed the Russians were interested in discovering Germany's desires and in maintaining contact with Berlin.[60]

The German Foreign Office was baffled and irritated by Molotov's coolness. For the time being the Ambassador at Moscow was instructed to do nothing more. The Nazi leaders became ever more firmly convinced that the British-French-Soviet negotiations would succeed, yet they could not

[60] Nazi-Soviet Relations, 21-27. We have used also the interesting tels. from Grummon (Moscow) of June 9 and July 1, 1939.

decide how to parry that blow. In the words of one Nazi official: "We could not drag Molotov and Mikoyan to Berlin through the Brandenburg Gate." Matters remained at dead center until suddenly, on July 22, 1939, the Soviet press announced that trade talks with the Germans would be resumed at Berlin. Apparently the Germans were surprised by this abrupt change, but agreeably so. A telegram was hastily sent to the German Embassy at Moscow stating that the Berlin Government was prepared to make substantial concessions because it desired a trade agreement for broader reasons. The Ambassador was told that the period of watchful waiting was over and that he might spin the thread of negotiation on. As of this date, then, the Nazis began to cast aside their reserve and systematically to pursue their objective.[61]

5. STALEMATE BETWEEN EAST AND WEST

While, during June and July, 1939, the Kremlin did little or nothing to encourage the Germans, it continued to negotiate actively with Britain and France, without, however, making much progress. The Soviet reply to the British-French note brought the prevalent optimism of London and Paris to an abrupt end (June 2, 1939), for the Moscow Government insisted not only that all reference to the League be omitted, but also that direct guarantees of the independence of Finland, Estonia and Latvia, as well as of Poland, Rumania, Turkey, Greece and Belgium, be written into the projected agreement. In addition, the Soviets now demanded that the political pact become effective only after the conclusion of a military convention.[62]

Even the sanguine and impatient French statesmen were shocked by the exorbitance of the Soviet demand. They bemoaned the fact that the negotiations had been so badly bungled and blamed the British for having rejected the original Soviet proposal. Now, they argued, things had progressed to the point where the Kremlin recognized that its support was indispensable to the democracies. The Paris Government still wanted the pact with Russia and refused to give up hope of it. On the other hand, it had got wind of the Soviet notes to Estonia and Latvia and was simply appalled by their implications. According to French intelligence the Kremlin had informed the Estonian Government that the Soviet Union had an interest in preventing any other power from securing special political, military or economic privileges in that country and was therefore determined to defend Estonia against any such "aggression," whether Estonia requested aid or not. To French minds this left no doubt that Soviet armies might

---

[61] *Nazi-Soviet Relations*, 27-32. The tel. to Moscow of July 22, 1939, is not to be found in this collection, but is in the *Tokyo War Crimes Documents* (Defense Document 1633).

[62] Bonnet: *Fin d'une Europe*, 186-87; tels. from Grummon, June 3, 1939, from Bullitt, June 5, 1939, and from Kennedy, June 5, 1939.

march into neighboring states at any time on the pretext of having to "protect" them. Under the terms laid down in the Soviet note of June 2, 1939, Britain and France would, in such a case, be called upon to support the Soviet action. To quote M. Bonnet: "France and England could certainly not consent to giving the Soviet Union support for such an extension of Bolshevism in Eastern Europe. . . . Acceptance of the Soviet proposal would mean consent to the establishment of a Soviet protectorate over the states named in the note."[63]

If the French, who had previously been willing to guarantee the Baltic States, reacted in this fashion, the feelings aroused by the Soviet note in British Government circles can easily be imagined. Lord Halifax remarked that the Kremlin was taking the Western Powers "up a very dark road," while Mr. Chamberlain was so completely disillusioned that he questioned whether the Soviets had even the slightest intention of concluding a pact with the West. He would, so he said, make some concessions, but if they, too, failed to satisfy, he would be tempted to call the whole thing off.[64] Apparently the Soviet demands induced in Chamberlain and some of his associates a relapse into the mentality of appeasement. Both the Prime Minister and the Foreign Secretary, replying in public to Hitler's repeated charges of encirclement, again expressed their abhorrence of a division of Europe into potentially hostile camps and reiterated their complete readiness to consider German needs and claims, once an atmosphere of peace and confidence had been restored. The German Ambassador in London, intent on forestalling a hostile coalition against his country, exerted himself to the utmost to convert British statesmen to the idea of direct conversations with the Nazi Government.[65]

The problem of the Baltic States presented an almost insuperable obstacle to the success of the negotiations for a peace front. It seems reasonably clear that the Kremlin was genuinely apprehensive of German designs in that quarter. In Moscow the Finnish Government was regarded as anti-Soviet if not actually pro-German; indeed, that government was suspected of pressing for the refortification of the Åland Islands at the behest of Berlin. Nothing could dispel Soviet distrust, and at the end of June, 1939, the Kremlin notified the Finns that the Soviet Union could not agree to the refortification unless it were permitted to participate in the work on the same basis as Sweden. It is almost superfluous to add that the conclusion of

[63] Tels. from Bullitt, June 5 and 6, 1939.
[64] Tels. from Kennedy, June 7, 9, 1939; Feiling: *Life of Neville Chamberlain*, 409.
[65] *German Documents on the Outbreak of the War*, Nos. 305, 307, 308; and the Official Soviet publication: *Documents and Materials Relating to the Eve of the Second World War* (New York, 1949), Vol. II: *Dirksen Papers*. See further Noel-Baker in *New York Herald Tribune*, May 31, 1939; *Christian Science Monitor*, June 21, 1939; *Chicago Daily News*, June 9, 1939; Sir Arthur Salters: *Security, Can We Retrieve It?* (New York, 1939), 345 ff.; Arthur Krock: "How War Came" (*The New York Times Magazine*, July 18, 1943).

nonaggression pacts between Germany, Estonia and Latvia served only to enhance Soviet suspicions and fears.[66]

But for all that, there was more than sufficient reason for believing that the Soviet Government had territorial ambitions with regard to the entire frontier region lost to it in 1917 and the succeeding years. London and Paris were well aware of Soviet claims and hopes and therefore found themselves in an awkward if not impossible position when confronted with the Soviet note of June 2, 1939. Apart from their unwillingness to aid and abet the expansion of Communist power, they felt strongly that, after posing as the defenders of small states against aggression, they could hardly themselves take part in forcing upon the Baltic States arrangements which they definitely did not want and would not accept. Like Poland and Rumania, all these countries objected violently to a Soviet guarantee or indeed to any guarantee that would seem to align them with one or another of the opposing European blocs. Hardly had their Governments realized what was being proposed when they announced publicly and privately that they desired to remain neutral and that they would resist all efforts to invade or occupy them. Privately they let it be known that if the British-French-Soviet negotiations eventuated in such guarantees, Estonia and Finland would conclude a military alliance against Russia and might even call in the Germans, who, in the last analysis, were preferable to the Russians.[67]

Disheartened though the British Cabinet may have been, it felt impelled to seek a solution, partly because of the growing conviction of the Soviets' importance and partly because of the continued needling of the opposition. Churchill, for one, demanded action and wrote in the *New York Herald Tribune* (June 7, 1939):

Agreement is driven forward by irresistible forces overriding and shearing away serious obstacles and valid prejudices as if they were but straws. Personally . . . I have from the beginning preferred the Russian proposals to either the British or French alternatives. They are simple, they are logical and they conform to the main groupings of common interest.

[66] Tel. from Schoenfeld (Helsinki), June 10, 1939, and despatch of June 30, 1939; statement of the Soviet press chief, July 10, 1941 (quoted in Alexander Werth: *Moscow War Diary*, New York, 1942, 46); tels. from Wiley (Riga), May 31, 1939; Biddle (Warsaw), June 7, 1939; despatch from Leonard (Tallinn), July 8, 1939, reporting a conversation between Molotov and the Estonian Minister in Moscow in mid-June, 1939. See also Davies: *Mission to Moscow*, 548 ff., retracing Soviet apprehensions to at least 1937.

[67] Tels. from Schoenfeld, June 7 and 28, 1939; despatch from Leonard, June 8, 1939; despatches from Gufler (Kaunas), June 8 and 13, 1939; despatches from Wiley, June 30, July 11 and 17, 1939; despatch from Grummon, June 22, 1939. See also *The New York Times*, June 7 and 14, 1939 and July 2, 1939; Admiral Usborne, in *New York Herald Tribune*, June 14, 1939. Further detail in Eljas Erkko: "La neutralité et sa defense" (*Le Nord*, 1939, 271-75); F. W. Pick: "The Evidence Re-Examined" (*Baltic Review*, L, 1946, 154-60); Wuorinen: *Finland and World War II*, 49-50.

Why not guarantee the Baltic States? he queried. If the Germans invaded those states, Poland would have to fight. So would Russia and the Western Powers. Why, then, not declare the fact?

In view of the grave questions at issue, the London Government might have been well advised to send Lord Halifax to Moscow, as some suggested. But Mr. Chamberlain would not even accept Mr. Eden's offer to undertake the mission, and finally named Sir William Strang, at that time Chief of the Central European Division of the Foreign Office, to assist Sir William Seeds, the ailing Ambassador at Moscow. The Soviets were to complain later that this was to foist off on them a subordinate and politically unimportant official. They scornfully recalled that Mr. Chamberlain had personally betaken himself to Hitler and maintained that at least Halifax might have come to Moscow.[68]

Strang departed for Moscow in mid-June, 1939, bearing an assortment of proposals in the hope that at least one of them would prove palatable to the Kremlin. After prolonged discussions with his French colleague, he finally proposed to the Soviets that each of the three signatory powers should come to each other's assistance not only in case of direct aggression against any one of them, but also in the event of any one of them becoming involved in war on account of assistance against aggression afforded any state or states which any one of the signatories considered vital to its security. Aggression was defined as the crossing of frontiers with military forces. The states in question were not to be publicly named, but might be secretly listed. In return for this veiled guarantee of the Baltic States, the Western Powers requested that the Soviets guarantee Belgium, the Netherlands and Switzerland.[69]

Prone though they were to criticize the British Government's attitude toward Russia, the French had to admit that their colleagues had "fallen over" themselves in agreeing to some form of guarantee for the Baltic States. Yet the Kremlin professed to remain dissatisfied. On June 29, 1939, the official newspaper *Pravda* published an astounding article by Andrei Zhdanov, a member of the all-powerful Politburo. The author's statement that he was expressing merely a personal opinion was given as little credit as it deserved and the article was therefore taken as an official utterance. According to Zhdanov the purpose of the British and French might be other than the construction of a peace front, the suggestion being that Moscow suspected the British and French of using the threat of a triple alliance to frighten Hitler into a new deal.[70] Since the Western Governments

[68] Churchill: *The Gathering Storm,* 389; *Falsificators of History;* Wheeler-Bennett: *Munich,* 403-4.

[69] Tels. from Wilson (Paris), June 16, 21, 22, 1939, and from Bullitt, June 28, 1939; tel. from Grummon, July 2, 1939. See also Bonnet: *Fin d'une Europe,* 187-93.

[70] *The New York Times,* June 30, 1939.

entertained exactly the same misgivings about the Soviets, it is clear that the chances for a meeting of minds were slight.

Molotov, who had been conferring with the German Ambassador on the very day of the appearance of the Zhdanov article, lost little time in commenting on the latest British-French proposals. On July 4, 1939, he declared the veiled guarantee of the Baltic States inadequate and insisted that the guarantee should provide for cases of indirect as well as direct aggression. He indicated in this connection that Soviet Russia would take immediate action if a change of government in a Baltic State seemed to favor an aggressor. As for other items, the Commissar objected that the Soviets could not guarantee countries like the Netherlands and Switzerland, which had not even recognized the Soviet Government. At any rate, the Kremlin could not consider this question until it had concluded suitable pacts with Poland and Turkey. In conclusion, Molotov renewed his demand that the political agreement between the three Governments be made conditional on the prior signature of the proper military arrangements.[71]

London and Paris were alike disheartened by the constant enlargement of the Soviet terms. They would never, so they said, accept a definition of indirect aggression that would permit the Soviets to march into the Baltic States at their pleasure, nor would they agree to make the political accord dependent on military discussions which might take months of time and even then fail of success. But the French Government was much disturbed by reports that Hitler meant to take action against Poland in August, 1939, and that he would do his utmost first to neutralize Soviet Russia by striking a bargain with Stalin. M. Bonnet therefore renewed his efforts to induce the British to yield further. British public opinion aided him in his campaign, for demands were already being made on Mr. Chamberlain to include Mr. Churchill in his Cabinet. The Prime Minister was utterly unwilling to entertain such notions, for he had no use for the policy urged by the opposition and was furthermore convinced that Mr. Churchill could not deliver one tenth of what the public expected of him; on the contrary, his presence in the Cabinet would only make for war.[72]

The debate between London and Paris, and the concurrent discussions in Moscow, continued for fully three weeks. Eventually the British gave in on a number of points, excepting, however, the important matter of defining indirect aggression. They proposed that this be taken to mean an act which a guaranteed state might be forced to accept under threat and which

[71] Tels. from Kennedy, July 3 and 5, 1939; tel. from Bullitt, July 5, 1939; Bonnet: *Fin d'une Europe*, 193; Kuhn, in *The New York Times*, July 5, 1939.

[72] Letter of Ambassador Kennedy to the President, July 20, 1939 (*Roosevelt Papers: Secretary's File*, Box 44). See also Lloyd George's attack on the government in the *Sunday Express*, July 23, 1939. On the British and French attitudes we have used tels. from Bullitt, July 5, 7, 18, 24, 1939; and from Kennedy, July 8 and 14, 1939. Bonnet: *Fin d'une Europe*, 193 ff., treats the matter in detail.

might destroy its neutrality or jeopardize its independence. This, declared the British, was to be their last word. Their Ambassador to Moscow was instructed to make clear to Molotov that London's patience was running out and that it could not go on forever accepting endlessly increasing demands by the Kremlin.

At this juncture, as though to save a situation that was rapidly getting out of hand, Molotov on July 24, 1939, suddenly and surprisingly announced that the Soviet Government was satisfied. Substantial agreement, he said, had already been reached, for the differences with respect to indirect aggression were merely matters of nuance. There was no reason why military negotiations should not be initiated, so that both the political and military accords could be signed in the near future. The Commissar, indeed, accepted informally a draft agreement, of which the text has since been published. This draft reveals that the Moscow Government agreed to the retention of some mention of the League of Nations and accepted the British definition of indirect aggression as a basis for discussion. Furthermore, the Kremlin conceded that the political accord should become operative as soon as military arrangements were completed. British and French military missions were to be despatched to Moscow for this purpose. The guaranteed states, listed in a secret protocol, were to be Estonia, Latvia, Lithuania, Poland, Rumania, Turkey, Greece and Belgium.[73]

In London and Paris Molotov's unexpected tractability was taken to mean that the Soviets were really determined to sign a pact and that therefore the military negotiations could be wound up in a week or two. On July 27, 1939, it was publicly announced that special French and British military missions would depart for Moscow in the immediate future. The British public was jubilant. The long and arduous debates were seemingly at an end and the much-desired peace front appeared about to become a reality. After many nerve-racking months the heavens were clearing and the future once more took on a rosy hue.

However, in reviewing Molotov's extraordinary *volte-face* in the light of later developments it is hard to interpret it as anything but a cunning move in the Kremlin's complicated game of playing off the British and French against the Germans. On the assumption that the real objective of the Soviets was to strike a deal with the Germans that would enable them to keep out of a European conflict while at the same time furthering their own aims and interests in Eastern Europe, it was clearly advantageous for them to delude the Germans into thinking that they were about to join the front against aggression. Their purpose then must have been to prolong the discussions with the Western Powers as long as the situation seemed

---

[73] Text in Bonnet: *Fin d'une Europe*, 401-3. See also Hamilton, in *The New York Times*, July 25, 1939. We have used also tels. from Bullitt, July 24 and 25, 1939; from Johnson (London), July 27, 1939; and from Grummon (Moscow), July 25, 1939.

to require. During July, 1939, however, the negotiations had reached the point where there was danger of their breaking down. Thereupon Molotov, having tried the British almost beyond endurance, suddenly reversed himself and ostensibly agreed to their proposals in order to gain time.

It is altogether probable that during July, 1939, another factor entered into the Soviet calculations. About the middle of the month a German official of Goering's economic staff, Dr. Helmuth Wohltat, arrived in London to attend a whaling conference. He was approached almost at once by Sir Horace Wilson, the confidential adviser of the Prime Minister, and Mr. Robert Hudson, Secretary for Overseas Trade, both of them gentlemen to whom Nazi proclivities were attributed. They discussed with Wohltat proposals which, they said, had the approval of the Prime Minister, and spoke freely of a British-German nonaggression pact which would enable the British Government to rid itself of its commitments to Poland. It is unnecessary to examine these advances in detail, but there seems to be no question of their authenticity. Mr. Chamberlain, who was never happy about the guarantee to Poland and who was definitely averse to the negotiations with Russia, was, informally and without the support of the Foreign Office, feeling out the Germans with a view to reviving the appeasement policy.[74]

News of these doings soon leaked to the press, which printed distorted stories of a projected British loan of one billion pounds to Nazi Germany in order to enable that country to return to a peacetime economy. Actually the German Government showed no interest whatever in the British advances, but to the Kremlin, ever suspicious of Chamberlain's attachment to appeasement, it must have seemed that Britain and Germany were about to strike a bargain, perhaps at the expense of the Soviet Union as well as of Poland. If indeed that was the Soviet reaction, it would explain Molotov's sudden announcement on July 22, 1939, that trade discussions with Berlin would be resumed, and his equally surprising acceptance of the British-French proposals which a short time before he had rejected out of hand. To Soviet thinking, a British-German pact would have been disastrous. It had therefore become urgently necessary for the Kremlin to bait the Nazis, but equally necessary for them to salvage the negotiations with the democracies. It is interesting to note that the Germans, as well as the British and French, were taken in by the Soviet maneuvers. They, too, believed that the antiaggression front would become a reality. The last act of this tragicomedy was to reveal how the leaders of the Kremlin exploited the hopes and dreams of the hated "imperialists."

[74] Chamberlain later stated publicly that the talks had been carried on without his approval. The most important source for this episode is the Dirksen correspondence, which was captured in Germany by the Soviet forces and later published under the title *Documents and Materials Relating to the Eve of the Second World War* (New York, 1949), Vol. II: *Dirksen Papers*. See also Wheeler-Bennett: *Munich*, 405-6.

CHAPTER IV

Illusions of Security

1. AMERICA AND THE EUROPEAN DEMOCRACIES

In analyzing and evaluating the evolution of American foreign policy, it is well to bear constantly in mind that in 1939 both the public and the Administration were exceptionally well informed about the developments abroad reviewed in the preceding chapter. Though the United States still held aloof from all entanglement in the foreign crisis, that element of the public which was interested in more than purely local happenings was able to follow the dramatic events in Europe through the press and the radio. Meanwhile the President and his immediate advisers enjoyed the advantage of very full and often highly confidential diplomatic reports. Only against the rather detailed account of the European scene already provided can one trace intelligently the reaction of American policy makers.

In view of the great importance attached to the American industrial potential it need cause no wonder that the British and French Governments took special pains to keep United States representatives fully informed and to enlist their Government's support. Ambassador Kennedy was sympathetic to the Chamberlain Government and its policies and tended to project his isolationism to the European problem. For the United States he prescribed complete abstention from the conflict brewing in Europe and urged that every effort be made to arm in self-defense against all eventualities. In substance he recommended a similar attitude for the British, for he was convinced that Hitler and the Nazis would pursue their objectives with the utmost ruthlessness and that any effort to stop them would probably mean war. To his mind the British had little to gain by fighting on continental issues and would be well advised to avoid at all costs a conflict which would reduce Europe to ruins and almost certainly prepare the triumph of communism. He favored appeasement as long as it held any promise of success and presumably would have welcomed a revival of the Four Power Pact,

122

which would have united Western Europe against the subversive force of the Soviet Union. Since these ideas were closely akin to those of Mr. Chamberlain, it was natural that the two men should have maintained an intimate and sympathetic relationship. The Prime Minister communicated to the Ambassador almost every step taken and discussed with him at length the British Government's reaction to each new development. From Ambassador Kennedy the President and the State Department therefore received prompt and full reports of British plans for a peace front and of the intricate course of the negotiations with the Kremlin.

Ambassador Bullitt's position in Paris was equally strong and probably more influential. In contrast to his colleague in London, Mr. Bullitt tended to be optimistic with respect to the role the United States could play and far from defeatist even with regard to the chances of the European democracies. A man whose experience in diplomacy went back to the First World War and whose interest in international affairs was extensive and keen, Mr. Bullitt could always be relied upon to keep himself exceptionally well posted and to pass every scrap of news on to the President. In view of his imagination, courage and energy it was inevitable that, in the midst of the confusion and uncertainty, he should have played a central role in Parisian politics and diplomacy. He was on intimate terms with Premier Daladier, whom he greatly admired, but also received the confidences of Foreign Minister Bonnet and the high officials of the Quai d'Orsay. In a sense Mr. Bullitt transcended his particular assignment and served as an Ambassador at Large. Representatives of the lesser powers in Paris confided in him and sought his advice or assurance. Consequently his reports, crisp, direct and forceful, supplied a rich and varied fare of intelligence and interpretation, and make fascinating reading even after the passage of years.

Ambassador Bullitt's views were as clean-cut as Mr. Kennedy's, but in many respects quite divergent. He detested the Nazi dictatorship, regarded it as a menace to Western civilization, and believed that if Hitler were not checked he would ultimately attempt to extend his power even to the New World. The effort to appease the Fuehrer, in his opinion, was entirely futile; therefore the only hope of salvation lay in taking a strong stand and uniting the forces in Europe opposed to the spread of Nazism. Mr. Bullitt had no extravagant conceptions of British and French military power and for that reason approved the efforts of the democracies to draw Soviet Russia into the peace front, despite his strong dislike and invincible distrust of the Communist regime. In July, 1939, he faithfully reported remarks of Premier Daladier with which no doubt he fully sympathized: "The basic policy of the Russians was to involve themselves as little as possible in war in Europe so that after England, France, Poland, Germany and Italy have torn each other thoroughly to pieces, the Russians might advance and conquer all

Europe in the interest of Bolshevism."[1] But clear though the handwriting on the wall may even then have been, the plight of the democracies was piteous and Mr. Bullitt agreed with Daladier and Bonnet that the attempt must be made to sup amicably with the devil, despite the need for a long spoon.

In the critical summer of 1939 the reporting from Berlin and Rome was of relatively lesser importance. Ambassador Wilson had not been returned to his post and the United States was therefore represented in Berlin only by a Chargé d'Affaires, who in any case would have been unable to play the role of an Ambassador. In this instance it mattered little; for Hitler, who made all the important decisions, was inaccessible to foreign diplomats and in fact chose for the most part to ignore his own. Berlin was constantly seething with excitement and rumor, but the dearth of reliable information was almost complete. In Rome the situation was not quite so bad, but nevertheless obscure and baffling. Ambassador Phillips, like other diplomats with the exception of the Germans, saw Mussolini only on the rarest occasions. The Foreign Minister, Count Ciano, was by contrast easily accessible and unusually voluble. In retrospect one can see that much of what he told Mr. Phillips was substantially correct, but Ciano's reputation for truthfulness and integrity was not of the best and his communications were therefore looked upon with a certain skepticism.

The truly remarkable feature of American diplomacy at this time was the flow of secret information on German and Soviet policy, about which otherwise nothing more than the merest inkling could have been expected. Events have shown that Hitler's distrust of professional German diplomats was fully justified. Within the German Foreign Office and throughout the Foreign Service there were men of the old school who disapproved of the Nazi regime and feared that Hitler's policy was fast leading their country to perdition. In the case of some this feeling was so strong that they considered themselves obligated to counteract the official policy and even to warn Hitler's opponents to prepare for the worst.[2] Among the diplomats as among German military leaders there were those who looked to foreign powers to create the conditions for a Nazi defeat.

The highly intelligent and generally respected German Ambassador in Moscow, Count Friedrich Werner von der Schulenburg, though an ardent champion of the close, traditional German-Russian friendship, was at heart an anti-Nazi and eventually paid with his life for his complicity in the plot against Hitler of July, 1944. From certain members of his staff the American Embassy in Moscow received full and accurate reports of the entire Nazi-

---

[1] Telegram from Bullitt, July 18, 1939.

[2] Ulrich von Hassell: *Vom andern Deutschland* (Zurich, 1946); Ernst von Weizsäcker: *Erinnerungen;* and Erich von Kordt: *Nicht aus den Akten* all have much to reveal on this subject.

Soviet negotiation. Virtually every step leading to the Nazi-Soviet pact was therefore known in Washington almost as soon as in Berlin, and President Roosevelt was far better informed on these matters than Paris or London. Because of the source of the information it was considered impossible to impart much of this intelligence to the British or French.[3] Occasionally broad hints were dropped to members of the British Embassy in Washington, but these, it might be added, were generally not taken very seriously.

It is doubtful whether any government in modern times could have been more effectively served with foreign intelligence than the American Administration in this critical period. Unhappily, however, there is no comparable body of evidence for reconstructing the reaction and attitude of the President and State Department to this vital information. The almost complete lack of records of internal discussions, either in the White House or the State Department, makes it unlikely that a fully satisfactory answer to this problem will ever be found. What was said between officials of the State Department, or between Secretary Hull and Under Secretary Welles and the President, or between the President and Ambassadors Kennedy and Bullitt in the course of frequent telephone conversations, will probably remain for the most part a mystery.

Nonetheless, the effort must be made to reconstruct the pattern of thought in Washington on the eve of the outbreak of war. By this time both the President and Mr. Hull had abandoned whatever sympathy for the policy of appeasing Hitler they may formerly have had. Like many American liberals the President was rather unsympathetic to the British "upper classes" and inclined to think that their policies were designed primarily to ensure their own class interests. It may be taken for granted that Mr. Roosevelt was not unaware of Prime Minister Chamberlain's disillusioned attitude toward the United States, and there is certainly evidence that at times he considered the British policy weak and inept. But he had a clear conception of the community of interest of the two English-speaking nations and within his capabilities he acted to support and strengthen the British position.[4]

An illuminating instance of the President's methods of procedure was his reinforcement of French pressure upon the British to introduce conscription. In view of the opposition of the Labour Party, Mr. Chamberlain consistently evaded action on this issue, though the French Premier redoubled his efforts after the Italian occupation of Albania. On April 19, 1939, Ambassador Bullitt, in reply to a question of his British colleague in Paris, stated that he was certain that Mr. Roosevelt believed it was of the highest

[3] Tel. to Steinhardt, August 25, 1939.
[4] See the record of the President's conversation with President Beneš of Czechoslovakia on May 28, 1939 ("Memoirs of Eduard Beneš," in *The Nation*, July 3, 1948), and James A. Farley: "Showdown with the Boss" (*Collier's Magazine*, July 12, 1948).

importance that Britain should adopt conscription, though obviously he could not instruct Ambassador Kennedy to say so. On learning of Bullitt's statement, the President had the following sanctimonious telegram sent the Ambassador:

The President has asked me [Under Secretary Welles] to let you know that while of course under existing conditions it would seem logical for every country which believed itself to be in danger of attack to take all possible steps to utilize in the most effective way its man and woman resources as well as its resources of other kinds, nevertheless, he believes that the question of conscription in England must be regarded as purely a question of British internal policy involving British decisions as to British national defense, and for that reason he does not consider it possible for him to express any opinion with regard thereto.[5]

Of at least equal importance was Mr. Roosevelt's attitude toward British-French efforts to include Soviet Russia in the peace front. Some of his State Department advisers shared to the full the distrust of the Kremlin so prevalent in European governing circles. The Soviet Government had not lived up to its engagements to the United States under the recognition agreements of 1933, and relations between the two countries were therefore cool and distant. Continued communist agitation in the United States aggravated the situation and led Assistant Secretary Berle to remark, in a memorandum of this period: "No one acquainted with the Russian Government will expect it to decline any opportunity to assist or foment revolution in the internal politics of any country with which it is in alliance."[6]

Mr. Roosevelt himself was at times highly irritated with the Soviets. In April, 1939, when asked to approve the appointment of the disagreeable Mr. Oumansky as Soviet Ambassador to Washington, he agreed, but jocosely issued instructions to "double the guard."[7] But in general his attitude toward Soviet Russia was a generous and open-minded one, for he had the feeling that the Bolshevik rule, for all its shortcomings, was an experiment designed for the improvement of the common man's lot. Although it is difficult to document matters of this kind, it seems that the President, who had begun his first term of office by putting through the recognition of the Soviet Government, continued to be influenced by the views of men like Assistant Secretary of State Messersmith and Ambassador Davies. Mr. Messersmith, who did so much to call attention to the menace of Hitlerism, held that Russia was a dictatorship of a somewhat different stripe. There was reason to believe that communism was being gradually transformed into a kind of

[5] Tel. from Bullitt, April 19, 1939; tel. from Welles to Bullitt, April 20, 1939. Mr. Bullitt has stated to the authors that the initiative came from the President.

[6] Memo for a State Department conference, April 2, 1939 (*Berle Diaries, MS.*). Scattered references in the *Moffat Diary (MS.)* show that the Soviet attitude and particularly indications of a Soviet-German *rapprochement* were watched with some anxiety.

[7] *F.D.R.: His Personal Letters,* II, 880.

state socialism, which might accommodate itself to the economic systems of the democracies. Politically, he argued, the Soviets had no territorial designs in Europe and only doubtfully in the Far East. The great need of the Kremlin was for peace, and it might therefore be wise to accept any coöperation the Soviets might proffer: "If there is a danger inherent in Russia for Europe and the world, it is a matter of the future and not of the present, while the three other dictatorships are actively today threatening that peace."[8]

In keeping with this interpretation the President had for a time contemplated the possibility of Soviet-American coöperation in checking Japanese expansion. In January, 1938, he had directed Ambassador Davies, who was about to return to his Moscow post, to explore with the Soviet leaders the possibility of military and naval liaison with an eye to exchange of information relating to Japan and the Far Eastern situation. According to Mr. Davies:

The President made it explicitly clear that it was not in his contemplation that there should be involved any pact of mutual support, or of aggression or defense, either directly or by the remotest implication; that it should be pointed out, however, that without any such commitment by either Government, it would be the part of prudence and wisdom on the part of each Government to familiarize the other with facts which might be of substantial value in the future by reason of similarity of purposes and necessities even though each power were pursuing separate and independent courses.

The Ambassador was not given much encouragement when he first broached this matter to Foreign Commissar Litvinov, but in June, 1938, he found Stalin and Molotov favorably disposed, on the understanding that such information should not go beyond the President, the Secretary of State, and their immediate advisers. The matter developed to the point where specific persons were discussed as prospective liaison officers, but for reasons still obscure no further action was taken by the President.[9]

Another illustration of Mr. Roosevelt's attitude may be derived from his treatment of a Soviet proposal, going back to 1936, that American shipyards build a battleship and a few destroyers for the Russian Navy. The story is far too complicated to be recounted in detail. Originally the Soviet Government projected a battleship of 62,000 tons, though it eventually agreed to one of 45,000 tons. Mr. Edison, the Acting Secretary of the Navy, was not averse to the project, though from the outset he encountered considerable

[8] Messersmith memo of October 11, 1937.

[9] Despatch from Davies (then at Brussels), January 17, 1939. The above section was omitted from the text as given in the appendix of Davies' book: *Mission to Moscow*. In January, 1939, Davies tried to revive the project, but evidently without avail (letter from Davies to Welles, January 17, 1939; letter from Welles to Davies, March 11, 1939; letter of Davies to the President, January 18, 1939).

opposition from high naval officers, who made an issue of the secrecy of American designs. The State Department took a consistently favorable attitude, the more so as the huge battleship envisaged was intended for service out of Vladivostok. Since little progress was being made in the negotiations, the problem was laid before the President for decision in June, 1938. In reply to a long series of questions, Mr. Roosevelt left no doubt that he desired the Navy Department to render friendly aid to the architects, shipbuilders and any Russian officers who might be sent to supervise the construction of a 45,000-ton ship. This decision was communicated to the American agents of the Soviet Government.

Despite the President's directive, little headway was made. The Soviet Government's interest shifted to the construction of destroyers of recent model and in the spring of 1939 it dispatched a naval mission to make arrangements. Several more months were spent in discussions of permissible designs and availability of secret equipment. Not until July, 1939, was substantial agreement reached and the designers enabled to get to work. The outbreak of war in Europe then intervened and after some soul-searching the Navy Department, through the State Department, explained that the huge orders for the United States Government would probably make it impossible for American shipyards to undertake construction for foreign Governments.[10]

Mr. Davies, though in the spring of 1939 no longer Ambassador to Moscow, continued to be concerned over what he considered dangerous ideas of Soviet Russia's weakness. Again and again he warned that if the Kremlin were cold-shouldered by the democracies, it might well seek a deal with Hitler. In April, 1939, as the British and French were beginning their negotiations with Russia, Davies offered to return to Moscow on special mission, but this suggestion was declined by the President lest it arouse public feeling and react adversely on the pending revision of the neutrality laws.[11] Nor did the Administration take any initiative with regard to the Soviet Government during the following summer months. Apart from occasional discussion of a debt settlement and of various aspects of trade relationships, there was little for the two Governments to talk about. Certainly the President took no direct hand in supporting the negotiations of the democracies for Russia's inclusion in the peace front. But since there is no evidence whatever of any objection from the American side to the effort

[10] The letter of the Secretary of State and the Secretary of the Navy to the President of June 8, 1938, reviewed the previous history of the project, while the President's annotations recorded his reaction. The further correspondence, between Mr. Green, of the Division of Controls, and the architects, is far too voluminous to itemize. The final stages were recorded in a State Department memo to Ambassador Oumansky, June 22, 1939; memo of conversation between Green and Oumansky, June 23, 1939; memos by Green, July 5, September 6, 1939; and memos of conversation between Mr. Green and Acting Secretary Edison, September 16, 1939.

[11] Tel. from Hull to Davies, April 18, 1939.

being made by London and Paris, one can only assume that Mr. Roosevelt approved the projected coalition and wished the European democracies success.

This conclusion seems warranted because the President's sympathy for the British-French cause was freely demonstrated. No doubt his conviction that the democracies were an essential European bulwark for the defense of the Western Hemisphere strengthened his sense of the common interest in opposing totalitarianism. Following Mr. Roosevelt's invitation of August, 1938, King George and Queen Elizabeth paid a state visit to the United States in June, 1939. Ostensibly the occasion had no political significance and the stress was put on the spiritual solidarity between the two countries. The King and Queen were warmly received in Washington and cordially greeted by the press from one coast to the other. They were then entertained by Mr. and Mrs. Roosevelt at Hyde Park, where, incidentally, the President had a good opportunity to canvass the international situation in privacy and confidence. Among other things, Mr. Roosevelt evidently expressed to the King his gratification over the firmer policy embarked upon by the London Government in the preceding months. The two men certainly saw eye to eye and established a relationship of genuine friendship. After the King's departure, he and the President, as well as Mrs. Roosevelt and the Queen, exchanged private letters from time to time. The visit was an unqualified success and contributed in some degree toward removing the animosity so long enshrined in the American attitude.[12]

2. DEFENSE OF THE NATION AND THE HEMISPHERE

The harrowing uncertainty of the European situation in the spring and summer of 1939 was fully reflected in the violent fluctuations of American public opinion. According to the opinion polls of early April, when the foreign situation was extremely tense, at least 51 percent of those queried believed that war would break out before the end of the year. But by May 19, 1939, this percentage had dropped again to 32. Considering that many prominent correspondents were at that very time reiterating their alarm over future developments, one can explain the American attitude only as wishful thinking, though great expectations were, no doubt, entertained of the projected peace front of Britain, France and Soviet Russia. The American people hoped almost against hope that a major conflict might be avoided, without as yet showing much disposition to face the possibility that the United States might become involved in the catastrophe.

[12] Based in part on the President's remarks to the French Ambassador, Count St. Quentin, and reported by the latter on June 14, 1939. This document was captured by the Germans and published in *Berliner Monatshefte*, February, 1943. The President's correspondence (*F.D.R.: His Personal Letters, passim*) bears eloquent testimony to the solicitude with which he supervised every item of the arrangements. For a detailed account of the visit see Eleanor Roosevelt: *This I Remember* (New York, 1949), Chapter XI.

One reaction, however, was prompt and firm: sensing the inherent threat to the country from events abroad, the American people was quite prepared to accept almost any measures deemed necessary for national or hemisphere defense. In this respect public sentiment to some extent outran the thinking of the Administration, which, in retrospect, can be charged with failure to grasp the magnitude of the effort that might ultimately be required, with laxity in coming to grips with important issues, and with having presented far too modest a program. At the time, however, the President's program appeared formidable and impressive enough and seemed adequate for all foreseeable contingencies.

The appropriations called for by the President for the fiscal year 1939-1940 were almost twice as large as those of the previous year, totaling about nine billion dollars, of which two billion were assigned to military needs. Public opinion supported this program with almost complete unanimity and Congress, though strongly economy-minded, raised little objection. The military appropriations were voted promptly and by comfortable majorities. On April 26, 1939, the President signed the regular military supply bill of half a billion dollars. A month later (May 25, 1939), he approved the naval supply bill of three quarters of a billion. Since Congress had reduced the original requests by only about $77,000,000, Mr. Roosevelt had every reason to be gratified, while the country at large was reassured.[13]

The experts of the War and Navy Departments were seemingly quite satisfied with the new appropriations. They now had the funds to put their immediate plans into operation and therefore turned to face the staggering tasks of extensive shipbuilding, Army expansion, airplane production, base construction and countless lesser requirements. Planning in government circles, military as well as civilian, was still on the traditionally modest and decidedly narrow plane. An excellent demonstration of the prevalent attitude was the failure to provide promptly and adequately for the stock-piling of essential strategic raw materials. For years Dr. Herbert Feis, the Adviser on International Economic Affairs of the State Department, had been urging the importance of this issue and had been conferring with officials of other government agencies in an attempt to block out an appropriate policy. In the spring of 1938 the Thomas Bill had been introduced in Congress, providing for the expenditure of $25,000,000 for the purchase of strategic raw materials during the fiscal year 1939 and each of the three succeeding years. But general apathy, combined with the pressure of private interests, had obstructed progress. In October, 1938, Secretary Hull had written the President, calling attention anew to the importance of the problem and requesting that it be considered in Cabinet meeting. But Mr. Roosevelt, evidently

---

[13] For a critical analysis of the program see Hanson W. Baldwin: "Our New Long Shadow" (Foreign Affairs, April, 1939), and the article entitled "America Arms for Peace" in the Christian Science Monitor, June 26, 1939.

influenced by the Director of the Budget, was unenthusiastic. He favored an initial appropriation of not more than $10,000,000 and refused to be bound by specific figures for the future. It was not until June, 1939, that Congress finally authorized the appropriation of $100,000,000 for four years, and not until August that it made the first $10,000,000 available. This sum was paltry indeed and therefore filled farsighted advocates of the program with despair. But it was not out of keeping with the restricted outlook of many high government officials. Congress was apparently ready to vote whatever sum the Administration considered necessary. It was primarily the President who insisted on reducing the initial outlay to a minimum.[14]

Another instance of slackness on the President's part had to do with the problem of gearing industry for war production. For years the War Department had been working on a War Mobilization Plan which was to provide for the adequate organization and administration of a war economy. Assistant Secretary of War Louis Johnson, who was charged by law with the direction of this program, had repeatedly urged Mr. Roosevelt to appoint an advisory board of industrial leaders to check the plans as they were periodically revised. But it was not until August 4, 1939, that the President suddenly established a War Resources Board, under the chairmanship of Edward R. Stettinius, Jr. It is highly probable that Mr. Roosevelt had deferred action on this matter while the question of revision of the neutrality law was still under debate. For obvious reasons he would have desired to avoid the impression that large-scale participation by the United States was being envisaged. Nevertheless, his delay in dealing with the matter would seem to indicate that the President was not thinking in terms of great urgency about the mobilization of American industry.[15]

The military appropriations for the fiscal year 1940 laid stress on air and naval power rather than upon the expansion of ground forces, and were clearly designed solely to strengthen the defense of the United States. But an important aspect of this problem, in the minds of military planners, was defense of the hemisphere against any type of attack from overseas. The subject is difficult to treat, not only because of the vast area involved, but because of the varying conditions and problems of the twenty American republics. In the present context a detailed analysis is impossible, but certain specific features may be briefly mentioned as illustrating the general policy.

[14] Details are superfluous in view of the authoritative treatment given by Feis in his book *Seen from EA* (New York, 1947). See also Brooks Emeny: "The Distribution and Control of Natural Resources and America's World Position" (*The Annals*, November, 1941). The President's attitude appears in a memo from Welles to Feis, January 16, 1939, and in a letter from the Bureau of the Budget to the Secretary of State, March 13, 1939.

[15] For details see Harold J. Tobin: "Preparing Civilian America for War" (*Foreign Affairs*, July, 1939); Alsop and Kintner: *American White Paper*, 50; and especially the official history: *Industrial Mobilization for War*, I (Washington, 1947), 3-6.

It will be recalled, from previous discussion, that by 1939 the American public had become keenly aware of the importance of Latin America for the national defense, and that even isolationists recognized the necessity for taking the hemisphere as a whole into consideration. Hence the general approval of the efforts made at the Lima Conference of 1938 to provide for Pan American solidarity and for common action not only against a military threat from abroad, but against subversive enemy activity. As the situation in Europe deteriorated, it became vitally important to avoid alienating any of the American powers and urgently necessary to provide all practicable economic support likely to cushion the shock of trade dislocation and thereby maintain the stability of the American states.

A striking example of the application of the Good Neighbor Policy to this end was the Administration's position in the dispute between the Mexican Government and the American oil companies following the expropriation of foreign oil properties in 1938. Despite heavy domestic pressure, the State Department held that the Mexican Government had the right to expropriate, provided adequate compensation were offered. Thenceforth the argument hinged on the widely disparate valuations of the properties in question. The Department made strenuous but unavailing efforts to further agreement. In August, 1939, the negotiations broke down, but Under Secretary Welles, at the special insistence of the President, issued a conciliatory statement urging further discussion. By no stretch of the imagination could the Administration be accused of having exerted pressure on Mexico in behalf of American interests. At no time was the oil issue permitted to embitter official relations between the two Governments. Indeed, Washington's stand in this matter could and was taken in Latin American capitals as a measure of its sincerity in espousing the Good Neighbor policy.[16]

Another demonstration of restraint was the negotiation of a new treaty between the United States and Panama. This pact, designed to replace the one-sided agreement of 1903, had been drawn in 1936, but had not been ratified by the United States Senate. Difficulty had arisen in connection with Article X, which appeared to provide for previous consultation between the two parties before either one of them could take measures to safeguard its interests, if these measures affected territory under the jurisdiction of the other. Since the Panama Canal was of crucial significance in any American plan for national or hemisphere defense, this proviso had potentially dangerous implications. Under Secretary Welles therefore arranged for an exchange of notes (February 1, 1939), which was to leave no possibility of misunderstanding. The salient passage read as follows:

[16] The controversial literature on this subject need not be analyzed here. Many of the key documents are printed in *Documents on American Foreign Relations*, II, 217 ff., and certain intimate information may be found in Josephus Daniels: *Shirt Sleeve Diplomat* (Chapel Hill, 1947), *passim*. See also Sumner Welles: *The Time for Decision*, 203 ff.

. . . in the event of an emergency so sudden as to make action of a preventive character imperative to safeguard the neutrality or security of the Panama Canal, and if by reason of such emergency it would be impossible to consult with the Government of Panama as provided in Article X of said treaty, the Government of the United States of America need not delay action to meet this emergency pending consultation. . . .

Furthermore, all negotiations for the purchase or lease of additional land for expansion of the Canal defenses were postponed until after the United States Senate had voted ratification of the treaty (July 26, 1939). Our relations with the Panamanian Government were bound to be delicate at best, and it is therefore understandable that Mr. Welles should have congratulated himself that the vital interests of the United States had been secured without loss of reputation as a Good Neighbor. The conclusion of the treaty gave promise that the relations between the Panamanian Government and the authorities of the Canal Zone would become more cordial than ever before.[17]

In the economic sphere the State Department tried to grapple with the needs of the Latin American countries for greater trade opportunities, capital investment and general financial aid. With these necessities in mind, the President had stated categorically in his Pan American Day address (April 14, 1939), that the United States would not only match force with force to defend the integrity of the hemisphere, but that, should the method of attack be that of economic pressure, the United States would give economic support "so that no American nation need surrender any fraction of its sovereign freedom to maintain its economic welfare." This was indeed a large order, but one assumed in all sincerity. During the visit of Foreign Minister Aranha of Brazil to Washington in February, 1939, a number of economic and financial agreements had been concluded and these were followed, in the course of succeeding months, by similar agreements with other states. Mr. Welles undertook to examine the requirements of the various American Republics seriatim and discussed with the Treasury Department the possibility of setting up a central clearing bank to facilitate exchanges between the United States and its neighbors to the South. It is true that by August, 1939, only a start had been made toward solving these complicated problems, but the pledge had been extended and, despite the enormous difficulties, the Administration was determined to redeem it.[18]

In the strictly military field the Washington authorities continued to in-

[17] The pertinent documents are in *Documents on American Foreign Relations*, II, 197 ff. We have used also a memo of conversation between General Strong and Mr. Briggs of the State Department, February 20, 1939; a letter of Secretary of War Woodring to Secretary Hull, June 19, 1939, and the reply, June 24, 1939; and the *Minutes of the Liaison Committee*, January 21 and July 26, 1939.

[18] *Documents on American Foreign Relations*, II, 129 ff. We have also the *Morgenthau Diaries (MS.)*, Volume 161, entry for January 20, 1939, and the State Department memo on *Economic Coöperation with Other American Republics* (October 9, 1939).

crease and strengthen American military and naval missions in Latin America in order to reduce the dependence of various Governments on German or Italian advisers. Furthermore, a bill was introduced in Congress in March, 1939, to permit the War and Navy Departments to make implements of war available to other American Republics at cost. Although there was reason to believe that no serious objection would be raised, the bill was not finally enacted into law until June, 1940. Nevertheless, the Administration's warm support of such legislation serves to illustrate the direction of its policy.[19]

A particularly ominous feature of the Latin American situation was the existence, in a number of states, of German or Italian controlled commercial airlines. Colombia, strategically located close to the Panama Canal, was eager to buy out the German Scadta Line, but could do so only if Panair (a subsidiary of Pan American Airways) would assume part of the financial and managerial burden. The State Department, as well as Mr. Spruille Braden, the United States Ambassador at Bogotá, was keenly aware of the danger presented by German-owned planes so near the Canal and did everything in its power to effect an agreement between the Colombian Government and Panair. But the company, which, as it turned out, held a substantial block of Scadta stock, was unwilling or unable to take on further responsibility and there was no way in which United States Government funds could be applied to the problem. This particular issue therefore hung fire for some time. Meanwhile a Special Interdepartmental Committee on Aviation was set up by President Roosevelt to coördinate the activities of various government agencies and to elaborate a general plan for the expansion of American aviation throughout the hemisphere. By June, 1939, this committee had completed a preliminary scheme, which became the basis for the further development of this American policy.[20]

Most important of these early steps to strengthen the defense of the hemisphere was the evolution of strategic planning to deal with the problem. Note has already been made, in an earlier chapter, of the fears of the War and Navy Departments lest Axis infiltration of Latin American countries eventuate in the overthrow of existing governments. With this danger in view, United States military leaders in the winter of 1938-1939 shelved most of the old, so-called "color" plans, providing for defense against attacks by specific nations. The planning divisions of the Services were then directed to study the requirements of hemisphere defense in a broader sense, with special reference to the problem of forestalling aggression from Europe or Asia. The result was the formulation of five concepts of possible future action known as the Rainbow Plans, the first of which was approved by the

[19] *Minutes of the Liaison Committee,* February 8, 1939. Essential papers are printed in *Documents on American Foreign Relations,* II, 173, 238-39.

[20] *Minutes of the Liaison Committee,* February 8, April 18 and 25, June 16, 1939; despatch from Braden, June 13, 1939. See further William A. M. Burden: *The Struggle for Airways in Latin America* (New York, 1943), 70.

Joint Board of the Army and Navy on August 9, 1939. This envisaged defense of the hemisphere at least as far south as 10° S.L., and assigned the Navy the task of interdicting all Axis communication with Latin America in the event of war. The plan recognized the real danger that Axis powers might establish themselves on the bulge of Brazil and stressed the absolute necessity for the United States to expel the enemy in such a contingency.[21]

Early planning for resistance to Axis attack at once brought to the fore the question of bases, a question which was to be for some time the key issue in United States relations with the Latin American states. In the Pacific the situation was reasonably satisfactory, since the United States held the potentially strong defensive triangle from Alaska to Hawaii to the Panama Canal. The military appropriations for 1940 provided for the construction of a number of new bases in that area which, it was believed, would make the American position unassailable. Therefore suggestions that the United States acquire by purchase or lease certain islands off the west coast of Latin America were put aside, the more so as such acquisitions would conflict with the recognized United States policy of seeking no territorial expansion and might, in fact, involve the Government in controversies which the Axis would be quick to exploit. Parenthetically it may be noted that discussion of these questions evoked in the President's mind an idea that was later to bear valuable fruit. Referring to one strategic island group, he had written to Mr. Welles in December, 1938, suggesting the possibility of "a joint trusteeship of the American Republics over the islands, whereby the islands would be administered as an international wild life reserve by a Board of the Pan American Union." This suggestion he repeated in March, 1939, expanding it to include several island groups, all of which would be "preserved for all time against colonization and for natural science." Finally, in August, 1939, the Byrd Antarctic Expedition led him to request Mr. Welles to consider the idea of joint Pan American sovereignty over territories lying to the south of the Americas, to be administered by an inter-American agency representing all the American Republics.[22]

More urgent was the need for additional United States bases on the Atlantic side, and particularly in the Caribbean, which, because of the Canal, was the critical area. The Caribbean islands were mostly in the hands of friendly European powers and it was almost axiomatic that the United States would never assent to the transfer of these territories from one non-American power to another.[23] The question was therefore merely how to

---

[21] We rely here on the study by Mark Watson: *Chief of Staff: Pre-War Plans and Preparations*, 101-4, and the MS. study by Captain Tracy Kittredge on *Anglo-American Naval Coöperation*.

[22] *Minutes of the Liaison Committee*, December 9, 1938, and the President's letters to Welles of March 25, 1939, and August 5, 1939 (*F.D.R.: His Personal Letters*, II, 871-72, 931-32).

[23] A. Lawrence Lowell: "Frontiers of the United States" (*Foreign Affairs*, July, 1939).

secure rights to use bases in the possessions of Britain, France or the Nether-lands. In March, 1939, Mr. Roosevelt had himself attended fleet maneuvers in the Caribbean designed to test the defenses of the Canal. As a result of these exercises the Navy Department was much concerned and reported: "This problem brings home the absolute necessity for a base of operations in or near the eastern extremity of South America in case the South Atlantic is to be controlled by any force." Admiral Andrews, commanding the de-fending fleet, wrote the President: "I hope that some means can be found to provide fortified and well-secured bases in this most important strategic area."[24]

Although no immediate solution seemed possible, the problem was of such transcendent importance that it was never lost from sight. In July, 1939, Admiral Leahy, then Chief of Naval Operations, handed the Presi-dent a memorandum analyzing the requirements of the Services. In order to carry out the missions assigned in the first Rainbow Plan, the Joint Board recommended that efforts be made to acquire limited base facilities at a large number of locations in British Caribbean possessions and in certain Latin American Republics as far south as Brazil and Ecuador, as well as air-fields in various Central American states.[25]

These far-reaching plans, though still a long way from realization, were admirable illustrations of the aims and objectives of the President and his advisers. At the outbreak of war in Europe the programs for both national and hemisphere defense were still embryonic and altogether inadequate for the requirements to be revealed later. But in 1939 they seemed impressively large and quite sufficient. The important point was that the defense pro-grams enjoyed the full support of the public, which thereby demonstrated that, even though determined to stay out of war, it was prepared for any sacrifices needed for the protection of its own shores and those of the hemisphere. Though the American people might still delude itself into thinking that it could remain aloof from a world conflict, it was taking no chances with the national security and was not at all blind to the fact that that security involved the safeguarding of the entire New World against the possibility of attack from abroad.

3. The Failure of Neutrality Revision

During the critical months of May, June, and July, 1939, the President and Secretary Hull still pinned their hopes of tipping the scales toward

---

[24] Letter of March 15, 1939 (*Roosevelt Papers:* Secretary's File, Box 41).

[25] *Minutes of the Liaison Committee,* July 26, 1939; Kittredge, MS. study on *United States-British Naval Coöperation,* memo of Admiral Stark to Mr. Welles, August 14, 1939; and letter of Admiral Anderson to the President, August 26, 1939 (*Roosevelt Papers:* Sec-retary's File, Box 52). For published discussion see the article by A. Lawrence Lowell, cited above, and George Fielding Eliot: "The Defense of the Americas" (*The Annals,* July, 1939).

peace on the revision of the neutrality laws and more particularly on the repeal of the arms embargo. They were firmly convinced that the United States could exercise an effective influence for peace only if, by Congressional action, it could make known to the world its determination to support the cause of the democracies by unstinted material aid. According to the public opinion polls, popular sentiment favored such a policy by a comfortable majority, but nevertheless opposition in Congress, especially in the Senate, ran high. From the discussion in Chapter II it may be recalled that Mr. Roosevelt, keenly alert to the personal animosities aroused by his domestic policies and fearful of provoking a debate that would do more harm than good, had entrusted the program for revision to Senator Pittman. The latter had mishandled it to such an extent that by early May, 1939, he had lost his original optimism and become so intimidated by the opposition that he recommended against the appearance of Secretary Hull before the Senate Committee on Foreign Relations lest the members ask embarrassing questions.[26]

Even before Pittman's admission of failure Mr. Roosevelt and Mr. Hull had carried on informal talks with Congressional leaders in an effort to make them realize the seriousness of the international situation and the urgent need to take a stand that might deter Hitler and aid in preserving the precarious peace. On the strength of reports from Ambassador Bullitt, the President warned that in the event of war the Nazis might win a quick victory and obtain control of the British and French Fleets, so that the United States and the whole New World might find themselves on the defensive "in our own back yard." In less elegant terms Mr. Hull argued that the anticipated clash in Europe would not be just "another goddam piddling dispute over a boundary line," but one of the greatest concern to the United States and the world. The existing neutrality legislation, he declared, had "substituted a wretched little bobtailed, sawed-off domestic statute for the established rules of international law," and conferred "a gratuitous benefit on the probable aggressors." But arguments and exhortations gave little promise of softening the opposition.[27]

Meanwhile another champion had offered his services. For some time Representative Sol Bloom, Chairman of the House Foreign Affairs Committee and a devoted supporter of the Administration's policies, had been eager to introduce a bill which would give the President more than his minimum requirements. Though Bloom was lacking in both knowledge and finesse, it was decided to let him try his hand. On May 10, 1939, the State Department supplied him with a draft which, after discussion with the

[26] Memo by Carlton Savage, May 8, 1939; *Berle Diaries (MS.)*, May 8, 1939.
[27] Tel. from Bullitt,. April 10, 1939; Alsop and Kintner: *American White Paper*, 41; Hull: *Memoirs*, I, 641 ff. Rauch: *Roosevelt: From Munich to Pearl Harbor*, 118 ff., supplies a good general account based on the published sources.

President, he used in shaping his own bill. This was to provide for repeal of the arms embargo, but made no mention of "cash and carry." It did, however, include prohibition of travel on belligerent ships and exclusion of American shipping from specified combat areas. On the whole it left the President greater discretion than the Pittman Bill. Had it been carried, it would have solved the whole problem to the President's satisfaction.[28]

Though there was less opposition in the House than in the Senate, the outlook for the Bloom Bill was none too good. Newspaper commentators thought it most unlikely that Congress would lift the arms embargo and predicted a revolt in Congress if the matter were pressed. Time and again it was pointed out that many people, in and out of Congress, suspected the President of desiring to steer the country into war and believed that only legislative restrictions could stop him. Far from giving the Executive wider discretion, the chances were that Congress would do everything to "clip his wings." On all sides there was talk of a filibuster if the issue were brought to the test.[29]

In the hope of forestalling defeat, the President invited a number of House leaders to confer with him at the White House on May 19. He spoke to them very frankly:

The President was emphatic in the view that every possible effort should be made to eliminate section 1 [i.e., the arms embargo] of the existing Neutrality Act. He believed that the elimination of section 1 would actually prevent the outbreak of war in Europe, or if it did not prevent the outbreak of war, the elimination of that provision would make less likely a victory for the powers unfriendly to the United States. The President was not seriously concerned about any other provision of neutrality legislation. He did mention, however, that he saw no objection to cash and carry provisions and that he inclined to the view that a war zone provision might really be useful.

With respect to the international situation the President employed the best arguments he knew:

He told them that in case of war there was at least even chance that Germans and Italians might win. In that case their first act would be either to seize the British Navy or put it out of action. Then they would establish trade relations with Latin America, put instructors in the armies, etc. They would probably not touch British, French or Dutch possessions in this hemisphere. But in a very short time we would find ourselves surrounded by hostile states. Further, the Japanese, who "always like to play with the big boys," would probably go into a hard and

[28] Memo by Carlton Savage, May 9, 1939; letter of Judge R. Walton Moore to the President, May 12, 1939, urging him to persuade Bloom not to propose excessive discretion for the President (*Roosevelt Papers:* Secretary's File, Box 42).

[29] Memo by Carlton Savage, May 15, 1939; *Moffat Diary (MS.)*, May 16, 17, 18, 1939; Alsop and Kintner: *American White Paper*, 43. For a detailed analysis of sentiment in Congress see the *Christian Science Monitor*, May 13, 1939, and the summary in D. F. Fleming: "America's Neutrality Dilemma" (*Events*, July, 1939).

fast alliance. The combined German and Italian Navies were about the equal of ours and the Japanese was about eighty percent of ours. Therefore, the temptation to them would always be to try another quick war with us, if we got rough about their South American penetration.

The President admitted that all this was merely a possibility, but it was, he added, one that no farsighted statesman could afford to tolerate. Yet the Congressmen remained skeptical about revision. They thought there was real danger of defeat for any measure involving repeal of the arms embargo, despite the fact that "the President made clear that there was no intent on his part to send American troops to Europe in case of a general European War." Mr. Roosevelt insisted that the fight be made and expressed the hope that by June 2 the House Committee might complete its hearings and report favorably on a bill which could be passed before the arrival of the British King and Queen on June 12.[30]

Mr. Hull hoped to further the cause by finally producing the letter in defense of revision, on which so many officials of the Department had labored so long. After yet another polishing it was sent to both Bloom and Pittman on May 27, 1939, thus providing the first formal statement of the Administration on this hotly contested issue. The document, which was closely reasoned, began by carefully describing the various proposals thus far advanced as "intended to aid in keeping the United States from becoming involved in war." The Administration, it continued, aimed to pursue this objective "within the limits of our traditional policy of non-involvement in overseas affairs." Attention was, however, called to the fact that "no matter how much we may wish or try to disassociate ourselves from world events, we cannot achieve disassociation. The simple fact of our existence as a great nation in a world of nations cannot be denied . . ." It was therefore inevitable that legislation adopted by the United States would influence other countries:

The problem for us is not whether we shall help any foreign country or any group of foreign countries. Nor is it that of passing judgment upon or interfering in other people's controversies. Rather, it is that of so conducting our affairs and our relations with other peoples, both before and after the outbreak of war elsewhere, that we shall be more, and not less, secure; so that we shall not become parties to controversies; and so that our attitude and actions will encourage other people to avoid, rather than to become engaged in, controversy.

[30] Memo by Carlton Savage, May 19, 1939, who attended as special assistant to Secretary Hull. Savage records as present Mr. Hull and Congressmen Bankhead, Rayburn, Bloom, Richards and Shanley. See also Hull: *Memoirs*, I, 641-44. We have used further the President's remarks to Berle (*Berle Diaries, MS.,* May 26, 1939) and a letter from Judge Moore to the President, May 19, 1939, expressing some optimism about Congressional action and urging that in any case the fight be made (*Roosevelt Papers:* Secretary's File, Box 42).

Having thus reassurred his isolationist critics that the Government's objectives were no different from their own, the Secretary warned against depriving the Executive in advance of all freedom of action in the attainment of these aims. He recommended that, so far as possible, our neutrality legislation should represent a return "to traditional concepts of international law." While this required that the neutrality measures adopted by the United States should apply equally to all belligerents, it did not require an embargo on arms to belligerents. In any case, if we were to have an embargo, it would be well to be logical and embargo everything, since in modern warfare the distinction between munitions of war and other exports had lost all relevancy. Since clearly we could not embargo all exports to belligerents, it would be best not to shackle ourselves in advance by drawing up a rigid list of prohibited articles. Besides, the most likely cause of involvement would not be lack of an embargo but, as experience had shown, the loss of American lives. Therefore it would be wise not to restrict our rights under international law by any self-imposed embargo, but rather to restrict the rights of our nationals to send their ships or expose their persons in areas of danger. By no means, of course, should we *abandon* any of our rights as neutrals, but we should, in our own interest and by our own domestic legislation, restrict them.

After reiterating his "firm conviction" that the arms embargo should be eliminated, the Secretary ended by listing a number of specific suggestions for "the most effective legislative contribution at this time toward keeping the country out of war." They were:

To prohibit American ships, irrespective of what they may be carrying, from entering combat areas;

To restrict travel by American citizens in combat areas;

To provide that the export of goods destined for belligerents shall be preceded by transfer of title to the foreign purchaser;

To continue the existing legislation respecting loans and credits to nations at war;

To regulate the solicitation and collection in this country of funds for belligerents;

To continue the National Munitions Control Board and the system of arms export and import licenses.[31]

On May 29, 1939, Mr. Bloom introduced a joint resolution embodying these points, but in addition assigning to the President wide discretionary powers in invoking the act and in administering it after finding belligerency to exist. One can only conclude that efforts to check the sponsor's ardor had failed. Mr. Bloom was optimistic, like Pittman before him, and assured Secretary Hull that he and his friends had enough votes to put through any measure the Administration desired.[32] For a few days the situation appeared

[31] Text in *Documents on American Foreign Relations*, I, 536-39, and in *Peace and War*, 461-64. We have used also Hull: *Memoirs*, I, 644, and the *Moffat Diary (MS.)*, May 23, 25, 26, 27, 1939.

[32] *Moffat Diary (MS.)*, May 31, 1939.

rosy, but before long the opposition began its attack on the discretionary powers proposed for the President, which Bloom had so blithely included. These powers were described as "supernatural" and the equivalent of a free hand to maneuver the country into war. The State Department did its best to reassure the legislators and to bolster the Administration forces. Even the War and Navy Departments were pressed into service to demonstrate that the embargo reduced the orders for American munitions and so hampered the expansion of industrial facilities upon which the Services depended for their own supply. But hope was growing dim and Bloom's leadership was proving disappointing.[33] It is true that on June 13, 1939, the Foreign Affairs Committee reported the Bloom Bill favorably, but the vote was on strictly party lines (twelve Democrats in favor, and eight Republicans opposed), and the minority report boded no good for the future. This report stated bluntly:

> No neutrality law at all would be better than this resolution which, in the name of neutrality, and under the guise of preventing provocative acts of American citizens, gives the President additional powers to be unneutral. . . . No President has ever had such powers before. . . . We are opposed to the President's policy of using the threat of our power to preserve a balance of power in Europe. We do not believe that the President is deliberately provoking war, but we believe that the way to peace is for us to be neutral, not biased; friendly, not threatening. . . .[34]

The House began debate on the bill in the midst of the British royal visit. Amendments were at once proposed and considered, and the closeness of the votes upon them indicated that the fate of the bill was unpredictable. Meanwhile the cause of the Administration was ill served by the French Foreign Minister, M. Bonnet, who stated in a speech of June 25, 1939, that "the United States perhaps holds the keys to peace or war. If the United States makes it clear that they are on our side when the conflict starts, the specter of war would be banished definitely." By way of explanation, if such were needed, an American correspondent added: "The logical Frenchmen do not understand why if, first, the Americans believe war is coming; if, second, they wish to keep out; and if, third, they believe that if war comes they will probably become involved; then, fourth, the Americans do not prevent the war by taking a stand now."[35] This was perfectly valid

---

[33] *Moffat Diary (MS.)*, June 5, 6, 9, 10, 1939.

[34] One of the best analyses of the issue is F. O. Wilcox: "The Neutrality Fight in Congress, 1939" (*American Political Science Review*, October, 1939, 811 ff.), but see also Shepardson and Scroggs: *The United States in World Affairs, 1939*, 75 ff.; Beard: *American Foreign Policy in the Making*, 225 ff.; Rauch: *Roosevelt: From Munich to Pearl Harbor*, 118 ff. For some of the detail we have used a letter from Judge Moore to the President, June 2, 1939, and the reply, June 7, 1939 (*Roosevelt Papers:* Secretary's File, Box 42), and a note from the President to the Speaker of the House, June 6, 1939 (*ibid.*, Box 46), as well as the *Berle Diaries (MS.)*, June 1, 12, 17, 1939, and memos by Carlton Savage, June 17, July 1, 1939.

[35] Mowrer, in *Chicago Daily News*, June 26, 1939. See also *The New York Times*, June 25 and 26, 1939.

argument, and to the "interventionist" made excellent sense. But since the very idea of aligning the United States with any foreign power was anathema to the isolationist, Bonnet's remarks were widely interpreted as a revelation of the President's real intent.

The Bloom Bill passed the House on June 30, 1939, by a vote of only 200 to 188, and only with the inclusion of the anomalous Vorys Amendment, which provided for an embargo on the shipment of "arms and ammunition," but not of "instruments of war." In other words, the House had cut the heart out of the bill and thereby struck the Administration with consternation. Secretary Hull at once issued a statement expressing regret and disappointment and pleading for the enactment of the unamended bill which, he maintained, was "not only best calculated to keep this nation out of war in the event war comes, but also, what is all-important at this time, best calculated to make a far greater contribution than could the present law or its equivalent toward the discouragement of the outbreak of war." The President himself wrote to a friend: "I honestly believe that the vote last night was a stimulus to war and that if the result had been different it would have been a definite encouragement to peace."[36]

Since the chances of favorable reconsideration of the bill by the House were almost nil, the President cast about for some other means to achieve his end. The reaction of European capitals was alarming. Everywhere it was felt that the Administration had suffered a terrific setback, that American aid was not to be counted on, and that failure to repeal the embargo would encourage Hitler to embark on further ventures.[37] Mr. Roosevelt and Mr. Hull considered it essential to the cause of peace that erroneous impressions be corrected. Some members of the official family argued that since the President had the constitutional right to conduct foreign affairs, he could not be bound by legislation which infringed his constitutional powers. This was rather questionable reasoning, but the situation was desperate. On July 1, 1939, the President therefore turned to the Attorney General with the query: "If we fail to get any Neutrality Bill, how far do you think I can go in ignoring the existing act—even if I did sign it?"[38] Whether this inquiry was ever replied to is not known, but since nothing further was heard of this approach, it may be assumed that it was abandoned as too daring and as politically hopeless.

The only recourse was to turn once more to the Senate. On July 5, 1939, the Committee on Foreign Relations began reconsideration of the Pittman Bill. Once again Mr. Pittman was buoyant and optimistic. Mr. Hull's

[36] *F.D.R.: His Personal Letters* II, 900-01 (letter to Caroline O'Day, July 1, 1939). Hull's statement may be found in *Peace and War*, 465. See also Hull: *Memoirs*, I, 646.

[37] Circular tel. of the Department to various European missions, requesting reports, July 2, 1939. The replies are conveniently summarized in Hull, *Memoirs*, I, 646.

[38] Note to the Attorney General, July 1, 1939 (*F.D.R.: His Personal Letters*, II, 899-900).

assistant reported (July 10) that "in general the Senator appeared to feel well convinced that there was really no doubt of favorable action by the Committee at tomorrow's meeting," and that therefore it would be inadvisable for the Secretary to submit any further statement.[39] Yet on the very next day the committee voted 12 to 11 against further consideration of neutrality measures until the next session of Congress. Among those voting to defer were five Democrats, including two (Gillette and George) whom the President had attempted to "purge" in 1938.

Since both Houses had now acted, in one way or another, the President might well have dropped the matter, leaving the responsibility where it belonged. But reports from Europe foreshadowed a crisis in August, 1939, and Mr. Roosevelt and his advisers were convinced that the only chance of forestalling it lay in a demonstration of American readiness to give the democracies at least material support.[40] The one ray of hope was that the Senate itself might be induced to overrule its committee and reopen the discussion. In preparation for this eventuality Secretary Hull on July 14 sent to Congress, with the President's endorsement, a long message reviewing the problem. In the attempt to dispel what he described as the "astonishing amount of confusion and misunderstanding" regarding the issue, the Secretary analyzed the pros and cons of the Administration program and reiterated his conviction that it offered "a far broader and more effective set of provisions, which in no conceivable sense could breed trouble but which to a far greater extent than the present act would both aid in making less likely a general war, and, while keeping strictly within the limits of neutrality, reduce as far as possible the risk of this nation being drawn into war if war comes." He pleaded for a spirit of collaboration between the Executive and the Legislature, lest peace and other vital interests of the country be jeopardized, and urged that so crucial a matter be kept outside the range of partisanship.[41]

Preliminary to the final effort the President and Secretary Hull conferred with Senate leaders of both parties at the White House on the evening of July 18, 1939. The story of this dramatic meeting has long been known, but will well bear repetition. The President opened the discussion by observing that prayer might be in order: "Our decision may well affect not only the people of our own country, but also the peoples of the world." Reviewing the alarming news from Europe and his past efforts in behalf of peace, Mr. Roosevelt remarked that in his opinion revision of the neutrality laws was essential: "I've fired my last shot. I think I ought to have another round in my belt."

[39] Memo by Carlton Savage, July 10, 1939.

[40] For the shock of the Senate Committee's action on Paris and London see Churchill's article in the *New York Herald Tribune* and Chamberlain's report from Paris in *Christian Science Monitor*, July 14, 1939.

[41] Text in *Peace and War*, 468-74, Hull: *Memoirs*, 648-49.

From the very outset, however, Senator Borah made clear that he personally and many of his colleagues were unalterably opposed to repeal of the arms embargo and that he for one did not believe that war would come in the near future. At this point Mr. Hull went over the ground again, positively predicting war by the end of summer and stating categorically that repeal of the embargo would reduce the chance of war by at least half. Yet Borah remained unconvinced: "No one can foretell what may happen. But my feeling and belief is that we are not going to have a war. Germany isn't ready for it." Mr. Hull invited him to come to the State Department and read the cables, which would undoubtedly change his views. But to this the doughty Senator, who did most of the talking for the opposition, replied emphatically: "So far as the reports in your Department are concerned, I wouldn't be bound by them. I have my own sources of information which I have provided for myself, and on several occasions I've found them more reliable than the State Department."

This brutal reflection on the Foreign Service and the State Department was too much for the Secretary, who was struck dumb with indignation and despair. Fearful of exploding, he refused to say more. Vice President Garner tried to smooth matters over by asking first Senator Barkley and then others whether there were enough favorable votes in the Senate to get the revision through. The answers, without exception, were negative, whereupon Mr. Garner turned to the President and remarked: "Well, Captain, we may as well face the facts. You haven't got the votes, and that's all there is to it." The President took the verdict with good grace, adding only that he had done his best and that the Senate must now assume responsibility. Borah's parting shot was that there would be "no difficulty about that."[42]

Borah's conduct on this occasion was unbelievably arrogant and opinionated. American diplomatic reporting at the time was full and accurate, and the least the Senator could have done was to convince himself of the fact. But his inexcusable presumption should not be allowed to obscure the further fact that his views were shared by thousands of Americans. The belief that war would be avoided was general and in Borah's case was probably reinforced, not only by the private and supposedly well-informed newsletters that proliferated in Washington and London, but also by American diplomats who disapproved of the President's policy. The question may also be raised whether in fact Mr. Roosevelt and Mr. Hull did not overstate the probability of war. By mid-July the newspapers were still reporting hopefully on the prospects for a British-French-Soviet peace front, and even

[42] Among the best accounts of this historic meeting are those of Alsop and Kintner: *American White Paper*, 44-46, and of Hull: *Memoirs*, I, 649-51, neither of which has been seriously challenged by any of the participants. See further the President's press conference statement of July 21, 1939, and his later reflections (*Public Papers and Addresses*, VIII, xxxvi and 389 ff.). Present at the conference were Vice President Garner and Senators Barkley, Pittman, Borah, McNary and Austin.

the cables from Europe, as quoted by Mr. Hull in his *Memoirs*, forecast an acute crisis rather than war. The President evidently said nothing to the Senators of the possibility of a Nazi-Soviet pact, and indeed there was as yet no certainty that such a deal would be concluded. It might be argued, therefore, that Mr. Roosevelt "laid it on too thick" and thereby created the suspicion that he was protesting too much.

On the morrow of the fateful White House conference Mr. Roosevelt publicly put the responsibility for the consequences of nonrevision of the neutrality laws on the Senate. The statement reporting the most recent developments read as follows:

The President and the Secretary of State maintained the definite position that failure by the Senate to take action now would weaken the leadership of the United States in exercising its potent influence in the cause of preserving peace among other nations in the event of a new crisis in Europe between now and next January.

Senator Barkley said: "The consensus of opinion on the part of those members of the Senate present was that no action on neutrality legislation can be obtained in the Senate at the present session and that a majority of the Senate would concur in this view."

Senator McNary expressed the same belief.

They agreed that a majority of the Senate would consider neutrality legislation at the beginning of the next session.[43]

Therewith ended, for the time being, the depressing story of almost eight months of discussion of neutrality revision, which was, by any standard, the key issue in the delineation of American policy in the immediate prewar period. Political commentators were at a loss for an adequate and convincing explanation of what had happened. A majority of the citizenry had come to favor the sale of arms and munitions to the European democracies and, more generally speaking, it was believed that, as the European situation became more explosive, isolationism was giving ground. Yet Congress nullified every effort to repeal the arms embargo. It appears, therefore, that the difficulty lay less in the defects of the Pittman or Bloom Bills than in the relations between the Executive and the Congress. The Republicans were, almost without exception, in opposition, and were reinforced by about a quarter of the Democrats, mainly from the anti-New Deal ranks. This coalition was chiefly concerned with obstructing the President's policy, and Mr. Roosevelt knew it. For that reason he at first left the matter entirely to Congress and himself observed scrupulous noninterference, later on trying to give the impression that the policy was Mr. Hull's rather than his own. For that reason, too, his opponents throughout laid the emphasis on the issue of discretionary power to the President.

Other considerations, however, also played a part. Isolationism was by

[43] Text in *Documents on American Foreign Relations*, II, 547.

no means dead and much pressure was brought to bear on Congress by the followers of Father Coughlin and by other extreme "nationalist" groups. These people, convinced that the United States should keep out of other nations' affairs and that Europe's troubles need not affect the country if the Government abstained from "meddling," suspected the President of believing that the country must take part and of maneuvering to "get us in." In such quarters it was felt that even if the existing legislation was unsatisfactory, it was still necessary as a means of keeping the President out of war.

Possibly a more heroic stand by the Administration would have saved the day. On this score Mr. Roosevelt and Mr. Hull, both of them extremely sensitive to movements of opinion and to Congressional attitudes, were grievously misled. The Secretary seems to have sensed, at a fairly early date, the necessity for taking a firm stand, but he, like the President, fell a victim to the timidity and false optimism of Pittman and the theatrical exuberance of Bloom. When the real gravity of the situation became obvious, it was already too late for a successful shift in tactics. In arguing for its program the Administration then made the most of the threatening crisis in Europe and the importance of repeal as a deterrent to political aggressors, but thereby came up against a new obstacle: the suspicions of Borah and many others that the danger of war was being exaggerated in order to serve the President's ulterior motives. The final decision hinged largely on this consideration, and for the record Mr. Roosevelt made the most of it. Again and again he referred to the fact that a solid Republican minority and a small Democratic minority gambled on the chance that there would be no war before January, 1940: they had "bet the Nation, made a large wager with the Nation which may affect, if they lose it, about a billion and a half human beings. . . . If they are not right and we have another serious international crisis, they have tied my hands, and I have practically no power to make an American effort to prevent such a war from breaking out."[44]

Before leaving the subject something may be said of the significance of Congress's action as it appears in the light of later information. It is reasonably clear that the President sent his strong message to Hitler and Mussolini (April 15, 1939) in the full expectation that he could soon buttress his words with the demonstration that the United States would provide material support to the democracies. During the debate on revision of the neutrality law he carefully abstained from further utterances or overt acts in the foreign field. The question may therefore be asked whether the failure of revision made any real difference—whether the friendly Governments of Europe were right in asserting that the President's defeat actually encouraged Hitler to attack Poland. A final answer is difficult, the more so

[44] Press conferences of July 21 and August 8, 1939 (*Public Papers and Addresses*, VIII, 392, 428-29). Good contemporary analyses of the situation are those of Davis in the *Christian Science Monitor*, July 11 and 13, 1939; of Hinton in *The New York Times*, July 16, 1939; of Krock in *The New York Times*, July 20, 1939; and of Kirchwey in *The Nation*, July 29, 1939.

as the voluminous German documents captured during the war contain little evidence of Hitler's evaluation of the United States. From what is known of his European policy, however, it seems unlikely that the American attitude would have had a decisive influence with him. He banked heavily on the aversion of the American people to war and had a low opinion of America's ability to mobilize its war industry in sufficient time to be effective. No doubt he reckoned on some American aid to the democracies in the event of war, but he was convinced that it would be too little and too late. Furthermore, he speculated on Japan's distracting the United States and probably hoped that the Western Powers, if deprived of the prospect of American support, might find it expedient not to oppose him with armed force. In any event, his plans had been laid long before Congress reached its decision. The chances are that he would have proceeded with them come what come might and that nothing short of an effective British-French-Soviet coalition would have deterred him. Americans may derive some slight and wholly unmerited consolation from these considerations. But the fact remains that at the time the President, as well as many other statesmen, believed sincerely that a potent weapon for peace had been thrust aside.[45]

4. THE UNITED STATES AND JAPAN

Hard upon the deadlock over American policy toward Europe, as reflected in the conflict over revision of the neutrality legislation, came an unexpected and spectacular move of the Administration which prepared the way for the eventual imposition of economic sanctions on Japan. On July 26, 1939—hardly more than a week after the fateful White House Conference—Tokyo was given the required six months' notice of the termination of the commercial treaty of 1911. The closeness of the two dates was not accidental and serves well as a reminder of the constant interplay of the crises in Europe and the Far East.

By June, 1939, Hitler's ambitious project for a military alliance with Japan had all but foundered on Tokyo's refusal to commit itself to military action against the Western Powers or the United States as well as against Soviet Russia. Although the Nazi Government had consoled itself by concluding a "Pact of Steel" with Mussolini's Italy (May 22, 1939), efforts continued to be made to persuade the Japanese of the attractions of the larger combination. Negotiations dragged on desultorily throughout the summer, punctuated from time to time by new proposals and counterproposals. But by August 18, 1939, the German Ambassador at Tokyo was obliged once more to report a deadlock.[46]

The Japanese Army leaders had remained as passionately eager for the

[45] On the German attitude toward the United States see Ribbentrop's remarks to the Hungarian Prime Minister, April 29, 1939 (*Nazi Conspiracy and Aggression*, VII, D-737), and Erich Kordt: *Wahn und Wirklichkeit* (Stuttgart, 1947), 139-40.

[46] *Ciano's Diplomatic Papers*, 286; Toscano: *Le Origini del Patto d'Acciaio*, 148 ff., 176 ff.; Wiskemann: *The Rome-Berlin Axis*, 143 ff.; Feis: *The Road to Pearl Harbor*, 31 ff.

alliance with Germany as ever. To them it seemed the ideal combination to neutralize Russia and at the same time forestall action by Britain and France in opposition to Japanese expansion. No doubt the military men were much disturbed by reports of the British-French-Soviet negotiations and looked upon a military alliance with Germany as the only means of discouraging such a coalition or at least of counterbalancing it. Rumors reaching Tokyo in July, 1939, of discussions between Berlin and Moscow must have caused even greater uneasiness, for of all possible alignments a Nazi-Soviet pact was necessarily least desirable from the standpoint of Japanese aspirations.

The Japanese Cabinet, however, continued to oppose the projected alliance with Germany, and was supported in its stand by the naval authorities and the big business interests. These elements were far from convinced by the Army's reasoning that a German-Japanese pact would render the British and French helpless in the Far East and would frighten the United States into complete abstention from international commitments. The Navy chiefs doubted Japan's ability to defeat the United States and dreaded the economic sanctions that the United States might impose in reaction to a German-Japanese alignment. Since American trade was vital to Japan, a rupture of the economic relationship might well prove disastrous.[47]

During the summer of 1939 the tension in Tokyo Government circles remained extreme. Civilian members of the Government lived in constant fear of assassination and there was an ever-present danger that the Army would force the resignation of the Hiranuma Cabinet, by withdrawing the Minister of War, and then set up a military regime. Presumably it was only the firmness of the Emperor that deterred the High Command from such desperate expedients.[48]

But the Japanese Army, though unable to impose its will on the Government with respect to the military alliance with Germany, at least had its way in all other matters. On the Manchurian border it carried on prolonged hostilities against the Soviet Union (the famous Nomonhan "Incident"), while in China it engaged freely in highhanded and exceedingly provocative activities. Japanese troops blockaded the British and French concessions at Tientsin and subjected British nationals to unheard-of indignities. Military arrogance and defiance did not even respect American rights and interests. There were insistent demands for the "reorganization" of the International Settlement at Shanghai, to say nothing of the chronic and ever increasing attacks on American properties in the zone of Japanese

---

[47] Tel. from the German Ambassador at Tokyo, July 5, 1939; Diary of Marquis Kido (*Tokyo War Crimes Documents*, Defense Document 1632W-29).

[48] *Diary of Marquis Kido*, August 4, 1939 (as cited above); *Saionji-Harada Memoirs*, August 2 and 8, 1939.

military operations. Despite official American protests and official Japanese assurances, the air raids on Chungking, for example, became more frequent and more destructive. During the great attacks of July 6-7, 1939, bombs fell within two hundred yards of the USS *Tutuila*, anchored in the Yangtze far from any military target. Only the most naïve and trustful could blink the conclusion that these attacks were deliberate.[49]

The "tough" policy of the Japanese commanders in China was clearly designed to further political ends. The assault on the Soviet front was intended as a warning against an alliance of the Kremlin with the Western democracies, while the intense pressure on the British, French and even Americans represented an effort to exploit the European crisis to force a cessation of Western aid to the Chinese Nationalist Government and to drive foreign interests out of Japan's projected Greater East Asia Co-Prosperity Sphere. If the latter objective could be attained, it was believed in Army circles that the prestige of the High Command would rise to the point where opposition to an alliance with the Nazis could be overruled. If it could be demonstrated that nothing was to be feared from the British, French and Americans, the main argument of the Army's opponents would fall away.[50]

The design of the Japanese military was not only logical, but promising. Both the British and French felt that with war threatening in Europe, it was utterly out of the question for them to accept Japan's challenge in the Far East. Devoid of all hope of successful resistance, the London and Paris Governments impressed upon the American Government that a conflict in the Far East would only smooth the way for further Nazi aggression in Europe. Unless the United States took a firm stand against Japan, they argued, the Western Powers would have no alternative but to surrender to Tokyo's demands.[51]

The Washington authorities, equally reluctant to be distracted from European issues, were still anxious to avoid commitments. Fully aware of the cleavages in Tokyo circles, they desired to avoid any move that might be interpreted as provocative, lest thereby they weaken the position of the Japanese moderates. Their attitude was well illustrated by the continuing but always inconclusive discussions of the advisability of denouncing the commercial treaty. Even more revealing was their hesitancy about strengthening the American strategic position in the Pacific. In February, 1939, Congress had debated an appropriation of $5,000,000 to construct harbor works on the island of Guam. Eventually the item was stricken, with the result that Congress has frequently been charged with blindness and negli-

---

[49] The essential documents on these innumerable incidents may be found in *Foreign Relations of the United States: Japan, passim.*

[50] Tel. from the German Ambassador at Tokyo, June 20, 1939.

[51] Tels. from Wilson (Paris), June 16 and 21, and from Bullitt, July 31, 1939.

gence in failing thus to provide for American defenses against Japan. The truth of the matter was that complete fortification had not been contemplated and, more importantly, that it was primarily the President and the State Department who opposed even the modest construction envisaged, on the score that such a step might be interpreted as a violation of the Washington Treaties of 1921-1922. Furthermore, the War Department, though it suspected the Japanese of having refortified their mandated islands, objected to any move that might involve the United States in major operations, even defensive ones, in the Western Pacific.[52]

With regard to the Far East, the War Department had long held the view that the Philippines became a military liability when Japan acquired Germany's Pacific islands in 1919, and that therefore the United States was in no position to carry a war into the Far East until after the mandated islands had been reduced. Even a cautious strengthening of places like Guam might be interpreted as a challenge to Japan which the United States would not be capable of following up. The War Department therefore supported the State Department in opposing the Guam project. Nor did the Navy take a much different position. In June, 1939, it had suggested to the President that the United States lease from France the island of Fakarava in the Tuamotu Group, on the theory that if Germany, Italy and Japan became involved in war with Britain and France, the Japanese would surely seize the British and French islands in the Pacific and might make Fakarava a formidable submarine base for attack on the Panama Canal. Despite reservations of the State Department, the President accepted the proposal and the French Premier, Daladier, readily gave assent. Yet the final steps were never taken. For obscure reasons the Navy Department postponed action and after the outbreak of war in Europe the whole project was dropped, much to the embarrassment, irritation and disappointment of Ambassador Bullitt.[53]

In adhering to its cautious and patient policy toward Japan, the State Department was certainly intent on avoiding any move that might upset the moderate Tokyo Government and so clear the field for some form of military dictatorship. There were at least some indications that the Japanese Cabinet was desirous of improving relations with the United States. In mid-May, 1939, just before Ambassador Grew left Tokyo for an extended

[52] Shepardson and Scroggs: *The United States in World Affairs, 1939*, 120 ff.; Samuel E. Morison: *The Rising Sun in the Pacific* (Boston, 1948), 32-34; and particularly the discussion of this issue in *Pearl Harbor Attack*, Report, 266V and 266W, and Part V, 2454 ff.

[53] Memo of Admiral Leahy to the President, June 21, 1939; memo of the Far Eastern Division to Welles, June 28, 1939; letter of Welles to Bullitt, August 4, 1939; tel. from Bullitt, August 12, 1939; tel. to Bullitt, August 14, 1939; tels. from Bullitt, October 30, November 8, 10, 13, 1939; tel. of the President to Bullitt, November 16; tel. from Bullitt, November 17, 1939; tel. from Welles to Bullitt, November 18, 1939. This matter was dealt with in the utmost secrecy. *The Minutes of the Liaison Committee*, August 3 and 9, 1939, indicate that fear of provoking Japan was constantly in mind.

leave at home, Foreign Minister Arita had given him assurances with regard to Japanese negotiations with Germany, but had explained that Japan might have to agree to some such pact if the European democracies tied themselves to Soviet Russia. Japan's real objective, he added, was to maintain strict neutrality as between the democracies and the totalitarian states. Having conveyed his veiled warning, the Foreign Minister then entrusted the Ambassador with a personal message from the Prime Minister, Baron Hiranuma, to Secretary Hull. This reminded the Secretary of Japan's earnest desire to prevent the outbreak of war in Europe and of the duty incumbent on Japan and the United States, as the two great powers outside the scope of conflict, to exert themselves to the utmost to stave it off. According to Baron Hiranuma, it was "the ardent desire of Japan that nations should have their own proper places in the world," such being the best guarantee that world peace would be established and maintained. Since the United States no doubt cherished similar aspirations, the two Governments had an opportunity to work together toward the same end. A few days later (May 23, 1939) the Prime Minister amplified this message by confiding to the American Chargé d'Affaires, Mr. Dooman, that if a "world conference" could be arranged, the China problem would be submitted to it along with other issues; and that if President Roosevelt were willing to sound out Britain and France on the subject, he (Hiranuma) would be willing to approach Germany and Italy.[54]

It is quite likely that this proposal was intended sincerely by Baron Hiranuma, who seems to have thought that through a world conference he might be able to overcome the opposition of the Japanese High Command to any settlement of the China Incident and to circumvent the distasteful Army project for a military alliance with Germany.[55] But it was almost a foregone conclusion that his overtures should receive a cool reception in Washington, where the course of Japanese policy was viewed with much suspicion. While the Japanese forces in China were trampling American rights and interests underfoot, the soft words of the Premier could not ring true, the more so as the suggestion that all nations be assured their "proper places in the world" sounded like an invitation to concede the demands of the "have-not" states. The Hiranuma message had the appearance of an attempt to exploit the known American desire to avoid embroilment in war and to assuage distrust of Japanese designs. One high official of the State Department took the view that the importance of a German-Japanese pact was being exaggerated and that, since there was

[54] Grew's report of May 18, 1939 (*Foreign Relations of the U.S.: Japan*, II, 1 ff.); Hull: *Memoirs*, I, 631 ff.; tel. from Dooman, May 23, and despatch, June 7, 1939; *Pearl Harbor Attack*, XX, 4132 ff., 4139, 4144 ff.; memo of conversation between Mr. Max Bishop and Baron Hiranuma, November 11, 1945 (transmitted in despatch from Acheson [Tokyo], December 14, 1945).

[55] Statement of Hiranuma to Mr. Bishop in 1945, as cited above.

grave doubt whether in any case the Japanese Cabinet would be able to withstand the pressure of the High Command, it would be futile to stake much hope on such negotiations as were proposed.[56]

The overbearing and ruthless procedure of the Japanese commander at Tientsin certainly served to underline such arguments. American opinion, already much wrought up by the indiscriminate bombing of Chungking and other Chinese cities, was deeply outraged by the indignities visited on British subjects by the Japanese soldiery. Public protests were mingled with demands that the United States Government should, at the least, put an end to the selling of war materials to the Japanese. Since Japan was dependent on the United States for more than half its requirements of such materials, it was reasonable to ask why America should continue to aid and abet the brutal Japanese aggression against Chinese and Europeans. Many Americans found it impossible to explain the Government's allegedly immoral policy except by supposing pressure from heartless business interests. The Gallup polls of the period reveal that 66 percent of those questioned were prepared to join in a boycott of Japanese goods, while 72 percent favored an embargo on the export of arms and munitions to Japan. The popular reaction seems to have been that the Japanese were behaving just as badly as the Nazis and that it would be an easy matter to put a stop to Japanese atrocities simply by withholding American supplies.

Those who advocated this course certainly tended to overlook the fact that economic sanctions might lead to war. Being so very dependent on American trade, the Japanese might choose to fight rather than face economic starvation. Ambassador Grew had already warned of this possibility and the Washington Administration was certainly keenly alert to it. In view of the fact that American military men were not entirely sure that Japan might not start a war even before Hitler moved again, and that an assault might not be made on the Philippines or Guam, to say nothing of a possible surprise attack on the United States Fleet, one can easily understand the caution of the State Department.[57]

By mid-June, 1939, the situation at Tientsin had become so serious that the British were appealing to Washington to permit the American Consul General to extend his good offices in the dispute. For the moment this proposal was evaded and on June 16, 1939, the whole Far Eastern situation was reviewed in a conference between Mr. Hull and Mr. Welles on the one side, and the highest military authorities on the other. The Chief of Staff (General Craig) and the Chief of Naval Operations (Admiral Leahy) were both of the opinion that the foreign concessions in China could not be

[56] Memo of Hornbeck to Hull, May 11, 1939; memo of the Far Eastern Division to Hornbeck, May 22, 1939 (*Pearl Harbor Attack*, XX, 4134); Hull: *Memoirs*, I, 631 ff.

[57] Reference to the meeting of the Joint Board on May 6, 1939, in the Kittredge MS. study on *United States-British Naval Coöperation*.

defended if the Japanese chose to force the issue. They agreed also that the Japanese, once they had forced the British out, would probably turn on the French and Americans. All those present understood that the British, since they could spare none of their warships from the Mediterranean, desired the United States to assume responsibility for checking aggression in the Pacific. But, it was pointed out, such a policy might involve the country, virtually single-handed, in a Far Eastern war, and would therefore be rejected by the American public. Accordingly, Mr. Hull, as usual, counselled caution, as did General Marshall, the newly designated Chief of Staff, a few days later. Without matériel, said General Marshall, one cannot fight. With recent Congressional appropriations the United States should be in a position, within eighteen or twenty-four months, to play a decisive role in any conflict. But for the time being there was nothing practical the United States could do in the Far East and for that reason pressure from the British must be resisted.[58]

Though unwilling to support the British in the Tientsin crisis, the State Department was nevertheless quite prepared to resort to the well-established technique of verbal warning. On June 19, 1939, Mr. Hull issued a statement to the press in the hope of disabusing the Japanese of any notion that the United States was disinterested in the events at Tientsin. At the same time the American Chargé in Tokyo was instructed to warn the Japanese Government that it would be gravely miscalculating if it imagined that by avoiding insults to American nationals in Tientsin it could induce the American public to ignore the shocking treatment accorded the British. Referring to the Japanese bombings of Chungking, the President directed that a statement be requested of the Tokyo Foreign Office, while Mr. Hull admonished the Japanese Ambassador that "something serious in the way of injuries to other nationals and their properties would inevitably occur," if the reckless bombings continued. But these warnings had long since been proved ineffectual and it is unlikely that much hope was founded upon them. At any rate, the Japanese were leisurely in replying and their answer, as usual, was thoroughly unsatisfactory.[59]

Meanwhile the State Department continued to grapple with the problem of how to impress and perhaps deter the Japanese without at the same time provoking a crisis or precipitating war. The idea of sending the Fleet from San Diego to Pearl Harbor was considered but rejected. Instead, Secretary Hull and his advisers concluded that the time had come to send a long and plain-spoken note to Tokyo which, while taking off from the Tientsin situation, would raise the "whole issue of the Japanese 'new order' in

[58] Memo of conversation between Mr. Mallet (Counselor of the British Embassy) and Mr. Hamilton, June 13, 1939; memo from Hamilton to Mallet, June 13, 1939; tel. to Caldwell (American Consul General at Tientsin), June 13, 1939. For the conference of June 16, 1939, we have relied on the *Berle Diaries (MS.)*, June 16-19, 1939.

[59] *Foreign Relations of the U.S.: Japan*, I, 652, 656 ff., 665 ff.

China." This document was ready on June 29, 1939, and was approved by the President on July 1, 1939. In sixteen typewritten pages it reviewed all the issues between the United States and Japan. First reiterating that American rights and interests were involved in incidents like those at Tientsin, Amoy and elsewhere, the State Department raised the question whether the objective of the Japanese was to block off large areas and close them to normal relationships with the rest of the world. Reference was made to the discriminatory measures imposed in China and inquiry made whether Japan meant to assert the right to dominate a large part of Asia, to set up and control governments in that area, and to claim monopoly of benefit and advantage despite treaties to which Japan was committed; and further, whether the Tokyo Government intended that American nationals, goods and ships should enter Chinese waters only on Japanese sufferance. If that were indeed the case, continued the note, the United States and other nations might have to reconsider measures necessary for their self-protection. Therefore the American Government felt impelled to state candidly, though in all friendship, its concern about the situation and to remind the Japanese Government that the United States could not acquiesce in any such "new order" as that apparently envisaged by Japan.[60]

Mr. Dooman, when consulted by cable, was definitely opposed to presenting this note to Tokyo at this juncture. He was skeptical of the idea of strengthening the Japanese Government as against the military because, he argued, all Japanese elements, though they might differ as to methods and timing, were in substantial agreement as to objectives, which were to assure their country sources of raw materials and markets for their products. The projected note would be taken as a challenge to Japanese policies and actions in China and as an indication of American intention to align with the British. The only non-Asiatic nation that still enjoyed respect in Tokyo was the United States. If, then, the American Government were to take a firm stand and insist that Japan modify its policies and actions to conform with its treaty obligations, a situation might arise which in the end could be resolved only by force. Furthermore, any such statement as that contemplated would create responsibilities toward the British which the United States could not lightly shirk if the Tientsin negotiations broke down.[61]

Mr. Hull was not entirely persuaded by Dooman's evaluation of the situation and referred the whole matter to Ambassador Grew, who was vacationing in New Hampshire. A letter to Grew conveyed the Secretary's conviction that an endeavor should be made "to keep alive to the Japanese

[60] Draft note of June 29, 1939; tel. to Dooman (Tokyo), July 1, 1939. See also *Pearl Harbor Attack*, XX, 4168, where reference is made to this draft. The *Berle Diaries (MS.)*, June 26 and 29, 1939, throw some light on the evolution of the document.

[61] Tels. from Dooman, June 15, 26, July 3, 1939.

and to our own people our continued belief in certain fundamental principles which we are convinced furnish the only basis for healthy relationships
among nations. We believe in those principles, we can't ignore their disregard in one half of the world, and we consider that they should be regarded as applicable to all parts of the world." But Grew's reply was
negative. He thought there was no need to restate the American position
either with respect to the Tientsin situation or to the broader issue of Japanese policy, for this position had been made perfectly clear on many occasions. He warned that:

Unless we are prepared and willing to proceed to forceful measures, we have
more to gain and less to lose by resting our case *for the present* on the goodwill
of the Japanese Government. We should await an appropriate time for the
adjustment by friendly negotiations of all outstanding problems. That time is
not yet. . . .

Such a note at this time would tend to agitate the military extremists against
us, would risk the application to American nationals and interests of the same
measures that are now being applied to British nationals and interests, and would
tend to mislead the British into believing that we are now going to support them,
thereby making them more recalcitrant and creating an implication of responsibility
which it would be difficult for us to fulfill.[62]

The Ambassador's statement clinched the matter, at least for the moment.
Further work was done on the draft note, of which refined versions were
completed on July 31 and August 10, 1939. But it was never formally submitted to the Tokyo Government. During July, 1939, Chargé Dooman was
instructed to evade British efforts to draw the United States into the discussions of the thorny Tientsin issue, but to make clear to the Japanese
authorities that the United States was gravely concerned lest the antiforeign
agitation being whipped up in China lead to attacks on Americans and
create new tensions.[63] The records suggest that there was much sentiment
in the State Department for presenting something like the draft note in
order to recapitulate and emphasize American grievances and to restate the
principles by which Mr. Hull and his associates put so much store. But the
Department could not bring itself to go beyond warnings and "oral" statements, for the simple reason that there was no obvious solution to the
dilemma in which American policy was enmeshed. Nothing but a firm
stand and perhaps identification of American with British interests would
have sufficed to give the Japanese military leaders pause. But to assume
such a position might, it was feared, drive Japan into alliance with Germany or in fact provoke a crisis that might conceivably eventuate in war.

[62] Letter of Hamilton to Grew, July 4, 1939; memo of a telephone conversation with
Grew, July 6, 1939.
[63] Tels. from Dooman, July 20, 23, 28, August 7, 1939; tels. to Dooman, July 21, 25,
August 1, 1939.

Since armed conflict was far beyond anything the Washington Government was prepared to contemplate, its sphere of action was necessarily limited to protest and remonstrance.

For the same reasons the proposed reply to Baron Hiranuma's message presented endless difficulty. A draft had been sent off to Mr. Dooman on July 7, 1939, but only produced another long series of cables debating questions of timing and raising doubts as to the propriety of making specific mention of Hiranuma's most secret suggestion of a world conference. Meanwhile Mr. Hull conveyed the substance of the projected reply to the Japanese Ambassador in Washington (July 10, 1939), adding for good measure some of the items of the abortive note of July 1, 1939. After discussing various specific issues and voicing American disapproval of all policies of conquest and economic discrimination, the Secretary had this to say about the Hiranuma proposal:

I said that the single test of my Government in dealing with other Governments relates to the question of peace; that we consider the preservation of peace so supremely important to the future of all nations that we draw the line between honest, law-abiding, peaceful countries and peoples, without reference to their form of Government, on the one hand, and those who are flouting law and order and officially threatening military conquest without limit as to time or extent; that we will work in a friendly spirit with every peaceful nation to promote and preserve peace, without serious thought as to who they are; that while we have not the slightest alliance, or secret or other understandings with any nation on earth, and do not propose to have any, we will keep thoroughly armed and prepared to take care of our interests and rights; that we have, in the spirit I was describing, made every kind and character of plea to the countries of Europe to indicate a willingness for the peaceful settlement and adjustment of their economic and other relations, and we have indicated our readiness to coöperate in every feasible plan to restore international trade and finance to a normal basis; that, notwithstanding these earnest pleas (which the Japanese Government itself might well have been making, if it had not been doing so, or might well make now and persistently in the future), nations perhaps could not but take notice that Japan herself is engaged in military operations for the purposes of conquest, and that this situation might well call for an ending, if Japan were to exercise her fullest influence along with the United States and other countries in efforts to compose threatened military conquest in other parts of the world.[64]

Long before the official reply to Baron Hiranuma's message was presented to the Japanese Foreign Office on August 8, 1939, the Premier was therefore fully aware that the American reaction would be negative. In view of the Japanese Government's inability to control the actions of the Army in China, the Premier may have been disappointed, but could hardly have been surprised. It was clear that there was little if any chance for

[64] *Pearl Harbor Attack*, XX, 4181-90. All the documents bearing on the reply to Hiranuma are in the same volume, 4169-4208. See also Hull: *Memoirs*, I, 633.

healthy collaboration between Japan and the United States for any purpose so long as Japan continued its aggression against China.

Meanwhile the State Department had at last taken an important, positive step, the genesis of which is even now not entirely clear. During July, 1939, the British attempted to reach agreement with the Japanese with respect to Tientsin, only to find that the Japanese insisted on treating the issue solely within the larger framework of their Chinese claims. Though fully aware that such a larger settlement might involve a "Far Eastern Munich," the British felt helpless without American support, which was denied them. They therefore felt obliged to yield. On July 24, 1939, the British Ambassador in Tokyo accepted the so-called Craigie-Arita formula, by which the British recognized "that hostilities on a large scale were proceeding in China; that the Japanese Army was responsible for security and the maintenance of law and order in the areas occupied by its troops; and that British consular officers would not impede the measures considered necessary by the Japanese military authorities for this purpose." The British Government might warmly deny that this formula involved a change of policy, but the Japanese were agreeably surprised by the ease of their victory and vociferous in celebrating it. Certainly as a matter of prestige they had scored a great success.[65]

The news of the Craigie-Arita formula, coming so soon after the Administration's setback in the matter of neutrality revision, clinched the decision for some positive action. The long-debated question of terminating the commercial treaty of 1911 with Japan was quickly taken in hand again. There was no doubt that the country, much wrought up about Japan, would not only approve but welcome the treaty's end. Congressional sentiment was equally favorable. The Senate Foreign Relations Committee had before it the Pittman Resolution of April 27, 1939, and the Schwellenbach Resolution of July 1, 1939, both of which called for some sort of arms embargo against Japan. Nothing had been done about these measures because of doubt whether or not they would violate the commercial treaty. But Senator Pittman was eager to get on with his project, arguing that Japan had already violated the Nine-Power Treaty of 1922 and therefore had no grievance. Secretary Hull was consulted on the matter, but as late as July 21 suggested that perhaps it had better be deferred. Meanwhile, on July 18, Senator Vandenberg, at that time a prominent isolationist, submitted a resolution calling for abrogation of the commercial treaty. This new proposal was discussed in committee on the morning of July 26, at which time there was some indication that the Democratic majority disliked supporting a measure introduced by a Republican.

At this point the President and Mr. Hull took matters into their own

---

[65] Sir Robert Craigie: *Behind the Japanese Mask* (London, 1946), 75; report of the German Ambassador in Tokyo, July 26, 1939; Hull: *Memoirs*, I, 635.

hands. The Vandenberg Resolution would have suited their purposes exactly, for they were now convinced that some spectacular move must be made to dampen the ardor of the Japanese. But they feared that final action by the Senate might be impossible before adjournment, that the vote might not be sufficiently impressive, and that there might be some undesirable debate. Having authority to take action on his own and perhaps eager to pay back the snub he had recently suffered from the Senate, the President on the evening of July 26, 1939, made known that the required six months' notice of termination of the treaty was being given to Japan. In substance this was a warning that after January 26, 1940, the United States Government might, if it thought proper, impose economic sanctions. Politically speaking, the President's decision was designed to satisfy the popular clamor for action of some sort—short of war—but more particularly to serve notice on Tokyo that this Government, at least, had no intention of weakening. The announcement was bound to encourage the British and the Chinese and it furthermore helped to counteract the impression, created by the failure of neutrality revision, that the United States would stand aloof at all costs.[66]

The Administration was convinced that its action would, as Mr. Welles remarked, have a "tremendous" effect, and so it did. The public applauded and even Senator Borah expressed approval. As ever, the country was much more ready to take a strong stand against Japan than against Germany. In the words of Mr. Berle: "It is a curious fact that the United States, which bolts like a frightened rabbit from even remote contact with Europe, will enthusiastically take a step which might very well be a material day's march on the road to a Far Eastern War." Naturally the British were greatly cheered by this sign of American firmness and thenceforth took a less yielding attitude in their discussions with Japan. The Chinese, too, were enthusiastic. They had been urging Washington to take its stand by Britain's side and had been deeply discouraged by the "appeasement" reflected in the Craigie-Arita formula. Now there seemed, after all, to be some prospect of definite American action to check Japanese expansion.

To Tokyo, accustomed to a diet of verbal protests, the announcement from Washington came as a sudden and disagreeable surprise. The Japanese realized at once that if only economic considerations had underlain the denunciation of the treaty, there would have been preliminary discussion between the two Governments. The political implications were therefore inescapable, but their exact nature was not at all clear. Efforts were made

[66] There is a good general account in Shepardson and Scroggs: *The United States in World Affairs, 1939*, 91, and a detailed analysis in Hull: *Memoirs*, I, 635 ff. For the rest we have relied on the long memo of the Far East Division dated April 30, 1940, reviewing all the steps in the development of the problem; also *Minutes of the Liaison Committee* July 26, 1939; *Berle Diaries, (MS.),* July 27, 1939; memo by Carlton Savage, July 10 1939; *Moffat Diary (MS.),* July 26, 1939.

to discover from the State Department what further steps were in contemplation, but Secretary Hull refused to elaborate. After all, the advantage of the American step was that it would deter the Japanese by keeping them in uncertainty.

The Tokyo militarists took the denunciation of the commercial treaty as a further argument for the need of an alliance with Germany as a counterweight to the United States. War Minister Itagaki made desperate efforts to force the issue, but in the crucial Cabinet meeting of August 8, 1939, he was again voted down. The Army leaders talked loudly of turning out the Government and setting up a military dictatorship, while Itagaki himself resorted to all kinds of devious methods in the attempt to gain his point. But time was running out: on August 23, 1939, came the shocking news of the Nazi-Soviet pact, which completely upset Japanese calculations and soon ushered in an entirely new phase of Japanese policy.[67]

[67] Reports from Dooman, in *Pearl Harbor Attack*, XX, 4191 ff.; *Foreign Relations of the U.S.: Japan*, II, 189 ff.; *The New York Times*, August 5, 1939; Hull: *Memoirs*, I, 637-38. On the final phase of the German-Japanese negotiations see the contemporary chronicle in G. N. Steiger: "Japan and the Axis" (*Events*, October, 1939), and the digest of the captured Japanese documents in Joseph W. Ballantine: "Mukden to Pearl Harbor" (*Foreign Affairs*, July, 1949).

CHAPTER V

The Agony of Peace

1. A MESSAGE TO MOSCOW

The reports reaching the President from European capitals in late July, 1939, indicated, almost without exception, that the crisis between Germany and Poland would probably come to a head within a month or six weeks. Whether the crisis would eventuate in war remained, of course, uncertain. That would depend largely on whether the peace front of Britain, France and Soviet Russia materialized or whether, failing that, the Western Powers, deprived of Soviet support, recognized the hopelessness of trying to succor Poland and therefore agreed to another "Munich." Fully cognizant of the vicissitudes of the British-French-Soviet negotiations, and also of German efforts to strike a bargain with the Kremlin, Mr. Roosevelt concluded that the time had come for heroic efforts to save the situation. He remarked to Mr. Berle that there probably would be war in Europe and that September 10 might be the date. But, he added, "I get this by being psychic; if other statesmen are allowed that luxury, I don't see why I should'n't."[1]

The President's thought, on this as on other occasions, was to throw his personal influence into the scales. He began by reviewing the situation with Ambassador Oumansky as the latter was preparing to leave for Moscow, and requested the Ambassador "to tell Stalin that if his Government joined up with Hitler, it was as certain as that night followed day that as soon as Hitler had conquered France, he would turn on Russia and that it would be the Soviets' turn next." The substance of these remarks was at once sent by Mr. Welles to Laurence Steinhardt, the newly appointed American Ambassador to Moscow. The message was cabled to Paris, but from there was taken to Moscow by special courier in order to obviate any chance of interception. The text read as follows:

[1] *Berle Diaries (MS.)*, August 4, 1939.

The President has asked me to send you these urgent lines, which will reach you as soon as I can get them to you, to let you know that in a conversation had with Oumansky just before the latter left Washington, the President gave him to understand that while he was making no suggestion, much less any official indication of any desire on the part of this Government, he nevertheless wished to make clear that this Government was viewing the present situation in an objective manner. The President said that if war were now to break out in Europe and in the Far East, and were the Axis powers to gain a victory, the position of both the United States and of the Soviet Union would inevitably be immediately and materially affected thereby. In such event, the position of the Soviet Union would be affected more rapidly than the position of the United States. For these reasons, while he was, of course, in no position either to accept any responsibility or to give any assurances as to the possible course which Great Britain and France might undertake in connection with their present negotiations with the Soviet Union, the President could not help but feel that if a satisfactory agreement against aggression on the part of the other European powers were reached, it would prove to have a decidedly stabilizing effect in the interest of world peace, in the maintenance of which, of course, the United States as well as the Soviet Union had a fundamental interest.

The President believes that it would be desirable for you at this juncture to reiterate to Mr. Molotov at the first opportunity the views which he so expressed, with the understanding, of course, that the transmission of these views shall be regarded as absolutely and completely confidential.

Please do not refer to the subject matter of this letter in any telegram which you may send to the Department. I suggest that when this message is delivered, you send me a personal telegram referring to the date of this personal letter to you and merely add "message delivered."[2]

Before receiving this instruction, Ambassador Steinhardt had already paid an informal call on Mr. Molotov (August 10) and had presented his credentials to President Kalinin (August 11). These high officials of the Kremlin had by this time received a telegraphic report from Oumansky and were therefore prepared. Some importance may therefore be attached to the lengthy remarks of Kalinin, unusual on such an occasion. The Soviet President spoke frankly and cordially, but about the Far Eastern situation rather than about the European. He stressed Russia's peaceful intentions with respect to Japan but at the same time made it clear that the Soviet Government was determined, if necessary, to resort to force to defend its interests. Steinhardt got the impression that the Kremlin regarded Japan as a real menace, while feeling relatively secure in Europe. It was the Ambassador's belief that the Soviet Government would be glad to coöperate in any measures to restrain Japan and that it tended to look to the American Government sooner or later to take the lead, with British, French and Russian support.

[2] Letter of Welles to Steinhardt, August 4, 1939; see Hull: *Memoirs*, I, 656-57, for a summary; Davies: *Mission to Moscow*, 450.

As for Europe, Steinhardt felt there was room for serious doubt whether the Kremlin would take affirmative action beyond the purely defensive:

> In view of the broad guarantee which has been accorded Poland and Rumania by Britain and France, the Soviets do not appear to regard themselves as under any imminent threat in Europe and they thoroughly appreciate the fact that Germany cannot attack Russia without inevitably involving either Poland or Rumania, or probably both. They thus seem to feel that they are assured of Anglo-French military assistance in the event of a world war and appear to be disposed on this front to sit back and await developments.

This, continued the Ambassador, would explain the halting progress of the negotiations with Britain and France. Unless there were a material change in the situation before the first of October, the Kremlin would probably keep the discussions alive and hold them over Hitler as a threat, but would avoid far-reaching commitments, in the hope of stalling off war for the current season. By way of conclusion the Ambassador reported:

> They [i.e., the Soviets] are fully aware of the fact that if war can be averted this fall, it is most unlikely to break out until the spring and they doubtless shrewdly calculate that by that time the Japanese will be further involved in China and materially weakened by the passage of another six months. They doubtless hope that a European War can be averted until the Japanese threat to Russia in the Far East has been minimized by Japan's economic exhaustion, and it is not improbable that they hope that the winter will see an embargo by the United States on exports to Japan. All in all, it is my opinion that the Soviet authorities are playing a very shrewd game in international politics, that from the point of view of their interests they are playing the game intelligently and successfully, and that they are likely to play a steadily increasing rôle in world politics, both in Europe, by reason of their potentialities and studiously concealed military forces, and in the Far East, by reason of their steadily expanding military strength as that of Japan grows weaker.[3]

Before commenting on this estimate of Soviet policy it will be well to adduce the record of the Ambassador's talk with Mr. Molotov on August 16, 1939, the day after his receipt of the Welles letter. Having listened to a verbal communication of the President's message, the Foreign Commissar spoke at some length. In the words of Steinhardt:

> He started by saying that the views I had just conveyed to him were of great interest and value to his Government, which considers the situation in Europe at the present time to be most serious, and that in consequence his Government was attaching great importance to the pending negotiations with Great Britain and France. He then said that he well understood that the United States was "aside" from taking any "immediate" part in European affairs, but that he knew that President Roosevelt held close to his heart a deep interest in and desire for the preservation of world peace, and that for this reason his Government would

[3] Despatch from Steinhardt, August 16, 1939.

attach the greatest interest and the utmost importance to the views just expressed. He continued, that from the start of the negotiations with Britain and France his Government had been unwilling that the negotiations should end "in merely general declarations"; that he did not regard general declarations as sufficient; that for this reason at the beginning of the negotiations and "even now" his Government had been and was insisting that any agreement must deal with "obligations of mutual assistance in order to counteract any possible aggression in Europe." He then stated categorically: "We are not interested in declarations. We are desirous that the present negotiations lead to a determination of the action to be taken under specific conditions or circumstances—and that there shall be mutual obligations to counteract aggression." He observed that the mutual obligations to be undertaken were to be of a defensive character in Europe, and "we would not go into any agreement aiming at an attack on anybody."

He stopped at this point, indicating that he had nothing further to say; and, in the hope of encouraging him to continue, I asked to have his last two or three comments restated. As restated, these comments read: "All of the negotiations with Britain and France which have taken place thus far we value, in so far as they may lead to an agreement for mutual defensive assistance against direct or indirect aggression in Europe."

I then asked him whether it was a fair question for me to request his personal opinion as to the probable outcome of the negotiations. To this he replied: "We have spent much time negotiating—this shows we expect the negotiations to succeed—but we are not to be blamed for the delay—the delay has not been caused by us alone. At present I cannot say any more to you than I have already said: what the outcome of the negotiations will be depends on others as much as on us. Much has already been done towards success and, as you know, the negotiations are continuing."

Ambassador Steinhardt was new at his post and was far too shrewd to think he had the key to Soviet policy. In his report he made careful reservations on this score, but ventured the personal opinion that the Soviet authorities were genuinely desirous that peace should be preserved and particularly anxious to avoid being drawn into any European conflict, at least in the beginning, if only because of internal problems and difficulties. Under the circumstances their guiding principle was to assure nonviolation of their frontiers. As for the rest:

They are deliberately carrying on negotiations with the French and British on the one hand and the Germans on the other, in the hope of thereby avoiding the outbreak of war before the beginning of October; that with this object in view they are intentionally dragging the negotiations out with the hope of finding Japan in a weaker position by next spring, the British and French rearmament progressed to the point where they need no longer fear Germany and can then take advantage of these developments by expanded commercial relations with Germany—which would be much to their advantage—while at the same time presenting a more aggressive front to Japan in the Far East. In all my interviews thus far with various higher officials of the Soviet Government, I have been forcibly struck by their active interest in and their repeated references to the situation in the Far East and their apparent indifference to the European situation.[4]

The high interest of these records should be immediately apparent and no excuse is needed for quoting them at such length. For the purposes of this study they serve as an ideal introduction to the great enigma of Soviet policy in the summer of 1939, a subject bound to occupy scholars for years to come. In Chapter III the opinion was ventured that by the end of July, 1939, if not sooner, the Soviet Government had given up whatever plans it may have had for a military alliance with Britain and France and that, in all likelihood, the decision had by then been made to strike a bargain with Nazi Germany. If that be so, the announcement made in late July that substantial agreement had been reached between the Kremlin and the Western Powers, and the Soviet invitation to those powers to send military missions to Moscow, can be interpreted only as cunning devices to impress the Germans and induce them to offer the Soviets favorable terms. This conjecture is to some extent borne out by an incident connected with President Roosevelt's message to Molotov. On August 11, 1939, when as yet Ambassador Steinhardt knew nothing of the coming message, the Nazi party newspaper *Voelkischer Beobachter* reported from Moscow that Steinhardt had called on Molotov and had handed him a long letter from Mr. Roosevelt. The German paper added the comment that "Roosevelt is obviously trying to spring to the side of his democratic comrades in London and Paris in the matter of the Moscow negotiations." Meanwhile the Soviet official news agency delayed fully three days before denouncing this report as "a complete invention." It is impossible to explain this extraordinary episode other than as a maneuver of the Soviet Foreign Office. Having received the cabled report of Oumansky of his talk with the President, the Kremlin itself inspired the story in the German press in order once more to emphasize to Hitler the strength of its position.[5]

The best test of Molotov's asseverations and Steinhardt's impressions will be found in the record of Soviet negotiations. For the moment, the British and French military missions can be disregarded, for these missions did not arrive in Moscow until August 11, 1939. To the surprise of contemporary journalists and the disgust of some later historians, they traveled leisurely by ship. Why, it has been asked, were they not sent by air, considering the supposed urgency of the situation? Part of the answer seems to be that the British did not have a plane available for so long a journey. But the more important part of the answer is no doubt to be found in a telegram from the French Ambassador in Moscow (July 24, 1939) reporting

[4] Letter of Steinhardt to Welles, August 16, 1939, received in Washington, August 29, 1939.

[5] Telegram from Kirk (Berlin), August 11, 1939; telegram from Steinhardt, August 14, 1939.

Molotov's statement that it would suit him very well if the missions arrived within eight or ten days.[6] This remark would seem to be another item of evidence that Molotov, as suggested by Steinhardt, was intent on protracting the negotiations as long as possible.

2. HITLER'S ESTIMATE

The course of the conversations between Berlin and Moscow in August, 1939, can be properly viewed only against the background of Hitler's objectives in the East and the deterioration of German relations with Poland. The Fuehrer's immediate design was to secure Danzig for the Reich and to acquire the territory necessary to link East Prussia with the rest of Germany. By the spring of 1939 it had become clear to him that these objectives could not be attained without war against Poland. Plans for such a war were initiated at once and all dispositions were to be completed by September 1, 1939. Meanwhile the Nazis were actively engaged in subverting the situation in Danzig. A succession of "incidents" had brought German-Polish relations to a stage of crisis by the beginning of August. At any moment Hitler could precipitate hostilities by provoking further "incidents."[7]

Unfortunately for them, the Polish leaders refused, almost to the very last, to believe that Hitler would resort to war. They were convinced that the Fuehrer would hesitate to provoke action by Britain and France, and, besides, they had an altogether exaggerated idea of their own military power. The Polish General Staff was so completely deluded that it decided, in case of war, not to stand on the defensive, but to use its mobile forces (cavalry) to carry the war into Germany.[8] By contrast, Hitler and his generals were convinced that Poland could offer no effective resistance. Six to eight weeks, they thought, would suffice to dispose of Poland. The sequel was to demonstrate how accurate their estimate was.[9]

It was not, then, the attitude of Poland that troubled Hitler, but rather the position of the great powers. Had the Nazi-Japanese military alliance materialized, Soviet Russia, Britain and France would all have been neutralized. Some years later Ribbentrop was to explain to visiting Japanese officers that it was the failure of the projected German-Japanese alliance that obliged Germany to seek an agreement with Soviet Russia: if a German-

[6] Bonnet: *Fin d'une Europe*, 203; tels. from Bullitt, July 24, 25, 31, 1939; tel. from Grummon (Moscow), July 28, 1939.

[7] The development of the German-Polish friction need not be analyzed in detail for purposes of the present study. Among recent treatments see Hans L. Leonhardt: *The Nazi Conquest of Danzig* (Chicago, 1942); Namier: *Diplomatic Prelude*; and Wheeler-Bennett: *Munich*.

[8] Memo of conversation between Welles and the Polish Ambassador, recently returned from Warsaw, August 9, 1939: *Moffat Diary (MS.)*, August 18, 1939, recording the "unreasoning optimism" of the Ambassador and the Polish inclination to underrate their opponents.

[9] The *Halder Diary* contains much evidence on this point.

Italian-Japanese pact had existed in 1939, Soviet Russia would have adopted a neutral attitude and would scarcely have dared attack Germany.[10] Since the Japanese had proved recalcitrant, the Fuehrer had to turn to Moscow in order to frustrate a British-French-Soviet alliance which, in all likelihood, would have represented a coalition of forces too formidable for even Hitler to challenge.

Even if his daring plan to buy off the Kremlin were to succeed, the Nazi leader would still have to face the question whether Britain and France would honor their obligation to support Poland. This question was patently a vital one for the Germans, yet their evaluation of it is still veiled in some obscurity. Postwar studies of German capabilities, based on Nazi records, show that Nazi military power and war production in 1939 were greatly overestimated by the democracies. There can now be little doubt that the Germans in 1939 were far from prepared for a long war on a large scale. Their current war production was inferior to that of the combined British and French and they had remarkably little in the way of reserves. Of the hundred divisions they put in the field against Poland only three were mechanized and none completely motorized. In a word, the Germans were equipped for a two-month *Blitzkrieg*, such as they waged in Poland. They were by no means ready for the type of war in which they became involved.[11]

Hitler and his military chiefs were therefore bound to consider the probable course of British and French policy, even if Soviet Russia were successfully neutralized by agreement. The Germans had concluded with Italy (May 22, 1939) the Pact of Steel, but this alliance, despite its grandiloquent title, was of little military value. The Italians had made it perfectly clear throughout that they would not be ready for a major war for several years. The Germans, on their side, were probably more interested in keeping Italy from a peaceful arrangement with Britain and France than they were in any potential Italian military contribution. They therefore assured the Duce that they too foresaw no large-scale hostilities for years to come and expressed full confidence that the Danzig issue could be solved by negotiation.[12] Hence the problem narrowed down to whether the Germans could localize the conflict with Poland or whether they must envisage the intervention of Britain and France.

Throughout the summer of 1939, as the Danzig issue came to a head, the

---

[10] Memo of conversation between Ribbentrop, General Oshima and General Okamoto, May 19, 1943 (*Department of State Bulletin*, XV, September 15, 1946).

[11] Hanson W. Baldwin: "Hitler's Power in 1939," which summarizes a U. S. Army report entitled *Foreign Logistical Organizations and Methods* (*The New York Times*, May 9, 1948).

[12] This topic is of only marginal interest, so the details may be omitted. The chief sources are the *Ciano Diaries* and *Ciano's Diplomatic Papers*. The best treatments, utilizing the available material, are Mario Donosti: *Mussolini e l'Europa* (Rome, 1945); Wiskemann: *The Rome-Berlin Axis,* Chap. IX; and Toscano: *Le Origini del Patto d'Acciaio,* Chap. IV.

British and French Ambassadors at Berlin repeatedly warned the German Foreign Office against delusion that the Western Powers would fail to keep their engagements to Poland.[13] It is quite likely that the professional diplomats of the German Foreign Service recognized the danger and used such influence as they had to deter the extremists.[14] But in high Nazi circles their admonitions fell on deaf ears. Ribbentrop enjoyed Hitler's confidence and posed as the authority on British and French policy, despite the fact that, according to Goering, he knew France only through champagne and England only through whisky. It was Ribbentrop's unshakable conviction that the Western Powers, whatever they might say, would never fight for Poland, if only because they were too weak and unprepared. Hitler may from time to time have had some doubts on the subject, but the evidence is fairly conclusive that in general he was persuaded that if he could square the Russians, the British and French would not dare intervene or, if they did, would be incapable of lending Poland effective aid.[15]

It must be confessed, however, that a number of statements made by the Fuehrer in the closing days of August, 1939, tended to contradict each other. They may have reflected his uncertainty, or they may have been tempered to satisfy his various listeners. Thus, on August 11, 1939, Hitler received Dr. Karl Burkhardt, the League High Commissioner for Danzig. Expecting, no doubt, and rightly, that his remarks would soon be relayed to Paris and London, Hitler struck a haughty note in referring to Danzig and the arrogant attitude of the Poles. If the latter, he said, were to make the slightest move, "he would fall on them like lightning with all the powerful arms at his disposal—of whose might the Poles had not the slightest idea." In a few days all would be over. In response to Burkhardt's warning that this would mean a general war, the Fuehrer admitted it, saying that he would prefer to wage it then rather than later and that he would wage it with every means at his disposal. But of the chances of his opponents he spoke most disparagingly. He felt sure, so he said, that he could count on Italy and Japan, and he could easily hold the West Wall against Britain and France. As for the Russians, he knew them well and was convinced that they had no offensive power: "France and Britain will not give me goose-flesh by threatening me with the Russian army."[16]

On the next day Hitler took a very different line in speaking to Count Ciano, who had come to learn the terrible news that an attack on Poland was to be launched in the immediate future. To cushion the shock, Ribben-

[13] See *British Blue Book*, Nos. 36, 48; *French Yellow Book*, Nos. 149, 150, 194; *German White Book*, Nos. 449, 450, 451.

[14] Weizsäcker: *Erinnerungen*, 237 ff.; Kordt: *Nicht aus den Akten*, 322.

[15] The postwar State Department interrogations of Goering, Neurath, Ribbentrop, Dirksen and Kordt throw considerable light on this problem.

[16] This report was published in 1940 (see *The New York Times*, April 16, 1940). It became known almost at once to the French Foreign Office, where it made a deep impression (see Bonnet: *Fin d'une Europe*, 266-72).

trop assured him that "Europe will be an impassive spectator of the merciless destruction of Poland by Germany," and that his (Ribbentrop's) information and, above all, his "psychological knowledge of England" made him certain that armed British intervention was ruled out. Hitler said substantially the same thing, stressing the unpreparedness of the Western Powers. "France and England," he remarked, "will certainly make extremely theatrical anti-German gestures, but will not go to war." Neither would Russia move, so that actually it would be unnecessary for Germany to turn to Italy for support.[17]

Both these interviews have been much quoted, each to argue the case one way or the other. Actually they demonstrate only that Hitler, through Burkhardt, intended to frighten off the British and French; while, through Ciano, he attempted to reassure the anxious Italians that such trouble as there might be would be strictly localized. Of much greater historical value is the record of Hitler's talk with his generals on August 14, 1939. It is quite possible that his remarks even on this occasion were meant to veil his real views and that he was trying to reassure those who were worrying about a war on two fronts. But it is reasonable to suppose that his comments to his generals were franker than his statements to outsiders; after all, this was a serious matter and misleading statements might well produce grave consequences. At any rate, Hitler expressed himself positively to the members of his High Command: England would not go to war, at least not into what might be a long war: "The men whose acquaintance I made at Munich will not engage in another world war." What should Britain fight for? "One does not give one's life just for an ally." The British were not prepared and could not stand the financial strain of a long war. Besides, they had not made a loan to Poland, which seemed to indicate that they were not serious about aiding that country. And if the British did decide to fight, what could they do? It was most unlikely that they would risk an attack on the West Wall, and an attack through the Low Countries gave no promise of early victory: "Everything points to the fact that England and France will not intervene, the more so as there is nothing to force them to do so." Neither would Russia take action, for the Soviets were patently intent on avoiding war and would certainly not shed their blood for the democracies: "a defeat for Stalin would be just as dangerous as a victorious army. His interest is at most restricted to the Baltic States." In a word, Poland would receive aid neither from the West nor the East, and everything would be over in a few weeks.[18]

---

[17] *Ciano's Diplomatic Papers* (Odhams Press, 1948), 296 ff.; Pietro Badoglio: *L'Italie dans la guerre mondiale* (Paris, 1946), 28-29; *Nazi Conspiracy and Aggression*, VIII, TC-77; Wiskemann: *The Rome-Berlin Axis*, 155 ff.; Paul Schmidt: *Statist und diplomatischer Bühne* (Bonn, 1949), 438-40.

[18] *Halder Diary*, August 14, 1939. See the similar statement of State Secretary Weizsäcker to the British Ambassador on August 16, 1939 *(British Blue Book, No. 48)*.

Pending further evidence, one must therefore assume that Hitler discounted heavily the possibility that Britain and France would fight for Poland. The Fuehrer probably calculated that even if the Western Powers intervened, they would be unable to prevent a German victory, and that once Poland was liquidated, they would accept the accomplished fact rather than embark on a prolonged conflict. The key item in the reckoning, however, was the abstention of Soviet Russia, to the assurance of which Hitler thenceforth applied himself.

3. Nazi-Soviet Negotiations

When, on July 22, 1939, the Soviet press agency announced the resumption of trade talks with the Germans and when, a few days later, it became known that British and French military missions were to go to Moscow, Hitler and Ribbentrop lost no time in going into action. The Kremlin had given them an opening, time pressed, and there was no knowing how seriously to take the new departure in the Soviet negotiations with the West. On the evening of July 26, Herr Schnurre, one of the high officials of the German Foreign Office, invited the Soviet Chargé d'Affaires, Mr. Astakhov, to dinner. Once again the question of improved relations was considered and Schnurre stated that he envisaged as the final stage:

The establishment of good political relations, either a return to what had been in existence before [Berlin Treaty] or a new arrangement which took account of the vital political interests of both parties. This stage three appeared to me [reported Schnurre] within reach, because controversial problems of foreign policy, which would exclude such a relationship between the two countries, did not, in my opinion, exist in the whole area from the Baltic Sea to the Black Sea and the Far East. In addition, despite all the differences in *Weltanschauung* [i.e., ideology], there was *one* thing in common in the ideology of Germany, Italy, and the Soviet Union: opposition to the capitalist democracies. . . . Therefore, it would appear to us paradoxical if the Soviet Union, as a Socialist State, were to side with the Western democracies.

Astakhov agreed, but emphasized that a *rapprochement* could only come gradually. Probably with some relish he rehearsed Soviet grievances against Nazi Germany, particularly the Anti-Comintern Pact with Japan. Schnurre attempted to explain everything and assured his guest that the Germans were perfectly ready to respect Soviet interests in the Baltic States and Poland. As for the German relationship to Japan, that was not directed against Russia, but against Britain. Of course, if the Soviet Government should decide to make an alliance with England, Nazi-Soviet friendship would become impossible. Then, making a special plea, Schnurre asked:

What could England offer Russia? At best, participation in a European War and the hostility of Germany, but not a single desirable end for Russia. What could we offer, on the other hand? Neutrality and staying out of a possible European conflict and, if Moscow wished, a German-Russian understanding on mutual interests which, just as in former times, would work out to advantage of both countries.

Astakhov listened sympathetically and promised to report to his Government. But he left Schnurre with the impression—almost identical with that of Steinhardt somewhat later—that the Kremlin had not yet made up its mind: "It looks as if Moscow, for the time being, is following a policy of delay and postponement toward us as well as England, in order to defer decisions the importance of which they understand completely." At the same time Schnurre cherished no illusions; he realized that Soviet distrust of Germany was comparable to Soviet lack of faith in Britain and France.[19]

It is neither possible nor necessary, in the present context, to review in detail the further course of the discussions. The Germans did what they could to force the pace. The record of the Schnurre-Astakhov conversation was sent without delay to Schulenburg, the Ambassador at Moscow, with the explanation that since the British-French-Russian negotiations seemed to be moving to a successful conclusion, Germany would have to abandon its previous reserve. Schulenburg was to see Molotov and repeat the assurances already given to Astakhov. With regard to Japan he was to suggest that Germany might do something to alleviate the tension between Moscow and Tokyo. As for Poland, Russia's interests were to be taken into account. Militarily Poland presented no problem, and the military decision would be reached so quickly that Britain and France would be unable to intervene. Why should Russia want to join the Western Powers? The British could not offer the Soviets an adequate *quid pro quo*. They could not act effectively even against Japan. Obviously they were only looking for someone to pull the chestnuts out of the fire for them. In a further communication Schulenburg was told that there was great concern in Berlin about Russia, that the Foreign Office had had a succession of conferences with Ribbentrop, who, in turn, was in constant touch with Hitler. Ribbentrop regarded an immediate agreement with the Soviets as essential and was eagerly awaiting the results of Schulenburg's conference with Molotov.[20]

Unfortunately for the Germans, the Russians were in no particular hurry, finding themselves in the enviable position of being wooed from all sides. Ribbentrop tried his hand with Astakhov on the evening of August 2, but made no progress. On August 3 Schulenburg had his all-important talk with Molotov. He found the dour Commissar somewhat less reserved than usual, but by no means tractable. In reply to the German suggestions he expressed some interest. In fact, he admitted that the Kremlin desired an

[19] *Nazi-Soviet Relations,* 32-36.
[20] Instructions to Schulenburg, July 29; Schnurre's letter to Schulenburg, August 2, 1939 (to be published).

improvement in relations. But he was pointed in his comments on past Nazi policy, especially its encouragement of Japan. With respect to Soviet negotiations with the West he remarked that "The present course taken by the Soviet Union aimed at purely defensive ends and at the strengthening of a defensive front against aggression. In contrast to this, Germany had supported and promoted the aggressive attitude of Japan by the Anti-Comintern Pact and in the military alliance with Italy was pursuing offensive as well as defensive aims." The Ambassador felt obliged to report to his Government his impression "that the Soviet Government is at present determined to sign with England and France if they fulfill all Soviet wishes." To a friend he wrote a little more optimistically: "I believe that we put a few good fleas in the ears of the Soviets, anyhow. At every word and at every step one can see the great distrust toward us."[21]

For another ten days the Germans tried in vain to induce Molotov to specify Soviet interests in the Baltic States and in Poland, which the Germans had expressed readiness to respect. Finally, on August 12, 1939, Astakhov was instructed to state the Kremlin's willingness to discuss various problems, but only by degrees or stages. The Russians proposed that the conversations take place in Moscow, but left open the question whether the Germans should send a special negotiator. On the strength of this exciting news Hitler told Ciano on the same day: "In the last few days there has been a Russian request for the despatch of a German plenipotentiary to Moscow to negotiate the friendship pact." The Fuehrer had suddenly become convinced that "the sending of the Anglo-French military mission to Moscow had only one purpose, i.e. to conceal the catastrophic position of the political negotiations."[22]

Although it will be necessary at some later point to examine the validity of this last assertion of Hitler's, it is advisable, in the interests of clarity, to pursue the story of the Nazi-Soviet negotiations a little further before turning to other aspects of the situation. On August 14 Schulenburg was directed to see Molotov again and to restate the German position at length. The urgency of the matter was heavily underlined. The Ambassador was to say

---

[21] *Nazi-Soviet Relations*, 37-44; tel. from Grummon (Moscow), August 6, 1939. The negotiations, as they appear from published sources, have been frequently analyzed. See Harold C. Deutsch: "Strange Interlude: the Soviet-Nazi Liaison of 1939-1941" (*The Historian*, Spring, 1947); George Denicke: "The Origins of the Hitler-Stalin Pact" (*Modern Review*, March-April, 1948, 204-9); Alexander Dallin: "The Month of Decision: German-Soviet Diplomacy, July 22–August 22, 1939" (*Journal of Central European Affairs*, IX, April, 1949, 1-32); A. Rossi: *Deux ans d'alliance germano-soviétique* (Paris, 1949); E. H. Carr: "From Munich to Moscow" (*Soviet Studies*, I, June, October, 1949); Peter Kleist: *Zwischen Hitler und Stalin* (Bonn, 1950), 45 ff.; L. B. Namier: *Europe in Decay* (London, 1950), 259-80. Vice Admiral Kurt Assmann: "Stalin and Hitler. I. The Pact with Moscow" (*U.S. Naval Institute Proceedings*, LXXV, June, 1949, 639-53) makes use of the records of the British-French military missions, which had been captured by the Germans.

[22] *Ciano's Diplomatic Papers*, 302. See also *Nazi Conspiracy and Aggression*, VIII, 525; *Nazi-Soviet Relations*, 48-49.

that Ribbentrop himself could come to Moscow with full powers to settle outstanding issues in short order, but that an extended conference between Schulenburg and Stalin would be a prerequisite for such a trip.

Hitler and his Foreign Minister waited at Berchtesgaden on pins and needles while Schulenburg conferred at length with Molotov on the evening of August 15. The Soviet Commissar was "unusually compliant and candid." He expressed himself as much gratified by the clear statement of the German program and professed to recognize the need for prompt action. On the other hand, he thought the visit of Ribbentrop would have to be carefully prepared and that therefore some time would be required. The Soviet Government would have to know first whether the Berlin Government saw any real possibility of influencing Japan in the direction of better relations with the Soviet Union, whether Germany would agree to a non-aggression pact with Russia, and whether Germany would contemplate a joint guarantee of the Baltic States. All these things, he opined, could be better handled in the first instance through regular diplomatic channels. The suggestion of a conference between the Ambassador and Stalin was passed over in silence.[23]

In this interview of August 15 Molotov had, for the first time, indicated the Soviet desiderata. In the form he used they appeared modest and innocuous. Ribbentrop therefore cabled back at once, suggesting a twenty-five-year nonaggression pact, a suitable *démarche* in Tokyo and the proposed joint guarantee of the Baltic States. But the burden of his message dealt with his projected journey to the Soviet capital. Schulenburg was to say that Germany was determined not to endure Polish provocation indefinitely and that "serious incidents" might occur any day. He was to propose to Molotov that the visit take place within a few days.

There was, however, no hurrying the Soviet Commissar. On August 17 he handed Schulenburg the formal reply of the Kremlin to the proposals of August 15. This document began with yet another rehearsal of past Soviet grievances and then outlined the following procedure: first, conclusion of the economic accord; second, signature of a nonaggression pact or reaffirmation of the neutrality treaty of 1926; third, simultaneously with the nonaggression pact, conclusion of "a special protocol which would define the interests of the signatory parties in this or that question of foreign policy and which would form an integral part of the pact." Molotov suggested that the Germans try their hand at drafting these agreements. As for the projected Ribbentrop visit, he remarked that the practical work could be done without much ceremony and that the Kremlin did not like the publicity attaching to such a visit.

Champing at the bit as the date for the attack on Poland drew near, Hitler agreed to everything. The trade discussions were hastily concluded

---

[23] *Nazi-Soviet Relations,* 50-57; tel. from Steinhardt (Moscow), August 16, 1939.

on August 18 and a draft nonaggression treaty was despatched at once to Moscow. The Ambassador was to remind Molotov again that German-Polish relations were becoming more acute from day to day and might make the outbreak of hostilities unavoidable. A "historic turning point" had been reached and the Ribbentrop visit should take place as soon as humanly possible. But Molotov remained unmoved. He insisted that time was required to study the terms of a political agreement and submitted his own draft of a nonaggression pact, to run for only five years. Only after what the German Ambassador conjectured must have been intervention on Stalin's part did the Foreign Commissar agree that Ribbentrop might come to Moscow on August 26 or 27, provided the conclusion of the economic agreement were published at once.

By ordinary standards the discussions were progressing not only at a reasonable but at an unusually rapid rate. But for Hitler every day counted. On August 20 he sent a personal message addressed to Mr. J. V. Stalin, Moscow, concurring in everything and urging that, because the tension between Germany and Poland had become "intolerable," Ribbentrop be received on August 22 or at the latest on August 23 to sign the nonaggression pact and the secret protocol. This telegram was handed to Molotov on the afternoon of August 21 and Stalin replied at once in a message "to the Chancellor of the German Reich, A. Hitler." The Soviet leader raised no further objection and consented to Ribbentrop's arrival on August 23. Molotov informed the German Ambassador that the Soviet Government would like Hitler's concurrence in the publication next morning of a communiqué announcing the coming conclusion of the nonaggression pact and the projected visit of Ribbentrop. This was given at once.[24]

Soviet acceptance of the Ribbentrop visit brought the maneuvering to an end and provides a convenient opportunity for review and summary of the Nazi-Soviet relationship. Although by August 12, 1939, the Soviet decision for a deal with Hitler had certainly been made, the Kremlin continued to temporize for another ten days. Stalin and Molotov were obviously making every effort to prolong the discussions and to postpone the Ribbentrop visit as long as they dared. Their main preoccupations at this time seem to have been with alleviation of the tension in Soviet relations with Japan and with the attainment of Soviet objectives in the Baltic States. Constant German references to the Polish problem and reiterated expressions of readiness to take account of Soviet interests in Poland elicited almost no response. Molotov hardly brushed this question, though he must have been as aware as anyone of the acute danger of a German-Polish clash. One is tempted to believe that at first Stalin and Molotov were envisaging a pact much less profitable to them than the agreement presently to be concluded. Only

---

[24] *Nazi-Soviet Relations,* 58-69; see also Erich Kordt: *Wahn und Wirklichkeit* (Stuttgart, 1947), 160-64.

when they began to realize that Hitler felt unable to act against Poland without a pact with Russia did they see the possibility of securing a secret protocol involving much more extensive political settlements. In this connection it is worth noting that when Ribbentrop landed at the Moscow airfield he still had no clear idea of the prospective Soviet demands. The Germans were prepared for concessions in the entire area from the Baltic to the Black Sea. The Kremlin was in the position to make the most of the situation. Once Ribbentrop had openly committed himself to the pact, he could hardly reject even the most extravagant demands. However, before Stalin could close with Ribbentrop, he had to dispose of the British-French military missions, of whose sad fate something must now be said.

4. The Military Missions in Moscow

The British and French military missions arrived in the Soviet capital on August 11, 1939, just as the conversations between Russia and Germany were entering upon their crucial stage. The French mission was led by an able staff officer, General Joseph Doumenc, but the British, strangely enough, was headed by a naval officer, who, even if able, could hardly have hoped to impress the Russians. The British Government must have been aware of this fact, but, for whatever reason, the London authorities appear to have had difficulty in finding a suitable Army officer and felt obliged to fall back on the Royal Navy. Their choice was a man whose name appears to have meant little even to the British public, excepting as a source of amusement, for the admiral in question was Sir Reginald Aylmer Plunkett-Ernle-Erle-Drax, reputedly the possessor of the longest name of any British naval officer.[25]

The Soviet Government, in its postwar polemic, has dealt harshly with the story of the military missions and has accused the Western Governments of "utter lack of seriousness" in treating the issue of the military agreement. To quote a salient passage:

It took those missions an unusually long time to get to Moscow, and when they did get there, it transpired that they were composed of men of secondary importance who, furthermore, had not been authorized to sign any agreement. That being the case, the military negotiations proved as futile as the political ones. The military missions of the Western powers demonstrated at once that they even had no desire to carry on serious conversations concerning means of mutual assistance in the event of aggression on the part of Germany. The Soviet military mission proceeded from the fact that, since the U.S.S.R. had no common border with Germany, it could render Britain, France and Poland assistance in the event of war only if Soviet troops were permitted to pass through Polish territory. The Polish Govern-

[25] Tels. from Bullitt, July 24, 25, 31, 1939; tel. from Grummon, July 28, 1939; Hamilton, in *The New York Times*, July 25, 1939.

ment, however, declared that it would accept no military assistance from the Soviet Union, thus showing that it feared the growth of the strength of the Soviet Union more than Hitler's aggression.

Both the British and French missions supported Poland's position. In the course of the military negotiations, the question also came up as to the strength of the armed forces which should be put in the field at once by the parties to the agreement in the event of aggression. The British named a ridiculous figure, stating that they could put in the field five infantry divisions and one mechanized division. That was what the British offered at a time when the Soviet Union declared that it was prepared to send to the front against the aggressor one hundred and thirty-six divisions, five thousand medium and heavy guns, up to ten thousand tanks and whippets, more than five thousand war planes, etc.[26]

The truth or falsity of these charges will appear presently. If the chiefs of mission did in fact lack full powers to conclude a military convention, there was nothing unusual in this circumstance, the more so as in this instance the military arrangements were to be so closely integrated with the political agreements. To suggest that the British and French Governments did not take the missions seriously is altogether wide of the mark. The British mission went to Moscow richly supplied with instructions and documents, and fully prepared to discuss concrete military dispositions. Among other items it had a detailed review of the international situation in which essential factors were soberly analyzed. Poland and Rumania, it was pointed out, were both of them weak in war matériel, for which reason Poland would be unable to mobilize more than forty divisions or maintain its supplies for more than three months. Since Britain and France would be unable to reach Poland or Rumania in time of war, Soviet aid to those countries would be decisive. It was thought that the Soviet Army had been much weakened by recent purges and that it would be hampered by poor communications, but it would at least be able to furnish essential supplies to Poland and Rumania. A basic difficulty was that the Poles feared that if Soviet forces entered their territory, it would later prove impossible to get them to withdraw or to prevent the Bolshevization of Poland.

Under these circumstances the mission was instructed to negotiate and to proceed slowly until the political agreement should have been consummated. It was to make clear to the Soviets that the pact should apply only to Europe, and was to be careful not to reveal British plans in the Far East or in fact anywhere. If the Soviet negotiators insisted that steps be taken to bring Poland and Rumania into line, the mission was to refer the matter to London and at the same time was to try to induce the Soviets to handle the problem directly with Warsaw and Bucharest. The instructions, in short, revealed full awareness of the difficulties, but ended with an expression of

[26] *Falsificators of History.*

belief that the Moscow Government really desired both a political and a military pact and that a settlement would prove feasible.[27]

The Kremlin had appointed its highest military authority, General Klimenty Voroshilov, the Chief of Staff, to conduct the discussions on the Soviet side. Voroshilov received the foreign missions with much pomp and circumstance and the meetings opened on August 12-13, 1939, in an atmosphere of warm cordiality which left the French convinced that the Russians meant business. To be sure, the Soviet chief was disappointed to learn that Admiral Plunkett and General Doumenc were authorized only to negotiate, but he agreed that a start should be made by having each delegation provide a statement of its country's military capabilities. The British and French did so, confessing in the process that the Polish Army, unless heavily supplied, could not last long. To this Voroshilov replied by raising the question of how the Soviets could aid. On August 14 he answered his own query by stating categorically:

> . . . that the first condition for Soviet military coöperation with France and England was that the Polish Government should announce to the Soviet Government its willingness to permit the Red Army to enter Poland by way of Vilna in the North and by way of Lemberg on the South for the purpose of combatting the German armies in case France, England and Poland should become involved in war with Germany.

According to their instructions, the British and French negotiators urged that the Soviet Government take up this matter directly with Warsaw and Bucharest. In any event, they said, this was a political question which they would have to refer to their Governments. General Doumenc made heroic efforts to persuade Voroshilov to continue the talks without reference to the problem of passage, but the Soviet general stood his ground. Probably in order to impress his hearers with the strength of the Soviet position, he stated on August 15 that the Russians were prepared to put 120 infantry and sixteen cavalry divisions into the field, and that they had 5000 planes.[28]

The cards were now on the table. The British and French were squarely faced with the ever-recurring problem of the passage of Soviet troops through Polish territory. The Soviet Government, as noted above, raised the question why the London and Paris Governments had not settled this issue before sending the military missions to Moscow. The answer is not easy, but part of it rests on the fact, clearly expressed in the instructions to the missions, that the British and French held very definite views on the military

---

[27] Instruction to the British military mission, August 5, 1939.

[28] Tel. from Bullitt, quoting Bonnet, August 16, 1939; Records of the Moscow military conversations; Bonnet: *Fin d'une Europe*, 275 ff.; Paul Reynaud: *La France a sauvé l'Europe*, I (Paris, 1947), 586 ff.; General Joseph Doumenc's account in *Carrefour*, May 21, 1947; and the article based upon it by Alexander Dallin: "The Month of Decision" (*Journal of Central European Affairs*, IX, April, 1949, 1-32).

situation in Eastern Europe. They had a poor opinion of the Soviet Army and therefore put little store by its active participation. On the other hand they believed that the Polish Army, if given adequate equipment and supplies, would be a first-rate fighting force. Therefore all they desired of the Russians was the provision of needed matériel to the Poles. The Soviet insistence on doing more than they contemplated was a matter of grave embarrassment to the British and French.

Certain other aspects of the Polish problem undoubtedly influenced the situation also. In May, 1939, a Polish military mission had visited Paris and had proposed the conclusion of a political-military agreement to supplement the existing guarantee. With much reluctance the French General Staff had consented to arrangements which assured the Poles that within sixteen days of the outbreak of hostilities the French Army would launch a major attack on the German frontier. But at the last moment Foreign Minister Bonnet refused to sign the complementary political agreement, on the plea that the British had not yet done likewise. It seems likely that Bonnet had convinced himself that the Germans would make war, if necessary to gain their objectives in Danzig, and that he therefore wished to avoid any accord which involved recognition of any change in the status of Danzig as a legitimate cause for Poland's going to war. The details are still obscure, but the end result of this imbroglio was much irritation with Bonnet in French Government circles and violent recriminations between the Polish Ambassador and the French Foreign Minister.[29]

The British were hardly more successful in their efforts to grapple with the Polish problem. A military mission had been sent to Warsaw in late May, 1939, and had reported fully on Poland's serious shortages in equipment and supplies. Thereupon the Poles began negotiations in London for a credit and a loan. Apparently British financial circles were chary about further large investments. The Poles, indeed, had the feeling that they still cherished hopes of a deal with Hitler. More important, however, was the fact that Britain was already under heavy financial strain, that Britain needed for its own use the very military items which Poland required, and that a loan threatened too great a drain on gold reserves. The discussions dragged on for weeks and eventuated, on August 2, 1939, in a credit agreement in the sum of eight million pounds, the French extending a comparable credit. Actually, however, practically no equipment reached Poland from Britain prior to the outbreak of war. The military agreement between the two countries had been deferred pending the financial negotiations, and was not finally concluded until August 25, 1939. Clearly there were real difficulties in the way of implementing the guarantee extended to

[29] Tels. from Bullitt, May 19, 22, 23, 25, 30, 1939; General Gamelin: *Servir* (Paris, 1946), II, 413 ff.; Bonnet: *Fin d'une Europe*, Chapter XI; Namier: *Diplomatic Prelude*, 456 ff., 463 ff.

Poland in March, 1939, but it is not surprising that Hitler regarded the endless delays on the part of the British as evidence that they did not intend to take their guarantees seriously.[30]

There is no reason to believe that after the discussions of March, 1939, either the British or the French made efforts to induce the Poles to agree to the passage of Soviet troops. The attitude of Warsaw was well known and, as aforesaid, it was thought that Russian aid in the form of supplies was all that would be necessary. Voroshilov's uncompromising demand on August 14 therefore struck like a bombshell. Nonetheless, General Doumenc considered the Soviet demand justified and took it to mean that the Kremlin did not intend to "remain on the balcony," but really to get into the fight. He asked and received permission from Paris to send an emissary to Warsaw in the effort to convert the Polish General Staff. Meanwhile Bonnet raised the issue with the Polish Ambassador as a matter of greatest urgency, and the British and French Military Attachés in Warsaw were instructed from home to bring pressure on the Polish High Command. But the Poles refused to yield. Foreign Minister Beck expressed doubt whether the Germans would make war, at least before the end of September, and asserted his country's ability to resist. Threats of a Nazi-Soviet pact left him unmoved. The Soviet demand for passage of troops, he said, "is nothing less than a new partition, which we are being asked to subscribe to. If we are partitioned, we shall at least defend ourselves. There is nothing to guarantee us that the Russians, once they are installed in our country, will participate actively in the war." Marshal Rydz-Smigly voiced his sentiments even more bluntly: "With the Germans we risk losing our liberty; with the Russians we lose our soul." Hours were spent in argument, the French insisting that it would be utter folly to reject the Soviet offer of genuine military support and offering to send two French divisions to assist the Soviet forces. Again and again they assured the Poles that the French and British could get from the Kremlin absolute guarantees of eventual evacuation and that they would give Poland "absolute guarantees of those guarantees." Nothing would avail. By August 20 the Poles had made only one slight concession: Colonel Beck had agreed that the French mission at Moscow "might approve [passage of Soviet troops through Poland] as though no question had been put to Poland."[31]

In retrospect one must sympathize with the Poles, headstrong though

[30] Despatches from Biddle (Warsaw), June 3, July 15, 18, 28, August 3, 1939; tels. from Kennedy (London), June 28, July 10, 20, 25, August 3, 1939; tels. from Bullitt, July 13, 27, 28, 1939. See also *Poland in the British Parliament* (New York, 1946), 103, 121, 124, 140.

[31] Bonnet: *Fin d'une Europe*, 275-84; Reynaud: *La France a sauvé l'Europe*, I, 586 ff.; Léon Noël: *L'Agression allemande contre la Pologne* (Paris, 1946), 420 ff.; Gafencu: *Derniers jours de l'Europe*, 218 ff.; Namier: *Diplomatic Prelude*, 205 ff., quoting the account of the Polish Ambassador in Paris. We have used also the records of the military conversations and tels. from Bullitt, August 16 and 18, 1939, and from Steinhardt, August 23, 1939.

they may have been in some respects. There was no assurance that the Soviet armies, once they had moved into Poland, would actually engage the Nazis, and, with regard to the eventual withdrawal of the Russians, Polish apprehensions were surely not without foundation. Nevertheless, the French were infuriated with the Poles. Evidently M. Bonnet did not seriously question the good faith of the Soviet Government, while in Moscow the French Ambassador, M. Naggiar, pressed for a conclusion on any terms. On the other hand, the French Counselor of Embassy, M. Payart, put no trust whatever in the Russians and regarded the entire negotiation as a terrible hoax. His views were shared by other experienced diplomats in Moscow, but made no impression on his superiors.

Premier Daladier, taking full advantage of the opening suggested by Beck, on August 21, 1939, instructed General Doumenc to agree in principle to the passage of Soviet troops through the Vilna and Lemberg corridors. At the same time both chiefs of mission were sent full powers to conclude the military convention. On the very next day they communicated these happy tidings to Voroshilov, but only to meet with a cool reception. The Soviet general was annoyingly scrupulous in analyzing the agreement regarding passage of Soviet troops. He wanted to know whether the British Government concurred in the French statement and whether the Governments of Warsaw and Bucharest had given their approval. Without such approval, he observed, nothing could be done. Remarking significantly that the British and French had dawdled so long that "certain political events" might intervene, the Soviet chief excused himself and went duck-shooting.[32]

Events had indeed outrun the course of the military conversations. On August 20, 1939, had come the announcement of the conclusion of a Nazi-Soviet trade agreement. Then, on the evening of the eventful August 22, 1939, the Soviet press agency elucidated Voroshilov's cryptic utterance by reporting that Ribbentrop would arrive presently for the negotiation of a Nazi-Soviet nonaggression pact. The capitals of Europe reeled under the blow while Bonnet, in a last desperate move, appealed once more to Warsaw. On the afternoon of August 23, just as Ribbentrop arrived in Moscow, the Polish Government finally gave qualified consent to the French demand:

The Polish Government agrees that General Doumenc should make the following statement: "We have come to the conviction that in case of common action against German aggression, coöperation between Poland and the U.S.S.R. is not to be excluded (or is possible), under technical conditions to be determined. The British and French General Staffs consider that therefore all hypotheses of collaboration should be immediately studied."

[32] Tel. from Steinhardt, August 18, 1939; records of the military conversations; Bonnet: *Fin d'une Europe*, 284; Reynaud: *La France a sauvé l'Europe*, I, 586 ff.; Namier: *Diplomatic Prelude*, 291-92, quoting Daladier's speech in the French Assembly, July 18, 1946; Dallin: "The Month of Decision," as cited above.

There was little if any prospect that the exigent Russians would regard this evasive statement with favor. Voroshilov, when informed of this new turn, simply reiterated his previous stand and insisted that the British and French Governments guarantee the agreement of Warsaw and Bucharest.[33]

Though further discussion had by this time become obviously futile, the Western Powers still grasped at straws. One of these was a statement by an official Soviet spokesman with reference to the forthcoming Ribbentrop visit: "We want to regularize commercial arrangements with Germany. We want to conclude a proper agreement with the democratic powers to restrain further aggression by the Fascist powers. We see nothing incompatible in the simultaneous pursuit of both aims."[34] The British Ambassador called at once on Commissar Molotov and requested clarification of this statement. The ensuing conversation was plain-spoken on both sides. Sir William Seeds inquired about the nature of the proposed Nazi-Soviet pact and asked whether it would contain the so-called "escape clause," characteristic of Soviet nonaggression pacts with other countries, which would render the agreement inoperative if either party committed aggression against a third state. But Molotov was evasive: the official communiqué, he insisted, contained the facts and for the rest the British would have to "wait and see." In reply to the Ambassador's suggestion that the Kremlin was acting in bad faith, the Commissar disputed any British claim to sit in judgment on Soviet policy and reminded Sir William that he had repeatedly charged the British with complete insincerity. The height of this insincerity, he continued, had been reached when the military missions arrived without powers to discuss such basic issues as the passage of Soviet troops through Poland and Rumania. The Soviet Government had therefore been forced to the conclusion that it was being "diddled" and that it had best close with the Nazi offers. The Ambassador did his utmost to defend British-French policy and took the occasion to recall all the concessions that had been made to the Soviet viewpoint. Molotov asserted that he had little interest in the past, yet closed with the suggestion that the military missions remain in Moscow until the outcome of the German-Soviet negotiations were known. That is, he invited the British and French to cool their heels at the door while Ribbentrop was being received within.[35]

Molotov's contentions and the postwar Soviet apologia both show that from the outset the Soviet Government attempted to blame the British-French military missions for the breakdown of negotiations and for the conclusion of the spectacular Nazi-Soviet pact. Yet the merest comparison of dates disproves this thesis. The Kremlin had agreed with Berlin on August 12, 1939, that is, before the beginning of the military conversations, to dis-

---

[33] Bonnet: *Fin d'une Europe*, 289-90; records of the military conversations.

[34] Gedye, in *The New York Times*, August 22, 1939.

[35] Tel. from Kennedy, August 23, 1939, giving the substance of Seeds's report. The French Ambassador also called on Molotov, but his visit, too, was barren of results (tel. from Bullitt, August 23, 1939).

cuss concrete political problems. Furthermore, Stalin had consented to Ribbentrop's visit before the British and French had made a final statement on the issue of the passage of Soviet troops through Polish or Rumanian territory. All the evidence indicates that the Soviet leaders desired the coming of the military missions partly to impress and soften the Germans and partly in order to keep the door ajar in case an agreement with Hitler proved impossible. By August 22 they certainly had reason to suppose that the Germans would pay dearly for a pact, yet even then Molotov made the strange suggestion that the missions remain until the Kremlin had made doubly sure of its prospective gains. Viewed in this light, the much discussed obduracy of the Poles in refusing assent to the passage of Soviet troops loses most of its significance. That issue was really nothing more than a convenient instrument by which the Soviet negotiators managed to protract the discussions. All in all, the Soviet policy in this latter phase was one of shameless deception.

5. The Nazi-Soviet Pact

August 22, 1939, was a red-letter day in the annals of even a career like Adolf Hitler's. Having heard that Stalin was prepared to receive Ribbentrop and conclude a nonaggression pact, the Fuehrer felt completely free to loose the attack on Poland, scheduled for the morning of August 26. In great elation he summoned his generals to a conference at Obersalzberg. Though there are disparities among the records of his remarks, the general tenor and content of the various versions are the same. They leave no doubt that the session was one of the most extraordinary and dramatic of all history. The Fuehrer began by recalling his original plan to attack the West in two or three years. This plan, he said, had been abandoned when, in the spring of 1939, it became clear that Poland could not be trusted at Germany's rear and therefore would first have to be liquidated. The Nazi dictator pointed out that time pressed since the German economic situation was deteriorating. Besides, he added, with exuberant self-conceit, the future depended so much upon himself: "Probably no one will ever again have the confidence of the whole German people as I do. There will probably never again be a man with more authority than I have. My existence is therefore a factor of great value. But I might be eliminated at any time by some criminal or idiot." The same, in lesser degree, was true of Mussolini and Franco. By contrast neither Britain nor France had the leadership to enable them to embark on a long life-and-death struggle: "Our enemies are little worms. I saw them at Munich." Britain and France were in decline and their much vaunted rearmament did not as yet amount to much. Germany therefore had much to gain and little to lose. The probability was great that the Western Powers would not interfere. In any case, Germany must accept the risk and act with reckless resolution.

At this point the Fuehrer broke the great news: the coming deal with

Soviet Russia. Stalin, he declared, was one of the three great statesmen of the world: "Stalin and I are the only ones that see the future. So I shall shake hands with Stalin within a few weeks on the common German-Russian border and undertake with him a new distribution of the world." But, he hastened to add, this would be only a temporary expedient. When the time came, the Soviet Union would be dealt with like Poland: "After Stalin's death (he is seriously ill), we shall crush the Soviet Union." However, for the moment the international situation was extraordinarily favorable. By the agreement with Russia the weapons of the democracies would be dashed from their hands and Poland would be maneuvered into the position needed for German success. Some propaganda reason could readily be found for starting the war: "The victor will not be asked later on whether he told the truth or not. In starting and waging war, not the Right is what matters, but the Victory." The struggle, he directed, was to be waged with the utmost brutality and the Poles were to be exterminated without mercy: "Only in this way will we win the living space that we need. . . . Eighty million people shall get what is their right. Their existence has to be secured. The strongest has the right." His one great fear, concluded Hitler, was that at the last minute some "dirty dog" like Chamberlain would bring up proposals for mediation. In that case he would be kicked downstairs.[36]

The notes taken by Hitler's listeners record that after this exultant outburst Goering led the cheering. He jumped upon the table and offered bloodthirsty thanks while he danced like a savage. Only a few doubtful officers remained silent. Perhaps some of the old-line soldiers had grave misgivings about the course of Nazi leadership. But the moment was hardly propitious for objection and protest. Some undercover effort was made to forestall the fateful decision, but the key men of the Army refused to cooperate and plans for organized opposition had to be abandoned.[37]

To what extent Hitler's bravado may have been designed to win over his uneasy generals one cannot say, but in any case his remarks provide an interesting if unedifying commentary on the negotiations of Ribbentrop in Moscow. The Foreign Minister reached the Soviet capital about noon on August 23, 1939, accompanied by a large staff. It seems likely that he expected long wrangling on details, but, as it turned out, his Foreign Office experts were not needed at all and only one of them, the legal adviser, took any part in the discussions. Ribbentrop had a long conference with Stalin and Molotov on the afternoon of his arrival. Almost nothing is known of

[36] *Nazi Conspiracy and Aggression,* III, 798-PS, 1014-PS; VII, L-3: *Halder Diary,* August 22, 1939.

[37] State Department interrogation of General George Thomas. The rather profuse but scattered evidence is collated in Franklin L. Ford: "The Twentieth of July in the History of the German Resistance" (*American Historical Review,* LI, 1946, 609-26); Allen W. Dulles: *Germany's Underground* (New York, 1947), Chap. IV; and in Maxime Mourin: *Les complots contre Hitler, 1938-1945* (Paris, 1948), 82-83.

the conversation, but Stalin inquired first of all whether the Germans were prepared to disinterest themselves in Estonia and Latvia to the extent of giving up claims to the seaports of Libau and Windau. This question was referred to Hitler by telephone and an affirmative reply was received that same evening. Ribbentrop came away from the first conference with the feeling that the hoped-for deal could be successfully arranged. In the evening the principals reassembled for a second session, lasting from 10 P.M. to 1 A.M. Stalin having been told of Hitler's compliance in the matter of the Baltic States, the atmosphere became warm and cordial. The agreement on the nonaggression pact presented little difficulty, save for the fact that Stalin objected to a flowery preamble celebrating Nazi-Soviet friendship. After all, he remarked, the Nazis had for years poured such "buckets of filth" upon the Soviet Government that the latter could hardly be expected publicly to proclaim its friendship. But this was by the by. On matters of substance agreement was easy, for the Germans assented to everything. With regard to Japan, Stalin admitted that the Kremlin desired better relations, but made it clear that if Japan wanted war, it could have war. Ribbentrop offered to do what he could to eliminate friction, but Stalin—no doubt anticipating the effect of the Nazi-Soviet pact on Tokyo—was anxious to have it understood that his Government would not take the initiative. There was some discussion of the position of Italy and of Turkey, and both sides indulged in some caustic remarks about the weakness and presumption of Britain.

Turning then to the terms of the secret protocol, which was to be an integral part of the agreement, Ribbentrop left no doubt that the Germans would not put up with Polish "provocation" any longer. He and the Soviet chiefs thereupon proceeded to plan the partition of Poland, the respective spheres to be defined by the courses of the Pisa, Narew, Vistula and San Rivers. Finland, Estonia and Latvia, "in case of a politico-territorial change," were assigned to the Soviet sphere, and Lithuania to the German. The Soviet Government "emphasized" its interest in Bessarabia, and the Nazi envoy declared Germany's complete "political disinterestedness" in southeastern Europe. The agreements were signed at about 1 A.M. on August 24, though dated August 23, 1939. Stalin was elated and "did not hide from Ribbentrop the fact that he had long been in favor of a Soviet-German *rapprochement.*" He drank a toast to Hitler and to "the revival of the traditional German-Russian friendship." Ribbentrop reciprocated. The "tremendous political overturn," as Hitler described it, had been accomplished. By noon next day Ribbentrop was able to report to the Fueher the details of his brilliant achievement at Moscow.[38]

All that is known of this spectacular transaction comes from German

[38] The essential materials are all in *Nazi-Soviet Relations,* 71-78. An earlier and substantially accurate account is to be found in Kordt: *Wahn und Wirklichkeit,* 175-77. At the Nürnberg trials the Soviet prosecutor repeatedly objected to the submission of the secret protocol as evidence, but the text leaked out and was published in British and

sources. The Kremlin, in its reply to the publication of the German documents by the American Government, added nothing to the facts there revealed, but countered only with the accusations, already discussed above, that in view of the insincerity of the British and French, the Soviet Government had had no other alternative than to accept Hitler's offers. Thereby it assured itself of a further period of peace during which it could complete its preparations for resistance to an eventual German attack, whereas rejection of the Nazi proposals would have permitted "war provocateurs" of the Western Powers to involve the Soviet Union singlehanded in war with Germany. The pact, then, "was, after all, the best of all possible ways out." And furthermore, so runs the Soviet apologia, what could be wrong with a nonaggression pact? Had not many other powers concluded such agreements with Germany, not excepting the British and French, who had exchanged assurances with the Germans after Munich? Should the Soviet Union alone have been denied this privilege?[39]

To this it may be replied that the Nazi-German pact was unusual and ominous in two respects. In the first place it failed to contain the so-called escape clause characteristic of almost all other Soviet nonaggression agreements. This meant that the Kremlin knowingly put no obstacle whatever in the way of Nazi aggression against a third power, such as Poland. Secondly, Article IV provided that "neither of the two High Contracting Parties shall participate in any grouping of powers whatsoever that is directly or indirectly aimed at the other party." This might be taken to mean that the Germans insisted on the termination of Soviet negotiations with the British and the French, though it is highly likely that the Kremlin intended it to apply at least equally to the German project for an alliance with Japan. Apart from all this, however, it should be pointed out that exception was taken abroad not so much to the nonaggression pact as to the secret protocol arranging for a division of the spoils. The German press discussed freely the coming partition of Poland and there was little room for doubt that a deal on spheres of influence had been arrived at, however secret the very existence of the protocol was kept. Looked at from the Soviet standpoint one can understand Stalin's relief and joy at learning that the Germans were prepared to concede everything demanded by the Kremlin with respect to the Baltic States. This was undoubtedly the crux of the matter for the Soviet leaders, and throughout it overshadowed the Polish issue. Stalin and Molotov found themselves in the rare and enviable position of being

---

American newspapers in very loose translation. It may now be found in *Nazi-Soviet Relations* in translation, and in *Die Beziehungen zwischen Deutschland und der Sowjet-Union, 1939-1941* (Tübingen, 1949), 90-92, in the original German text. For the narrative of the conferences we have used also the detailed and authoritative tel. from Steinhardt, August 24, 1939.

[39] *Falsificators of History.*

able to get more than they could have reasonably asked. It is hardly surprising that they helped themselves to all that was offered.[40]

There remains the problem of the Soviet attitude toward the Western Powers. Not only before, but after the Ribbentrop visit it was publicly stated by Soviet spokesmen that a pact with Germany would not preclude agreement with Britain and France, and it may be recalled that Molotov, in his talks with Ambassadors Seeds and Naggiar on August 22, had suggested possible continuation of the talks. It appears from the record that the Ambassadors put too much stock in these remarks. Sir William Seeds deluded himself into thinking that Ribbentrop would become involved in possibly futile negotiations and cherished the notion that a Nazi-Soviet non-aggression pact would not necessarily prevent an alliance of Russia with the West. Ambassador Steinhardt, who was fully aware of the realities, tried to warn his British colleague that the essentials had been settled before Ribbentrop's arrival, but Seeds remained incredulous and rather patronizingly thanked Steinhardt for his "opinion."[41]

It was not until August 25, when Admiral Plunkett and General Doumenc had their final meeting with Voroshilov, that the hopelessness of the situation became fully apparent. Asked whether there was any point in continuing the military conversations, the Soviet Chief of Staff replied in the negative. He blamed the Poles for the failure of the negotiations and remarked: "Were we to be expected to conquer Poland in order to give aid, or to get on our knees to the Poles?" Molotov took the identical line in reviewing the situation with the French Ambassador, carefully abstaining from recrimination and indeed expressing regret that the projected peace front had foundered on the obstinate blindness of the Poles.[42] Clearly nothing more was to be done. On August 26 the military missions packed their bags and departed for home.

6. Preparations for the Worst

In Washington the sultry month of August, 1939, recorded no developments either in government policy or in popular attitude commensurate with the inexorable march of Europe down the road to war. The President and his advisers followed virtually every stage of that dismal progress. Shortly after Molotov on August 3 had indicated to Schulenburg his willingness to entertain the idea of a political understanding, the significant details reached the President at Hyde Park. It may be recalled that at that juncture he had sent the message to Molotov indicating the American in-

---

[40] Tel. from Steinhardt, August 24, 1939. See also Tolischus in *The New York Times,* August 25, 1939.

[41] Tel. from Steinhardt, August 24, 1939.

[42] Records of the Moscow military conversations; Voroshilov's interview in *Izvestia,* August 26, 1939 (*The New York Times,* August 27, 1939); Bonnet: *Fin d'une Europe,* 290-92.

terest in the success of the British-French-Soviet negotiations. The reply, though naturally of great interest, could not be expected for some time, since for security reasons it had to be sent by courier. Actually Steinhardt's report did not reach Washington until August 29, by which date it could serve only as a sorry commentary on the tortuous ways of power politics.[43] In the interval, while the American public was pinning its hopes on the success of the British-French military missions, day-by-day reports from London, Paris and Moscow kept the State Department on tenterhooks. By the time the military missions arrived in Moscow, Mr. Welles was already telephoning the President that in his opinion war was a matter of only a week or ten days.[44]

Sharing the fears of the State Department, Mr. Roosevelt began to take steps to meet the impending emergency. On August 9 the creation of a War Resources Board, under the chairmanship of Edward R. Stettinius, Jr., was announced. This board, composed primarily of prominent industrialists, was to review and appraise the Industrial Mobilization Plan which had been worked out by the Services over the years; was to draft a program for price controls; and was to study problems of raw materials, labor, and industrial facilities. Apparently it was intended that, if the country became involved in war, the Board should be transformed into a War Resources Administration with comprehensive executive control over the national war effort. The Board held its first meeting on August 17 and threw itself at once into its important task.[45]

At about the same time, in mid-August, the President gave instructions for the completion of all regulations and measures necessary for the proclamation and maintenance of American neutrality in the event of war abroad. Most of these papers had originally been drafted in March and April and therefore required little more than revision. Under the chairmanship of Acting Secretary Welles an important meeting was held on August 17, with high officials of the State, War, Navy, Treasury and Justice Departments participating. After reviewing the situation, this group examined relevant legislation and considered many aspects of the international economic and financial picture. At its own request, the President constituted the group as an Interdepartmental Committee to devote continuing attention to these problems.[46]

In contrast to this practical work on the home front there was almost nothing the President could hope to do diplomatically to influence the

---

[43] Note of Welles to the President, transmitting Steinhardt's report, August 29, 1939.
[44] Alsop and Kintner: *American White Paper,* 54.
[45] For details see the official history: *Industrial Mobilization for War* (Washington, 1947), I, 6-11.
[46] *Berle Diaries (MS.),* August 17, 21; *Morgenthau Diaries (MS.),* August 17, 23, 1939 (Vol. 206).

course of events abroad. It was all but inevitable that Hitler, once he had bought off the Soviets, would attack Poland, without much concern for the decisions of the British and French. The only conceivable way to stay his hand would be to induce his Italian partner to exert influence for peace. The effort promised little, but it was known in Washington that Ciano had come back from his meeting with Hitler shocked by the news of the German plans and altogether disgusted by the Fuehrer's failure to take his ally into his confidence at an earlier date. Ambassador Phillips was convinced that Ciano was doing his utmost to put on the brakes and reported that "Everywhere throughout Italy there is outspoken condemnation of the policy of the military alliance with Germany, and nothing that Mussolini could do would be more unpopular than to drag Italy into the maelstrom on the side of Germany, and particularly at this moment when Danzig is the objective." In the light of these reports, the President and his advisers decided to draft a message, not to Mussolini, but to King Victor Emmanuel himself, and perhaps to send similar messages to King George of England and to President Lebrun of France. Several drafts of the message were made on August 16-17 and forwarded for comment to the President at Hyde Park. Mr. Roosevelt himself made some changes and then kept the text in readiness for transmission as soon as the situation seemed to warrant.[47]

At this point the announcement came (August 20) of the conclusion of the Nazi-Soviet trade agreement, and then (August 22) of Ribbentrop's coming visit to Moscow to conclude a nonaggression pact. Along with these dramatic items came a report from Berlin that Hitler had fixed on August 24 or 25 as the day for attack on Danzig and the Corridor. This in turn was followed by a long cable from Ambassador Bullitt reporting Premier Daladier's reactions. The French statesman was convinced that war was imminent and that Japan would take part in it. He hoped profoundly that "the President would issue a declaration stating that war seemed imminent and summoning all the nations of the earth to send delegates immediately to Washington to try to work out a pacific solution." Even though he feared Germany would reject the proposal, it should be spread on the "moral record." Daladier bemoaned the collapse of the effort to build up a peace front, feared that the Poles would go under in a short time, that Britain and France would be unable to give them much assistance, and that thereafter Hitler would fall on France. Daladier found himself faced by the terrible alternatives of either at once staking the lives of all able-bodied Frenchmen in a war of doubtful outcome or of abandoning Poland only to face later the onslaught of a Germany controlling most of Europe. Like many other

[47] *Berle Diaries (MS.)*, August 16, 17; *Moffat Diary (MS.)*, August 16, 17, 19, 1939; letter from Phillips to the President, August 18, 1939 (*Roosevelt Papers:* Secretary's File, Box 45); Alsop and Kintner: *American White Paper*, 51, 55.

Frenchmen, the Premier felt bitter about the Poles but unwilling to countenance the moral turpitude of deserting them.[48]

The State Department, having had the benefit of full and accurate intelligence on the course of events, was less surprised than either the French or British Foreign Offices. The Nazi-Soviet pact was looked upon as a very cynical piece of business, but with this redeeming feature: that countries like Italy and Spain might shake loose from Germany, and, what was more important, that Japan might abandon all thought of a Nazi military connection. On the other hand, there was the danger that Britain and France might lose heart and relapse into a policy of appeasing Hitler at Poland's expense. This was the gnawing fear of Ambassador Bullitt, among others. In any case it was thought imperative that the United States do something before the stupefaction of the European chancelleries resulted in undesirable decisions. The President evidently gave little consideration to Daladier's suggestion that he call a conference. Instead, he issued instructions that the message to Victor Emmanuel be despatched and that appeals to Hitler and to President Mościcki of Poland be drafted. Mr. Hull, like the President, hurried back to Washington, the former arriving on August 23, the latter on August 24.[49]

The appeal to the King of Italy was sent off on August 23, just as Stalin and Ribbentrop were putting the final touches to their agreement. Considering the amount of effort devoted to it, the message was not an impressive document. After calling attention to the danger of war and expatiating on the dire consequences of conflict, the President expressed his belief that the Italian King could do much to avert the catastrophe. He then rehearsed the terms of the American offer of April, 1939, and assured His Majesty of "the earnest sympathy" of the United States for anything he might do to further a peaceful solution along those lines.[50]

Since Mussolini had not even troubled to make a formal reply when the same proposal was submitted to him in April, 1939, it is hard to imagine why the President should have expected Victor Emmanuel to be able to overrule the Duce. In the State Department there was general agreement that the move was a weak one, but there was not much else to be done. The reaction from London was unfavorable, too. Ambassador Kennedy telephoned that the message was "a complete flop." Yet the President insisted on making

[48] Tels. from Bullitt, August 21, 22, 1939, the latter already published by Arthur Krock in *The New York Times Magazine*, July 18, 1943. See further Hull: *Memoirs*, I, 661, and the reports of Tolischus from Berlin and of Gedye from Moscow in *The New York Times*, August 21, 1939.

[49] *Berle Diaries (MS.)*, August 22; *Moffat Diary (MS.)*, August 21, 22, 1939; Alsop and Kintner: *American White Paper*, 55-56; *The New York Times*, August 21, 1939; memo of conversation between Welles and the Polish Ambassador, August 22, 1939.

[50] Text in *Peace and War*, 475-76.

further efforts by addressing Hitler and President Mościcki. Perhaps he
shared the view of Assistant Secretary Berle, who noted:

> My private opinion is that these messages will have about the same effect as a
> valentine sent to somebody's mother-in-law out of season; and they have all that
> quality of naïveté which is the prerogative alone of the United States. Nevertheless,
> they ought to be sent. The one certain thing in this business is that no one will
> be blamed for making any attempt, however desperate, for preserving peace.[51]

The messages to Hitler and Mościcki were drafted by Welles and Berle,
and were sent off on August 24. They consisted not only of renewed offers
in terms of the April message, but embodied also an appeal to refrain from
hostilities "for a reasonable and stipulated period" and proposals to settle
the difficulties between the two countries either by direct negotiation, or by
submission to impartial arbitration, or through conciliation, "selecting as
conciliator or moderator a national of one of the traditionally neutral states
of Europe, or a national of one of the American Republics, which are all of
them free from any connection with or participation in European political
affairs." Thus, the President offered himself as conciliator, though on the
understanding that, whatever method might be chosen, each nation to the
dispute should agree "to accord complete respect to the independence and
territorial integrity of the other." Nor did the President neglect the opportunity to remind Hitler of the opposition of the American people to policies
of "military conquest and domination," and of their unanimous rejection
of the "thesis that any ruler or any people possess the right to achieve their
ends or objectives through the taking of action which will plunge countless
millions of people into war . . ."[52]

To wind up the story of these appeals and proposals, it ought to be added
that the message to Victor Emmanuel had to be taken by hand to the royal
shooting box near Turin. It was delivered by Ambassador Phillips in person
on August 25, and the King's reply, a brief though polite negative, was not
received in Washington until August 30. President Mościcki, on his part,
responded at once (August 25), expressing appreciation and accepting either
direct negotiation or conciliation. The proposal for arbitration was passed
over in silence. Since nothing had been heard from Berlin, a second message
was dispatched to Hitler, communicating Poland's readiness for negotiation
or conciliation and appealing to the Fuehrer "to agree to the pacific means of
settlement accepted by the Government of Poland." "All the world," concluded the President, "prays that Germany, too, will accept."[53]

[51] *Berle Diaries (MS.)*, August 24, 1939; *Moffat Diary (MS.)*, August 24, 1939; Krock in
The New York Times, August 25, 1939.

[52] Texts in *Peace and War*, 477-79.

[53] Texts in *Peace and War*, 479-80; Alsop and Kintner: *American White Paper*, 55-57;
Hull: *Memoirs*, I, 662-63. We have used also a letter from Phillips to the President, reporting delivery of the message to Victor Emmanuel, August 25 *(Roosevelt Papers:*

Despite the urgency of the matter, Hitler maintained silence. Not until August 31 did Dr. Thomsen, the German Chargé d'Affaires in Washington, present a note to Secretary Hull stating that his Government had directed him to say that the President's messages had been received and were "greatly appreciated" by the Fuehrer. Hitler's real response, of course, was the attack on Poland the next day. Long before that, however, it had become clear to Mr. Roosevelt and his advisers that nothing whatever was to be hoped from their efforts. The controlled press of Italy and Germany characterized the messages as nonsensical if not comical—hardly worth talking about. The organ of the German Foreign Office commented:

The President appears devoted to the illusion that his person or his government is fit for suitable mediation as the representative of a "disinterested republic of the Western Hemisphere, distant from the territory and causes of the present crisis." Roosevelt must understand that he has forfeited his authority as a nonpartisan on the basis of his own methods.[54]

The net effect of the appeals, then, was precisely the failure which the State Department and probably the President himself had anticipated. There remained, however, the forlorn satisfaction of having entered the last item of German guilt on the record. Without a doubt this was one of the main objectives from the beginning. As Mr. Roosevelt remarked when the second message to Hitler was despatched: "This puts the bee on Germany, which no one did in 1914."[55] And the President's messages were in fact warmly and gratefully received by the American public, devoted as ever to good deeds, however futile. An editorial in the *New York Herald Tribune* (August 26) summed up the situation succinctly:

Americans are faced once more with the lesson which they refused to learn in the World War—that a nation armed to the teeth and bent on war . . . can be checked only by the use or threat of force greater than its own. Mere pleas, mere appeals to reason, count for nothing. . . . Yet such is the temper of the American people that they are glad that the President made his appeals. They would have felt, had he not made them, that perhaps he had overlooked a chance to preserve peace. The fact that his proposals have fallen on deaf ears in no sense detracts from their sane soundness . . .

Admission that the President had done what any decent and responsible statesman would have felt compelled to do under the circumstances did not,

Secretary's File, Box 45). Mościcki's reply was telegraphed to Paris and relayed by telephone from Bullitt to Washington (memo of telephone conversation with Bullitt, August 25, *ibid.*, Box 43).

[54] Matthews from Rome, and Tolischus from Berlin, in *The New York Times*, August 26, 1939.

[55] *Moffat Diary (MS.)*, August 24, 1939; *Berle Diaries (MS.)*, August 25, 1939. The remark is somewhat more elegantly phrased in Alsop and Kintner: *American White Paper*, 57.

however, imply that Americans felt he should have done more, nor indeed that they themselves had clear notions of what to do next. News of the Nazi-Soviet pact had taken the public completely by surprise and left it utterly bewildered. Editors of sober newspapers and journals tried to whistle in the dark. Some thought the whole act a "grandstand play" which would prove short-lived. Stalin, it was reasoned, may have used the device of the pact merely to extract greater concessions from the British and French and might well end by concluding the alliance with the democracies. Journals of the Left were particularly reluctant to believe that the Socialist Fatherland could make as realistic and hardheaded an appraisal of national interests as any capitalist state. It seemed incredible that the Soviet Union should not take its stand with the West. Ironically, *The Nation,* as late as August 26, 1939, published a letter signed by four hundred prominent American liberals demonstrating the "basic points in which Soviet socialism differs from totalitarian fascism." *The New Republic,* indeed, went so far as to commiserate with Stalin as the victim of an Eastern Munich.[56]

One spark of humor, however, shone through the prevailing gloom. This was provided by the American Communists, who were caught completely off base by the shocking reversal of the Kremlin. In accord with the party directive, the Communists had long denounced Fascism and demanded full American participation in the effort to check Hitler's aggression. Earl Browder, who had declared in the early summer that there was about as much chance of an agreement between Hitler and Stalin "as of Earl Browder being elected President of the American Chamber of Commerce," was now obliged to find a new line. He began by denying the agreement; then he presented it as a clever move by which Stalin had tricked Hitler and supported the democracies; later he celebrated it as a positive aid to peace; and finally he hailed it as an exposure of the iniquitous plans of the capitalist democracies to foist the cost of an imperialist war on the Soviet Union. The *Daily Worker,* never noted for consistency, had no trouble in glorifying the Soviet achievement:

The Soviet Union has made one of the most valuable contributions to the peace of the United States and the world. . . . By compelling Germany to sign a non-aggression pact, the Soviet Union not only tremendously limited the direction of the Nazi war aims, but thereby bolstered the possibilities for the peace of the world.

But the intellectual organs of communism, like the *New Masses,* exhausted themselves in the struggle to find the proper line. On September 5 it wrote justifying the pact as:

. . . a burglary insurance policy which Soviet diplomacy has been forced to take out against the threat of another and more dangerous Munich. Burglary insurance

---

[56] A good review of the American press reaction may be found in Meno Lovenstein: *American Opinion of Soviet Russia* (Washington, 1941), 150 ff.

is no substitute for a vigorous drive to stamp out crime, but when so many con-
victed diplomatic criminals are on the police force, aiding and abetting crime,
it is an indispensable precaution.

Yet a week later the same unhappy journal was still appealing for sympathy and aid for a Poland, which was on the eve of invasion by the Soviet
armies: "A swift, decisive victory over German fascism," it declared, "is
America's best guarantee that it will keep out of war."[57]

The German attack on Poland came before a balanced evaluation of the
Nazi-Soviet pact could emerge among students of European affairs. The
diplomatic revolution and the acute crisis abroad served, if anything, to
strengthen American opinion along established lines. The Nazi-Soviet
partnership reinforced the hatred of totalitarianism by reviving all the
latent aversion to communism. At the same time it evoked strong sympathy
for the British and the French, who were exhorted to stand firm and not
retreat from their commitments to Poland. Here and there prominent advocates of all-out aid to the democracies pointed to the threat now presented,
even to the United States. Lewis Mumford, for example, urged that we back
Britain and France to the hilt: "The real danger lies in the fact that either
France or England may submit to the Fascists or be conquered by them.
Either of those events might put their combined Fleet, with terrific power
of attack, in the hands of the Fascist barbarians." But these were voices
crying in the wilderness. The more general reaction was "What else could
be expected from such gangsters?" The great mass of the American people
were isolationist and no doubt felt with Oswald Garrison Villard when
he wrote: "The lesson for us Americans is clearer than ever: to keep out of
this ungodly, revolting mess in Europe, in which one can have respect for
neither side in the power-politics struggle for the control of Europe."[58]

Yet thoughtful Americans, however sick at heart, could not ignore the fact
that one of the pillars of their faith was collapsing: the belief that there
would be no war in Europe in 1939. Most of them clung more desperately,
therefore, to the belief that they must at all costs avoid involvement. They
seemed less rather than more willing to face the question which was forever
plaguing them: whether an aggressor could be stopped by anything less than
force. But events, which, more than words, influence opinion, were conspir-
ing to prove the question an inescapable one. Once confronted with war,
that calamity could not longer be put aside as incredible. The chances were
that American sympathy for the democracies, greatly strengthened by the
agreement of the "gangsters," would force a gradual revision of attitude
and policy as soon as the duel between democracy and totalitarianism was
fairly joined.

---

[57] Browder interview in *New York Herald Tribune*, Augugst 24, 1939; *Daily Worker*,
August 25, September 7; *New Masses*, September 5, 12, 1939; Louis Fischer: *Men and
Politics* (New York, 1941), 605 ff.
[58] Both quoted in *New York Post*, August 22, 1939.

7. THE OUTBREAK OF WAR

Hardly more than a week intervened between the conclusion of the Nazi-Soviet pact and the opening of Hitler's *Blitzkrieg* against Poland. These few days were, of necessity, filled with hectic efforts on the part of British-French diplomacy to avert the calamity which we now know to have been inevitable. The main lines of the story have been fixed for some time and have recently been analyzed in some detail in the light of the German evidence contained in captured documents.[59] It would be quite superfluous, therefore, to go over familiar ground in connection with the present study. Nothing is needed but a brief consideration of certain aspects of the crisis which had significance for American policy and opinion.

One such aspect was the Far Eastern question, in which the United States was necessarily deeply interested. Occasion has been taken before to say that this phase of the world situation has been rather generally slighted and that for the most part attention has been devoted to the European scene. It must be remembered that in August, 1939, discussions of a military alliance between Germany, Italy and Japan were still under way, and that Soviet Russia was bound to view such a coalition as a major threat to its security. If the Japanese had had their way, the alliance would in fact have been directed primarily against the Soviet Union. Under the circumstances it is no wonder that Stalin and Molotov made so much of this issue in their discussions with the Germans. Indeed, it is not beyond the bounds of possibility that the unwillingness of the British to include the Far Eastern problem in their own negotiations with Moscow may have played a part in the failure of the peace front.

It stands to reason that the precipitate conclusion of the Nazi-Soviet pact was felt in Tokyo, more than in almost any other capital, as a major blow— a blow not only to Japanese interests but also to Japanese dignity and self-respect. It was only on the very eve of Ribbentrop's departure for Moscow that General Oshima, the Japanese Ambassador in Berlin and one of the most ardent advocates of the German-Japanese alliance, had been informed of the new turn of affairs. Though he at once expressed fears lest Russia, if relieved of anxiety in Europe, increase its support of China, Oshima was easily persuaded that Germany might be able to bring about an improvement in Soviet-Japanese relations and that, as a matter of fact, Japan's chief enemy, like Germany's was really not Russia, but Britain. But the reaction in Tokyo was utterly different. After a brief period of confused and generally hopeful speculation, the Cabinet on August 24, 1939, evidently with the approval of the Army, decided to drop all negotiations for an alliance, to lodge "an earnest protest" in Berlin, and for the time being to adopt a foreign policy of independence and neutrality. Oshima attempted, reluc-

---

[59] Namier: *Diplomatic Prelude,* Chap. VIII, contains the best single treatment now available.

tantly, to carry out instructions to submit a written protest to the German Foreign Office, only to find himself involved in unpleasant recriminations. The details of this extraordinary incident need not detain us. The important thing was that the Tokyo Government had been struck with consternation at being so unceremoniously deserted in favor of its traditional enemy. The Nazi-Soviet pact involved an intolerable loss of face. On August 28 the Hiranuma Cabinet resigned.[60]

The British, fearing at first lest the Nazi-Soviet pact be followed by a Soviet-Japanese agreement, and then realizing the discomfiture of the Tokyo Government, were eager to exploit the grievance. They proposed to try for a settlement with Japan in the hope of drawing that power to the side of the democracies. The French chimed in and both Governments suggested to the United States that it help, among other things, by mediating between Japan and China. But these ideas were at once discouraged by the State Department, where it was felt that any suggestion of interference in Tokyo would be resented. The chances were that the Japanese Government would of its own accord adopt a new policy more friendly to the democracies. Therefore, when Ambassador Horinouchi on August 26 informed Mr. Hull that his Government would probably initiate a new policy, the Secretary gave the news a friendly reception and assured his visitor of the American desire for good relations with Japan on a basis of "live and let live."[61]

It soon turned out that the State Department attitude was, in this instance, well founded. Had it attempted to use influence in Tokyo, the Japanese would probably have done no more than they did. On the other hand, the Chinese Government would have been seriously estranged. Chiang Kai-shek soon learned of the British project for mediation and was horrified, realizing no doubt that agreement of the democracies with Japan would involve settlement of the China Incident to Japan's satisfaction. The Generalissimo spoke in the strongest terms to the American Ambassador, urging that the United States warn Britain against appeasing Japan and suggesting instead that Washington attempt to associate Soviet Russia with a firmer anti-Japanese policy. The latter idea, though a novel one, hardly held much promise. The State Department therefore confined itself to reassurances: the British would scarcely do anything that would offend American opinion, and as for the United States, its traditional foreign policy was unchanged

---

[60] Memo of conversation between Weizsäcker and Oshima, August 22, 1939 (*Nazi-Soviet Relations,* 70-71); German Foreign Office memo, August 26, 1939 (*Department of State Bulletin,* June 16, 1943); Weizsäcker: *Erinnerungen,* 249-50; tels. from Dooman, August 23, 24, 26, 1939; Kido Diary, August 28, 1939 (*Tokyo War Crimes Documents,* No. 1632W); see also Byas, in *The New York Times,* August 26, 1939, and the official Japanese statements in *Bulletin of International News,* XVI (2), 1939, pp. 957, 968; Feis: *The Road to Pearl Harbor,* 32-35.

[61] Tel. from Kennedy, August 25; tel. from Dooman, August 25 and reply; memo by Hornbeck, August 26; tel. from Bullitt, August 29; memo of conversation between Hull and Horinouchi, August 26, 1939 (printed in *Peace and War,* 480-82).

and was well known to other powers. Therewith the period of hectic confusion in the Far East came to a temporary end. Thenceforth all depended
on the line to be followed by the new Japanese Cabinet.[62]

If there was danger of a British-French effort to appease Japan, there
was also a genuine possibility that when it came to the showdown, London
and Paris, deprived of the prospect of Soviet support, might relapse into
appeasement, this time at Poland's expense. The records of the French War
Council of August 23, 1939, for example, leave no doubt that Foreign
Minister Bonnet desired that France's obligations to Poland be reviewed
in the light of Russia's defection and Poland's alleged responsibility therefor.
His recommendation was that France, rather than embark on a life-and-
death conflict, should press Poland to accept a compromise on Danzig and
the Corridor. The contrary decision was taken, partly no doubt because of
the moral issue involved, but chiefly because General Gamelin, the Chief of
Staff, was convinced that Poland could hold out until spring, by which time
Britain could give effective support to France.[63]

With regard to the British there was likewise much apprehension lest
the Chamberlain Government attempt to solve its problem by reverting to
appeasement. The Poles and to some extent the French were filled with
anxiety on this score, while the American Government was positively dismayed when Ambassador Kennedy reported that the British wanted only
one thing of America; namely, that it bring pressure to bear on the Poles.
This seemed like a request that the United States assume responsibility for
another Munich, an idea which the Persident rejected out of hand.[64] Even
the Soviet leaders, when they concluded the pact with Hitler, seem to have
believed that the British would yield and accept another Munich, in which
case the agreement with Hitler would ensure the Kremlin of an invitation
to the feast. As late as August 31, 1939, Molotov declared in a public speech
that the Nazi-Soviet pact meant that "the danger of a military clash in Europe
is narrowed, if not eliminated." The Russians encouraged the Poles to hope
for Soviet material aid in the event of a German attack. On September 3,
1939, Molotov admitted to the Polish Ambassador that Germany had committed aggression, but expressed skepticism of British or French intervention.
Not until September 8 did the Soviet Government go back on its promise
of supplies to Poland, and then on the strange plea that when the promises

---

[62] Tel. from Johnson (Chungking), August 30, 1939, reporting a long discussion with
Chiang Kai-shek, Mme. Chiang, and the Foreign Minister; message from Chiang to the
Chinese Embassy in Washington and Hornbeck's covering memorandum thereto, September 1; letter of the President to Chiang Kai-shek, November 10, 1939, recalling assurances
given on September 5, 1939.

[63] On this high controversial matter see Gamelin: *Servir*, 23 ff.; Bonnet: *Fin d'une
Europe*, 300 ff.; Reynaud: *La France a sauvé l'Europe*, I, 589 ff.

[64] *Moffat Diary (MS.)*, August 24-27, 1939. On the Polish and French fears, a memo
of conversation between Welles and the Polish Ambassador, August 22, 1939, and a tel.
from Bullitt, August 26, 1939.

were given, the Kremlin could not know that the Western Powers would enter the war.[65]

Actually there is no reason to suppose that the British Cabinet, or Mr. Chamberlain himself, contemplated a change of policy as a result of the Nazi-Soviet pact. The Prime Minister, returning from a vacation, was utterly discouraged and felt that all his work had come to naught. The only possible way of avoiding a war seemed to him to be in Polish negotiations and concessions to Berlin. Mr. Chamberlain would doubtless have been delighted if the United States had encouraged Warsaw to proceed along this road, but he felt that matters would only be made worse if the British attempted to do so. Having no illusions about American intervention, he had lost all hope: "He says," reported Ambassador Kennedy, "the futility of it all is the thing that is frightful; after all they cannot save the Poles; they can merely carry on a war of revenge that will mean the destruction of the whole of Europe . . ."[66] In forlorn hope, therefore, the Prime Minister and the Cabinet devoted their efforts, after August 23, 1939, toward two ends: first, to induce the Germans and Poles to negotiate with a view to voluntary concessions on Poland's part; second, to leave no shred of doubt in Hitler's mind that in the event of a Nazi attack on Poland, the British would honor their engagements. No other program would have been tolerated by the British public, which, as the German Ambassador in London reported, was tired of being described as weak and degenerate, and which was determined to fight rather than again retreat. Furthermore, a policy of resistance was bound to enlist the moral support of the United States, while any relapse into appeasement would certainly have lost Britain all sympathy in America.[67]

For purposes of the present study it is quite unnecessary to retrace what Mr. Chamberlain described as the "final, long drawn out agonies that preceded the actual declaration of war." The main theme was the relationship of Britain and Germany. Hard on the announcement of Ribbentrop's coming visit to Moscow, Mr. Chamberlain wrote a personal letter to Hitler warning him against believing that a Nazi-Soviet pact would produce any alteration in British policy:

No greater mistake could be made. Whatever may prove to be the nature of the German-Soviet agreement, it cannot alter Great Britain's obligation to Poland,

[65] Molotov's address to the Supreme Soviet, August 31, 1939; tel. from Biddle (Warsaw), August 28; tels. from Steinhardt, August 28, September 6, 1939; *Polish White Book*, Nos. 170, 171, 172, 184; see also "Memoirs of Eduard Beneš" (*The Nation*, July 10, 1948).

[66] Tels. from Kennedy, August 23 and 24, 1939. The British Ambassador to Paris, returning from London, told Mr. Bullitt that both Chamberlain and Halifax were "absolutely determined to support Poland in case of war between Poland and Germany" (tel. from Bullitt, August 24, 1939).

[67] *Cf.* the Dirksen memo of August 18, 1939 (*Documents and Materials Relating to the Eve of the Second World War*, II, *Dirksen Papers*, 138); Kuhn, in *The New York Times*, August 20, 1939.

which His Majesty's Government have stated in public repeatedly and plainly, and which they are determined to fulfill.

Sir Nevile Henderson carried this message to the Fuehrer at Berchtesgaden on August 23, only to evoke a violent outburst of rage and invective against the Poles and against the British for backing them. Hitler took a high and mighty attitude, dispelling all doubt that he was determined to "settle" the Polish question in any case and admonishing the British that if there were to be war between Britain and Germany, the British and not the Germans would be the losers. Nonetheless, he gave Henderson a well-reasoned written reply and suggested that if once the Polish issue were solved he would be glad to make a deal with Britain, including a guarantee of the British Empire. This was to be his approach to the London Cabinet throughout the ensuing days.[68]

British statesmen were tempted to think that the Fuehrer might genuinely wish for an agreement, but they were utterly unwilling to leave him a free hand against Poland as a preliminary. In order to underline their position, they hastily concluded the treaty of mutual assistance with Poland and published the essentials of the text on August 25, 1939. This was undoubtedly a severe blow to Hitler, who promptly countermanded orders to attack Poland on the morning of August 26. It may be that a letter from Mussolini on the same day, announcing that Italy would not be able to take part in a war at that time, also contributed to Hitler's decision, but it is likely that of the two developments the reaffirmation of the British obligation to Poland was the more important.[69]

From August 25 onward Hitler made a real and systematic effort to hold off British and French intervention. He appealed directly to Premier Daladier and ultimately pretended to Sir Nevile Henderson that he would receive a Polish emissary empowered to negotiate a settlement. At the same time Goering commissioned a Swedish businessman, Birger Dahlerus, to flit to and from London in a desperate effort to persuade the British to accept another Munich.[70] The sole result of these efforts was to lead British and French statesmen to think that the Fuehrer was drawing back. It was conjectured that the Nazi-Soviet pact might have aroused opposition even in Nazi circles, and that Hitler might have been impressed by the Italian

---

[68] *British Blue Book,* Nos. 57, 58; *German Documents on the Outbreak of the War,* Nos. 453, 454, 455; tel. from Kennedy, August 25, 1939.

[69] *Ciano Diaries,* entries for August 14-27, 1939; *Nazi Conspiracy and Aggression,* IV, 1822-PS, 1823-PS; V, 2817-PS, 2834-PS; Wiskemann: *The Rome-Berlin Axis,* 166 ff., and especially the careful analysis in Namier: *Diplomatic Prelude,* 328-31. The secret protocol of the British-Polish agreement was not published until 1945 (Cmd. 6616). In effect it merely specified that the term "European Power" meant Germany. The agreement obligated Britain to aid Poland in the event of an attack on Danzig.

[70] Birger Dahlerus: *The Last Attempt* (London, n.d.); Kordt: *Wahn und Wirklichkeit,* 197 ff.; Feiling: *Life of Neville Chamberlain,* 416-17.

stand as well as by the firmness of the Western Governments. As late as August 30 Ambassador Kennedy could report that the British Cabinet felt that it had "Hitler on the run," and that Lord Halifax thought it necessary to tone down a note to Berlin for fear of provoking Hitler and making the Poles recalcitrant. Premier Daladier, too, was convinced that the Fuehrer was now bluffing, and that he would not dare throw down the gauntlet to the British and French.[71]

Throughout these tense days the London Government kept Washington fully informed of every move and submitted to the State Department copies of all important diplomatic papers. For a moment American officials, like the British, thought the Nazis might retreat.[72] From our present knowledge of German records it is clear that these hopes were utterly vain. Hitler was indeed anxious to shake the opposition of the democracies, but he was absolutely determined on the conquest of Poland and had fixed September 1 as the new date for attack. He obviously realized that there was a possibility that Britain and France would intervene, but he found it hard to believe that they would actually do so "just for Poland," and seems to have thought that in any case they would prefer, after the liquidation of Poland, to recognize the accomplished fact and accept a settlement rather than face a prolonged war. Anyway, it was a chance that he had to take, inasmuch as he could wait no longer if military operations were to be undertaken that autumn. When, on the evening of August 30, Ribbentrop rattled off to Henderson in German the so-called sixteen-point program for German-Polish discussions, and at the same time indicated that it was already too late to embark upon them, the die had clearly been cast. On the morning of September 1 the Nazi divisions opened the assault on Poland.[73]

Even after the beginning of the German invasion of Poland, hopes that a general war might be avoided were kept alive. The British Government was eager to declare war as quickly as possible, but the French Cabinet, partly for parliamentary and partly for military reasons, desired to delay for a few days. While this important matter was being debated between London and Paris, an Italian proposal for a European conference further complicated the situation. In view of the known unpreparedness of the Italians for war, efforts had been made by London as well as by Washington to induce Mussolini to repeat the role he had played at the time of Munich. Lord Halifax had suggested the idea of a conference to Rome as early as August 21, and Count Ciano had been working on a plan by which Danzig

---

[71] Tels. from Kennedy, August 27, 30, 1939; tel. from Bullitt, August 31, 1939.

[72] *Berle Diaries (MS.)*, August 28, 1939.

[73] Tel. from Kirk (Berlin), August 31, giving Henderson's account of his midnight conference with Ribbentrop; tel. from Kennedy, August 31, on last-minute efforts to induce the Poles to negotiate; tel. from Biddle (Warsaw), August 31, 1939, on the suspicious and stiff-necked attitude of the Poles; *Fuehrer Conferences, 1939* (U.S. Navy Department, 1947), 1, on Hitler's calculations.

was to be turned over to the Reich as a preliminary condition for a "great peace conference." This idea was clearly unacceptable and for a time the conference proposal remained in abeyance while attention centered on the hoped-for German-Polish negotiations.

Finally, as a forlorn hope, Mussolini proposed to Britain and France on August 31 that a conference meet on September 5 "for the purpose of reviewing those clauses of the Treaty of Versailles which disturb European life." The French Foreign Minister, Bonnet, espoused and supported the idea with enthusiasm, since he firmly believed that it was up to the Poles to pay the price of European peace. But M. Daladier, backed by Reynaud, Mandel, Campinchi and others objected vigorously, on the plea that Hitler was bluffing and that the whole plan was nothing more than a device to extricate him from the impossible position into which he had maneuvered himself. More important, however, was the reaction of London. The British from the outset refused to negotiate under pressure. On August 31 they insisted that the Germans first demobilize. After the invasion of Poland they made the withdrawal of Nazi forces a condition for acceptance of the conference proposal.[74]

Though he disliked interference with his plans, Hitler evidently saw in the Italian proposal a possible means of deterring the democracies from military action. He received the plan with ostensible cordiality, but did nothing to follow it up. Only when the British-French declarations of war on September 3, 1939, had destroyed whatever value the scheme might have had, did the Fuehrer send a reply to Rome. In this he thanked his colleague for the efforts he had made and remarked that he himself might have accepted the conference plan had he a guarantee that it would be successful! But, he continued, now that the German forces had advanced so far into Poland, it seemed best to push on while the Germans still had a crushing superiority.[75]

The British and French ultimatums to Berlin on September 3, 1939, brought the tragic story of the August crisis to an end. Hitler's policy during those critical days is generally regarded as diabolically clever, and his conclusion of the pact with Stalin as a masterpiece of Machiavellian practice. But at bottom the Fuehrer made a terrible miscalculation and one that was ultimately to prove fatal: throughout he had gambled on the abstention of the British and French, believing that they were unprepared for war, that

[74] Tels. from Johnson (London), August 21, and from Bullitt, August 23, 31, 1939; *Ciano Diaries*, entries for August 23, 28-31, 1939; Ciano: *L'Italia di Fronte al Conflitto* (Milan, 1940), where all the documents are assembled. On the French side see Bonnet: *Fin d'une Europe*, Chap. XIX; Reynaud: *La France a sauvé l'Europe*, I, 597 ff.; Wiskemann: *The Rome-Berlin Axis*, 171 ff.; Georges Suarez and Guy Laborde: *L'Agonie de la paix* (Paris, 1942), 211 ff., 219 ff.; Pierre Lazareff: *De Munich à Vichy* (New York, 1944), 153 ff.

[75] *Ciano Diaries*, entries for September 1-3, 1939; *Nazi Conspiracy and Aggression*, IV, 1831-PS; Kordt: *Wahn und Wirklichkeit*, 211.

they would recognize their inability to aid Poland, and that they would not be rash enough to stake their national existence on support of a distant ally. His estimate was entirely mistaken and he was much shaken by realization of his error. When the British ultimatum was submitted to him, he lapsed into deep thought and then turned to Ribbentrop, who had done so much to mislead him: "Well, what now?" he queried. Ribbentrop had no answer, but Goering, more realistic and extrovert than his master, sensed the full force of the blow and threw up his hands with the exclamation: "Heaven help us, if we lose this war."

CHAPTER VI

The United States and the War

1. PRELIMINARY MOVES

In the small hours of Friday morning, September 1, 1939, the President was awakened by a telephone call from Ambassador Bullitt in Paris, informing him that the German armies had just crossed the frontiers of Poland. A few hours later Americans everywhere were listening to the sobering news over their radios, or reading it in their morning newspapers. Apart from a few Communists, and even fewer Nazi sympathizers, the nation was united as rarely before when confronted by shattering events abroad. Sympathy and admiration for Poland were universal. Nearly everyone held Adolf Hitler responsible for the catastrophe which had now occurred. Hope was therefore general that Britain and France would fulfill their obligations to the Poles, and that together the Allies would defeat the Germans, the more so since the public at large could not wholly suppress the nagging suspicion that any other outcome might conceivably force the United States itself into eventual participation.[1] As to the nation itself entering the conflict at once, American opinion was extraordinarily united. Everything possible, it was agreed, should be done to keep the nation out of war. A poll taken during the first weeks of hostilities confirmed the vitality of this conviction, although, significantly, 44 percent of those consulted already thought American armies should be sent to European battlefields if it appeared that Britain and France were in danger of being defeated. Our national sympathies, then, were crystal clear. We were not really blind to the grave implications for ourselves of the German invasion of Poland; nevertheless, we steadfastly shrank from facing the issues. For the time being, at least, Americans remained determined to steer clear of foreign quarrels, which they had been

[1] The most recent public opinion polls (late August) had indicated that 76 percent of those queried professed to believe that the United States was likely to be drawn into a great war. Sixty-one percent favored an economic boycott of dictators who resorted to arms.

thoroughly conditioned to suspect and condemn ever since the end of the last war.[2]

Despite the strong inference of a friendly biographer that Mr. Roosevelt became convinced when the Hitler-Stalin pact was signed that this nation would be obliged eventually to enter the war, the present authors doubt whether, in the light of so much contrary evidence, the inference can be accepted as more than a natural but passing expression of anxiety.[3] In general they believe that the President shared the attitudes prevalent in the nation, though he and his advisers were naturally better informed than the public at large. Moreover, Mr. Roosevelt was certainly more keenly aware than most of his fellow countrymen of this nation's stake in the conflict which now began to engulf Europe. His aversion to Hitler and his associates was second to none. His hopes for a victory of the democracies were as lively, if by no means as sure, as those of most Americans. Such sentiments were significantly illustrated by the moves the President made just before, as well as just after, the receipt of Ambassador Bullitt's announcement. In order to prevent the great German liner *Bremen* from eluding her British pursuers in her dash for home and safety, he gave instructions that she was to be held at her New York dock on one pretext or another for a minimum of forty-eight hours.[4] Similarly he gave much thought during the final days of August to ways and means by which even after the impending invocation of the Neutrality Act it might still be possible to transfer certain types of war supplies to the friendly nations without violating the letter of the law.[5] For the rest, the President, according to Assistant Secretary Berle, wanted to postpone issuing the required neutrality proclamation as long as possible, and remarked as early as August 26 that "now is the time to shoot the gun towards getting our neutrality laws changed."[6]

The first shot was actually fired by Assistant Secretary of War Louis Johnson in Boston on August 28, with a speech which, though approved by the President, was more notable for forcefulness than for tact.

[2] The above statement scarcely requires specific documentation, but see the contemporary review in D. F. Fleming: "America Faces the Issue" (*Events*, October 1939, 264-70), and the digests of opinion in the *New York Post*, September 4, and in *The New York Times*, September 8, 10, 1939. For subsequent and more penetrating appraisals of public sentiment see John Crosby Brown: "American Isolation: Propaganda Pro and Con" (*Foreign Affairs*, October 1939), and Raoul de Roussy de Sales: "America Looks at the War" (*Atlantic Monthly*, February 1940).

[3] Alden Hatch: *Franklin D. Roosevelt* (London, 1947), Foreword and pp. 250 ff. Even Professor Beard in his *President Roosevelt and the Coming of the War* (New Haven, 1948), 414 f., admits that Mr. Hatch's statement will be "discounted by critics" unless "supported by authentic documents." We have been unable to find either supporting documents or supporting opinions among those close to the President at this stage.

[4] *Morgenthau Diaries (MS.)*, Vol. 206 (August 28, 1939). The flustered port officials managed to carry out orders even though this involved holding up the *Normandie* to save appearances.

[5] Memo describing the Cabinet meeting of August 25, 1939 (*Morgenthau Diaries MS.*, Vol. 206).

[6] *Berle Diaries (MS.)*, August 26, 1939; *Moffat Diary (MS.)*, September 1, 2, 3, 5, 1939.

If there is much, then, to establish the fact that the President emphatically shared the national desire to assist Britain and France by every safe expedient, there is equally valid evidence that he recoiled from the prospect of war, was determined to spare no effort to keep this nation out of it, and devoutly hoped that by one means or another he would succeed. Thus, at the Cabinet meeting held on the afternoon of September 1, Mr. Roosevelt, in a remarkably somber mood, coupled his intention of summoning a special session of Congress to repeal the arms embargo with expressions of confidence that America would keep out of the war. He recalled the similarity between the current crisis and the hectic hours when the United States entered the First World War. His great concern with measures to prevent economic dislocation and high prices, as well as proposals for discouraging profiteers, "those jackals of war," suggest not merely how closely he shared popular hopes of continued peace, but even how far he was himself the victim of popular prejudices against the "munitions makers."[7]

It would be hazardous indeed to accept the views of any member of the President's official family as an expression of Mr. Roosevelt's own feelings. Yet Assistant Secretary Berle's thoughts after leaving the last meeting of the "death watch over Europe" at Mr. Hull's office on September 3 were probably influenced as well as shared by many other Administration officials.

In this war [wrote Mr. Berle], we cannot, so far as I can see, count on a military victory of Britain, France and Poland. Should they be on the eve of defeat, the square question would be presented to us whether to enter the war using them as our outlying defense posts; or whether to let them go, treble our navy, and meet the ultimate issue between us and a Russo-German Europe bent on dominating the world, somewhere in the Middle Atlantic. My mind is rather running on the latter. This is brutal, and depends on a consideration of national interest. Matters may not get to this point. The Russian-German domination would be huge, impressive, and in appearance terribly powerful. Yet it reverses the processes of men's minds in a way which I do not believe can be permanent. Winning or losing, that combination must eventually break up. Even if it is victorious, we should be in a position to hold a powerful and almost impregnable line for a few years; and those years ought to see this tremendous combination tear itself to pieces internally; after which Europe will tend to re-emerge. But they will be ghastly years.[8]

[7] Hull: *Memoirs*, I, 674 f. We have also used Secretary of the Navy Edison's recollections of the President's remarks at this meeting (*F.D.R.: His Personal Letters, 1928-1945*, II, 915-17), and a memo of Carlton Savage describing the meeting of the State Department on the morning of September 1, 1939, referred to by Mr. Hull. Alsop and Kintner in their *Postscript* to the *American White Paper* (New York, 1940), p. 82a, assert that the alternatives which governed the Administration's choices of policy at the outbreak of the war did not include the possibility of a complete German victory.

[8] *Berle Diaries (MS.)*, September 3, 1939. Berle's pessimism was shared by Pierrepont Moffat, to whom the issues involved appeared "so terrible, the outlook so cloudy, the probability of ultimate Bolshevism so great, and the chances of a better peace next time . . . so remote that if one stopped to think one would give way to gloom" (*Moffat Diary, MS.*, September 1, 1939).

In any event, when, on the evening of the same day, a few hours after the British and French had declared war on Germany, the President delivered his fireside chat, he confided to the American people what we believe were his private sentiments. It was, to be sure, a circumspect utterance, wholly devoid of accusation and recrimination. It contained a solemn warning as well as a cautious assurance:

It is easy for you and me, to shrug our shoulders and to say that conflicts taking place thousands of miles from the whole American Hemisphere do not seriously affect the Americas—and that all the United States has to do is to ignore them and go about its own business. Passionately though we may desire detachment, we are forced to realize that every word that comes through the air, every ship that sails the sea, every battle that is fought, does affect the American future.

Let no man or woman thoughtlessly or falsely talk of America sending its armies to European fields . . .

This nation will remain a neutral nation, but I cannot ask that every American remain neutral in thought as well. Even a neutral has a right to take account of facts. Even a neutral cannot be asked to close his mind or his conscience.

I have said not once, but many times, that I have seen war and that I hate war. I say that again and again.

I hope the United States will keep out of this war. I believe that it will. And I give you assurance and reassurance that every effort of your Government will be directed toward that end.

As long as it remains within my power to prevent, there will be no blackout of peace in the United States.[9]

The actual course of hostilities was by no means precisely what had been anticipated. For years the world had lived in dread that a new war would mean the immediate bombardment of the great cities of Western Europe from the air, with the resulting massacre of thousands of civilians. Under this threat the British and French Governments had at once begun large-scale evacuations from London and Paris, and almost the first action of the President (September 1) was to appeal to all the belligerents to renounce air attacks on the civilian population or upon unfortified cities, with the understanding that both sides would scrupulously observe the same rule. Favorable replies were received almost immediately from the Germans as well as from the British and French. Nonetheless, in less than a week's time reports began to come in describing the *Luftwaffe's* savage attacks on Polish towns, and before long the Poles were clamoring to the Western Powers for reprisal attacks upon Germany. The British in particular rejected these demands on the plea that American opinion would be estranged. A not less cogent reason, perhaps, was Britain's recognition of German air superiority and relief that London had thus far been spared. Nevertheless, the President's appeal may have had some slight deterrent force even at the begin-

[9] Text in *Public Papers and Addresses*, VIII (1939), 460-64. For the drafting see Hull: *Memoirs*, I, 676.

ning, and later on it was to provide the basis for imposing moral embargoes on powers like Russia which ignored it.[10]

The outbreak of war brought out at once a series of Presidential proclamations, which had been prepared well in advance. On September 5, Mr. Roosevelt proclaimed the traditional neutrality of the United States "pursuant to general international law," as well as the ban on the export of arms, ammunition, and implements of war as specifically required by the neutrality legislation of 1937. He followed this up on September 8 with a proclamation of the existence of a state of limited national emergency and a number of routine measures.[11] The effect, of course, was to embargo automatically the export of all the airplanes and other instruments of war on order for Great Britain and France, though they and all other powers remained free to purchase in the United States a great variety of raw and semi-finished products. With the Allies in practical control of the Atlantic, and the Administration intent on avoiding friction with them over their blockade of Germany, it was only the existing neutrality legislation that threatened to deprive them of these advantages, and to frustrate the manifest desire of the American people to aid them against Hitler.[12] In short, the country was now face to face with precisely the fantastic situation Mr. Roosevelt had foreseen and tried to avoid in the preceding months. Obviously the issue became critical the moment war was declared. Thenceforth repeal of the arms embargo became, of necessity, one of the President's first objectives. Before turning to his efforts to achieve it, however, we must examine yet another basic ambition of the Administration, namely, to ensure the solidarity and to safeguard the defenses of the Western Hemisphere. Our security, the President had told the people in his address of September 3:

. . . is and will be bound up with the safety of the Western Hemisphere and the seas adjacent thereto. We seek to keep war from our own firesides by keeping war from coming to the Americas. . . . It is serious enough and tragic enough to every American family in every state in the Union to live in a world that is torn by wars on other continents. Those wars today affect every American home. It is our national duty to use every effort to keep them out of the Americas.

A fortnight later, when the German liquidation of Poland was completed by the Soviets, and German-Russian domination was "unchallenged from the Rhine to the Pacific," hemisphere solidarity had attained the highest priority in the minds of influential American officials. "It seems to me," wrote

[10] The President's appeal and the replies to it are printed in *Documents on American Foreign Relations*, II, 352. See also Hull: *Memoirs*, I, 677 f. We have used, in addition, telegrams from Bullitt, September 6, 9; and from Kennedy, September 12, 1939; *Moffat Diary (MS.)*, September 9, 1939.

[11] The texts are printed in *Public Papers and Addresses*, VIII (1939), 464-79, 488 f.

[12] Hull: *Memoirs*, I, 679 f.

Assistant Secretary of State Berle to the President, "that in any event we shall have to intensify our South American policy to the limit."[13]

2. THE PANAMA CONFERENCE

In an earlier context some attention was given to the progress of the Good Neighbor Policy and to the achievements of the Buenos Aires and Lima Conferences of 1936 and 1938 respectively. At the former it had been agreed that "every act susceptible of disturbing the peace of America affects each and every one of them [American Republics] and justifies the initiation of the procedural consultation provided for in the Convention for the Maintenance, Preservation and Re-establishment of Peace." The Declaration of Lima, in turn, had provided for implementation of this consultative system by specifying that whenever the peace of the hemisphere was threatened, the foreign ministers of the twenty-one Republics should meet and deliberate on measures to be taken. Thus, when the conflict broke in Europe, the principle of solidarity was already recognized and the means of achieving it already available.

Mr. Roosevelt, firmly convinced of the inevitability of serious repercussions of the war in Europe on all other countries, was fully persuaded that the security of the United States was closely bound up with the security and welfare of the entire hemisphere. He was also keenly aware of the peculiar vulnerability of many Latin American nations, whose well-being depended in large measure on trade with Europe. War in the Old World was bound to create profound economic dislocations in the New, and there was an immediate and real danger that the Axis powers would exploit the distress for their own purposes. As pointed out before, there was much concern in Washington, notably in military circles, over the constant flow of Axis propaganda to Latin America, over the threat of Axis economic pressure, and especially over the prospect of political overturns engineered by hostile agents. Some eighty German ships lay in Latin American ports and might well be used to service Axis submarines or even to supply shock troops for the seizure of bases along remote stretches of the coast. In view of the widespread German intrigues in Latin America during the First World War it was only reasonable to expect even greater subversive activity during the new conflict.[14]

Under the circumstances the President and his advisers had long since decided to call a conference of American Foreign Ministers the moment war broke out. The aim of the meeting would be to establish united action for the preservation of neutrality; to take such measures as might be neces-

---

[13] Memo of Berle to the President, September 18, 1939 (*Roosevelt Papers:* Secretary's File, Box 42).

[14] *Minutes of the Liaison Committee,* September 13; warning of the British Government to Latin American Governments, September 14 (*The New York Times,* September 14); memo of Division of American Republics (Duggan), September 21, 1939.

sary and feasible for keeping the hemisphere, excepting for Canada, free of conflict; and to provide for economic stability and coöperation. The matter was taken in hand immediately after Britain and France declared war on September 3, on which date Argentina, Brazil, Chile, Colombia, Cuba, Mexico, Panama and Peru were asked to join in an invitation to the other Governments to meet in conference at Panama on September 21. Agreement was reached at once, even the Buenos Aires Government making only a feeble effort to have Uruguay included among the inviting Governments before accepting the proposal in good faith. Invitations were sent out by the Panamanian Government on September 5 and a suggested agenda was submitted by the United States Government the next day. This found ready acceptance and was adopted by the Governing Board of the Pan American Union on September 12. On September 23 the conference formally opened at Panama City.[15]

The President designated Under Secretary of State Welles to represent the United States at the conference. Prior to Welles's departure the vital issues were discussed at considerable length and drafts of the proposed measures were elaborated.[16] These, particularly as they bore on military and economic matters, deserve some analysis.

During the First World War several of the Latin American Governments had put forward suggestions for a neutral zone around the American coasts capable of being extended far out into the Atlantic and Pacific. Nothing had come of these proposals, but in the interval between the wars the United States Government had been much concerned over the inadequacy for defense purposes of the three-mile limit recognized by international law. The issue had arisen in connection with rumrunning in the days of the prohibition law, and more recently with respect to Japanese fishing activities off the Pacific coast. The President had toyed with the idea of declaring coastal waters as far out as the edge of the continental shelf under American jurisdiction. He had likewise asked the State Department to search out precedents which might justify action to prevent foreign hostilities in the vicinity of the Americas, or which might tend to show that the object of the Monroe Doctrine had actually been to keep war away from this hemisphere. An example of such a precedent might be the United States' action against France in the undeclared war of 1798-1800, when, according to the President, our newly created Navy had put an end to the destruction of commerce in the Caribbean.[17] It is even probable that the

---

[15] Hull: *Memoirs*, I, 688-9, and Alsop and Kintner: *American White Paper*, 68 ff., for the preliminaries, supplemented by tels. to the inviting governments, September 3, 4, and tel. and despatch from Armour (Buenos Aires) September 5; proposed agenda September 6, 1939.

[16] *Berle Diaries (MS)*, August 30, 1939.

[17] President's press conference, March 7, 1939 (*Public Papers and Addresses*, VIII (1939), 154-57; conversation of the authors with Mr. Sumner Welles, May 27, 1947; *Berle Diaries (MS.)*, August 26, 1939.

President was well aware of the advantages which the establishment of such a zone might confer on the British, since in the course of the royal visit of June, 1939, there was some informal discussion of Atlantic patrols and bases.[18]

By the end of August Mr. Roosevelt's ideas on the subject had begun to crystallize. What he had in mind, he explained to Mr. Berle and other State Department officials, was action to prevent an attack on any European colony in the New World, all the way from Canada to Guiana. He would patrol that line and warn the belligerents to keep their warships on the further side of the Atlantic. Since the boundary of the New World, he argued, was no longer the three-mile limit, obviously it had to be somewhere in the middle of the Atlantic. Otherwise airplanes might upset the American peace. He would therefore propose that each side agree to keep outside that line. Britain and France, he believed, would undoubtedly agree; the Germans and Italians would not. "He would then direct the Navy to make sure that no vessel came on this side of the Atlantic."[19]

The upshot was the President's decision, when war broke out, to propose a neutrality zone at the forthcoming Panama Conference. In consultation with Secretary of the Navy Edison and Mr. Welles, the President elaborated plans for patrolling the western Atlantic over an area extending several hundred miles from American shores. Secretary Hull was highly skeptical of the proposal from the outset, insisting that it was without precedent in international law and would meet with valid objections from the belligerents. Mr. Roosevelt, however, persisted in an idea which was his own brain child, and when Mr. Welles left for Panama he carried with him the draft of the document presently to be known as the Declaration of Panama.[20]

As for the economic problem, the President and his advisers had vivid recollections of the desperate situation of Latin American countries during the First World War. They realized that all hope of political solidarity would be illusory unless supported by adequate financial and trade arrangements. In his address to the Board of Governors of the Pan American Union in April, 1939, the President had anticipated this aspect of the problem and had promised that the United States would "give economic support, so that no American nation need surrender any fraction of its sovereign freedom to maintain its economic welfare." In the six months following this speech remarkable progress was recorded in developing measures designed to redeem the President's promise. By early October, indeed, the State Department was confident that it had finally succeeded in drafting for Congressional approval a formal program of economic coöperation covering the

---

[18] *Roosevelt Papers:* Secretary's File, Box 82.

[19] *Berle Diaries (MS.),* August 26, 1939.

[20] Hull: *Memoirs,* I, 690; *American White Paper,* 61 ff.; memo of Mr. Berle to Secretary Hull, September 2; *Berle Diaries (MS.),* September 6, 30, 1939; tel. from Welles to Hull, September 19, and from Hull to Welles, September 21, 1939.

extension of financial assistance, the conclusion of trade agreements, the loan of civilian experts, and plans for increasing the United States market for the exports of the other American Republics.[21] Reciprocal trade agreements had already been concluded with a number of Latin American states, and on August 23, 1939, Under Secretary Welles had announced that negotiations for such an agreement would be initiated with Argentina. Conclusion of such an agreement, he declared, would be "one of the most important accomplishments of this Administration in the field of international relations." There had been no revision of trade arrangements between the two countries since 1855, and the competition of their products had contributed more than a little to the traditional lack of understanding between them. There can be no doubt that the opening of trade negotiations at so critical a moment made a favorable impression in Buenos Aires and helped assure the coöperation of the Argentine Government at the Panama Conference.[22]

The new program of economic aid to Latin America was complicated by a number of difficult factors. Several of the Latin American countries were still in default on public and private debts and in some cases, notably that of Mexico, disputes were going on over compensation for confiscated American properties. Furthermore, the only suitable agency for government lending by the United States was the Export-Import Bank. It had already made some small loans, but was rigorously limited as to funds. The President and Mr. Welles felt strongly that in an emergency like the existing one, technicalities should be put aside. They considered setting up a stabilization fund of some two hundred millions and were prepared to make modest commitments to Latin American countries where it seemed essential. Congress could be approached later for the required funds. Secretary of the Treasury Morgenthau at once raised objections. While agreeing completely with the President's long-range objectives, he did not share the State Department's view that arrangements should now be made on a bilateral basis and advantage taken of the opportunity to induce individual governments to settle their past obligations. In view of the Treasury attitude, and the possibility of unfavorable reactions in Congress, Mr. Welles was obliged to confine his assurances at Panama to very general statements. In his address to the conference he said:

I am authorized to state that the United States Government wishes to coöperate with all other American Republics in such efforts of each to develop the resources

[21] Tel. to Welles at Panama, September 29; memo of the Division of American Republics (Collado): "A Program for Economic Coöperation with the Other American Republics," October 9, 1939. This lengthy document is vital to the understanding of the State Department's early planning for economic coöperation under the impetus of the Panama Conference.

[22] Tel. from Armour (Buenos Aires), August 26, 1939; for a succinct treatment of the general problem, see C. H. Haring: *Argentina and the United States* (Boston, World Peace Foundation, 1941).

of its country along sound economic and non-competitive lines. When desired it will assist in making credit available to them through the services and facilities of its privately-owned banking system as well as its Government-owned agencies when the latter have funds available for such purposes.[23]

The Panama Conference completed its work in eight days, concluding its deliberations on October 3, 1939. Despite the presence of the German Minister to Central America and a number of German newspapermen, all of whom spread the word that the meeting was nothing but the latest effort of the United States to make the whole hemisphere its protectorate, the conference was, from the outset, marked by unusual cordiality. Mr. Welles has recorded the extraordinary feeling of inter-American unity and the complete absence of the customary animosity and bickering:

There was not the slightest divergence of views as to the moral issues involved in the European contest; nor was there other than a deepseated feeling that the triumph of the Axis powers would result in a curtailment of the liberties of the American peoples and inevitable peril to the integrity of the hemisphere.

As an American correspondent pointed out, the truly epoch-making feature of the meeting was that the Latin American nations were seeking, rather than resisting, closer relations with the United States. Even the Argentine delegation made no difficulties, giving full support to the program of common action.[24]

The Panama Conference agreed unanimously on sixteen resolutions or declarations, none of which had the force of law, but all of which reflected a common view and in actual practice resulted in continuing consultation and uniformity of action.[25] One group of resolutions embodied a "General Declaration of Continental Neutrality," affirming the "unanimous intention" of the American Republics "not to become involved in the European conflict," and restated the standards of conduct to be followed. Since these were in general consonance with the recognized rules of international law, they need not be analyzed in detail. Several, however, were of particular interest

[23] *Report of the Delegate of the United States of America to the Meeting of the Foreign Ministers of the American Republics* (Washington, 1940), Appendix IV, p. 36; *Morgenthau Diaries (MS.)*, Vol. 209, September 6; Vol. 210, September 12; Vol. 211, September 13; and an excellent analytical memo to Mr. Morgenthau from Joseph P. Cotton, Jr., October 10, 1939 (*Morgenthau Diaries MS.*, Vol 216); tel. to Welles at Panama. September 29; *Berle Diaries (MS.)*, September 30, 1939; and memo of the Division of American Republics (Collado), October 9, 1939.

[24] *Report of the Delegate of the United States of America to the Meeting of the Foreign Ministers of the American Republics*, 18-19; Sumner Welles: *The Time for Decision*, 211; *Christian Science Monitor*, September 23; *The New York Times*, September 24, 1939; H. Banta Murkland: "Pan American Peace Drive" (*Events*, November 1939, 388-92). Secretary Hull formally thanked the Argentine Government for its coöperation (tel. from Welles at Panama, October 3, and tel. to Armour, October 5, 1939).

[25] Texts in the *Report of the Delegate of the United States of America to the Meeting of the Foreign Ministers of the American Republics*, 49 ff., and excerpt in *Documents on American Foreign Relations*, II, 100 ff.

and new importance. It was agreed, for example, that the transfer of merchant ships from one American flag to another should not be regarded as unlawful. Further, it was decided that merchant ships, if not armed with more than four six-inch guns on the stern, should not be considered warships. The American Governments were left free to exclude belligerent submarines from the waters adjacent to their territories or to admit them under whatever regulations each government might prescribe. Finally, the conference set up an Inter-American Neutrality Committee, composed of seven experts in international law, which was, for the duration of the war, to make continuing recommendations for uniform action in defense of neutral rights. With commendable foresight the conference added Resolution XVI, which stated:

> That in case any geographic region of America subject to the jurisdiction of any non-American state should be obliged to change its sovereignty and there should result therefrom a danger to the security of the American Continent, a consultative meeting such as the one now being held will be convoked with the urgency that the case may require.

In the economic field, the importance of which was keenly and generally felt, no less than twenty-seven projects were submitted to the conference. But the complexity of the issues were such that immediate solutions were impossible.[26] It was therefore decided to set up, before November 15, 1939, an Inter-American Financial and Economic Advisory Committee, on which each of the American Governments would be represented, to study and make recommendations concerning monetary relationships, foreign exchange management and particularly trade dislocations. The general objective was to liberalize trade regulations and develop a more balanced economic relationship, as well as to plan for close financial coöperation.

Most novel and spectacular of the resolutions of the Panama Conference was Number XIV, the Declaration of Panama, which established a neutrality zone around the entire hemisphere, with the exception of Canada. This Declaration was adopted practically in the version suggested by the United States Government, and the proposal met with general acceptance from the outset. In his introductory address to the delegates Mr. Welles had stated:

> I believe that the time has come when the twenty-one American Republics must state, and state clearly and in no uncertain terms, to all of the belligerents, both as a right of self-protection, and as a right inherent in their position as peaceful and independent powers, constituting an entire continent remote from the causes of the hostilities which have broken out, that they cannot agree that their security, their nationals, or their legitimate commercial rights and interests should be jeopardized by belligerent activities in close proximity to the shores of

[26] Tels. from Welles, September 26, 27, 30; tel. to Welles, September 26, 29, 1939.

the New World. This assertion of principle, I believe, must be regarded as constituting a declaration of the inalienable right of the American Republics to protect themselves, so far as conditions in this modern world make it possible, from the dangers and the repercussions of a war which has broken out thousands of miles from their shores, and in which they are not involved.

In keeping with this viewpoint, the preamble of Resolution XIV declared:

. . . there can be no justification for the interests of the belligerents to prevail over the rights of neutrals causing disturbances and suffering to nations which by their neutrality in the conflict and their distance from the scene of events, should not be burdened with its fatal and painful consequences.

The resolution itself read:

As a measure of continental self-protection, the American Republics, so long as they maintain their neutrality, are of inherent right entitled to have those waters adjacent to the American Continent, which they regard as of primary concern and direct utility in their relations, free from the commission of any hostile act by any non-American belligerent nation, whether such hostile act be attempted or made from land, sea, or air.

Thereupon a zone averaging three hundred miles in breadth was marked out around North and South America, excluding Canada and "the undisputed colonies and possessions of European countries." It was further provided that the American Republics should endeavor, through joint representation to the belligerents, to secure compliance with the declaration, and that the governments, whenever they deemed necessary, should consult to determine upon measures which they might take collectively or individually in order to ensure observance of the declaration. For the duration of the war the American Governments assumed the right, if the need existed, to patrol the waters adjacent to their coasts, either individually or collectively as might be agreed upon by common consent.

The Declaration of Panama evoked a good deal of criticism both within and without United States Government circles. Secretary Hull still feared that if effective efforts were made to prevent belligerent action within this huge zone, the result might well be our own involvement in hostilities. The Navy Department, which apparently had not been consulted on the technical details, was appalled by the prospect of patrolling so vast an area. As Mr. Hull had predicted, protests were lodged by the belligerents even before any decision was reached by the Panama Conference, and these protests were the more significant inasmuch as the British Government hastened to base its case squarely on the established doctrine of freedom of the seas. But the President refused to listen to objections and ordered the Navy to commission eighty destroyers at once and block out the general outlines of the patrol. Its purpose, as Mr. Hull stated publicly on October 4, was for information only.[27]

From the standpoint of international law, the Declaration of Panama appears to have aroused rather less objection than was anticipated by Secretary Hull. A view widely held was expressed by *The New York Times*: "A neutral's rights in wartime are as broad as the power which that neutral is willing and able to exert in order to preserve those rights." Eminent international jurists, at least on the American side, pointed out that the "principle of protective jurisdiction" was well recognized in international law and had been embodied in the recommendations of the League of Nations Committee for the Progressive Codification of International Law as recently as 1926 and 1930. In the committee's discussions there had been much disagreement over the purposes for which jurisdiction beyond the traditional three-mile limit might be recognized, but security to the littoral state was generally accepted as one such purpose. In general, the consensus of opinion of international lawyers was that every nation had the right "to defend its laws and security from threatened violations, under varying circumstances, in the waters contiguous to the conventional three-mile limit, within which municipal law is supreme." Neither the width of the zone nor the problem of enforcing respect for it had any bearing on the validity of the principle, which was regarded as unassailable.[28]

The difficulty with the Declaration of Panama, therefore, was less legal than practical, the more so as the signatory powers recognized from the outset the need for securing the assent of the belligerent powers and envisaged no measures of enforcement pending further consultation. Actually the problem of securing compliance proved very serious, and Mr. Welles has confessed that the whole project was perhaps conceived in too great optimism and born of a naïve belief that the war could be won by the forces of freedom without its becoming universal.[29]

The Declaration was unofficially rejected, first by the British, then by the French Government. While averring its eagerness to assist the American Republics in keeping hostilities from their shores, the British Admiralty insisted:

. . . it is now generally recognized that no country can properly claim jurisdiction over large areas of ocean nor the right to control or exclude the movements of foreign ships on the high seas. . . . The width of the general belt of territorial

[27] *Berle Diaries (MS.)*, September 30, October 4; tels. to Welles, September 27 and 29; *The New York Times*, October 3, 1939, reporting editorial comment in the London *Times*, same date; Hull: *Memoirs*, I, 691.

[28] *The New York Times*, October 5, 1939; Philip M. Brown: "Protective Jurisdiction" (*American Journal of International Law*, XXXIV, 1940, 112-16); C. G. Fenwick: "The Declaration of Panama" (*ibid.*, 116-19). See also Charles Warren: "Lawless Maritime Warfare" (*Foreign Affairs*, April, 1940).

[29] *The Time for Decision*, 212; statement of Mr. Welles to the authors, May 1947.

waters is now widely accepted as being three miles. Great Britain in common with many other countries has long refused to recognize claims to a territorial belt of greater width.[30]

These flat-footed statements at once aroused the fears of American isolationists, who, despite Mr. Hull's assurances, had visions of our interfering by force to prevent belligerent action within hundreds of miles of our shores. Mr. Alfred M. Landon described the Declaration as setting up "a hazy new zone on the high seas" which raised many questions "full of peril to our neutral position." The United States, he went on, did not come near possessing the ability to enforce the Declaration and it was certain "that the duty of enforcement falls solely upon us and our navy." The whole thing, he asserted, was an illustration of the President's "enthusiasm for new and dramatic things. . . . W ehave no law and are considering no bill which is as full of dangerous possibilities as this one."[31]

Mr. Hull continued unhappy over the whole transaction, and as late as October 8 was considering going on record with the President in opposition to the Declaration. At the same time both he and Mr. Welles were kept busy explaining to ambassadors and to the press that the project was not as formidable as it sounded; that the United States had no responsibility for patrolling anything but its own coasts; that the purpose of the patrol was primarily to secure information; and that nothing more would be undertaken without further consultation between the American Republics.[32]

For all the public controversy, the implications were really not so grave. Mr. Churchill, then First Lord of the Admiralty, was sympathetic to the scheme from the start. While reserving the general question of international law, he told the United States Ambassador that if the American Governments could induce all the belligerents to observe the zone, Britain would agree at once. He had no faith in the capacity of the weaker powers to patrol their coasts effectively, but would be glad to have the United States police the zone as far south as possible. The main objective, he concluded, must be to prevent the enemy from using the zone as a sanctuary.[33]

Of course Mr. Roosevelt and his advisers also recognized the importance of effective patrol if the neutrality zone were to mean anything. The President was extremely anxious to keep the entire Caribbean area under strict

[30] Statement of the British Admiralty, October 13 (*The New York Times*, October 14); see also Frank R. Kelly, in *New York Herald Tribune*, October 6, and *The New York Times*, October 6, 1939.

[31] Landon, quoted in *The New York Times*, November 2, 1939.

[32] *Berle Diaries (MS.)*, October 8; memo of conversation between Hull and the French Ambassador, October 7; Welles's statement in *The New York Times*, October 11; statement issued by the Department of State, November 3; radio address by Welles, November 13, 1939.

[33] Tel. from Kennedy, October 5, 1939; Winston S. Churchill: *The Gathering Storm*, 513-16. The U.S. reaction to Mr. Churchill's views is given in a memo of conversation between Welles and Lothian, November 14, 1939.

surveillance. In part this reflected a desire to keep track of the eighty German merchant vessels tied up in American ports. Having ordered the State Department to investigate what action the United States had taken with respect to German vessels in its ports when war broke out in 1914, he learned that we had prevented them from escaping to be converted into armed raiders by the simple device of withholding sufficient fuel. Thereupon he instructed Mr. Welles to pass on the information to the Mexican and other Latin American Governments, with the advice that they resort to this same expedient.[34]

The President was also concerned lest the small states of Central America prove unable to prevent the Germans from supplying submarines and raiders from bases in the Caribbean area. The Dominican Republic was urging the United States Navy to patrol its waters, and reports of suspicious activities were already coming in from Brazil, Haiti, and Peru.[35] Under the circumstances, Mr. Roosevelt evinced considerable impatience with the delays in getting the patrol under way. On October 9 he issued orders for the rapid overhaul of forty destroyers built during the earlier war, and made it clear that ships and planes which sighted submarines or suspicious surface craft within the limits of their zone were to maintain contact and report their sightings not in code but in plain English. "In this whole patrol business," he observed, "time is of the essence and loss of contact with surface ships cannot be tolerated."[36] Finally, on October 11, United States consulates throughout Latin America were instructed to report in clear language the movements of all belligerent merchant ships which had taken refuge in American ports. The State Department had some misgivings about these methods, fearing that they would result in the drying up of information sources. The Navy Department, in turn, refrained for the time being from taking advantage of the President's suggestion.[37]

Even more delicate was the question of actual sea and air patrol by the United States Navy in Central America, the Caribbean area and along the adjacent coasts of South America. Apparently this matter, which had been raised by the Navy Department even before the opening of the Panama Conference, was discussed by Mr. Welles with some of the other delegates.[38]

[34] Memo of the President to Welles, September 7, 1939 (*F.D.R.: His Personal Letters*, II, 917-18).

[35] Letter of Acting Secretary of the Navy Edison, to Hull, September 16; report from the Military Attaché in Brazil, September 22; despatch from Dreyfus (Lima), October 5; letter from Mayer (Port au Prince), October 27, 1939. London again warned the Latin American Governments on this score (*aide-mémoire* of the British Embassy, Washington, October 4, 1939).

[36] Samuel E. Morison: *The Battle of the Atlantic* (Boston, 1947), 14 ff.; memo of the President, October 9, 1939 (*F.D.R.: His Personal Letters*, II, 936-37).

[37] *Morgenthau Diaries (MS.)*, Vol. 217, October 9; *Minutes of the Liaison Committee*, October 16, 1939.

[38] Letter of the Acting Secretary of the Navy (Edison) to Mr. Hull, October 3; and Mr. Hull's reply, October 12, 1939.

At any rate, on his return to Washington the Under Secretary reported that he anticipated no difficulty in negotiating satisfactory arrangements with the Central American Governments. Furthermore, he stated, the Colombian Government was quite ready to discuss collective patrolling, the Venezuelan Government was prepared to take up the matter, too, and Ecuador was actually anxious to make some provision. Mexico, however, was a more delicate case, since German propaganda was strong there and the Government had to be careful not to expose itself to criticism. Negotiations on this subject were carried on with the Latin American Governments concerned, and by December, 1939, satisfactory agreements were being reached. Thenceforth United States warships and planes were generally able to carry on reconnaissance as necessary without first asking permission. It was agreed, however, that the governments concerned should be notified in advance whenever the circumstances of the case permitted.[39]

A strenuous effort, then, was made by both the State and the Navy Departments to implement the Declaration of Panama by establishing effective, coöperative patrolling of the vital Caribbean area. To this effort the Central American Governments contributed to the limit of their slender resources. As for the others, it was hoped that Mexico, Brazil, and Argentina would presently be able to take adequate measures along their own littoral. In any case, no serious violation of the neutrality zone occurred until mid-December, 1939, when the German pocket battleship *Graf Spee* was attacked by British cruisers off the coast of Uruguay and compelled to seek refuge in the harbor of Montevideo. Having been refused permission for a prolonged stay, which, as the United States and other Latin American Governments quickly pointed out, would constitute a violation of international law, the commander of the *Graf Spee* consulted his Fuehrer, scuttled his ship, and blew out his brains.[40]

The dramatic end of the *Graf Spee* came as a great relief not only to the Uruguayan Government, but also to Washington and other American capitals. Nevertheless, the episode represented a flagrant violation of the Declaration of Panama. Clearly the American Governments were either obliged to take a stand or else allow the whole project of a neutrality zone to go by default. Some officials in the State Department, like Assistant Secretary Berle, thought it would be impossible to adhere to a broad interpretation of the Declaration, since strict enforcement had proved impossible. Mr. Berle

---

[39] Memo of Admiral Stark to the President, September 4, 1939, announcing that bases for "routine training flights" had been obtained at Bermuda, St. Lucia and Trinidad (*Roosevelt Papers:* Secretary's File, Box 44). Memo of Secretary of the Navy Edison to Secretary Hull, September 16; *Minutes of the Liaison Committee*, October 16, November 6, December 7; memo of the Under Secretary's liaison office, October 19; memo of the Division of American Republics, November 1; memo of Mr. Hull to the Secretary of the Navy, November 4, 1939.

[40] Hull: *Memoirs*, I, 692; *Fuehrer Conferences on Matters Dealing with the German Navy* (Washington, 1947), Vol. I (1939), 60 ff. (This compilation of German documents will henceforth be cited as *Fuehrer Conferences*.)

therefore suggested to Secretary Hull that a more modest objective be adopted, and that the American Republics declare only against such belligerent activities in the zone as interfered with neutral rights and trade.[41] The same viewpoint was reflected in responsible newspapers like *The New York Times*, which took the line that the American Republics had simply bitten off more than they could chew. Senator Robert A. Taft, indeed, went so far as to assert that the security zone could not be enforced short of war, and characterized the whole scheme as "a joke," as "perfectly indefensible and ridiculous," and as tending to involve the country in "disputes with other states that might conceivably lead to war."[42]

But the President and Mr. Welles were not prepared to let the incident pass without at least an effort to restate the "rights" of the American Republics. While the *Graf Spee* was still at Montevideo, the United States Government on December 15 suggested to the other governments the desirability of issuing a joint statement in accordance with the principles enunciated at Panama. The replies were favorable and certain Argentine suggestions were quickly accepted to avoid delay. As a result the President of Panama was able within a week of the sinking of the *Graf Spee* to send to the belligerents a joint protest. This note called attention to this and other violations of the Declaration and protested against them all. It added that with a view to preventing similar incidents in the future the American Governments would commence consultation "in order to strengthen the system of protection in common through the adoption of adequate rules among them which would prevent belligerent vessels from supplying themselves and repairing damages in American ports, when the said vessels have committed warlike acts within the zone of security established in the Declaration of Panama."[43]

Although the sanctions here suggested would have borne much more heavily on the Germans than on the British, who had bases of their own in the Atlantic and the Caribbean, the London Government at once manifested great concern over the implications of the neutrality zone. Mr. Churchill, designating himself "former naval person," sent a message to the President on Christmas Day pointing out that the British had refrained from sending submarines into the zone, but adding that they could not always avoid stopping German ships within it. He begged the President to bear in mind the strain under which Britain was laboring and, in general, to put the best possible construction on its actions.[44]

The official British reply to the joint protest was not received in Washing-

---

[41] *Berle Diaries (MS.)*, December 20; memo of Berle to Hull, December 21, 1939.

[42] *The New York Times*, December 21, 26, 1939; January 3, 1940.

[43] State Department circular instructions to missions in Latin America, December 15, 18, 20, 1939. The joint note of protest was published at once (*Documents on American Foreign Relations*, II, 121-22).

[44] Tel. from Johnson (London), December 25, 1939; memoranda of conversation between Secretary Hull and Lord Lothian, December 27, 1939; and between Welles and Lothian, January 8, 12, 1940.

ton until January 15, 1940, and the French and German replies came even later. None of them need be considered in the present context, for whatever resolution the Administration had mustered to compel the belligerents to respect the zone was hopelessly shaken by the blows which Adolf Hitler rained upon Britain beginning in April, 1940. Let us turn back, therefore, to consider the next manifestation of American policy after the outbreak of war: the repeal of the arms embargo. Like the neutrality zone itself, this action, it was confidently expected by the President, would serve the dual purpose of aiding the democracies and keeping the United States out of the conflict.

3. REPEAL OF THE ARMS EMBARGO

The strengthening of the program of inter-American solidarity was the Administration's first move following the outbreak of hostilities in Europe. The major objective, as we have seen, was to build a solid neutral front, and to contrive, as far as possible, the insulation of the New World from the Old. This policy reflected American determination, both official and popular, to keep clear of the war, the dominant feature of public opinion in the United States when the conflict commenced. In the main, to repeat, the President shared this feeling, and he is reliably reported to have informed his advisers and his Cabinet again and again that the country would not go to war. No matter what happened, he insisted, we would not send armies abroad. "We need only think of defending this hemisphere."[45]

Second only to this conviction, both in the President's and in the public's mind, was, of course, the desire to see the Axis quickly defeated and to contribute to that end insofar as dangers of involvement could be safely avoided. Accordingly, from the moment war broke out, revision of the existing Neutrality Law, at least to the extent of dropping the arms embargo, jostled with hemisphere solidarity for top priority in the Administration's policy. The lightning speed with which the European dictators liquidated Poland enhanced the President's doubts as to the certainty of an Allied victory, as it reinforced his belief that the existing legislation played into the hands of the aggressors.[46] Mr. Roosevelt lost no time, therefore, in deciding to call a special session of Congress with the sole object of revising the neutrality legislation and so enabling Britain and France to capitalize on the advantages of sea power. Since popular sentiment was so

[45] Alsop and Kintner: *American White Paper*, 64-65.
[46] The Gallup and Fortune polls showed that in the second half of September, 83 percent professed to desire the victory of the Western Powers, but that only 15 percent favored American entry into the war. At that time the Fortune poll reported 65 percent convinced that Britain and France could win. The Gallup poll recorded 82 percent of that conviction. Only 44 percent believed that we should intervene to prevent their defeat. By October 6 only 5 percent favored our entry, and by October 20, only 29 percent spoke for this course even if Britain and France were in danger of defeat.

overwhelmingly favorable to the democracies, the President anticipated no insuperable difficulty with the Congress. "My own personal conviction," he wrote to Judge Moore of the State Department, "is that we can get the votes in the House and Senate, but that the principal difficulty will be to prevent a filibuster in the latter." To Prime Minister Chamberlain he was even more reassuring: "I hope and believe," ran his message of September 11, "that we shall repeal the embargo within the next month and this is definitely a part of the Administration policy."[47] This was no mere wishful thinking. A careful check had revealed as early as September 7 that some sixty Senators were likely to support a "cash and carry" neutrality act; that twenty-five would oppose it; while the remainder were on the doubtful list.[48]

There is little doubt that both the President and Mr. Hull would have preferred the repeal of all special neutrality legislation and an immediate return to the practices of traditional international law. So far as one can determine the President's thoughts on this point, he believed the existing law was "miscalled" a Neutrality Act, and "in every case puts us on the side of the offenders."[49] Quite apart from sharing the popular anxiety to avoid assisting Hitler, he was by no means as sure as many people that the British and French could defeat the Axis. Nor, now that the die was cast, were the British and French Governments, who made no bones about their eagerness to purchase war matériel in the United States. In Paris, Premier Daladier bluntly informed Ambassador Bullitt early in September that "If we are to win this war, we shall have to win it on supplies of every kind from the United States. We can hold for a time without such supplies, but England and ourselves cannot possibly build up sufficient production of munitions and planes to make a successful offensive possible."

The Ambassador not only emphatically agreed, but added, in reporting this statement to the President, that American military men in Paris doubted even whether the British and French could hold out until trans-atlantic production could be brought to bear. On September 20 Bullitt warned that "every Frenchman who is in a position to know the facts" was convinced that if the embargo provision were not eliminated, "German victory would be certain."[50]

[47] Letter of the President to R. Walton Moore, September 11, in reply to the latter's memo of September 8 noting the disposition of many members of Congress to reverse their attitude of the previous summer (*F.D.R.: His Personal Letters*, II, 919); message of the President to Chamberlain, September 11, 1939 (*ibid.*, 919).

[48] Memo of Stephen Early to the President, September 7, 1939 (*F.D.R.: His Personal Letters*, II, 918).

[49] Chit of the President, outlining ideas on repeal, perhaps in anticipation of his address to Congress, in longhand and undated, but presumably circa September 13, 1939 (*F.D.R.: His Personal Letters*, II, 923).

[50] Letter of Bullitt to the President, September 8, 1939 (*Roosevelt Papers:* Secretary's File, Box 43); tel. from Bullitt, September 20, 1939.

The verdict from London was much the same. Kennedy reported Church-ill's comment on how "terribly discouraging" the neutrality provisions then seemed, and Prime Minister Chamberlain's remark that he

... never had the slightest suspicion that the United States contemplated coming to their rescue with men . . . but he felt the benefit of buying goods, paying for them, and carrying them away should be received by Britain. . . . The passage of a bill permitting England to buy and carry goods would be . . . the greatest psychological lift they could have at this time. . . . It would be a sheer disaster for England and France if such a bill failed to pass.[51]

The President's initial optimism about repealing the entire neutrality legislation was soon chilled by a shower of isolationist agitation. Prominent Congressional leaders were already warning the country that if the manage-ment of American neutrality were left wholly to the President's discretion, the result would presently be our involvement in war. As early as August 24 Senator Nye had pointed out:

In that question is embodied the real nub of the neutrality controversy. It is a question of presidential power, presidential discretion, presidential chance to commit the country in a way that makes staying out of war exceedingly difficult. . . . If America really means to stay out of foreign war, she needs to remember how easy it is to get in. We need the neutrality law. We need restraints upon a President.

On September 14, Senator Borah, the recognized leader of the isolationist forces in the Senate, took up the cry in a radio broadcast: "Force," he in-sisted, "is gradually undermining and destroying freedom everywhere. If we are not going to wholly surrender to a world governed by force, then we must establish somewhere a great power which speaks for and represents in act and deed the things which make for reason and justice." European wars, the Senator remained convinced, were "wars brought on through the manipulation and unconscionable schemes of remorseless rulers." If we decided to sell them arms, we would be taking sides, and that would be the first step to active intervention. He could entirely understand the popular condemnation of foreign ideologies, "but it is not hatred of another country but love of our own which makes for wisdom and justice in the formation of national policies."[52]

In the face of such evidence of the unimpaired vitality of the isolationists, even after the shock that blasted their illusions of continued peace, the President felt compelled in this second effort to revise the 1937 law to avoid the errors of the first attempt.[53] A number of eminent men had already been approached as spokesmen to reply to the dreaded Borah and to other

[51] Tels. from London, September 8, 15, 18, 1939. On the representations of the British and French to the same end in Washington, see Hull: *Memoirs*, I, 692 f.

[52] *The New York Times*, September 15, 1939.

[53] On this point see Arthur Krock, *The New York Times*, August 31, 1939.

influential isolationists like Senator Vandenberg and Colonel Charles A. Lindbergh.[54] Beyond that, Mr. Roosevelt decided not only to take a hand in the battle, but to attempt, so far as possible, to have the issue fought out on nonpartisan lines. Thus, in his telegram of September 13 to the majority and minority leaders of the House and Senate, announcing the special session, to convene on September 21, he expressed the hope that they could reach Washington a day in advance "for an informal conference with me."[55] Finally, it seems to have been the President's hope to heal the breach with Congress, and to remain in close touch with its leaders even after adjournment of the special session. "This plan," commented Mr. Thomas W. Lamont, "will emphasize your attitude that you described to me over the telephone that you are seeking no enhancement of the President's powers, but that it is your wish to share the heavy burdens of the hour with members of Congress without regard to party."[56]

Mr. Lamont, who was to become one of the most loyal supporters of the Administration's foreign policy, hoped for straight repeal of the existing Neutrality Law. The State Department, however, in marshaling its arguments for the special session, was already restricting its aims to the elimination of the arms embargo. A long memorandum, reviewing all the pros and cons of the existing law, emphasized particularly the fact that in 1914-1917 munitions and implements of war constituted only 10 percent of our total exports to the Allies. In short, merely to prohibit the export of such items would offer no assurance against America's economic involvement in the war. Only a complete embargo of all trade with the belligerents could conceivably provide such assurance, but in all probability only at the cost of a new and more severe depression. So long as we sent any supplies whatever to the British and French, our ships would be in danger of being sunk, because the contraband lists of the belligerents were so inclusive that no cargo would be exempt. The only safeguard against involvement on this score would be to keep American ships out of combat zones, no matter what they were carrying, and to provide for transfer of title to goods before they left our ports.

As for the familiar isolationist argument that repeal of the embargo would be tantamount to taking sides, the State Department memorandum restated the equally cogent thesis that to retain the embargo also meant taking sides. The prime objective of the United States Government being

[54] Memo of S. T. Early to the President, September 14, 1939, noting contacts with Landon, Knox, Stimson, President Conant of Harvard, and President Compton of Massachusetts Institute of Technology (*F.D.R.: His Personal Letters*, II, 921); *Berle Diaries (MS.)*, September 22, 30, 1939. Senator Byrnes was selected to lead the fight for the repeal of the embargo in Congress; and Messrs. Dunn, Moffat, and Savage of the State Department were charged with preparing the necessary material (*Moffat Diary (MS.)*, September 12, 15, 17, 1939).

[55] *Roosevelt Papers:* Official File, 1561, Box 2.

[56] *Ibid.*: Secretary's File, Box 47 (September 16, 1939).

to keep out of war, it would be manifestly in our interest to avoid facilitating victory for the Germans, who were the best prepared and best supplied among the belligerents. If Britain and France were defeated and their colonies were to fall into German hands, the United States would be menaced in every corner of the world, and the danger of its involvement enormously enhanced. Obviously, it would be in our own interest, then, to prevent the annihilation of the democracies.[57]

With these thoughts in mind, the President met on the afternoon of September 20 with a bipartisan group from Congress, fortified by the addition of the Republican leaders, Alfred M. Landon and Colonel Frank Knox. The discussion hinged almost exclusively on the most effective political strategy for securing repeal of the embargo. All agreed that the issue ought to be treated on an entirely nonpartisan basis. The Congressmen, however, left no doubt in the President's mind that outright repeal of the existing neutrality legislation would be impossible. In the words of Senator McNary: "The trouble is that people would think, if we repealed the whole Neutrality Act, that we were repealing our neutrality." The Congressional leaders, therefore, insisted that repeal of the arms embargo must be balanced by restrictive legislation such as "cash and carry," and the prohibition of credits to the belligerents. Mr. Roosevelt on his part accepted the necessity of compromise. He appears by this time to have become thoroughly sympathetic to the idea of "cash and carry," or at least to the "carry" part of it. American ships had been running the German blockade with all kinds of contraband supplies for Britain and France. It was probably largely owing to Hitler's reluctance to antagonize the United States that an "incident" had thus far been avoided. Furthermore, as we have seen, the President had been considering the desirability of warning American shipping to avoid danger zones. The Administration, accordingly, was quite willing to accept exclusion of American merchantmen from combat areas. The moot question was whether such regulations should be included in the new law, or left to the discretion of the Executive.[58]

The President's initial effort to repair his long-standing breach with Congress was emphatically continued in his address to the Senators and Representatives in the House Chamber on September 21, 1939. As usual, many minds had contributed to marshaling ideas and drafting this vitally important speech, notably Hull, Berle, Norman Davis, and the ever-present Judge Samuel Rosenman of New York. Although the Secretary of State favored a

[57] Memo of the Division of Controls, State Department, September 18, 1939. We have also used the memo of Carlton Savage to Mr. Hull, September 19, analyzing the shortcomings of the Bloom resolution passed by the House on June 30, 1939. On the general subject of preparations see Hull: *Memoirs*, I, 682 f.

[58] Alsop and Kintner: *American White Paper*, 73 ff.; Hull: *Memoirs*, I, 682; *Berle Diaries (MS.)*, September 20, 1939; *Christian Science Monitor*, September 21, 23, 1939. On the German official caution see *Fuehrer Conferences* I (1939), 3 ff.

message heavily laced with concrete if rather defensive argument, the President's actual remarks were general and mild.[59] Clearly he desired to reduce controversy to a minimum, and to permit Congress a wide choice of alternatives if it dropped the embargo. It is significant that no trace of the popular desire to aid the democracies, nor of the President's anxiety on this point, was allowed to creep into his address. Indeed, the keynote of the entire message was that everyone belonged to the "peace bloc." The Administration's objectives were "such measures as will protect the neutrality, the safety, and the integrity of our country, and at the same time keep us out of war."

At some length, but without a trace of rancor, the President reviewed the history of the neutrality legislation and his efforts to prevent the outbreak of the European conflict. He expressed regret that Congress had passed and that he had signed the Neutrality Act in the first place, for he was now convinced that the best course for the country would be to return to the traditional neutrality which accorded with the precepts of the law of nations. With regard to the arms embargo, he emphasized its inconsistencies: the present law prohibited the sale of completed implements of war, but permitted the sale of many varieties of unfinished weapons and other supplies. Even from a purely material point of view, it was better to employ our own people in the processes of complete manufacture and so strengthen our production for national defense.

Warned by Mr. Hull and his other aides that his speech must contain a reply to the contention that repeal of the embargo during the course of war would be an unneutral act likely to bring the country closer to war, the President voiced his "deep and unalterable conviction . . . that by the repeal of the embargo the United States will more probably remain at peace than if the law remains as it stands today."[60] This he felt to be all the more true since he believed that the Government should insist that American citizens and American ships keep out of combat zones; that American citizens be forbidden to extend credits to the belligerents; and that belligerents take title in this country to goods purchased here. While such objectives could be "substantially achieved by executive proclamation," the President went on to state that "the Congress, of course, should make its own choice of the methods by which these safeguards are to be attained, so long as the method chosen will meet the needs of new and changing day-to-day situations and dangers."

[59] *Berle Diaries (MS.),* September 20; *Moffat Diary (MS.),* September 18, 19, 20, 1939; Hull: *Memoirs,* I, 683; Alsop and Kintner, *op. cit.,* 72 ff.

[60] Letter of R. Walton Moore of the State Department to Stephen Early, September 21, 1939, enclosing a memo of Mr. Hull's views on this point (*Roosevelt Papers:* Secretary's File, Box 49). Mr. Hull also summarized his position in his public statement issued September 21, 1939 (*Documents on American Foreign Relations,* II, 655).

On this note of danger and uncertainty, and on the need of a nonpartisan stand in facing the future, the President concluded his address:

These perilous days demand coöperation among us without trace of partisanship. Our acts must be guided by one single hard-headed thought—keeping America out of war. . . . I should like to be able to offer the hope that the shadow over the world might swiftly pass. I cannot. The facts compel my stating, with candor, that darker periods may lie ahead. The disaster is not of our making; no act of ours engendered the forces which assault the foundations of civilization. Yet we find ourselves affected to the core; our currents of commerce are changing, our minds are filled with new problems, our position in world affairs has already been altered. In such circumstances our policy must be to appreciate in the deepest sense the true American interest.[61]

The battle was now joined. We may certainly doubt whether Mr. Roosevelt even then was quite as single-minded, not to say hard-boiled, as he would have had his audience believe. Secretary Hull has confessed that the thought really uppermost in the President's mind, as in his own, was the assistance which repeal of the arms embargo promised to give to Britain and France. Conversely, there is no valid reason to doubt that, as the situation then appeared, the President and the Secretary of State were, in Mr. Hull's words, "sincere in our belief that the new legislation would afford us a better chance of keeping out of war than the old legislation because, if Britain and France won the war, we could remain at peace, whereas if Germany won, there was every likelihood that we should soon have to fight."[62] That Mr. Roosevelt refrained from stating this in so many words is candidly explained by the Secretary as stemming from fear of the isolationists. When it was reported to him that even Senator Borah thought it a good speech and expressed himself privately as favoring cash and carry, the President may well have thought that some sacrifice of candor was worth while![63]

Senator Pittman, Chairman of the Foreign Relations Committee, was almost solely responsible for the actual writing of the Neutrality Bill of 1939. This came before the committee in the form of an amendment to House Joint Resolution 306, passed by the House of Representatives the previous summer.[64] Apparently unchastened by his unhappy experience of the past spring, the Senator was in no mood either to accept advice in this task from the State Department or to brook interference from the Executive

[61] Text in *Public Papers and Addresses*, VIII (1939), 512-22, and in *Documents on American Foreign Relations*, II (1939), 6-11. On the circumstance of delivery see the account in *American White Paper*, 76-77.

[62] Hull: *Memoirs*, I, 684.

[63] Memo of General Watson to the President, September 21, 1939, reporting Borah's alleged approval but also the Senator's determination to "make some kind of fight . . . so as to keep the President from leading us into war" (*Roosevelt Papers:* Secretary's File, Box 49).

[64] *Congressional Record*, 76th Congress, 2nd Session, Vol. 85, Part I, 58 ff.

Branch in guiding the course of the legislation. Pittman's bill did, of course, provide for elimination of the arms embargo, but Secretary Hull was little short of aghast at the price Pittman felt it necessary to pay for this concession. Besides a number of "oddities," the Senator envisaged very severe restrictions on American shipping, commerce, and neutral rights in general, which threatened to produce a new law as thoroughly isolationist in character as any of its predecessors.[65] It proved impossible to induce him to accept the more elastic substitutes suggested by the State Department. Indeed, he informed the White House on September 25 that "in the nature of things we had to make some compromises in the Committee." He added, however, that "we had got as much as we could" and that the bill would be reported out immediately and carried to the floor of the Senate. This, at least, proved correct. On September 28, 1939, the bill was reported out of committee by a vote of 16-7. Only one Republican, Senator White of Maine, voted with the majority.[66]

During the interval the returning members of Congress had been deluged with tens of thousands of telegrams and letters, many of them, as usual, being form appeals inspired by organized groups and the great majority vigorously objecting to repeal of the embargo.[67] Working on behalf of repeal were the American Union for Concerted Peace Efforts (composed of the representatives of such organizations as the League of Nations Association, the World Alliance for the International Friendship through the Churches, the Institute of International Education, the American Youth Congress, the General Federation of Women's Clubs, etc.) and the newly founded Non-Partisan Committee for Peace Through Revision of the Neutrality Law, of which William Allen White assumed the chairmanship.

Among the organizations ranged in opposition were the Anti-War Mobilization, the Women's International League for Peace, the National Council for the Prevention of War, the Keep America Out of War Congress, and World Peaceways.

Although in Congress the Republicans were preponderantly against repeal, popular sentiment on the neutrality issue cut across many accepted political lines. The Middle West was rather more pronouncedly isolationist than the East, and notably more so than the South. The influence of foreign-language elements, even the German, was much less marked than in 1914-1917. In the same way big business interests, stung by the charge of major responsibility for our entry into the earlier war, professed to be much opposed even to economic involvement. Churchmen were widely divided, but the marked hostility to repeal of many Roman Catholics, especially

[65] Hull: *Memoirs*, I, 693 f.

[66] Memo of General Watson to the President, September 25, 1939 (*Roosevelt Papers: Secretary's File*, Box 48).

[67] *The New York Times*, October 1; *Life*, October 2; L. E. Gleeck: "96 Congressmen Make Up Their Minds" (*Public Opinion Quarterly*, March 1940, 3ff.).

those of Irish origin, and of followers of Father Coughlin in Boston, Brooklyn, and Philadelphia, gave the Administration some concern, and induced the President to seek the advice of well-disposed prelates like Cardinal Mundelein of Chicago and Archbishop Spellman.[68] The intellectual classes, especially along the eastern seaboard, were perhaps most ardent in arguing for support of Britain and France in our own national interest. In the political realm it was noteworthy that some of the most violent New Dealers were suspicious of the President's foreign policy and espoused a narrowly nationalist viewpoint. Conversely, many conservatives who loathed the President's domestic program tended to support his attitude on international affairs. By and large, as the debate in the Senate opened, public opinion was about evenly split on repeal of the embargo, though the President's message to Congress momentarily increased the sentiment in favor. But, as the hundreds of thousands of messages which poured in on Congress testified, the all-important question for the average man was how to keep out of war. Those who opposed the Pittman Bill did so largely because they feared that its passage would constitute the first step toward American involvement.[69]

So faithfully did the debate in Congress reflect the national preoccupation with keeping out of war, that it would seem unprofitable, not to say tedious, to devote much space to the speeches which consumed the month of October.[70] Almost without exception they commenced with the sage observation that this country detested war and that the sole objective was to find the surest means of avoiding it. Characteristic of the line faithfully pursued by the Administration's supporters in Congress were these words of Representative Sol Bloom: "The aim of all neutrality legislation has been to keep the country out of war. No matter how many points are covered, no matter what is put in or left out, no law is good if it falls short of what law can do to keep us out of war."[71] Those who supported the bill took their cue from the President himself. They argued not that repeal of the embargo promised effective aid to the democracies, but that its retention was illogical and ineffectual, whereas the new "cash and carry" provisions provided much better safeguards. The opposition, with similar unanimity,

[68] *Roosevelt Papers:* Secretary's File, Boxes 46, 47 and 49.

[69] This fact was much commented on at the time: *Christian Science Monitor*, September 21, November 6; *The New York Times*, September 27, October 1; *Life*, October 2, 1939. *Cf.* Philip E. Jacob: "Influences of World Events on U. S. 'Neutrality' Opinion" (*Public Opinion Quarterly*, IV (1940), 45-66). On the subject of business opinion, see the release of the Opinion Research Corporation, November 6, 1939, and *The New York Times*, September 15, 20, 21, 27, and October 6, 1939.

[70] For those desiring to avoid the ordeal of reading the *Congressional Record*, the selections quoted by Beard in *American Foreign Policy in the Making*, 237-61, can be recommended.

[71] *Congressional Record*, 76th Congress, 2nd Session, Vol. 85, Part I, 1119 ff. Bloom refers very briefly to the debate in his *Autobiography* (New York, 1948), 237.

harped on the theme that repeal was tantamount to taking sides in a struggle that did not concern us, and that it would gradually lead the country to the point where "cash and carry" would have to be abandoned. We should then find ourselves back in the morass of 1917. Since all but a handful of the speeches amounted to no more than variations on these well-rehearsed themes, we need note only a few of the most authoritative recordings.

Senator Pittman introduced the bill on October 2 with a speech that was largely a repetition of the President's message. He went to great lengths to prove that it was not the munition-making interests that took us into war in 1917, and then argued that if there was to be an embargo it should include everything needed in war as revealed in the extensive contraband lists. The new bill, he pointed out accurately enough for the most part, meant a tightening up of the 1937 legislation rather than the reverse, and yet at the same time promised an expansion of our foreign trade: "The condition with regard to industry and labor in this country today is so deplorable that further obstructions to our exports would bankrupt large sections of our country." The "cash and carry" provisions of the bill, he concluded, would bring us business without risk.[72]

The other side of the case was expounded by Senator Borah on the same day. After repeating the well-worn thesis that we could not undertake to right the wrongs of Europe and that our first task should be to maintain liberty and free institutions here, he argued that a step in this direction was to maintain the embargo and give neither help nor encouragement to either side. The demand for repeal, the Senator insisted, came not from the American people, but from "the war hounds of Europe." The whole purpose of the demand was clearly to help Britain and France and, that being the case, "cash and carry" would mean nothing. If it was necessary to help the democracies, it would ultimately be imperative to give them credit and even to make them outright gifts. In the end we would be sending armies as well as arms, all of which would be well enough if this were a war for democracy. But in the Senator's view it was not that at all: "I look upon the present war in Europe," he concluded, "as nothing more than another chapter in the bloody volume of European power politics," and he fearlessly predicted that in the final settlement there would not be a word about Nazism or Communism.[73]

This, of course, was the old familiar line, echoed in the Senate by Senators Nye, La Follette and Hiram Johnson, who foresaw that if the embargo were repealed "we will be pushed about and shoved along by those wily men who play the game of power politics in which some of our people, some of those who are snobbish, imagine they can play better than the diplomats

[72] *Congressional Record*, 76th Congress, 2nd Session, Vol. 85, Part I, 50 ff.
[73] *Congressional Record*, 76th Congress, 2nd Session, Vol. 85, Part I, 69 ff.

of Europe."[74] Meanwhile, outside Congress, former President Hoover was assuring the country that the democracies could not be beaten; that they controlled the seas and could sit still until the enemy was exhausted. He proposed that instead of repealing the embargo completely, we permit the sale of defensive weapons but continue the prohibition of offensive implements. Colonel Lindbergh supported this proposal and also adopted the happy suggestion of Senator Lundeen that we seize the possessions of foreign nations in the New World in payment of their war debts: "As long as European powers maintain their influence in our hemisphere, we are likely to find ourselves involved in their troubles."[75]

As aforesaid, the Administration forces concentrated on refutation of the idea that repeal would be a step toward war, and on scotching the familiar charge that the President was intent on maneuvering us into the conflict. Outside Congress Colonel Henry L. Stimson, in a broadcast of October 5, characteristically called a spade a spade and warned the country "that Britain and France are now fighting a battle which, in the event of their losing, will, whether we wish it or not, become our battle. . . . In the interests of our own safety we should repeal this foolish and dangerous embargo and return to the wise policy of our forefathers."[76] But in Congress the question of aid to the democracies was glossed over, and the emphasis was put on the hoped-for effectiveness of "cash and carry" in keeping us out of trouble. The new bill, declared Senator Tom Connally:

. . . makes sacrifices, it makes sacrifices of our shipping and entails sacrifices upon our people greater than have ever been made by any people in all the history of warfare. . . . We are doing it willingly; we are doing it as a domestic regulation; we are doing it in order to save the necessity for facing the issue as to involvement or noninvolvement in the war. We want to stay out of the war, and we are going just as far as any people can go in this legislation to stay out of war.[77]

To top it all, the President himself, in a radio address to the New York Herald Tribune Forum on October 26 went the limit to dispel popular fears:

In and out of Congress we have heard orators and commentators and others beating their breasts and proclaiming against sending the boys of American mothers to fight on the battlefields of Europe. That I do not hesitate to label as one of the

[74] *Ibid.*, 630 f.

[75] Herbert Hoover in the *World-Telegram*, October 3; Colonel Charles Lindbergh in a radio address, October 13. Many of the speeches are abstracted or summarized by Denna F. Fleming: "Arms Embargo Debate" (*Events*, November, 1939, 339-46) and "The End of the Arms Embargo" (*ibid.*, December, 1939, 413-21), as well as in Charles A. Beard: *American Foreign Policy in the Making*, 238 ff. A competent and dispassionate foreign study is that of Pierre Monniot: *Les Etats-Unis et la neutralité de 1939 à 1941* (Paris, 1946), 57 ff.

[76] For Stimson's position, see H. L. Stimson and McGeorge Bundy: *On Active Service in Peace and War* (New York, 1947), 316 f.

[77] *Congressional Record*, 76th Congress, 2nd Session, Vol. 85, Part I, p. 92.

worst fakes in current history. It is a deliberate setting up of an imaginary bogey man. The simple truth is that no person in any responsible place in the national administration in Washington, or in any state Government, or in any city Government, or in any county Government, has ever suggested in any shape, manner or form the remotest possibility of sending the boys of American mothers to fight on the battlefields of Europe. That is why I label that argument a shameless and dishonest fake. . . . The fact of the international situation—the simple fact, without any bogey in it, without any appeals to prejudice—is that the United States of America, as I have said before, is neutral and does not intend to get involved in war.[78]

The initial advice allegedly given by Vice President Garner to the Senators entrusted with steering the Pittman Bill through the Senate was succinct enough:

Tell Barkley, Sherman Minton, and Jim Byrnes to do two things: (1) To keep their mouths shut and to shut off debate. (2) To keep the ball going at least six hours a day for a week. If, at the end of a week, a filibuster starts, have night sessions . . . Tell them we are going to take care of neutrality first . . .[79]

Actually it had become clear, at the end of the first two weeks of debate, that the Senators in question had not found the advice useful, and had certainly ignored it. There had been more than enough talk, and everything possible had been said at least several times. Interest in the debate had dwindled to the point where the galleries were sparsely populated and the floor of the Senate almost empty. As Mr. Arthur Krock acidly observed, the Senate had bored both itself and the country at large.[80] Yet Senator Pittman continued to fear for the outcome and apparently communicated some of his anxiety to the President. In view of the fragmentary character of the evidence, it is impossible to establish how far Mr. Roosevelt sought to influence the course of the bill through the Senate. It would seem, however, that he regarded cordial relations between himself and Congress as so crucial for the conduct of foreign policy in the coming months, and the repeal of the embargo as of such vital importance to the democracies, that he restricted his interference to a minmum. On October 5 he wrote Lord Tweedsmuir: "I am almost literally walking on eggs and, having delivered my message to the Congress, and having good prospects of the bill going through, I am at the moment saying nothing, seeing nothing and hearing nothing."[81] In any case, just prior to his meeting with Secretary Hull on October 15 to "draft our final recommendations," he was warned of the necessity of certain amendments to the Pittman Bill. Senator Bailey urged one which would

[78] *Public Papers and Addresses*, VIII (1939), 556-57.
[79] Memo to the President, reporting Mr. Garner's views, September 21, 1939 (*F.D.R.: His Personal Letters*, II, 924).
[80] *The New York Times*, October 29, 1939.
[81] *F.D.R.: His Personal Letters*, II, 934.

delimit a zone in the Atlantic from which American ships would be barred, though he disapproved Pittman's suggestion that we likewise prevent American ships from carrying arms to belligerents by way of the Pacific.[82] Similarly the Acting Secretary of the Treasury, John W. Hanes, counseled the President that it wasn't worth a fight to include in the new law short-term credit provisions to the belligerents, if their elimination would help passage. In this judgment, Secretary Morgenthau had himself anticipated Mr. Hanes.[83]

At the meeting with Secretary Hull the President was given a State Department redraft of the "cash and carry" section of the bill and sent it on to Pittman. The latter rejected it out of hand, as he had most of the other suggestions from that quarter. There is no evidence that Mr. Roosevelt was inclined to force the issue, although it is possible that he had a hand in inducing Pittman on October 19 to introduce a series of amendments to his own bill, one of which, Secretary Hull notes, slightly liberalized the drastic restrictions that were to be imposed on American shipping. For the rest, however, the Secretary was left to do what he could to influence the views of individual Senators and Representatives, and to meet the mounting objections of both the Allied and the neutral governments.[84] However considerable the sacrifices entailed, the President's cautious tactics were undoubtedly successful. Among the numerous converts to the amended Pittman Bill was even Senator Bridges of New Hampshire, an isolationist stalwart, who was reported on October 18 as having "come around almost completely to the President's line of thought," and as going to work on the House, where the greatest danger was thought to lie.[85]

The debate in the Senate came to an end on October 26, when Senator Byrnes informed the White House that "everything is all right" and the leaders thought they "can get the vote by tomorrow night." On the following day indeed, the Senate passed the Pittman Bill, 63-30, thus exceeding even the two-to-one margin which Secretary Hull had anticipated.[86]

Thereafter, with the anticipated difficulties in the House failing to materialize, progress was rapid. By noon on November 1 the President was informed that the conferees of the Senate and House had reached agreement. On the following day the House passed the Pittman Bill 243-181.

[82] Memo of the President to Mr. Hull, October 14, 1939, enclosing a letter from Senator Bailey (*Roosevelt Papers:* Secretary's File, Box 47).

[83] Memo of John W. Hanes to the President, October 14, 1939 (*ibid.*, Box 47); *Morgenthau Diaries (MS.)*, Vol. 217 (October 13, 1939).

[84] Hull: *Memoirs*, I, 694 f.

[85] Memo of General Watson to the President, October 18, 1939, reporting the views of Thomas Lamont (*Roosevelt Papers:* Secretary's File, Box 47).

[86] Memo of Carlton Savage, October 8, 1939; Hull: *Memoirs*, I, 695-97; memo of General Watson to the President, October 26, 1939, reporting a telephone call from Byrnes (*F.D.R.: His Personal Letters*, II, 947).

The final vote on the conference report, November 3, was 55-24 in the Senate and 243-172 in the House. The margins were very gratifying to the Administration, though they promised little for the nonpartisan approach to problems of foreign policy. The voting was throughout heavily along party lines, only six Republicans finally voting for the Pittman Bill in the Senate, and only nineteen in the House, a proportion which scarcely reflected the sentiments of Republicans throughout the country. The President signed the bill on November 4, 1939, and therewith opened a new chapter in the bizarre history of American neutrality.

4. "Cash and Carry" Neutrality

Secretary Hull's public statement, issued the day the Neutrality Act of 1939 became law, betrayed neither the extreme annoyance he felt over many of its provisions nor his genuine gratification that the planes and munitions piled up in American ports could forthwith be dispatched to Britain and France:

> I desire to repeat with emphasis, what I have consistently said heretofore to the effect that our first and most sacred task is to keep our country secure and at peace, and that it is my firm belief that we shall succeed in this endeavor. I am satisfied that the new act will greatly assist in this undertaking.[87]

In any event and despite a now rather absurd conspiracy of silence, in which the American people and their Congress avidly joined with the Administration, the repeal of the embargo involved a profound and obvious change in the relationship of the United States to the war in Europe. Under the old law Germany was favored, for the Germans were far more fully prepared for war, and their war production notably more advanced. Under the new act, Britain and France were enabled to purchase in the United States as much matériel as they had money to buy and ships to transport. From a state of affairs beneficial to the Germans, we had now shifted to one advantageous to the democracies. As Prime Minister Chamberlain observed to the President: "The repeal of the arms embargo, which has been so anxiously awaited in this country, is not only an assurance that we and our French allies may draw on the great reservoir of American resources; it is also a profound moral encouragement to us in the struggle upon which we are engaged."[88] Since public opinion was only slightly less favorable to this shift than the Administration itself, we suspect that this feature of the new legislation was in truth the one which contributed most to its enactment.

The repeal of the embargo likewise constituted a return to traditional American policy and to the concepts of international law. For the rest, how-

[87] Hull: *Memoirs,* I, 697.
[88] *Roosevelt Papers:* Secretary's File, Box 44 (November 8, 1939). Many entries in the *Moffat Diary (MS.)* for this period testify to the anxiety, occasioned by this shift, among proponents of strict neutrality within the State Department.

ever, the Neutrality Law of 1939 bore not even a remote resemblance to established practice, and largely continued the provisions of the Act of 1937. The cash and carry provisions of the earlier law, which had expired on May 1, were restored in the new act. When the President "found" a state of war among foreign powers, he was directed to single them out and apply the law. If he did not, Congress had authority to rectify the omission. American vessels were forbidden to carry either freight or passengers to belligerent ports. American ships might not be armed, and American citizens were prohibited from traveling on the ships of belligerents. The President was given authority to describe and proclaim combat zones which American ships and American citizens were forbidden to enter. The former prohibition of loans to belligerents by United States citizens was relaxed only to the point of permitting short-term (ninety-day) credits.[89]

All these provisions, and more particularly, of course, the "cash and carry" feature, stamp the Neutrality Act of 1939 as the very epitome of American isolationism, embracing every conceivable device to protect the country from the dangers to which it had been exposed in 1914-1917. The requirement of cash payment appeared in itself relatively unobjectionable, the more so since the Administration could take the view that the Johnson Act did not preclude loans by the United States Government to belligerent governments, for example, through the Export-Import Bank.[90]

Since, for the time being, both Britain and France had ample foreign exchange available, this provision became troublesome only at a later stage of the war. It was the *carry* requirement that represented the most drastic departure, for it meant the exclusion of American shipping from the combat zones promptly defined by the President on November 4 as covering the entire Baltic Sea and the whole Atlantic area from southern Norway around the British Isles, the Low Countries and France, leaving open only part of the northern coast of Spain for access to southern France.[91] It was estimated at the time that under this provision ninety-two United States ships would be withdrawn from the Atlantic and that eight trade routes, in which the Government had invested $195,000,000, would be abandoned. The United States merchant marine, it was expected, would lose an annual revenue of $52,500,000. This was indeed a heavy price to pay to avoid incidents, but

[89] Text in *Documents on American Foreign Relations*, II, 656-70.

[90] There was some uncertainty on this point, but for the moment the question was not pressing. The Treasury took the stand that the Johnson Act did not prohibit loans by the government and that Johnson himself had accepted this interpretation as far back as 1934. The Attorney General concurred in this opinion, but there was a flurry when Senator Pittman on October 27 made a statement in the Senate indicating that the drafters of the new legislation intended to forbid government loans to belligerents. (*Morgenthau Diaries, MS.*, Vol. 215, October 2; 219, October 25, 30, 1939.)

[91] *Documents on American Foreign Relations*, II (1939), 677 ff. Mr. Hull took a firm stand against State Department sentiment opposing the creation of combat zones (*Moffat Diary, MS.*, November 3, 1939).

there was more to it than that, for the withdrawal of American ships from the combat zones relieved Hitler of the threat of "clashes with the strongest neutral."[92] In the words of one contemporary writer: "By taking our ships off the seas the bill aided the German blockade of Britain as effectively as if all our ships had been torpedoed."[93] To Maritime Commission arguments favoring freedom of the seas, Secretary Hull had retorted: "That's all very well, but the important thing is that Congress doesn't and the public doesn't." The President supported Mr. Hull and overruled the Maritime Commission. Henceforth the Germans had only the lesser neutrals to confront. With the United States abdicating its neutral rights and deserting the principle of freedom of the seas, it was commonly predicted that Hitler would give the smaller neutrals short shrift, and that, following the rejection of his peace offer to Britain and France, unrestricted submarine warfare would commence in earnest. Unhappily these gloomy prognostications soon proved justified.[94]

Congress and the country, for all their anxiety to assist the democracies, were determined, so far as legislation could accomplish it, to keep the country out of war at almost any cost. The Administration itself was not far behind. A significant reflection of its attitude may be found in the record of a meeting held in the State Department on November 30, 1939, at which Senator Pittman and the legal advisers of several government agencies were present. The purpose of the meeting was to examine various obscurities in the Neutrality Act, in the hope of clarifying them. Pittman observed that wherever doubt as to the intentions of Congress appeared, the interpretation to be given was to be the one least likely to involve the United States in hostilities. The intent of Congress had been, he insisted, to enact a law which would avoid situations obliging the Government to make strong representations to any belligerent, or which would arouse public opinion. The new act, he continued, was passed in the "interests of peace." Congress was fully aware that its provisions would interfere seriously with our normal trade, but the Senator, at least, had no sympathy with American businessmen who would not sacrifice their trade practices to Congress's peace policy. These sentiments being resoundingly echoed by most of the others present, the general conclusion reached was that wherever the statute required interpretation, it was best to err on the side of safety.[95]

The Neutrality Act of 1939 was noteworthy, among much else, for the

---

[92] *Fuehrer Conferences*, I (1939), 35.

[93] D. F. Fleming: "Arms Embargo Debate" (*Events*, November 1939, 339-46). See also the admirable analyses by Allen W. Dulles: "Cash and Carry Neutrality" (*Foreign Affairs*, January 1940), by Shepardson and Scroggs: *The United States in World Affairs*, 1939, pp. 165 ff., and by Francis Deák: "The U. S. Neutrality Acts" (*International Conciliation*, No. 358, March 1940). Mr. Hull's exchange with the representatives of the Maritime Commission is recorded in *Moffat Diary* (MS.), September 26, 1939.

[94] *Fuehrer Conferences*, I (1939), 3-7, 9, 24, 27, 33, 35, 37.

[95] *Morgenthau Diaries* (MS.), Vol. 225 (November 30, 1939).

sheer obscurity of its phraseology. "Its tortuous language," wrote one eminent authority not long after the enactment, "and the involved inter-relationships of its exceptions to exceptions have already led to conflicting interpretations and to great confusion in business circles."[96] Under the circumstances it was inevitable that there should be "ghastly meetings" at the State Department in an effort to clear up the numerous moot points.[97] Into these details it is unnecessary to enter, since for the most part they involved matters of procedure rather than of policy. One point, however, deserves brief mention, as it reflects something of the Admin-istration's attitude. This was the issue of transferring American ships to foreign registry.

The single point in the Neutrality Act of 1939 on which the country was generally united was the demarcation of combat zones and the exclusion of United States shipping from such areas. Even so, it was with genuine regret that Americans contemplated this blow to their merchant marine. The idea had therefore been early advanced that a number of American ships be transferred to Panamanian or other neutral registry, perhaps with re-tention of actual ownership by American interests, or at least with some provision for repurchase of the vessels at the end of the war. Immediately after the passage of the Pittman Bill, this issue became acute. Not only private owners, but the United States Lines as well, applied to the Maritime Com-mission for permission to effect the transfers. The Commission was not averse to what one official described as a "dirty subterfuge." Secretary Hull, however, regarded such transactions as a plain attempt to evade the provisions of the new law and opposed them uncompromisingly. For the present, at least, the Secretary had his way, and a ruling was made that American ships could be transferred to foreign registry only in cases of bona fide sale.[98]

Nevertheless, the fixed determination of the American people to continue to enshrine in their laws a neutrality which did not exist in their hearts constituted an irresistible invitation to subterfuge. Since the Neutrality

[96] Philip C. Jessup: "The Neutrality Act of 1939" (*American Journal of International Law*, XXXIV (1940), 95-99). Among the many treatments of the new act, we have found the following most useful: Quincy Wright: "American Neutrality" (*ibid.*, No. 2); J. L. Kunz: "Neutrality and the European War, 1939-1940" (*Michigan Law Review*, 1940-1941); Guerra Everett: "The Neutrality Act of 1939" (*The Annals*, September 1940, pp. 95 ff.); Clyde Eagleton: "Revision of the Neutrality Act" (*American Journal of International Law*, XXXIII (1939), pp. 119 ff.). For a summing up of the pros and cons of American neutrality in general, see Charles G. Fenwick: *American Neutrality, Trial and Failure* (New York, 1940), and Edwin Borchard and W. P. Lage: *Neutrality for the United States* (New Haven, 1940).

[97] *Berle Diaries (MS.)*, November 16, 1939.

[98] *Berle Diaries (MS.)*, October 3, November 6, 11, 17; Arthur Krock in *The New York Times*, November 11, 1939; Hull: *Memoirs*, I, 697-700; *Moffat Diary (MS.)*, November 8, 1939. Letter of the President to William Allen White, November 13, 1939 (*F.D.R.: His Personal Letters*, II, 953-54).

Law of 1939—a monument to the deep but divided purposes which motivated United States policy at the outbreak of the war—was not seriously revised until just before Pearl Harbor, it was inevitable that long before that time evasion should have made much of the legislation a dead letter. All this, however, was for the distant future. Curiously enough, the repeal of the embargo, on which the democracies professed to count so heavily, resulted in no immediate increase in the orders they placed in the American arsenal now opened to them. This phenomenon, a reflection of the hesitation, confusion and false optimism with which Britain and France were to confront the first winter of war, must presently engage our attention. It was not wholly without reason that Senator Borah was to attach to these early months a characterization which they will doubtless never lose: the "phony war." Similarly, to describe as "phony neutrality" the initial American response to the war in Europe, especially as illustrated by the Neutrality Act of 1939, would not involve serious violence to the facts.

CHAPTER VII

The Phony War

1. THE LIQUIDATION OF POLAND

When the United States Congress met in special session on September 21, 1939, to consider revision of the neutrality legislation, the fate of Poland had already been decided. The world had been treated to the first of Hitler's spectacular military victories, to an ominous revelation of modern *Blitzkrieg*. Everything had gone according to Nazi calculations. In hardly more than a week's time the German air force had destroyed the Polish planes, many of them before they could leave the ground; had made the airfields unusable; and had wrecked the military communications. Meanwhile the Nazi Panzer divisions had rolled forward in great encircling movements, catching the Polish forces in their pincers and capturing hundreds of thousands of men. The self-assurance and valor of the Poles availed them nothing. They fought desperately, but were never given time to reform or readjust to the new conditions. By September 8 the Nazi forces were in the outskirts of Warsaw. The Germans avoided a frontal attack on the city and it did not yield to blockade until September 27. But by September 20 the major operations were over. The Government and what was left of the armed forces fled over the frontier into Rumania. Three weeks had sufficed to eliminate one of the larger states of Europe, a state which had been rated as the strongest military power in the East. Those who had talked so freely of Hitler's bluffing had been given much food for thought.[1]

During the short duration of the campaign neither Britain nor France did much to relieve the Nazi military pressure on their ally. In the words of Churchill: "We [the British] contented ourselves with dropping [over

[1] Military operations fall beyond the scope of the present study, but it may be remarked that Ambassador Biddle's analysis of the causes of Poland's defeat (forwarded by telegram from Bullitt, September 24, 1939) covered the situation admirably.

Germany] pamphlets to rouse the Germans to a higher morality."[2] But this must not be taken as reflecting unwillingness on the part of the Allies to honor oft-proclaimed obligations. Rather, it was due to confusion, lack of time, and unpreparedness. Originally, so it seems, the Allied strategy had been based on the supposition that Italy would enter the war at Germany's side and that it would be far easier to act effectively against Italy than against the heavily fortified German frontier. Even when, on September 1, 1939, it became known that Mussolini would stand aloof for the present, there was .some sentiment both in London and Paris for forcing the Italians to choose sides, though the idea was soon abandoned. Instead, a policy of placating the Duce and attempting to wean him from the German connection was adopted.[3]

There remained, then, only two ways of aiding the Poles. The first was to launch a large-scale air attack on Germany, in the hope of drawing the *Luftwaffe* back from the Polish front. The second was to advance vigorously in the West, where for the moment the Germans had only about twenty inferior divisions. Neither of these courses was followed, despite urgent appeals from the Poles. Apart from the generally defensive mentality that prevailed in both British and French military circles, the practical obstacles to immediate, effective aid seemed insuperable. An air attack on Germany, it was feared, might estrange American opinion. Furthermore, the German Air Force was rated much stronger than it actually was, so there was every reason to expect the most ruthless retaliation. Finally, the British were convinced that, in view of the weakness of France in the air, the first task of the Royal Air Force must be to protect French communications during the period of mobilization.[4]

It is doubtful whether in any case the bombing of German targets could have been more than what General Gamelin calls "a symbolic gesture." Genuine relief could have been given the Poles only through a large-scale land offensive on the Western Front, such as that promised the Poles in the abortive French-Polish military convention of May 19, 1939.[5] Hitler, counting on the rapid conquest of Poland, had taken the great risk of leaving

[2] Churchill: *The Gathering Storm*, 423; see also Sidney B. Fay: "How Serious Is German Unrest?" (*Events*, January, 1940).

[3] Tel. from Phillips, September 2; letter from Phillips to the President, October 18, 1939 (*Roosevelt Papers:* Secretary's File, Box 45); see also J. Paul-Boncour: *Entre deux guerres* (Paris, 1946), 163 ff.; Bonnet: *Fin d'une Europe* (Paris, 1948), 321; François Charles-Roux: *Huit ans au Vatican* (Paris, 1947), 335-36.

[4] Tels. from Bullitt, September 13; from Kennedy, September 14; memo by Biddle, February 3, 1940, on the Polish-German conflict; W. K. Hancock and M. M. Gowing: *British War Economy* (London, 1949), 95; General Gamelin: *Servir* (Paris, 1947), III, 51-53.

[5] This agreement was signed, together with the complementary political agreement, on September 4, but Gamelin claims that he was not even informed of the fact (Gamelin: *Servir*, III, 60). The text is printed in *Poland in the British Parliament* (New York, 1946), 256-57.

only about twenty divisions opposing France. Since the French were able to mobilize about forty-five divisions at once, they had a temporary superiority. When, at the Nürnberg war-crimes trials, General Keitel spoke of German surprise that the Western Powers had not attacked in force, he revived Polish complaints of having been left in the lurch, despite the solemn promises of the French.[6] Actually, however, the question is not as simple as it sounds. The French had promised to undertake an offensive in force only on the fifteenth day of war (for them, September 17). They did, in fact, begin an advance into the Saar on September 6 and continued it until September 12. By that date it was already clear that the Polish Army was finished and that the Germans were hastily transferring troops to the Western Front. There was real danger that the Nazi armies would launch an attack through Belgium while the French were committed in the Saar. Under the circumstances the Interallied Supreme War Council decided to suspend the advance, though offensive pressure was continued until September 21.[7]

In sum, then, the German victory in Poland came so quickly that, even with the best of Allied intentions, it was impossible to do anything substantial to aid the Poles. Furthermore, by September 10, reports of Soviet mobilization on the Polish frontier had begun to reach London and Paris. Exactly what this presaged was not clear, but it did raise the specter of Nazi-Soviet coöperation, with its ominous military implications. Actually the Soviet forces crossed the Polish frontier on September 17 merely to claim their share of the spoils. A fleeting glance at the development of the Nazi-Soviet relationship during these momentous weeks will help to illuminate the situation.

Reading backward, one is tempted to conclude that the real aim of the Soviet Government was to plunge Europe into war and, by itself remaining outside the conflict, prepare the way for the ultimate triumph of Communism. According to this interpretation it was the Kremlin's prime objective, in closing the deal with Hitler on August 23, 1939, to provoke a clash between Nazi Germany and the Western democracies, thereby assuring itself of huge territorial gains in Eastern Europe. It is significant, however, that in the summer and autumn of 1939 it was the considered opinion, not only of most British, French, and American observers, but likewise of German diplomats, that Stalin had postponed or abandoned his objective of world revolution and that he was now primarily intent on national aggrandizement. While it is difficult to draw conclusions where concrete and contemporary evidence is so scanty, it should be stressed that Soviet short-range and national aims were altogether compatible with the long-term imperialist objectives of world revolution, even though at a given moment this might not be plain from Soviet tactics.[8]

In the immediate situation, it appears that when Stalin and Molotov signed their pact with Germany, they probably did not expect Britain and France to honor their obligations to Poland. As a minimum, therefore, they looked forward to a new and bigger Munich compromise from which they could not be excluded and from which they could anticipate substantial gains. Even after the Nazi attack on Poland, Molotov expressed to the Polish Ambassador distinct skepticism about British-French intervention. At that time the Soviet Government was still pressing the Poles to ask for Russian supplies, ostensibly in the thought that thereby resistance to the Germans could be prolonged. It was only on September 8 that the Foreign Commissar changed his tune, saying that the participation of Britain and France in the war had changed the entire picture. The explanation no doubt was misleading. What chiefly produced the Soviet shift of policy was unquestionably the rapid and spectacular success of the Germans. When, on September 10, Molotov told the German Ambassador that the Soviet Government had been "taken completely by surprise by the unexpectedly rapid German military successes," he was probably telling the plain truth.[9]

The reputedly omniscient Kremlin, in short, was as much astonished and as little prepared as any other government. Immediate decisions were imperative, and these of necessity turned on the question of what to do about eastern Poland. By the agreement of August 23, 1939, the Germans had declared their disinterestedness in the entire area east of the "Four Rivers Line" (Pisa, Narew, Vistula, San), but the Soviets had not committed themselves to do anything specific about these territories. If the Germans had had their way, the Soviets would have marched at once when the Germans attacked Poland. Thereby the resistance of the Poles would have been crushed even more quickly and the danger to Germany from the West would have been correspondingly reduced. Such action was proposed to Moscow from the outset, Ribbentrop pointing out that unless the Soviets moved in, the German armies might have to pursue the Poles beyond the Vistula into the Russian sphere of influence. But Molotov replied (September 5) that the time had not yet come—that excessive haste might injure the common cause and promote unity among the opposing powers. Am-

[8] There is no need to retrace ground already covered, except to say that the German documents in *Nazi-Soviet Relations* leave no doubt of the opinions of men like Schulenburg. Mr. Loy Henderson, one of the keenest American diplomats, expressed the same views on his return from Russia (memo of Captain Puleston of a talk with Henderson, November 14, 1939, in *Morgenthau Diaries (MS.)*, Vol. 297, pp. 184 ff.).

[9] *Polish White Book,* Nos. 171, 172; *Nazi-Soviet Relations,* 91; Léon Noël: *L'agression allemande contre la Pologne* (Paris, 1946), 499-500; Max Beloff: *The Foreign Policy of Soviet Russia* (New York, 1949), II, 280.

bassador Schulenburg, in reporting this response, added his own opinion that the Soviet Government was having difficulty making the Nazi-Soviet pact palatable to the man in the street, who could hardly think of the Germans as friends and partners.[10]

Within another few days the Nazi armies had reached Warsaw. To defeat the Poles they would have to sweep on across the Vistula. In something of a panic, Molotov, while congratulating the Germans on their arrival at the Polish capital, announced to them that military action would be taken by the Soviets presently. The official news agency, Tass, explained to the Russian people that mobilization had become necessary because of the "ever wider and more threatening character of the German-Polish War." On September 10 Molotov confided to the German Ambassador that preparations might be somewhat delayed and that, in order to satisfy the Russian people, it would be necessary for the Kremlin to explain that the Polish State was disintegrating and that the Soviet armies would have to aid the Ukrainians and White Russians of Poland, who were being "threatened" by the Germans.[11]

One can readily understand that Hitler and Ribbentrop were not much edified by the Soviet suggestion. For some days Berlin and Moscow discussed the text of a projected joint communiqué, publication of which finally took place on September 18. Meanwhile the Soviet press was preparing the public. *Pravda*, in a revealing article on September 14, explained Poland's quick defeat by the "inner weaknesses and contradictions of the Polish State, which is a multinational state." Pointing up the fact that there were no less than eight million Ukrainians and three million White Russians under Polish rule, *Pravda* castigated the Polish "ruling circles" for their alleged maltreatment of these minorities. The same theme was developed in classic form in the note submitted by Molotov to the Polish Ambassador on September 17, the very day on which the Soviet armies finally began the occupation of eastern Poland. According to this note:

The Polish-German war has revealed the internal bankruptcy of the Polish State. . . . The Polish Government has disintegrated and no longer shows any signs of life. This means that the Polish State and its Government have, in fact, ceased to exist. Therefore the agreements concluded between the U.S.S.R. and Poland have ceased to operate. Left to her own devices and bereft of leadership, Poland has become a suitable field for all manner of hazards and surprises, which may constitute a threat to the U.S.S.R. For these reasons the Soviet Government, which hitherto has preserved neutrality, cannot any longer observe a neutral attitude towards these facts.

The Soviet Government further cannot view with indifference the fact that the

---

[10] *Nazi-Soviet Relations*, 86-89; *Halder Diary (MS.)*, September 1; tel. from Steinhardt, September 1, 1939, which is an excellent analysis of the Soviet position.

[11] *Nazi-Soviet Relations*, 89-91; tel. from Steinhardt, September 9, 1939; *Bulletin of International News*, XVI, 1028.

kindred Ukrainian and White Russian people, who live on Polish territory and are at the mercy of fate, are left defenceless.

In these circumstances, the Soviet Government has directed the High Command of the Red Army to order the troops across the frontier and to take under their protection the life and property of the population of Western Ukraine and Western White Russia.[12]

To the world in general Molotov spoke over the radio on the same day:

One cannot expect the Soviet Government to remain indifferent to the fate of our kindred Ukrainians and White Russians inhabiting Poland, whose status heretofore has been that of nations without any rights and who are therefore at present subjected to the will of chance. The Soviet Government deems it its sacred duty to extend a helping hand to our brother Ukrainians and brother White Russians who live in Poland.

It was left for General Timoshenko, commanding the invading Red forces, to strike the old note of revolutionary fervor, now so rare as to be almost refreshing. Just before the advance, Timoshenko called upon his brothers and sisters of the Ukraine to "fall upon Polish gentlemen with firearms, scythes, hayforks and axes," and to follow "the example the Russian people gave under Lenin's and Stalin's leadership in paying back the enemy."[13] The task of the Red Army was accomplished with such brutal despatch that there was no occasion for the "new feats of heroism and glory" which Molotov had called for. The one fly in the ointment was the fact that the German armies had already overrun almost half of the sphere assigned to the Soviets under the August 23 agreement. Hitler left no doubt whatever that the Kremlin might have all that had been promised, but the Nazi commanders, knowing nothing of the secret protocol, were little less than indignant at the idea of surrendering territories they had conquered. But Hitler's will prevailed and a temporary line of demarcation was settled upon.[14] The Germans did, however, make an effort to retain the valuable Borislav-Drohobycz oilfields in Galicia. Molotov rejected their request, but suggested (September 20) that the time had probably come to discuss the future structure of the "Polish area." Ribbentrop invited him to Berlin, but, in reply to Molotov's statement that it would be impossible for him to leave Moscow, readily agreed to pay another visit to the Kremlin. He arrived there on September 27 and departed on September 29. During that time he negotiated and signed a number of agreements, all dated September 28.[15]

[12] *Polish White Book*, No. 175. On the discussions regarding the communiqué, see *Nazi-Soviet Relations*, 92-100.

[13] *Bulletin of International News*, XVI, 986, 1098.

[14] *Nazi Conspiracy and Aggression*, V, 3047 P-S, and especially *Halder Diary (MS.)*, September 20, 21, 1939; *Nazi-Soviet Relations*, 98, 101.

[15] *Nazi-Soviet Relations*, 101 ff. The best secondary account of these events is in Beloff: *Foreign Policy of Soviet Russia*, II, 282 ff., though the treatment in David Dallin: *Soviet Russia's Foreign Policy* (New Haven, 1942), 69 ff., which was written before the documents were known, is still worth reading.

The background of these settlements was Hitler's plan to annex to the Reich those parts of Poland which it had possessed in 1914, and to organize the rest of the German sphere of Poland and perhaps the strictly Polish part of the Soviet zone as a self-governing but entirely dependent Polish state. This solution attracted him, partly because it would relieve the Germans of a heavy administrative burden, but chiefly because it was hoped that the Western Powers might be willing to settle for a rump Polish State, officially "independent." The Kremlin, however, declared against the scheme on the plea that a Polish State might cause friction between Germany and Russia. Instead, Stalin proposed that the German zone be extended eastward to the Bug River and that, by way of compensation, Lithuania be transferred from the German to the Soviet sphere. The Germans were most reluctant to give up the idea of a Polish State and the matter was left open for discussion at Moscow. But evidently the Soviets held their ground. Plainly their main objective was to secure Lithuania as part of their booty. Ribbentrop finally discussed the matter with Hitler by telephone and the Nazi leaders decided to concur. By the agreements of September 28 the line of demarcation was moved eastward from the Narew River to the Bug. Thereby the Germans took over almost all of the strictly Polish area, while the Soviets acquired the Ukrainian and White Russian districts. In a general way the new line was similar to the ethnic line (Curzon Line) proposed by the British Government in 1919, though actually the Soviets secured about 8000 square miles of territory to the west of that line. The transfer of Lithuania to the Soviet sphere of influence was part of the bargain.[16]

Ribbentrop was given a much more cordial and even enthusiastic reception on his second visit to Moscow than on his first. Without regard to democratic susceptibilities or world opinion, the Soviet bands played the Nazi "Horst Wessel Song," while the Soviet staffs displayed the swastika flag and gave the Nazi salute. Stalin was genial and Ribbentrop, as he was later to tell Ciano, felt as much at home as he did among his old party stalwarts.

The truth was that in the Polish War the Nazi-Soviet partnership, conceived in suspicion and born in fear, had weathered the first storm. That partnership was now a real one—a partnership in crime—with Russia, in the words of one newspaper, playing the noble role of hyena to the German lion. As evidence of this one might cite the various supplementary agree-

[16] On the question of a Polish State see *Nazi-Soviet Relations*, 102 ff.; *Nazi Conspiracy and Aggression*, V, 3047 PS; *Halder Diary (MS.)*, September 7, 1939; on the Moscow negotiations and agreements see also Kordt: *Wahn und Wirklichkeit*, 217 ff., and A. Rossi: *Deux ans d'alliance germano-soviétique* (Paris, 1949), 79 ff., who uses some unpublished German materials. On the new demarcation line and its relation to the Curzon Line, see statement of the British Government, October 18, 1939 (*Poland in the British Parliament*, 346), and James T. Shotwell and Max M. Laserson: *Poland and Russia* (New York, 1945), 22.

ments that accompanied the settlement of the Polish issue. Both sides undertook not to permit Polish agitation in their respective territories and both accepted arrangements for the repatriation of their nationals from the newly acquired areas. The Soviets engaged to supply the Germans with quantities of oil equivalent to those Germany would have gotten from the Galician wells, and committed themselves to a program of military aid to Hitler. Russian railways were to be at the disposal of the Germans for the transportation of goods from Rumania, Iran, Afghanistan and the Far East, and negotiations were to be initiated at once for an extensive program of trade involving Soviet supplies of raw materials in return for German machinery. Last but not least, the Soviet Government was to endorse and support Hitler's efforts to conclude peace with the Western Powers. No wonder that Ribbentrop returned to Berlin full of enthusiasm for the Soviet connection and that both he and Hitler convinced themselves that, since Stalin was pursuing a purely nationalistic and brutally realistic policy, it would be possible to do business with him for a long time. In public speeches on October 24 and 31, 1939, respectively, Ribbentrop and Molotov celebrated the Nazi-Soviet friendship, the latter going so far as to declare: "We have always held that a strong Germany is an indispensable condition for a durable peace in Europe."[17]

To the rest of the world the liquidation of Poland and the manipulations of the "terrible twins" came only as most unpleasant shocks. According to the American representative in Berlin, Mr. Kirk, even in Germany certain military and conservative business circles looked with some alarm on Hitler's gyrations, fearing the strategic and economic designs of Soviet Russia in the Baltic States and in the Danubian area, to say nothing of the danger of expanding communism.[18] These sentiments were certainly shared in Italy, where the Duce and his associates were already much piqued by Hitler's failure to keep them informed. Mussolini could see the sense in using a small person to kill a large one, but thought it a mistake to call in a large one to despatch a small one. Hitler, he was sure, would rue the day when he brought the Russians into the heart of Europe. Ciano, likewise, considered the Berlin-Moscow combination "a monstrous union against the letter and spirit of our [i.e., the German-Italian] pact," and described it as a return to barbarism. When, belatedly, he was invited to Berlin on October 1, it was chiefly to hear Hitler's glowing account of the campaign and Ribbentrop's rhapsodical effusions about the Russians.[19]

---

[17] Texts of the agreements in *Nazi-Soviet Relations*, 105 ff. For the rest see the conversations of Ciano with Hitler and Ribbentrop, October 1, 1939 (*Ciano's Diplomatic Papers*, 309 ff.); Dallin: *Soviet Russia's Foreign Policy*, 79; and Rossi: *Deux ans d'alliance germano-soviétique*, 89-90.

[18] Tels. from Kirk (Berlin), September 30, 1939.

[19] *Ciano Diaries*, September 24-26, 1939; *Ciano's Diplomatic Papers*, 309 ff.

In France and Britain the assault on Poland evoked universal horror. Léon Blum in the *Populaire* (September 18) denounced Stalin as "a bloody accomplice in the most monstrous iniquity," while on both sides of the Channel the press exploded in terms like "cowardly," "murder," "dastardly," "hyena," and "stab in the back."[20] The British Cabinet seethed with indignation at the Soviets' "double-crossing" and at their "callous, brutal policy." However, Mr. Churchill, as he himself has told us, could not convince himself that the "profound and quenchless antagonism" between Germany and Russia was at an end. He pointed out that Germany, now having a common frontier with the Soviet Union, would be obliged to keep a substantial number of troops in the East. Under the circumstances the British Government decided to put the best face possible on the situation. On September 20 the Prime Minister, though he suggested that it was too early to pronounce a final verdict, remarked that "for the unhappy victim of this cynical attack the result has been a tragedy of the grimmest character." Ten days later (October 1) Mr. Churchill, in a radio broadcast, coined the description of Soviet policy as "a riddle wrapped in a mystery inside an enigma," but ventured the conclusion that it was probably dictated by national interest:

We could have wished that the Russian armies should be standing on their present line as the friends and allies of Poland instead of as invaders. But that the Russian armies should stand on this line was clearly necessary for the safety of Russia against the Nazi menace. At any rate, the line is there, and an Eastern front has been created which Nazi Germany does not dare assail.

He was certain that it could not be in Russia's interest for the Germans to overrun the Balkans and plant themselves on the shores of the Black Sea. In that regard Soviet interests were at one with those of France and Britain. Churchill as well as Chamberlain, who endorsed his statement, drew what comfort they could from the generally gloomy outlook. On advice of their Ambassadors in Moscow, the British and French Governments decided against breaking off relations with the Soviet Government, on the theory that such a move would only help Hitler without doing the Poles any good.[21]

The attitude of the United States Government developed along lines similar to the British and French. From the outset popular sympathy with the Poles was well-nigh universal, but there was little indeed that could be done to support Poland. Even the President's appeal to the belligerents to

[20] See W. P. and Zelda K. Coates: *A History of Anglo-Soviet Relations* (London, 1943), 622 ff.

[21] Tels. from Steinhardt, September 17, and from Kennedy, September 15, 17, 25, 30, 1939; Churchill: *Blood, Sweat and Tears*, 173 ff.; Churchill: *The Gathering Storm*, 448; Feiling: *Life of Neville Chamberlain*, 425; *Poland in the British Parliament*, 271, 356-57 (statements of Chamberlain and Halifax on October 26, 1939). We have also used a memo from Lord Lothian to Mr. Dunn, September 21, 1939.

abstain from ruthless air attacks on civilian populations did little if anything to mitigate the savagery of the Nazi assault. President Mościcki as well as Ambassador Biddle reported to the President on the Nazi terror bombings, to which Mr. Roosevelt could reply only by expressing sympathy for the victims. Of material support for Poland there could be no thought. Immediately following the German attack, the Polish Ambassador in Washington appealed earnestly to the State Department to omit Poland from the list of belligerents subject to the neutrality law, on the grounds that Germany had not declared war. But this proposal was put aside as an obvious violation of the intent of the law and as likely to strengthen opposition to repeal of the arms embargo. The whole question proved to be purely academic, for Poland went under long before any supplies could have reached it.[22]

Ambassador Steinhardt, who initially had been inclined to estimate Soviet military preparedness as wholly defensive in character, presently changed his mind and forecast the Soviet aggression against Poland. His reports caused the greatest uneasiness in Washington.[23] Further Soviet action against the Baltic States, Rumania and Turkey was foreseen and, as Mr. Berle noted: "This is a nightmare and recalls Jenghis Khan. It means that soon the Western World will be besieged in the two Americas."[24] The Polish Ambassador at once expressed the hope that the United States would join with Britain and France in protesting the "flagrant aggression" of Russia, but to the Administration it seemed best to proceed cautiously. The Kremlin had promptly informed the American and other Ambassadors that it proposed to remain neutral in the European War, and it therefore seemed ill-advised to antagonize the Soviets when there was no prospect of saving Poland. Mr. Hull and presumably the President shared Churchill's hope that Germany and Russia would not become full allies, and wanted to avoid anything that would drive Russia into Germany's arms. The result was that not even the provisions of the neutrality legislation were invoked against Soviet Russia.[25]

Nonetheless, everything possible was done to comfort the Poles in their tribulations. Every ounce of influence was used with the Rumanian Government to assure decent treatment for the refugee Polish Government and to secure permission for President Mościcki to come to the United States. The President took a personal interest in this matter, though with

[22] Mościcki's message to the President, September 16, and the latter's reply, September 18 (see Hull: *Memoirs*, I, 677 ff.); on the neutrality problem, memo of conversation between Moffat and Wonkowicz, September 4, and between Moffat and Potocki, September 5; tel. from Biddle, September 17, 1939.

[23] Tels. from Steinhardt, August 30; September 1, 5, 8, 9, 15, 1939.

[24] *Berle Diaries (MS.)*, September 13, 18; *Moffat Diary (MS.)*, September 17, 1939.

[25] Hull: *Memoirs*, I, 685; *Moffat Diary (MS.)*, September 18; memo of conversation between Dunn and Potocki, September 18, 1939.

limited success. Not until December, 1939, was Mościcki allowed to go to Switzerland. Meanwhile, on September 30, a Polish Government-in-Exile had been established in Paris, with Mr. Raczkiewicz as President, General Sikorski as Premier and Mr. Zaleski as Foreign Minister. The American Government at once (October 2) recognized this Government and took occasion to issue a public statement which completed the American record on the fourth partition of Poland:

> Poland is now the victim of force used as an instrument of national policy. Its territory has been taken over and its government has had to seek refuge abroad. Mere seizure of territory, however, does not extinguish the legal existence of a government. The United States therefore continues to regard the Government of Poland as in existence . . .[26]

2. HITLER'S OFFER OF PEACE

With the passage of time it seems likely that Hitler's miscalculation with respect to Britain and France will be set down as the most serious blunder committed on any side in the course of the Second World War. The Germany of 1939 was in no sense prepared for a general conflict extending over a term of years. Indeed, in his long-range planning the Fuehrer himself had reckoned on war with the West only in 1943 or 1944. The German land forces were, to be sure, formidable, but the naval preparations for war with Britain were woefully inadequate. Of submarines, only forty-five were available, while of the surface forces Admiral Raeder could remark: "They are so inferior in number and strength to those of the British Fleet that, even at full strength, they can do no more than show that they know how to die gallantly." Even the much-vaunted air fleets were unequal to really large-scale attacks on Britain. Not until the spring and probably not until the autumn of 1940 would they be strong enough to undertake that task successfully.[27]

In view of this situation Hitler could only hope that once Poland had been disposed of—once the solidarity of Germany and Soviet Russia had been paraded before the world—his enemies in the West would be willing to accept the accomplished fact and would conclude that a long and disastrous war would be suicidal. Actually, his hopes on this score were

---

[26] *Documents on American Foreign Relations*, II, 359; Hull: *Memoirs*, I, 686 ff.; tel. from Biddle, September 19; tel. to Biddle, September 20; tel. to Gunther (Bucharest), September 28, 1939, which was the beginning of a long and persistent effort in behalf of the Poles in Rumania. This effort, spurred on by Ambassadors Bullitt and Biddle, is described in the *Moffat Diary (MS.)*, September 20, 27, 1939.

[27] Raeder never tired of impressing these facts on Hitler. See *Fuehrer Conferences, 1939*, September 3, 23, 1939; Anthony Martienssen: *Hitler and His Admirals* (New York, 1949), Part I and Part II, Chap. IV; Morison: *The Battle of the Atlantic*, 4 ff. United States Air Forces officers were of the opinion that a massed air assault on Britain would be impossible before the summer of 1940 (*Morgenthau Diaries, MS.*, Vol. 297—report of Captain Puleston, November 25, 1939).

not altogether extravagant. The declaration of war by Britain and France had certainly been disillusioning and the Fuehrer could no longer blink the fact that in Britain, certainly, public opinion was in a most uncompromising mood. On the other hand, in France the war had been accepted with little more than resignation. Despite Premier Daladier's firm attitude, certain factions were known to be opposed to it and there was at least some reason to think that the French, once they saw the Nazi legions arrayed against them and realized that the brunt of the war's impact would fall upon them, would insist on an agreement that would spare the country another bleeding. The record shows that all through Hitler hoped to drive a wedge between the British and the French and induce at least the latter to accept his terms. One reflection of this hope was his order that the German Navy should not torpedo French merchantmen or even warships, and that nothing should be done for the present to mine French harbors.[28]

In high German circles there was much sentiment among diplomats and among the chiefs of the Army for a peaceful settlement. These men were under no illusions that a war against the West would be as simple as the *Blitzkrieg* against Poland. Furthermore, they were much concerned about Hitler's concessions to Russia and fearful lest a major conflict with the democracies leave communism triumphant in Europe. This divergence of view between Hitler and the High Command was not a new thing; in fact, it was the most serious internal problem the Fuehrer had to contend with. For even among his own close associates the Army viewpoint had its adherents. Marshal Goering, for example, had made a considerable effort to prevent the outbreak of war with the Western Powers. Having failed in this objective, he nevertheless persevered in his attempt to forestall irrevocable decisions and large-scale hostilities. Hopeful of enlisting President Roosevelt's mediation, Goering succeeded early in September, 1939, in establishing contact with the White House. The instrument was a certain W. R. Davis, who had been engaged in purchasing Mexican oil for the German Government, and who seems to have been introduced to the President by John L. Lewis. Davis himself had contacts with Goering through the German Embassy in Mexico City. At the outbreak of war Goering invited Davis to visit him in Berlin. Before leaving, Davis had an interview with Mr. Roosevelt. The latter was certainly intrigued by the possibilities suggested by his visitor, including reports that Goering might be planning to take over the German Government, or that the Army might engineer a *coup d'état* to oust Hitler. In any case, the President gave Davis to understand that he would consider the possibility of mediation, though only if the interested governments officially requested it.

---

[28] *Fuehrer Conferences, 1939*, September 7, 23, 1939; Maxime Mourin: *Les tentatives de paix* (Paris, 1949), Chap. I. Daladier's determination to fight on is recorded in telegrams from Bullitt, September 8, 9, 17, 26, 29, 1939.

Interpreting Mr. Roosevelt's cautious approach very broadly, Davis departed on his self-appointed mission to Germany early in September. In the course of his brief visit, which included a whirlwind tour of the Siegfried Line and of occupied Poland, Davis had a number of conversations, not only with his host, but with prominent officials of the German Army, Navy, and intelligence services. Upon his return to this country he again talked to the President and submitted two written reports. Their precise content is unknown to the authors, but they included Germany's terms for a peaceful settlement. Mr. Davis told the President that Goering and the German General Staff would like to have Mr. Roosevelt mediate peace on something like the basis of the sixteen-point program advanced by the Germans during the last days of the August crisis. He was convinced that the United States could "write the ticket," and that the President could, if he would, "force peace" on Europe. A few days later he reported a further message from Goering asking the President to desist from his efforts to revise the neutrality laws and to support the German peace offer in return for an absolutely free hand against Japan in the Far East. To all this the President listened attentively, as did Mr. Berle and Mr. Moffat when Davis subsequently repeated his story to them. But the President's response was a reiteration of his stand, that he could act only on a direct proposal from the German Government. Moreover, he added that the British would probably not be willing to accept any proposal based on the existing military situation.[29]

The State Department was likewise skeptical of the possibilities of Presidential mediation at this stage. Mr. Hull's response to the rumors current in Washington was negative. Not only would Mr. Roosevelt's mediation prove embarrassing to Britain and France; it might embroil us in Europe. Assistant Secretary Berle and Mr. Moffat in turn canvassed the possibility of mediation, only to conclude that the time was not ripe. The most they could conceive as opportune in the existing circumstances was to have the President set forth "certain broad principles on which ultimate peaceful relationships would have to be based."[30]

While these backstairs activities were under way, Hitler himself broached the matter of peace in a speech at Danzig on September 19. To all intents and purposes he urged the Western Powers not to pursue a barren policy of war, but to accept the realities of the German conquest of Poland. Together with this "offer" went the usual threats and warnings that Germany would get what it wanted one way or another. All in all, Hitler's words

[29] Our information on this episode is based upon a memo of conversation between Davis, Berle and Moffat, October 12 (*Moffat Diary, MS.*), and on *Berle Diaries (MS.)*. September 15, 19, 1939. On W. R. Davis see Josephus Daniels: *Shirt-Sleeve Diplomat* (Chapel Hill, 1947), 251 ff. A telegram from Kirk (Berlin), September 19, 1939, reported that Goering was regaining his paramount position in Nazi councils, but Davis held out little hope that Hitler would be overthrown.

[30] *Moffat Diary (MS.)*, October 7, 9, 1939.

were probably meant to exploit the confusion created by the Soviet inter-vention in Poland and to sound out sentiment in the West. The British Government felt unable to let it pass without some statement in reply.

On the outbreak of war the British Cabinet had been reorganized by Mr. Chamberlain so as to include dissident members of the Conservative Party and also representatives of the Liberals. The Labour Party still stood aloof, but the whole complexion of the Government was changed by the ad-vent of Winston Churchill as First Lord of the Admiralty. In all of Britain there was no more uncompromising opponent of Hitler and Nazism and no one more determined to prosecute the war vigorously to the end. Better than anyone else, Churchill represented the fighting mood of the British people. While the general mentality in military circles was a defensive one —based largely on the idea of blockade, gradual build-up of air forces, and ultimate destruction of German fighting power—Churchill from the outset began seeking possibilities of offensive action, preferably in the Baltic.[31] Without doubt Churchill exercised a profound influence on his Cabinet colleagues and stiffened the determination to see the war through.

Interesting light on the British position was thrown by Ambassador Kennedy's report on September 11 of a conversation with two high per-sonages. Both expressed great concern lest Hitler, as soon as he had cleaned up Poland (perhaps in three or four weeks), should propose to Britain and France that they call off the war. They feared that this might create a most serious contingency, for they recognized that there was little likelihood that the French could break through the German defenses and they dreaded the time when the French might demand that the British send their bombers to attack Germany. If the British yielded to French pressure, their bomber forces would soon be destroyed and German retaliatory attacks would hamper British production. On the other hand, if they refused, the French might begin to ask: "Why fight further to save Britain?" Yet it was thought out of the question for the British Government to entertain the idea of a deal with Hitler: any government that considered such a course would be at once turned out of power. To these reflections Ambassador Kennedy added his own interpretation: "It seems to me that this situation may crystallize to a point where the President can be the savior of the world. The British Government as such certainly cannot accept any agreement with Hitler, but there may be a point when the President himself may work out plans for world peace."

Mr. Roosevelt's reaction to this suggestion was immediate and definite. On the same day the following cable went off to the Ambassador from Secretary Hull:

[31] Churchill: *The Gathering Storm*, 461 ff., 533 ff., 692-94. For the prevalent defensive doctrine see Liddell Hart: *The Defence of Britain* (London and New York, 1939) and Max Werner: *The Battle for the World* (New York, 1941), Chap. IX.

The President desires me to inform you, for your strictly confidential information and so that you may be guided thereby without divulging this message to any one, that this Government, so long as present European conditions continue, sees no opportunity nor occasion for any peace move to be initiated by the President of the United States. The people of the United States would not support any move for peace initiated by this Government that would consolidate or make possible a survival of a regime of force and aggression.[32]

If the aim of the British was to smoke out the President, they succeeded. In replying to Hitler's speech of September 19 Mr. Chamberlain had to do little more than paraphrase the above-quoted cable. Speaking in Parliament (September 20) he added: "Our general purpose in this struggle is well known. It is to redeem Europe from the perpetual and recurring fear of German aggression and enable the peoples of Europe to preserve their independence and their liberties. No threats will deter us or our French allies from this purpose."

This would seem to have been clear enough, but Hitler had another card up his sleeve. As part of the bargain struck with the Kremlin on September 28 the German and Soviet Governments issued a joint declaration in this sense:

After the Government of the German Reich and the Government of the U.S.S.R. have, by means of the treaty signed today, definitively settled the problems arising from the collapse of the Polish State and have thereby created a sure foundation for a lasting peace in Eastern Europe, they mutually express their conviction that it would serve the true interest of all peoples to put an end to the state of war existing at present between Germany on the one side and England and France on the other. Both Governments will therefore direct their common efforts, jointly and with other friendly powers if occasion arises, toward attaining this goal as soon as possible.

Should, however, the efforts of the two Governments remain fruitless, this would demonstrate the fact that England and France are responsible for the continuation of the war, whereupon, in case of the continuation of the war, the Governments of Germany and of the U.S.S.R. shall engage in mutual consultations with regard to necessary measures.[33]

Here then, Hitler was drafting his partner to reinforce his own proposal, at the same time threatening his opponents with the specter of joint German-Soviet "measures" in the event of their continued refusal to recognize the establishment of "lasting peace" in Eastern Europe. From that day to this there has been much speculation about the Soviet participation in the German peace move. Much of it has been farfetched. There is no obvious reason to question the willingness of the Kremlin to see the dangerous general war brought to an early close, provided it could be

---

[32] Tel. to Kennedy, September 11, 1939.
[33] *Nazi-Soviet Relations*, 108.

done on the basis of Soviet as well as German gains. It is true there is no evidence that, after the failure of the peace effort, further measures were discussed. The fact remains, however, that presently the Communist Parties in all countries became insistent proponents of peace and that Molotov and other Soviet officials publicly castigated the British and French for their refusal to fall in line with Hitler's ideas.[34]

The materials now available throw some interesting light on Hitler's motivation at this time. On September 29 he held a long discussion with his generals, most of whom entertained the gravest doubts of success in case of an immediate attack on the West. They kept emphasizing that the campaign against Poland furnished no adequate recipe for war with France and Britain. Equipment was lacking and the troops required further training; besides, the season was a poor one, in view of the short days and the fog, which would hamper air operations. Hitler was not impressed. He affirmed his readiness for peace, but left no doubt that if the effort to negotiate should fail, he was determined to strike and strike hard.[35] Count Ciano, on his visit to Berlin on October 1, obtained the same impression. He found Ribbentrop highly skeptical about the peace project and champing at the bit to try a solution by force of arms. Hitler himself had no illusions about his proposed peace offer, but was anxious to put the burden of war responsibility on his opponents. He would be only too glad to make peace, concluded Ciano, but "if in order to reach it he had to sacrifice even to the smallest degree what seem to him the legitimate fruits of his victory, he would then a thousand times prefer battle."[36]

On the Allied side there was much deflation as a result of the Nazi-Soviet coöperation. From Paris Ambassador Bullitt reported that there was real fear lest the Soviet Government lend the Germans support, at least in air power, for an atack on France.[37] Ambassador Kennedy wrote the President on September 30 that the situation in London was glum. He quoted Sir John Simon as saying of the Soviets: "having double-crossed everybody, they will probably turn around and start all over again, so it is not known exactly what form the new tie-up with Germany might take." For himself, Kennedy favored getting out of the scrape as well and as quickly as possible. What, he asked Simon, are the British fighting for? They could not restore Poland, and even if Hitler were gotten rid of, chaos would ensue in Germany and the country might well go Communist. The whole business would leave England and France mere shells. But to

---

[34] See particularly Molotov's speech of October 31, 1939. On the Communist peace drive see especially Beloff: *The Foreign Policy of Soviet Russia*, II, 287-88, 291-92; Rossi: *Deux ans d'alliance germano-soviétique*, 92 ff., 112 ff.

[35] *Halder Diary (MS.)*, September 29, 1939.

[36] *Ciano's Diplomatic Papers*, 309 ff.; see also Wiskemann: *The Rome-Berlin Axis*, 176 ff.

[37] Tels. from Bullitt, September 27, October 2, 1939.

this Simon replied that there was no way of getting around the British public: "If they [the Government] were to advocate any type of peace, they would be yelled down by their own people, who are determined to go on." Kennedy's conclusions were depressing indeed:

I have yet to talk to any military or naval expert of any nationality this week who thinks that, with the present and prospective set-up of England and France on one side and Germany and Russia and their potential allies on the other, England has a Chinaman's chance. . . . England and France can't quit, whether they would like to or not and I am convinced, because I live here, that England will go down fighting. Unfortunately, I am one who does not believe that is going to do the slightest bit of good in this case.[38]

Goaded no doubt by British public opinion, the Prime Minister on October 3 took a stand with regard to the Nazi-Soviet declaration:

. . . . The passage in the Russo-German declaration about the liquidation of the war is obscure, but it seems to combine a suggestion of some proposal for peace with a scarcely veiled threat as to the consequences if the proposal should be refused.

I cannot anticipate what the nature of any such proposal might be. But I can say at once that no threat would ever induce this country or France to abandon the purpose for which we have entered upon this struggle.

Vigorously rejecting Hitler's effort to saddle the Allies with responsibility for the conflict, Mr. Chamberlain continued:

No mere assurances from the present German Government could be accepted by us. For that Government have too often proved in the past that their undertakings are worthless when it suits them that they should be broken. If, therefore, proposals are made, we shall certainly examine them and we shall test them in the light of what I have just said. Nobody desires the war to continue for an unnecessary day, but the overwhelming mass of opinion in this country, and I am satisfied also in France, is determined to secure that the rule of violence shall cease, and that the word of Governments, once pledged, must henceforth be kept. . . .[39]

In this statement the unwillingness of the British Government to deal with the Nazi regime, or at least with Hitler, was already implicit. It stands to reason that the Chamberlain declaration could not have been encouraging reading for the Fuehrer. Possibly it induced him to water down the relevant portions of his address to the Reichstag on October 6, 1939. This turned out to be an exceptionally long and tedious harangue. After reviewing the Polish campaign and celebrating the feats of German arms, the Fuehrer

---

[38] Letter of Kennedy to the President, September 30, 1939 (*Roosevelt Papers:* Secretary's File, Box 44). On Chamberlain's attitude at this time see also Feiling: *Life of Neville Chamberlain,* 523-24.

[39] Text in Louise W. Holborn: *War and Peace Aims of the United Nations* (Boston, 1943), 160-61. The attitude of Mr. Churchill and Lord Halifax is described in tels. from Kennedy, October 2, 4, 1939.

analyzed at length the reasons for Poland's collapse. He glorified the Nazi-Soviet partnership and predicted a long future for it. Indeed, he thought the other powers, if they were really desirous of peace, should be grateful to Germany and Russia for assuming the responsibility and burden of transforming the Polish hotbed into a zone of peaceful development. In any event, the Treaty of Versailles was now dead. He, Hitler, had devoted himself to the revision of this impossible settlement. It was not his fault if the last phase of revision had had to be effected by force. Anyway, it was gone beyond recall, and as a result of his efforts, "clear, stable and bearable conditions" had been established. Even in the inconceivable event of Germany's being defeated after a long war, a second Versailles would become only a source of fresh conflict. Why, then, should Britain and France want to continue? Hitler had made no demands on France, but on the contrary had done his utmost to bury the age-old enmity. As for Britain, he had no claims beyond the return of the German colonies, and even this claim he did not advance in the form of an ultimatum. He sincerely desired friendship with the Western Powers.

Coming finally to the point at issue, the Fuehrer raised the question:

Why should this war in the West be fought? For restoration of Poland? Poland of the Versailles Treaty will never rise again. This is guaranteed by two of the largest States in the world. Final reorganization of this territory and the question of reëstablishment of the Polish State are problems which will not be solved by a war in the West, but exclusively by Russia on the one hand and Germany on the other. . . .

What other reason exists? Has Germany made any demands of England which might threaten the British Empire or endanger its existence? On the contrary, Germany has made no such demands on either France or England. But if this war is really to be waged only in order to give Germany a new regime, that is to say, in order to destroy the present Reich once more and thus to create a new Treaty of Versailles, then millions of human lives will be sacrificed in vain, for neither will the German Reich go to pieces nor will a second Treaty of Versailles be made.

As consolation for the acceptance of the accomplished fact, Hitler dangled before the Western Powers the prospect of a Polish State "so constituted and governed as to prevent its becoming once again either a hotbed of anti-German activity or a center of intrigue against Germany and Russia." He opened also the prospect of arrangements for the revival of international trade and a reduction of armaments. To achieve the latter end, he declared, "The leading nations of this continent will one day have to come together in order to draw up, accept, and guarantee a statute on a comprehensive basis which will insure for them all a sense of security, of calm—in short, of peace." This would take time, but "If these problems must be solved sooner or later, then it would be more sensible to tackle the solution before millions of men are uselessly sent to death and milliards of riches destroyed."

Mr. Churchill and his ilk might interpret his suggestions as signs of weakness or cowardice, but if their opinion prevailed, this statement would be Hitler's last:

> Then we shall fight. Neither force of arms nor lapse of time will conquer Germany. There never will be another November 1918 in German history. It is infantile to hope for the disintegration of our people. Mr. Churchill may be convinced that Great Britain will win. I do not doubt for a single moment that Germany will be victorious. Destiny will decide who is right.
>
> One thing only is certain. In the course of world history, there have never been two victors, but very often only losers. This seems to me to have been the case in the last war. May those peoples and their leaders who are of the same mind now make their reply. And let those who consider war to be the better solution reject my outstretched hand.[40]

Hitler's "peace offer," ending with an invocation to the Deity, may have been designed in part to reassure the German population, which, according to all reports, was deeply disturbed by the prospect of a long war.[41] It is also quite likely that the Fuehrer had in view the possibility of confounding opinion abroad, which to a certain extent he surely did. But such evidence as we have seems to indicate that Hitler probably and his henchmen almost certainly cherished real hopes of success. The same was true of Mussolini, who would have been only too glad to extricate himself from a dangerous position.[42] Goering, for his part, appears to have done his best to put the wheels in motion and more specifically to enlist President Roosevelt in the good cause. Before turning to a consideration of the French and British reaction to the Fuehrer's speech, the repercussions of his move in Washington may well be examined.

It will be remembered that in mid-September Mr. Roosevelt had had a conversation with Mr. W. R. Davis, who was avowedly acting as an agent of Goering. Although the President had given him but little encouragement, it seems that Davis reported optimistically to Goering. This may explain the fact that immediately after Hitler's address, someone high in the Nazi councils approached our Chargé d'Affaires, Mr. Kirk, and suggested that the President send a confidential endorsement of the Fuehrer's views and ask for further details. Indeed, a Nazi press spokesman stated on October 9 that the German Government would accept a suggestion from the President for a truce, and intimated that it might be willing to take part in a conference, perhaps in Washington. Added to all this came a number of

---

[40] Text in *Der grossdeutsche Freiheitskampf: Reden Adolf Hitlers* (Munich, 1940), 67-100; English translation in *Adolf Hitler: My New Order* (New York, 1941), 721-57.

[41] *Cf.* William L. Shirer: *Berlin Diary* (New York, 1941), 228-36. Hitler's short address at the Berlin Sportpalast on October 10 certainly sounded like an attempt to bolster German morale.

[42] Kordt: *Wahn und Wirklichkeit*, 227-28; Wiskemann: *The Rome-Berlin Axis*, 179; despatch from Phillips (Rome), October 11; tels. from Phillips, October 7, 9, 1939.

messages from other capitals. From Brussels Ambassador Davies cabled the President that a high source (later revealed to have been King Leopold) had remarked that only the President could avert an assault on Western Europe and had expressed the hope that Mr. Roosevelt would renew his efforts for peace. Much the same appeal came from the Finnish Foreign Minister, who was already being subjected to strong Soviet pressure.[43]

The role of peacemaker was certainly congenial to Mr. Roosevelt. He desired that the possibilities at least be explored. On Sunday, October 8, the whole problem was thoroughly canvassed in a long meeting of the senior members of the State Department. Consideration was given to the draft of a possible American proposal asking the belligerents to state their terms and offering to act as intermediary. But there was little inclination to entertain the terms suggested by Hitler. It was clear that he would not give up Poland, much less Czechoslovakia or Austria. Could one ask the British and French to make a deal which would leave Hitler and the Nazis in power? Would it be fair or wise to put the democracies in the position of having to reject an American proposal? According to Assistant Secretary Berle:

> The consensus of the meeting was that while peace *ought* to be made, now was not the time. At least until the British and French have said something, we cannot. Furthermore, we cannot undertake to advise them. Still less can we undertake to back up Germany. For the moment, therefore, we must watch and we must wait, but the time might come and might come very soon.

By way of appendix Mr. Berle noted that in Berlin a false rumor of the fall of the British Government and the conclusion of an armistice had created a tremendous outburst of joy, which could only be regarded as a sign of breaking morale. As a matter of fact, some information of the dissension between Hitler and his generals had begun to seep through and there were even reports of rising German opposition to the Nazis. All this, together with intelligence on Germany's oil shortage and food difficulties, made it seem that spectacular developments might be expected. The decision, then, was to await the initiative of France and Britain.[44]

The reaction in those two countries has not yet been adequately studied, so that a definitive judgment is impossible. So much, however, seems certain: that among the French people the war was not uniformly popular and that it had been embarked upon in a feeling of disillusionment and resignation.

[43] Tel. from Davies, October 7; tels. from Kirk, October 7, 9; tel. from Schoenfeld, October 8, 1939, all summarized in Hull: *Memoirs*, I, 710 ff. We have used also the *Berle Diaries (MS.)*, October 13, 1939.
[44] Hull: *Memoirs*, I. 710 ff.; *Berle Diaries (MS.)*, October 8, 1939; report by Captain Puleston of a talk with Mr. W. F. Landis of the American Cyanamide Company, October 11, 1939 (*Morgenthau Diaries, MS.*, Vol. 297, p. 77). The rejoicing in Berlin and the subsequent letdown are recorded also in Shirer: *Berlin Diary*, 236.

Furthermore, a considerable number of French politicians (besides the Communists) had been opposed to the war and favored peace on any reasonable terms. Laval, Chautemps, Bonnet, De Monzie and others belonged to this circle and brought to bear such pressure as they could. The French Ambassador to Rome, M. François-Poncet, had been trying to interest the Italian Government in the idea of acting as mediator, and it was noted in French Government circles that the Pope seemed anxious to have the democracies examine proposals even if they involved acceptance of a truncated Poland. On September 13 Premier Daladier had recast his Cabinet and had taken over the Foreign Office from Bonnet. The latter, however, was given the Ministry of Justice. This political maneuver permitted certain people, like former President Beneš, to imagine, however erroneously, that Daladier himself was intent on not antagonizing the Germans and was dreaming of a compromise peace which would turn the Nazis against the Soviets.[45]

After close consultations with London as well as with Ambassador Bullitt, Premier Daladier gave his answer to Adolf Hitler in a radio broadcast on October 10. Speaking, as Mr. Bullitt noted, "with the simplicity and sincerity of a French peasant," Daladier declared:

> Certainly it has been and is our constant desire to see the establishment of sincere and loyal coöperation between peoples, but we are resolved never to submit to the dictates of violence. We have taken up arms against aggression; we shall not lay them down until we have sure guaranties of security—a security which cannot be called in question every six months.[46]

If these words did not quite quench the embers of Hitler's peace hopes, Prime Minister Chamberlain's statement in Parliament two days later did. The salient passages read:

> We must take it that the proposals which the German Chancellor puts forward for the establishment of what he calls "the certainty of European security" are to be based on recognition of his conquests and of his right to do what he pleases with the conquered.
>
> It would be impossible for Great Britain to accept any such basis without forfeiting her honor and abandoning her claim that international disputes should be settled by discussion and not by force. . . .
>
> I am certain that all the peoples of Europe, including the people of Germany, long for peace, a peace that will enable them to live their lives without fear, and

---

[45] Ambassador Bullitt's tel. of October 4 describes Daladier as "in a fine, serene fighting mood." "Memoirs of Eduard Beneš" (*The Nation*, July 3, 10, 1948), reporting a talk of Beneš with Daladier in October, 1939. The French situation is ably reviewed in Mourin: *Les tentatives de paix*, Chap. I, but see also the admirable analysis in Pierre-Etienne Flandin: *Politique française, 1919-1940* (Paris, 1947). We have also used a memo by Mr. Berle, November 8; and tels. from Bullitt, October 6, 7, and 10, 1939, pointing out the determination of the Daladier Government to reject the peace offer.

[46] Text in Holborn: *War and Peace Aims of the United Nations*, I, 560-61. Ambassador Bullitt interpreted the speech and the press reaction to it as convincing proof of French determination to fight (tel. from Bullitt, October 11, 1939).

to devote their energies and their gifts to the development of their culture, the pursuit of their ideals and the improvement of their material prosperity. The peace which we are determined to secure, however, must be a real and settled peace, not an uneasy truce interrupted by constant alarms and repeated threats. What stands in the way of such a peace? It is the German Government, and the German Government alone, for it is they who by repeated acts of aggression have robbed all Europe of tranquillity and implanted in the hearts of all their neighbours an ever-present sense of insecurity and fear. . . .

Past experience has shown that no reliance can be placed upon the promises of the present German Government. Accordingly, acts—not words alone—must be forthcoming before we, the British peoples, and France, our gallant and trusted Ally, would be justified in ceasing to wage war to the utmost of our strength. . . .

The issue is, therefore, plain. Either the German Government must give convincing proof of the sincerity of their desire for peace by definite acts and by the provision of effective guarantees for their intention to fulfill their undertakings, or we must persevere in our duty to the end. It is for Germany to make her choice.[47]

Chamberlain's uncompromising declaration certainly reflected the sentiment of his country. Lloyd George and George Bernard Shaw, to be sure, expressed some readiness to explore Hitler's offer, and the Prime Minister received considerable quantities of mail urging him to "stop the war." But the average Briton was sick of Hitler and Hitlerism and determined not to return to the uneasy, crisis-laden days of the prewar period. In Parliament even the Labour Party supported the Chamberlain statement, while Sir Archibald Sinclair, the leader of the Liberals, stated bluntly what the Prime Minister had only adumbrated: "The present German Government would have to resign. There would have to be some reparation for the wanton sufferings and miseries inflicted on the Polish people."

The British attitude was no doubt based in part on an altogether exaggerated notion of the difficulties confronting Hitler. The British Government was aware of a conspiracy among German military leaders to depose the Fuehrer, and as early as September 4, 1939, Lord Halifax had ventured the opinion that the war was most likely to end through the internal collapse of Germany.[48] Hence the British propaganda efforts to fan popular discontent in the Reich, and the ever more specific official statements that Hitler must go before peace could become possible. The failure of the Nazis to bomb the great cities of the West seemed another indication that Hitler was unable or unwilling to wage a general war. According to Mr. Chamberlain's biographer, the Prime Minister all through the autumn doubted that Hitler would stake everything on an attack in the West, or assume the odium

---

[47] Text given only in abstract in Holborn: *War and Peace Aims of the United Nations*, I, 162; full text in *Poland in the British Parliament*, 324-31.

[48] Allen W. Dulles: *Germany's Underground* (New York, 1947), 53 ff.; tel. from Kennedy, September 4, 1939. Interesting information on the British contacts of the German dissidents may be found in Erich Kordt: *Nicht aus den Akten*, 337 ff.

of violating the neutrality of Holland and Belgium. Chamberlain believed that Hitler's chief objective was the peace offensive, and he therefore concluded: "What we ought to do is just to throw back the peace offers and continue the blockade. . . . I do not believe that holocausts are required."[49]

Hitler, then, saw the door banged in his face by the French and British. Like the whole German nation, he was bitterly disappointed and indignant. An official statement of October 13, 1939, described the Chamberlain speech as "an unheard-of outrage." Thenceforth there was, in the Fuehrer's mind, no alternative to real war. Ribbentrop exultantly announced this fact to the German people in a speech at Danzig on October 24, 1939.[50] Goering, however, continued his approaches to London and Paris as well as his devious attempts to interest President Roosevelt in the role of mediator.[51] In the middle of October he informed Mr. James D. Mooney of the General Motors Export Corporation that if France and Britain would make peace, Germany would be prepared to restore part of Czechoslovakia and part of Poland. Thereafter, Soviet Russia would be ejected from Europe. The Nazis, added Goering, would be willing to get rid of Ribbentrop and Goebbels, but Hitler would have to stay. All this Mr. Mooney was asked to report to Ambassadors Kennedy and Bullitt, which he did in person to the latter. In like fashion Dr. Hjalmar Schacht, deposed head of the Reichsbank, who had become one of the conspirators against Hitler, did his utmost to arrange a visit to the United States and a conference with the President. But none of these maneuvers seemed promising to Washington, and it was with some relief that Ambassador Bullitt received instructions from Mr. Hull to refrain from urging the French Government to consider the proposals brought by Mr. Mooney. The peace problem continued to be discussed from time to time in the State Department, but the opportune moment did not present itself and action was continually deferred.[52]

In concluding this account it may be remarked that, as the autumn wore on, there seems to have been some mild activity in the Labour Party, in British Government circles, perhaps even in the Cabinet, in favor of renewed peace efforts. Speaking to Ambassador Kennedy at the end of October,

[49] Feiling: *Life of Neville Chamberlain* (Macmillan, 1946), 424-28. The skeptical attitude of the Foreign Office to the peace proposal was reported in telegrams from Kennedy, October 6 and 7, 1939.

[50] Kordt: *Wahn und Wirklichkeit*, 227 ff.; *Ciano Diaries*, October 12, 13, 1939; Mourin: *Les tentatives de paix*, 26-27.

[51] Tel. from Kennedy, October 16, 1939.

[52] Tel. from Bullitt describing his conversation with Mooney, October 23; tel. to Bullitt, indicating agreement with his assumption that the Department did not wish him or Kennedy to support Goering's proposals, October 23; despatch from Kirk (Berlin) reporting a conversation of Donald R. Heath (First Secretary of the Embassy) with Schacht, September 28, 1939; Hjalmar Schacht: *Abrechnung mit Hitler* (Hamburg, 1948), 26; Hull: *Memoirs*, I, 711; *Berle Diaries (MS.)*, November 15, 1939; *Morgenthau Diaries (MS.)*, Vol. 297 (report of Captain Puleston, December 8, 1939); *Moffat Diary (MS.)*, November 13, 1939; Alsop and Kintner: *American White Paper*, 85.

Lord Halifax confessed that the war was not popular, but that the British were determined not to let Hitler "get away with any more fast ones." A few days later the Ambassador reported that there was a group agitating for a declaration of war aims, in the thought "that when those aims are set forth, it will be apparent to the world, and particularly to the English and French, that they are fighting for something they probably never can attain." Everybody, added Mr. Kennedy, hated Hitler, but at the same time they did not "want to be finished economically, financially, politically and socially, which they are beginning to suspect will be their fate if the war goes on very long."[53]

We may well imagine that Churchill, at least, fought such tendencies tooth and nail, and, as it turned out, successfully. On November 7 Lord Halifax, in a radio broadcast, squelched talk of war aims by restating some familiar generalities, while Churchill himself, in a fighting speech on November 12, set forth a characteristically optimistic viewpoint and a thoroughly uncompromising program:

You may take it absolutely for certain that either all that Britain and France stand for in the modern world will go down, or that Hitler, the Nazi regime and the recurring German or Prussian menace to Europe will be broken and destroyed. That is the way the matter lies and everybody had better make up his mind to that solid, somber fact.

The Allies, he insisted, were much stronger than they had been even ten weeks earlier: "I do not doubt that time is on our side. I go so far as to say that if we come through the winter without any large or important event occurring, we shall in fact have gained the first campaign of the war." Italy, he continued, remained neutral and with the Japanese the British had no quarrel. Meanwhile Stalin, so Churchill felt, was barring the German advance to the East: "The left paw of the Bear bars Germany from the Black Sea; the right paw disputes with her the control of the Baltic. . . . Nazi Germany is barred off from the East, and has to conquer the British Empire and the French Republic or perish in the attempt." It was clear, he concluded, that Hitler was menacing Belgium and Holland, and there might well be rough weather ahead. Nonetheless, he was convinced that Germany was weaker than in the First World War and that Hitler's confederates were not sure of themselves. An examination of the other side of the shield will help in appraising the accuracy of the optimist's forecast.[54]

3. THE "WAR SCARE" OF NOVEMBER

There was never the slightest doubt in Hitler's mind that, if the Allies rejected his peace offer, the Germans must attack in the West with the least

[53] Tel. from Kennedy, October 31, 1939; letter from Kennedy to the President, November 3, 1939 (*Roosevelt Papers:* Secretary's File, Box 44).
[54] Churchill: *Blood, Sweat and Tears*, 173 ff., 189 ff.

possible delay. The Nazis were not ready for an all-out assault on Britain, nor equipped to carry on decisive submarine warfare against enemy commerce. They were bound to suffer severely from the Allied blockade and had to bear in mind the possibility that with time the Soviet attitude might change. For the moment, however, the Germans could muster at least as many divisions in the West as could the French and British. Hitler, as he told Ciano on October 1, felt "mathematically certain" that he could defeat the French armies, despite the Maginot Line. After all, he had a number of armored divisions, while the French had none. More important yet, he had a marked superiority in air power. If he could quickly defeat the French armies, there was a fair probability that the British would experience a change of heart and would agree to peace.

Added to these considerations was the Fuehrer's keen apprehension about the safety of the Ruhr, that great and concentrated industrial area of closely packed population on which the German war effort necessarily depended. If the British and French were permitted to establish air bases in the Low Countries, they would be so close to the Ruhr as to make devastating and probably demoralizing air attacks feasible. As far back as May 23, 1939, Hitler had explained to his generals:

England cannot deal with Germany and subjugate us with a few powerful blows. It is imperative for England that the war should be brought as near to the Ruhr Basin as possible. . . . The possession of the Ruhr Basin will determine the duration of our resistance. The Dutch and Belgian air bases must be occupied by armed force. Declarations of neutrality must be ignored. If England and France intend the war between Germany and Poland to lead to a conflict, they will support Holland and Belgium in their neutrality and make them build fortifications, in order finally to force them into coöperation. Albeit under protest, Belgium and Holland will yield to pressure. Therefore, if England intends to intervene in the Polish War, we must occupy Holland with lightning speed. We must aim at securing a new defense line on Dutch soil up to the Zuider Zee.[55]

Hitler never changed his views on this subject. He was not so foolhardy as to plan an assault on the Maginot Line, but was determined to get control of the Low Countries, partly from considerations of defense, partly in the conviction that the Allied armies could be sucked into Belgium and there defeated. The evidence shows that his calculations were exceedingly well grounded. The British and French High Commands were very much alive to the importance of the Low Countries, for the British were profoundly disturbed by the thought that the Nazis might secure control of Dutch and Belgian air bases, from which they could then bomb British industrial areas and British shipping; while the French, facing the fortified West Wall

[55] *Nazi Conspiracy and Aggression*, VII, L-79. On Hitler's views see further the testimony of his generals in B. H. Liddell Hart: *The German Generals Talk* (New York, 1948), 107 ff.

(from the Swiss border north to Trier), much preferred to meet the German armies in Belgium, where there would be greater space for maneuver and where the fighting could be done outside French territory. On September 1, 1939, the French Commander in Chief, General Gamelin, had pointed out to Daladier that an offensive to relieve Poland would be possible only through Belgium. As we have seen, the French Government was unwilling to do this.[56]

One might have thought that Belgium, and to a lesser extent the Netherlands, caught as they were between these great military powers, would for their own security have found it prudent to join one side or the other. As a practical matter, public opinion in both countries was decidedly hostile to the Nazis and strongly sympathetic to the democracies. If a choice had been made, it would have been in favor of Britain and France. After the First World War Belgium had been linked to these powers by defensive military agreements providing for mutual aid. But in October, 1936, following the rearmament of Germany and the reoccupation of the Rhineland, King Leopold of Belgium, evidently despairing of a strong policy on the part of Britain and France, had denounced the treaties of guarantee and had returned to a policy of plain and simple neutrality. The King was much criticized at the time and even more later for this departure, but the Belgian Government accepted his judgment and adhered to the policy of strict neutrality with unyielding obstinacy. Moreover, the Brussels Government must have felt reinforced in its stand when Britain and France proffered new assurances of aid in case of attack—assurances which were entirely unilateral and which, despite their value, cost the Belgians nothing. In the days just preceding the outbreak of war in 1939, the British and French renewed their promises, at which time Hitler, too, desiring for the moment nothing better than the maintenance of the neutrality of the Low Countries, voluntarily undertook "that Germany will in no circumstances impair the inviolability and integrity of Belgium (or Holland) and will at all times respect Belgian territory," on the explicit understanding, naturally, that the two countries should observe strict neutrality and not tolerate violation of their territory by a third power.[57]

Since the Nazi armies turned eastward against Poland, the Belgian Government, at the outset, was more concerned about Allied pressure than about German designs. As aforesaid, General Gamelin on September 1 had pointed out that an offensive against Germany could be successfully executed only through Belgium. If the Belgians deferred their appeal for aid until the Germans had actually begun an invasion, it would be too late for the Allies

---

[56] Reynaud: *La France a sauvé l'Europe*, I, 398 ff., 619; see also the extensive discussion in Gamelin: *Servir*, I, 82 ff.; III, 138 ff.

[57] *Belgium: The Official Account of what Happened* (London, 1941), Appendix VI; E. N. van Kleffens: *The Rape of The Netherlands* (London, 1940), 38, 41.

to save them, for the Belgian front would be broken before the Allied forces could reach the scene. Furthermore, Gamelin stressed the fact that from Belgian soil the Allies could launch an effective air attack against the Ruhr, the very move that was Hitler's bugbear.[58]

Although Daladier was highly skeptical of Belgian consent, both the French and British Governments made urgent representations at Brussels, suggesting at least defensive military discussions. But Leopold and his ministers were adamant. They suspected the Allies of being more interested in securing bases for an attack on the Ruhr than in protecting Belgium, and they therefore rejected all Allied proposals, while sticking by their promise to call upon the Allies if Belgium were attacked.[59] For a short time the matter rested there. On the Allied side it was felt that, however great the temptation, it would be impossible to assume the odium of violating Belgian neutrality. But when Hitler in mid-September began to move his divisions from Poland to the Luxembourg and Belgian frontiers, the problem again became a burning one. It was discussed at length at the meeting of the Supreme War Council on September 22. Both the British and French recognized that the Brussels Government would do nothing that might give the Germans a pretext for attack. On the other hand, it was agreed that if Belgium appealed for help only at the moment of German attack, it would be impossible for the French and British armies to advance beyond the line of the Scheldt. The Belgian Government was told that, without previous agreements, no support could be given east of that line.[60]

Meanwhile Hitler was concentrating his forces. At the end of September he informed his generals that, if his peace move failed, he proposed to attack as soon as possible. At once there was vigorous opposition from the military men, who argued that no safe conclusions could be drawn from the Polish campaign with respect to a war against an army like the French. They pointed out the lack of equipment, the need for further training, the likelihood of bad weather so late in the season, the danger of galvanizing the British into a full-scale effort. ("We know the British from the last war—how tough they are.") But the Fuehrer refused to be moved. He replied that Belgian neutrality was utterly insincere and that the Brussels Government would call in the British and French at the moment it considered opportune. Germany simply could not tolerate a hostile occupation of Belgium. The thing to do was to strike quickly, while the Nazis had a clear superiority. Besides, only by a daring offensive could Italy be brought

---

[58] Reynaud: *La France a sauvé l'Europe*, I, 618 ff.; tel. from Bullitt, September 20, 1939.

[59] Sir Robert Clive, in *London Times*, May 31, 1940; *Rapport de la commission d'information* (Brussels, 1947), 33; tel. from Bullitt, September 20, 1939; General van Overstraeten: *Albert I, Leopold III* (Bruges, 1950), 364.

[60] Gamelin: *Servir*, III, 138; Churchill: *The Gathering Storm*, 482; General van Overstraeten: *Albert I, Leopold III*, 368-71, 375-77.

to intervene. In his directive, issued shortly after his peace offer, Hitler wrote:

If it should become apparent in the near future that England and, under England's leadership, also France, are not willing to make an end of the war, I am determined to act actively and aggressively without much delay.

If we wait much longer, not only will Belgian and perhaps Dutch neutrality be lost in favor of the Western Powers, but the military strength of our enemies will grow on an increasing scale, the neutrals' confidence in a final German victory will dwindle, and Italy will not be encouraged to join us as a military ally.

The objective, therefore, must be to defeat as large a part of the French Army as possible and to gain "as large an area as possible in Holland, Belgium and northern France as a base for conducting a promising air and sea war against England and as a glacis for the vital Ruhr area." Finally, in connection with the offensive on land, the most vigorous and ruthless campaign against British shipping was to be opened: "Even the threat of America's entry into the war, which appears certain if the war continues, must not give rise to any restrictions. The earlier and more ruthlessly we commence, the sooner the effect and the shorter the duration of the war." After all, said the Fuehrer to Ciano, American aid to the democracies would be very small once the Germans had sunk the ships necessary for large-scale transport.[61]

The German generals did not dare disobey. Plans were therefore laid for a large operation to take place about November 10-15. The required forces were concentrated as rapidly as possible. By mid-October the Germans had some ninety to ninety-five divisions in the West, as against about ninety French and four British divisions. By that time an attack seemed to General Gamelin to be imminent. Ambassador Bullitt reported that the French Government expected the German assault within ten days.[62] But the more they planned, the more the German High Command became convinced that the French armies could not be defeated and that Germany was therefore courting disaster. Again and again the Commander in Chief, General Brauchitsch, and the Chief of Staff, General Halder, attempted to dissuade Hitler. But the latter remained firm. After all, he replied, if the weather is bad, it will hamper the enemy as much as the Germans. Besides, it will be bad in the spring, too. If the attack were delayed the enemy would only gain valuable time, "and one winter night England and France will be on the

---

[61] *Ciano's Diplomatic Papers*, 309 ff.; *Fuehrer Conferences, 1939*, October 10, 23, 1939; *Halder Diary (MS.)*, September 25, 29, October 7, 10, 1939; *Jodl Diary (MS.)*, October 25, 1939; State Department interrogation of General Walter Warlimont; Liddell Hart: *The German Generals Talk*, 107 ff. The text of the directive is in *Nazi Conspiracy and Aggression*, VI, C-62, and VII, L-52.

[62] Gamelin: *Servir*, III, 116; tels. from Bullitt, October 12, 1939.

Meuse without firing a shot and without our knowing it." Only through an attack could the Ruhr be protected.[63]

As matters stood at the beginning of November, the attack was still scheduled for November 15, the final orders to be given by November 5. Having failed to dissuade Hitler, some of the highest generals (Beck, Brauchitsch, Halder, Canaris, the Chief of Military Intelligence, and others) had decided that the only way to stave off an awful fate for the nation was to execute a coup, depose Hitler and then open negotiations for peace. With this program a number of influential civilians (Schacht, Hassell, Goerdeler, Gisevius, etc.) were associated. In short, the extraordinary and almost inconceivable situation had developed in which Hitler and the party chiefs (excepting Goering, who also opposed the offensive) were aligned on the one side, and the High Command of the armed forces on the other. In the first days of November Brauchitsch and Halder paid a visit to the Western front and passed the word around that on issuance of orders for the offensive, the coup against Hitler was to be executed.

For a moment at least there was a genuine possibility that the world would be spared much of the agony that was to follow. But on November 5 Brauchitsch had a conference with Hitler that ended in a terrific outbreak of fury on the Fuehrer's part. He accused the Army chiefs of misrepresentation and obstruction, and in general left the Commander in Chief completely unnerved. Thereupon Brauchitsch refused to have anything more to do with the conspiracy. Neither was any other general willing to assume the mantle of leadership. Some, in fact, had been troubled by the thought that an overturn might leave the country at the mercy of an Allied attack. They had therefore insisted that arrangements be made beforehand with the British.

At this juncture two very untoward events occurred. On November 8, 1939, the Gestapo succeeded in luring two British secret service agents into a trap. These agents had evidently been in touch with the German conspirators and were on their way to a secret conference when they were apprehended on Dutch territory, close to the frontier.[64] The second incident was the attempted assassination of Hitler in the Bürgerbräu Haus in Munich (November 9, 1939). The Fuehrer escaped through having left the hall just before the explosion of a time bomb. It is not improbable that the affair had been arranged by the Nazis themselves in order to demonstrate Hitler's enjoyment of divine protection and to rally the country on the eve of the projected offensive in the West. In any case, the conspiracy against Hitler

---

[63] *Halder Diary (MS)*, October 17; *Jodl Diary (MS.)*, October 25, 1939.

[64] For a compilation of the evidence on the so-called Venlo incident see the official *Enquêtecommissie Regeringsbeleid, 1940-1945*, Part II, a and b (The Hague, 1949), 34-47; and the account of one of the victims, Captain S. Payne Best: *The Venlo Incident* (London, 1950).

fell flat. In the wry words of one of the plotters: "These generals seem to want the Hitler Government itself to order them to overthrow it."[65]

The German preparations for an offensive could not, of course, be kept a complete secret. They were known in Washington as in other capitals, and naturally caused the greatest apprehension in the Netherlands and in Belgium. On October 21 the Dutch Minister in Washington transmitted a request of his Government that the President ask the German Government for an explanation. President Roosevelt agreed at once and Mr. Kirk was instructed to approach some high German official, expressing the concern of the American people and requesting assurances that the neutrality of the Low Countries would be respected. Unofficial explanations were given, but Mr. Kirk evidently had but limited confidence in their value. In his opinion it would have been better for the President to send a personal message to Hitler, though one may doubt whether much reliance could have been placed even on the Fuehrer's promise.[66]

Certainly there is no evidence that the Fuehrer was influenced by any intervention from abroad. In early November members of the German military opposition informed the Dutch and Belgian Governments that the offensive would be launched in the near future. For the moment it seemed that the attack might strike Holland rather than Belgium. There were rumors that the Germans had demanded of the Dutch permission to occupy the region along the lower Rhine. So acute was the crisis that King Leopold of Belgium on November 6-7 paid a hurried visit to The Hague. The two rulers agreed upon and issued a public appeal and sent to the belligerents an offer of mediation. Feeling themselves on the edge of the abyss, they evidently meant to demonstrate that as neutrals they were doing their utmost to initiate peace talks, and hoped at least to gain time until the season was too far advanced for major military operations.[67]

The various responses to the royal offer proved inconclusive. The British and French replied that they would be glad to entertain German proposals that promised a peace of real justice. President Roosevelt sent expressions

[65] The literature on this dramatic episode is extensive and scattered. See the critical review by Paul Kluke: "Der deutsche Widerstand, eine kritische Literaturübersicht" (*Historische Zeitschrift*, April, 1949). Most of the essentials may be found in Kordt: *Wahn und Wirklichkeit*, 227 ff.; Dulles: *Germany's Underground*, 53 ff.; Maxime Mourin: *Les complots contre Hitler* (Paris, 1948), 91 ff.

[66] Memo of conversation between Moffat and the Netherlands Minister, October 21; tel. to Kirk (Berlin), October 21; tel. from Gordon (The Hague), October 23; tels. from Kirk, October 24, 26; tel. to Gordon, October 24, 1939.

[67] On the German warnings to the Dutch and Belgians see Dulles: *Germany's Underground*, 53 ff.; and on the course of the crisis generally the abundant evidence in General van Overstraeten: *Albert I, Leopold III*, 407-15 and in *Rapport de la commission d'information*, 27 ff. We have used further tels. from Bullitt, November 7, 10, 16, 23, 27, 29, 1939; tels. from Davies (Brussels), November 8, 13, 22, 24, and despatch of November 8, 1939; memo of conversation between Hull and the Netherlands Minister, November 9, 1939; *Berle Diaries (MS.)*, November 17, 1939. See also Hull: *Memoirs*, I, 712 ff.

of American friendship, but avoided any suggestion of commitment. Ambassador Bullitt had raised the question whether the President might not send Queen Wilhelmina an encouraging message, but Mr. Roosevelt, though much perturbed and eager to express his views, nevertheless felt that there was nothing he could do for the time being.[68]

The action of the Dutch and Belgian rulers did, however, induce the Fuehrer to postpone the Nazi attack until the replies of the British and French were known. In fact, thenceforth he deferred the date of the offensive again and again, if only each time for a few days. The weather, which was very rainy, played the chief role in these postponements, but the continued recalcitrance of the German generals and the attitude of the various powers were probably also of importance. According to King Leopold, both the Italian and Spanish Governments expressed disapproval in Berlin and counseled against an unprovoked attack on the neutrals. It is at least conceivable that the repeal of the American arms embargo and the President's public stand in behalf of another small nation, Finland, may also have had some weight with Hitler.[69]

The war scare of November served to break down the negative stand of the Belgian Government in the matter of planning for Allied help. Inquiries were made of the French whether, in case of an emergency, the Allied forces could advance into Belgium as far as the Antwerp-Namur (i. e., the Meuse) line. After much conferring, the fateful decision was taken by the French and British, and approved by the Supreme War Council on November 17. The Brussels Government was told that the advance to the Meuse would be made if possible, and at the same time it was agreed that an Allied Army, the Seventh, should push forward rapidly on the extreme left wing to occupy the Dutch island of Zeeland. Militarily these decisions were fraught with risk, but, as General Gamelin states, the Allied authorities felt that after their failure to succor Poland, they could not afford to let Belgium go under. Furthermore, they calculated, if the Germans were stopped only at the Scheldt, they would already have possession of the air bases needed for operations against Britain. So the obligation was assumed and the Belgians, in turn, agreed to secret technical planning. Through a special liaison officer General Gamelin thenceforth sent to Brussels written "suggestions," to which the cautious Belgians made only oral replies. These communications, however, were strictly on the operational level. King Leopold remained deaf to any proposals for agreements that might in any way have compromised his country's neutrality.[70]

[68] Tel. from Bullitt, November 7, 1939; *Berle Diaries (MS.)*, November 11, 1939; *Moffat Diary (MS.)*, November 9, 1939; Hull: *Memoirs*, 1, 712 ff.; Mourin: *Les tentatives de paix*, 40-41.

[69] Tel. from Davies, November 21, 1939.

[70] Gamelin: *Servir*, I, 84, 92; III, 140-47; Reynaud: *La France a sauvé l'Europe*, I, 618 ff.; Churchill: *The Gathering Storm*, 482-83; *Rapport de la commission d'information*, 29; Hubert Pierlot, in *Le Soir* (Brussels), July 9, 1947.

Strange though it may seem, certain Allied authorities rather regretted that the showdown had not come at the time of the November crisis. Gamelin, reckoning that the Allies could, even without the Belgians, muster about the same number of divisions as the Germans, considered the chances of success excellent. Ambassador Bullitt reported him "extremely confident and entirely serene." He thought the Germans "in a most serious situation," and held that they had made a mistake in turning first on Poland. Their losses in the East had been heavy and their matériel was in bad repair. Now that the season was so advanced, they could no longer undertake operations in the West, especially as the Lord had sent such heavy rains. Gamelin thought it doubtful whether the Germans could launch an offensive before March, 1940.[71]

The optimism of the French High Command was not shared by British soldiers like General Ironside, but it was clearly reflected in the hopeful review of the military situation expounded by Mr. Churchill in his speech of November 22, 1939. This, he declared, was "a fortress war," a war of endurance, for which the British were notably well fitted. The enemy, in order to win, would have to break through the Allied defenses, and the French High Command was awaiting the result with confidence: "On our side we can afford to choose our opportunity."

By way of explaining the French estimate of their own strength, it is only fair to recall that the German generals, too, held a high opinion of the French Army. But they and the whole world had to deal with an extraordinary, unfathomable personality. Hitler's appreciation of French power was much more accurate than that of his generals or of the French Command itself. He had made his calculations and he had reached a decision. At the end of November he was still obstinately expounding his views to his generals and urging the necessity for early and vigorous action, lest time work against the chances of German success:

We have an Achilles' heel—the Ruhr. The progress of the war depends on the possession of the Ruhr. If England and France push through Belgium and Holland into the Ruhr, we shall be in the greatest danger. That could lead to the paralyzing of the German power of resistance. Every hope of compromise is childish: Victory or Defeat! The question is not the fate of a national-socialist Germany, but of who is to dominate Europe in the future. The question is worthy of the greatest efforts. Certainly England and France will assume the offensive against Germany when they are armed. England and France have means of pressure to bring Belgium and Holland to request English and French help. . . . If the French Army marches into Belgium to attack us, it will be too late for us. We must anticipate them. . . . It is a difficult decision for me. None has achieved what I have achieved. My life is of no importance in all this. I have led the German people to a great height, even if the world does hate us now. I am setting this work on a gamble. I have to choose between victory and destruction. I choose victory. . . . My decision is

[71] Gamelin: *Servir*, III, 116; tel. from Bullitt, November 13, 1939, reporting a long talk with Gamelin. We have used also a despatch from Davies, November 10, 1939.

unchangeable. I shall attack France and England at the most favorable and earliest moment. Breach of neutrality of Belgium and Holland is meaningless. No one will question that when we have won. We shall not bring about the breach of neutrality as idiotically as it was done in 1914. If we do not break this neutrality, then England and France will. Without attack, the war is not to be ended victoriously.[72]

So it was still the old story. The generals, as before, kept conjuring up objections. "Day of crisis," noted Halder in his diary after the meeting with Hitler on November 23. But the opposition, such as it was, proved impotent in the face of the Fuehrer's iron will. Dates for the offensive were set successively through December and into January, when another acute crisis developed. If Western Europe was spared the shock of the Nazi assault in the autumn of 1939, it was certainly not because of hesitancy or lack of determination on Hitler's part. Nor was the "phony war" any part of his program. More than the democracies knew, the threat of disaster hung over them.

[72] *Nazi Conspiracy and Aggression*, III, 789-PS; *Halder Diary (MS.)*, November 23; *Jodl Diary (MS.)*, November 23, 1939; see also Raymond Cartier: *Les secrets de la guerre* (Paris, 1946), Chap. VII.

CHAPTER VIII

Aspects of American Policy

1. THE PROBLEM OF DEFENSE

The pessimism and fear which temporarily paralyzed the American people at the outbreak of war and during the shocking liquidation of Poland soon gave way to misguided hopefulness as Europe settled down to the "phony" war in the winter of 1939-1940. Since Hitler followed up his initial success only with suggestions of peace, it was readily assumed that he was not prepared to carry the struggle further. Prominent military commentators, like George Fielding Eliot, and Hanson Baldwin, appeared convinced that the Allies were bound to win in the end and that, consequently, the United States had nothing to fear. In some of the highest circles of the Army it was thought that the French and Belgian fortifications guaranteed those countries ample security and that in any case the French Army was capable of taking care of itself in the face of any attack by the Germans.[1] On the radio the ever-popular General Hugh S. Johnson declared that Hitler could not muster sufficient sea power to threaten us even if he built warships for fifty years, and that, furthermore, the combined fleets of any conceivable coalition could not land in either North or South America against a well-prepared defense. Small wonder then that the Gallup polls recorded (September 17) that 82 percent of those queried believed that the Allies would win, and (November 14) 66 percent held the view that the German people were not supporting Hitler.

It is most unlikely that Mr. Roosevelt shared the popular optimism. Both Ambassador Kennedy and Ambassador Bullitt were sending him reports of the most lugubrious nature, and he was perfectly well aware of the imminence of a German offensive against the Low Countries scheduled for early November. Yet the President made almost no move during the autumn even

[1] First Biennial Report of General Marshall (*The War Reports*, 18); Report of Captain Puleston to Secretary Morgenthau, November 25, 1939 (*Morgenthau Diaries, MS.*, Vol. 297).

in the direction of strengthening the national defenses. By executive order, following the proclamation of a limited emergency (September 7), he authorized an increase of the Regular Army by 17,000 men, the National Guard by 35,000, and the Navy by 60,000. The Navy was in excellent condition and even the Army had received large appropriations for the fiscal year 1939-1940. The task, however, of translating these vast sums of money into equipment and of modernizing the armed forces was a tremendous one. By the dawn of the year 1940 the Army was still, in point of numbers, training, and equipment, hardly better than third rate. Much more had to be done, and had to be done much more quickly to meet the emergency. General Marshall urged upon the President (October, 1939) the need for a greatly expanded program, but Mr. Roosevelt would agree only to a supplementary War Department appropriation of $120,000,000.[2]

At the root of the President's reluctance to take drastic measures was his uneasiness about the domestic political situation. To him the first and foremost task was to secure the repeal of the arms embargo so that the Allies might be reinforced by American supplies. Until Congress had acted favorably on that proposal, Mr. Roosevelt was determined to avoid anything that might arouse "undue excitement" or in any way suggest plans for active participation in hostilities.[3] Nothing reflects this attitude better than his reaction to plans for industrial mobilization, which, after all, were basic to all preparations either for national defense or for systematic, large-scale aid to the democracies. The reader will recall that early in August Mr. Roosevelt had set up a War Resources Board under the chairmanship of Edward M. Stettinius, Jr. Although the chief assignment of this Board was to review the War Department's Industrial Mobilization Plan, the impression spread abroad that in the event of war it would be transformed into a powerful, centralized War Production Board. Whether such was ever the intention of the President may be doubted, for we find him at the end of August stating bluntly that the War Resources Board was merely a "study group," and suggesting to the Board itself that he planned to revive the dormant but not quite defunct Council of National Defense, supported by some kind of an advisory commission. He had in mind, so he said, a group of advisers who would deal respectively with production, labor, prices, materials, transportation and agriculture, and who would all report directly to him. It is reasonably clear from the record that the President was impressed by criticism of the Stettinius Board, much of which came from New Deal circles. The critics charged that the Board represented the Morgan interests and complained that labor organizations were completely unrepresented upon it. Beyond that, it should be added, the President had no

[2] Mark Watson: *Chief of Staff: Pre-War Plans and Preparations* (Washington, 1950), 155-62; Marshall's report in *The War Reports*, 18-20; Donald M. Nelson: *Arsenal of Democracy* (New York, 1946), Chap. II.

[3] Watson: *Chief of Staff: Pre-War Plans and Preparations*, 164.

stomach for a powerful, centralized war production agency. He certainly wanted to retain effective control himself, and did not fancy approaching a strongly isolationist Congress with proposals which envisaged rigorous wartime controls of American economic life.[4]

Mr. Stettinius and the members of his Board raised no objection to the President's desires. On October 12 the Board's report was completed. Contrary to the myths that soon grew up about it, the document was relatively innocuous. It rejected the idea of a superagency to control the war economy and recommended instead that a number of strictly wartime agencies be set up, which could be promptly disbanded at the end of the emergency. A War Resources Administration was to have charge of industrial mobilization, "coördinating America's productive capacity with the requirements of the Army and Navy and of the civilian population." In addition to this agency there were to be six others: a Public Relations Board, a Selective Service Board, a War Labor Board, a War Finance Board, a Food Administration, and a Price Control Authority—all told, a completely rational program which, on the face of it, should have been perfectly acceptable to the President. On Mr. Roosevelt's own copy he himself evidently marked the following passages:

> Obviously, final plans for war will depend in a large measure on the character of the war and the extent of the preparation for defense and national preparedness. . . .
>
> Final responsibility for policies and for the coördination of the war program must be vested in the President. We would urge that the number of emergency agencies reporting directly to the President be kept at a minimum, so as to simplify the President's task and to remove administrative bottlenecks.

Despite its modest proposals, the War Resources Board was dealt with in somewhat cavalier fashion. Its activities were terminated and the report, classified as "secret," was impounded. Stories got about that it was a revolutionary document which, had it been adopted, would have shortened the preparation for war by eighteen months. When, finally, the report was released in September, 1946, it proved to be so harmless that the question at once arose as to why it had been guarded so scrupulously. Unfortunately we cannot, even now, supply the answer. Above all, we cannot explain the animus with which the President treated his own creation. From the existing

---

[4] On this general problem see the valuable official studies: *Industrial Mobilization for War*, I, 9 ff.; *Plans for Industrial Mobilization 1920-1939* (Army Industrial College, November, 1945); also Harold W. Thatcher: *Planning for Industrial Mobilization 1920-1940* (Quartermaster Corps Historical Studies, No. 4, 1943). Important for the controversy over the War Resources Board are the *Hearings of the Special Committee Investigating the National Defense Program* (Part 42, "Industrial Mobilization Plan," Washington, 1948). Further comment is provided by the statement of General Robert E. Wood, a member of the War Resources Board, in *The New York Times*, February 21, 1947. We have also used the *Morgenthau Diaries (MS.)* for September 4, 7, 14, 1939 (Vols. 210, 211), and the MS. study of Troyer Anderson: *History of the Under Secretary of War's Office* (Department of the Army: Historical Division).

record we can only conclude that he was highly irritated by all the talk of his dictatorial propensities; that he was afraid, pending repeal of the arms embargo, to publish any plans for war time control of the national economy; and that, in general, he concluded that all these matters could wait. From his conversations with Secretary Morgenthau and others it becomes perfectly clear, furthermore, that he was much concerned by the charges of big business influence and troubled by the political problem of integrating labor with the other national forces. Discussing future tax legislation with Secretary Morgenthau, Mr. Roosevelt suggested that nothing be done beyond preliminary study, pending the repeal of the arms embargo. He then emphasized that fiscal policy could play a large part in the protection of democratic institutions:

We must therefore map out a fiscal policy which strengthens, not weakens, our basic institutions. One of the dangers to our institutions would be a fiscal policy which overlooks the interests of underprivileged groups and at the same time permits overprivileged groups to attain special gains. We must help maintain the unity of the great mass of Americans by curbing the extremes of excessive suffering and excess profits. . . .

The program I have in mind is not a program of war taxes. It is a program of national defense for a neutral country in a war-torn world. I have in mind a tax program which will help keep us neutral—one that will facilitate the adjustment necessary for the preservation of neutrality.

The President's thought, then, centered on ways and means of checking war profits and inflated prices, of protecting the interests of the common man. It would almost seem that he regretted ever having appointed a Board composed of business and industrial leaders. Of course, if the worst came to the worst, these men would be indispensable to the war effort. But Mr. Roosevelt was determined not to abandon control to them and appears to have still confidently hoped that the United States could remain neutral. The only reasonable conclusion seems to be that the President considered repeal of the arms embargo a sufficient program for the moment, that he thought this measure about all the public would accept, and that he based his policy of military and economic preparedness on the belief that the Allies would be able to hold the fort in Europe at least for some time to come.[5]

2. THE LATIN AMERICAN PROGRAM

In view of the President's temporizing attitude toward national preparedness, it was hardly to be expected that any really drastic action should have been taken on the larger problem of hemisphere defense. However, the State,

[5] In addition to the sources noted above, we have used a letter of Secretary Morgenthau to Under Secretary of the Treasury Hanes, September 20, 1939 (*Morgenthau Diaries, MS.*, Vol. 212); memo of Lauchlin Currie to the President reporting a talk with Stettinius, October 12, 1939 (*Roosevelt Papers:* Secretary's File, Box 41); and the original of the War Resources Board Report (*ibid.*, Box 63).

War and Navy Departments were all agreed that everything possible should be done to meet the immediate needs of the other republics, and the Panama Resolutions had laid down a fairly inclusive program for economic coöperation. To complete the picture, at least a summary account of Pan American developments during the autumn of 1939 and the ensuing winter ought to be given here.

Military questions continued to be discussed regularly by the so-called Liaison Committee, consisting of Under Secretary Welles, General Marshall as Chief of Staff, and Admiral Stark as Chief of Naval Operations. Through coördinated action, measurable though modest progress was made in this field. The establishment of the neutrality patrol zone, especially in the Caribbean area, provided a convenient opening for naval and air coöperation. By the spring of 1940 arrangements had been made with all the Governments of the Caribbean region to provide for the defense of their ports, airfields and other vital installations. While Mexico declined to enter into any general defense agreement with the United States, in specific instances coöperation was invariably forthcoming.[6]

Of particular concern to the War Department was the fact that Italian and German military and aviation missions were scattered through Latin America, including Brazil and Argentina. It was urgently necessary to eliminate these influential groups, which, as a matter of fact, the Latin American Governments were only too ready to dispense with, provided they could secure American missions to take their places. The difficulty was that both the United States Army and Navy lacked officers of appropriate training and rank. Nonetheless, heroic efforts were made to solve the problem. By the spring of 1940 the United States military and naval representation in Latin America had been increased by about 50 percent. By that time, too, there were military missions in Brazil and Haiti, aviation missions in Argentina and Colombia, and naval missions in Brazil, Argentina, Colombia and Peru, with individual Army officers assigned also to Nicaragua and Guatemala. Reciprocally, more and more Latin American officers were brought to the United States and an increasing number of student officers enrolled in our service schools.[7]

Among the most trying and urgent problems of hemisphere defense was the extraordinarily complicated issue of German control of many Latin American airlines. This matter has been referred to in an earlier chapter and need not be recapitulated here. Though it was not to be satisfactorily settled for some time to come, one aspect of the problem brooked no delay after the outbreak of war in Europe. In Colombia the Scadta Line was operating planes within three hundred miles of the Panama Canal. The

[6] Memo by the Division of American Republics, February 23, 1940.

[7] *Minutes of the Liaison Committee,* September 13, 1939; memo of the Division of American Republics, February 23, 1940.

manager, a certain von Bauer, was reputedly a confirmed Nazi who maintained personal contact with such men as Goering. The chief officials of the company, as well as its pilots and maintenance men, were almost exclusively Germans, though some of them had acquired Colombian citizenship. It was known that the company had an elaborate radio service and photographic survey. In short, the potentialities for evil were manifest and the American Embassy at Bogotá was much disturbed by reports, in late August, 1939, that some of the younger pilots proposed, if war broke out in Europe, to make names for themselves through some signal exploit. It seemed hardly credible that they should attempt an attack on the Canal, but it certainly was not beyond the realm of possibility that they should try a coup against the important oil refineries at Aruba.[8]

Ambassador Braden had long viewed this situation with suspicion and apprehension, feelings that were fully shared in the State and War Departments. The Ambassador found the Colombian authorities full of understanding and eager to eliminate German control. Their idea was to buy out the German interests, set up a new national airline (Avianca) and arrange for Panair, the American company, to take over the management of the new line and the training of Colombian pilots during a transitional period. Panair was already part owner of the Scadta company, and negotiations were therefore initiated in January, 1939, looking toward a reorganization. But in the course of long and tedious discussions it gradually emerged that Panair owned no less than 80 percent of Scadta, that it was involved in extremely complicated business arrangements with the German interests, and that for financial reasons, if for no other, it was reluctant to get rid of von Bauer and his compatriots. Added to this was the further fact that there was always danger of political difficulty if it became known that the Germans, who had given altogether satisfactory service, were to be replaced by Yankees.

It would be tiresome and not very profitable to review the details of this imbroglio. As a matter of policy, the United States Government considered it a point of the utmost importance that the Germans be removed. On the other hand, it was thought advisable that the Government avoid the appearance of interfering directly in these business affairs. Accordingly both the State Department and Ambassador Braden restricted themselves to encouraging the Government of Colombia and bringing pressure on Panair. Negotiations really got under way when, on September 5, 1939, a competent representative of Panair arrived in Bogotá. By the end of October substantial agreement had been reached. But when it came to the implementation

---

[8] Tel. from Braden (Bogotá), August 27, 1939. The published facts of the situation may be found, for the most part, in Oliver J. Lissitzyn: *International Air Transport and National Policy*, (New York, 1942), 332 ff.; 345, and in William A. M. Burden: *The Struggle for Airways in Latin America* (New York, 1943), 68, 72-73, 128.

there was so much misunderstanding and confusion that the final settlement was not achieved until the end of February, 1940. Even then it was to take several more months before the German personnel of the now defunct Scadta company was entirely replaced by Americans and Colombians. Throughout the whole tedious affair, the attitude of Colombia was, from the inter-American standpoint, above reproach. Immediately after the outbreak of the European war all planes and airfields were placed under military control. Time and again, notably on February 22, 1940, Ambassador Braden was given the most explicit assurance of coöperation in all matters touching the defense of the Canal. The State Department hastened to express its own and the War and Navy Departments' gratification over this policy. No doubt the Washington authorities shared to the full Ambassador Braden's relief, as expressed in a closing despatch of March 20, 1940:

I feel that, from the defense angle, the situation is well under control and in as favorable position as could possibly be hoped for under the circumstances. Moreover, conditions should steadily improve. . . . While, as I have previously stated, we must continue on the alert, it would seem that the major difficulties have been removed, the German influence can in due course be entirely eliminated, the safety of the Canal insured, and a mutually beneficial collaboration between the Colombian authorities and Panair be developed.[9]

Mention should be made of one other vexing military problem: that of supplying war materials to Latin American countries. These countries were not, under the law, subject to the restrictions of the arms embargo. They were free to buy in the United States whatever they could find available. On the other hand, there was no legal way of supplying them with United States Army or Navy equipment unless it had first been declared obsolete and surplus, and unless there existed no market for it in the United States. Both the War and Navy Departments, deeply concerned for hemisphere security, were eager to make available anything that could be spared. The Administration had therefore proposed to Congress a measure that would have authorized the War and Navy Departments, at the President's discretion, to release from current stocks or to manufacture for any Latin American Government, coast-defense and antiaircraft equipment and the ammunition therefor, as well as ships of war with armament. A resolution to this effect had passed the House, but was still lodged in the Senate, where it was not approved until May 28, 1940.

[9] Despatch from Braden, March 20, 1940. The records on this matter are extremely voluminous. Among the most important are telegrams or despatches from Braden, September 12, October 25, December 28, 29, 31, 1939, and January 3, 5, 10, 19, 30, 31, February 1, 3, 4, 6, 15, 19, 21, 22, March 14, 20, 1940; letter from Braden to Briggs, December 1, 1939; tels. to Braden, February 26, March 16, 1940; memo prepared for Mr. Welles, reviewing the course of the discussions, January 9, 1940; memo of conference of State and War Department representatives with representatives of Pan American Airways, February 28, 1940.

Under these circumstances it was impossible for the time being to meet Latin American requests for war materials. An appeal from the President of Mexico for small arms and ammunition had to be refused. This was embarrassing, but less important than a Chilean request for two cruisers, two destroyers, artillery and antiaircraft guns. The Chilean military establishment was notoriously weak, and therefore of much concern to American military leaders. The country had a large German element and in the past had usually turned to the British or Germans for military advice and supplies. Mr. Welles therefore urged upon General Marshall and Admiral Stark the great importance of doing something for Chile: "This is really the last link in our South American chain. If we can get Chile in coöperation with us—both Army and Navy—then the chain is complete." General Marshall could only reply that neither his conscience nor the law would permit him to declare as surplus, materials which the United States Army itself badly needed. A few items—chiefly small-caliber guns and coast-defense artillery —were made available and, in the course of the winter, were supplied not only to Chile, but to Brazil, Colombia and one or two other countries. These were mere token contributions, valuable only insofar as they indicated good will and forecast the policy that was later to be implemented on a larger scale.[10]

In the crucial field of economic aid there was more scope for action. Administration circles fully appreciated the need to cushion the shock of the European war on the highly dependent Latin American economies. Most of the Republics were now cut off from their extensive trade with Germany and, because of Allied blacklists and contraband regulations, from most of their commerce with European neutrals as well. During the First World War the situation had been somewhat alleviated by heavy purchases of food and raw materials by the belligerents, but in 1939 all hopes of a greatly expanded trade with Britain soon proved illusory. It was clearly to be a "poor man's war," with the British drawing as much as possible on their own Empire resources and holding down food consumption through drastic rationing.[11]

In Washington it was thought desirable to clear the decks of old issues so as to plan intelligently for a program of extended aid. The chronic and

[10] *Minutes of the Liaison Committee,* September 13, November 6, December 7, 1939; memo by the Division of American Republics, February 23, 1940; and the War Department records cited in Mark Watson: *Chief of Staff: Pre-War Plans and Preparation,* pp. 301-4.

[11] The literature on this problem is almost endless, but the main features were all well analyzed by Percy W. Bidwell in "El Dorado Beckons" (*Foreign Affairs,* January, 1940), and in his book *Economic Defense of Latin America* (Boston, 1941). Edward L. Korey and Edmond J. Runge: "How to get South America's business" (*Events,* March, 1940) is also a good statement. We have used further an exhaustive memorandum by Harry White of the Treasury Department, dated March 12, 1940 (*Morgenthau Diaries, MS.,* Vol. 246, pp. 388 ff.).

highly bothersome question of private debt adjustments was tackled with new vigor and satisfactory arrangements were presently arrived at with Brazil and Colombia. By the spring of 1940 only six countries still remained in default and these to the extent of only half a billion dollars. Of such countries only Mexico and Peru were major problems. Mexico alone accounted for half of the outstanding indebtedness, to say nothing of the still pending claims of the expropriated owners of agricultural and petroleum properties. Immediately after the outbreak of war President Roosevelt had addressed a letter to President Cárdenas suggesting "that all the matters of difference pending between the two Governments, some of long standing, should be adjusted, so that all the problems operating to disturb harmonious relations be removed." President Cárdenas was personally well disposed and ready to coöperate, but there was some opposition in the Mexican Congress to the whole program of inter-American action, and good will on the part of the chief executive was not in itself enough to settle the heated dispute between American companies and the Mexican Government.[12]

The main problem and the most urgent one, however, was to ease the crisis in Latin American exports and to provide financial relief. In October, 1939, the Department of Commerce arranged a meeting of United States businessmen with representatives of Latin American producers, at which time the latter were encouraged to undertake for the United States trade, the manufacture of certain items, such as linens, woolens, glassware and rugs, which were normally imported from Europe. The State Department, having already announced that negotiations for a trade agreement with Argentina were under way, added that similar discussions would be initiated with Uruguay and Chile. Meanwhile the Export-Import Bank, despite its limited funds, extended a loan of five million dollars to Chile.[13]

While emergency relief of one kind or another was being provided, the State Department was wrestling with the larger question of how to save the financial structure of the Latin American countries and how to approach the overriding problem of their surpluses. It was felt that, whatever might be done to meet sudden, short-term requirements, large-scale assistance should be based on a long-term program which was sound in a business sense and which might help to remedy the underlying economic difficulties of the various countries.[14] Because of the great variety and complexity of the

[12] Letter of Ambassador Daniels to the President, September 12, 1939 (*Roosevelt Papers:* Secretary's File, Box 45); despatch from Daniels, December 12, 1939; *Berle Diaries (MS.),* December 13, 1939. On all this see also William O. Scroggs: "Mexican Anxieties," (*Foreign Affairs,* January, 1940).

[13] H. Banto Murkland: "The Hispanic-American Scene" (*Events,* December, 1939); memo by Joseph P. Cotton, Jr., dated October 10, 1939 (*Morgenthau Diaries, MS.,* Vol. 216).

[14] All aspects of this problem were carefully canvassed in a memo by Leo Pasvolsky, dated October 6, 1939; and in the long memo by Mr. Collado, same date, entitled *Program for Economic Coöperation with the Other American Republics.*

issues involved, much hope was placed on the establishment of the Inter-American Financial and Economic Advisory Committee, provided for by the resolutions of the Panama Conference. This body, on which each of the American Republics had one representative, opened its meetings in Washington on November 15, 1939, with Under Secretary Welles in the chair. Its mandate was to consider "everything under the sun" so far as economic affairs were concerned, but with special reference to monetary problems, foreign exchange, trade dislocations, tariff reductions and financial investment.

The range of problems was so great that the committee was from the outset almost swamped. Its task was rendered particularly arduous by the lack of coördinated action among the government agencies concerned with these matters. The State Department insisted that it must have the lead in all discussions and thereby irritated the Secretary of the Treasury and to some extent the Governor of the Federal Reserve Bank. Mr. Jesse Jones, Director of the Export-Import Bank, tended to stand by the State Department, which, on the whole, enjoyed the support of the President also. Secretary Morgenthau, however, remained wedded to his basic conviction that satisfactory economic relations among the American Republics as well as the long-term interests of private American bondholders could best be served "by a policy of financial coöperation which aims at an increase in the long-run productivity of those countries."[15] Furthermore, the four-man interdepartmental committee, which, upon Mr. Morgenthau's recommendation, the President had established at the outbreak of the war to deal with requests for assistance from Latin American Governments, soon found itself rent by the jurisdictional strife to which such committees are prone.[16]

These unedifying disagreements came to a head in connection with the abortive project for setting up an Inter-American Bank, to be the clearinghouse for financial transactions and especially for loan agreements. The idea of such a bank was not new. In fact, it had been specifically recommended by the Seventh Conference of American States in 1933. Nothing had thus far come of it, and President Roosevelt urged that now the problem be tackled in earnest. With regard to Latin America, he remarked to one of his subordinates, he was prepared to "shoot the works," and to agree not only to an Inter-American Bank but to a new inter-American currency. After some weeks of interagency friction and argument, he finally called in Secretary Morgenthau and secured his promise to coöperate. Nonetheless, one of the President's staff thought it necessary some weeks later

[15] Letter of Mr. Morgenthau to Mr. Welles, August 1, 1939.
[16] Letters of Mr. Welles to Messrs. Jesse Jones and Marriner Eccles, September 8; letter of Welles to the President, November 20; memo of Feis to Welles, September 13, 1939. The interdepartmental committee consisted of Morgenthau, Welles, Jesse Jones, and Eccles.

to warn him that all was not rosy: "As you know, the main 'headache' of our coöperation with South America has been the faultiness of our internal mechanism—in other words, the clash of personalities and the disagreements between the interested agencies of our Government."[17]

It is unnecessary to review here the details of the planning. Many weeks were spent over the Bank project, which was finally approved by the Inter-American Financial and Economic Advisory Committee on February 27, 1940. The plan called for an institution to be chartered by the United States Government. The capital was to be one hundred million dollars, divided into one thousand shares. Each participating government was to subscribe to a minimum number of shares, based upon the volume of its foreign trade. The Bank was to begin operating as soon as the agreement had been ratified by at least five governments which together had subscribed to at least 145 shares. On May 10, 1940, the convention was opened for signature, on which day the United States, Mexico, Bolivia, Colombia, the Dominican Republic, Ecuador, Nicaragua and Paraguay subscribed. Brazil joined on May 13, but no other governments did so and ratifications were never deposited. Few of the major Latin American Governments showed sustained interest in the project, and Washington, where the question never got out of the Senate committee, was as ineffective as the others. The whole scheme was thus stillborn. It can perhaps be most charitably dismissed as an earnest of the Administration's good intentions which at least did nothing to interfere with economic coöperation along more immediately practical lines.[18]

It goes almost without saying that common action in the economic field involved many hitches and setbacks. For example, it was announced on January 8 and 9, 1940, that negotiations for trade agreements with Argentina and Uruguay had broken down. Worse yet, the Buenos Aires Government on January 13 issued a communiqué openly blaming the United States Government for having been unwilling to make concessions at the expense of American producers. Even though this was part of the story, and a familiar part, other factors had contributed to the failure of the negotiations. Somewhat later a United States Tariff Commissioner told a committee of Congress that the Argentine Government had refused to grant the United States equality with Britain and France. In any event, trade relations between the United States and Argentina were by nature difficult, and a satisfactory agreement was almost more than could be hoped for. Unhappily, the

[17] Note to the President, January 24, 1940 (*Roosevelt Papers:* Secretary's File, Box 58); *Morgenthau Diaries (MS.)*, October 18 (Vol. 218) and November 30, 1939 (Vol. 225); *Berle Diaries (MS.)*, November 17, 27, 28, December 4, 11, 13, 15, 19, 20, 26, 1939.

[18] *Morgenthau Diaries (MS.)*, January 9 (Vol. 234), February 21 (Vol. 242), February 27, 1940 (Vol. 243). The pertinent documents may be found in *Documents on American Foreign Relations*, II, 147 ff., and an excellent summary account in Samual F. Bemis: *Latin American Policy of the United States* (New York, 1943), 353-54.

Argentine Government, and then the Uruguayan, promptly concluded trade agreements with Japan on February 21, and other Latin American Governments were in process of doing the same thing. In these matters we were clearly up against fundamental economic divergences. At most we could hope only to prevent them from crystallizing into suspicion and antagonism.[19]

3. NEUTRALITY AND BLOCKADE

It was a foregone conclusion that war between Britain and Germany would raise countless troublesome questions of neutral rights. During the First World War British blockade procedures had occasioned so much interference with American trade that the discussions between Washington and London ultimately reached a pitch of unprecedented acrimony. Shortly after, German unrestricted submarine warfare had provoked the active intervention of the United States in the war. Many of the old issues were still unresolved, and there was every reason to expect another series of incidents and another outburst of recrimination, if nothing worse.

The expectancy was all the greater because it was perfectly well known in Washington that the British Government staked its hopes of success largely on an ironclad blockade of Germany. It will be recalled that the basic principle of British strategy was to strangle Germany economically and so gain time to build up a huge bomber force which ultimately could deliver the *coup de grâce*. With this in mind Prime Minister Chamberlain had announced blandly on September 9 that Britain was preparing for a three-year war. All arrangements had been made for keeping the sea and supply lines to Britain open and at the same time choking off German trade with the rest of the world. Immediately after the declaration of war, a Ministry of Economic Warfare was set up to coördinate action and so provide for concentrated effort. An extremely comprehensive list of absolute contraband was published at once, followed by blacklists of undesirable traders. The Ministry might assert that "no blockade of Germany in the formal sense has been declared," but there could be no shadow of doubt that the British proposed to strike at German trade in every practicable way. Neutral ships were stopped on the high seas and in many instances taken for examination to control ports, where contraband cargo, including even mail addressed to Germany, was removed.[20]

Hitler's Reich was certainly vulnerable to this type of warfare, for Germany was dependent on imports for such important materials as iron-ore, man-

[19] *Documents on American Foreign Relations*, II, 479 ff.; *Berle Diaries (MS.)*, December 24, 1939.

[20] On the British position generally see W. H. Hancock and M. M. Gowing: *British War Economy*, 95 ff., and the review of contraband and blockade measures in *Bulletin of International News*, XVI (2). An excellent account of the situation is to be found in Shepardson and Scroggs: *The United States in World Affairs, 1939*, Chap. IX.

ganese, alloy metals, edible fats and especially petroleum. There had been some stockpiling, though probably not as much as the British supposed. Furthermore, the German position was not apt to become desperate for some time, because the channels of trade to the Scandinavian countries were still open, the products of the entire Balkan area were available, and through the agreement with Moscow the prospect of extensive supplies of raw materials from the East was opened up. From the German standpoint, then, it was at first not so much a question of breaking the Allied blockade as of blockading Britain itself. After all, Britain could not live without tremendous imports. If these could be cut off, victory would be certain.

During the first four months of war the advantage certainly appeared to rest with the Allies. With command of the sea, they were able to keep some four to five hundred German vessels immobilized in foreign ports and to capture about one million tons of goods destined for Germany. To be sure, the Germans for their part succeeded in sinking about 250 Allied and neutral ships, but these losses were markedly smaller than the British had anticipated. The explanation, as we now know, was a twofold one. In the first place, the Germans had far too few submarines to carry on extensive maritime war, the more so as the British had at once instituted the system of convoy. In the second place, Hitler was genuinely reluctant to embark upon unrestricted submarine warfare. Until mid-October, that is, until he was convinced that a negotiated peace was impossible, he had insisted on rigid observance of the rules of international law and had tried scrupulously to avoid provocation of the United States. Admiral Raeder, the Commander in Chief of the German naval forces, had argued with the Fuehrer again and again in the effort to convince him that Britain, as the main enemy, must be fought with all available means. In a basic memorandum of October 15 he had pointed out that the Nazi aim must be "to cut off all imports into and exports from Britain," whether carried in enemy or in neutral ships. International law should be observed when possible, but anything that might interfere with the success of the blockade must be disregarded:

Every protest by neutral powers must be turned down. Even threats of further countries, including the United States, coming into the war, which can be expected with certainty should the war last a long time, must not lead to a relaxation in the form of economic warfare, once embarked upon. The more ruthlessly economic warfare is waged, the earlier it will show results and the sooner will the war come to an end.

Hitler agreed in principle. But as a matter of policy he hesitated to incur the hostility of the neutrals, especially of the United States. In a speech at Danzig on October 25, his henchman, Ribbentrop, went out of his way to reassure the United States. The Reich, he declared, desired a large trade with the Americas and had always respected the Monroe Doctrine. Germany had no designs on American territory and "only a pathological imagination could imagine points of conflict or of opposition between her and the United States."[21]

Hitler's forbearance certainly simplified the problem, in the beginning, so far as the United States was concerned. Prior to the Neutrality Act of 1939 (approved by the President on November 4), there was nothing to stop American ships from trading with belligerent powers. On September 14 and on October 4 Secretary Hull had warned American flag vessels to keep out of dangerous areas, but the trade went on until the combat zones were marked out after November 4. It was little short of a miracle that no United States ships were sunk during the initial period.[22]

The Administration was determined from the outset to take an indulgent attitude toward the conduct of the blockade by the British, and above all to avoid bitter arguments over neutral rights such as had taken place in 1916. As early as September 4 Secretary Hull had reviewed these matters with the new British Ambassador, Lord Lothian. Having suggested the possibility of reintroducing the British "navicert" system of the earlier war, the Secretary summed up his point of view in these words: "Let's simplify in every possible way the relations between our two countries as they may be affected by British interference with American commerce." Naturally the Ambassador was delighted by this approach and readily agreed that points at issue should be dealt with in friendly discussion rather than by public protest. Mr. Hull entrusted the conduct of conversations on the American side to the Economic Adviser of the State Department, Mr. Herbert Feis, who could be counted on to give the British the benefit of every doubt. In the first two months of war the Allies detained forty-four American ships and removed contraband from ten of them. American shippers might complain of the loss of time and other inconveniences, but initially the State Department restricted itself chiefly to exhortation of the British to be as little troublesome as possible.[23]

Officially and publicly the stand of the United States Government was

[21] Tel. from Kuykendall (Danzig), October 25, 1939. For the rest see *Fuehrer Conferences, 1939*, especially the entry for October 10, and *Nazi Conspiracy and Aggression*, VIII, UK-65, for the detailed memorandum of October 15, 1939. In a long interview granted to a representative of the Amsterdam *Algemeene Handelsblad* on September 19, 1939, Admiral Raeder had explained in detail the German adherence to the precepts of international law (tel. from Kirk, September 19, 1939).

[22] *Documents on American Foreign Relations*, II, 650; Hull: *Memoirs*, I, 679-80; *Berle Diaries (MS.)*, September 18, 1939.

[23] Memos of conversation between Hull and Lothian, September 4, 11, 1939; Hull: *Memoirs*, I, 679-80; Shepardson and Scroggs: *The United States in World Affairs, 1939*, 214-15; State Department memo, September 13, 1939. The whole problem is well reviewed by David H. Popper: *American Neutrality and Maritime Rights* (Foreign Policy Reports, XV, No. 20, January 1, 1940). On navicerts see H. Ritchie: *The "Navicert System" During the World War* (Carnegie Endowment for International Peace, Monograph 2, Division of International Law, New York, 1938).

simply that it did not abandon any of its rights under international law: "This Government, adhering as it does to these principles, reserves all rights of the United States and its nationals under international law and will adopt such measures as may seem most practical and prudent when those rights are violated by any of the belligerents."[24]

In practice, however, the Administration leaned over backward to accommodate the Allies. We made no difficulty about permitting defensively armed Allied merchantmen to use our ports, and subscribed to the Panama Declaration (October 3), which provided that merchantmen should not be regarded as warships if they did not carry more than four six-inch guns on the stern, if their lateral decks were not reinforced, and if, in the judgment of the local authorities, there existed no other circumstances indicating that the vessels could be used for offensive purposes.[25] At the same time we prohibited the entry of belligerent submarines into our ports except in cases of *force majeure*, and then only under drastic safeguards. In short, we saw to it that Allied ships might "carry" supplies purchased in the United States, despite the fact that they were armed and might, on occasion, use their armament offensively. Conversely, we made sure that submarines (and only Axis submarines could come in question) would not be able to supply themselves or secure repairs in American ports. Even more: as part of the patrol of the neutrality zone set up at Panama, we informally exchanged information with the British on the movements of German naval units and received from the British Admiralty detailed reports on procedures and technical developments.[26]

Unfortunately the lesser European neutrals were not so favorably situated as the United States. In order to prevent countries like Belgium and the Netherlands from serving as channels for German imports, the Allies from the beginning rationed their trade, in general restricting it to peacetime proportions. The neutrals might protest, but to no avail. At the same time they were exposed to heavy pressure from Berlin. The Nazi Government quickly warned them that if they accepted British regulations, they could no longer be looked upon as neutral. By early October the Germans were threatening to take over protection of Belgian and Dutch neutrality themselves. So stiff was the Nazi attitude that the French and British concluded that Hitler must be seeking a pretext for attack, with the objective of getting control of neutral gold stocks, raw diamonds and such alloy metals

[24] Hull statement of September 14, 1939, in *Memoirs*, I, 681. State Department sentiment is analyzed in *Moffat Diary (MS.)*, September 13, 1939.

[25] Memo by Mr. Gaston, of the Treasury, September 20, 1939 (*Morgenthau Diaries, MS.*, Vol. 212); *Moffat Diary (MS.)*, September 26, 1939. See also Edwin Borchard: "Armed Merchantmen" (*American Journal of International Law*, XXXIV, 1940, 107-12), and Pierre Monniot: *Les Etats-Unis et la neutralité de 1939 à 1941* (Paris, 1946), 87 ff.

[26] Kittredge MS.: *United States-British Naval Coöperation, 1939-1942*.

as tungsten. It was suggested that perhaps the American Government could arrange to take possession of these stocks in Europe and transfer them to safekeeping in the United States. But such proposals were deemed impracticable. Indeed, while the European neutrals were looking to the United States to champion the cause of nonbelligerents, the Washington Government cautiously refrained from anything more than expressions of sympathy. When, for example, the rulers of the Scandinavian States met at Stockholm on October 18, 1939, to consider the problems raised for them by the war, the American Governments, at the suggestion of the Argentine Foreign Minister, all sent identical messages to King Gustav, expressing their support of "the principles of neutrality and order for which the nations represented at the Stockholm Conference have, throughout their history, taken a consistent stand." Even more characteristic was the President's reply to a message from King Leopold of Belgium, transmitted through a special emissary, M. Theunis. In a letter to the King dated November 3, just as the fear of a German onslaught was reaching its climax, the President said:

I am in entire agreement with your belief that peace-loving nations, like your own, cannot be satisfied that their mission ended with the outbreak of war. The search for a lasting peace based on justice must go on; indeed, the neutral nations are charged with a greater responsibility before the human race than previously since they, more than any others, can express the desire for a world in which order in law has once more been restored.

We cordially agree that while the conflict continues, those nations still at peace must attempt to minimize the effects of economic warfare, to keep commerce flowing where possible, and to insist that the carrying on of war does not set up any right in belligerents to deprive neutral nations of the necessary economic basis for the continuance of their normal existence.

The Government of the United States is ready to discuss measures with M. Theunis to achieve this end, and to examine with great care any suggestions he may have to offer. The economic position of Belgium is well understood; it is fundamentally unjust that any nation should be forced into idleness and famine because it refuses to make war; the humanitarian grounds which Your Majesty asserts are of the highest; and you may be assured that this Government will not be indifferent to the appeal which you have made.

The Government of the United States will, therefore, take great pleasure in actively searching for ways and means by which the end you seek may be brought about.[27]

[27] Letter of the President to King Leopold, November 3, 1939. For the rest, tels. from Davies, September 18, October 7, 14; despatches from Davies, October 15 and November 16; tel. from Bullitt, October 4, 1939; memo of conversation between Hull, the Belgian Ambassador and M. Theunis, October 31, 1939. On the message to King Gustav, tel. from Tuck (Buenos Aires), October 14, 1939; Hull: *Memoirs*, I, 703-4; *Moffat Diary (MS.)*, October 16, 1939.

Despite these resounding assurances, little of significance was done beyond cautious efforts to warn the Germans of American displeasure in the event of an attack on the Low Countries. With few exceptions, American officials, intent on avoiding friction, and anxious above all not to interfere with the success of the economic warfare on which the Allies staked so much, ensconced themselves behind the Neutrality Act of November 4, and showed little disposition to enter the arena as the champion of the hard-pressed neutrals. On November 17, after repeated proddings from the London Embassy, the State Department finally instructed Ambassador Kennedy to present a note to the British Foreign Office (November 20). It had been drafted two weeks earlier, but so violent was the disagreement it engendered that nothing had been done in the interval. Moreover, the note scarcely did more than inform the British Government that we expected "minimum" interference in our trade with neutrals, and "appropriate" reparation for injuries to Americans in violation of their rights under international law. Not until the beginning of December did it seem necessary for the American Government to take a further stand. By then the situation had been complicated by a new development.[28]

In November the Germans had produced a new weapon in the form of magnetic mines, which were sown loose at the entrance to British harbors and soon began to take a heavy toll of shipping. It was not until November 23 that the Admiralty recovered one of these mines intact, and so was able to devise means for rendering them harmless. The German practice was not only illegal, but was contrary to agreements which the Germans themselves had signed. However, Hitler was now determined to take advantage of any weapon available. From the German records we know that he hoped for quick, decisive results from the magnetic mine.[29] The British, on their part, were for a time in a serious predicament. They hastily began to work out plans, suggested by Churchill, for sowing mines in the River Rhine, though this operation would not be possible until March, 1940, at the earliest. Meanwhile the British decided to take advantage of the German mine-laying to put into effect the long-considered blockade of German exports. This again was contrary to international

[28] Tel. from London, October 19; tel. to Kennedy, November 17, containing the U.S. note presented on November 20. On these issues we have also used despatches from Johnson (London), November 20, 21, 1939. The emergence of sentiment within the State Department favoring a stronger position on neutral rights against the British may be traced in the *Moffat Diary (MS.)*, November 2, 6, 7, 22, 23, 1939. Opposition to the policy of acquiescence centered in the Office of the Legal Adviser, but included other influential officers. On this point we have used memos of Mr. Feis to Mr. Welles, November 20; of Mr. Berle to Mr. Hickerson, November 16; and of Mr. Hunt to Mr. Hackworth, December 8, 1939. The British reply to the U.S. note of November 20 was sent in tel. from Kennedy, December 29, 1939.

[29] Note by General Thomas, December 1, 1939 (*Nazi Conspiracy and Aggression,* VII, EC-615). See also Churchill: *The Gathering Storm,* 505 ff.

law, but it was made more palatable by announcement at the same time (November 21) that the system of navicerts, by which neutral ships could secure clearance of their cargo before beginning their voyage, would be instituted. The blockade of German exports was put into effect on November 28, and the navicert system introduced on December 1, 1939.[30]

The new British policy was extraordinarily far-reaching, for it provided not only that any ship sailing from an enemy port or any port under enemy occupation or control might be required to discharge in an Allied port any goods laden in an enemy port, but also that any ship sailing from a non-enemy port but having on board goods of enemy origin or ownership might be required to discharge such goods. In other words, goods shipped from one neutral country to another were subject to seizure if they had been originally bought in Germany, or even if materials that had gone into their manufacture had come from Germany. Under these regulations American property located, let us say, in Belgium could on shipment be seized by Allied authorities if any element of German origin were involved.

The new British departure at once evoked a howl of protest from neutrals like Japan, Soviet Russia and Italy, to say nothing of the more circumspect remonstrances of the lesser states of Western Europe. It might have been expected that the United States, too, would now take a very strong line. Advocates of this course, however, again failed. No doubt Secretary Hull and many of his associates felt strongly about the growing tendency of the British to circumvent international law and to impose on American good will. On the other hand, the majority felt that a real protest would be unrealistic. After all, we wished the British all success in the campaign against Hitler and we could argue that in terms of dollars and cents little was at stake so far as we were concerned. German exports to the United States, which in October, 1938, had been valued at some $13,000,000, had dropped to a paltry $40,000 in October, 1939. Since, under the Neutrality Act, American ships were barred from most of the ports of Western Europe, it was most unlikely that German exports would be part of their cargo. It was decided, therefore, to reiterate publicly that the United States reserved all its rights, and to make no issue of the British measures excepting as concrete cases arose. As Pierrepont Moffat summed up the issue: "We all agreed that there was nothing we could do to stop it, as the war, from Britain's point of view, had become a war to block every avenue of foreign exchange. On the other hand, we all felt that, having preached the doctrine of respect for international law, to allow continued British

---

[30] Churchill: *The Gathering Storm*, 508 ff.; *Documents on American Foreign Relations*, II, 705; Shepardson and Scroggs: *The United States in World Affairs, 1939*, 216 ff.; Kelley, in *New York Herald-Tribune*, November 7; Daniels, in *The New York Times*, November 22; see also the legal opinion of Professor Edward S. Corwin in *The New York Times*, November 22, 1939.

infringements to go by default without protest, would be very ill-advised."[31] Accordingly it was agreed that another note should be sent to London, if only out of consideration for the other American Republics. Even so, the American note of December 8 was mild. It included no protest and made no demand. It simply stated, after rehearsing some of the implications of the British Order in Council and pointing out their possible effect on American interests, that the United States Government could not "view with equanimity" the measures contemplated, and requested "that measures adopted by the British Government shall not cause interference with the legitimate trade of its [i.e., United States] nationals."[32]

The American note was given no special publicity and no official emphasis. It was clearly designed primarily for the record, and was so taken by the country. The important metropolitan newspapers expressed understanding and approval, *The New York Times* pointing out that the note was a good reflection of our position toward Britain. On the one hand, it was remarked, we were neutral and vitally interested in the maintenance of respect for international law. On the other hand, our sympathies were all with the Allies in their effort to use the blockade to end German aggression. The *Christian Science Monitor*, too, let out a sigh of relief:

The carefully laid foundations of the American moral and economic support of the Allied cause may now be said to have successfully passed the most important test of their strength since the repeal of the arms embargo. . . . The willingness of Mr. Hull to moderate his protest stands, therefore, as the most striking evidence to date of the support of this country for the Allied cause.[33]

This was certainly a long cry from the sharp and even threatening notes of the Wilson era. Unfortunately in late December incidents began to crop up in regard to which the Washington Government finally felt obliged to take a sterner line. These matters can be dealt with more appropriately in another connection. What should be emphasized here is that during the first four months of the war the Administration, while "reserving all its rights," carefully abstained from making any real issue of British procedures and practices or of uttering any strong protest against Allied violations of international law. The truth was, of course, that the Government was stretching every point in the effort to be of service to the

[31] *Moffat Diary (MS.)*, November 23, 1939.

[32] Text in *Documents on American Foreign Relations*, II, 707-8; *Berle Diaries (MS.)*, December 6, 1939; Shepardson and Scroggs: *The United States in World Affairs, 1939*, 218 ff. See also the statements of Secretary Hull and Under Secretary Welles in *Christian Science Monitor*, November 22 and in *The New York Times*, November 22, 1939 (especially the editorial). The American note was communicated at once to the other American Governments (circular tel., December 8, 1939).

[33] *The New York Times*, December 9; *Christian Science Monitor*, December 9, 1939.

Allies. The repeal of the arms embargo was designed for that purpose, and the refusal to take cognizance of British blockade measures had the same end in view.

4. AID TO THE DEMOCRACIES

In retrospect, one of the most amazing features of the period of the "phony war" was certainly the leisureliness of the Allied preparations for the future. The British and the French, whatever their ultimate potentialities, lagged far behind the Germans in their preparedness for war, yet they took their time in gearing for the great effort to come. In Britain there were still more than a million unemployed workers and labor was not yet registered. In France there was not even a Ministry of Munitions until October, 1939. Both countries were making strenuous moves to increase their airplane production, but even in this respect they jointly still lagged behind the enemy. It is no part of our task to examine these matters at length, but it is worth stating once more that both the French and British were thinking in terms of a three-year, slow-moving war, based largely on the conception of economic attrition. Both were much concerned about the shortage of dollar exchange and the need for husbanding their financial resources. The British, in particular, were far too optimistic about their shipping situation, and in general seemed to feel that it would be both unnecessary and undesirable for them to purchase finished munitions in the United States. Their policy, then, was to confine their imports from the United States to essential materials and machine tools, together with some aircraft.[34]

It stands to reason that American aid to the Allies was contingent on their requirements and, prior to the repeal of the arms embargo on November 4, 1939, was restricted by domestic legislation. Good will there was aplenty. According to the Gallup polls of October 22, 1939, about 62 percent of the population favored all possible assistance to the Allies short of war. The President and his advisers felt at least as strongly as the majority of their fellow citizens. As soon as war broke out, Mr. Roosevelt made it clear that he favored sale to the Allies of everything they needed, within the limits of the neutrality legislation. He and Secretary Morgenthau, in fact, hatched out a plan by which the United States was to buy the liners *Normandie* and *Queen Mary* in order to provide the Allies with ready cash. This idea, needless to say, made no appeal to the parties in question, and was therefore dropped.[35]

In anticipation of the repeal of the arms embargo and consequently of a

[34] Far and away the best treatment of all this is to be found in Hancock and Gowing: *British War Economy*, 105 ff., but see also John F. Kennedy: *Why England Slept* (New York, 1940), 208 ff., and Pertinax: *The Gravediggers of France* (New York, 1942), 115 ff.

[35] *Morgenthau Diaries (MS.)*, Vols. 209, 210 *passim*; tel. from Kennedy, September 7; tel. to Kennedy, September 7, 1939.

flood of Allied orders, the President was much preoccupied not only with the problem of increasing American production, especially of planes and plane engines, but also with ways and means of coördinating Allied orders and meshing them with United States Army requirements. He was particularly opposed to any revival of the British connection with Morgan or any other American bank, and made it clear that both the British and French should set up purchasing commissions or corporations to deal directly with the Washington authorities. These ideas fitted in admirably with those of the French economist, Jean Monnet, who was exerting his best efforts to induce the British and French Governments to set up an organization, recommended by Mr. Bullitt, to coördinate all aspects of the Allied economy. It is unnecessary to enlarge on these matters beyond saying that early in November the President named the Director of Procurement (Treasury Department), the Quartermaster General (War Department) and the Paymaster General (Navy Department) to serve as an informal liaison committee to scrutinize foreign orders in the light of domestic requirements. About a month later (December 6), the Allies finally reached an agreement and set up an Anglo-French Coördinating Committee under the chairmanship of M. Monnet. As part of the organization of this committee an Anglo-French Purchasing Commission, under Mr. A. B. Purvis, was established in Washington. At the same time the informal American committee mentioned above was regularized under the name President's Interdepartmental Committee. To all intents and purposes the scene was now set for large-scale aid to the Allies, the whole to be closely integrated with American requirements.[36]

Mere organization, however, was not enough to solve the underlying problem. Both Ambassador Bullitt and Ambassador Kennedy were highly skeptical of Allied chances of success and thought that Britain and France should take advantage of the repeal of the arms embargo to place large orders in the United States. Mr. Bullitt lived in mortal fear lest the Nazi *Luftwaffe* prove strong enough to defeat France and Britain before those nations were in a position to offer effective resistance. He kept urging upon the French the need for a long-term program and for getting started on it. At the same time he kept impressing on the President the desirability of a vast expansion of the airplane industry to meet Allied requirements, pointing out that even if the Allies were defeated, the United States would benefit from a going war industry and from the planes previously ordered from abroad.[37] The question still remained, however, how to

[36] Hancock and Gowing: *British War Economy*, 106, 179 ff.; *Industrial Mobilization for War*, I, 51; *Morgenthau Diaries (MS.)*, September 12 (Vol. 209), 19 (Vol. 212), October 24 (Vol. 219), November 7 (Vol. 221), November 10 (Vol. 222); letter of the President to Ambassador Bullitt, November 23, 1939 (*F. D. R.: His Personal Letters*, II, 959-60).

[37] Letter of Bullitt to the President, October 18, 1939 (*Roosevelt Papers*: Secretary's File, Box 43).

bring about this expansion. American capacity for building air frames was at about 18,000 annually, but engine production lagged far behind, and it stood to reason that private interests hesitated to invest heavily in what presumably would be a temporary venture. As a partial solution the President instructed Secretary Morgenthau to work out a policy of depreciation allowances by which the abnormal investment required for plant expansion might be absorbed over the period of the contracts. He furthermore requested Mr. Morgenthau to consult with Congress to devise a program whereby the facilities thus created would become a permanent part of the national defense establishment.[38]

Even so, the foreign orders were slow in coming. On the face of it, the dilatoriness of the Allies was hard to understand, for they then had gold and securities with which to pay over a considerable period.[39] But as aforesaid, the British felt impelled, in view of the Johnson Act, which precluded American loans, to spend as few dollars as possible. They were convinced, furthermore, that they could themselves build as many planes as they could train pilots for. Their policy, then, was to buy in the United States chiefly food, cotton, petroleum and machine tools, and incidentally to counterbalance these purchases by a reduction of imports of such items as tobacco, fruits and meats. The result was that during the first five months of war American sales abroad increased only about 30 percent—those to Britain only about 10 percent.[40]

In the key matter of plane orders the figures were strikingly modest. As of January 1, 1940, the French had ordered 2095 planes, of which only 617 had been delivered, and 7372 engines, of which 1397 had been delivered. The British, on the other hand, had ordered only 1450 planes, of which they had received 650. It was not until the very end of the year 1939 that they came forward with a more extensive program. This envisaged, for the year 1940, 10,000 planes and 20,000 engines, two thirds of the planes to be bombers and one third pursuit planes. In addition, they were now prepared to sink large sums of money into the financing of American plant expansion. At long last, the sluggish Allied war effort seemed to be picking up momentum. But the immediate result was to precipitate further difficulties. It would take many months to complete American plant expansion, and it was fairly obvious that the Allied needs could be met at first only at the expense of the American defense program.

[38] *Morgenthau Diaries (MS.)*, October 24 (Vol. 219), November 7, 8 (Vol. 221), November 9, 10, 1939 (Vol. 222).

[39] On the Allied financial position see Hancock and Gowing: *British War Economy*, 107 ff. The estimates of the United States Treasury arrived at much the same figures (memoranda by Harry White, November 21, 1939, and February 5, 1940, in *Morgenthau Diaries, MS.*, Vols. 223, 239).

[40] Hancock and Gowing: *British War Economy*, 106; memo by Harry White, February 21, 1940 (*Morgenthau Diaries, MS.*, Vol. 242); report of Captain Puleston, March 27, 1940 (*ibid.* Vol. 298).

This issue had been coming to a head for some time and now precipitated a major crisis in the War Department. Secretary of War Woodring, supported by a number of high military men, was definitely opposed to foreign commitments which would interfere with American requirements, and was equally hostile to making recent American models and devices available to foreign nations. Assistant Secretary Louis Johnson, who was charged by law with the task of industrial mobilization for war, took the opposite view and held, with the President and Bullitt, that for the long term nothing could be more advantageous for the national defense than to induce the Allies to pay for the expansion of American facilities.

The President, as was his wont, did everything possible to avoid openly taking sides in the dispute, though in December he was evidently on the point of asking for Mr. Woodring's resignation. In the end he changed his mind. On January 17, 1940, he called a conference to thrash out the issue. He urged upon his subordinates the need for expediting deliveries to the Allies, and finally got them to agree that, to meet the situation at least in part, the French should be given a percentage of the United States Army orders as they were completed. The French were, for example, to receive twenty-five of the first eighty-one P-40's, which were due by June 30, 1940. Later on, it was decided further that the War Department would defer delivery in this country and permit the sale abroad of any plane as soon as an improved type became available. Under this system the Army released three hundred additional P-40's at the end of March. And so began, slowly and haltingly, the vast expansion of American plane and engine factories. It came much too late to save the French from disaster, but it was to play a role of major importance in the defense of Britain and also in the development of the American defense program. Secretary Morgenthau was speaking very much to the point when he remarked on March 1, 1940: "From the standpoint of national defense, the best thing that has happened to this country was when the French came in here and gave us the money with which to build up these engine factories."[41]

5. Impasse in the Far East

If the diplomatic revolution of August 23, 1939, and the resultant Nazi-Soviet pact boded no good for the democracies, it had at least one redeeming feature: it put an abrupt end to the ominous German plan for a military alliance between Berlin, Rome and Tokyo, a combination that was of as much concern to the United States as to Britain and France. It

---

[41] Of the Woodring-Johnson feud more will have to be said later, but see Woodring's press release of November 10, 1947, and Harold L. Ickes: "My Twelve Years with F. D. R." (*Saturday Evening Post*, June 5, 1948). For the rest, by far the best source is the *Morgenthau Diaries (MS.)*: November 8 (Vol. 221); December 29, 1939 (Vol. 232); January 4-5 (Vol. 233); January 8 (Vol. 233); January 17 (Vol. 236); March 1 (Vol. 244); March 14 (Vol. 247); March 25, 1940 (Vol. 249).

may be recalled, from the discussion in Chapter IV, that the shock of the German "betrayal" had led at once to the downfall of the Hiranuma Cabinet and to the formation of a new government under General Abe, who for the moment took over the Foreign Ministry also. The new Premier was in no sense a prominent figure. He had been selected only after plans for a cabinet under Koki Hirota, or under Prince Konoye with Hirota as Foreign Minister, had foundered. Abe had had little political experience, but at any rate had not been involved in the heated disputes about the projected alliance with Germany and therefore enjoyed the advantage of being a "new face." His Cabinet from the outset lacked character and strength, and perhaps was never thought of as anything more than a caretaker government. Its main function was to tide over affairs until Japan could adjust to the new situation created by the Nazi-Soviet partnership and the war in Europe.

Under the circumstances, it was hardly likely that the Far Eastern situation would take a spectacular turn during the "phony war." For our purposes it will suffice, therefore, to sketch the broad outline of developments and to examine in greater detail only their implications for United States policy.

Turning first to the Tokyo scene, the reader should be warned that authentic source material on Japanese policy in this period is still extremely scanty and that consequently the historian, while he may offer his impressions, is hardly in a position to speak with authority. Nonetheless, it is reasonably certain that in Tokyo Government circles most of the blame for Japan's discomfiture was laid at the door of those elements in the Army which had pressed for the alliance with Germany. According to Prince Saionji, the last survivor of the Elder Statesmen, Japanese foreign policy had proved a greater failure than ever before in the national history. Having always had his doubts about an alliance with Germany, the old Prince greatly resented the power of the Army and felt strongly that something should be done to bring it to heel and to reëstablish the rightful authority of the Foreign Office. The Emperor himself shared these views and even went so far as to challenge the right of the Army to nominate the new Minister of War. He wanted a man of his own choice, one who would coöperate with the Prime Minister and who would purge the Army of rebellious elements. Happily, General Hata, on whom the choice fell, was acceptable to the Emperor and to the Army chiefs as well.

This did not mean, however, that the aggressive groups of younger officers in the Army were completely under control. During the entire month of September, 1939, the course of Japanese policy hung in the balance. Ribbentrop, enamored as ever of the scheme for an alliance with Japan against Britain and France, was at infinite pains to convince the Japanese Ambassador, General Oshima, that it was to Tokyo's interest to ally itself

with the new Nazi-Soviet bloc: "If Germany were defeated in this war,"
he argued, "an extensive world coalition of Western democracies would
quickly form itself, which would oppose any expansion of Japan and would
in particular again take away her position in China." Germany, he continued, would be only too happy to mediate a settlement between Japan
and Soviet Russia:

If that should succeed, Japan would be able to freely extend her power in East
Asia toward the South and there penetrate further. According to our conviction,
this is the direction in which Japan's vital interests lie. . . . Of course, it was important that this [settlement] should happen quickly, so that the above-mentioned
power constellation might yet be realized during our present conflict with England,
which is decisive for the world politics of the future.[42]

General Oshima, whose Nazi sympathies were notorious, was taken into
camp completely. He assured Ribbentrop that the Japanese Army would
probably be favorable to the idea, and promptly began to advocate this
new course in his reports. As he had predicted, the scheme evoked an immediate response from the restless military elements. Almost at once there
was agitation in government circles "to strike at England with the military alliance between Japan, Germany, and Russia." It seems that at first
Premier Abe himself was not wholly averse to the idea, though he soon
abandoned it. The forces which had blocked the projected military alliance
before August 23 were still united and in a stronger position than ever.
They smarted under the indignity Japan had suffered at Nazi hands and
did not put the slightest trust in Soviet Russia. The Emperor would hear
nothing of Ribbentrop's scheme, Prince Saionji objected vigorously, the
Navy leaders and representatives of business interests were opposed, and
finally Admiral Nomura, selected as Foreign Minister on September 18,
registered his veto. These circles warmly advocated that Oshima, who provoked one complication after another, be recalled. At a Cabinet meeting
of September 21 it was decided, at least for the time being, to abandon
discussion of the project.[43]

Of this entire matter it should be remarked, by way of parenthesis, that
Russia, whether Imperial or Soviet, was Japan's traditional enemy and that,
in September, 1939, the forces of the two powers were engaged in what
amounted to an undeclared war on the Manchurian border. These hostilities had apparently been provoked by the Kwantung Army command
without reference to the Tokyo Government and had assumed unexpectedly
large proportions. Worse yet, the Soviet forces had demonstrated a marked
superiority, especially in artillery, and the Japanese were getting distinctly

[42] Tel. of Ribbentrop to Tokyo, September 9, 1939 (*Tokyo War Crimes Documents*, No.
4034A). *Cf.* also Ribbentrop's interview with Japanese correspondents in Berlin, published
also in the Moscow press (tel. from Steinhardt, October 7, 1939).
[43] *Saionji-Harada Memoirs*, September 3, 8, 19, 21, 27, 1939.

the worst of it. The new Abe Government was therefore only too ready to follow up the Army's suggestion that a truce be sought. On their side the Soviets had every reason to end complications in the Far East. Agreement was quickly arrived at and a truce concluded on September 16, 1939.[44] Nevertheless, this settlement did not portend a radical departure in Japanese-Soviet relations. The Tokyo press was still violent in its denunciations of "Red imperialism," and the Japanese Government made a point of denying that the agreement had anything to do with German good offices or in fact had any significance except as part of Japan's policy of peace in China.[45]

In brief the situation between Soviet Russia and Japan was this: in view of the European war both sides desired to minimize friction and conflict. Both were quite prepared to eliminate specific issues and to adjust chronic disputes over such matters as the fisheries, the Sakhalin concessions, and railroad interests in Manchuria. Beyond that, neither party trusted the other, and the basis for a general settlement was lacking. Among other things, an alliance would have been worthless to Tokyo unless the Soviets were willing to abandon the policy of aiding Nationalist China. For the time being, at least, there was not the slightest prospect that the Kremlin would leave Chiang Kai-shek in the lurch or allow China, the best guarantee against a Japanese attack on the Russian Far East, to go under. That being so, the outlook for a Soviet-Japanese pact was dim indeed.

The Japanese policy, as publicly announced by the new Abe Cabinet, was to concentrate on the settlement of the burdensome "China Incident." So long as the Japanese armies were tied up in China, it would be utterly impossible for the Tokyo Government to take advantage of opportunities presented by the European war for further expansion either to the North or to the South. There can be little doubt that in the autumn of 1939 a really concerted effort was made by the Tokyo Government to clear the decks so far as China was concerned. The discussions which went on continuously with members of Chiang Kai-shek's own entourage, as well as with Wang Ching-wei, who had deserted the Generalissimo, were extraordinarily involved. It will be a long time, if ever, before the details can be known. Fortunately they need not concern us here beyond requiring note of the decision, arrived at in Tokyo in October, to strike an agreement with Wang Ching-wei and set up a puppet government at Nanking. Concurrently the military campaign against the Nationalists was resumed with vigor, though with indifferent success.

[44] Dallin: *Soviet Russia's Foreign Policy*, 224 ff.; Harriet L. Moore: *Soviet Far Eastern Policy* (Princeton, 1945), 112 ff.; Dallin: *Soviet Russia and the Far East* (New Haven, 1948), 43-44; *Saionji-Harada Memoirs*, September 24, 1939; tel. from Steinhardt, September 15, 1939.

[45] *Bulletin of International News*, XVI (2), 1017, 1152; *The New York Times*, September 21, 1939.

At the heart of the China problem, as the Japanese realized so well, was the fact that Chiang Kai-shek enjoyed for differing reasons the moral and material support of many powers, at this time more especially of Soviet Russia, but also of Britain, France and the United States. It was only natural that the Generalissimo should have viewed the international scene from the angle of continued aid and that therefore he should have lived in mortal fear lest the Soviets and the Japanese reach an agreement at his expense. Almost equally alarming to him was the prospect that Britain and France, once they were engaged in war in Europe, would find it necessary to make their peace with Japan, even if it meant abandoning China to its fate.

So far as the Kremlin was concerned, Chiang's fears were soon revealed as groundless. It appears that by mid-September the Soviet Government had given explicit assurances that no nonaggression pact was being negotiated with Tokyo and that Russia proposed to continue its "sympathetic assistance" to the Chungking Government. A trade mission was dispatched to China and, so far as one can determine, the flow of supplies continued and perhaps even increased.[46] But with regard to the British and French the situation was necessarily different. The British were fully convinced, after the acute Tientsin crisis of the summer of 1939, that the Japanese Army was initiating a systematic drive to force the British and French out of China. They were furthermore deeply impressed by the possibility that Russia might join forces with Germany and Japan for a concerted attack on the Allied position in the Far East. Under the circumstances they were understandably eager to take advantage of the change of government in Japan to embark on a policy of appeasement, and were insistent in their suggestions to the United States Government that it use its influence to mediate a settlement of the China Incident that would satisfy Japan.[47]

In the State Department the situation was viewed with greater detachment. Neither Ambassador Steinhardt nor Mr. Dooman, the Chargé d'Affaires in Tokyo, believed that a Soviet-Japanese pact was likely, and their opinion was largely shared by the State Department. Indeed, the prevailing view was that Tokyo, under the impact of the Nazi-Soviet deal and if left alone, would reorient its policy and seek to establish better relations with the Allies and with the United States.[48]

The general plan of the State Department, then, was to eschew any

[46] Note from the Chinese Embassy to Secretary Hull, September 14; tels. from Bullitt, September 14, October 26, 1939.
[47] See above, Chapter IV. For the rest see Hull: *Memoirs*, I, 720; memo of conversation between Welles and the French Ambassador, August 30, 1939.
[48] Tels. from Dooman, August 25, 28; tel. from Steinhardt, September 8; tels. to Dooman, August 30, 31; tel. to London, September 19; Hull: *Memoirs*, I, 720; note of Hornbeck to Hull, September 2; the *Moffat Dairy (MS.)*, September 8, 1939, indicates some worry over the possibility of a Soviet-Japanese pact.

effort to bring pressure on the Tokyo Government, but to stand firm in its established position and to give no encouragement to British desires to withdraw. Unhappily a test case arose almost at once and gave much food for thought. On September 5, 1939, the Japanese Government handed to the British, French, German and Polish Ambassadors a note offering the "friendly advice" that, as a voluntary act, they withdraw their naval vessels and troops from areas of China under Japanese military control. Japan, according to the note, planned "to avoid becoming involved in that war [in Europe] and to devote its energies to settling the China Incident." It therefore feared that the presence of "naval vessels and troops belonging to powers participating in that conflict might result in unfortunate incidents and in a condition of affairs ill-adapted to Japan's non-involvement policy."[49]

Since neither Germany nor Poland had any warships or troops in China, it was fairly clear that the note was one more move in Japan's unrelenting effort to eliminate foreign influence from China. A copy of the note having been given the American Chargé "for information," Mr. Dooman was certainly safe in concluding that United States ships and forces were envisaged along with the rest. Washington read the note in the same way and at once accepted the challenge. While the British and French were ready to withdraw in order to avoid humiliating expulsion, Secretary Hull took up the matter with the Japanese Ambassador. In a series of outspoken conversations he told Mr. Horinouchi that the Japanese note directly affected the rights and interests of the United States, inasmuch as Allied withdrawal from Shanghai, for example, would leave the American forces in an impossible position:

> The American Government cannot and does not admit any right on the part of any power to force it out. The rights of the United States have in many ways been impaired by acts of Japanese authorities during recent years. There are many ways in which the United States is capable of taking action of retaliation. . . . This Government must make clear its conclusion that the purpose behind the Japanese notice to the British and French is not a mere innocent, friendly purpose, but a purpose further to exclude first one set of nationals of another country, and then another set of nationals of still another country, until the Shanghai situation would be on a parity with the Yangtze situation and others like it. . . . How does your Government expect us to prevent the Congress and country, if we should attempt to do so, from taking up the question of our monetary and financial and trade relations with your country and dealing with it in a way that you can well imagine in the light of all the circumstances?

The Ambassador was clearly taken aback, but neither at the time, nor a week later, after he had heard from his Government, was he able to give anything beyond the weakest assurances that there was no intention of

[49] Text in *Foreign Relations of the U. S.: Japan*, II, 9 ff.

compelling the American forces to leave. To these assurances Mr. Hull replied by reiterating that the United States Government could not "bring out its guards on the basis of an unwarranted suggestion or threat by another Government."

The American stand induced the British and French not to withdraw their forces for the time being. Whatever they thought of Mr. Hull's suggestion that no reply be made to the Japanese note, it is clear that London and Paris did not consider the United States position sufficiently affirmative to enable them to defy Tokyo. The point was discussed for several weeks until, on September 27, the Secretary informed the British definitely that the United States proposed to leave its own forces in China, and in the places where at the time they were stationed. While the British and French did not reconsider their plans for eventual evacuation of their own forces, for the moment at least Tokyo decided not to force the issue. So the matter rested.[50]

The Japanese note of September 5 would seem to have been enough to dispel any ideas that Tokyo would seek better relations with the democracies. It is particularly important to realize, therefore, that the whole business seems to have been an ill-considered move engineered by the Chief of the Asia Section of the Tokyo Foreign Office, a man evidently completely subservient to the demands of the Army. The step was taken, moreover, at a time when Premier Abe had not yet appointed a Foreign Minister and when the entire Foreign Office was in a state of confusion. It is therefore understandable that the issue aroused opposition even in Japanese Government circles, which probably accounts for the fact that, after the vigorous American reaction, nothing more was done about it.[51]

The situation looked far more hopeful when Admiral Nomura presently assumed charge of the Japanese Foreign Office. As a younger man the Admiral had served, during the First World War, as Japanese Naval Attaché at Washington. He spoke the English language and was well acquainted in American circles. Even more than other Japanese naval leaders he was firmly opposed to any conflict with the United States and anxious to find some reconciliation of the existing antagonism. In Japanese circles, too, he was looked upon as a man of character and sound common sense. Those elements which were opposed to an alliance with Germany welcomed his appointment and were gratified to have him put the quietus on talk of concluding an agreement with Soviet Russia and Germany against

[50] Memos of conversation between Mr. Hornbeck and Mr. Mallet of the British Embassy, September 9; between Mr. Hull and the British Ambassador, September 19; between Mr. Hull and the French Ambassador, September 20; between Hornbeck and the British and French Ambassadors, September 27, 1939. *Foreign Relations of the U. S.: Japan*, II, 12 ff. The episode is treated in some detail in Hull: *Memoirs*, I, 718-22. See also Feis: *The Road to Pearl Harbor*, 39.

[51] *Saionji-Harada Memoirs*, September 5, 1939.

Britain and France. At a Cabinet meeting on September 21 it was evidently agreed that, in view of Japan's economic situation (referring no doubt to the expiration of the commercial treaty with the United States in January, 1940), it was imperative for the Government to reëstablish more cordial relations with Britain and especially with the United States.[52]

In Washington there was deep satisfaction at Nomura's appointment. According to a Japanese source, for which no corroboration has been found in the American records, the President himself sent a message to the new Foreign Minister, recalling their mutual acquaintanceship of World War I days and ending with the phrase: "I pray for your success." To this Nomura is alleged to have replied: "To have received Your Excellency's cordial message through Horinouchi at this time, when we are expending our utmost efforts towards the betterment of diplomatic relations between the United States and Japan, is indeed gratifying and I am deeply impressed."[53] But it was to be some weeks before Nomura was in a position to devote attention to the key problem of relations with the United States. He found the Tokyo Foreign Office rent by internal dissension and in practical revolt over the projected transfer of trade questions to a new Ministry of Overseas Trade. It must have taken several weeks to restore a modicum of discipline and morale.[54]

Meanwhile President Roosevelt and his advisers had come to what, under the circumstances, was a rather unusual decision, namely, to put the American position plainly before the Japanese people. Ambassador Grew was about to return to Tokyo after a furlough of five months. He had had ample opportunity, while at home, to convince himself that the American public felt strongly about Japanese policies and procedures, that it thoroughly approved of the denunciation of the trade treaty, and that, further, it would probably welcome the imposition of economic sanctions if the Japanese persisted in violating American rights and disregarding American interests. He had found, too, that the President and Secretary Hull, however desirous they might be of better relations with Japan, had not the slightest intention of retreating from the essential position which had so often been expounded to Tokyo. Ambassador Grew himself raised the question whether it might not be useful for him on his return to Tokyo to make a public report on American sentiment and policy as one way of clearing the atmosphere for further discussion and of inducing action on the part of the Japanese Government. It was decided that the Ambassador should do this in an address to the America-Japan Society, of which many prominent Japanese were

[52] *Saionji-Harada Memoirs,* September 5, 17, 21, 1939; tels. from Dooman, September 26, 28, 1939, reporting Nomura's assurances of his eagerness to work for better relations.

[53] Statement of Vice Foreign Minister Tani to Harada (*Saionji-Harada Memoirs,* December 17, 1939).

[54] *Saionji-Harada Memoirs,* September 27, 1939; Sir Robert Craigie: *Behind the Japanese Mask* (London, 1946), 80.

members. The text of his speech was carefully considered in the State Department, and Mr. Grew took a draft with him when he set out for his post. Interestingly enough, the Ambassador, after surveying the ground in Tokyo and finding the Japanese authorities better disposed than he had anticipated, requested and received permission from the Department to tone down some of the passages in his address. Nonetheless, as he delivered it on October 19, 1939, it was still an unusually plain-spoken review of the situation, most appropriately referred to as the speech "straight from the horse's mouth."

The Ambassador began his address not only with the amenities ordinarily expected of a diplomat, but with all the extra graces required by the peculiar Japanese sense of propriety and form. Thereupon he launched upon a discussion of American public opinion, the stuff of which it was made and the interest and information on which it was based. This intelligent and articulate opinion, he stressed, was a force which the American Government could not "possibly overlook" and, indeed, would have to reflect in its policies and actions. With respect to Far Eastern affairs he, the Ambassador, had found American opinion "very nearly unanimous" in resenting "some of the things that Japan's armed forces are doing in China today, including actions against American rights and legitimate interests in China."

Turning then to examine the reasons for American resentment, the Ambassador made no attempt to draw up a "bill of particulars." He did make a special point, however, of refuting the idea, prevalent in Japan, that the American approach to Far Eastern problems was purely "legalistic." He reviewed the cardinal principles of American policy: the maintenance of peace through orderly processes in international dealings, respect for the sovereign rights of other peoples, reliance on equality of economic opportunity, etc. Again and again Mr. Grew stressed the American belief that wars could not be localized and that therefore they were the concern of all nations. He made it as clear as he could that in the view of his country and his Government there need be no conflict with Japan, and that he personally proposed to expend his every effort in the attempt to arrive at agreement. But certain things, he felt, must be said, notably with regard to Japan's plans for the New Order in East Asia, a program which the Japanese were constantly charging Americans with misunderstanding:

The American Government and people understand what is meant by the "new order in East Asia" precisely as clearly as it is understood in Japan. The "new order in East Asia" has been officially defined in Japan as an order of security, stability and progress. The American Government and people earnestly desire security, stability and progress not only for themselves but for all other nations in every quarter of the world. But the new order in East Asia has appeared to include, among other things, depriving Americans of their long established rights in China, and to this the American people is opposed.

There followed a more elaborate statement regarding Japanese violation of American rights as well as of international agreements and then, by way of peroration, the pointed statement:

In short, the American people, from all the thoroughly reliable evidence that comes to them, have good reason to believe that an effort is being made to establish control, in Japan's own interest, of large areas on the continent of Asia and to impose upon those areas a system of closed economy. It is this thought, added to the effect of the bombings, the indignities, the manifold interference with American rights, that accounts for the attitude of the American people towards Japan today.[55]

It is always extremely difficult to appraise the effect of such unorthodox moves as Mr. Grew's address. The President, the State Department and the Ambassador were all at one in thinking that, after abandoning the idea of sending another strong and comprehensive note to the Japanese Foreign Office, it was desirable to restate the American position and the determination of the Administration not to recede from it. The whole speech was, in a sense, based on the belief that many high officials in Tokyo were unaware of what was going on in China and ignorant also of the American reaction to the violations of foreign rights and interests. It was realized that the Japanese might well resent the Ambassador's proclaiming American grievances in public, but Washington thought the time had come to put the cards on the table, and the President, for one, had no regrets. In a message to Grew he said: "I liked your address and the Secretary and I agreed that you did it in the right way and at the right time."[56]

In Tokyo the repercussions were mixed. The newspapers referred to the address as "arrogant" and "impertinent" and expressed doubts whether the American public, which construed a few unintentional "accidents" as wholesale depredations, really understood the situation or appreciated the objectives of the New Order. The same line was taken by a Foreign Office spokesman, Yakichiro Suma, who told foreign correspondents that it was difficult to agree with Mr. Grew's statement that the American public had a correct grasp of the facts, and added: "From my own experiences in America, there has been deplorable ignorance among the people concerning conditions in the Far East—American views with regard to the Far East are completely directed by emotion. The American Government should pay full attention to actual facts of the situation and their opinion should be more constructive and practical." On the other hand, the Ambassador was told by one of his liberal Japanese friends, who claimed to have discussed

[55] Text in *Foreign Relations of the U. S.: Japan*, II, 19-29. See also Joseph C. Grew: *Ten Years in Japan* (Simon and Schuster, New York, 1944), 288-97; Hull: *Memoirs*, I, 723; and Feis: *The Road to Pearl Harbor*, 42.

[56] The President to Ambassador Grew, October 23, 1939. *F. D. R.: His Personal Letters*, II, 945.

the matter with the highest officials, that the address had made a deep impression, that it had started the ball rolling at precisely the right moment, and that a number of influential people would form a team to keep it rolling in the right direction.[57]

The truth of the matter was probably that the "horse's mouth" speech had both favorable and unfavorable effects. The rift in Japanese Government circles between the militarist, pro-German elements and the more circumspect moderates was perfectly well known and, as it appears from the records, was a real and important factor. It is essential, however, to bear in mind that for the most part all factions in Japan had the same objective, differing only in their conceptions as to how the expansion of the Empire, which they all deemed vital, could best be attained. It is important, too, to realize that the division in Japanese counsels was not simple and clean-cut. For example, there were military men, like General Hata, the War Minister, who favored better relations with the United States and Britain. On the other side, there appears to have been a noisy group within the Foreign Office which sided entirely with the High Command and favored a coalition with Germany against the democracies. Certainly the Government did very little to check the violent anti-British demonstrations in Tokyo, which probably underlay the disappointing decision taken by London and Paris in late October to withdraw all but token forces from Peiping and Tientsin. Obviously the British and French rated the military influence in Tokyo higher than that of its opponents and genuinely feared an outright attack upon the Allied positions.[58]

The situation as it presented itself at the beginning of November was substantially this: The Japanese High Command was gradually recovering its confidence and was again bringing much pressure to bear in favor of a deal with Germany and Russia. Shiratori, the Japanese Ambassador to Italy, who had recently returned from his post, was agitating for the same move and was rallying an active group of younger officials in the Foreign Office, a group of which Yakichiro Suma was one of the most aggressive.[59] On the other hand Foreign Minister Nomura, supported by the Prime Minister, the Minister of War, the Minister of the Navy and, most importantly, by the Emperor, was determined to try for better relations with both Britain and the United States.

To this group the question of the day was not whether Japan should combine with other powers for further conquest, but rather how Japan could ward off the threat of American economic sanctions following the expiration of the commercial treaty in January, 1940. It is impossible to

[57] *Foreign Relations of the U. S.: Japan*, II, 29-30; Grew: *Ten Years in Japan*, 288, 297-98.
[58] The decision was announced early in November. See Hull: *Memoirs*, I, 722; and G. Nye Steiger: "Japan Resumes the Initiative" (*Events*, January, 1940).
[59] *Saionji-Harada Memoirs*, November 2, 16, 1939; Hallett Abend: "Japan Picks on Uncle Sam" (*Saturday Evening Post*, November 25, 1939).

emphasize too forcefully that Japan was dependent on the United States for the great bulk of its vital imports, notably of scrap iron and petroleum. There was no way in which Japan, if deprived of this trade, could long continue military operations, even in China. The military men themselves, excepting the most rabid, could not fail to see the transcendent importance of this issue. We must suppose that they gave at least grudging approval of the efforts of the Abe-Nomura Cabinet to find some substitute for the doomed trade treaty with the United States. On the other hand, it is reasonably clear and should be carefully noted that the military, while agreeing to Nomura's bargaining, were never willing to give him anything substantial to bargain with. Certain basic objectives of Japan, especially in China, were regarded as beyond debate. That was the root difficulty all the way through and it was recognized as such on the American side. A State Department memorandum of October 25, 1939, laid it down as a "basic certainty" that Japan was committed "to its program of establishing a 'new order in East Asia,' which meant the establishment of Japanese political and economic hegemony in China and the corollary elimination of American and other Western influences."[60] Ambassador Grew held much the same view and even then looked upon the situation with serious concern. In his diary he noted on November 1:

> The next two months, in my opinion, are going to be the most critical in the history of American-Japanese relations. Unless we can get concrete results *promptly* and not only negative but positive steps to show the American people that Japan desires and intends to respect the interests and rights of the United States in China, the pressure for an embargo against Japan next winter is going to be great and Congress may demand it. . . . If and when we impose an embargo, we must expect to see American-Japanese relations go steadily down hill; it will then be too late for any possible hope of improvement, and that is why the coming months will be critical.[61]

The discussions, which began under such a cloud of well-justified pessimism, need not long detain us. On November 4 Ambassador Grew left with Nomura three memoranda. The first was a necessarily incomplete chronological statement of the Embassy's written protests and representations since 1937, indicating which had been answered or at least acknowledged. The second was an inevitably lengthy collection of excerpts from the Ambassador's previous conversations with Japanese Foreign Ministers, comprising the assurances that American rights and interests in China would be

[60] Memo by the Far Eastern Division, October 25, 1939.
[61] Grew: *Ten Years in Japan*, 299; also letter of Grew to the President, November 6, 1939 (*Roosevelt Papers:* Secretary's File, Box 45); *Saionji-Harada Memoirs*, November 5, 1939; and the interesting Japanese press release after the Cabinet meeting of October 27, 1939 (*Foreign Relations of the United States: Japan*, II, 30-31). The differences of American official opinion on the issue of sanctions against Japan in the autumn of 1939 are clearly outlined in Feis: *The Road to Pearl Harbor*, 38-46.

respected. The third consisted of certain passages which Mr. Grew had deleted from his "horse's mouth" speech before delivering it. By way of explanation the Ambassador pointed out that "there is at present in the United States a strong demand for an embargo against Japan when our Treaty of 1911 expires next winter, and it is my earnest hope that steps will be taken by Japan which will relieve this pressure of public opinion." The first thing needed was to clear the atmosphere, to which end he suggested that Japan cease the bombings, indignities and flagrant interferences with American rights and interests in China, and give some concrete evidence of readiness to improve relations. The opening of the Yangtze River to American commerce would be an appropriate step of a positive character. In response to this Nomura could only protest that there was "a misunderstanding on the part of the United States that Japan intends to drive American interests out of China." He asked the Ambassador to bear in mind that "Japan's paramount object in China is to convert an anti-Japanese China into a China sympathetic to Japan. . . . If third powers help China to antagonize Japan, stabilization will be impossible." He hoped that "the United States will give better appreciation of the extent to which Japanese authorities in China are endeavoring to protect American property in China."[62]

In all this discussion there was not even the slightest suggestion that the gulf between the two Governments created by the China Incident could be bridged. During the ensuing weeks both sides, on the contrary, strove earnestly to reinforce their positions in China. The Japanese pushed on with their arrangements for a new regime under Wang Ching-wei and notified Washington of their intentions. The State Department was assured that the new government would not be a puppet government, though the Japanese would feel obliged to keep troops in China to aid in combatting communism. They did not ask for *de jure* recognition of the new regime, but hoped that foreign governments would coöperate with it. The American reply to this must have been expected. Secretary Hull hastened to dispel any shadow of doubt about his attitude:

It is our opinion that the proposed regime, if set up, would be a purely artificial creation, and that its existence would depend upon Japanese armed support; that the regime would lack any spontaneous or genuine broad support on the part of the Chinese public; and that it would be designed primarily to serve the special purposes of Japan which, as in the case of the regimes established during recent years under Japanese auspices in Manchuria, Inner Mongolia, at Peiping and at Nanking, would result in depriving the people and the Government of the United States, and the people and governments of other third countries of long-established rights of equal opportunity and fair treatment in China which are legally and justly theirs. We could not regard the setting up of such a regime as evidence of a

[62] *Foreign Relations of the U. S.: Japan*, II, 31-34.

disposition on Japan's part to pursue a course in and with regard to China which would be in accord with fundamental principles and policies in which this Government believes. The setting up of such a regime would therefore in our opinion serve to render more difficult rather than to facilitate an adjustment of American-Japanese relations.[63]

Far from lending countenance to the Japanese designs, the United States Government was determined to continue its support of Chiang Kai-shek and the Nationalist Government. It will be recalled that after the conclusion of the Nazi-Soviet pact, the Generalissimo was deeply apprehensive lest the British and French abandon their position in China and appease Japan as best they might; further, lest Soviet Russia and Japan come to an agreement that would involve the discontinuance of Soviet aid to China. For a time it had seemed to Chiang Kai-shek that the only solution to the impasse would be for the United States to impose economic sanctions on Japan which would oblige the Japanese militarists to accept a conference and a settlement of the China Incident on the basis of the Nine-Power Treaty. These were ideas born of desperation, which were soon abandoned when it became clear that the United States Government would stand firmly by China and would use its influence with the British and French toward the same end.[64] There remained, however, the problem of further financial support for the Chungking regime. Need for a further loan or credit had been impressed upon the President by the Chinese Ambassador at the end of September and Mr. Roosevelt had instructed Secretary Morgenthau "to do everything we can that we can get away with." What the Chinese desired was a further credit of $75,000,000, but this could be handled only through the Export-Import Bank, whose funds were extremely limited and which in any case would require some return. The obvious arrangement would have been to have China export some such strategic material as tin, but such a plan at once opened the further question of how this was to be gotten out of China. At best a solution of the problem would take time, despite the abundance of good will in Washington. In high circles there was much feeling that "any help we give to China will repay us by relieving the next generation of Americans from facing a triumphant Japan dominating Eastern Asia," but the ways and means of giving effective support were ever something of a mystery.[65]

[63] *Foreign Relations of the U. S.: Japan*, II, 34-35.

[64] In addition to what has been said in Chapter IV, reference should be made to the letter of Chiang Kai-shek to the President, dated July 20, 1939. This letter, the substance of which was completely outdated when it became known to the Department on October 14, was not actually delivered to the President until November 2. In reply, November 9, 1939, the President could only renew the assurances given early in September. This whole episode is well treated in Hull: *Memoirs*, I, 723-24.

[65] Reports of Captain Puleston, after talks with Admiral Yarnell and Mr. Hornbeck, November 8, 15, 1939 (*Morgenthau Diaries, MS.*, Vol. 297). Further data on the loan project is to be found in the same *Diaries*, for September 26 (Vol. 213), October 4 (Vol. 215), and November 22, 1939 (Vol. 223).

The month of November went by without further word from Nomura, but with another crop of rumors regarding a Japanese-Soviet pact. On November 6 a new Soviet Ambassador arrived at Tokyo, a post that had been vacant since 1938. A few weeks later it was announced that the two powers had agreed to negotiate a trade treaty as part of their effort to solve outstanding issues. This was enough to give the British and French another attack of nerves. On November 21 the British Ambassador, Lord Lothian, once again expounded to Mr. Welles the British view of the Far Eastern problem. The Allies, he reiterated, could do nothing if the Japanese decided to destroy their position in China. Hence, if Britain were simply to consult its own selfish interests, the obvious course would be to seek direct agreement with Japan. On the other hand, the American public would be bound to regard such a policy as a sellout. Accordingly, it seemed to the British to be in the interest of all the democracies to help Japan and China arrive at a settlement, which of necessity would involve concessions by both sides.

To this argument the Under Secretary took strong exception. He could not, so he said, conceive of a Soviet-Japanese agreement to partition China, and he was convinced that without an agreement on such terms Japan would be unable to disregard Russia and turn southward against the British, French and even Dutch possessions. Indeed, Welles added that it seemed to him "fantastic to believe that the Japanese Government, from its own selfish standpoint, would undertake an adventure of this character, knowing perfectly well that Russian policy in the Far East was inevitably antagonistic to Japanese policy and knowing equally well that no reliance could be placed by Japan upon any agreement which might be proffered by the Soviet Government." In any case, the United States Government refused to be intimidated. It would not, said Welles, agree to any settlement in China that left Japan in a special military or economic position. It would continue to insist on its legal and treaty rights, and on equality of opportunity for all nations in China. It was doubtful whether Chiang Kai-shek would negotiate on any other basis, and it was equally doubtful whether Japan would negotiate even on that basis. To Lothian's inquiry whether, in case an equitable peace could be arranged, the United States would still refuse to recognize Japanese domination of Manchuria, the Under Secretary replied that on this subject the American attitude was "well-known."[66]

It seems altogether likely that the Tokyo Government itself propagated rumors of a coming agreement with Russia in order to soften the democratic governments. On November 24 the Japanese Ambassador, in the course of a general discussion with Mr. Hull of Japanese-American relations, stressed the desire of the liberal and business interests in Japan for an improvement of those relations and then dropped the ominous remark: "If no means of obtaining economic coöperation from the United States were found, these elements in Japan would possibly find it necessary to look elsewhere for

[66] Memo of conversation between Welles and Lord Lothian, November 21, 1939.

these means of economic coöperation, and the arrangements between Japan and Soviet Russia for economic coöperation might consequently be the inevitable result." Although the Ambassador's remarks were restricted to "economic coöperation," they at once brought forth an acid retort from Mr. Hull: "Whatever surprise might be created in the United States by the development of closer relations between Japan and another power, it would not be equivalent to the surprise which was created when Hitler entered into closer relations with that same foreign power."[67]

Although the British and French Governments continued to plead the acute danger of a Japanese-Soviet pact unless something were done to satisfy the Tokyo Government, the State Department refused to be taken in by the flood of rumor. After carefully analyzing the matter, Mr. Welles, the first week in December, handed the Allied Ambassadors a long memorandum restating his conviction that a Soviet-Japanese pact was unlikely and that therefore important concessions to Japan were uncalled for. Russia and Japan might reach agreement on a number of minor problems; they might in fact achieve a commercial treaty and even some sort of vague political accord. But, even if taken together, such agreements would not add up to great material advantages. The result, therefore, would at best be psychological. The fundamentals of the situation, on the other hand, would not be changed. As for concessions necessary to divert Japan from a Russian course, these could only lead to disaster; for at bottom they would involve nothing less than the complete abandonment of all Western rights and interests, the cessation of all aid to China, and, conversely, accordance of a free hand to Japan in settling the China Incident:

> It is this Government's view that we should not compromise our principles or surrender any of our material interests in an attempt to dissuade Japan from reaching an accord with the Soviet Union. Japan is employing the idea of such an accord as a threat to wrest from the democracies concessions such as those outlined above.

If we were to yield, continued the memorandum, we should end all hope that Japan might ultimately realize that it cannot forever disregard treaties and international law. If Japan actually tried for a full-scale *rapprochement* with Russia, it would mean not that the "extremists" would secure control, but that they were already in the saddle. Accordingly, "this Government continues to believe that the principles of policy to which it adheres in regard to the Far Eastern situation are fundamentally sound and that they should not be deviated from."[68]

---

[67] *Foreign Relations of the U. S.: Japan*, II, 36-39.

[68] The text of this memorandum is filed with a covering memo of the Division of Far Eastern Affairs, December 7, 1939. On the British and French warnings: tel. from Grew, November 27; tel. from Bullitt, November 28; Hornbeck memo to Hull, December 2; Hull tel. to Bullitt, November 30. We have also used a memo of conversation between Welles and Lothian, December 6, 1939.

This memorandum has been quoted at length because, even though it did not convince London and Paris, it was a clear formulation of the American position on the eve of the resumption of the Grew-Nomura talks. The outlook for any substantial progress was indeed dark, and somber were the Ambassador's comments on December 1:

Nothing in international affairs can be more mathematically certain . . . than that Japan is not going to respect the territorial and administrative integrity of China, now or in future; has not the slightest intention of doing so and could be brought to do so only by complete defeat. . . . There does not now appear on the horizon the possibility of such a defeat. . . . Even an American embargo could not stop the drive in China. . . . To await the hoped-for discrediting in Japan of the Japanese Army and the Japanese military system is to await the millennium. The crux of Japanese-American relations lies in the fact that while the Government is prone to give us soothing assurances, no individual or group in Japan is strong enough to bring about the full implementation of those assurances. . . .[69]

On December 4, 1939, Foreign Minister Nomura at last reopened discussions of Japanese-American relations with Ambassador Grew. Since the differences between the two countries were so fundamental and agreement so unlikely, the substance of the negotiations was as usual blanketed under a mountain of verbiage. No good purpose would be served in going over the ground step by step. Suffice it to say that the conversations were conducted in an atmosphere of cordiality. On the American side there was never the slightest doubt of Nomura's sincerity, though there was, of course, the greatest skepticism with respect to the Foreign Minister's ability to meet the American requirements. In the discussion of December 4 Nomura was at great pains to explain away the many American protests and representations, more than half of which had not been answered or even acknowledged. But the chief burden of his remarks was a series of assurances: the Japanese had no intention of driving American interests out of China; every effort was being made to put an end to indiscriminate bombings, violations of American rights, and offenses and indignities of all kinds; interferences with American property and trade were due entirely to military operations; they would cease as soon as peace could be made. All of this was clearly intended as a preface to what for the Japanese was the immediate, burning issue: what would the United States do when the commercial treaty of 1911 expired on January 26, 1940? Nomura hoped "there will be no cause for the people of both countries to get excited about," but hinted that if Japan's all-important trade with the United States were impaired, Japan would have to seek other commercial channels. In reply to this implied threat, the Ambassador could only repeat what Secretary Hull had already told the Japanese Ambassador, that "logically and legitimately" it was up

[69] Despatch from Grew, December 1, 1939; Grew: *Ten Years in Japan*, 298 ff.

to the Tokyo Government to take the initiative in removing the obstacles to friendly relations.[70]

Certainly there was nothing in this first interchange to revive the drooping hopes of the American authorities. In the State Department it was felt that "only the fringes of the problem" had been touched upon. Or, in the words of Mr. Hull, the conversations "were disposing only of chicken-feed."[71] The Secretary was indeed in a quandary in deciding what to do. On the one hand he continued to be badgered by the British and French Ambassadors, who were sure that if the United States refused to conclude a new trade agreement with Japan, the Abe-Nomura Cabinet would be swept aside by the military, which would proceed forthwith to strike a bargain with the Soviets and with Germany.[72] On the other hand, the Japanese made no secret of their intention of setting up a Chinese puppet regime and, far from indicating any readiness to discuss basic issues, let it be known that "there was little that could be done now in the way of examining principles of policy, such as the territorial and administrative integrity of China."[73] Among the senior advisers of the State Department there were some who favored a coldly realistic attitude: since nothing short of serious pressure would ever induce the Japanese military to draw back, the sensible course would be for the United States to make use of the effective weapon it had to hand, that is, to impose economic sanctions after the expiration of the commercial treaty, or at the very least to keep the Japanese in suspense as to the future policy of the United States.

Secretary Hull, sharing Ambassador Grew's feeling that we should avoid discouraging the Japanese moderates, chose the less heroic course. On December 11 he recommended to the President that after the expiration of the commercial treaty the United States should not impose on Japanese ships and goods the additional tonnage and import duties which American law permitted. The President concurred, but wanted it made clear to the Japanese that this decision was strictly temporary, designed "to show that we have no desire to push them into a corner or bear down on them unduly as long as there is any reasonable possibility of reaching a new commercial treaty."[74]

Ambassador Grew was informed of this decision on December 18 and was

[70] Foreign Relations of the U. S.: Japan, II, 36 ff.; 40 ff.; Grew: Ten Years in Japan, 305-9; Hull: Memoirs, I, 725.

[71] Foreign Relations of the U. S.: Japan, II, 52; Berle Diaries (MS.), December 10, 1939.

[72] Despatch from Grew, December 11; Berle Diaries (MS.), December 10; memo of conversation between Hull and Lothian, December 15; memo of conversation between Welles and St. Quentin, December 21, 1939.

[73] Memo of conversation between Mr. Yoshizawa, Chief of the American Section of the Japanese Foreign Office, and Mr. Dooman, December 6, 1939 (Foreign Relations of the U. S.: Japan, II, 43-46).

[74] Memo of Hull to the President, December 11, and the latter's reply, December 14, 1939 (Roosevelt Papers: Secretary's File, Box 52); Hull: Memoirs, I, 726.

instructed as to the attitude he was to take toward further Japanese suggestions for a temporary arrangement (*modus vivendi*). He was not to commit himself on this point, but was to make clear to Nomura that Japan's failure to observe the principles of nondiscrimination in trade was a serious obstacle to any new arrangement. He was further warned that discussions of commercial relations did not mean that the United States Government had "in any way modified its position with regard to other aspects of American-Japanese relations." Our notes of October 6 and December 30, 1938 were still valid.[75]

Before these instructions reached Tokyo, the Ambassador had had a second conversation with Nomura (December 18). The upshot of this discussion was that the Foreign Minister announced the intention of the Japanese military authorities to open the lower Yangtze, as far as Nanking, in about two months time. This step had been suggested earlier by Mr. Grew as an appropriate indication of Japanese readiness to take "positive" measures to improve relations. Nomura took pains to point out that the Japanese expected something in return: "It goes without saying that more than anything else the termination of the Treaty of Commerce and Navigation casts the darkest shadow over American-Japanese relations." In short, the Foreign Minister proposed a *modus vivendi* and expressed the hope that negotiations to this end could be started before Christmas.[76]

Ambassador Grew felt strongly that the United States Government should at least agree to negotiate, if only in order to bolster the Tokyo Cabinet as against the Army. But Secretary Hull, with the concurrence of the President, stood by his earlier position: the matter of future trade relations was to be kept open. As he explains it in his *Memoirs*:

We were not convinced that the Tokyo Government was any less interested than the Army in building up a greater Japan ruling the eastern half of the world. Previous Japanese Governments had not lagged many steps behind the Army in staking out claims to an overlordship of the Orient. . . . Moreover, Japanese Governments were fragile affairs. Just about the time we got to understand a Japanese Government, it would fall and be replaced by another. The Army was almost always too strong for the Government, and if the Government's policies, domestic and foreign, did not suit the Army, the Government got into trouble.[77]

The Ambassador, therefore, had no choice but to communicate to Nomura the decision of his Government, cushioning the shock, however, by the statement that the United States "sincerely appreciates the efforts made by the Japanese Government to remedy the conditions which adversely affect Japanese-American relations and the indication of the intent of the Japanese Government to persist in those efforts." Of more importance was the

[75] *Foreign Relations of the U.S.: Japan*, II, 190-193; Hull: *Memoirs*, I, 726.
[76] *Foreign Relations of the U.S.: Japan*, II, 49-52; Grew: *Ten Years in Japan*, 309-11.
[77] Hull: *Memoirs* (Macmillan, 1948), I, 728.

announcement Grew was instructed to make: that after January 26, 1940, no discriminatory charges would be levied on Japanese ships or goods— "until such time as further instructions shall be issued."[78]

In the following couple of weeks the Tokyo Government made several more attempts to reopen the question through its Ambassador in Washington, and protested particularly when the American Government imposed a "moral embargo" on the shipment to Japan of equipment needed for oil refineries. But all these last-ditch efforts left the Washington authorities unmoved. Indeed, this phase of Japanese-American relations was already drawing to its close as the Abe-Nomura Cabinet began to totter. The reasons for its fall on January 14, 1940, are not known, but it is not unlikely that failure to stave off the expiration of the trade treaty played an important part. The Cabinet had never been a strong one, and the wonder is less that it should have collapsed than that it should have survived so long. In any event, its doom was sealed by the end of December and at least a shimmer of light is thrown on its fate by Premier Abe's remarks that it was hopeless to go on "when there seem to be two nations, one being the Army and the other something else."[79]

The facts of the Japanese-American relationship in the autumn of 1939 are so patent as to make a concluding summary almost superfluous. The Japanese militarists had unquestionably suffered a severe, even though only a temporary, setback as a result of the Nazi-Soviet pact, which to many had seemed to demonstrate the complete duplicity of the Germans. Ribbentrop, to be sure, had blandly applied himself to the task of luring the Japanese into the new combination, and among the extremists in Tokyo there was much sentiment for burying the past and climbing on the bandwagon of victory. But so far as the scanty evidence shows, there was never serious danger that the Emperor and the Cabinet would countenance such a step. Much of the talk of a coming Japanese-Soviet agreement was no doubt allowed to get about in the thought that it might frighten the democracies into making concessions. The most immediate problem of the Tokyo Government was to forestall a rupture of trade relations with the United States. That was the task to which Abe and Nomura applied themselves, with the tolerance if not the qualified approval even of the High Command. But it must be clearly understood that the Japanese Cabinet itself probably never envisaged abandonment of Japanese plans for hegemony in the Far East, and that, if it did, there was never the slightest chance that it would be able to overrule the Army, backtrack on the China issue, renege on the

[78] Foreign Relations of the U.S.: Japan, II, 193-96.

[79] Saionji-Harada Memoirs, December 28, 1939, January 14, 1940. On the moral embargo see Hull: Memoirs, I, 729. The various discussions leading to the expiration of the trade treaty are systematically reviewed in a memorandum of the Far East Division entitled Termination of the 1911 Treaty of Commerce and Navigation Between the United States and Japan: Narrative of Developments from July 26, 1939 to January 26, 1940.

program for a Greater East Asia Co-Prosperity Sphere, or in general accept the principles laid down by the United States Government as the only possible basis for an understanding. Compared to the larger issues at stake, the Grew-Nomura conversations were indeed concerned with mere "chicken feed." No one in Washington Government circles ever had any illusions about them, or ever expected the Japanese to meet the American requirements to such an extent as to warrant the abandonment of the one effective instrument of pressure—short of war—which remained to the United States Government. The threat of economic sanctions therefore remained suspended over the Tokyo Cabinet. It was a formidable threat indeed, and it may safely be assumed that if, in the autumn of 1939, the "phony war" in Europe was not followed by real war in the Far East, the firm position of the American Government more than anything else served as an effective deterrent.

CHAPTER IX

The Soviet Advance

1. Turkey and the Balkans

Foreign Minister von Ribbentrop, recalling to Adolf Hitler in June, 1940, the circumstances which resulted in the division of Eastern Europe into German and Soviet spheres, took pains to emphasize the "still very vague German-Russian relationship" as of August, 1939.[1] He had in mind especially Bessarabia and the Balkans, but the reference applies with equal force to nearly every aspect of the Nazi-Soviet partnership. Vagueness and mutual suspicion thus provide the first clues for penetrating the "enigma" of subsequent Soviet policy throughout Eastern Europe. Doubtless the Kremlin was somewhat reassured by the good grace with which Hitler handed over to the Russians their due share of the Polish booty. The fact remained, however, that the pact of August, 1939, had been concluded in obvious haste and had provided no definition of long-term relationships between the two accomplices. Uncertain what even the immediate future might bring, and now enjoying a common border with the former Nazi enemy, Stalin felt it wise to "cash in" as rapidly as possible on the promissory notes which, in an hour of need, this enemy had flung about so prodigally. The first objective was to assure the security of the Soviet Union against Germany by obtaining control of the border areas clearly assigned to the Soviet sphere of influence. Beyond that the Russians waited to see what further concessions they might, in the course of a long war, extract from a necessitous partner without themselves being obliged to enter the conflict.

Accordingly, almost simultaneously and before the fate of Poland was itself wholly decided, the Soviet Government had formulated demands involving Turkey, the Balkans, the Baltic Republics, and Finland. The present chapter will sketch briefly the evolution of Soviet policies in each of these areas, together with such American reactions as they evoked. A

[1] *Nazi-Soviet Relations*, 157 ff.

beginning may be made with Turkey and southeastern Europe. While this region was not as immediately vital as the Baltic States and Finland to the defense of the Soviet Union against Germany, it was the area in which hostilities between Germany and the Allies seemed most likely to involve Russia's ultimate interests, as well as to risk its embroilment in the war.

To few governments had the announcement of the Soviet-German pact come as a greater shock and surprise than to the Turkish. Wary and generally well informed, the Ankara authorities professed to have had not the slightest intimation from Moscow of this development, which struck at the foundations of a foreign policy which Turkey had been constructing since 1920. From the moment of its birth the new Turkish Republic had concentrated on friendship with the Soviet Union. The latter had seemed to respond in kind.[2] When Italian aggression against Ethiopia, Spain and Albania posed a threat to Turkey on its Balkan-Mediterranean flank, Ankara had turned naturally to Great Britain and France for support. London- and Paris warmly welcomed the Turkish approach, especially after their "Stop Hitler" policy had hardened into the guarantees of Greece and Rumania and they had begun to explore the possibility of erecting a Balkan front against the Nazis. This was a major aim of the preliminary Anglo-Turkish agreement of May 12, 1939, and of the similar Franco-Turkish understanding of the following month.[3] Although the Turks were somewhat concerned over contemporary Anglo-French attempts to enlist Italian support against Hitler in the Balkans, and were aware also that the Soviets would prefer their friendship with the Turks to be exclusive, it was only after August 23, 1939, that Ankara grasped the fact that its effort to pursue a policy mutually acceptable to the Soviet Union and to the democracies was probably based on illusion.

Hitler was convinced that the mere announcement of his pact with Stalin would compel Turkey to revise its entire position as well as prevent Rumania from taking part in any war against the Axis.[4] In case a dramatic coup did not quickly doom Allied hopes of making Turkey the leading member of a Balkan "encirclement" pact against the Reich, the Germans

[2] Cevat Açikalin: "Turkey's International Relations" (*International Affairs*, XXIII (1947), 477 ff.) The author, a Turkish diplomat, notes, however, an alarming approach by Litvinov shortly after the signature of the Montreux convention, July 20, 1936, for the conclusion of a joint Soviet-Turkish pact of defense for the Straits.

[3] On the genesis of the Anglo-Turkish alliance see, in addition to Açikalin's article cited above, the accounts by Nihat Erim Kocaeli: "The Development of the Anglo-Turkish Alliance" (*Asiatic Review*, N.S. 42, October 1946, 347-51); Harry N. Howard: "Germany, the Soviet Union and Turkey During World War II" (*State Department Bulletin*, July 18, 1946, 63-64), and Sir Hughe Knatchbull-Hugessen: *Diplomat in Peace and War* (London, 1949), 146 ff. The attempts of German Ambassador von Papen to counter this "encirclement" effort at Ankara are recorded in his State Department interrogation, November 1, 1945.

[4] Letter of Hitler to Mussolini, August 25, 1939 (*Nazi-Soviet Relations*, 80-81).

clearly hoped that Soviet pressure on Ankara would be all that was necessary to ensure the complete neutralization of Turkey and the ruin of Anglo-French strategy in the Eastern Mediterranean. Stalin and Molotov had indicated to Ribbentrop a dislike of the "vacillating policy" of the Turks, and on the day after the German invasion of Poland, Molotov had informed Schulenburg that the Soviet Government was ready to work for the permanent neutrality of Turkey "as desired by us." From this Schulenburg deduced that Moscow shared Berlin's conception of Turkey's position in the conflict.[5]

Actually, this was by no means precisely the case. As the Germans suspected, and Molotov confirmed, the Soviet Government had already begun negotiations with Ankara looking to the substitution, for the nonaggression pact then in existence, of a pact of mutual assistance between Turkey and the Soviet Union. Molotov was quite prepared to agree with the Germans that, in view of rumors that the British were putting pressure on Rumania to take an active part in the war and that British and French troops might be sent by sea to Rumania's assistance, it would be desirable to prevail on the Turks to close the Dardanelles completely.[6] On the other hand, there were also reports that when Hitler had finished with Poland he might turn his attention to Rumania. Needless to say, the prospect of German armed intervention in the Balkans was no whit more pleasing to the Soviet Government than was the possibility of Anglo-French operations there. The Soviet Government had its own plans for southeastern Europe, encompassing, as in northeastern Europe, centuries-old Tsarist ambitions. It could for the moment advantageously share German anxiety to keep Turkey neutral and to exclude Anglo-French influence from the Balkans, but it had no inclination to see that influence eventually replaced by German.[7] Observing how quickly the Germans were overrunning Poland, and estimating that they would soon be free to move into the Balkans if they chose, the Soviet Government decided it was high time for the Turkish Foreign Minister, Sükrü Saracoglu, to visit Moscow in order to hasten the conclusion of the mutual assistance pact. This, so the Soviets told the Germans on September 17, the Turks had originally suggested.[8]

Saracoglu's observation to American Ambassador MacMurray that he was going to Moscow to clarify his own mind, if for no other reason, is understandable enough.[9] On the one hand, Turkey's alliance with Britain and France was all but complete and awaited only final approval. Generals Weygand and Wavell had visited Ankara between September 9 and 13, 1939,

[5] *Nazi-Soviet Relations*, 73, 85 f.

[6] *Ibid.*, 87 f.

[7] A. Rossi: *Deux ans d'alliance germano-soviétique*, 100 f.; Beloff: *The Foreign Policy of Soviet Russia*, II, 298; Dallin: *Soviet Russia's Foreign Policy*, 106-8.

[8] *Nazi-Soviet Relations*, 97.

[9] Despatch from MacMurray (Ankara), September 16, 1939.

and the Turks were presumably aware of tentative Allied plans for moving troops from Syria to the Balkans (Salonika) in the hope of anticipating German moves in that direction, or even of setting up a second front in that area.[10] On the other hand, it was now evident to Ankara that the conclusion of the treaty with Britain and France might not only invite German retaliation against Turkey but would also incur Moscow's displeasure. The Soviet Government had not been impressed by the Turkish suggestion that the mutual assistance pact contain a restrictive clause whereby Turkey's aid to the Soviet Union should involve no action directed against Britain and France.[11] In any case, disillusioned by the cavalier treatment accorded his country by the Soviet Government, but trusting that Russia was none the less anxious to keep war away from the Balkans and the Black Sea, Saracoglu left for Moscow on September 22, still hopeful of satisfying the Soviet Union without wholly abandoning Turkey's obligations to Great Britain and France.[12]

The Turkish Foreign Minister's lengthy sojourn in the Soviet capital—from September 26 to October 17, 1939—is sufficiently well known to require but a brief summary. Received at once by Molotov, Saracoglu soon discovered the difficulties of charting a satisfactory course between Turkey's obligations to Britain and France on the one hand, and the desires of the Soviet Union on the other. The Soviet Government professed no interest in a mutual assistance pact containing the reservation that the U.S.S.R. could demand no aid from Turkey against the British and French. Moreover, Molotov at once signified his desire that Turkey enter into arrangements for joint defense of the Dardanelles and guarantee that warships of non-Black Sea powers be denied passage through these straits.[13] Saracoglu reaffirmed his desire to conclude a mutual assistance pact along the lines originally proposed by Ankara, but refused the demand that the Dardanelles be closed to Allied war vessels and rejected other proposals plainly at vari-

[10] These plans, which, of course, did not eventuate in action, are referred to in a memo of Admiral Darlan of September 11, 1939; a memo of unknown authorship of September 18; a message from French Ambassador Corbin in London to Leger of the French Foreign Office, September 7, and in the report of General Weygand's visit to Ankara. These documents were subsequently captured by the Germans. On these plans see J. Weygand: *The Role of General Weygand: Conversations with His Son* (London, 1948), 33-34; and General Gamelin: *Servir*, III, 110 ff. On French efforts to interest the Italians in preventing the supposed German advance into Rumania, see *Ciano's Diplomatic Papers*, 306-9.

[11] *Nazi-Soviet Relations*, 97. The highly suspicious Germans were informed of the Turkish proposal by the Soviets on September 17 and replied on the next day approving the mutual assistance pact with certain qualifications.

[12] Telegrams from MacMurray, September 18, 23, 1939. The British and French were informed of the Soviet proposals by the Turks.

[13] Açikalin: "Turkey's International Relations" (*International Affairs*, XXIII (1947), 481); Harry N. Howard: "Germany, the Soviet Union and Turkey in World War II" (*State Department Bulletin*, July 18, 1948, 65 f.); Dallin: *Soviet Russia's Foreign Policy*, 108; Beloff: *The Foreign Policy of Soviet Russia*, II, 298-301.

ance with the Montreux convention, or with Turkey's commitments to Great Britain and France.[14]

Despite the willingness of the British and French to agree to a revision of their forthcoming treaty with the Turks so as to eliminate any obligation on the part of the latter to go to war with the Soviet Union, it proved in the last analysis impossible to reconcile Turkey's obligations to the Allies with the demands of the Soviet Union and the requirements of Germany as presented by the Soviet Government.[15] It is apparent that the essential causes for the final failure of Saracoglu's negotiations at Moscow were two Soviet demands, already once rejected by the Ankara Government, but raised afresh by Stalin and Molotov. The first called for wording the mutual assistance pact in such fashion as to preclude all possibility that the Soviet Union could become involved in war with Germany as a result of lending assistance to Turkey. The second was Stalin's firm insistence that Turkey undertake to close the Dardanelles to the fleets of non-Black Sea powers, whether or not Russia were at war. For the rest, the Soviet leaders asked for assurance that Ankara would agree to suspend all its obligations under the treaty with Britain and France if Russia became involved in war with them, and, finally, Stalin demanded that Turkey remain neutral in the event that the Soviets seized Bessarabia, or revisionist Bulgaria seized the Dobrudja from Rumania.[16]

Saracoglu did not fail to penetrate this thinly veiled attempt of the Kremlin to conceal its anxiety over Germany's intentions by emphasizing its fear of the Allies. He suspected that, in turn, Stalin and Molotov realized that the Ankara Government was equally anxious to forestall German aggression in the Black Sea areas and the Balkans. Nevertheless, the Turkish Foreign Minister could not but be alarmed at what he regarded as the completely opportunistic and imperialist character of Soviet policy.[17] Clearly, a mutual assistance pact which specifically freed Russia from any obligation to assist Turkey in case of German attack was of slight value compared with an alliance with Britain and France. Saracoglu pointed out the willingness of London and Paris to respect Turkey's determination to avoid war with the Soviet Union. As for the Balkan issues raised by Stalin, the Turks, with British approval, agreed to stand aside if the Soviets seized Bessarabia, since this would not involve an inter-Balkan frontier and, accordingly, Turkey's

[14] Dallin: *op. cit.*, 108-9; tel. from Steinhardt (Moscow), October 3, 1939.

[15] German pressure on the Soviets to compel Turkey to abandon its alliance with France and Britain and to close the Dardanelles to their war vessels is recorded in *Nazi-Soviet Relations*, 110-11, 113, 117-18, 120.

[16] Tels. from Kennedy (London), October 14, 19; tels. from Steinhardt, October 17, 19; tel. from MacMurray (Ankara), October 26, 1939; A. Rossi: *Deux ans d'alliance germano-soviétique*, 100.

[17] Tel. from Steinhardt, October 19, 1939.

obligations under the Balkan Entente. However, should Bulgaria try to seize the Dobrudja, Turkey would stand by Rumania.[18]

To all this reasoning Stalin turned a deaf ear and eventually Saracoglu returned to Ankara. Significantly, however, the Tass Agency observed that the negotiations had been conducted in a friendly atmosphere and that both parties would continue to maintain contact. From all this the Ankara Government deduced that the Soviet Union was reasonably content with the position Saracoglu had maintained. True, the Kremlin had not succeeded in bending the stubborn Turks to the point desired by the Germans and, even more, by the Russians themselves. Yet three weeks of negotiation had at least established Turkey's peaceful intentions toward the Soviet Union, and the outcome permitted the Kremlin to inform Berlin that it had done its best to forestall the Anglo-French-Turkish treaty and had failed. The Ankara Government strongly suspected that Stalin, in presenting demands which he knew the Turks could not accept, was deliberately creating an excuse for suspending negotiations until in more opportune times an agreement with Ankara could be reached excluding both German and Allied interests.[19]

Two days after Saracoglu's return to Ankara, on October 19, 1939, the Turkish Government concluded its long-prepared treaty with Britain and France. In its final form American experts were disposed to regard the document as a meshwork of subtleties.[20] The British and French were obligated to lend Turkey "all aid and assistance in their power" in case Turkey were attacked by any European nation. Turkey, on the other hand, was similarly obligated toward Britain and France only if the conflict extended to the Mediterranean area, or if these powers became involved in hostilities as a result of their guarantees to Greece and Rumania of April 13, 1939. Even so, the terms relieved the Ankara Government from any commitments to its allies which might involve Turkey in war with Russia.

Special economic and military agreements accompanied the conclusion of the alliance, as well as a secret protocol leaving wide discretion to Turkey in discharging its obligations. None of these was published. All in all, as London well realized, the effectiveness of the treaty depended on Turkish good faith, as well as upon Anglo-French ability to provide Ankara with

---

[18] The Turks may not have been aware that the U.S.S.R. was pressing a mutual assistance pact on Bulgaria (*Nazi-Soviet Relations*, 124). They suspected, however, Soviet discussions with Bulgaria looking to joint action by which Bulgaria should get the Dobrudja from Rumania with a naval base reserved for the U.S.S.R. (tel. from Steinhardt, November 2, 1939).

[19] Tel. from MacMurray, October 26; tel. from Bullitt (Paris), October 18, 1939.

[20] Memo of the Division of Near Eastern Affairs, State Department, December 15, 1939. The published text of the treaty is printed in the *State Department Bulletin*, November 11, 1939, pp. 544-46.

the credits and war matériel necessary for effective resistance to the Germans.[21]

The Soviet reaction to the announcement of the treaty's signature was sharp, but took the now well-established line that Britain, not Germany, was the real villain of the piece.[22] Molotov, in his public review of Soviet policy on October 31, 1939, referred to the Russian negotiations with Turkey at some length. He insisted that the real question at issue had been the conclusion of a bilateral pact of mutual assistance limited to the regions of the Black Sea and the Straits. Russia, he declared, could not conclude such a pact if it involved taking actions which might lead to armed conflict with Germany. Moreover, the Soviet Union had sought from Turkey a guarantee, in view of the war danger, that Turkey would not allow warships of non-Black Sea powers to pass through the Straits. The Turks, complained Molotov, had definitely discarded a "cautious policy of neutrality," preferring to enter "the orbit of the expanding European war." Whether or not Turkey would regret her action the Soviet Commissar modestly refrained from guessing.[23]

The President of Turkey himself presently replied to these strictures in words of cautious moderation. But his comments were followed, on November 3, by a semi-official statement giving the lie to Molotov's implication that the Soviet Union had not in fact demanded changes in the Montreux convention which would have conflicted with Turkey's international obligations under that instrument.[24]

Thus ended the first episode in the play for position among the Germans, the Soviets, and the democracies in southeastern Europe. While most observers then regarded the Kremlin as having suffered a serious diplomatic rebuff at the hands of the Turks, it appears in retrospect that only the Germans were complete losers in this first skirmish. The Soviets, it is true, had been compelled to accept the disturbing fact of a Turkish alliance with Britain and France which might lead to a second front in the Balkans. Yet, they could derive satisfaction from Turkey's opposition to German penetration of the peninsula. The Allies, in turn, had been forced to recognize that the Turks would not fight Russia unless attacked, but they believed they could count on Turkish support against Germany and Italy. Thus, it was Berlin alone which, surveying the record, and looking to the future, could derive no satisfaction whatever from the Ankara Government's stubborn stand.

2. THE BALTIC STATES AND FINLAND

Well before the denouement of Moscow's devious negotiations with the Turks, the Soviet Government had successfully completed the first and most

[21] Tel. from Kennedy, October 19, 1939.
[22] Tass report (Bulletin of International News, XVI (1939), 1224).
[23] Quoted in Dallin: Soviet Russia's Foreign Policy, 111.
[24] Bulletin of International News, XVI (1939), 1291.

urgent phase of its program for establishing the security of its northern borders. This ruthless calculation involved the absorption, in graduated stages, of the Baltic Republics: Estonia, Latvia, and Lithuania. Since all three had been indisputably assigned to the Soviet sphere of influence by the agreement of August 23, 1939, or, in the case of Lithuania, by subsequent revision of that pact, their collective fates were quickly decided, and without possibility of resistance. Soviet divisions had taken up positions along their borders simultaneously with the entry of the Red Army into Poland. On September 25, Stalin informed Berlin that with its consent, indeed in anticipation of its unstinting support, he would proceed at once to the "solution of the problem of the Baltic countries." Berlin quickly agreed. Significantly, however, operations on the first victim, Estonia, had already begun.[25]

In a matter of hours thereafter the Estonian Foreign Minister was compelled by the threat of imminent attack by Russia, and in the face of German refusals to interfere, to accept a mutual assistance pact with the Soviet Union (September 28, 1939). This cynical arrangement was accompanied by secret agreements handing over to the U.S.S.R. naval and air bases in Estonian territory, and providing for Soviet garrisons of some 25,000 men. Despite virtuous denials by the Kremlin of any intention to interfere in the internal affairs of Estonia, opinion everywhere, and not least of all German opinion, accepted the treaty as marking the first stage of the absorption of Estonia into the Soviet Union.[26]

The pattern so swiftly set by the Kremlin in establishing effective control over Estonia was followed without significant variation in Moscow's subsequent dealings with Latvia and Lithuania.[27] The former succumbed to its pact of mutual assistance on October 5, Lithuania on October 10, 1939.[28] Lithuania's hopes of preserving a precarious independence were prematurely raised by the unexpected acquisition of its ancient capital, Vilna, seized by the Soviets from the Poles. Momentarily the Lithuanians sensed the German irritation over the Kremlin's crude effort to make Russia appear the

[25] *Nazi-Soviet Relations*, 102 f. In addition to the accounts of the reduction of the Baltic States given in the studies of Dallin and Beloff, cited earlier, the reader will find those of John Scott: *Duel for Europe* (Boston, 1942), 62 ff., and of K. R. Pusta: *The Soviet Union and the Baltic States* (New York, 1942) of value and interest.

[26] The published text of this treaty, as well as of the subsequent pact with Latvia (October 5, 1939), is printed in *State Department Bulletin*, November 11, 1939, pp. 542-44. The Department was informed of the content of the secret arrangements in tels. from Wiley (Tallinn), October 6, and (Riga), October 10, 1939. The frantic but futile efforts of the Baltic States to enlist German support against the U.S.S.R. are recorded in *Nazi-Soviet Relations*, 103, 104 ff., 115, 116 ff., 118 ff. *Cf.* A. Rossi: *Deux ans d'alliance germano-soviétique*, 135 ff.

[27] The case for Latvia is presented in *Latvia in 1939-1942* (Washington, 1942). This study, published by the Latvian Legation, refutes the Soviet apologia: "The Soviet Union and the Baltic Staties" (*Soviet War News*, London, 1941).

[28] The published text of the Lithuanian pact is printed in the *State Department Bulletin*, December 16, 1939, pp. 705 ff.

benefactor and Germany the robber in this territorial transfer.[29] The difference, however, was quickly composed. For the rest, the Soviet Government had no valid grounds for complaint at the fashion in which Berlin acquiesced in the advancing control of Russia in the Baltic. Nor did Ribbentrop and Hitler allow the obvious misgivings of many German officials to poison the seeming harmony of the new partnership. Even the subsequent repatriation of thousands of old-established Baltic Germans from the Soviet sphere, humiliating though it might be, was accomplished with a minimum of friction.

Germans of the military caste were already convinced that Soviet policy was aimed "uniquely" at Germany. They admitted with some candor that the Reich was being forced to permit Soviet moves into the Baltic because it could not then risk a war on two fronts. Their chief consolation was derived from the equally strong conviction that, even with its newly acquired outposts, the Red Army was too weak to constitute a serious threat to Germany in the East, and the Soviet Government too dependent on Berlin to contemplate the risk.[30] For his part, Stalin made singularly little effort in the course of his "negotiations" with the Baltic officials to disguise the fact that his demands were motivated, in the first instance at least, by anxiety over Berlin's immediate intentions. Though Soviet worries over alleged Anglo-French designs in the Baltic may be partially discounted, the fact remains that the Soviet Union was seeking protection there, as elsewhere, from every eventuality and from every combination of enemies in the long war which Stalin now professed to foresee.[31] In the Baltic States the Kremlin had by the end of October extracted from the complacent Germans that degree of Soviet control which had been refused by the more scrupulous Allies during the negotiations of the previous summer.

Partly because London and Paris grasped the import of these Soviet moves, partly because there was literally nothing they could do to forestall them, indignation over the fate of the Baltic States was tempered by satisfaction over this latest check to Hitler's success. It gave rise, indeed, to premature hopes that the Soviet Union might presently be detached from its detestable liaison.[32] The American reaction was much the same. *The New York Times* spoke for nearly all Americans in observing that "the swift and cold-blooded manner in which sovereign states are summoned one by one to hear what their future status is to be, shows Stalin to be more than an apt imitator of Hitler."[33] The United States Government, however, did nothing. As Mr. Hull has since remarked, the Baltic States

[29] *Nazi-Soviet Relations,* 112-14.

[30] Despatch from Norem (Kaunas), October 7, 1939; despatch from Wiley (Tallinn), November 16, 1939; *Nazi Conspiracy and Aggression,* VI, 978-79.

[31] Tel. from Wiley (Tallinn), October 23, 1939; *Latvia in 1939-1942,* 95 ff.

[32] Helen Kirkpatrick (from London) in *Chicago Daily News,* October 14, 1939.

[33] Editorial, October 3, 1939.

remained nominally independent and there was no diplomatic step our Government could take. Meanwhile, the Secretary shared Allied hopes that at some future time Russia might "veer away from her apparently close relationship to Germany."[34] So Russia ultimately did, but hope that the veering would soon occur all but vanished in the unfolding of the next Russian move. The Finns were not to be subjugated so easily, and, before the Kremlin gave up the effort, war between Russia and the Western Powers was but narrowly averted. In the course of the same development, Soviet-American relations sank to their lowest point since 1933.

In seeking German support and approval on September 25, 1939, for "solving" the problem of the Baltic States, the Russians, as Berlin noted, made no specific mention of Finland.[35] Nevertheless, the Nazi-Soviet agreement of August 23, so far as can be ascertained, assigned that country to the Soviet sphere without reservation. Thus no surprise was occasioned when, in the course of its demands on the other Baltic Governments, the Kremlin summoned the Finns to Moscow to discuss certain "concrete" questions. Quite apart from the warnings emanating from Estonia, the Finns had long since had a foretaste of the claims likely to be advanced.[36] Foreign Minister Erkko could scarcely doubt that Molotov's invitation of October 5, 1939, presaged a renewal of the demands for Finnish territory which had been previously rejected. The Finnish Government at once alarmed Berlin, stating that, desirous as it was of improving its relations with Russia, it would never accept the fate of Estonia.[37]

In Washington Mr. Procopé, the Finnish Minister, had been pressing for a loan which would enable his country to finance the purchase of war materials.[38] On learning that the Soviet Government had proposed the reopening of conversations, the Minister hurried to the State Department, "in a high state of tension." He predicted that Russia would request Finland to take the path of ultimate destruction already trodden by the Baltic Republics, and besought Secretary Hull to intervene with the Moscow Government in Finland's behalf. Mr. Hull gave him little encouragement, reminding him that the United States could not mix in controversies between other powers and suggesting that in this particular instance intervention by the United States would probably only irritate the Kremlin. But Procopé was not willing to rest his case. "Thinking out loud" with Assistant Secretary Berle, he

[34] Hull: *Memoirs*, I, 701.

[35] *Nazi-Soviet Relations*, 102 ff.

[36] See the treatment of the earlier demands in Chapter III, above; further, John H. Wuorinen, ed.: *Finland and World War II* (New York, 1948), 41-48, and Herbert Elliston, in *Christian Science Monitor*, January 15, 1940.

[37] Tels. from Schoenfeld, September 23, October 3, 6, 1939; tel. from Steinhardt, October 4, 1939; *Nazi-Soviet Relations*, 104.

[38] Memo of conversation between Hull and Procopé, September 15, 1939; *Morgenthau Diaries (MS.)*, Vol. 211 (September 15) and Vol. 217 (October 11, 1939); *Berle Diaries (MS.)*, October 9, 1939.

proposed an ingenuous device by which Washington could acquaint the Kremlin of its concern without appearing to interfere. The President could telephone directly to Ambassador Steinhardt, telling him in plain English of American anxiety. Berlin and Moscow would surely listen in, and would thereby be informed, without any embarrassment to the President.[39]

The Soviet invitation to the Finns soon produced a crisis, for the Helsinki Government had no intention of capitulating. The instructions given to the Finnish delegation, headed by Mr. J. K. Paasikivi (at that time envoy to Sweden) and by Mr. Vaino Tanner (the Minister of Finance), were quite as stiff as the American and British Ministers to Finland had anticipated.[40] Having failed in their appeals to their Scandinavian neighbors for support, the Finns began to mobilize. Simultaneously the Soviets began massing troops on the Finnish border. In this crisis atmosphere the Finnish delegates arrived in Moscow on October 11, rightly expecting the worst.[41]

The one hope of salvation was still in persuading President Roosevelt to take a hand. On October 10, 1939, the Swedish Minister tried to enlist the aid of Secretary Hull, only to be told that American intervention would probably do more harm than good. Thereupon the Minister repaired to the White House, to present a personal appeal from the Swedish Crown Prince to the President urging him to use his influence in Moscow to counteract any possible attempts of an aggressive nature toward Finland. Mr. Roosevelt replied that his influence with the Kremlin was just about zero, but finally agreed that he might, after consulting Mr. Hull, send a message to Ambassador Steinhardt instructing him to tell Molotov that it was the President's hope that Russia would not make war on Finland. The Minister observed that Molotov would probably point out that Russia had not made war on Estonia or Latvia and had no intention of making war on Finland. He suggested that it might be better to phrase the message to the effect that the President hoped Russia would not make demands on Finland which would seriously threaten that country's integrity and independence. Once again Mr. Roosevelt assented, but only on the understanding that he would first consult Mr. Hull, who was temporarily absent in New York. Later in the day the Finnish Minister called on Mr. Roosevelt and evidently found him more ready than ever to send a message.[42]

[39] Memos of conversation between Hull and Procopé, October 5 and 7, 1939; *Berle Diaries (MS.)*, October 6, 1939; *Moffat Diary (MS.)*, October 7, 1939; Hull: *Memoirs*, I, 702.
[40] *The Finnish Blue Book* (New York, 1940), 46 ff.; tel. from Schoenfeld, October 9, 1939.
[41] Tel. from Steinhardt, October 9, 1939; tel. from Sterling (Stockholm), October 9, 1939. Though many German officials were much concerned over the fate of Finland, the Nazi Government expressed its disinterestedness (*Nazi-Soviet Relations*, III, 121-24; tel. from Schoenfeld, October 11, 1939).
[42] Memo of conversation between Hull and the Swedish Minister, October 10, 1939; letter of the Crown Prince of Sweden to the President, submitted October 10, 1939; memo of conversation between Moffat and the Swedish Minister, October 11, 1939; *Berle Diaries (MS.)*, October 11, 1939; *Moffat Diary (MS.)*, October 10, 11, 1939; Hull: *Memoirs*, I, 702 ff.

Mr. Roosevelt himself drafted the text of a proposed message to Soviet President Kalinin and showed it to Secretary Hull on the latter's return to Washington on the afternoon of October 11. Mr. Hull was not at all pleased with what had occurred in his absence. He pointed out to the President that intervention in this instance would create a precedent that was sure to plague the Government in the future. But in view of the President's commitments, there was little the Secretary could do but tone down the text and persuade Mr. Roosevelt not to publish the message or even tell the Swedish or Finnish Ministers what had been done. The text was cabled to Ambassador Steinhardt on the evening of October 11, in the hope that it could be transmitted to President Kalinin before the opening of the Soviet-Finnish discussions, scheduled for the late afternoon of October 12. The message read, in part:

> While the United States is taking no part in existing controversies in Europe, the President wishes to call attention to the long-standing and deep friendship which exists between the United States and Finland. . . .
> Such being the case, the President expresses the earnest hope that the Soviet Union will make no demands on Finland which are inconsistent with the maintenance and development of amicable and peaceful relations between the two countries, and the independence of each. . . .[43]

In sending the message to Kalinin, Mr. Roosevelt could be sure of eventual popular approbation. American public sentiment was manifestly favorable to some action in support of "brave little Finland" which, through the years, had so conscientiously made payments on its debt to the United States while most of the world defaulted. Senators Pittman, Bankhead and Connally, as also Congressman Bloom, at once expressed approval when the message became known. Among the Scandinavian-American elements of the Middle West, otherwise strongly isolationist, the President's move was bound to arouse enthusiasm.[44]

Molotov's reaction, on the other hand, was anything but cordial. To Ambassador Steinhardt he observed acidly that he had anticipated "American sentimental interest in Finland." The United States would do well, he added, to remember that Finland had received its independence from Russia. The treaties recently concluded with the Baltic States were "proof" that the negotiations with Finland need not involve loss of territory or independence. Molotov categorically denied any desire on Russia's part to impair Finnish independence even "in the slightest degree." Finnish Foreign

---

[43] The message leaked out almost at once, and so had to be released by the Government (Hull: *Memoirs*, I, 703). The text may be found in *Public Papers and Addresses*, VIII, 538-39. For the narrative we have relied on the tel. to Steinhardt, October 11, 1939; *Berle Diaries (MS.)*, October 11, 1939; *Moffat Diary (MS.)*, October 11, 1939.

[44] Saville Davis, in *Christian Science Monitor*, October 12, 1939; *The New York Times*, October 13, 1939; Krock, in *The New York Times*, October 16, 1939.

Minister Erkko, when told of this statement, considered it a significant commitment, since Molotov had made it to the United States Ambassador, and not to the Finns themselves. Later Mr. Erkko was to revise drastically his favorable view of the effects of Mr. Roosevelt's message.[45]

Mr. Steinhardt would have subscribed to the President's estimate that American influence on Soviet policy was just about zero. Kalinin's prompt reply and Molotov's public remarks bore out the opinion. Kalinin's response at least observed the diplomatic amenities, but Molotov, in his address of October 31, 1939, made no effort to conceal the Kremlin's irritation:

> One might imagine [said the Foreign Commissar], that the relations between the United States of America and, let us say, the Philippines and Cuba, which have long been demanding their independence without getting it, are better than those between the Soviet Union and Finland, which long ago received its liberty and independence from the Soviet Union.[46]

Mr. Procopé, elated at having induced the President to take so important a step, was presently back in Secretary Morgenthau's office seeking a loan to facilitate Finnish preparations for self-defense. The Secretary promised to bring the matter to the attention of the President and Mr. Hull at the next meeting of the Cabinet. But on that occasion he discovered that there was not "very much enthusiasm." A private loan to Finland would have been all right, but it was no secret that Congress did not like foreign loans for armaments, even when they were not prohibited by the Johnson Act. The only solution, thought Mr. Morgenthau, would be a credit from the Reconstruction Finance Corporation, for the President could hardly leave Procopé "high and dry." But this proposal, again, posed a serious problem for Mr. Jesse Jones, the Director of the RFC, who was disinclined to act until some clear line of policy had been laid down.[47]

It was precisely this clear line of policy which the President found it difficult to adopt. For all the sympathy for the Finns, it seemed prudent not to raise the question of an armaments loan at the very time when Congress was considering repeal of the arms embargo. Mr. Morgenthau minced no words in explaining to Procopé: "We are not going, with this bill pending on the Hill, to take any risks. The whole picture is *so* important for you and for everybody else, the *whole* picture." So the Finns had to reconcile themselves to delay, trusting the while that Mr. Roosevelt's message and the widespread interest in Finland's cause would yet deter the Kremlin from extreme demands or drastic measures.

On the afternoon of October 12, 1939, the Finnish delegation to Moscow

[45] Tel. from Steinhardt, October 12, 1939; tel. from Schoenfeld, October 15, 1939.

[46] *The New York Times*, November 1, 1939. The text of Kalinin's reply is printed in *Documents on American Foreign Relations*, I, 383. See further John Scott: *Duel for Europe*, 95, and Dallin: *Soviet Russia's Foreign Policy*, 117 ff.

[47] *Morgenthau Diaries (MS.)*, Vol. 218 (October 19, 1939).

heard from Stalin, Molotov and Potemkin the first version of the Soviet Union's demands. As described to Ambassador Steinhardt, these consisted of:

1. A pact of mutual assistance.
2. An "arrangement" with respect to the Finnish islands in the Gulf of Finland off Kronstadt.
3. Cession of Finnish territory on the Rybachi Peninsula in Northern Finland.
4. Lease of the port of Hangö to the Soviet Union as a naval and air base with the right to garrison it with not more than 5,000 men.
5. Cession to the U.S.S.R. of four Karelian districts along the Gulf of Finland between Leningrad and Viborg.[48]

By way of compensation Russia offered Finland territorial cessions in the central and southern areas of Soviet Karelia, and abandonment of its objections to the fortification of the Åland Islands, provided this was done by Finland alone. Stalin was affable. There was no note of threat. In short, the Finns, while unwilling to enter into a mutual assistance pact with Russia, and absolutely rejecting the lease of Hangö, believed that if Stalin did not insist upon these two demands a satisfactory settlement could be reached.

Unhappily for the Finns, on October 14, when the Soviet Government committed its minimum demands to writing, it was precisely on Hangö that it insisted most strongly. While the Kremlin was willing to modify its demand for the mutual assistance pact, in deference to Finland's desire to remain strictly neutral, it demanded the complete demilitarization of the Finnish-Soviet border and the demolition of the vital "Mannerheim Line" fortifications. Paasikivi, the head of the Finnish delegation, returned to Helsinki to consult his Government. On October 23 he presented the Finnish counterproposals in writing.[49] In brief, the Finns professed understanding for Soviet anxiety to render the defenses of Leningrad secure. Finland believed, however, that the maintenance of strict neutrality would constitute Finland's most effective contribution to the maintenance of peace in northern Europe, as well as to the security of the Soviet Union itself. Accordingly the Finns again rejected the demand for a Soviet lease of the port of Hangö, or for such far-reaching territorial concessions in Karelia as would deprive their country of effective means for resisting Soviet attack. As for the Soviet suggestion that, in lieu of a mutual assistance pact, each state agree not to enter into any alliance directed against the other, the Finnish Government expressed the belief that it would be sufficient to reaffirm the existing treaty of nonaggression between the two countries.[50]

---

[48] Tels. from Steinhardt and from Schoenfeld, October 13, 1939.
[49] *Finnish Blue Book*, 51 ff. We have also used an unpublished tel. of October 15, 1939, from Schulenburg to Ribbentrop, reporting Molotov's account of the negotiations.
[50] *Finnish Blue Book*, 54 ff.

The Kremlin rejected the Finnish counterproposals on the very day they were presented. It deemed Soviet control of Hangö, situated at the entrance to the Gulf of Finland, as essential if the Germans were to be barred from the eastern reaches of the Baltic and Leningrad made secure. Similarly that city's defense could not be adequately safeguarded by land if the Finns persisted in refusing to hand over the nearby territory which contained the Mannerheim defenses. Having themselves made some concessions to Helsinki, Stalin and Molotov expected the Finnish delegates to accept them gratefully and make no further trouble. From this point on, however, no real progress attended the lengthy discussions, though a complete impasse was avoided until November 13.

No useful purpose would be served by following in detail a record which is already well known.[51] Clearly Finland was already finding itself impaled on the horns of a tragic dilemma, from which it has not yet extricated itself, the inescapable dilemma of the small state which finds it impossible to preserve its own security because it is situated between two great powers professedly anxious to expand theirs. Even if the Helsinki Government had believed Stalin's protestations that he was concerned solely with the defense of Leningrad and the Gulf of Finland, it could not have met his specifications without destroying Finland's own vital defenses. In any case, the Finns felt unable to put such faith in the Soviet leader's fair words.

On the other hand, Stalin, obsessed with the idea of leaving no opening in the massive walls with which he was surrounding the Soviet Union against future contingencies, defensive or offensive, was unwilling to tolerate the genuine independence of the Finnish State. It is hardly worth while to argue whether Finnish opinion was in the main pro-Allied or pro-German. The immediate threat to Finnish democracy came from the Soviet Union, and the Finnish people, whatever else be said of it, was all but unanimous in its dread of the Russians. Under these circumstances Finland's effort to continue its Nordic neutrality policy in conjunction with the Scandinavian powers was as futile as it was well-intentioned. Neutrality, without collective security, had become a meaningless concept and an untenable position. In the uncertain state of German-Soviet relations, and in the certain sympathy of powerful friends, it seemed as good a gamble to accept war with the Soviet Union as to accept demands which were incompatible with continued Finnish neutrality and independence.

The issue was not long in doubt. Molotov's unfriendly references to the Finnish negotiations in his speech of October 31, 1939, touched off a Soviet

<hr/>

[51] Dallin: *Soviet Russia's Foreign Policy*, 115 ff., offers a lucid and lively account, as does John Scott: *Duel for Europe*, 95 ff. *Cf.* Beloff: *The Foreign Policy of Soviet Russia*, 304 ff. See also Mr. Paasikivi's own account of his negotiations in *Life*, March 4, 1940, and the judicious presentation of Finland's case in J. Wuorinen, ed.: *Finland and World War II*, 52 ff. We have also used the tels. and despatches of Minister Schoenfeld at Helsinki and Ambassador Steinhardt at Moscow.

press campaign against Finland which became particularly ominous after the virtual suspension of the negotiations on November 14. Rarely had the world been treated to such an exhibition of Marxian invective. The Finnish leaders were described as "bandits of capitalism," or "rapacious bands of Finnish kulaks, armed by capitalism." Premier Cajander was a "clown." Nor were Finland's friends spared. Members of the Swedish Government, for example, were abused as "lackeys of British and American capitalism." Only the Germans wholly escaped the effects of this barrage, which lasted throughout the remainder of November. The climax was approached on November 26 when the Soviet Government accused the Finnish Army of having fired across the border, killing four Red Army soldiers and wounding nine. The Finnish Government categorically denied the charge and it is quite pointless to pursue the question of its authenticity. It simply served notice on Helsinki, as the Germans had been warning the Finns, that the Kremlin was determined on their capitulation and was ready to use force to encompass it.[52]

Accordingly, on November 28, Molotov informed the Finnish Minister in Moscow that the Soviet Union considered itself "released" from its obligations under the 1932 pact of nonaggression. In vain did that official attempt to reach Molotov with a belated Finnish acceptance of Russia's demand that Finnish troops be withdrawn from the border areas near Leningrad. On November 29 the Soviet Union severed diplomatic relations with Finland. At once a radio broadcast, apparently emanating from the town of Terijoki, just inside the Finnish border, was heard proclaiming the creation of a Finnish revolutionary government. In the early hours of the following morning, units of the Red Army invaded Finland and Soviet planes bombed Helsinki.

Finland's friends and neighbors found it almost impossible to credit what was happening in the final hours before the Red Army marched. The Swedes and the French refused to believe that the Kremlin would actually resort to war against its small neighbor. The United States Government shared this incredulity. Even Ambassador Steinhardt believed that the severance of diplomatic relations itself was but the last stage in a war of nerves.[53] Minister Procopé, however, was more forehanded. As soon as he learned of the border incident, he was at the State Department begging for a last-minute effort by the United States to try to save the situation. "Thinking out loud," as he again expressed it, Procopé appealed to this Government to proffer its good offices to prevent war.[54]

[52] *Finnish Blue Book*, 75 f.; Dallin: *Soviet Russia's Foreign Policy*, 123, 131; tel. from Wiley (Tallinn), February 15, 1940.
[53] Tels. from Sterling (Stockholm), November 28; from Bullitt (Paris), November 27, 28; and from Steinhardt (Riga), November 30, 1939.
[54] Memo of conversation between Procopé and Mr. Moffat, November 28, 1939.

American officials did not disguise how forlorn they held this hope to be. Quite apart from the outspoken sympathy of the American people for Finland and their open contempt for Soviet methods, relations between the American and Soviet Governments had been embittered by an incident which bore no relation to Finland. The American freighter, *City of Flint*, had been captured by the Germans on October 9 while en route to Britain with contraband cargo. Sailed by a prize crew to the Norwegian port of Tromsö, the *City of Flint* reached the Russian port of Murmansk on October 23, 1939. There, with Soviet connivance, she remained until October 28, in violation of the rules of maritime warfare. Not only did the Soviet Government fail to answer Washington's inquiries about the vessel; it even refused Ambassador Steinhardt permission to visit her crew. The American Government finally decided to ignore what Mr. Hull describes as the Soviet Government's "somewhat specious" explanations of November 4, but the acrimonious exchanges could not be regarded as presaging a receptive attitude on the part of the Soviet Government toward any fresh American *démarche* on behalf of Finland.[55]

Nevertheless, the President and Mr. Hull agreed to try. Mr. Berle, even as he and Mr. Welles were drafting another message, was convinced that the Russians intended "to mop up Finland as soon as the lakes freeze." "All we are doing," he added, "is making the record." The job the Russians were going to do in Finland would be accomplished as cynically as that earlier in Poland.[56] On November 29, the American offer was handed to the Finnish and Soviet Governments: "Without in any way becoming involved in the merits of the dispute," it ran in part, "and limiting its interest to the solution of the dispute by peaceful processes only, this Government would, if agreeable to both parties, gladly extend its good offices."[57]

The United States offer met precisely the fate predicted by those who had drafted it. Accepted with alacrity by the Finns, it was blandly rejected by the Soviet Union on the ground that there was no occasion whatever for mediation.[58] Russia was not at war with the "Finnish Peoples Government," which had conveniently materialized at Terijoki under the leadership of the exiled Finnish Communist, Otto Kuusinen, but only, as the Soviets alleged, with the reactionary elements in Finland. In a last desperate effort to appease the unappeasable, the Finns formed a new Cabinet, with Risto Ryti as Premier and Vaino Tanner as Foreign Minister. With Mr. Roosevelt's approval, the State Department officially informed the Soviet Government of this move. It was all of no avail. Molotov, indeed, blamed the failure of

[55] On the incident see Hull: *Memoirs*, I, 704 ff. The *Moffat Diary (MS.)*, October 24, 26, 27, 28, 1939, records Mr. Hull's indignation and fury, and reveals the hours of effort devoted to this incident. *Cf. Documents on American Foreign Relations*, I (1939), 700-705.

[56] *Berle Diaries (MS.)*, November 29, 1939.

[57] *Documents on American Foreign Relations*, I (1939), 384. *Cf.* Hull: *Memoirs*, I, 706; *Moffat Diary (MS.)*, November 29, 1939.

[58] *Documents on American Foreign Relations*, I (1939), 384-85.

the negotiations primarily on Tanner, and informed Ambassador Steinhardt that he hoped for an early settlement with the Kuusinen regime. Naturally he was not disappointed.[59]

The last-minute efforts of other interested powers to avert war between Finland and Russia failed as dismally as those of the American Government. Finland's sympathetic but apprehensive Scandinavian neighbors, under Swedish leadership, found themselves unable to induce Russia and Finland to compose their differences peacefully, yet were too frightened of Germany and Russia to cast their lots boldly with their Finnish neighbor. Indeed, in the face of German threats and in order to prevent war from engulfing all of Scandinavia, the Swedish Government counseled Finland to take a conciliatory attitude. Such also was Berlin's advice to Helsinki.[60] Evidently many Germans were chagrined at the unexpected course of Russia's quarrel with Finland, but for the time being the necessity as well as the advantages of supporting the Soviets overbore all other considerations. Admiral Raeder anticipated securing German bases in Norway "with Russian help," and as early as October 10 the Soviets had offered Hitler "a well-situated base near Murmansk" (Polyarny).[61] So complete, in fact, was the apparent triumph of the Ribbentrop policy that on the outbreak of hostilities the Wilhelmstrasse strictly enjoined all German diplomats abroad "to avoid any anti-Soviet note" in their discussions of the event.[62] Accordingly, earnest efforts by the Helsinki Government to reopen negotiations on December 4 and December 15 came to nothing, and the "Winter War" began its course.[63] As it seemed to Ambassador Steinhardt, the immediate Soviet objectives were to secure strategic positions promptly in order to assure Russia a dominant position in the Baltic. The haste of the Russian action, he advised, stemmed from anxiety to liquidate the Finnish question so that Russia might be free to meet the developments it anticipated in the Balkans, as well as generally to strengthen its position vis-à-vis Germany.[64]

3. THE "WINTER WAR"

Returning to Washington from Warm Springs "in the midst," as he expressed it, "of this dreadful rape of Finland," Mr. Roosevelt obviously shared the furious contempt and indignation of all his fellow Americans

[59] Tels. from Shantz (Helsinki) and Schoenfeld, December 1; from Steinhardt, December 2; from Sterling (Stockholm), November 30, December 2, 1939.

[60] Tels. from Schoenfeld, October 28, November 26; from Sterling (Stockholm), October 31; from Steinhardt, October 26, November 7; and from Kirk (Berlin), October 21, 1939.

[61] Nazi Conspiracy and Aggression, VI, 978 f. (October 3, 10, 1939). Cf. Vice Admiral Kurt Assmann: "Stalin and Hitler" (U.S. Naval Institute Proceedings, LXXV, July 1949, 759-74).

[62] Nazi-Soviet Relations, 127-30.

[63] Tel. from Steinhardt, December 5, 1939.

[64] Tel. from Steinhardt, December 1; Berle Diaries (MS.), December 11, 1939. Similar views were entertained by the British Foreign Office (tel. from Johnson, December 1, 1939). On Soviet insistence that the Germans limit their naval operations in the Baltic to the western half of that sea (20° E. long.), see the article of Vice Admiral Assmann, cited above.

save only the Communists.[65] The latter had at long last completely adjusted to the official Moscow line, as was perfectly indicated by the headline in the *Daily Worker* announcing the Soviet invasion: "Red Army Hurls Back Invading Finnish Troops." But the President, and probably, as he claimed, 98 percent of all Americans, felt differently. According to the *New York Herald Tribune*, "in bold, crude, barefaced mendacity, the Government of the Soviet Union" had "no peer in history." Even the most inflexible isolationists were strangely moved. Herbert Hoover, denouncing the invasion as "butchery," put himself at the head of a private organization to assist the Finns, which was ultimately to collect more than two million dollars in cash for relief purposes. On December 15, when the Finnish Government once again met the installment due on its debt to this country, Secretary Morgenthau announced that the money would be placed in a special account in accordance with the President's instructions. If Congress approved, it would be returned to Finland. Mr. Berle's words, "the neutrality of this country is not as solid as a week ago," constituted an egregious understatement.[66] American moral indignation had in fact reached a peak of intensity probably unequaled since the German invasion of Belgium in the First World War.

In the circumstances, and with the repeal of the arms embargo safely behind him, the President was not condemned, as in the case of Poland, to mere gestures on Finland's behalf, though in the end the Administration remained almost as parsimonious in deeds as it was prodigal in words. Immediately upon receipt of the news of the bombing of Helsinki by Soviet planes, Mr. Roosevelt stated publicly that "all peace-loving peoples . . . will unanimously condemn this new resort to military force." This was at once followed by an appeal, tactfully issued to both powers, not to bomb civilian populations or unfortified cities, and requesting an immediate reply. The Soviet Government was prompt enough. The American appeal, it insisted in brief, was the result of a misunderstanding. The Soviet Air Force had not bombed any Finnish towns and had no intention of doing so![67]

This was so plainly at variance with the facts that the Administration did not hesitate to invoke, by way of reply, the well-known "moral embargo" against Russia. In the President's public statement of December 2, expressing the hope that American manufacturers would not export airplanes or airplane equipment to "nations obviously guilty of such unprovoked bomb-

[65] Letter of the President to Lincoln MacVeagh, December 1, 1939. (*F.D.R.: His Personal Letters*, II, 961).

[66] *Berle Diaries (MS.)*, December 5, 1939.

[67] Tel. from Steinhardt, December 1, 1939; *Moffat Diary (MS.)*, December 1, 1939. Texts in *Documents on American Foreign Relations*, I (1939), 384-87; Hull: *Memoirs*, I, 706.

ing," the Soviet Union was not singled out by name.[68] The statement was, in point of fact, directed also against Japan for its indiscriminate bombings of Chinese towns and cities.[69] There is no question, however, that the blow was aimed primarily at the Soviet Union and that the President and Mr. Hull intended the embargo to include all materials used in the manufacture of planes. At the Cabinet meeting of December 4, Mr. Roosevelt said to the Secretary of the Treasury: "You see that they stop buying aluminum." When Mr. Morgenthau pointed out that the large Soviet purchases of aluminum and molybdenum were perfectly legal and that he could not stop them, the President replied impatiently that more difficult problems had been solved before.[70] Thereafter, aluminum, molybdenum, nickel, tungsten, and machinery for producing aviation gasoline were all added to the moral embargo list, and Secretary Morgenthau used his influence with American manufacturers to make the embargo effective. The President kept himself fully informed as to the efficacy of the measure (less than he hoped), and was annoyed that no means could be found to add other items to the list.[71]

Having made these preliminary statements and decisions, the Administration was compelled to abandon the empyrean of rhetoric and get down to earth. It had failed to prevent Soviet aggression against Finland. It had no reason to suppose that the Soviet Union would conduct its war against Finland in accordance with bourgeois conceptions of civilized warfare. The American Government had invoked a moral embargo against the Soviets. However, no decisive results were to be anticipated from such pressures, either in assisting the Finns, or in deterring the Russians. Meanwhile, to the astonishment of the entire world, and most of all no doubt of the Kremlin, the Finnish Army was putting up a magnificent fight.[72]

It is now abundantly clear that the Soviet leaders absurdly miscalculated and mismanaged the initial phase of the war against Finland. In the face of evidence which should have convinced any but the most doctrinaire Communist of the contrary, the Soviet authorities appear to have believed that large numbers of Finns would rally round Kuusinen's puppet regime and open the door to the Soviet comrades. Even Soviet citizens were discreetly

[68] Text in *Documents on American Foreign Relations*, I (1939), 725 f.

[69] Memo. of Mr. Joseph Green (State Department), December 20, 1939. This, together with a collection of other documents on moral embargoes, is in *Morgenthau Diaries (MS.)*, Vol. 257 (April 26, 1940). *Berle Diaries (MS.)*, December 15, 18, 1939.

[70] *Morgenthau Diaries (MS.)*, Vol. 226, pp. 261, 264. The Soviets had purchased over three million dollars worth of molybdenum and aluminum in the U.S. since October 24, 1939.

[71] *Ibid.*, Vol. 229, p. 241 (December 15, 1939); Vol. 230, p. 408 (December 19, 1939); Vol. 240, p. 283 (February 13, 1940). On the last date the Secretary of the Treasury provided the President with statistics indicating that for the period November, December and January, U.S. exports to the U.S.S.R. amounted to 29 million dollars, more than double those of a year before. On the moral embargo in general see Hull: *Memoirs*, I, 706 f.

[72] Tels. from Steinhardt, December 8 and 18, 1939.

amused by the blunder. In any case, this example of stereotyped thinking explains the admitted failure of the Kremlin to make adequate military preparations. Despite the generally low opinion of the Red Army prevalent at the time, military men never doubted that Russia could complete the occupation of Finland within a few months.[73] But the Soviet leaders counted on Finland's collapse in the course of about five days, and therefore deluded themselves into thinking that the resources of the Leningrad military district would suffice for the purpose. It is interesting to note that on this occasion the Soviet leaders were operating with strictly Leninist concepts, though at the time most of the world, the Germans included, was convinced that the revolutionary doctrine had been discarded and that the Kremlin was acting in the spirit of nationalism and imperialism.[74] For the United States and other governments friendly to Finland, however, the unexpected and valiant resistance of the Finns reopened the whole question of the extent and kind of aid that might be accorded the victim of aggression. A major policy decision now loomed before the President.

In the political sphere, the Soviet attack on Finland at once raised the issue of severing diplomatic relations with Moscow. Under Secretary Welles was heartily in favor of an immediate break, if only as a demonstration of opposition to Nazi-Soviet partnership. For some days the matter was debated in the Department. It was pointed out that such action would not aid Finland, that it would deprive the United States of the advantages of having full representation in an important capital, and that it would mean surrendering in advance all opportunities to exercise influence. Secretary Hull advocated caution and the President agreed with him. The question was allowed to lapse, but the very fact that it was carefully considered provides an eloquent illustration of the depths to which American relations with Soviet Russia had sunk.[75]

Despite strong feeling on the Finnish issue and popular demand for a definite stand against Moscow, the Administration proceeded with caution. It avoided associating the United States with other powers in further condemnatory words or actions. A suggestion of the Ecuadorean Government that the twenty-one American Republics join in a protest against Soviet aggression was initially supported by the State Department but later evaded on the plea that all the other Governments were not likely to participate. Anything short of unanimity was judged detrimental to hemisphere solidar-

[73] This was American military opinion also (*Morgenthau Diaries (MS.)*, Vol. 297, December 13, 19, 1939).

[74] Tel. from Steinhardt, December 7, 1939; Dallin: *Soviet Russia's Foreign Policy*, 133-45; Scott: *Duel for Europe*, 101 ff.

[75] *Moffat Diary (MS.)*, November 30, December 2, 4, 1939; *Berle Diaries (MS.)*, December 1, 4, 5, 1939; memo of conversation between Moffat and Procopé, December 5, 1939. Tels. from Schoenfeld, December 7, 12, 1939, advocated a break, on the theory that Britain and France would probably follow suit and that the effect on Russia and Germany would be great. See also Hull: *Memoirs*, I, 707-9.

ity, which in such cases was always difficult to attain. Many American Governments protested individually, but the United States abstained.[76]

Purely domestic considerations probably underlay the refusal of the American Government to associate itself with the move to expel the Soviet Union from the League of Nations. Ambassador Bullitt strongly advocated American participation. Having himself been instrumental, behind the scenes, in getting Finland's case before Geneva, Bullitt urged Mr. Hull to contemplate American support and share in the League's deliberations and verdict.[77] Again the Secretary balked. With the President's approval, he replied that the United States Government had already expressed sufficiently to the world its low opinion of the Soviet attack on Finland. It could not, however, as a nonmember of the League of Nations, urge a specific course of action on the British and French, who were members. Apart from such considerations, Hull added that both he and the President felt that "at the present moment we should be especially careful to avoid any connection with any political developments either within the League or which contemplated its use."[78]

Without visible American support, and in the face of Molotov's pronouncement that the "Soviet Union is not at war with Finland and does not threaten the Finnish people," the League convened on December 11. It proposed a commission to study the Finnish charges against Russia, but experienced difficulty in adequately staffing its membership. Most of the European neutrals were in terror of either Germany or Russia. The British Government was as yet decidedly reluctant to take any step which might result in still closer Russo-German collaboration. Accordingly, it was chiefly among the member states far removed geographically from the scene of the crime that genuine zeal for action was shown, though Premier Daladier strongly favored sanctions against Russia.[79] In the end the Council of the League adopted a resolution (December 14) to the effect that, by its aggression against Finland, the Soviet Union had expelled itself from the League. Thus, what was to prove the final meeting of that ill-fated organization came to an end. Its farewell gesture of defiance did something to redeem the League's tarnished reputation for virility, but the expulsion of Russia unhappily provided no tangible assistance to Finland.[80]

The Soviet press greeted the League's decision with fresh cascades of in-

---

[76] Tels. to Panama, December 5, 27, 1939; memo of the Division of American Republics, December 20, 1939; memo by Welles, December 21, 1939. The Ecuadorean suggestion was based on Article IV of the Declaration of Panama (Resolution X).

[77] Tel. from Bullitt, November 30, 1939. Conversations of the authors with Mr. Bullitt.

[78] Tel. to Bullitt, December 4, 1939.

[79] Tel. from Bullitt, December 11, 1939. Gamelin (Servir, III, 190-91) suggests that the French Government shared London's doubts, but was impelled to take a stand by the force of popular antagonism to the U.S.S.R.

[80] On this episode see Dallin: Soviet Russia's Foreign Policy, 148 ff.

vective and the ludicrous contention that the fast-vanishing Kuusinen regime truly represented the people of Finland. Meanwhile the Finns, assured of virtually unlimited moral support throughout the nontotalitarian world, were seeking munitions and money in any quarter—even Italy—which offered nope of success. Foreign Minister Tanner realized that, however valiant and successful Marshal Mannerheim's forces were proving to be, the outcome of the war could not be long in doubt unless concrete help were quickly forthcoming.[81] In view of the hesitation displayed by the Allies, and particularly by the Scandinavian Governments, and Washington's own reluctance to take any step which might antagonize Russia irrevocably, the prospects of financial, not to say military, assistance were far from bright.

Apart from foreign factors, Procopé's efforts throughout December to persuade the Administration to release war matériel to Finland, and to supply adequate credits with which to purchase it, encountered heavy obstacles occasioned by domestic politics. The arms embargo had, of course, been repealed, and the Neutrality Law had not been invoked against Russia and Finland. Furthermore, Mr. Roosevelt had been quoted as stating that Finland had a "perfect right" to borrow money in this country.[82] Nevertheless, the President was clearly intent on avoiding any quarrel with Congress as well as on calming the fears of the isolationists. Accordingly Minister Procopé met heavy going in his persistent attempts to get favorable action on the list of implements of war which the Helsinki Government submitted, together with a request for an American loan of sixty million dollars. Mr. Welles informed him that the consent of Congress would be necessary for the loan, and the most that the Treasury and Federal Loan Agency officials felt able to offer "within our policy and under the terms of existing law" was three or four millions. Although the President himself got the amount raised to ten millions, there was a proviso that none of these funds could be used to purchase munitions.[83]

As Procopé explained somewhat impatiently, what he required was not "guarded assistance in the way of surplus supplies but cold cash which he could use to buy arms in Sweden.[84] Mr. Hull offered no objections to Procopé's discussing the matter with the War and Navy Departments, but there was little to spare from American stocks of weapons nor were funds readily available in Federal agencies to provide Finland with the consider-

[81] Tel. from Schoenfeld, December 13, 1939.

[82] *The New York Times*, November 18, 1939. Having paid its debts, Finland was not bound by the terms of the Johnson Act.

[83] *Moffat Diary (MS.)*, December 4, 9, 11, 1939; memo of the Finnish Legation, December 5; letter of Mr. Welles to the President, December 6; memo of Welles to Moffat, December 6; *Morgenthau Diaries (MS.)*, Vol. 235 (December 5, 1939).

[84] *Berle Diaries (MS.)*, December 11. Specifically Finland wanted $20,000,000 worth of U. S. matériel, guns, shells, and fifty planes (*Morgenthau Diaries, MS.*, December 11, 1939).

able amount of cold cash and cold steel it vitally needed.[85] Throughout the remaining weeks of 1939, the State, War, Navy and Treasury Departments vainly strove to make up their minds whether or not it was legal to sell or transfer arms to Finland if, indeed, any could be spared. Perhaps, they speculated, the whole issue of a policy to aid Finland should be handed to Congress. The President, meanwhile, assured the American Minister at Oslo, Mrs. Harriman, that "we are literally doing everything we can without legislation to help the Finns."[86] Concretely, however, the best that Minister Procopé was able to extract by way of military assistance was a promise from the Navy of some forty American planes, and assurances from the President and Mr. Hull that they had no special objection to Finland's plan to use its ten-million-dollar credit to buy agricultural products in the United States, sell them in England, and use the proceeds to purchase munitions. Arrangements along these lines were actually completed in the course of January, 1940.[87] However genuine, therefore, the President's concern for Finland, he found himself hampered at every turn by existing laws and regulations. The only remedy for this situation would have lain in an appeal to Congress. But this, evidently, Mr. Roosevelt was unwilling to make. The struggle over the repeal of the arms embargo was still fresh in Administration minds and there was no desire to revive the debate on America's position with respect to foreign conflict. In view of the fact that throughout December the Finns continued to do very well in their campaign against the invader, the question did not appear urgent. For the Finns, however, it was a sorry story. They were fully aware that without aid from abroad on a large scale they would not be able to withstand Soviet pressure for long. One can therefore understand the biting remark of Foreign Minister Tanner, that the Soviets, through the equipment captured by the Finns, had themselves furnished more military supplies than any of the friendly powers.[88]

4. AMERICAN AID TO FINLAND

Mr. Procopé, the emotional Finnish Minister in Washington, was not the man to allow the all-important issue of American assistance to Finland to fall into oblivion. Aside from the fact that the Finns probably needed funds and that they certainly needed various types of military equipment, the

[85] Memoranda of conversation between Procopé and Moffat, December 5; between Hull and Procopé, December 14; and between Hull and the British Ambassador, Lord Lothian, December 15; note of the Finnish Legation, December 14, 1939; Hull: *Memoirs*, I, 707.
[86] *F.D.R.: His Personal Letters*, II, 972.
[87] *Morgenthau Diaries (MS.)*, Vol. 236 (January 17, 1940); *Berle Diaries (MS.)*, December 19, 1939; tel. to Schoenfeld, December 29, 1939, summing up the negotiations for aid; memo of conversation between Welles and Lothian, January 8, 1940; memo of conversation between Moffat and Procopé, January 16, 1940.
[88] Tel. from Schoenfeld, January 8, 1940.

political aspect of the question was undoubtedly of the utmost significance to them. If the United States Government could be induced to align itself officially with the Finnish cause, there was at least some chance that the Soviet Government might abate its demands. The credit thus far extended, which specifically excluded the purchase of arms and munitions, was wholly inadequate for Finnish purposes. So also were the existing facilities for acquiring munitions. A number of contracts had been placed with American manufacturers, but these covered only minor items which could quickly be supplied. What the Finns really needed were airplanes, heavy artillery, and antitank and antiaircraft artillery. These items would take many months to produce and could therefore become immediately available only if the War Department were to declare them surplus and therefore legally salable.

On December 28, 1939, Mr. Procopé reopened his earlier proposal for a loan of $60,000,000, and at the same time presented two memoranda listing Finland's most urgent requirements in planes and arms.[89] Both the President and Secretary Morgenthau were eager to give Finland whatever financial support was possible, Mr. Roosevelt suggesting the idea of a loan equivalent in amount to what Finland had paid on its debt to the United States after other nations had suspended payments.[90] But Secretary Hull was much concerned over the political storm that might be raised over this issue. True, Soviet Russia and Finland were not officially at war, but there was a high probability that the isolationists in Congress would seize upon financial and military aid to a country actually engaged in hostilities as an indication of Administration plans to assist Britain and France.[91]

Of the intragovernmental discussions of the ensuing days little is known. On January 8, 1940, Senator Brown had introduced a bill providing for an unrestricted loan of $60,000,000 to Finland. This bill had been referred to the Senate Committee on Banking and Currency. The President might well have given it wholehearted support, but was evidently persuaded by Mr. Hull not to expose himself to Congressional attack. Some such decision must have been taken before January 10, for on that date Secretary Morgenthau, at Mr. Roosevelt's suggestion, conferred with Congressmen Taylor and Doughton, Chairmen respectively of the House Appropriations and Ways and Means Committees. The Secretary told them quite frankly that the President had no precise program for aiding Finland and suggested that Congress decide for itself what assistance should be given. Privately Mr. Morgen-

---

[89] Note from Procopé to Secretary Hull, December 28, 1939; letter of Mr. Hull to the President, December 29, 1939; memo from Berle to Moffat, December 28, 1939, enclosing two memoranda from Procopé.

[90] Memo from the President to Mr. Hull, January 2, 1940.

[91] Moffat Diary (MS.), January 5, 1940.

thau hoped that Congress would authorize a loan of $50,000,000, which he was sure would be spent to excellent advantage.[92]

A few days later (January 16) the President, warned again and again by Mr. Hull that the opposition was "laying for the Administration," took a position altogether in consonance with that outlined by Morgenthau. His message to Congress was diluted to a degree that surprised even State Department officials. In identical letters to the Vice President and the Speaker of the House, Mr. Roosevelt thus stated the case:

Last month, when the Republic of Finland paid the regular installment of her debt to the United States, I directed the Secretary of the Treasury to place the money in a separate account pending such action, if any, as the Congress might desire to take with respect to it. There is without doubt in the United States a great desire for some action to assist Finland to finance the purchase of agricultural surpluses and manufactured products, not including implements of war. There is at the same time undoubted opposition to the creation of precedents which might lead to large credits to nations in Europe, either belligerents or neutrals. No one desires to return to such a status. The facts in regard to Finland are just as fully in the possession of every member of Congress as they are in the Executive Branch of the Government. There is no hidden information; and the matter of credits to that Republic is wholly within the jurisdiction of the Congress. . . .

An extension of credit at this time does not in any way constitute or threaten any so-called "involvement" in European wars. That much can be taken for granted.[93]

This was indeed an unheroic statement of the situation and amounted to little more than a political maneuver to put the responsibility for action or inaction directly on Congressional shoulders. Minister Procopé was utterly distraught when he read the message and was certain that it did not reflect Mr. Roosevelt's sentiments.[94] But his outbursts failed to move Mr. Hull, who on January 22, 1940, told the Minister in so many words that in his judgment there was no chance of a direct loan to Finland for the purchase of arms.[95]

Even the diluted proposal of the President, with its proviso restricting the projected loan to nonmilitary expenditures, was bitterly attacked in Congress. The Senate Banking and Currency Committee, after brief hearings, on January 24, 1940, reported out a bill that did not even mention Finland, but provided for raising the capital of the Export-Import Bank from $100,000,000 to $200,000,000, with the reservation that the Bank should not make any loans "for the purchase of any articles listed as arms, ammuni-

[92] *Morgenthau Diaries (MS.)*, Vol. 234 (January 10, 1940).
[93] Text in *Documents on American Foreign Relations*, I, 390. For the background we have relied on the *Moffat Diary (MS.)*, January 15 and 16, 1940.
[94] Memo of conversation between Moffat and Procopé, January 16, 1940; *Moffat Diary (MS.)*, January 16, 1940.
[95] *Moffat Diary (MS.)*, January 22, 1940.

tions, or implements of war by the President of the United States in accordance with the Neutrality Act of 1939," and that no loan of more than $30,-000,000 should be made to any one country.[96] Well-wishers of Finland were frankly embarrassed by the modesty of this program. The *New York Herald Tribune*, describing it as "unheroic," condemned as insincere the refusal to offer the Finns the one commodity, "arms," of which they stood in desperate need.

Yet even this innocuous measure was subjected to prolonged debate in Congress. The Senate passed it on February 13, 1940, by a vote of 49 to 27, at the very time when the Red Army at last breached the Mannerheim Line. Throughout the deliberations the isolationists attacked the bill as a foretaste of Administration policy to support countries at war. According to Senator Capper, he was "strong for Finland," but much opposed to lending American money "to any country engaged in war," including such a country as Finland, which was putting up such a "glorious fight against unprovoked and brutal attack by Soviet Russia."[97]

Two more weeks were required before the House passed the measure on February 28, 1940. The vote, 168 to 51, was decidedly favorable, but by that time entirely safe, for the Soviet-Finnish War had already entered its closing phase. In its final form the bill provided for the increase of Export-Import Bank funds and allocated twenty million to Finland, fifteen million to Sweden, and ten million to Norway, none of it to be used for the purchase of munitions. As the Finns themselves pointed out wryly, when acknowledging America's good intentions but tardy performance, the year 1940 was an election year, which certainly explained a good deal.

The kindred issue of making available to the Finns United States Army surpluses of artillery and other items proved equally ill-starred. In mid-January, 1940, Minister Procopé had renewed his requests for such supplies, stressing, as ever, that the element of time was of the essence and suggesting that the matter be laid before Congress.[98] On January 22, 1940, he left with Secretary Hull another memorandum outlining Finland's chief needs. But again, Mr. Hull left the Minister no illusions. Reporting the conversation the Secretary noted:

I then made clear to the Minister and his two associates the entire improbability of this Government selling arms, ammunition or implements of war to the Government of Finland. I said that I did not want them to be misled for a moment. They sought to bring up the technical law in the matter. I replied that wherever fighting was taking place and whatever it might be called in technical law, the one matter

[96] Memo by Carlton Savage, January 24, 1940; tel. to Schoenfeld, January 30, 1940.

[97] A concise summary of the debate may be found in Shepardson and Scroggs: *The United States in World Affairs, 1940*, (New York, 1941) 36 ff.

[98] Memo of conversation between Hull and Procopé, January 16, 1940; memo of conversation between Green and Procopé, January 20, 1940.

of concern in this country is that this Government does not engage in acts or utterances that might materially endanger its peace and safety by causing it to be drawn into war. In these circumstances, I stated that, in my opinion, it need not be expected that this Government would sell arms, ammunition and implements of war to the Government of Finland.[99]

Not even this explicit statement sufficed to dispose of the matter. Mr. Procopé conveniently forgot about Mr. Hull's statement and a week later was reopening the issue, declaring roundly that "if this Government refused to sell arms to his Government at this juncture, the decision would be tantamount to signing a death warrant for his country."[100] At this point the situation became utterly confused, for on the one hand General Marshall declared that the War Department had only some eight-inch howitzers with ammunition and some British-type 75-mm guns without ammunition that could reasonably be pronounced surplus. The General was greatly relieved to learn from Mr. Hull that according to the latter's understanding the President had ruled against the sale of arms to foreign governments. Yet shortly afterward a message arrived from the White House suggesting to the General that the next move in supplying the Finns was up to him.[101]

State Department officials agreed that they had never seen the Secretary feel so strongly on any matter as on this. He telephoned to the President, only to find him unrepentant. Why, he asked, could this matériel not be sold to some neutral country like Sweden for resale to the Finns?[102] At the suggestion of Secretary of War Woodring, Mr. Hull proposed a White House conference to clarify the situation. This conference appears to have taken place on February 7, 1940. Under combined pressure, Mr. Roosevelt seems to have yielded, for on the very next day Mr. Hull notified Minister Procopé that the United States Government, in the existing circumstances, could not sell arms, ammunition and implements of war to the Government of Finland.[103]

There remained the possibility of selling such surplus stocks as were available to Sweden, "not a pretty solution," according to Mr. Welles, who bemoaned the Government's unwillingness to aid Finland with more than words. Negotiations with Sweden were undertaken early in March, 1940, but were not consummated until after the conclusion of the Soviet-Finnish War. Thereafter there were no further obstacles to Finland's purchasing

[99] Memo of the Finnish Legation, January 22, 1940; memo of conversation between Hull and Procopé, January 22, 1940.

[100] Memo of conversation between Green and Procopé, January 29, 1940.

[101] Memo of conversation by telephone between Green and General Marshall, January 25, 1940; memo of Green to the Secretary, January 29, 1940; *Moffat Diary (MS.)*, January 29, 1940.

[102] *Moffat Diary (MS.)*, January 30 and 31, 1940.

[103] Memo by Green to the Secretary, formulating the questions to be discussed, January 29, 1940; memo by Green to the Secretary, reviewing the issues, February 6, 1940; note of Secretary Hull to the Finnish Legation, February 8, 1940.

what it could directly. The Swedish Government therefore abandoned its claims and the Helsinki Government proceeded to close the deal for 32 eight-inch howitzers and 200 75-mm field guns.[104]

Thus ended the unimpressive record of the Administration with respect to aid for Finland. The President, like Secretary Morgenthau, was evidently eager to take a positive stand from the outset and it is quite possible that he led Minister Procopé to expect more than proved feasible. In view of the strong and widespread sympathy for the Finns throughout the country, one must suppose that the President could have mustered sufficient support to put his policy over. But he came up against the adamant opposition of Secretary Hull, who seems to have been motivated entirely by political considerations. It may be true that the isolationists in Congress were "laying for the Administration," and that the effort to put through a program of substantial aid might have aroused passions and conflict that would have been unmanageable later on. Secretary of War Woodring supported Mr. Hull to the hilt, though for his own isolationist reasons, while General Marshall opposed the sale of surplus arms chiefly because he felt that nothing could be spared from the requirements of self-defense. The upshot of it all was that the issue was thrown into Congress, the Administration refusing steadfastly to go beyond the President's message of January 16, 1940. Congress acquitted itself no more nobly than the Administration. In the end, the Government and the country cut a sorry figure, and one can easily understand the poignant remark of Mr. Erkko on March 16, 1940, when, speaking of the sympathy of the United States and indeed of the whole world, he observed that this sympathy was so great that "it nearly suffocated us."[105]

The part played by the United States Government in the conclusion of peace between Finland and the Soviet Union had better be left for later treatment, but it is apposite to note here that the period of the Winter War, during which the democracies showed themselves so ineffectual, marked the high point in the Berlin-Moscow partnership. The Kremlin's decision to invade Finland certainly increased the misgivings of conservative German groups about the Ribbentrop-Stalin pact. Under Goering's influence military supplies of German and Italian origin were permitted to reach Finland for some time.[106] The Soviets were well aware of this fact and aired their displeasure through the Tass Agency. Ribbentrop at once explained and secured from Hitler instructions to the Naval Command to put an end to

---

[104] Note from the Swedish Minister, March 7, 1940; memo by Green, March 11, 1940; letter from Secretary Woodring to Secretary Hull, March 18, 1940, and reply, March 21, 1940; memo by Green, March 26, 1940; letter from Woodring to Hull, March 26, 1940, and reply, March 30, 1940.

[105] Quoted in *The New York Times,* March 17, 1940.

[106] *Berle Diaries (MS.),* December 11 and 15, 1939. As late as January 8, 1940, Finnish officials admitted that German supplies were still arriving by way of Sweden (tel. from Schoenfeld, January 8, 1940).

all Axis arms deliveries to the Finns.[107] The present advantages of abiding strictly by the letter of the agreement with Russia were too great to jeopardize because of aversion to the Kremlin's activities. For the rest, the opening weeks of the Soviet campaign against the Finns produced the same scornful judgment of Soviet military potential in Berlin as elsewhere.[108]

Nevertheless, this triumph of Ribbentrop's *Realpolitik* subjected the entire German nation, including even Hitler himself, to a strain which left a permanent mark upon Berlin's sentiments toward Moscow. Coöperation with the Soviets had been relatively easy against Poland. Soviet moves against the Baltic States, especially Lithuania, were distinctly unpalatable. Finland, however, was the bitterest pill that German pride had yet swallowed, since Berlin's abetment of Moscow in the subjugation of Finland was not only abhorrent to German sentiment, but even contrary to what many Germans deemed the national interest.[109] The Italian attitude was an additional cause of embarrassment to the Germans, as it was a source of hope to the Allies. Mussolini made little effort to disguise his sympathy for Finland. The Italian press was rabidly anti-Soviet, freely predicting that when the Soviet Union had absorbed Finland, it would turn rapidly upon the Balkans, a sphere in which any action was of direct interest to Italy. Ciano allegedly informed the Finnish Minister at Rome that Italian aid to Finland was limited solely by the necessity of avoiding open offense to Germany.[110] Thus if the Nazis were able to persevere throughout the Winter War in something remarkably close to the letter of the law in their relations with Russia, the effort constituted enough of a strain to open the first slight fissures which months later were to broaden into dangerous gaps and ultimately into an unbridgeable chasm of hostility.[111]

For its part the policy of the Soviet Union revealed no such symptoms of incipient schizophrenia. While its attitude toward the ever-present German threat remained one of vigilance, the Kremlin may well have come to fear that, as 1939 drew to its close, the plans of the Allies might be a greater threat to its peace and profit than were any likely moves of the Germans. Already suspicious of Allied designs in the Balkans, to say nothing of the dangers of Allied operations against the oil wells of the Caucasus, the Soviet Government had now to face the possibility that France and Britain would intervene in Finland's favor to the point of engulfing all Scandinavia in the zone of hostilities. This, as we shall see, probably accounts in large measure for the Soviet Union's willingness to accept a peace with Finland

---

[107] *Nazi-Soviet Relations*, 130-31 (December 11, 1939); *Fuehrer Conferences*, I (1939), 55 (December 12, 1939).

[108] Vice Admiral Kurt Assmann in *U.S. Naval Institute Proceedings*, Vol. LXXV (July 1949), 759-74 (end of December 1939).

[109] Tel. from Sterling (Stockholm), December 28, 1939.

[110] *Bulletin of International News*, XVI, 1408; tel. from Schoenfeld, December 12, 1939.

[111] State Department interrogation of Marshal Goering.

which provided Russia with only what it deemed its minimum objectives, though no doubt anxiety to avoid provoking Berlin by a complete absorption of Finland was also a consideration. All in all, then, despite the initial military miscalculation, Soviet policy in Finland, as elsewhere in Eastern Europe, gave promise of proving more effective, more realistic, and more brutally successful than that of any of Russia's competitors.

CHAPTER X

The Phony Peace

1. THE PEACE ATMOSPHERE IN WASHINGTON

Earlier in this narrative note has been made of the devious efforts of certain German personalities, supported by appeasement-minded Americans, to induce President Roosevelt to undertake the role of mediator between the belligerents.[1] It might have been supposed that the Allies' stiff rejection of Hitler's October peace offer and their highly optimistic predictions of eventual victory would have ended all speculation, in Washington or elsewhere, on the possibility of a negotiated peace. On the contrary, when in November Hitler's anticipated attack in the West failed to materialize, and when the only marked deviation from the pattern of "phony" war was provided by the Soviet invasion of Finland, latent interest in the possibilities of peace quickly revived. Thereafter the subject remained one of lively concern to the American people and their Government, until all illusions were finally dispelled by the Nazi descent upon Norway in April, 1940.

It is now plain that the several manifestations of this concern for peace—the appointment of Mr. Myron Taylor to represent the President at the Vatican, projects for an organization of neutrals, the premature blueprints of postwar policy and, finally, the Welles Mission—all in some degree reflected an American aberration. These efforts must not be judged solely on their patent failure to forestall the outbreak of "real" war. The interest of the President and the American people in the eventual peace and in the organization of the postwar world, thus early and somewhat naïvely manifested, was never thenceforth to fade out completely. As the London *Economist* sagely observed at the time (February 17, 1940), the paradox of the United States was that it did not want to be drawn into the war, but at the same time it did not want to be left out of it. In reflecting the dawning conviction that America must take part in the organization of the peace, if

---

[1] *Supra,* Chapter VII, Section 2.

not in the prosecution of the war, the account of the first steps to this end obviously forms a vital if confused chapter in the evolution of American thinking and policy.

It was doubtless natural that many Americans, observing the continued stalemate in the West and listening to the reassuring predictions of victory by Prime Minister Chamberlain, should have deduced that this was indeed the psychological moment for America to intervene, not only to stop the war, but even to assure a just and permanent settlement. The view was widely held that "neutrals were parties at interest in a modern war" and that they had a claim in the shaping of the world in which they had to live.[2] In the press there were frequent demands for studies of peace possibilities, and in December a Commission to Study the Organization of Peace was actually established under the chairmanship of President Neilson of Smith College. Earlier still, and with the blessing of the State Department the Council on Foreign Relations had inaugurated long-range studies on economic, financial, and territorial problems; limitation of armaments; and American membership in a world political organization. All of these issues, it was clear, must one day engage the attention of the peacemakers. If the mistakes of Versailles were to be avoided, it was thought, no time should be lost in entering on the task.[3]

In the State Department, Assistant Secretary Berle, among others, was turning over the problem in his mind and exploring the possibilities of reorganizing Europe along regional lines. He had long felt the necessity for a statement of war aims, had discussed that point with Mr. Welles, and had proposed as soon as convenient to broach it to the President.[4] At intervals Mr. Roosevelt himself seemed receptive. Early in December, for example, he told Berle and Morgenthau that he "proposed to make peace next spring on the basis of having everybody produce everything they could; take what was needed; and put the rest into a pool; and let the countries which needed the balance draw it as needed through the cartels." All this, thought Mr. Berle, sounded a little like Huxley, but he was ready to concede that conventional methods seemed to be leading nowhere. The President's idea might be as good as any other.[5]

In Mr. Roosevelt's case, concern with the problem of a negotiated peace stemmed at least as much from fear of Allied defeat as from hope of early

---

[2] Alsop and Kintner: *American White Paper*, 85, and especially the President's letter to King Leopold, November 3, 1939, quoted in Chapter VIII, Section 3.

[3] Memo of conversation between Assistant Secretary Messersmith and Hamilton Fish Armstrong and Walter Mallory of the Council on Foreign Relations, September 12, 1939. This aspect of the Council's work is succinctly described in a pamphlet: *The War and Peace Studies of the Council on Foreign Relations 1939-1945* (New York, 1946). See also the official State Department account: *Postwar Foreign Policy Preparation 1939-1945* (Washington, 1950), 18 ff.

[4] *Berle Diaries (MS.)*, November 3, 15, 1939.

[5] *Berle Diaries (MS.)*, December 4, 1939.

victory. It has already been noted that American diplomats like Ambassadors Bullitt and Kennedy were far from sharing the optimism of many Allied leaders and were profoundly impressed by the weaknesses of Britain and France. By contrast, the United States Consul General in Berlin, Raymond Geist, returned to Washington late in November with a disheartening report on the strength of the German situation. It was a mistake, he maintained, to think that the German people would not follow Hitler, and an even more dangerous error to believe that the German generals would overthrow him. In all seriousness Mr. Geist reported a conversation he had recently had with Goering, who had urged that the President try to engineer peace on the basis of the *status quo*. As Mr. Berle noted, the Germans steadily "moved up a little."[6]

An even more depressing note was struck by Ambassador Kennedy on his return home in December. The peoples of Britain and France, he reported, were low in spirit and yearned for an early peace. Economic conditions in both countries were so bad that the Germans might well be able to outlast them. On the military side the Germans were building submarines faster than the British could destroy them, and their production of airplanes, too, continued to outrun the British. In London a Nazi attack on Belgium or on the Maginot Line was generally expected in the spring. Mr. Kennedy doubted whether Britain could stand the strain beyond another year: "By the end of this year, if not before, people in England and France, and all over Europe, would be ready for communism . . ."[7] To top it all, Ambassador Bullitt arrived in Washington in February, 1940, and reported to the President in detail on a visit he had paid to the French front lines in December. His observations had only strengthened his fears that France might go down before a Nazi air attack. The Ambassador therefore used every ounce of his influence to speed up the supply of American planes to the French.[8]

Mr. Kennedy's deduction from the facts was that we should reinforce our own position to the point of being able to withstand the shock of ruin in Europe. Under no circumstances should we allow ourselves to be drawn in. Mr. Bullitt, on the other hand, insisted that in our own interest it was essential to do all we could to bolster the Allies against the anticipated attack. The President himself was evidently greatly concerned, but decidedly at a loss to know what precisely he could do. As aforesaid, he had already exerted himself to assist the democracies, but in the larger political sense he was more or less at sea. Even in the program of aiding Finland he had felt obliged to defer to strong isolationist feeling throughout the country.

[6] *Berle Diaries (MS.)*, November 28, December 26, 1939.
[7] Report of Ambassador Kennedy to a group of Army and Navy officers, December 15, 1939 (*Morgenthau Diaries MS.*, Vol. 230, pp. 3 ff.); *Moffat Diary (MS.)*, December 8, 15, 1939.
[8] Conversation of the authors with Mr. Bullitt, January 1946.

In offering Colonel Knox of the *Chicago Daily News* the post of Secretary of the Navy on December 10, 1939, he had combined dire predictions of the chaos which would reign in Europe if Germany won (he thought the chances fifty-fifty) with hints of possible American participation in shaping the postwar world. In this connection, Colonel Knox recorded the President's disquisition on what he called "four freedoms," perhaps the first reference to this subsequently famous formula.[9]

It is, however, a letter from Mr. Roosevelt to William Allen White that most clearly reveals the anxieties and confusion which the "phony war" engendered even in the President's mind. After thanking White for the services he had rendered in the fight to repeal the arms embargo, Mr. Roosevelt urged him to spend a night at the White House in mid-January:

Here [he continued], is the thought for you to devote thought to. Taking things in their broadest aspect, the world situation seems to me to be getting rather progressively worse as the weeks go by. No human being, with the best of information, has the slightest idea how this war is going to come out. But the fact remains that there are four or five possibilities, each leading to greater chaos or to the kind of truce which could last only a very short period.

As you know, I do not entertain the thought of some of the statesmen of 1918 that the world can make, or we can help the world to achieve a permanently lasting peace. . . . On the other hand, I do not want this country to take part in a patched-up, temporary peace which would blow up in our faces in a year or two.

There are several schools of thought about the Russian-German arrangement. One thinks that Germany took hold of the Bear's tail to keep England and France out of the war and that Germany today is much concerned over Russia's unexpected policy of action. . . .

The other school of thought, with equal reason, believes that there is a fairly definite agreement between Russia and Germany for the division of European control and with it the extension of that control to Asia Minor, Persia, Africa, etc., etc.

If that latter is true and Germany and Russia win the war or force a peace favorable to them, the situation of your civilization and mine is indeed in peril. Our world trade would be at the mercy of the combine, and our increasingly better relations with our twenty neighbors to the south would end—unless we were willing to go to war in their behalf against a German-Russian dominated Europe.

What worries me, especially, is that public opinion over here is patting itself on the back every morning and thanking God for the Atlantic Ocean (and the Pacific Ocean). We greatly underestimate the serious implications to our own future and I fear most people are merely going around saying "Thank God for Roosevelt and Hull—no matter what happens, they will keep us out of war."

The Lord and you know perfectly well that Roosevelt and Hull fully expect to

[9] Memo of conversation with the President, December 10 (*Knox Papers*, December 12, 1939).

keep us out of war—but on the other hand, we are not going around thanking God for allowing us physical safety within our continental limits.

Things move with such terrific speed these days that it is really essential to us to think in broader terms and, in effect, to warn the American people that they, too, should think of possible ultimate results in Europe and the Far East.

Therefore, my sage old friend, my problem is to get the American people to think of conceivable consequences without scaring the American people into thinking that they are going to be dragged into this war. . . .[10]

Mr. White's response to this revealing letter serves only to emphasize that perceptive men of good will fully shared the President's dilemma. "I fear," wrote White on December 22, "our involvement before the peace, and yet I fear to remain uninvolved, letting the danger of a peace of tyranny approach too near."[11] Such, then, was the background against which must be viewed the steps which the President and his advisers presently took along the only road on which the American people seemed then prepared to follow—the blind alley of a just and permanent peace.

2. A Special Mission to the Vatican

Among the many conflicting diagnoses of what was really wrong with an ailing world, there was at least one to which the President and his advisers all subscribed. The crisis which had produced war was at bottom moral and spiritual. "The President," wrote Berle, "is convinced that there is something more than merely mechanics wrong with Europe." Unless the "underlying philosophical necessities of the situation" were met, nothing would really be accomplished in the ultimate peace settlement.[12] The President had made the acquaintance of Pope Pius XII when, as Cardinal Pacelli, he had visited the United States in 1936. In that same year Mr. Roosevelt had first conceived the idea of establishing closer relations with the Vatican. Nothing, to be sure, had come of it prior to the advent of the war. During the summer of 1939 the problem had been discussed by the President with Mr. Hull and his other advisers, including Ambassador Phillips at Rome.[13] With the actual outbreak of hostilities, the President took up the problem in connection with relief measures in off-the-record conferences with Archbishop Spellman of New York. The latter was heartily in favor of establishing direct contact between the President and

[10] Letter of the President to William Allen White, December 14, 1939 (F.D.R.: His Personal Letters, II, 767-68); Walter Johnson: The Battle Against Isolationism (University of Chicago Press, Chicago, 1944), p. 60.
[11] Letter to the President (Roosevelt Papers: Secretary's File, Box 51), printed in Walter Johnson, ed.: Selected Letters of William Allen White (New York, 1947), 402 f.
[12] Berle Diaries (MS.), December 26, 1939.
[13] Letter of Welles to the President, August 1, 1939 (Roosevelt Papers: Secretary's File, Box 54); memo of the President to Mr. Hull, October 2, 1939 (F.D.R.: His Personal Letters, II, 931-33); Berle Diaries (MS.), December 26, 1939; Hull: Memoirs, I, 713.

the Holy See. Although there is little evidence on the specific objectives Mr. Roosevelt entertained, we need not doubt that his all-embracing aim was that described by Mr. Myron C. Taylor as: "a world order built upon firm moral and political foundations, upon the principle of the Good Neighbor, upon economic progress and social justice, upon the essential human freedoms, and upon respect for the dignity of the human soul."[14] In short, the President was moved by the laudable if rather tenuous hope of pooling his influence and joining his efforts with those of the Pope in preventing the spread of the war and providing for a just peace. Obviously of immense practical value to the American Government would be the un-paralleled wealth of information available to the Vatican from areas and sources more or less closed to American reporting. Finally, the President fully shared the Pope's anxiety to deter Mussolini from dragging Italy into the war at Hitler's side.[15]

Mr. Roosevelt encountered some opposition to his plan among State De-partment officials, but Secretary Hull thought well of it. On December 13, 1939, therefore, Mr. Hull asked Mr. Berle to draft a Christmas letter from the President to the Pope, "designed to lay something of a moral foundation for an ultimate peace."[16] The President himself revised the draft and ex-panded it to include the proposal that he appoint a personal representative to the Vatican. Just before Christmas Archbishop Spellman was again in-vited to the White House. Through him and through the Apostolic Dele-gate in Washington, Archbishop Cicognani, the letter was transmitted to the Vatican. At the same time similar letters were addressed to Dr. George A. Butterick, President of the Federal Council of the Churches of Christ in America, and to Rabbi Cyrus Adler, President of the Jewish Theological Seminary. The main object, however, was to establish the post at the Vati-can, to which Mr. Roosevelt would name Mr. Myron C. Taylor as his per-sonal representative. The Apostolic Delegate would have preferred a full diplomatic mission, but the President proposed to keep the matter on a "slightly tentative line." Taylor was to have the rank of Ambassador, but was to serve without pay and to defray his own expenses.[17]

The President's message to Pius XII was couched in exalted phraseology. It recalled that the world had previously gone through Dark Ages, but that such periods had invariably brought in their train a rebirth of order, cul-ture, and religion.

[14] Introduction to *Franklin D. Roosevelt and Pius XII: Wartime Correspondence,* with introduction by Myron C. Taylor (New York, 1947).

[15] Conversation of the authors with Mr. Welles, May, 1947; Hull: *Memoirs,* I, 713; Maxime Mourin: *Les tentatives de paix,* 57-8. On Vatican policy in relation to the Taylor Mission, see François Charles-Roux: *Huit ans au Vatican* (Paris, 1947), 364 ff.; and Camille M. Cianfarra: *The Vatican and the War* (New York, 1944), 207-8.

[16] *Berle Diaries (MS.),* December 13, 1939.

[17] In addition to the entries in the *Berle Diaries (MS.),* December 13, 20, 26, we have also used tel. to Phillips (Rome), December 23, 1939.

In their hearts [wrote the President], men decline to accept, for long, the law of destruction forced upon them by wielders of brute force.

I believe that while statesmen are considering a new order of things, the new order may well be at hand. I believe that it is even now being built, silently but inevitably, in the hearts of masses whose voices are not heard, but whose common faith will write the final history of our time. They know that unless there is belief in some guiding principle and some trust in a divine plan, nations are without light, and peoples perish.[18]

So pleased was the President with what Mr. Berle considered to be a careful approach to the Vatican that he seriously contemplated similar appeals and missions in the cause of peace to the Patriarchate of the Orthodox Church at Istanbul and even to various Moslem personalities. His idea was to send Mr. Lincoln MacVeagh, the United States Minister to Greece, on a special mission to the Patriarch of Constantinople and perhaps other Orthodox Patriarchs, "in order to confer with them on the general subject of peace, much as Myron Taylor has been conferring in Rome." But these extravagant ideas had to be abandoned in the light of numerous difficulties pointed out by the State Department: the Balkan States, fearing ecclesiastical encroachment, might resent appeals to the Patriarchs. As for a mission to the Moslems, to whom should it be sent? If a Sunni leader were chosen, Iran and Iraq would be estranged; yet if King Ibn Saud were selected, the Egyptians might object.[19]

Added to these difficulties was the growing chorus of protest against the establishment of "diplomatic relations" with the Pope. Protestant organizations throughout the land demanded angrily by what authority the President undertook to spend the taxpayers' money for such a reprehensible purpose. Technically the answer was simple: the President had full power to appoint personal representatives, and Taylor was to spend his own, not the public's, money. Nonetheless, criticism of the President's move was lively and insistent.[20] If he stuck to his guns, it was undoubtedly only because he was jealous of his prerogatives and convinced of the righteousness of his purpose. Taylor set out for Rome at the end of February, 1940, and thereby initiated the first of the President's moves in the interest of peace. As he wrote, in acknowledging Archbishop Spellman's "sincere and powerful work" in the good cause, Mr. Roosevelt felt sure that the special mission to

[18] The President's letter of December 23, 1939, and the Pope's reply of January 7, 1940, are printed in *Franklin D. Roosevelt and Pius XII: Wartime Correspondence*, Nos. 1 and 2; the preliminary drafts of the message are in *Roosevelt Papers*: Secretary's File, Box 45.

[19] Letter of the President to Berle, March 27, 1940 (*F.D.R.: His Personal Letters*, II, 1010); memo of the Division of Near Eastern Affairs, March 18, 1940; Hull: *Memoirs*, I, 715-16.

[20] See the President's reply to Senator Bailey, January 12, 1940 (*F.D.R.: His Personal Letters*, II, 988-89). On February 27, 1940, Dr. Buttrick wrote the President, calling attention to the "misgivings among Protestants" (*Roosevelt Papers*: Secretary's File, Box 58). The State Department files are full of letters of protest.

the Vatican would be "of deep and growing significance." So, indeed, it proved to be.[21]

3. An Organization of Neutrals: Postwar Plans

Having, in his messages to the Pope and to the American religious leaders, given expression to the importance he attached to the moral basis of an ultimate peace, the President at once turned his attention to the more mundane considerations with which the problem fairly bristled. At his request, Secretary Hull undertook to create, at the end of December, 1939, a special State Department committee to study questions of peace terms and postwar reconstruction. Initially, at any rate, there was considerable confusion as to the President's precise objectives. Mr. Welles, favorably impressed by the research programs of private organizations such as the Council on Foreign Relations, believed that the new committee should likewise devote itself to the study of the long-range issues and "formulate recommendations upon the problem of the bases for peace so that these recommendations and the results of these studies may be available when the war terminates."[22] Mr. Berle, on the other hand, privately believed that the President's mind was still "working towards trying to summon a general peace conference before the beginning of the spring drives," and concluded that there was no reason to suppose that "the situation is any worse for making a just peace now than it would be later." The State Department's Economic Adviser, Mr. Herbert Feis, in turn, saw little sense in trying to do anything at all until it was clear who was to be the victor. However, it was thought, the United States should be ready with a positive program if an opportunity presented itself, and Mr. Welles was appointed temporary chairman of the new committee on December 28, 1939.[23]

Such was the confused status of American peace efforts as the first New Year of the war rolled round. Secretary Hull, pressed for a statement, disclaimed all knowledge of what the future might bring, but suggested the possibility

. . . that, even during the coming year, *all* nations may find in themselves sufficient strength of conscience, of reason, of the very instinct of self-preservation to return—before the forces of destruction have been loosed in all their fury—to the tried and proven road of friendly and peaceful international relations, along which

---

[21] Letter of the President to Archbishop Spellman, December, 1939 (*Roosevelt Papers: Secretary's File*, Box 45). On the beginnings of the Taylor Mission see also Charles-Roux: *Huit ans au Vatican*, 370 ff.

[22] Memo of Welles to Hull, December 18, 1939; *Postwar Preparation*, 19-22.

[23] *Berle Diaries (MS.)*, December 28, 29, 1939; conversations of the authors with Mr. Berle, November 1947, and with Mr. Pasvolsky, January 1949; *Moffat Diary (MS.)*, December 27, 1939.

alone the human race can move in the direction of material advancement and spiritual progress.[24]

The President, in his State of the Union Speech of January 3, 1940, was even more insistent than Mr. Hull in urging the necessity for Americans to interest themselves in the organization of the future peace. In words far stronger than he had used in his letter to William Allen White, he denounced those

. . . who wishfully insist, in innocence or ignorance or both, that the United States of America as a self-contained unit can live happily and prosperously, its future secure, inside a high wall of isolation while outside, the rest of civilization and the commerce and culture of mankind are shattered.

He could understand, said Mr. Roosevelt, the feelings of those who would never consent to sending American youth to fight in Europe. However, he added, no one had asked them to consent, since no one expected such an undertaking:

But there is a vast difference between keeping out of war and pretending that this war is none of our business. We do not have to go to war with other nations, but at least we can strive with other nations to encourage the kind of peace that will lighten the troubles of the world, and by so doing help our own nation as well.

The President therefore urged his fellow citizens to look ahead and consider carefully what it would mean to their country and its future if the world were to be dominated by force in the hands of a few. He recalled the achievements of our own Good Neighbor Policy and pointed to the hopeful results of our trade agreements program. Along such lines, he concluded, lay the hope of the future.[25]

The President's utterances before the Joint Session of Congress inevitably aroused controversy. It soon became evident that the country at large was far from prepared to draw the desired conclusion from his warnings. At the end of the year isolationist sentiment was running stronger than at any time since the outbreak of hostilities. Opinion polls published in February, 1940, revealed that the percentage of those who thought America would ultimately be drawn into the conflict had fallen to 32, while the percentage of those who believed we should take part in the war as a last resort to save Britain and France had fallen to 23.[26] The President's remarks were therefore frequently dismissed as a "hankering to put the world aright— to succeed where Woodrow Wilson failed."[27]

[24] January 1, 1940 (Text in Documents on American Foreign Relations, II, 32-33). Cf. Hull: Memoirs, I, 731 f.

[25] Text in Documents on American Foreign Relations, II, 34 ff.

[26] See also the address of Sir Frederick Whyte, Director of the American Division of the British Ministry of Information, as reported in the London Times, January 23, 1940.

[27] Alvin Adey: "Does President Roosevelt Want War?" (Events, February 1940, 102-5).

Prominent isolationists again took to the stump, with vigorous warnings against involvement by Senator Vandenberg at St. Paul, Minnesota, February 10, and by Senator Taft at New York on March 2. An optimistic speech by the British Ambassador, Lord Lothian, at Chicago on January 4, was hardly calculated to shake the popular belief that Britain and France could successfully resist the attack which Lothian predicted for the coming spring.[28]

The President, however, would not allow himself to be deterred in his efforts to further the cause of peace and to stake out an American claim to a voice in its formulation, even, it must be supposed, if this were to involve negotiation with the existing German Government. On January 8, 1940, Mr. Hull issued a public statement announcing the creation of the Advisory Committee on Problems of Foreign Relations.[29] Mr. Welles continued as chairman and the fifteen members were drawn almost exclusively from the Department of State. By January 15, its economic subcommittee had already drawn up an outline for an economic settlement which, as Mr. Hull observes, the Administration proposed to offer as a basis for discussion with the neutral powers.

This latter project, the first envisaging concrete action by the United States Government, was submitted to the President by Chairman Welles on January 12, 1940, in the form of a memorandum entitled *Organization of Neutrals*.[30] As Welles explained to Mr. Roosevelt, the aim of the proposed organization of neutrals was twofold: "to determine the best means of strengthening moral and economic coöperation between them during the duration of the war," and to obtain their judgment "as to the most effective means, upon the conclusion of the war, of securing a stable world order based upon international law and a sound international economic system." If the replies of the neutral governments proved favorable, the President would convoke a congress of representatives of these governments in Washington. The Latin American Republics would choose five delegates; the Oslo Powers, one; Turkey, Iran and Iraq, one; and the other neutrals, one each.[31]

The President seems to have been well impressed with this proposal.[32] However, in the course of subsequent discussion, the plan was profoundly

---

[28] *Vital Speeches*, VI, 197 ff.

[29] *Documents on American Foreign Relations*, II, 374-75; Hull: *Memoirs*, I, 732; II, 1626-27.

[30] Letter of Welles to the President with enclosed memo on *Organization of Neutrals*, January 12, 1940 (*Roosevelt Papers:* Secretary's File, Box 62; file copy in State Department).

[31] Letter of Welles to the President, with enclosed memo, January 12, 1940 (*Roosevelt Papers:* Secretary's File, Box 62).

[32] Letter of the President to Oswald Garrison Villard, January 18, 1940 (*Roosevelt Papers:* Secretary's File, Box 67). Villard had written urging the President to request the belligerents to state their war aims before the anticipated spring offensive should begin (*ibid.*, Box 67).

modified. The proposed strong reassertion of the superiority of neutral rights vis-à-vis the belligerents was deleted, and ultimately nearly all else not strictly related to postwar conditions was omitted.[33] The motives behind these changes are not clear, but it may be assumed that the President was still laboring to reconcile irreconcilables. While he wrote Berle (the leading proponent of the neutral bloc idea) that "this particular time (end of January) may be a turning point . . . toward unofficial considerations in the direction of peace," he could not, as we have seen, persuade himself to accept the idea of a patched-up truce with the aggressor powers.[34]

Beyond the desire to avoid embarrassing London and Paris by seeming to sponsor the idea of a settlement with Hitler which these Governments had repudiated, there were other grounds for caution. Presumably the organization of an effective neutral front would have involved something akin to the extension of the hemispheric bloc to include the European neutrals. This, in turn, might lead to further blockade difficulties, not to mention increased friction with Germany, which by this time was destroying neutral shipping with little or no compunction. In sum, the organization of a neutral front on the scale originally envisaged presupposed a readiness on the part of the United States to face precisely those international complications which our neutrality legislation was designed to avoid.[35]

At any rate, when Secretary Hull finally announced on February 9 that Washington was opening diplomatic conversations with the neutral governments on the "establishment of a sound foundation for a lasting world peace," he was careful to specify that "matters involving present war conditions" were to form no part of these conversations.[36] Since the President chose the same day to announce Under Secretary Welles's forthcoming mission to four major European capitals—news that was certain to create anxiety in London and Paris—Mr. Hull, in his press conference next day, reiterated that the agenda of the conversations was to be restricted to postwar problems.[37]

While, as Mr. Hull has pointed out, two thirds of the neutral nations approached signified their willingness to coöperate, several of the most powerful among them were reserved in their responses, precisely because they believed that nothing of importance could be accomplished toward disarmament and economic renovation without the collaboration of the

[33] Memo of Welles to the President, February 1, 1940, enclosing a draft of the proposed message to neutral governments (*Roosevelt Papers:* Secretary's File, Box 62).

[34] Memo of the President to Mr. Berle, January 27, 1940 (*Roosevelt Papers:* Secretary's File, Box 62).

[35] Alsop and Kintner: *American White Paper*, 85-86.

[36] *Documents on American Foreign Relations*, II, 375.

[37] Hull: *Memoirs*, I, 738; II, 1628; tel. to neutral capitals (omitting Moscow, Helsinki, Tokyo, and Chungking), February 10, 1940. We have also used the draft of a second circular telegram to the neutrals, April 2, 1940, not actually sent.

powerful belligerents.[38] In the blunt language of the Spanish Foreign Minister, who had expected peace overtures, the proposal of the Washington Government "seemed of a romantic and platonic character," most unlikely to lead to the "achievement of any practical result."[39]

Conceived in confusion, and stillborn in the catastrophes which began in April with Hitler's invasion of Norway, nothing was ever to come of this grandiose scheme for an organization of neutrals. It stands simply as a remarkably picturesque manifestation of American indecision in the face of a war which the people and Government of the United States could neither wholly ignore nor resolutely embrace. However, the more modest efforts of the State Department Committee on Problems of Foreign Relations survived the convulsive end of the phony war and in due course were to produce fruitful studies of both the war aims and peace aims of the United States and the United Nations.[40]

It is a commentary on the state of mind of Washington in the final weeks preceding the German descent on Norway that even in its efforts on behalf of peace, the Administration desired to avoid the appearance of too close collaboration with Britain. When Lord Lothian informed the President that the British Government had itself just established a semi-official committee to study the problems of peace, Mr. Roosevelt offered no objection to an informal exchange of ideas with the American committee, but warned Welles against allowing an impression to arise that we were collaborating with the British for common peace terms.[41] Beyond this, and as a further manifestation of the paralysis which seemed to overtake American policy in the last stages of the phony war, we may glance briefly at the developing misunderstandings between London and Washington. Initiated by conflicts over neutral rights, these Anglo-American differences were exacerbated by British anxiety over Washington's nebulous peace plans, and especially by the announcement of Mr. Welles's approaching European mission.

4. ANGLO-AMERICAN FRICTION

Writing to thank Winston Churchill for his lively account of the destruction of the *Graf Spee*, the President put his finger very neatly on the major reason for the friction between Britain and the United States which came to a head early in 1940:

---

[38] Tel. to Santiago, March 23, 1940, commenting on Chilean objections. The forty-three replies are analyzed in a State Department memo of May 23, 1940.

[39] Tel. from Weddell (Madrid), February 14, 1940. Doubts and reservations were also expressed by Portugal, Greece, Yugoslavia, and Hungary.

[40] Hull: *Memoirs*, II, 1628 ff.; *Postwar Foreign Policy Preparation*, Part I. The committee was ultimately extended to include eminent private citizens like Hamilton Fish Armstrong, Mrs. Anne O'Hare McCormick, Isaiah Bowman, and others (*Berle Diaries, MS.*, 1941).

[41] Tel. to Welles (London), March 2, 1940.

At the time of dictating this I think our conversations in regard to search and detention of American ships are working out satisfactorily—but I would not be frank unless I told you that there has been much public criticism here. The general feeling is that the net benefit to your people and to France is hardly worth the definite annoyance caused to us. That is always found to be so in a nation which is 3,000 miles away from the fact of war.[42]

Our earlier easygoing acquiescence in what we deemed to be violations of our neutral rights and interests by Great Britain had been based not only on sympathy for the Allied cause, but on the assumption that London's economic warfare tactics were temporary expedients designed to assure a speedy and bloodless victory. When, however, at the close of the year, no victory was yet in sight and the British Government resorted to increasingly stringent measures to insure the success of its blockade, it was inevitable that friction should develop. Doubtless the final sentence of the President's letter to Mr. Churchill went directly to the heart of the matter. Yet one must explore somewhat more fully the circumstances which induced the Administration to cease winking at London's tactics. and to adopt instead a new attitude of rather fretful complaint.

One item in this bill of particulars was the very subject on which Mr. Churchill had written to the President—the tracking down of the *Graf Spee*. This exciting episode had filled the British people with elation, leaving little room for worry about the crass violation of the American neutrality zone. The official British reply to the joint protests of all the American Republics did not reach Washington until January 15, 1940, though the British Ambassador had given previous notice of its probable content.[43] As anticipated, the British note proved to be little more than a restatement of the British view of the neutrality zone as originally expounded in October. The London Government, it repeated, appreciated the anxiety of the American Governments to keep the war away from their shores, but trusted that they would make no effort to enforce observance of the zone by unilateral action. The Declaration of Panama, it was recalled, involved the abandonment of legitimate rights by the belligerents, and therefore required their specific concurrence. To obtain this it would at least be necessary for the American Governments to give assurance that the zone "would not provide German warships and supply ships with a vast sanctuary from which they could emerge to attack Allied and neutral shipping." Similarly German warships must not be permitted "to pass with impunity from one ocean to another through the zone," or otherwise to engage in activities "depriving the Allies of the fruits of their superiority at sea."

The British Government furthermore repudiated any idea that it had

[42] Letter of the President to Mr. Churchill, February 1, 1940 (*F.D.R.: His Personal Letters*, II, 995).

[43] Memo of conversation between Lord Lothian and Mr. Welles, January 8, 1940.

acted in such fashion as to justify punitive measures, and pointed out that the effort to impose sanctions might well lead to serious and deplorable friction. It suggested that "the only effective method of achieving the American object of preventing belligerent acts within the zone would be, firstly, to ensure that the German Government would send no more warships into it." In view of the fact that so many German ships had taken refuge in ports of the Americas, it would seem necessary that the American Governments take over these vessels for the duration.[44]

The German Government carefully refrained from taking any stand until after publication of the British and French notes. It then sent a positively unctuous reply. Declaring Germany's complete sympathy with the aims of the American Governments, Berlin nevertheless rejected as firmly as London the right of those Governments to introduce sanctions by unilateral decision and in violation of international law. Stressing the advantages enjoyed by Britain and France in the possession of territories in the New World, which, incidentally, the note described as "exceptions to the Monroe Doctrine," Berlin went on to submit that this inequity "might perhaps be eliminated to a certain extent if Great Britain and France would pledge themselves, under the guaranty of the American states, not to make the possessions and islands mentioned the starting points or bases for military operations." Extraordinary as was this reasoning, the root of the matter, so far as Berlin was concerned, was the obvious unwillingness of the British and French Governments "to take up seriously the idea of the security zone." Until the Allied Governments had fundamentally revised the position taken in their notes, the German Government could profess no confidence whatever in the security zone plan.[45]

For once American authorities found themselves in something like theoretical agreement with a German position. Several State Department officials, after subjecting the unaccommodating replies of London and Paris to painstaking analysis, deemed them unsatisfactory and concluded that the Allies had had from the outset no intention of respecting the zone. Some, however, were frankly favorable to the Allied arguments. Others confessed that the zone was larger than hemisphere trade interests required and too large to be effectively patrolled. The least the American Governments could do was to inaugurate measures to prevent German ships in their ports from engaging in "undesirable activities."[46]

---

[44] Text in *Documents on American Foreign Relations*, II, 122-25. The French reply, dated January 23, 1940, contained much the same arguments and added nothing in the way of substance (*ibid.*, 125-27).

[45] Text in *Documents on American Foreign Relations*, II, 127-31. Hitler, "in view of the psychological effect on the U.S.A.," continued to refuse to sanction the operations within the zone recommended by the German Admiralty (*Fuehrer Conferences*, I (1940), 13).

[46] Memoranda of Hackworth and Bonsal, January 29, February 1 and 28, 1940, analyzing the belligerents' replies.

If there was thus no real disposition to go to the mat with London and Paris on this issue, neither did it seem desirable to abandon all effort to secure the compliance of the belligerents with the Declaration of Panama. Indeed, as Mr. Ellis Briggs, an official of the State Department, had already stated in public, that pronouncement was no "limp scarecrow to be knocked flat by the first gust of wind, and then to be forgotten." The important thing, said Briggs, was the solidarity of views among the American Republics, which was bound to acquire increasing weight as time went on.[47] On this basis the State Department elected to proceed. Under Secretary Welles suggested that the whole problem be dumped into the laps of "Fenwick and the Inter-American Neutrality Committee." Accordingly this body, which convened at Rio de Janeiro on January 15, 1940, was instructed to study the replies of the belligerent powers and to come up with recommendations. No response was to be made to the Allied notes in the interval, which in fact extended to April 24, by which time the issue had lost much of its practical importance.[48]

Meanwhile, unhappily, even more troublesome issues had arisen to plague an Administration which was still trying valiantly to chart a course between the demands of neutrality and the desire to assist Britain. On December 14, 1939, the State Department despatched a new note to the Foreign Office in reply to a British note of November 9, which had been interpreted in Washington as implying a threat to violate the Neutrality Law of November 4 by reserving Britain's right to force American ships into control ports located within the now-forbidden combat zones. This new note, however, still reflected Mr. Hull's consistent efforts to smooth the path of Anglo-American relations, and once again ended on a minor key.[49] Although the British had not forced any American vessels into combat zones since the passage of the Neutrality Act, they showed no disposition to renounce their right to do so, and took Mr. Hull's latest remonstrance with the usual grain of salt. As a result pent-up American irritation overflowed to cover the whole area of Britain's economic warfare procedures. By the end of the year yet another American note had been drafted, objecting this time to what the State Department contended were unilateral innovations in the

---

[47] Address of Mr. Ellis O. Briggs, January 4, 1940 (*State Department Bulletin*, January 6, 1940).

[48] Memos of conversation between Lothian and Welles, January 31, April 22, 1940. The text of the Inter-American Neutrality Committee's statement of April 24 is printed in *Documents on American Foreign Relations*, II, 133 ff. See especially the detailed account of the last phases by a member of the committee, Charles G. Fenwick: "The Inter-American Neutrality Committee" (*American Journal of International Law*, XXXV, January 1941, pp. 12-40).

[49] *Supra*, Chapter VIII, Section 3. Text in *Documents on American Foreign Relations*, II, 710-11. We have also used memos of conversation between Mr. Moffat and Mr. Hoyar Millar of the British Embassy, November 4; and between Mr. Hickerson and Mr. Foster of the Embassy, November 9, 1939. In these conversations the American officials took a much stronger line than had been used previously.

navicert procedures hitherto agreed upon between London and Washington. The point had been reached, thought the American authorities, where the British were granting or withholding navicerts "at their good pleasure." The bringing of the American vessel *Mooremacsun* into Kirkwall early in January seemed to bear out the State Department's worst suspicions.[50]

Nor did the American Government take kindly to a misguided British proposal whereby American ships lacking navicerts could be inspected for contraband without being forced into a combat area. Mr. Roosevelt instructed Welles to inform Lord Lothian that the United States Government could not even "tacitly acquiesce" in the taking of American ships to Halifax for inspection, since the Nova Scotia port lay within the hemisphere neutrality zone from which all belligerent activity must be excluded. Saint John's, Newfoundland, might do, but if that port were selected, Lothian was to be told that the United States would hold Britain accountable for all damage incurred by the diversion of American vessels from their normal courses.[51]

Some balm for these wounds was provided by Mr. Churchill's assurance, as First Lord of the Admiralty, to the President that Great Britain would cease the practice of inspecting American vessels in combat zones.[52] But by then, unhappily, still other instances of friction had arisen. It was, in fact, British interference with American mails which produced the angriest public reaction in this country and induced the State Department to despatch its first really sharp protest to London. As Mr. Berle had observed when Washington first got wind of the British plan to censor air mail as it passed through Bermuda: "I suppose they have the right to, but our people will dislike it intensely."[53] The British persisted, however, in exercising what they regarded as rights already clearly recognized by the United States in the years 1916-1918. Moreover, in their reply to the American protest (January 17), they insisted that the United States mails were being used not only for the transfer of funds and the transmission of military intelligence, but even for the shipment of contraband like industrial diamonds.[54]

[50] *Berle Diaries (MS.)*, December 29, 1939; *Moffat Diary (MS.)*, January 5, 1940; memo of Assistant Secretary Grady, January 2, 1940, containing an oral statement made to the British Ambassador; memoranda of conversations between Mr. Moffat and the French Ambassador, January 23, and with Lord Lothian, January 25; memo of conversation between Lord Lothian and Mr. Berle, February 14, 1940. On the general problem see Hull: *Memoirs*, I, 735-36.

[51] Memoranda of conversations between Lothian and Welles, January 12; between the President and Welles, January 15; and between Lothian and Welles, January 31, 1940.

[52] Tels. from Mr. Churchill to the President, January 29, 30, 1940; Hull: *Memoirs*, I, 733.

[53] *Berle Diaries (MS.)*, December 20; *Moffat Diary (MS.)*, December 26, 1939.

[54] Text in *Documents on American Foreign Relations*, II, 713 ff.; Hull: *Memoirs*, I, 734. See especially Clyde Eagleton: "Interference With American Mails" (*American Journal of International Law*, XXXIV, 1940, pp. 315-20).

When to these American grievances was presently added London's decision to curtail British imports of American agricultural products, notably tobacco, the public resentment predicted by Mr. Berle became a matter of genuine concern, both to Secretary Hull and to Lord Lothian. The British move was prompted by a natural desire to conserve dollars by purchasing within the sterling area, as well as to assist the necessitous Turks and Greeks by assuring them a market for their tobacco. On the other hand, any curtailment of British purchases of American cotton or tobacco was mathematically certain to touch off bitter resentment among hard-pressed American exporters. Lord Lothian was therefore frankly warned that we felt the British were presuming on our friendliness. While Mr. Hull professed to understand Britain's plight, he left the Ambassador in no doubt that both the American people and their Government regarded certain of Britain's economic warfare tactics as "unnecessary, unreasonable, and injurious restrictions to trade and other interests." Quite apart from the danger that these practices might be carried over into the postwar period, the Secretary warned that they would soon prove more harmful than helpful to Britain's war effort.[55]

Puzzled and hurt by the increasingly anti-British tone of sections of the American press, and dismayed by Washington's decision to make public its protests to London, Lothian was at great pains to expound his Government's position and to emphasize the crucial importance it attached to the blockade as the chief weapon of victory. Great Britain was prepared, he concluded, to defer to American sensibilities wherever possible, but not to the point of abandoning any course of action which it deemed vital to the successful prosecution of the war.[56] In reply, the American authorities reiterated their fear that Britain's war regulations would prove harmful to the United States in postwar competition, and pressed Britain to refrain from "minor practices" which proved so annoying to this country.[57] With both Governments thus sticking to their guns, the rash of anti-British sentiment in this country spread sufficiently to fill Ambassador Kennedy with misgiving as he was about to return to his London post.[58] The French Ambassador, in turn, was provoked to the point of forgetting himself, and inquired irritably whether the Government of the United States was trying "to stir up trouble with Great Britain." Lothian himself confessed that he was worried about what

[55] Tel. to Johnson (London), January 26; *Moffat Diary (MS.)*, January 20, 1940; Hull: *Memoirs*, I, 748-49.

[56] Memoranda of conversations between Lord Lothian and Messrs. Moore and Moffat of the State Department, January 25; between Lothian and Hull, January 30; and between Lothian and Welles, January 31, 1940; Hancock and Gowing: *British War Economy*, 226.

[57] Memo of conversation between Hull and Lothian, February 14, 1940; Hull: *Memoirs*, I, 734.

[58] Memoranda of conversation between Kennedy and Breckinridge Long of the State Department, February 15; and between Kennedy and Berle, February 15, 1940. The *Moffat Diary (MS.)*, February 13, 1940, indicates Ambassador Bullitt's concern.

might represent a concerted campaign against his country. Although Secretary Hull scouted such fears, which were indeed exaggerated, the dangers of friction became manifest when Berlin proceeded to fish in the troubled waters.[59]

The German Government, obviously greatly cheered by the prospect of any deterioration in Anglo-American relations, announced unofficially in mid-February that it would regard neutral ships that called at Gibraltar, a British contraband-control port, as no longer neutral and therefore subject to attack. The stir was immediate. Senator Gillette of Iowa described the Berlin Government's position as "hardly open to criticism." While but few members of Congress agreed with him, many did hold the British at least partly responsible for the threat. There was, moreover, much grumbling over the patent failure of the latest Neutrality Law to remove every last element of danger to American shipping.[60]

It is possible that the German move unwittingly contributed to the *détente* which, in any event, presently set in. Both the American and British Governments had the good sense to appreciate the danger of allowing a misunderstanding over practice to harden into a genuine clash of principle. Though the belated British reply (February 21) to our original protest (December 8) against interference with exports from Germany struck one high official of the State Department as a "combination of misstatements of international law and propaganda," he recommended against further argument and suggested instead that we "press for favorable action in individual cases."[61] This the British had insisted from the beginning they would be glad to accord us. More than that, the much-worried Allied Governments in early March sent to Washington special emissaries to review the entire field of blockade difficulties and, if possible, to find a mutually satisfactory solution. These gentlemen, Mr. F. Ashton-Gwatkin of the British Ministry of Economic Warfare, and M. Charles Rist of the French Ministry of Blockade, were received by the President on their arrival and subsequently conferred at length with appropriate American officials. They promised to do their utmost to reduce the inconveniences being caused to neutral trade "so long as this does not lessen the effect of the contraband control in all its branches." Likewise they calmed American fears that Allied wartime restrictions might be prolonged into the postwar period, stating

. . . categorically that the restrictive measures rendered necessary by the war were of an entirely temporary character and that at the earliest possible moment the French and British Governments would return to liberal commercial policies based

---

[59] Memoranda of conversations between Moffat and Saint-Quentin, January 23; and between Lothian and Hull, February 23, 1940. Hull: *Memoirs*, I, 734 f.

[60] *The New York Times*, February 15, 17, 1940.

[61] Memo of Mr. Hickerson, February 29, 1940. The American note of December 8, 1939, had been followed by another (tel. to London, January 12, 1940).

on the principle of the progressive reduction of trade barriers and to world trade conducted on a multilateral basis.[62]

Whatever misunderstandings still remained after the departure of the Allied emissaries were swallowed up in the wave of disaster which engulfed the Allied nations in April and May. With the advantages of hindsight one is tempted to charge American critics of Britain with having exhibited a hypersensitive, stiff-necked, and generally unrealistic attitude throughout the whole unhappy contretemps of the winter. It now seems utterly preposterous that Americans should have lost sleep over the danger of Anglo-French postwar trade practices when, in fact, Britain and France were standing on the brink of disaster. Our rather academic defense of neutral rights and liberal trade policies can only be explained, in the final analysis, by the President's sage observation that it largely reflected our national insulation from direct contact with the war in Europe. Yet, in partial vindication of the Washington stand, it should be emphasized that London and Paris, too, remained optimistic about their chances of victory through economic warfare until their complacency was abruptly shattered by harsh realities. In short, like other manifestations of the American concern for orderly process, for a just peace, and for postwar prosperity, the debate with Britain sprang from tragic illusions fostered on both sides of the Atlantic. At the very least, then, it is no cause for wonder that President Roosevelt, whose own fond hopes alternated with dark misgivings, should have felt it necessary to send a special emissary to Europe in a supreme effort to penetrate the veil of uncertainty.

5. THE WELLES MISSION

On February 9, 1940, in the midst of the tension with Britain, the President announced that at his request Under Secretary Welles would presently visit Europe "solely for the purpose of advising the President and the Secretary of State as to present conditions in Europe." Mr. Welles was to visit Rome, Berlin, Paris and London, but was to make "no proposals or commitments in the name of the United States Government."[63] Evidently this terse announcement did not exhaust all the possibilities the President had in mind in sending Mr. Welles abroad. Yet, in the light of what has already been revealed about Mr. Roosevelt's interest in peace, there is no need to suspect hidden or ulterior motives behind this final manifestation of that interest. We have it on Mr. Welles's own authority that the President wanted

---

[62] State Department press release, April 26, 1940 (*Documents on American Foreign Relations*, II, 501 ff.); Hull: *Memoirs*, I, 735. On the final phases of the disagreement we have also used a tel. from Johnson (London), February 28, various memoranda of conversations between American officials and Messrs. Ashton-Gwatkin and Rist, and between Mr. Hull and Lord Lothian, March 20, 1940.

[63] Text in *Documents on American Foreign Relations*, II, 376.

to ascertain "what the views of the four Governments might be as to the present possibilities of concluding any just and permanent peace."[64] Furthermore, an early and discarded draft of the President's announcement stated baldly that its object was to ascertain whether the belligerent powers "will state for the confidential information of the President the basis upon which they would be prepared to make peace."[65]

While the President hastened to reassure the alarmed heads of the Allied Governments that he hoped the forthcoming exchange of views might prove "of real value towards a peace which is neither 'inconclusive nor precarious,'" Mr. Welles is again our authority for stating that Mr. Roosevelt was at least willing to contemplate a peace with Hitler if, forlorn as the chances seemed, the Fuehrer would submit acceptable terms.[66] Finally, if Mr. Welles was to refrain from making any "proposals" or "commitments," it has been asserted on good authority that he was empowered "at his discretion" to discuss peace on the "old basis of disarmament and an opening of trade."[67] We may safely assume, then, that besides the desire to obtain first-hand knowledge of European developments, and to influence Italy to remain out of the war, it was a major objective of the Welles Mission to explore peace possibilities even with a Nazi Government.

No useful purpose would be served by trying to ascertain whether the President requested Mr. Welles to undertake the mission or was persuaded to the idea by Welles himself. It is plain enough that the Secretary of State disliked the proposal and equally clear that, if the inspiration was not the President's, Welles, as a seasoned diplomat and chairman of the State Department committee on peace problems, was the logical choice.[68]

Mr. Hull was not alone in disapproving of Welles's forthcoming visit to Europe. Prime Minister Chamberlain, in messages to the President, made no effort to disguise his initial dislike of such "sensational intervention." While he professed appreciation of Mr. Roosevelt's motives, and was pleased to observe that the President was aware that the nub of the peace problem was a German guarantee against renewed aggression, he said he was not sure that Berlin's threats of a coming offensive were more than propaganda or

[64] Welles: *The Time for Decision*, 74.

[65] This undated draft of early February, 1940, is found in *Roosevelt Papers:* Secretary's File, Box 62.

[66] President's longhand letters to the Pope, Mussolini, Chamberlain and Daladier, to be presented by Welles, February 14, 1940 (*F.D.R.: His Personal Letters*, II, 1000-1002); conversation of the authors with Mr. Welles, May 27, 1947. Mr. Leo Pasvolsky has informed the authors that to the best of his knowledge there was no idea of a "compromise peace" behind the Welles Mission (conversation, January 25, 1949).

[67] Alsop and Kintner: *American White Paper*, Appendix, p. 85. The fact that Mr. Welles carried with him memoranda outlining the familiar American position on liberalization of trade lends substance to this claim. An accurate text was made public in a State Department press release, May 3, 1940.

[68] Hull: *Memoirs*, I, 737-38; Welles: *The Time for Decision*, 74-5.

that peace would be any more difficult to secure later. He doubted whether, on the one hand, suitable guarantees could be extracted from the existing German regime, and, on the other, whether the British and French peoples would accept any settlement with Hitler. "I must frankly admit," he added, "to a good deal of anxiety lest the effect of this move, however carefully presented, should be to cause embarrassment to the democracies, from which Germany, still unconvinced of the failure of the policy of force, will reap advantage." Specifically, he explained in another message, he was worried lest the Welles Mission ruin the Allies' current plans for operations in Scandinavia by enabling Norway and Sweden to say that peace was on the way and Finland could be saved without an Allied expeditionary force.[69]

Before Welles actually reached Europe, Mr. Chamberlain seems to have experienced a change of heart. In a speech on peace aims (February 24) he concluded: "We for our part should be ready to seek a settlement with any Government that had subscribed to those aims and given proof—proof that can be relied upon—of their sincerity."[70] Unhappily for the peace-minded, Adolf Hitler chose the same day to make a speech declaring his determination to break Britain's power.

To the decidedly mixed reception thus accorded the President's scheme by two of the principal parties was added also some chilling domestic criticism. American isolationists denounced the proposed mission as yet another of Mr. Roosevelt's interventionist maneuvers, while the interventionists were fearful that it was Welles's sinister objective to force appeasement upon the Allied Governments. In short, as the American Under Secretary of State debarked at Naples, in company with Mr. Myron Taylor and Mr. Pierrepont Moffat, the cause looked rather hopeless.[71]

Yet in Rome the Under Secretary's visit was viewed with considerable satisfaction, if for no other reason than that for once Italy had been accorded priority over Germany in the itinerary of an influential foreign statesman.[72] Welles arrived in the Italian capital on February 25 and had a first conversation with the Foreign Minister, Count Ciano, on the next day. The two men were evidently well impressed with each other. Ciano spoke with apparent frankness, making no secret whatever of his intense dislike for Ribbentrop and his distrust of Hitler and the whole Nazi program. Welles expressed appreciation for the efforts made by the Italian Government to prevent the outbreak of war, and tactfully stressed the role it could continue

[69] Letters from Mr. Chamberlain to the President, undated, but apparently of early February, 1940 (*Roosevelt Papers*: Secretary's File, Box 62). For the anxious reaction of British public opinion see "Mr. Roosevelt's Dove" (*Economist*, February 17, 1940) and R. Daniell in *The New York Times*, February 22, 1940.

[70] Holborn: *War and Peace Aims of the United Nations*, I, 178 ff.

[71] Welles: *The Time for Decision*, 74, 77; Hull: *Memoirs*, I, 738-39; tel. from Kennedy, March 9, 1940.

[72] Tel. from Phillips, February 10, 1940.

to play as a prominent neutral. With regard to the possibilities of peace, the Under Secretary averred that his function was simply to report on the chances for "a stable and lasting peace—that was the only kind of peace in which my Government was interested." Ciano judged the chances slim, but indicated that in any event the Italians were determined to keep both the Germans and the Russians out of southeastern Europe. The Foreign Minister was particularly bitter about the Russians and the Hitler-Stalin pact. He expressed his conviction that the ultimate objective of the Soviets was "to bring about the hegemony of Soviet influence in every part of the world."[73]

On the afternoon of the same day (February 26) Welles and Ambassador Phillips were received by the Duce in the presence of Ciano. The Under Secretary was astonished to find the Italian dictator looking weary and moving sluggishly. His aloofness reflected the fact that Mussolini (though not his chief civilian and military advisers) was convinced that the Germans would win the war and that the only sound policy for Italy was to stand by them, no matter how irritating and unpopular they were. Welles began by presenting President Roosevelt's personal letter, reviving the idea that the two leaders might meet for a conference at some such place as the Azores.[74] Mussolini, touched in his vanity, was obviously gratified, but reserved his decision for a later date. Conversation then turned to questions of Italian-American trade relations and the future economic order, Welles submitting his memorandum on the American program. To this Mussolini raised no specific objection, merely emphasizing that economic agreements would be impossible until a sound political peace had been established. The prerequisite for this was Allied recognition of Germany's "just" claims in Central Europe, which, as the Duce described them, amounted virtually to acceptance of the *status quo*. Italy's claims would likewise have to be granted. He would not go into these in detail, but he gave Welles clearly to understand that there could be no peace so long as Italy remained a prisoner in the Mediterranean. Even so, the Duce by no means excluded all hope of peace negotiations if the Allies moved before real war began. The conversation closed with an agreement that Mussolini should see Welles again after his return from the other capitals.[75]

Certainly the most difficult part of Mr. Welles's assignment was his visit to Berlin, where he arrived on March 1, 1940. The mere announcement of

[73] Mr. Welles's *Report to the President* on his return. By arrangement, Welles rarely reported his conversations by cable or despatch, for reasons of security. Moreover, the account given in Welles: *The Time for Decision,* Chap. III, is both accurate and detailed, omitting only certain passages which at the time could not safely be published.

[74] Text in *Roosevelt Papers:* Secretary's File, Box 62.

[75] Welles's *Report:* tels. from Welles, February 27, and from Phillips, February 28; Welles: *The Time for Decision,* 78-88; *Ciano Diaries,* February 26, 28; *Ciano's Diplomatic Papers,* 335 ff.

his coming had produced much speculation in German official circles. As early as February 12 the Berlin Foreign Office had reached the tentative conclusion that, beyond seeking information, Mr. Welles would try to prepare the way for a negotiated peace. It was thought that his terms would certainly involve the restoration of a Polish State and the reconstruction of Czechoslovakia "in the sense of the Munich agreement." But there would be no claims for endless reparations payments nor interference in German internal affairs. The American contribution to the settlement would probably consist of financial and economic measures to put European trade back on its feet. Very shrewd, indeed, was the German guess at the reasons which had prompted Mr. Welles's mission. These consisted, thought Berlin, of surprise and confusion in America over the course of the war to date; apprehension that the United States might be unable to avoid involvement; the approaching collapse of Finland; and the probable reaction in America to military developments in the Balkans and Near East. Nor did these German speculations overlook the fact that 1940, an election year, was appropriate for dispatching an "angel of peace" to Europe. In general, the Germans tended to link up the Welles Mission (perhaps correctly) with Mr. Hull's approach to the European Governments on forming a neutral bloc in which even the Pope would play a part.[76]

Whatever Mr. Welles's motives and whatever the peace terms he might offer, Hitler decided in advance to reject them. On February 29 he issued a directive for all German officials to follow the same line in their discussions with Welles. This directive reviewed the Nazi historical argument and concluded on an altogether negative note:

All references are to be avoided which . . . could be construed as indicating that Germany has any interest at present in the exploration of possibilities of peace. It is requested rather that Mr. Sumner Welles be not left in the slightest doubt that Germany is determined to conclude this war victoriously. . . .[77]

This *mot d'ordre* was, of course, unknown to the Under Secretary as he commenced his interviews with leading German officials. It was not long, however, before he strongly suspected its existence. The whole atmosphere of Germany was repugnant to the Under Secretary, and his first conversation —with Foreign Minister von Ribbentrop—did nothing to mitigate his aversion. Sitting in his chair with eyes closed, Ribbentrop proceeded to treat his guest to a two-hour tirade on German policy since Hitler's advent to power. His account was a tissue of gross inaccuracies and misstatements,

[76] Ernst von Weizsäcker: *Erinnerungen* (Freiburg, 1950), 276 ff.; *Halder Diary*, February 12, 1940; Mr. Feis, former Economic Adviser to the State Department, believes that Mr. Welles's mission initially had as a major purpose the forging of the neutral bloc (conversation with the authors, December, 1946).

[77] Text in "German Documents on Sumner Welles Mission, 1940" (*Department of State Bulletin*, March 24, 1946, 459 ff.).

punctuated, reported Welles, with the words "England, England, England" sounding like the toll of a funeral bell. The burden of the disquisition was that cordial relations with Britain had been the keystone of the Fuehrer's policy, but that the English had scornfully rejected all advances. As for the United States, the Foreign Minister insisted that German policy in no way conflicted with American interests. Far from desiring to interfere in the affairs of the American Republics, the German Government fully understood the Monroe Doctrine. It merely desired recognition of its own right to a Monroe Doctrine for Central Europe. Germany, of course, wanted peace, but Ribbentrop could see no way to secure this boon "except through complete and total German victory."

When Ribbentrop had at last exhausted himself, Welles was able to interject a few observations. He wished to avoid any acrimony which would prejudice the results of his forthcoming interview with the Fuehrer. Nevertheless he did feel compelled to state that the deterioration in German-American relations was not the result of propaganda, but of real American indignation over the persecution of the Jews and over Germany's aggression against other nations. Furthermore, he put Ribbentrop straight on the difference between the Monroe Doctrine and German demand for a sphere of influence in Central Europe. Lastly he reiterated the urgent desire of the United States for a durable peace, based on a return to more liberal trade policies and a reduction of armaments. To this plea Ribbentrop responded that peace could be attained solely through a German victory. Ribbentrop's mind, concluded Welles, was not only closed, but empty of everything but hatred of England. "I have rarely seen a man I disliked more."[78]

On March 2 the Under Secretary had his crucial interview with Hitler. By contrast, he found the Fuehrer dignified, cordial and composed. Welles renewed his plea for a lasting peace before the belligerents embarked upon a war of annihilation from which no real victors could emerge. Hitler's reply was to repeat Ribbentrop's lecture of the previous day. Though he manifested some interest in the eventual reduction of armaments and the ultimate liberalization of international trade relations, he added that Germany would have to insist upon a preferential economic position in eastern and southeastern Europe, and could not tolerate the existence on her borders of states like Czechoslovakia, which constituted threats to her security. In conclusion the Fuehrer expressed the conviction that the British were bent on the annihilation of Germany. Like his Foreign Minister, Hitler could see no hope of a lasting peace "until the will of England and France to destroy Germany is itself destroyed."[79]

[78] The account in Welles: *The Time for Decision*, 90 ff., faithfully reflects that given in Welles's contemporary *Report*.

[79] Here again Mr. Welles's book provides an accurate account, to which his unpublished *Report* adds little of significance. We have also used a tel. from Berlin, March 2, 1940.

The Under Secretary came away from his interview with Hitler depressed by the realization that the important decisions had probably already been made. Furthermore, his conversations with foreign diplomats in Berlin convinced him that Hitler had nothing to fear from internal opposition and dissension, and that Germany was far better prepared for a sustained military effort than was generally believed in London and Paris.[80] There was really nothing more for him to learn in Berlin, since it was so evident that everybody was following the same line. Nevertheless the Under Secretary kept his appointments with the Deputy Fuehrer, Rudolf Hess; with Field Marshal Goering; and with other prominent Germans. Hess, who impressed Welles as a man "of the lowest order of intelligence," simply parroted the formulas of Ribbentrop and Hitler. Goering, on the other hand, made a quite different impression, for, though ruthless to the last degree, he at least possessed intelligence and a knowledge of the outside world. Nevertheless, Goering's conclusions followed substantially the familiar line of the Fuehrer's directive. Germany must and would win even if the war were prolonged for five or ten years. Of the United States, added Goering, "it is needless for me to say to you that Germany has no ambitions of any kind other than those I have indicated to you, and least of all any ambitions which could affect the Western Hemisphere."[81]

Before leaving Berlin Mr. Welles had one more interview, and of markedly different character. At the house of the American Chargé d'Affaires, Mr. Alexander Kirk, he met privately Dr. Hjalmar Schacht, the German financier who had lost favor with Hitler a year before. Schacht informed Welles of the movement among German officers to remove Hitler and supplant the regime, adding that if he could get out of Germany, preferably to the United States, he could promote the conspiracy much more effectively. The German generals, he indicated, could stall the offensive in the West for a time, but not indefinitely. In conclusion he described Hitler as the "greatest liar of all time," but all the same, "a genius, amoral and criminal."[82] As we now know, there was some truth in Schacht's account of the military opposition to the Fuehrer. At the time, however, the evidence seemed too slight to warrant taking seriously the statements of an individual who enjoyed everywhere the reputation of being slippery. In any event, Mr. Welles refused to allow himself to become involved in an intrigue, and ignored the communications from Schacht which continued to reach him for some months.[83]

The Under Secretary was decidedly low in spirits as he left Germany. The

[80] Welles: *The Time for Decision*, 109.

[81] Tel. from Berlin, March 3, 1940; Welles: *The Time for Decision*, 113 ff., which reproduces the substance of Welles's subsequent *Report*. The lengthy German record (*Department of State Bulletin*, March 24, 1946, 460 ff.) is also substantially accurate.

[82] Welles *Report*.

[83] *Ibid.*; conversation of the authors with Mr. Welles, May, 1947.

glimmer of hope which he had detected in Rome had been virtually extinguished in Berlin. There could no longer be much doubt that Hitler had made up his mind and that before long the storm would break over Western Europe. As Welles himself wrote subsequently:

> There was only one power on earth which could give Hitler and his associates pause. That would be their conviction that, in a war of devastation forced upon Europe by Germany, the United States, in its own interest, would come to the support of the Western democracies.[84]

Since, however, Welles was aware that there was not the "remotest chance" that the American Government could, with popular approval, issue such a warning to Berlin, there seemed no alternative to allowing matters to take their course. At Berlin the Under Secretary had played his trump card by indicating that the United States was ready to explore the possibilities of a peace settlement even with the Nazi regime. Beyond that it was impossible for him to go. Hitler had rejected the bid and made it abundantly clear that the only road to peace lay through a decisive German victory. To all intents and purposes, therefore, the major object of the Welles Mission had failed of attainment when the Under Secretary left the German capital.

It made but little difference, therefore, what the British and French leaders might say, though their appreciation of the situation is obviously of great historical interest. In Paris, at least, Mr. Welles found little to restore his depressed spirits. "Among the innumerable persons with whom I talked," he wrote later, "only in the rarest instances, outside of a few governmental departments, did I obtain the impression of hope, or vigor, or even, tragically enough, of the will to courage."[85] After a brief call on President Lebrun, Welles had his first interview with Premier Daladier, whom he described as "lucid, vigorous, and realistic." Daladier was frankly critical of French and particularly of British policy toward Italy during the preceding two years. Personally, he insisted, he had been quite prepared to make concessions to Rome. The trouble had really been between Britain and Italy until the Duce had finally stirred up the agitation for Corsica and Nice, which made further discussion impossible. As for the present, Daladier believed that neither France nor Britain could agree to any peace which did not provide for an independent Poland and for the restoration of Czechoslovakia. He had no objection to the unification of the German people, was ready to acknowledge that Danzig was a German city, and even that the Sudetenland and Western Poland should be incorporated in the Reich. He feared, however, that Hitler aimed at much more: the domination of the continent of Europe. Nevertheless, the Premier did not consider political or territorial adjustments as insuperable obstacles to peace. Nor would he refuse to deal even

[84] Welles: *The Time for Decision,* 119.
[85] Welles: *The Time for Decision,* 121.

with the Nazi Government, provided France obtained security. The crux of the problem was how to get assurance that Germany and Italy would live up to engagements they might make. The only solution, thought Daladier, would be for some great neutral power, like the United States, to assume the responsibility or to organize an international air force for police purposes.[86]

Following his conversation with the Premier, Mr. Welles made use of every opportunity to discuss the situation with other French statesmen and politicians. For the most part these interviews yielded nothing new, though they served to emphasize the willingness of the French Government to discuss political and territorial issues with the Nazi leadership, provided the crucial problem of France's future security could be resolved. On this score they professed scant hope. The only possible solution seemed to lie in the military defeat of Germany, yet even this could be accomplished only at the price of Europe's ruin. Men like Herriot and Blum were profoundly sad, and indeed the whole atmosphere of Paris was one of "corroding discouragement."

The interval from March 11 to March 13, 1940, found the Under Secretary in London. There he sensed an entirely different attitude—one of determination, not to say of overweening confidence. Now reassured that the Welles Mission did not have as its purpose "putting over a peace plan,"[87] Prime Minister Chamberlain and the Foreign Secretary, Lord Halifax, both took the firm line that no lasting peace was possible so long as the Nazis remained in control of Germany. Chamberlain, recounting with "a white-hot anger" how Hitler had deceived him, reminded Welles that he had gone on record publicly that Britain was determined to destroy the Nazi Government. On the other hand, he was willing to give positive assurances to President Roosevelt "that England had no intention of destroying the German people, nor of impairing the integrity of the German Reich." With respect to political and territorial issues, he continued, the British could not even consider a peace settlement which did not include the complete independence of Poland and the restoration of Czechoslovakia as a free and independent state.

Other Cabinet ministers and military leaders echoed Chamberlain's views, or in some cases presented the British position in even more uncompromising terms. Winston Churchill, who treated the American emissary to a "cascade of oratory, brilliant and always effective, interlarded with considerable wit," insisted that Germany's objectives had not changed in twenty years. It still aimed at world supremacy through military conquest. Moreover, he went on, German aims endangered the United States as much as the British Empire:

[86] Welles *Report;* tels. from Welles, March 9, 1940; Welles: *The Time for Decision,* 123 ff.
[87] Tel. from Kennedy, March 9, 1940.

There could be no solution other than outright and complete defeat of Germany; the destruction of National Socialism, and the inclusion in the new peace treaties of provisions which could control Germany's course in the future in such a way as to give Europe and the world peace and security in the days to come, at least for a hundred years.[88]

On the military side Mr. Churchill was full of confidence. Britain had mastered the submarine and mine menace. In a few months, he was sure, Britain and France would have mastered the threat from the air as well.

London, then, displayed a remarkably intransigent attitude, which lent some color to Hitler's fear of Britain's determination to destroy the German Reich, as it also explained Chamberlain's initial anxiety lest Welles try to induce Britain to accept a settlement based on appeasement of the Nazi regime. It is even possible that the Prime Minister may have thought that the British position had been stated too uncompromisingly, for in his final talk with Welles he reiterated his willingness to make a unilateral declaration to Mr. Roosevelt that Britain did not intend to destroy Germany. Furthermore, he added, if the miracle should happen and Hitler should offer a practicable plan for security, he would not discard it just because the Nazis remained in power. But the British would have to insist that Hitler give an earnest of his sincerity by evacuating Poland, Bohemia and Moravia. In the final settlement, London would not be intransigent regarding the future frontiers of Poland or the reconstituted Czech state. Indeed, Danzig and German Poland might go to Germany, and the fate of Austria be decided by a plebiscite. However, the Prime Minister anticipated grave difficulties in the way of disarmament, security, international police arrangements and the like. Recollecting his interviews in Berlin, the Under Secretary knew that there was no hope of successful negotiations on this basis. He did not, it seems, even submit to the British Government his memorandum on economic policy.[89]

Although Washington had received but fragmentary accounts of the Under Secretary's conversations, the President and Mr. Hull by this time had themselves apparently concluded that a settlement with Hitler was impossible. Furthermore, Mr. Hull believed that the flood of rumors, which inevitably followed in the wake of Welles's progress, was doing decided harm to the Allied cause. Accordingly, the President in a broadcast of March 16 did his utmost to dispel the idea that the American Government was seeking a peace of appeasement:

Today we seek a moral basis for peace. It cannot be a real peace if it fails to recognize brotherhood. It cannot be a lasting peace if the fruit of it is oppression,

88 Welles: *The Time for Decision*, 133-34.
89 Welles *Report;* Welles: *The Time for Decision*, 130 ff.; despatch from London, April 15, 1940. On Mr. Chamberlain's attitude toward Welles, see Keith Feiling: *The Life of Neville Chamberlain*, 428 f.

or starvation, or cruelty, or human life dominated by armed camps. It cannot be a sound peace if small nations must live in fear of powerful neighbors. It cannot be a moral peace if freedom from invasion is sold for tribute. It cannot be an intelligent peace if it denies free passage to the knowledge of those ideals which permit man to find common ground. It cannot be a righteous peace if worship of God is denied.[90]

Not content with this, Secretary Hull took the added precaution of warning Welles of the dangers of allowing himself to become a "go-between" among the belligerents, and of the narrow limits within which he was authorized even to comment on any peace proposals.[91] This was hardly necessary, since, as aforesaid, the Under Secretary returned to Rome on March 15 in a most pessimistic mood. While still in London he had heard the news of Ribbentrop's sudden appearance in Rome and of his conferences there both with Fascist leaders and with the Pope.[92] Initial hopes that Ribbentrop's visit to Rome presaged fresh German interest in peace negotiations lasted only as long as Count Ciano required to inform Mr. Welles of the contrary. In fact, Ribbentrop in his conversations with Ciano and Mussolini dismissed Welles's Berlin visit as largely a reflection of America's dislike of war. Even though undertaken "in good faith," it had produced nothing new, and, as Mussolini suggested, was best understood as an "internal American matter." The danger that the United States would enter the war could thus be discounted. Roosevelt, it was supposed, had been obliged to modify his views considerably in face of the determination of the American people to avoid involvement.

Ribbentrop reported that the Germans were determined to launch a great offensive in the near future, that they were confident of victory, and that they proposed to settle the war by a dictated peace. The Foreign Minister considered success possible within as short a time as five months. He did not press Mussolini to name the date when Italy would join in hostilities, remaining content with the Duce's assurances that this would occur at "the given moment" and that in the meantime the Duce would work to bring about a progressive deterioration of Italy's relations with the democracies. Beyond this, Ribbentrop's chief concern was to urge the Italians to come to an agreement with the Soviets. He rhapsodized about Germany's own relations with Russia and spoke of Stalin, reported Ciano, as of a second

---

[90] Text in *Documents on American Foreign Relations*, II, 48 f.; *cf.* Hull: *Memoirs*, I, 739; Shepardson and Scroggs: *The U.S. in World Affairs (1940)*, 9 ff.

[91] Hull: *Memoirs*, I, 740.

[92] The conversations between Ribbentrop, Mussolini and Ciano (March 10, 11) are recorded in *Ciano's Diplomatic Papers*, 339-59, and in the *Ciano Diaries*. On Ribbentrop's unhappy interview with the Pope, see Charles-Roux: *Huit ans au Vatican*, 374-76; Cianfarra: *The Vatican and the War*, 208-11; and Mourin: *Les tentatives de paix*, 61 ff. In general on Welles's visit to Rome, see Wiskemann: *The Rome-Berlin Axis*, 194 ff.

Christ. Mussolini consented to meet Hitler at the Brenner Pass on March 18.[93]

All this boded ill not merely for peace but likewise for Mr. Welles's aim of influencing Italy to remain outside the war. The only hope seemed to lie in Ciano's contempt for Ribbentrop, his hatred for the Russians, and his persistent doubt whether the Germans could so easily win their victory. Like many others, Ciano believed that if the democracies could hold defensively, the Germans would ultimately be beaten. As for the future, he still dreamed of a four-power pact (Britain, France, Italy and Germany) as the best guarantee of security and the best bulwark against the Bolshevik East.

This all-important question of security was discussed by Welles with Mussolini at an evening meeting on March 16. The American emissary asserted that in the course of his visits he had found the Western Powers by no means intransigent. Everywhere, however, he had noted the primary desire for security based on disarmament. Territorial and political questions seemed secondary and certainly not insoluble. Mussolini then informed Welles of his forthcoming meeting with Hitler at the Brenner Pass. A German offensive, he predicted, was clearly on the way and might occur in a matter of hours. In that case all hope of a negotiated peace would be killed. The Duce professed himself prepared to do his utmost to persuade Hitler to postpone action, but he could do so only if he could report to the Fuehrer that Welles had found the British and French not unreasonable. To this the Under Secretary replied that he would have to consult President Roosevelt by telephone, since he had promised to maintain secrecy with respect to his talks in London and Paris. Mussolini agreed, but stressed the lateness of the hour. However, he requested the Under Secretary to postpone his departure by one day so that he could report to him the results of the Brenner meeting with Hitler.[94]

That evening, over the telephone, Mr. Welles recommended to the President against authorizing any statement by Mussolini to Hitler on the basis of Welles's "inadequate" impressions gleaned in London and Paris. Actually Welles feared that if his mission were brought into the Italian-German discussions, "the impression would inevitably be created that the President was participating in the determination of such bases for a practical peace as might be offered." Having publicly repudiated any such suggestion, Mr. Roosevelt agreed with Welles's advice but requested him, nevertheless, to tell Mussolini that the President regarded security as the fundamental issue. Furthermore, the Under Secretary was to stress the President's

[93] Ciano's Diplomatic Papers, 339-59; Welles Report; Welles: The Time for Decision, 137; Wiskemann: The Rome-Berlin Axis, 199 ff.

[94] Welles Report; Welles: The Time for Decision, 138 ff.; Ciano's Diplomatic Papers, 359-60; Ciano Diaries, 222. For Mr. Welles's correction of the entries in the Diaries for March 16 and 17, 1940, see his article "Count Ciano's Diary" (Washington Post, July 11, 1945). We have also used tels. from Welles, March 16, 17, 1940.

confident belief "that the Allied Governments did not hold as an objective the destruction of Germany nor of the German people, but that they did want a real guaranty that war would not be forced upon them every generation."[95]

While Mussolini and Ciano were off to their meeting with Hitler and Ribbentrop, Welles paid a visit to the Vatican. He found that the Pope did not consider peace discussions practicable for the moment, but at the same time Vatican authorities doubted the likelihood of an early German offensive in the West. In the meantime both the Pope and Cardinal Maglione, his Secretary of State, expressed the earnest hope that the President would do his utmost to prevent an undecided Mussolini from leading Italy into the war. It was likewise obvious that the danger of the spread of communism was very much on the mind of the Pope and his advisers. All felt that Hitler's pact with Stalin had been a grave mistake.[96]

On his return to Rome on March 19, Count Ciano at once reported to Mr. Welles the substance of the brief conference at the Brenner. Happily, the meeting had effected no startling change in Axis relationships and had not altered Italy's status of nonbelligerency. Neither had Hitler attempted to apply pressure to force an Italian-Russian *rapprochement*. In fact, thought Ciano, the Fuehrer did not seem to share Ribbentrop's illusions about the Soviets, creating in Ciano's mind, at least, the impression "that Hitler was using the Russian arrangement to his own interest, with the expectation that the time would come when he could turn against Russia and secure back from Russia the positions Germany had given away in the Baltic States and through the cession of Finnish territory to the Soviets." While the Fuehrer, continued Ciano, had been silent on the subject of peace proposals, he had at least made it clear, in contrast to Ribbentrop, that no military offensive would be undertaken on the Western Front in the immediate future.[97]

Therewith Welles's reconnaissance of the European scene came to an end. Having issued a statement to the press denying that he had given or received "any peace plan or proposals," and asserting that his mission had been solely to gather information for the President, the Under Secretary embarked at Naples on March 20, 1940.[98] The information he would bring home on the prospects for peace was grim enough, but Welles left Italy

[95] Welles *Report;* Welles: "Count Ciano's Diary" (*Washington Post,* July 11, 1945); *cf.* M. Mourin: *Les tentatives de paix,* 65.

[96] Welles *Report;* tel. from Myron Taylor, March 19; Welles: *The Time for Decision,* 142; *cf.* Charles-Roux: *Huit ans au Vatican,* 376-77.

[97] Tel. from Welles, March 19, 1940. The Welles *Report* adds little to the account given in his *The Time for Decision,* 143 ff. The stenographic report of the Brenner meeting (*Ciano's Diplomatic Papers,* 361-66) is, however, less optimistic than Ciano's account to Welles or his comments in his *Diary* (March 19).

[98] *Documents on American Foreign Relations,* II, 379.

with the renewed conviction that none of its people, save the rabid Fascists, were in favor of joining Germany in the war. The Royal Family, the Army, the great business interests, and, above all, the Church were vigorously opposed to intervention. Ciano himself distrusted the Germans and was exerting all his influence on the Duce to keep Italy out.[99] Evidently the American Government should do all in its power to assist the forces aligned against Italian participation. Welles, however, was under no illusions. Mussolini was clearly Italy's boss, and the Duce was at heart, reported Welles, a peasant—vindictive, amoral, and enamored of force and power. He would never forget nor forgive the British policy of sanctions during the Ethiopian crisis. Now he was convinced of German power and confidently hoped to secure from the forthcoming Nazi victory everything that Italy had unsuccessfully sought from Britain and France. Accordingly, if Germany won some rapid victories, such as the occupation of the Low Countries, opined Welles, Mussolini would probably force his country into the war.

The conclusions of Mr. Welles's confidential report to Mr. Roosevelt and Mr. Hull were perforce altogether depressing:

I do not believe [he wrote], there is the slightest chance of any successful negotiation at this time for a durable peace if the basis is made the problem of political and territorial readjustment—the "just political peace" insisted upon by Mussolini —or the problem of economic adjustment.

The basic question, Welles was certain, was security inseparably linked to disarmament:

If the great powers of Europe—even exclusive of Russia—could be shown a practical means of obtaining security and disarmament, neither the political peace required nor the essential basis for a real peace would, in my judgment, offer any insuperable obstacles.

But the initiative could not come from Europe. It could only come from the United States, supported by the other neutral states, especially those of the New World. If the moment should come when the United States felt it possible to move, Mussolini and the Vatican would probably support such an initiative.[100]

That moment never came, or, to be more precise, it had come and gone. The long and short of it was that the British, like the Germans, were now convinced that only military victory could achieve their ends. The two major antagonists were ready, and in a sense, even eager to face the ordeal. It is, therefore, far from likely that even a drastic American intervention would at this late hour have deterred Hitler. He had, as we know, an alto-

[99] Wiskemann: *The Rome-Berlin Axis*, 203-4.
[100] Conclusion of the Welles *Report;* Welles: *The Time for Decision,* 145 ff.

gether low opinion of our ability to act effectively in time to frustrate the rapid victory on which he counted. In any event, there was not the remotest possibility of the United States committing itself to any positive or far-reaching intervention in Europe.

Mr. Welles's mission, last of the series of Mr. Roosevelt's peace initiatives, reveals more clearly than any of its antecedents the illusions prevalent in this country in the final weeks of the phony war—illusions which prompted Ambassador Bullitt to describe the mood of the United States in the late winter of 1940 to be that of England before Munich. Not the least of the merits of Mr. Welles's mission was to shatter this illusion in high Washington circles. After reading the Welles *Report*, the President and Mr. Hull could scarcely have been unprepared to face the forthcoming catastrophe in Europe. Unhappily, as much could not be said of the heads of the Allied Governments. In the account which follows of their wholly inadequate preparations to meet what Hitler had in store for them will be found the principal justification for Mr. Roosevelt's belief that a peace negotiated with Hitler was at least preferable to a peace dictated by him. Beyond that, the President's summation on March 29 of the fruits of the Under Secretary's mission applies with equal force to all the other efforts toward peace which a bewildered Administration had sponsored:

Finally, even though there may be scant immediate prospect for the establishment of any just, stable, and lasting peace in Europe, the information made available to this Government as a result of Mr. Welles's mission will undoubtedly be of the greatest value when the time comes for the establishment of such a peace.[101]

[101] *Documents on American Foreign Relations*, II, 380.

CHAPTER XI

Girding for Action

1. ALLIED PLANS FOR THE SOVIET-FINNISH WAR

While Under Secretary Welles was engaged in his forlorn effort to canvass the possibilities of peace in Europe before major military operations should have dispelled all thoughts of a compromise settlement, the principal antagonists were all busily applying themselves to the elaboration of plans which they hoped would produce a military decision. The general setting of these plans was necessarily the war between Russia and Finland, which had provoked an altogether unforeseen crisis in European affairs. It will be remembered that the Soviet attack on its small and inoffensive neighbor had called forth a storm of indignation throughout the world. The Germans themselves, who had played so effective a part in securing independence for the Finns, found it extremely exasperating to stand by and abet the aggression of their Soviet partner. In other countries, even in those attached to Nazi Germany, there was less obligation to observe restraint. The Italian Foreign Minister, Count Ciano, had already delivered himself, on December 16, 1939, of a plain-spoken and patently critical review of German policy. This was to be followed, on January 4, 1940, by a long and extraordinarily frank letter from Mussolini himself to Hitler. Though admittedly aware of German displeasure with Ciano's speech, the Duce took his stand firmly by his Foreign Minister, whom he disarmingly described as "one of the most convinced partisans of German-Italian friendship." Having disclaimed any idea of Italian sympathies with Britain and France, the Duce devoted himself to a review of the European situation. He made no secret whatever of Italian sympathies for Finland, of desires to see a Polish State reconstituted, and of hopes for peace. But the very heart of the letter was Mussolini's castigation of the Nazi connection with the Kremlin, which, as he pointed out, involved the abandonment of the anti-Bolshevik crusade for which such sacrifices had been made. The Duce felt impelled to add that "one step farther in your relations with Moscow would have catastrophic repercussions in Italy," where sentiment was absolutely and unshakably anti-Bolshevik, especially among the Fascist rank and file. "The solution of your problem of living space," he reminded Hitler, "is in Russia. . . . The mission of Germany is to defend Europe against Asia."[1]

Hitler was surely not blind to the great upsurge of sympathy for Finland and hatred for Russia, and it was therefore superfluous to call his attention to the deleterious effects of his pact with Stalin on countries like Spain, Portugal, Hungary and Rumania. There could, however, be no thought of scrapping the advantages of the Nazi-Soviet pact. Under the circumstances, the Fuehrer could only hope that the whole unhappy episode of the Soviet invasion would soon be brought to a close.

The Allies, on the other hand, could hardly fail to regard the Finnish War as a great opportunity. The sentiment of the world was with the Finns and, by decision of the League of Nations, all members were morally obligated to give the victim of aggression such aid as they could. The democracies might, of course, restrict themselves to a policy of furnishing volunteers and supplies to the valiant Finns, and eventually that proved to be all they were able to do. But in the early weeks of the war the prospect of more drastic action—military action—loomed as a God-given opportunity. From the very beginning of the European War, men like Churchill in England and Daladier and Gamelin in France had been casting about for secondary lines of attack on Germany by which an offensive against the Low Countries might be forestalled and other countries brought into the fray. During September, 1939, Churchill had been assiduously at work laying plans for action in the Baltic or Scandinavia, and more particularly developing schemes for cutting the supply routes from the important North Swedish iron-ore fields to Germany. These early plans are now of little more than academic interest, since the neutrality of the Scandinavian powers was, for the time being, an apparently insurmountable obstacle.[2]

The Soviet-Finnish War put an entirely new complexion on these embryonic schemes. Sentiment in Norway and Sweden being generally pro-Allied and of course deeply stirred by the attack on a sister nation, it was not unreasonable to suppose that the Scandinavian States might be willing to coöperate to afford the Finns military assistance. An expeditionary force would be, from the Allied standpoint, a most attractive proposition. Quite apart from the relief it might provide the Finns, it could incidentally cut the Norwegian-German ore route and perhaps lead to the occupation of the Swedish iron fields themselves; finally, it might provoke the Germans

---

[1] *Les lettres secrètes échangées par Hitler et Mussolini* (Paris, 1946), 47-58; Wiskemann: *The Rome-Berlin Axis*, 187 ff. *Cf.* also, on Italian hostility to Russia, Beloff: *The Foreign Policy of Soviet Russia*, II, 303.

[2] Churchill: *The Gathering Storm*, 461 ff.; 533 ff.; 692-94; Gamelin: *Servir*, III, 206 ff.

into counteraction which would enable the Allies to fight the war on Scandinavian soil. Every one of these motives played its part in the plans and developments of the first quarter of 1940. The emphasis was now on one, now on another, with the result that the main outlines were often obscured. Though it is necessary to try to unravel this tangled skein, it should be remembered that confusion and indecision were so typical of the period that any attempt to reduce the problem to simple terms must involve serious distortion of the historical development.

Before pursuing the subject further, it should be noted that any Allied action in Scandinavia carried with it the probability of a conflict with Soviet Russia. This consideration, too, was an integral part of the issue, and in fact produced a rather basic divergence of opinion between London and Paris. The British Government throughout was most reluctant to abandon hope of ultimately weaning the Soviets from their Nazi connection, and was therefore loath to adopt a policy which might lead to hostilities. The French, on the other hand, saw no disadvantage in exploiting the almost universal detestation of Communist Russia and had no fears whatever of Soviet military power. It is worth repeating here what has already been stressed in an earlier chapter: that after the great purges of 1937 and 1938, Soviet capabilities were rated very low indeed by almost all experts. The Red Army, for all its size, was thought equal at best to no more than a defensive war. In the summer of 1939 the British and French had held it far inferior to the Polish Army, and a fortnight before the Soviet attack on Finland, General Gamelin had described it as "extraordinarily bad."[3]

It stands to reason that the poor showing made by the Soviet forces in the initial phase of the Finnish War served only to fortify these opinions. Mr. Churchill was unquestionably expressing a general conviction when, in a radio address of January 20, 1940, he declared of the Finns:

> They have exposed, for all the world to see, the military incapacity of the Red Army and of the Red Air Force. Many illusions about Soviet Russia have been dispelled in these few fierce weeks of fighting in the Arctic Circle. Everyone can now see how Communism rots the soul of a nation; how it makes it abject and hungry in peace, and proves it base and abominable in war.[4]

Even the German General Staff, usually well informed, held substantially the same views. In an evaluation dated December 31, 1939, the Red Army was thus described:

> In quantity a gigantic military instrument. Organization, equipment and means of leadership unsatisfactory. Principles of leadership good; leadership itself, however, too young and inexperienced. Communication system bad; transportation bad;

---

[3] Tel. from Bullitt, November 13, 1939; Gamelin: *Servir*, III, 194. See also the interesting article by Earl Reeves: "The Red Army Myth" (*Events*, February, 1940).

[4] Churchill: *Blood, Sweat and Tears*. 213 ff.

troops not very uniform; no personalities. Simple soldier good-natured, quite satisfied with very little. Fighting qualities of the troops in a *heavy* fight, dubious. The Russian "mass" is *no* match for an ,army with modern equipment and superior leadership.[5]

In the light of later Soviet performance against the Germans, much has been made of these "shocking" miscalculations. It is true that the Red Army was undervalued in 1940, but probably not by much. After the great purges of 1937 and 1938 it was badly demoralized and seriously deficient in training and equipment. Presumably that was one of the reasons for the Kremlin's effort to avoid involvement in war in 1939 and 1940 through the pact with Hitler. During the term of the Nazi-Soviet partnership desperate attempts were made to put the forces into better shape. But even by the summer of 1941 the Red Army was far from being the instrument which it became under the pressures developed by the first catastrophic reverses. All told, the Allied and German estimates of 1940 were not very wide of the mark.

The lead in promoting military intervention in Scandinavia was taken by Premier Daladier, who had already suppressed the Communist Party in France and who, aside from his personal aversion to Soviet Russia, appears to have hoped that a break with the Kremlin would serve to rally the disillusioned French public to more vigorous support of the war. The Premier had in hand a report from the French Ambassador in Moscow, declaring that Nazi-Soviet coöperation was complete and that Germany was gaining all the advantages of a military alliance without having its associate involved in a general war. Retailing this information to Ambassador Bullitt, Daladier remarked that if Norway and Sweden would coöperate, the French Government would send the Finns not only planes and munitions, but an expeditionary force as well.[6]

Daladier lost no time in submitting his proposal to the Allied Supreme War Council at its meeting on December 19, but elicited only a lukewarm response from the British. The latter were definitely averse to challenging the Russians, and even Mr. Churchill, who for months had been attracted by the possibilities of Scandinavia, was as much interested in cutting the German iron-ore route from the Norwegian port of Narvik as in aiding the Finns. As he says in his memoirs, referring to the projects for succoring Finland: "I welcomed this new and favorable breeze as a means of achieving the major strategic advantage of cutting off the vital iron-ore supplies of Germany." In a memorandum of December 16 he had expounded his ideas at greater length:

If Germany can be cut from all Swedish ore supplies from now onwards till the end of 1940, a blow will have been struck at her war-making capacity equal

---

[5] *Nazi Conspiracy and Aggression,* VI, 981-82.
[6] Documents captured by the Germans; telegram from Bullitt, December 11, 1939.

to a first-class victory in the field or from the air, and without any serious sacrifice of life. It might, indeed, be immediately decisive. . . . It is not seen how, even if retaliation by Germany were to run its full course, we should be worse off for the action now proposed. On the contrary, we have more to gain than lose by a German attack upon Norway or Sweden.

There was, to be sure, the question of Scandinavian neutrality, but to this Churchill responded by observing: "Small nations must not tie our hands when we are fighting for their rights and freedom. The letter of the law must not in supreme emergency obstruct those who are charged with its protection and enforcement."[7]

But neither Daladier nor Churchill was able to carry along Mr. Chamberlain or Lord Halifax. The Supreme Council ended with a decision that was in reality no decision: "If Norway and Sweden should wish to support Finland by military action, France and England would support Norway, Sweden and Finland with all the forces at their disposal." The London Cabinet agreed, on December 22, that the Chiefs of Staff should plan a landing at Narvik as part of the program of aiding Finland, but the only concrete action that emerged from the inter-Allied discussions was a joint note to Norway and Sweden of December 27. This, in effect, stated that the Allies were "disposed to afford unofficially to Finland . . . all the indirect assistance in their power," and expressed the hope that the Scandinavian Governments would do likewise. The conclusion, however, was the salient passage, stating that Britain and France were "prepared to consider in what circumstances and in what form assurance could in practice be given to Sweden and Norway of Franco-British help against the possible consequences to those countries of giving such direct or indirect assistance as they might afford to Finland."[8]

This was, to all intents and purposes, an invitation to the Scandinavian Governments to go the limit in support of Finland, on the assurance that if Germany or Russia intervened, the Allies would come to the aid of the Northern States. It is reasonably certain that Germany, and entirely certain that Russia, had already warned Sweden and Norway against overstepping the bounds of unofficial aid.[9] In any case, neither Oslo nor Stock-

---

[7] Churchill: *The Gathering Storm*, 544-47; Reynaud: *La France a sauvé l'Europe*, II, 24 ff.; tel. from Bullitt, December 20, 1939.

[8] Text in the Swedish official publication: *Förspelet till det Tyska Angreppet på Danmark och Norge* (Stockholm, 1947), 10-12; tel. from Bullitt, December 30, 1939; see also the excellent study of Norwegian policy by Arne Bergsgard, which forms supplement III of the official inquiry report: *Instilling fra Undersøkelseskommisjonen av 1945* (Oslo, 1947), especially pp. 209 ff.

[9] The German policy was ambiguous at least until the end of 1939. According to American reports, the Swedish Government was warned that "official aid" to Finland would not be tolerated. In the meanwhile, under Goering's influence, the Germans "unofficially" supplied Sweden with war materials, knowing full well that they would replace Swedish supplies "unofficially" transferred to the Finns (tels. from Sterling, December 11, 15, 22, 28, and from Schoenfeld, December 15, 1939).

holm could be oblivious to the danger of becoming a European battlefield. Even hard-pressed Finland seems to have been more interested in reopening peace negotiations with Moscow than in provoking intervention from outside. It was to be expected, therefore, that the replies from Sweden and Norway would be evasive and negative. Deliberately avoiding any reference to the Allied offer of aid, the Northern Governments made it clear that they would not consent to the passage of Allied troops through their territories.[10]

From the scant evidence now available it appears that Lord Halifax was positively relieved by the negative response of the Northern Powers, fearing lest the sending of an expeditionary force provoke hostilities with Soviet Russia.[11] But this did not affect Mr. Churchill's scheme for cutting the German ore route from Narvik by closing the strip of Norwegian territorial water along the coast (the Leads). On January 5, 1940, the British Government sent a stiff note to Norway (notified also to Sweden), pointing out that since the Germans were making illegal use of these waters, the British felt obliged to make "appropriate dispositions to prevent the use of Norwegian territorial waters by German ships and trade. To achieve this purpose, it would be necessary for His Majesty's naval forces at times to enter and operate in those waters." The reply from Oslo and Stockholm was to insist anew on respect for Scandinavian neutrality and to plead with London not to precipitate a crisis. Under strong pressure from Moscow, and presumably from Berlin, the Northern Governments found themselves on the horns of a hopeless dilemma. What saved them for the moment was the lack of agreement in British Government circles and the distracting effect of a threatened German attack on the Low Countries in mid-January.[12]

The French, however, were not content to let the matter rest. A special emissary returned from Finland early in January with a project advanced by Marshal Mannerheim, involving the landing of an Allied force at Petsamo, the Arctic port of Finland. When the British objected to the idea, Daladier proposed that Polish forces, strengthened by some French detachments, be used for the purpose and that in any case renewed pressure be brought on Norway to close the Leads. The evidence leaves little doubt that Daladier thought the Germans would retaliate, thus giving the Allies a pretext for occupying the Norwegian ports and opening a new front in Scandinavia. To the British he argued that the Allies were suffering a moral setback and that soon they might see all Scandinavia in German and Russian hands. The

---

[10] References to Scandinavian sources as in previous note; in addition tels., from Schoenfeld (Helsinki), December 23, 28, and from Johnson (London), January 4, 1940; Halvdan Koht: *Norway, Neutral and Invaded* (Macmillan, New York, 1941), 27 ff.

[11] Tel. from Johnson (London), January 4, 1940; report of the Swedish Ambassador in London, January 5 (*Förspelet till det Tyska Angreppet*, 17); Churchill: *The Gathering Storm*, 554.

[12] *Förspelet till det Tyska Angreppet*, 24-35. For the situation within the British Government see the biting note of Churchill of January 15, 1940 (*The Gathering Storm*, 554).

British Government, while ready to support the Northern States against Germany, still objected that the Norwegian ports could not be seized without Norwegian consent. In the end no action was taken beyond the dispatch of yet another note (January 19, 1940) warning the Scandinavians of their probable fate if the Allies were defeated and calling upon them to find ways and means of helping rather than hindering the cause in which they themselves had so direct an interest:

His Majesty's Government trust that the Swedish Government are under no misapprehension as to their view on where the balance of equity lies in this matter, or their conviction that the present situation cannot be tolerated indefinitely, and that, if the Swedish Government are so anxious that no action shall be taken which might be dangerous or embarrassing for them, then it is for them to suggest an alternative which will not leave the Germans free to break all the rules of war and yet obtain vital supplies from Scandinavia for carrying on a war in which their success would be as fatal to Sweden as to the Allies themselves.[13]

The whole issue was thrashed out in Allied military conferences on January 31 and again in the Supreme War Council meeting of February 5, 1940. Daladier put his case as forcefully as possible, repeating that a conflict with Russia was a matter of no account and that German retaliation would be a positive advantage to the Allies. The British concurred in the latter point, but continued to be dubious about antagonizing Russia. They discarded the idea of an expedition to Petsamo, but agreed to examine the project for occupying Narvik, which would at one and the same time enable them to cut the ore route and open a line of advance to Finland. It was decided to prepare an expeditionary force of "volunteers" in the style of the Spanish Civil War, to consist of two British divisions, backed by French and Polish contingents. This was to be ready by mid-March, at which time it was reckoned the Finns would have reached the end of their tether and would be ready to appeal for aid. The British hoped that under such circumstances the Norwegians would consent to operations in northern Scandinavia, trusting that these would not provoke counteraction by the Germans. No decision was made as to the course of action to be taken if Norway and Sweden persisted in refusing passage. The substance of these discussions was at once communicated to President Roosevelt for his information.[14]

While Allied plans and preparations were under way, the outward calm was broken on February 16, when the British destroyer *Cossack* was sent

13 *Förspelet till det Tyska Angreppet*, 24-35; Gamelin: *Servir*, III, 195-96; Reynaud: *La France a sauvé l'Europe*, II, 24 ff.; Daladier's tel. to London, January 17 (published by the Germans in *Geheimakten des französischen Generalstabes*, Berlin, 1941, No. 18); tels. from Bullitt, January 15, 25, 1940.

14 Churchill: *The Gathering Storm*, 560-61; Gamelin: *Servir*, III, 199-202; Reynaud: *La France a sauvé l'Europe*, II, 24 ff.; message from Chamberlain to the President, n.d. (*Roosevelt Papers*: Secretary's File, Box 62).

into Norwegian territorial waters to remove captive British sailors from the German prison ship *Altmark*. This act was clearly contrary to international law, though there was certainly moral justification for it, and the Norwegian protest was weakened by the admitted negligence of the Norwegian inspectors.[15] Dramatic though this episode was, it involved no new issue of policy. Churchill was probably quite right in thinking that its effect was to hasten German preparations for counteraction in the event of the Allies taking further measures. The temptation for the British to do so was certainly strong, and Premier Daladier continued to urge his allies to make use of their opportunity. Disregarding the problem of aiding Finland, he proposed that the Allies announce to Norway that they would protect its territorial waters. The Oslo Government would undoubtedly refuse, whereupon the Allies should override the objection and occupy the ports nevertheless. Fear of German retaliation might then induce the Swedes to accept Allied aid and open the route to Finland. This was simply another version of Daladier's oft-repeated argument, and the British answered it in the usual way: they felt unable or unwilling, in the face of world opinion, to violate flagrantly the neutrality of Scandinavia, and they continued fearful of a conflict with Russia.[16]

Finally, at the end of February, there emerged a momentary possibility that the Allied plans might yet be put into effect. The Finnish military situation, essentially hopeless from the start, had become desperate as the invigorated Red Army pressed its offensive. Aid from the Scandinavian States and from the Allies, though not inconsiderable, was far from sufficient to save the situation. What the Finns required was a large, organized force of 50,000 to 100,000 men. In mid-February they warned Stockholm that unless direct military aid were forthcoming, they would have to appeal to the Allies.[17] This they did, in an informal way, on February 28, asking whether 50,000 men could be sent at once. London and Paris gave assurances that the first of some 57,000 troops could be embarked by mid-March, and immediately turned to the Norwegian and Swedish Governments for permission to pass through their territory. In their note of March 2 they assured the Northern Governments that they would intervene with all their might if those states became involved in war with Russia or Germany as a result of their aid to Finland. The British and French Govern-

[15] On this episode see Churchill: *The Gathering Storm*, 561 ff.; Koht: *Norway, Neutral and Invaded*, 37 ff.; and the detailed review of the incident in Appendix IV of the Norwegian official *Instilling fra Undersøkelseskommisjonen*. The legal aspects were examined by Edwin Borchard: "Was Norway Delinquent in the Altmark Case?" (*American Journal of International Law*, XXXIV, 1940, 289-93).

[16] Daladier's tel. to London (*Die Geheimakten des französischen Generalstabes*, No. 21); Reynaud: *La France a sauvé l'Europe*, II, 24 ff.; Churchill: *The Gathering Storm*, 564. The well-informed Swedish reports from Paris in this period are given in *Förspelet till det Tyska Angreppet, passim*.

[17] Tel. from Sterling (Stockholm), February 19, 1940.

ments, it was stated, were prepared to occupy not only Narvik but Trondheim, Stavanger and Bergen within four days if only Norway would consent. In a personal message to King Gustav of Sweden, Premier Daladier laid his cards on the table: France was ready to despatch 50,000 men to Finland by way of Narvik, as part of a larger plan for an attack on Russia. Swedish involvement was not desired and if necessary the troops could be sent without arms![18]

The Norwegian Government returned a negative reply (March 4), which it evidently expected the Allies to ignore, and decided that in such event it would confine itself to protests and perhaps some show of passive resistance. But the Swedish Government remained adamant (March 3). The Foreign Minister made it perfectly clear to the Allied representatives that Sweden could not regard the project as a program of aid to Finland. It was patently part of a plan to engage Russia and Germany, and so forestall a Nazi attack on France. The Swedes flatly refused to permit the passage of foreign troops, and King Gustav appealed to Daladier not to pursue the matter further.[19]

These replies must have been anticipated, but Daladier felt that politically he could hardly survive the defeat of Finland. The Helsinki Government was therefore invited to make a formal appeal, on the understanding that the Allies would then intervene despite the opposition of Norway and Sweden. March 5 was fixed as the final date, by which time, however, the Swedes had at last succeeded in arranging with the Soviet Government for peace negotiations with Finland. The Finns, realizing that in any event Allied help could not arrive for several weeks, decided to make terms as best they could, and therefore never made the formal appeal for aid which the Allies regarded as indispensable to their intervention. And so the first phase of the Scandinavian crisis came to an end.[20]

In retrospect the entire Allied project appears to have suffered from inherent contradictions. For one thing it should be obvious from the foregoing that the issue of aiding Finland was not the primary consideration. Both the British and the French were intent on luring the Germans into Scandinavia and on opening a new front on distant soil. Furthermore, they were anxious to cut the iron supply route along the Norwegian shore and if possible to occupy the Swedish iron fields themselves. But while the British were at no time ready to violate the neutrality of the Northern States or to risk a conflict with Soviet Russia, Daladier, under heavy pres-

[18] *Förspelet till det Tyska Angreppet*, 120-22; Bergsgard, in Supplement III of *Instilling fra Undersøkelseskommisjonen*, 221 ff.; John H. Wuorinen, ed.: *Finland and World War II*, 71.

[19] *Förspelet till det Tyska Angreppet*, 120-24; Bergsgard, as cited above; record of the Norwegian Cabinet meeting of March 2, as published by the Germans in *Britain's Designs on Norway*, No. 27.

[20] Tels. from Schoenfeld, March 4 and 7, 1940; Wuorinen: *Finland and World War II*, 71; tel. from the Swedish Ambassador in Paris, March 4, 1940 (*Förspelet till det Tyska Angreppet*, 125).

sure from the activists at home, discounted the hostility of the Soviets and had no compunctions about ignoring the rights of neutrals. In behalf of the Swedes it should be said that they gave the Finns such "unofficial" support as they could afford. They could hardly have been expected to oblige the Allies to the extent of providing the battlefield in a war from which they wanted above all to stand aloof. As they pointed out repeatedly, it was not in the least certain that the Allied project would serve to rescue Finland. Certainly it would seem, in the light of later developments, that an Allied landing of 50,000 or even 100,000 men in Norway at that time would have resulted in a disaster quite beyond the conceptions of the men who advocated the plan.

2. ALLIED PLANS FOR THE NEAR EAST

Closely related to the Allied projects for intervention in Scandinavia, and likewise based on the strategy of opening diversionary fronts against Germany, were the schemes of the British and the French involving the Balkans and the Near East. None of these schemes ever advanced beyond the embryonic stage or ever had much influence on American policy, but they deserve at least brief mention as illustrations of the confusion which prevailed during the first quarter of 1940 and as indications of the relations of the great powers to each other. For after all, the United States Government was profoundly interested in the major alignments, especially as they touched Soviet Russia, and the Administration in fact took a direct hand in certain phases of the problem, which, for that reason if for no other, calls for some attention.

The Balkan side of the picture, interesting though it was, need not long detain us. It may be recalled that in the spring of 1939 it was generally feared that Hitler might direct his advance to the rich wheat and oil fields of Rumania, while his henchman, Mussolini, might apply himself to settling old scores with Yugoslavia or Greece. Even after the Nazi conquest of Poland it was fervently hoped in London and Paris that Hitler might send his victorious divisions to the southeast rather than concentrate them in the West. In that case the Allies would induce the Balkan States to resist. An expeditionary force could be landed at Salonika and Nazi power drained in long and indecisive campaigns. During September, 1939, this aspect of the situation was discussed at length by Allied military authorities, and on September 22, 1939, the Supreme Council decided that an effort should be made to create a Balkan bloc, which could command about one hundred divisions and which, with Turkish and Allied support, might offer formidable resistance to both German and Russian designs.[21]

---

[21] Gamelin; *Servir*, III, 206 ff., 211; P. A. Bourget: *De Beyrouth à Bordeaux* (Paris, 1946), Chap. I; J. Weygand: *The Role of General Weygand* (London, 1948), 33; General Maxime Weygand: *Mémoires: Rappelé au service* (Paris, 1950), 19 ff.

Logical though this project might appear, it was bound to meet with numerous and, in several cases, insurmountable obstacles. First, each and every one of the Balkan States lived in mortal fear of Germany, Russia or Italy. In view of the fate of Poland, they had no desire but to avoid disaster. Second, the traditional antagonisms of the Balkan States were more alive than ever. The feud over Transylvania kept Hungary and Rumania at daggers drawn, while Hungarian revisionism created acute tension between Budapest and Belgrade. Bulgaria, in turn, had stood aloof from the Balkan Entente (Turkey, Greece, Rumania, Yugoslavia) and maintained uncompromisingly its territorial claims against Rumania and Greece. Even if it were to prove possible to bring all or most of these states into one camp, there emerged the question of Italy's position. Supposedly the Italians were also interested in a Balkan bloc to frustrate Soviet designs, but what the Duçe envisaged, of course, was a bloc under Italy's aegis. It was not to be expected that, as the ally of Hitler, he would look with equanimity upon Allied leadership in this area. And finally, the Turks, though bound by alliance to Britain and France and eager to consolidate the Balkans in resistance to Hitler, Mussolini or Stalin, were not apt to take a strong lead unless they could count on substantial Allied military support. Of this there was little if any in prospect, for, even though the newspapers were given to understand that France had concentrated an army of some 400,000 to 500,000 men in Syria, this force actually numbered hardly one tenth of these figures. We must take it for granted that the governments involved in these matters were fully aware of that fact.[22]

Our knowledge of the discussions between the Allied representatives and the Balkan Governments during the winter of 1939-1940 is fragmentary, but it is reasonably clear that they made little if any progress. On December 11, 1939, the whole problem was examined in detail by the Allied General Staffs, in consultation with Generals Wavell and Weygand, the commanders in the Near East. The result was wholly negative, for it was agreed that intervention in Thrace would be impossible without Turkish consent and that a landing at Salonika would require not only Greek but also Italian approval. In general, no operations in the Balkans could be undertaken without the benevolent neutrality of Italy. Military conversations with the Balkan Powers were to be continued, but obviously without much hope of success.[23] Somewhat later, at the beginning of February, 1940, the Turks made a valiant effort, at a meeting of the Balkan Entente powers, to overcome the opposition of the Bulgarians and to bring the various states to-

[22] Weygand: *The Role of General Weygand*, 32, 35; Weygand: *Mémoires*, Chap. II.

[23] Gamelin: *Servir*, III, 212-13; Weygand: *The Role of General Weygand*, 34; Weygand: *Mémoires*, 47 ff. A long retrospective memorandum by Gamelin, March 10, 1940, shows that he preferred operations in the Balkans to intervention in Scandinavia, but that he recognized the difficulties presented by Italy's attitude (*Die Geheimakten des französischen Generalstabes*, No. 23).

gether in one front, but again without success.[24] The attitude of the Balkan Governments was probably well expressed by Prince Regent Paul of Yugoslavia when he remarked to the American Ambassador that the Allies must be crazy to try to form an eastern front which would provoke an invasion of the Balkans by the Germans.[25]

While the scheme of a Balkan front remained an alluring dream, the Soviet-Finnish War opened up new and equally attractive vistas. Although, as we have seen, certain British leaders persisted in deluding themselves with hopes that the Nazi-Soviet pact would break down and that the Kremlin might yet be brought into the Allied camp, the French considered such speculations "idiotic" and insisted that Germany and Russia were firmly bound to each other, and that the Soviets as well as the Nazis must be looked upon as enemies. Parenthetically it may be remarked that the French in this matter held the sounder view. From the present evidence one must conclude that at this time both Hitler and Stalin looked upon their agreement as a desirable and feasible one. There was genuine collaboration all along the line, culminating in the all-important commercial agreement of February 11, 1940. This agreement had been in negotiation for months and had proved difficult because of the technical problems involved in supplying to the Soviets the machine tools, machines and manufactured products which they demanded in return for raw materials. The deadlock was finally broken by a personal message from Ribbentrop to Stalin (February 3) appealing for understanding on broader grounds. What finally emerged was more than an ordinary trade agreement; it was rather what Stalin called it—a treaty of mutual aid. Over a period of eighteen months Russia was to send Germany huge quantities of raw materials (during 1940 alone, 900,000 tons of petroleum, 100,000 tons of cotton, 500,000 tons of phosphates, 300,000 tons of manganese, 800,000 tons of feed grains, 200,000 tons of bread grains, 600,000 tons of iron-ore, 100,000 tons of chrome, etc.). Over a period of twenty-seven months the Germans were to supply Russia in return with some forty-three items of an industrial nature, including armaments. Perhaps even more significant than these terms were the provisions that Russia would facilitate free transport over its territories of German trade with the Middle and Far East, and that Russia would actually purchase abroad, on behalf of the Nazis, such materials as were vitally needed by the German war machine, to circumvent the Allied blockade.[26]

Fully convinced, then, that the Nazis and the Soviets were tarred with the

---

[24] Sir Hughe Knatchbull-Hugessen: *Diplomat in Peace and War* (London, 1949), 154-57; Beloff: *The Foreign Policy of Soviet Russia*, II, 304.

[25] Tel. from Lane (Belgrade), December 30, 1939.

[26] *Nazi-Soviet Relations*, 131-34; Beloff: *The Foreign Policy of Soviet Russia*, II, 293-96. We have used also a memo by Weizsäcker, November 1, 1939, and Ribbentrop's message to Ritter, for transmission to Stalin, February 3, 1940.

same brush, and deeply impressed with the Red Army's poor showing in the Finnish War, Daladier and his advisers took the stand that to strike at Soviet Russia would be not only safe, but also sane, for it would in effect be the same thing as striking at Germany. Just as the projected intervention in Scandinavia represented a medley of motives (cutting the iron-ore supply lines; striking at Russia; luring the Germans into Sweden), so there was now hatched a new scheme, the objective of which was to deprive Russia, and through Russia Germany also, of that vital war material —oil.

Daladier was by no means the only statesman to indulge in such thoughts. President Roosevelt, sharing in full his countrymen's detestation of Soviet policy, was alert to the rapidly rising volume of Soviet purchases in the United States, consisting mostly of strategic materials, such as oil, copper, brass and molybdenum. On January 27, 1940, he penned a note to Assistant Secretary Berle in these terms:

> I think it is time to give serious consideration to the definite curtailment of gasoline shipments to Russia and also possibly shipments of scrap iron. This particular time may be a turning point when one or two comparatively minor matters may tip the scale toward unofficial considerations in the direction of peace.

The upshot of it all was that, in an unobtrusive way, the Maritime Commission put a stop to the chartering of American vessels by the Soviet Government, "on good and sufficient domestic reasons." In addition to the moral embargo introduced in December, 1939, every effort was made to reduce Soviet purchases of war materials in the United States.[27]

The Kremlin was quick to sense the gradual congealing of the American market, the one remaining major source of supply for the materials needed so urgently by itself and its Nazi ally. On February 1 the ill-tempered Soviet Ambassador, Oumansky, retailed to Secretary Hull a number of real or alleged grievances, including "the breach of the gasoline contract between American citizens and Soviet agencies." Needless to say, he got no satisfaction but only caustic remarks from Mr. Hull. The temper of American Government circles was revealed by the President's address to the American Youth Congress on February 11, when he remarked that he had originally been sympathetic toward the Soviet revolution, but that his earlier hopes had been shattered or put in storage against a better day. Soviet Russia, concluded the President, was run by a dictatorship as absolute as any in the world, and was allied with another dictatorship.

[27] Memo of the President to Berle, January 27; memos of Berle to the President, February 1, 20 (*Roosevelt Papers:* Secretary's File, Box 62). The Treasury watched every transaction and shipment with eagle eye, and reported them to the President. See *Morgenthau Diaries (MS.),* January 8 (Vol. 233), January 9 (Vol. 234), early February (Vol. 238-39 *passim*), February 5 (letter of Vincent Astor to the President, Vol. 240), memo of February 13, reflecting discussion at the previous Cabinet meeting (Vol. 240).

At the very end of February 1940, Foreign Commissar Molotov tried another tack in an effort to remedy the situation. He actually gave a luncheon in honor of the American Ambassador, on which notable occasion he unburdened himself with regard to the world scene. Among other things he spoke of Japan as Russia's enemy and remarked that it would not surprise him if one day the Red Army and the United States Navy were to coöperate in destroying this common foe! But even this enticing suggestion called forth no cordial response. By the end of March the Soviets were back with their usual complaints. Both in Moscow and in Washington they presented long lists of grievances: hostile utterances by American officials, "humiliations" endured by Soviet citizens detained at Ellis Island, the "moral embargo," the exclusion of Soviet engineers from American airplane factories, the refusal to charter American vessels to the Soviet Union, etc., etc.

Ambassador Steinhardt had cogent and telling replies to all of these points, but Secretary Hull declined to discuss them in detail with Oumansky, on the plea that he had no time for "small complaints." The issues, he added, were larger, and the United States Government was tremendously disappointed by the general accumulation of Soviet moves leading up to the existing situation. Not knowing what the Soviet Government would do next, there was no reason why the United States should assist Russia with materials needed for American defense. When Oumansky reported that his Government was following a policy of neutrality and was merely determined to stay out of war, Mr. Hull inquired dryly whether he meant only wars which the Kremlin desired to avoid, or whether he included wars of aggression, like that against Finland. Clearly discussions of this tenor were entirely bootless. By the spring of 1940 American-Soviet relations were, in the words of Mr. Welles "only nominal," and the Washington Administration was adhering to its policy of doing everything possible to cut down the export of strategic materials to Russia and, through Russia, to Nazi Germany.[28]

But to return to the Allied plans for obstructing the Soviet and indirectly the German oil supplies: Daladier's idea, as it emerged in mid-January, 1940, was that Allied submarines should be sent into the Black Sea to attack oil tankers and possibly to bomb the Soviet oil-shipping center of Batum. At the same time Allied bombers, based on Syrian or Iraqi fields, should attack and destroy the Soviet oil fields in the Caucasus, at Baku, Grozny and other localities. Finally, an effort should be made to stir up the Moslem populations of the Caucasus, so as to create additional difficulties

---

[28] For the foregoing we have used memo of conversation between Hull and Oumansky, February 1; tel. from Steinhardt, February 28; memo by Loy Henderson, commenting on this telegram, March 2; tel. from Steinhardt, March 28; memo of the European Division for Mr. Hull, April 1; memo of conversation between Hull and Oumansky, April 2; tel. to Steinhardt, commending him for his replies to Soviet complaints, April 4, 1940; see also Hull: *Memoirs*, I, 743-45.

for the Moscow Government. However, when this program was submitted to London, it was received with little enthusiasm. As in the Scandinavian affair, the British were disinclined to being drawn into conflict with the Soviet power.[29] Nonetheless the French, encouraged by reports of the growing anti-Russian and Pan Turanian feeling in Turkey, continued to study the project. On February 22 the French General Staff was ready with a report setting forth the requirements in detail and arguing that the operation, if successful, might be a decisive blow at Soviet military and economic power and might even lead to complete Soviet collapse, thereby depriving Germany of essential support.[30]

Although this entire project did not reach a practical stage until after the conclusion of the Soviet-Finnish War, it seems best to pursue it to its inglorious end before turning to other themes. By early March the British Government must have indicated some readiness to join in the enterprise, for the British Air Command at Cairo asked French permission to engage in reconnaissance flights from Syrian airfields. From Moscow Ambassador Steinhardt reported the Soviet Government sufficiently worried to send additional troops to the Caucasus region. Finally, at Ankara the French Ambassador, M. Massigli, tentatively broached the subject to the Turkish Government, finding it not averse to letting Allied planes fly over the national territory providing the Turkish Government were not officially approached for permission. The new French Cabinet, under M. Reynaud, was more ardent for action than even that of his predecessor. At the meeting of the Supreme War Council on March 28, 1940, the subject was raised anew and the decision made to study it jointly, with special reference to the attitude of Turkey and the probable reaction of Russia. Meanwhile, preparations were to be started, so the plan could be put into execution when it seemed advisable.[31]

The rest of the story can be told in few words. With considerable gusto Premier Reynaud summoned General Weygand from Syria. There was much talk of the need for more energetic action in the Balkans, even of measures to obstruct the supply of oil from Rumania to Germany. But the main topic for discussion was the Caucasus project. Exuberant estimates suggested that with a hundred Allied planes, each mission carrying some seventy tons of projectiles, the oil fields and port facilities could be one third destroyed in six days. The Turks were discreetly told what was up

[29] Gamelin: Servir, III, 211; Weygand: The Role of General Weygand, 36; French General Staff paper, January 19, 1940 (Geheimakten des französischen Generalstabes, No. 19); tels. from Bullit, January 15, 25, 1940. This entire subject is reviewed, on the basis of the French documents published by the Germans, by P. Iurev: "Podgotovka Anglii i Frantsii k napadeniio na sovyetskii soiuz s iuga v 1939-1940 gg." (Voprosy Istorii, 1949, No. 2, 101-8).

[30] Die Geheimakten des französischen Generalstabes, Nos. 20, 22; French Staff memo of February 29, dealing particularly with the possibilities of Moslem unrest in the Caucasus.

[31] Geheimakten des französischen Generalstabes, Nos. 26, 27, 28, 30; Gamelin: Servir, III, 216, 293-98; Churchill: The Gathering Storm, 576 ff.; Weygand: The Role of General Weygand, 36; tel. from Steinhardt, March 9, 1940.

and steps were taken to assemble the planes and supplies. But on sober examination it emerged that these preparations would take from forty-five to fifty days, leaving out of account the time required to train pilots for the operation. All told, it became clear that action could hardly be undertaken before the end of June, or early July, 1940. Meanwhile the Germans had already begun the occupation of Norway. On April 23, 1940, the Supreme War Council, meeting at Paris, reviewed the project for the last time. The British declared that they needed all their long-range bombers in Norway, and the French agreed that little could be spared for the Near East in view of the probability of attack on the Low Countries and France.[32] The plan was therefore adjourned indefinitely. Looking back upon it and recalling the readiness of the French to challenge the supposedly feeble Soviet power, the scheme appears somewhat fantastic. Perhaps the kindest comment to be made was that of a discerning critic, Max Werner: "The entire plan was no more than a flight from inherent weakness into grandiose adventure."[33]

3. Hitler's Preparations

In striking contrast to the fumbling efforts of the British and French to agree on a course of action against Germany or Russia, or both, was the single-minded and determined program of the Fuehrer. Ever since the conquest of Poland his mind had been fixed on one objective, and one objective only, namely the great offensive in the West. At least until the outbreak of the Soviet-Finnish War, Scandinavia played only a minor role in his thinking. From his conversations with Ciano in mid-August, 1939, it is clear that he expected the Northern countries to remain neutral in the coming conflict and that he considered the occupation of countries as large as Norway and Sweden to be impracticable.[34] To be sure, after the declaration of war by Britain and France, German admirals began to impress upon him that Britain was the chief enemy, and that, in view of Germany's relative weakness at sea, his only hope of success lay in prosecuting the economic war with the utmost ruthlessness and, where necessary, without regard to international law or the protests of neutrals. For the conduct of the submarine war it would be of the greatest importance to have a good base on the Norwegian coast. Trondheim would be ideal for the purpose, though Narvik too would be highly desirable. Hitler promised to consider the matter, but evidently was too engrossed by his plans for attack in the West to give the subject much attention.[35]

[32] Gamelin: *Servir*, III, 310-11, 361.

[33] Max Werner: *The Battle for the World* (New York, 1941), 99. On the final phase of the project see also *Die Geheimakten des französischen Generalstabes*, Nos. 32, 34, 37, 38; *The Private Diaries of Paul Baudouin* (Eyre & Spottiswoode, London, 1948), 8.

[34] *Ciano's Diplomatic Papers*, 296 ff.

[35] *Fuehrer Conferences, 1939*, 12 ff.; *Nazi Conspiracy and Aggression*, III, 19-27; IV, 104-6. The development of German plans regarding Norway is well reviewed in Peter de Mendelssohn: *Design for Aggression* (New York, 1946), 109 ff., and in Anthony Martienssen: *Hitler and His Admirals* (New York, 1949), 43 ff. There is an excellent monographic

By mid-December, 1939, the situation had matured somewhat. The attack in the West had been postponed and the Finnish War had necessarily distracted German attention to the North. It was at this juncture that the Norwegian Nazi leader, Colonel Vidkun Quisling, arrived in Berlin. Alfred Rosenberg, the official "philosopher" of the Nazi party, had long been in contact with Quisling, who, even before the outbreak of war, had repeatedly called attention to the importance of Norway in any struggle between Britain and Germany. Rosenberg in turn had suggested to Admiral Raeder the possible usefulness of Quisling and his diminutive though vigorous Norwegian following. On December 11 Raeder and Rosenberg had a long conference with Quisling and his aides. The Norwegians made much of the pro-British sentiments of their countrymen and especially of the "Jew Hambro," who was President of the Norwegian Parliament. They talked of a secret British-Norwegian treaty and made great play of the pressing danger of a British occupation. The remedy, they thought, was to stage a political overturn and seize power. Thereafter the victorious Norwegian Nazis would put their country's ports at the disposal of Germany.

Raeder, though somewhat distrustful and skeptical, was well impressed by a scheme which would cost the Germans little and might net them much. He put the matter up to Hitler, who twice received Quisling to hear his story. The Norwegian must have presented a strong case, for Hitler was evidently intrigued with his plan. True, the Fuehrer still maintained that from his standpoint it would be best if the Northern countries observed strict neutrality. He had no desire or intention, he said, to extend the theater of war or to draw other nations into the conflict. On the other hand, "if the enemy were preparing an enlargement of the zones of war with the aim of further throttling and threatening the Greater German Reich, then, of course, he would be obliged to arm against such steps." The upshot was that he promised Quisling financial and other support and ordered that a special military staff be set up to study the problem in all its aspects.[36]

At the end of the year 1939, when the Allies were already seriously considering an expeditionary force to succor Finland, the Germans were still

study, based on unpublished German materials and Norwegian records, by Helge Sivertsen: "Tysklands Planer om Overfall på Norge" (Supplement I of *Instilling fra Undersøkelses-kommisjonen*). Harald Jörgensen: "Det diplomatiske Forspil til det Tyske Angreb på Norge og Danmark" (*Nordisk Tidskrift*, XXIV, 1948, 86-94) provides a good digest of the records published by the Swedish Government. See also the discussion of the War Crimes Tribunal's treatment of this matter in Lord Hankey: *Politics, Trials and Errors* (Chicago, 1950), Chap. IV.

[36] The story of these conferences leaked out at an early date and was published by Ronald Scarfe: *In the Norwegian Trap* (London, 1940), 58 ff. For the documentary evidence see *Fuehrer Conferences, 1939*, 54, 56, 58; *Nazi Conspiracy and Aggression*, VI, 884-92; *Jodl Diary*, December 13, 1939; *Halder Diary*, December 14, 1939. Sivertsen's study, cited above, is very full on Quisling's role.

on the fence so far as any Scandinavian plans were concerned. It was to their interest to keep Norway neutral, if possible, and even though they were supporting Quisling, they had made no definite commitment to him. They realized that the Norwegian Nazis were an insignificant group and they probably had grave doubts of Quisling's ability to deliver the goods. Conversely, they knew from the Allied press of the extravagant plans that were being hatched, and they were now keenly aware of the dangers of a British descent on Scandinavia. The German attitude was well stated in a memorandum from Raeder to Hitler on December 30: "It is essential that Norway does not fall into British hands. There is danger that volunteers from Britain, in disguise, will carry out an unobtrusive occupation of Norway. Therefore it is necessary to be prepared and ready." But apparently Hitler did not yet consider the threat a serious one. It was to be some time yet before he made a decision. Meanwhile he was still preoccupied with his plans for the attack in the West.[37]

It was undoubtedly the prolonged bad weather that induced Hitler to postpone repeatedly the date for the great offensive against the Low Countries, but during December, 1939, a new and important factor was introduced which required further time for the revision of plans. This was the proposal, attributed in the first instance to General Manstein, to scrap the original project for a great sweep by the German left wing through Maastricht, a plan which was essentially a modified version of the famous Schlieffen Plan of 1914. Manstein argued that this operation was too obvious, and that greater surprise and effect might be attained by concentrating the German armored divisions for a thrust through the difficult Ardennes country, toward Sedan. If the breakthrough there should succeed, the German tanks, supported by dive bombers and infantry, could cut across France and make for the Channel at Abbéville, thus cutting off the Allied forces in Belgium. The conception was as brilliant at it was daring and made a strong appeal to Hitler. As usual, many of his generals had reservations. They were frightened by the idea of sending their armor across France without the traditional artillery and infantry support. But once again Hitler overruled all opposition. The idea was adopted and the plans were modified accordingly.[38]

At this point the highly dramatic events of January, 1940, intervened. On December 28 Hitler had decided that if the weather were to prove bad in mid-January, it would be better to defer the great offensive until the

---

[37] Tel. from Kirk (Berlin), January 4, 1940, discussing German knowledge of Allied plans. For the Raeder memorandum see *Fuehrer Conferences, 1939*, 62, and for German hesitation, *Halder Diary*, January 1, 1940.

[38] B. H. Liddell Hart: *The German Generals Talk* (New York, 1948), 112 ff., who places the change in January, 1940. The *Halder Diary* gives indications of it much earlier (December 7) and would seem to show that it was pretty well complete by December 27. General Warlimont (State Department interrogation) also dated it "late in 1939."

spring. Two weeks later (January 10) his forecasters reported the prospect of excellent winter weather for ten days or a fortnight following January 15. Thereupon Hitler announced that he would fix the day of attack for January 17.[39] But on the next day (January 11) the German High Command received shocking news of a most extraordinary episode. A German air officer, carrying important plans of the invasion, had disobeyed his orders to travel by rail from Münster to Cologne. Having been delayed through his own fault, he boarded a plane which, when obliged to make a forced landing, found itself on Belgian territory. Despite his efforts to burn his papers, most of them fell into the hands of the Belgian police. One can well imagine the horror in German military circles when news of the incident arrived. Hitler's first reaction was to give orders that the attack be made on January 17, nevertheless, in the hope that if the papers had not been destroyed he could strike before the enemy had time to take countermeasures. But by January 14-15 reports of Belgian concentrations were pouring in and the conclusion was inescapable that at least part of the German plans had been revealed. Not only that, the weather forecast became unfavorable—fog was to be expected by January 16 and air operations would be impossible. Under the circumstances there was no alternative to further postponement, first to January 20 and then tentatively until March.[40]

The Belgian authorities could not, of course, be certain that the papers they had captured were not part of a ruse. But they appeared to be authentic, and the Brussels Government had already been warned by its Ambassador in Berlin that an attack was to be expected in the near future. The Belgian forces were therefore quickly ordered to readiness and copies of the captured documents were at once sent to the British and French. Gamelin and his colleagues, being unable to examine the originals, were skeptical about the whole business, though on the British side Churchill at least seems to have felt that there would have been no point in the Germans arranging such a plant. In any event, the Belgians rightly feared an immediate assault and King Leopold opened discussions with the British liaison officer, Admiral Keyes, as to what should be done. Keyes assured him that the Allies would give the Belgians full support, provided they were summoned in good time. Evidently Leopold considered the possibility of inviting the Allied forces to cross into Belgium then and there, but Keyes's report to London, when relayed to Paris, gave the impression that the King had already made the decision. The French High Command, while still dubious about the imminence of a German attack, decided to take advantage of the situation. In the night of January 14-15, during a heavy

---

[39] *Jodl Diary*, December 28, 1939, January 10, 1940; *Halder Diary*, January 10, 1940.
[40] *Jodl Diary*, January 11-21; *Halder Diary*, January 12-20, 1940; see also Kordt: *Wahn und Wirklichkeit*, 227 ff.

snowstorm, the French forces were concentrated on the Belgian frontier. Only on the evening of January 15 did Daladier and Gamelin learn that the deal was off, the King having failed to persuade his Ministers of the need for calling in the Allies. It was another case of bungling, but it had at least the advantage of paving the way for closer contacts between the Allied and Belgian Governments and for better coördination of plans. On the other hand, the French troop movements were observed by the Germans, who thenceforth knew with complete certainty that the Allied forces would march into what the Germans hoped to make the Belgian trap.[41]

During the ensuing two months the situation in the West was calmer than it had been since October. This was due less to any German respect for the Welles Mission than to the bad weather and the need for time to revamp the Nazi plans. By mid-February the German High Command was congratulating itself that the documents captured by the Belgians had revealed nothing of the projected Ardennes breakthrough and the lightning advance to the Channel. The longer Hitler pondered this plan, the better he liked it. Indeed, he was now rubbing his hands in gleeful anticipation and even speculating that the shock to the Allies would be so great that they might decide not to fight at all: "After half a day the news from Holland and Belgium may be so threatening that he [the enemy] will decide to stand still."[42]

In the interval the Germans became more and more uneasy about Allied designs in Scandinavia, the substance of which was freely available in the French press. Nothing had come of the Quisling coup, which had been promised for mid-January, and it gradually became evident that military action might be necessary to forestall an Allied occupation of Norway. This idea was not entertained with any enthusiasm by the Germans, for it was realized that even if they occupied the Norwegian ports, it would be extremely difficult to protect the coast against British raids. As late as February Hitler and Raeder were agreed that continued Norwegian neutrality would be best for Germany. But they were deeply concerned, after the *Altmark* affair (February 16), about British designs against Narvik and the iron-ore route. A British occupation, they concluded, must be prevented at

---

[41] Gamelin: *Servir*, III, 155-62; Reynaud: *La France a sauvé l'Europe*, I, 623 ff.; Churchill: *The Gathering Storm*, 556 ff. On the Belgian side the fullest and most richly documented account is that of General van Overstraeten: *Albert I, Leopold III* (Bruges, 1950), 445-88, but see also *Belgium: the Official Account of What Happened, 1939-1940* (London, 1941), 22-23; *Rapport de la Commission d'Information* (Brussels, 1947), 30 ff.; Hubert Pierlot, in *Le Soir* (Brussels), July 9, 1947; Theodore Draper: *The Six Weeks' War* (New York, 1944), 18 ff. The German documents captured by the Belgians are printed in *Nazi Conspiracy and Aggression*, VIII, 423-29. We have used also a tel. from Cudahy (Brussels), January 18, 1940, reporting the initiation of military conversations with the Allies.

[42] *Jodl Diary*, February 13, 1940. Hitler's ideas were too much for Jodl, who noted: "I don't believe it."

all costs. The Fuehrer therefore ordered plans drawn up so that the operation could be undertaken as soon as the offensive in the West was well in hand.[43]

From this point onward the German plans ripened quickly. Hitler undoubtedly had wind of Allied efforts to persuade the Norwegians and Swedes to grant them passage and he undoubtedly warned the Finns against making an appeal for Allied aid. In any case, the situation was tense and brooked no delay. Therefore the Fuehrer on March 1 issued a directive for the occupation of both Denmark and Norway, with the objectives of preventing Allied encroachment, of making secure the iron-ore route from Narvik, and of acquiring better naval and air bases for use against Britain. The whole action was, however, to be presented as a peaceful one, designed to give military protection to Scandinavian neutrality. Force was to be used only if necessary. In view of the urgency of the matter, Hitler now decided that the Scandinavian operation should precede the offensive in the West by a few days and set March 15 as the date for the occupation of Denmark and Norway. The Navy was to carry the main share of the burden, though the Army and Air Force were to make their contributions. Admiral Raeder, anxious though he was to get a footing in Norway and to shut out the British, seems to have grown ever more dubious about the operation as the plans matured. The whole undertaking, he pointed out, was contrary to naval theory, since the Germans lacked command of the sea and the one hope therefore lay in the element of surprise.[44]

By this time the conclusion of peace between Russia and Finland was already in the offing. On both the Allied and the German sides all plans for Norway were ready. In reconsidering them one is inescapably struck by the fact that while the British and French found themselves stymied by the recalcitrance of the Norwegians and Swedes, and by their dependence on an appeal by the Finns, Hitler was not hampered by any considerations of neutrality or of world opinion, nor was his action in any way contingent on what the Finns might do. The Fuehrer had convinced himself of the reality of the Allied threat and had decided to anticipate it without squeamishness or hesitation. But the conclusion of peace in the North was bound to upset the Allied plans and thereby make necessary a reconsideration of the entire program. Before turning to this final phase of the question, it will be well to examine the circumstances of the Soviet-Finnish peace negotiations and the role of the United States in these developments.

[43] *Fuehrer Conference, 1940 (I),* 14, 18; *Halder Diary,* January 8, February 19, 21, 1940; Martienssen: *Hitler and his Admirals,* 48-49. The study by Sivertsen, cited above, gives a great deal more detail, especially on the relationship to Quisling.

[44] The directive is printed in *Nazi Conspiracy and Aggression,* VI, 1003-5. For the rest see *Fuehrer Conferences, 1940 (I),* 20; *Jodl Diary,* February 26, March 3, 5, 7; *Halder Diary,* March 2, 3, 6, 1940.

4. END OF THE "WINTER WAR"

Despite its initial military successes, the Finnish Government never shared the delusion, so prevalent throughout the world, that it might ultimately defeat the Soviet armies. To make a Finnish victory even possible would have required official armed intervention by Sweden and Norway, full military support of those countries by Britain and France, and substantial aid in money and munitions from the United States. As previously pointed out, hopes of such support were never bright. With the coming of the new year, it is true, the Allies seemed finally to be girding for action, but as their project for intervention ripened, the obstruction of the Swedes and Norwegians became more determined. By February the Finnish forces, which had held the field without relief much longer than anyone had expected, were rapidly becoming exhausted. The Soviets, on the other hand, had at last marshaled some of their best divisions and had moved up armor and heavy artillery to batter down the Mannerheim Line. Without large-scale aid from the outside, the Finns could not hope much longer to continue the unequal struggle.

Foreseeing the inevitable outcome, the Helsinki Government had begun at an early date to sound out the possibilities of a negotiated settlement. Its ideal solution would have been to have some powerful neutrals, like the United States and Italy, take the lead in mobilizing the other powers for concerted action in Moscow. Even the Germans, it was fondly hoped, would recall their traditional friendship for Finland and throw their weight into the scales. A suggestion of this nature was made to the American Minister by the Finnish Prime Minister on December 28, 1939, but was rejected as "inopportune" after Ambassador Steinhardt had cabled from Moscow warning that the Soviet Government was now too deeply committed in the Finnish affair even to consider such a plan. Prime Minister Ryti, while agreeing reluctantly that the time was perhaps not yet ripe, nevertheless held to his conviction that it was up to the United States Government to take the lead in ending not only the Finnish war but also the entire European conflict. This, of course, was a matter of opinion. The Washington Administration was not only ready but eager to do what it could to bring about a European settlement. But the matter of timing was important. As yet there was no reason to suppose that the Soviets, after their miserable military showing, would be ready to come to terms before redeeming their reputation.[45]

By the end of January the position of the Finns was already becoming desperate. They made no secret of the fact that while, with the aid of

[45] Tel. from Schoenfeld, December 28, 30, 31; tel. from Steinhardt, December 31, 1939; tel. to Schoenfeld, January 3; tel. from Schoenfeld, January 9, 1940. See also Hull: *Memoirs*, I, 741.

100,000 foreign troops, they thought they could defeat the Red Army, without such support they would not be able to hold out more than another six or eight weeks. Marshal Mannerheim was urging the despatch of an Allied expeditionary force to Petsamo, and it was at this juncture that the British-French plans for intervention finally began to take shape (Supreme War Council decision of February 5). Faced with the prospect of dangerous developments, the Swedish Government now made real efforts to mediate, but its approaches to Moscow gave little hope of success. Molotov told the Swedish Minister that the Kremlin would not deal with Ryti and Tanner, the men who had made the war, and added, by way of good measure, that in any case the Soviet demands would be higher than those discussed in November. The Finns indicated readiness to discuss even on this basis, but Molotov remained cold.[46]

Concurrently with the Swedish *démarche*, though no doubt quite independently, the United States Government renewed its own efforts. Ambassador Steinhardt was instructed to find out from Molotov "whether an approach . . . looking towards a cessation of the present conflict between the Soviet Union and Finland would be given serious consideration by the Soviet Government and would be received in the friendly spirit in which it would be made." The Ambassador discussed the matter with the Foreign Commissar on February 2, 1940, and reported:

Molotov . . . denounced the Finns for "provocative" acts and blamed them for the war. He admitted that Finnish resistance was stronger than expected. He cited as proof of the correctness of the Soviet attitude throughout the fact that Finland was now equipped to serve as a base of operations "for other powers."

He said twice that it would be impossible to negotiate with the Ryti-Tanner-Mannerheim Government, but he studiously avoided giving any indication as to whether the Soviet Government would be prepared to negotiate with any independent Finnish Government. On the other hand, he did not once reaffirm the previous Soviet position that the Kuusinen Government was the only legal government with which they would deal.

I was unable to obtain from Molotov any clear statement as to the attitude of his Government towards an approach from my Government.

In other words, the Ambassador met only with evasion. His conclusion was that the Kremlin was not interested at the time in negotiations to end the conflict, though it was possible that at some future date it might consider American good offices.[47]

It is reasonable to suppose that the Soviet Government, at last in a position to crush Finnish resistance, was determined to fight to the end as

---

[46] Tel. from Bullitt, January 25; tel. from Harriman (Oslo) January 30; tel. from Sterling (Stockholm), February 8, 1940. By far the best account, clearly based on Finnish records, is that of John Wuorinen, ed.: *Finland and World War II* (New York, 1948), 73 ff.

[47] Tel. to Steinhardt, January 27; tel. from Steinhardt, February 2, 1940; *Moffat Diary (MS.)*, January 26, 1940.

a matter of prestige if for nothing else. The Finns, on their side, finding it impossible to open negotiations, had no choice but to redouble their efforts to get foreign aid. Foreign Minister Tanner arrived in Stockholm on February 13 and told the Swedes that unless they were prepared to send volunteers in complete units, the Finns would have to call upon the Allies, which in turn would involve the Northern States in war. Nonetheless, the Swedes remained firm. On February 19 King Gustav announced publicly that Sweden could give no official assistance and somewhat later the Stockholm Government rejected a Finnish plea for permission for the passage of Allied troops. The reply to the Allied request, shortly afterward, was of the same tenor, as the reader may recall.[48]

Providentially for the Swedes as well as for the Finns, the Soviets now suddenly reversed their attitude. According to Molotov's later explanations, they harkened to the Finnish appeal for terms and consulted with Kuusinen, the head of the Soviet-sponsored but still phantom Finnish Communist Government, with which the Kremlin had concluded a formal treaty. One can readily understand that Kuusinen yielded to the importunities of Stalin and Molotov and counseled negotiations for peace with the existing Helsinki Government; but one may well ask why the Soviets, who had not yet reached their primary objective of Viipuri, suddenly decided to eat their words, drop Kuusinen, and agree to discuss a settlement. The simple answer in this case is probably the correct one: for, all statements to the contrary, it is highly probable that the Kremlin was genuinely concerned by Allied plans to bomb the Caucasus oil fields, and more particularly by the prospect of Allied landings in Scandinavia. All the evidence supports the idea that the Soviets were far from prepared to face a hostile coalition, which leads to the conclusion that they had come to consider it essential to get out of the Finnish morass as quickly and as profitably as possible. Molotov, in his above-mentioned speech, gave clear indications of Soviet motivation when he remarked: "What was going on in Finland was not merely our collision with Finnish troops. It was a collision with the combined forces of a number of imperialist states most hostile to the Soviet Union."[49]

On February 22 the Soviet Commissar handed the Kremlin's terms to the Swedish Minister, with a warning that if the Finns rejected them, harsher demands would follow. Four days later the same terms were sent, oddly enough, to London, with the request that they be transmitted to Helsinki. The British Government declined, on the plea that the terms were exorbitant. Thenceforth the Swedes, ardently desirous of ending the dangerous conflict on any even remotely decent terms, served as the chief intermediaries. It must have been some comfort to them to note how urgently the

[48] Wuorinen: *Finland and World War II,* 75-76.
[49] Molotov's speech as reported in *The New York Times,* March 30, 1940.

Soviets now pressed the settlement. On February 28 Molotov called for a Finnish reply within forty-eight hours.[50]

For the moment, at least, the shoe seemed to be on the other foot. The Helsinki Government was faced with a really difficult decision. Mannerheim and the soldiers, it appears, were ready to continue the struggle, hoping for early and effective assistance from the Allies. As late as March 1 the Marshal sent a message to President Roosevelt requesting urgently the dispatch of 150 fighter planes and 36 fast bombers, with volunteer crews.[51] We may assume that he and his subordinates were intrigued by the Allied proposal that the Finns call upon them for help before March 5, in the belief that then the Allies would act even in the face of Norwegian and Swedish opposition. Yet it must have been perfectly obvious that Allied aid, even if invoked, would plunge all Scandinavia into hostilities and probably reach Finland too late to be of practical value. For several days the issue hung in the balance. The Helsinki Government played for time by asking for further information concerning the Soviet terms. On March 5 the Soviet Government replied that it would wait a few more days, but that further delay would mean more drastic demands, if not a definitive agreement with the Kuusinen Government. By this time, however, the Finns had evidently made their decision for peace, even though they knew the Soviet terms to be more far-reaching than those of November, 1939. They therefore accepted in principle and on March 6 despatched a mission consisting of Prime Minister Ryti, Minister Juho K. Paasikivi, and General Walden to Moscow by way of Stockholm. The Finnish delegation reached the Soviet capital in great secrecy by Swedish plane on the evening of March 7.[52]

It is understandable that, having made their decision, the Finns should attempt to mobilize support for themselves in Moscow. From the British and French nothing was to be expected. Although Prime Minister Chamberlain disarmingly told the American Ambassador that he personally would be glad if the Soviets and Finns reached agreement, in both London and Paris there was much indignation over alleged Swedish pressure on the Finns to make peace, this pressure being attributed to German influence. The Germans, however, seem to have evaded Finnish suggestions that they themselves use their good offices in Moscow, being clearly unwilling to compromise their relations with the Soviets.[53] There remained, then, aside

[50] Wuorinen: *Finland and World War II*, 75-76; tel. from Schoenfeld, March 8, 1940.

[51] Tel. from Mannerheim to the President, March 1, 1940 (*Roosevelt Papers*: Secretary's File, Box 63).

[52] Wuorinen: *Finland and World War II*, 76-77, supplemented by the following American reports: tel. from Wiley (Tallinn), March 1; tels. from Schoenfeld, March 3, 4, 7, 8; tels. from Sterling (Stockholm), March 7, 8; tels. from Steinhardt, March 7, 8, 1940.

[53] Tel. from Kennedy, March 9, 1940, and the Swedish reports in *Förspelet till det Tyska Angreppet*, 140 ff.; tel. from Schoenfeld, March 8; tels. from Sterling, March 7, 8; tel. from Atherton (Copenhagen), March 8, 1940. The visit of the former Finnish President,

from such influence as the Swedes could exert, only the possibility of American support. On March 4 the Finnish Foreign Minister inquired of Minister Schoenfeld what assistance his country could expect from the United States, assuming that Finland decided to embark on negotiations. The Minister replied that his Government, as stated in January, would be glad to "take under benevolent advisement" any concrete suggestions the Finns might put forward.[54]

This cautious though friendly reply was quite in keeping with the Administration's attitude. From the President downward everyone favored the doughty Finns and was much soured on Moscow. Having received Marshal Mannerheim's plea for more planes, Mr. Roosevelt had at once instructed Secretary Morgenthau to get them from General Arnold "if it did not mean too much hot water." But, as on previous occasions, good will proved inadequate. There were no more planes to be disposed of as surplus. In fact, the first of the forty-four Brewster fighters originally sold were only just arriving in Finland after assembly and test flying in Sweden. Regretfully the President had to abandon the project.[55]

As for the Finnish request for support at Moscow, the Administration was glad to do what it could, short of mediation or actual involvement in the dispute. On March 7 Ambassador Steinhardt was instructed to see Commissar Molotov as soon as possible and tell him that while the United States did not propose to intervene directly in the discussions, any generosity the Soviets might show would make a deep impression on American opinion. Indeed, the Ambassador was authorized, if he thought wise, to imply that the moral embargo might be relaxed to the same degree to which the Soviets abated the severity of their demands on Finland. Steinhardt saw Molotov on March 8 and found him "effusively cordial." The Commissar expressed great appreciation of American interest in the restoration of peace and promised to call on the Ambassador "in case difficulties arose." In fact, he went so far as to outline the Soviet demands, adding that the Kremlin was interested in peace but not insistent, and not at all prepared to tolerate any "dragging of the negotiations."[56]

Molotov's cordiality was no doubt due to the earnest desire of the Kremlin to secure larger quantities of badly needed goods from the United States. But the Commissar's unwonted benevolence did not extend to the point of letting the Finns off easy. When the discussions started, on the

---

Svinhufud, to Berlin at this time was entirely unofficial. The strong German desire to see the war terminated was reflected in Ribbentrop's conversations with Mussolini and Ciano, March 10, 11, 1940 (*Ciano's Diplomatic Papers*, 345-50).

[54] Tel. from Schoenfeld, March 4, 1940.

[55] *Morgenthau Diaries (MS.)*, March 5 (Vol. 245, pp. 223, 230 ff.); March 7, 1940 (Vol. 246, pp. 50, 69); tel. from Schoenfeld, March 4, 1940.

[56] Tel. to Steinhardt, March 7; tels. from Steinhardt, March 8, 9, 1940; Hull: *Memoirs*, I, 742.

evening of March 8, the Finnish delegation was shocked to learn from Molotov, Zhdanov and General Vasilevski that the terms originally outlined to them had been raised. The Kremlin now demanded not only a lease of Hangö, the cession of the Karelian Isthmus, including Viipuri (Viborg) and the northern shore of Lake Ladoga, including Sortavala, but also part of the Rybachi Peninsula, a large area of territory in the vicinity of Salla and Kuusamo, and finally the construction of a railroad across the waist of Finland from Salla to Kemijarvi. Ambassador Steinhardt, who was authorized by Washington to urge magnanimous terms if the negotiations reached a suitable stage, joined with his Swedish colleague in appealing to the Soviets for moderation, but all in vain. The Finns had to decide for themselves whether to sacrifice 10 percent of their territory and 15 percent of their resources, or whether to attempt to continue the struggle.[57]

Their problem was certainly not simplified by the renewed efforts of the Allied Governments to induce them to appeal for aid. On March 8 Daladier had sent a message to Helsinki in these terms:

We have waited for several days for Finland to make her appeal, so that we can come to your aid with all the means at our disposal. It is difficult to understand why this request is still postponed. We know the pressure Sweden is exerting on you to make a peace which would leave you at Russia's mercy. We know Russia fears you will appeal to the Allies, because she fears that an Allied intervention will lead to a Russian catastrophe. To avoid the catastrophe, Russia is now ready to negotiate in order to be able to destroy you later. I assure you once more, we are ready to give our help immediately. The airplanes are ready to take off. The operational force is ready. If Finland does not now make her appeal to the Western Powers, it is obvious that at the end of the war the Western Powers cannot assume the slightest responsibility for the final settlement regarding Finnish territory. I request the Government to make its decision soon.

Orally Daladier stated that the request should be made not later than March 12, indicating that after that date the Allies would have to discontinue aid to Finland.[58]

At this crucial moment Marshal Mannerheim finally admitted that the Finnish military position on the Karelian Isthmus had become untenable and that in his opinion Allied aid would be inadequate and too late. This being so, it is hard to believe that the Helsinki Government could have seriously thought of continued resistance. If, during the next two days, it went through certain motions, these were probably intended chiefly to

[57] Wuorinen: *Finland and World War II*, 77-78; tel. from Sterling, March 10, 1940, reporting information from the Finnish representative in Stockholm; tel. to Steinhardt, March 9; tels. from Steinhardt, March 9, 12, 1940.

[58] Wuorinen: *Finland and World War II*, 78; tel. from Sterling, March 8, reporting Erkko's statement; tels. from Steinhardt, March 9, 10, reporting the futile efforts of the French representative to see the Finnish delegation on this matter; tel. from Murphy (Paris), March 12, 1940, relaying information from M. Leger.

impress the Soviets and induce them to agree to easier terms. On March 11 the Finns once again appealed to their Scandinavian neighbors to grant passage to Allied forces. At the same time they requested the Allied Governments to do likewise. This the British and French did on March 12, only to meet with the usual reply that to grant permission would involve the Northern Powers in the war and that therefore they must refuse.[59]

That these were mere tactical maneuvers would seem to be proved by the fact that the Finns did not await their outcome. On March 11 the Parliamentary Committee for Foreign Affairs voted to make peace on the Soviet terms. Last-minute discussions with the Soviets failed to modify their position. The Kremlin by this time clearly considered the talk of Allied intervention bluff. Accordingly the Finns had to yield. The peace treaty was signed about midnight on March 12 and hostilities ceased at noon on the following day, just after the Red Army had at last taken Viipuri.[60]

By the final settlement the Finns, despite their fortitude and losses, were obliged to give up more than the Soviets had demanded in October and November, 1939. Their only consolation lay in the fact that during the negotiations the Soviets had said nothing more about the ill-starred Kuusinen Government and had suggested no drastic curtailment of Finland's independence. On March 13 President Roosevelt issued a statement, which was formally communicated to the Helsinki and Moscow Governments, saying that "The people of Finland by their unexcelled valor and strong resistance in the face of overwhelming armed forces, have won the moral right to live in everlasting peace and independence in the land they have so bravely defended." Certainly the Finns had aroused the sympathy and admiration of the civilized world, but for them the fact remained that they had lost important territory and resources and above all that they were now strategically at the mercy of the Soviets. While, as they said, they were almost suffocated by expressions of good will from abroad, the aid and support they received, while not inconsiderable, was far from enough to affect the final outcome. By March, 1940, they certainly had no alternative but to yield. The point need not be labored, but it is still astounding that the Kremlin should have managed to get everything it regarded as immediately essential. After all, if the Soviet expectations had materialized—if Finnish resistance had collapsed within a week and the puppet Kuusinen Government had taken over in Helsinki—the whole Soviet-Finnish dispute would have been nothing more than a ripple on the turbulent waters of European politics. But prolongation of the struggle had stirred up all sorts of dangers and had whipped the waters into fury. Confronted with the real danger of an

---

[59] *Förspelet till det Tyska Angreppet,* 153 ff.; Wuorinen: *Finland and World War II,* 78-79.
[60] Text of the treaty in *Finnish Blue Book,* 115 ff. On the final negotiations we have used, in addition to Wuorinen, tels. from Steinhardt, March 12, 1940.

Allied invasion of Scandinavia and of an attack on the Caucasus, the Soviet leaders were realistic and clever enough to offer peace at the critical moment. Thereafter they simply gambled on the proposition that militarily the Finns could not go on, that the Swedes and Norwegians would refuse passage for Western troops, and that, if the Allies nevertheless invaded Scandinavia, the Germans would intervene before effective aid could reach the Finns. The Soviets won, it is true, but the price of their victory was a legacy of almost universal hatred which, if actually translated into action, might in the ensuing months prove extremely dangerous to the Soviet Union. For the Allies were not disposed to shelve the plans which appeared so promising. They simply revamped them to fit the new situation, but only to find themselves before long disastrously embroiled with the Germans in Norway.

INDEX

To Volume I